ALL OUT
WAR

ALL OUT
WAR

THE FULL STORY OF HOW BREXIT
SANK BRITAIN'S POLITICAL CLASS

TIM SHIPMAN

WILLIAM
COLLINS

William Collins
An imprint of HarperCollins*Publishers*
1 London Bridge Street
London SE1 9GF
WilliamCollinsBooks.com

First published in Great Britain by William Collins in 2016

1

Copyright © Tim Shipman 2016

The author asserts the moral right to
be identified as the author of this work

A catalogue record for this book is
available from the British Library

HB ISBN 978-0-00-821515-6
TPB ISBN 978-0-00-821620-7

Printed and bound in Great Britain by
Clays Ltd, St Ives plc

MIX
Paper from
responsible sources
FSC™ C007454

FSC™ is a non-profit international organisation established to promote
the responsible management of the world's forests. Products carrying the
FSC label are independently certified to assure consumers that they come
from forests that are managed to meet the social, economic and
ecological needs of present or future generations,
and other controlled sources.

Find out more about HarperCollins and the environment at
www.harpercollins.co.uk/green

For my mother, who taught me to read,
and my father, who taught me to think.

Above all, for my wife Charlotte,
who was there and who deserved to win.
By meeting her, I did.

CONTENTS

PART THREE: ALL OUT WAR
Leadership
June to August 2016

ACKNOWLEDGEMENTS

This book is based on more than eighty interviews conducted in person and on the telephone during July and August 2016. A number of people have been immeasurably helpful but understandably do not wish to see their names in print, particularly those who work for the civil service, the new prime minister or the Labour Party, whose discretion is a living concern. They know who they are, and I'm grateful. Many of the interviews included 'on the record' observations, but most of the time we spoke on the understanding that I would construct a narrative of events without signalling the parentage of every fact and quote. Where I have directly quoted someone, or attributed thoughts or feelings to them, I have spoken to them, the person they were addressing, someone else in the room, or someone to whom they recounted details of the conversation. This means that I have only provided references to quotes or information from published sources and broadcast interviews. Where matters are disputed I have been clear about who is making the claims.

While it is invidious to single anyone out for special thanks, I am immensely grateful to: Iain Anderson, Adam Atashzai, Steve Baker, Arron Banks, Eddie Barnes, Jake Berry, Gabby Bertin, Nick Boles, Peter Bone, Graham Brady, Andrew Bridgen, Chris Bruni-Lowe, Conor Burns, Alistair Burt, Paul Butters, Alastair Campbell, David Campbell Bannerman, Joe Carberry, Douglas Carswell, Max Chambers, David Chaplin, Bill Clare, Ryan Coetzee, Therese Coffey, Henry Cook, Andrew Cooper, Dominic Cummings, Ruth Davidson, Henry de Zoete, Oliver Dowden, Brian Duggan, Sir Alan Duncan, Iain Duncan Smith, Matthew Elliott, Nick Faith, Lord Falconer of Thoroton, Nigel Farage, Liam Fox, Mark Fullbrook, Nusrat Ghani, Ameet Gill, John Glen, Michael Gove, Chris Grayling, Damian Green, Gerry Gunster, Matthew Hancock,

Daniel Hannan, Richard Harrington, Michael Heaver, Patrick Heneghan, Kate Hoey, Richard Howell, Bernard Jenkin, Alan Johnson, Boris Johnson, Hermann Kelly, Daniel Korski, Brandon Lewis, David Lidington, James McGrory, Michael McManus, Lord Mandelson of Foy in the County of Herefordshire and of Hartlepool in the County of Durham, Katie Martin, Zack Massingham, Nicky Morgan, David Mundell, Jonathan Munro, Henry Newman, Brett O'Donnell, Sir Craig Oliver, George Osborne, Rob Oxley, Mike Penning, Mats Persson, Amy Richards, Lewis Robinson, Lord Rose of Monewden, Josh Simons, Keith Simpson, Anna Soubry, Paul Stephenson, Will Straw, Lucy Thomas, Gawain Towler, Laura Trott, Nick Varley, Will Walden, Ben Wallace, Graeme Wilson and Nick Wood.

I'm also grateful to several lobby colleagues for passing on anecdotes and advice, including James Lyons, Oliver Wright, Sam Coates, James Kirkup, Beth Rigby, Fraser Nelson, Matt Chorley and Rob Hutton. Laura Kuenssberg gave me prior sight of the transcript of her television documentary *Brexit: Battle for Britain*, which was broadcast on 8 August 2016. Andy Taylor made several helpful suggestions on structure.

A first-time author has more debts than they can possibly repay. Victoria Hobbs, my agent at A.M. Heath, has been a friend and a professional through various abortive projects, and quickly did the deal, mid-holiday, when this one came up.

At HarperCollins, my editor Arabella Pike embraced the project from the off, and was very understanding of a recalcitrant hack's flexible approach to deadlines. Special thanks to Robert Lacey, the best copy editor in the business, Joseph Zigmond for sorting the pictures, PR supremo Helen Ellis, and Essie Cousins who keeps the ducks in a row.

My greatest debt is to Gabriel Pogrund, without whom this project would never have been completed. When he got in touch to offer his services I envisaged a keen amanuensis, but he was so much more than that. He began by tirelessly transcribing my tapes, but was also quickly introducing me to key sources, conducting some interviews himself, and always fizzing with ideas. He has been an engine of great industry and insight, and does everything with good humour and judgement. Bénédicte Earl, George Greenwood, Hannah McGrath, Oliver Milne and Thomas Seal also provided invaluable assistance in transcribing more than half a million words of interviews. Hannah also shared some notes on one episode. Harriet Marsden gave me access to her Brexit project, including an interview with Andy Wigmore.

At the *Sunday Times* I'd like to thank the editor Martin Ivens, his deputy Sarah Baxter and Eleanor Mills, the magazine editor, for giving prominence to serious coverage of politics that also revels in the soap opera of SW1.

We are all products of our education, and I was fortunate to have inspirational teachers at Queen Elizabeth's Grammar School in Horncastle, Lincolnshire. None more than my English teachers David and Heather Slater, who taught me to appreciate a good sentence (though not how to write one) while nurturing the subversive aspects of my personality that best prepared me for journalism. At Cambridge, Christopher Andrew, the late Mark Kaplanoff, Joanna Lewis, Peter Clarke and Chris Clark nurtured my love of history. I hope that as a first draft this passes muster.

Whenever there is an election, people ask me who I would like to win. I have a stock answer, which is only partially facetious: 'My contacts – anyone who answers the phone.' In general elections your mates can theoretically all win their seats. But the EU referendum was a civil war. I had close friends on both sides. At least one journalist with a loved one on a campaign was banished from the marital bed as a result of something they wrote. By the end of it people I like and admire were looking for work. Others whose careers had been unfairly coasting were returning in glory. The public rarely considers the human cost that accompanies a political realignment. The referendum campaign represented a career-life-or-death situation for many involved. Yet under levels of sleep deprivation that would be regarded as torture if they were inflicted on an enemy combatant, they remained professional and helpful. To everyone who answered the phone, if I could vote for you all, I would.

Most of all I would like to thank my family. My parents raised me in a house of books and have always supported me unconditionally. My sister Hannah has been a rock and a wizard webmistress, despite sharing a nuclear family with a thermonuclear ego. My wife Charlotte makes everything complete, and has endured more absences than any spouse has a right to expect during this project. Memories of our wedding mean that the day this book is published will be only the second proudest of my life.

Tim Shipman
Camogli, Todi, San Niccolo and Blackheath,
October 2016

TIMELINE

1973
Ted Heath takes Britain into the EEC, or 'Common Market'

1975
British public backs EEC membership in referendum with 67 per cent
   voting to stay

2007
Sep – David Cameron gives a 'cast-iron guarantee' to hold a
   referendum on the Lisbon Treaty if he becomes PM

2009
Jun – Ukip demands a referendum and finishes second in the
   European elections with 16.5 per cent of the vote
Nov – Cameron rules out a referendum because the Lisbon Treaty has
   been ratified

2011
Oct – Largest post-war parliamentary rebellion on Europe as eighty-
   one Tories defy a three-line whip to back an in/out referendum on
   British membership
Dec – Cameron 'vetoes' EU fiscal compact treaty. Other twenty-six EU
   member states agree their own deal

2013

23 Jan – Cameron makes Bloomberg speech, promising to get 'fundamental reform' and then call an in/out referendum

5 Jul – James Wharton brings forward Private Member's Bill to enshrine referendum pledge in law

2014

15 Mar – In article for the *Sunday Telegraph*, Cameron outlines seven areas where he wants reform of the EU

22 May – Ukip wins European elections with 26.6 per cent of the vote

28 Aug – Douglas Carswell defects from Tories to Ukip

27 Sep – Mark Reckless becomes second defector to Ukip

28 Nov – Cameron lays out demands for a four-year ban on in-work benefits for EU migrants. He ditches plans for an emergency brake on numbers

2015

7 May – General election. Cameron wins first Tory majority since 1992 and vows to hold a referendum before the end of 2017

8 May – Nigel Farage resigns as Ukip leader after failing to win South Thanet, but returns three days later

6 Jun – Steve Baker and David Campbell-Bannerman launch Conservatives for Britain

25 Jun – Cameron outlines his broad-brush proposals at EU summit

9 Sep – Tory rebels and Labour MPs unite to defeat government over purdah rules

25 Sep – Nigel Farage announces Ukip will back Arron Banks's group Leave.EU, originally called 'The Know'

9 Oct – Vote Leave is officially launched with a video highlighting the £350 million-a-week cost of EU membership

12 Oct – Britain Stronger In Europe launches with Stuart Rose as chairman

9 Nov – Vote Leave activists disrupt Cameron's speech to the CBI

10 Nov – In a letter to Donald Tusk, Cameron sets out details of the 'four baskets' of reforms. In a speech to Chatham House he details plans for a sovereignty lock demanded by Boris Johnson

1 Dec – Alan Johnson launches Labour In For Britain

6 Dec – Vote Leave calls Cameron 'toxic' after he claims he will have to campaign to leave if he is ignored by Brussels

8 Dec – MPs overturn an attempt by Labour peers to lower the voting age to sixteen

17–18 Dec – European Council discusses Cameron's demands and agrees to push for a deal in February

2016

4 Jan – Cameron agrees that ministers will be allowed to campaign for Leave after Chris Grayling and Theresa Villiers threaten to resign

25 Jan – 'Coup' attempt to oust Cummings is repelled when other Vote Leave staff threaten to quit

2 Feb – Donald Tusk publishes draft agreement of a 'new settlement' between the EU and the UK

3 Feb – Steve Baker says the deal is 'polishing poo'

18–19 Feb – Cameron secures a new deal in Brussels, including an emergency brake on migrant benefits. George Galloway attends a Grassroots Out rally in Westminster

20 Feb – Cameron holds historic Saturday cabinet meeting. Michael Gove leads a 'gang of six' cabinet ministers to back Brexit

21 Feb – Boris Johnson announces that he too will campaign to leave

22 Feb – In a statement to Parliament Cameron says, 'I have no other agenda than what is best for our country', which is widely interpreted as an attack on Johnson's motives

12 Mar – ITV does a deal with Downing Street and Ukip to secure Cameron and Farage for a debate

15 Mar – Cameron accuses Johnson of 'literally making it up' for suggesting the UK should have a Canada-style trade deal with the EU

18 Mar – Iain Duncan Smith resigns as work and pensions secretary over cuts to disability benefits in the budget

31 Mar – Vote Leave submits its designation document to the Electoral Commission with just twenty minutes to go

13 Apr – Electoral Commission designates Vote Leave and Britain Stronger In Europe as the two official campaigns

18 Apr – First Treasury document claims Brexit will cost families £4,300 a year

22 Apr – On a visit to London, President Barack Obama says Britain will be 'in the back of the queue' for a trade deal with the US

26 Apr – During a crunch meeting in George Osborne's office, Tory chiefs on Stronger In rule out 'blue-on-blue' attacks on Johnson and Gove or any moves to tackle the immigration issue

5 May – In local elections Labour suffers the worst result by an opposition since 1982

6 May – Farage visits Vote Leave to discuss the ground campaign and the debates

8 May – Michael Gove tells the BBC's Andrew Marr that Brexit Britain would be outside the European single market

9 May – Cameron warns that Brexit could lead to war in Europe

15 May – Boris Johnson says the EU is pursuing the same superstate as Hitler, using 'different methods'

17 May – The *Sun* splashes on sex smears against Boris Johnson's wife. Michael Heseltine condemns Johnson's 'preposterous' claims

19 May – Eurosceptic rebels force Cameron to accept amendment to the Queen's Speech on transatlantic trade deal

21 May – Osborne claims house prices will be 18 per cent lower in the event of Brexit

25 May – Ryan Coetzee reports to Stronger In chiefs that the economic message is not working

26 May – Immigration figures are released showing net migration to the UK rose to 333,000 in 2015

27 May – Purdah period begins, preventing the government from publishing further pro-Remain documents. Downing Street staff move to Stronger In HQ

29 May – Gove and Johnson write to Cameron accusing him of 'corroding public trust' with his immigration pledges. Andrew Bridgen says Cameron is 'finished' as PM

30 May – In the first of a series of 'alternative government' pledges, Vote Leave says a Brexit administration would scrap VAT on household energy bills

1 Jun – Gove and Johnson announce that a Brexit government would introduce an Australian-style points system to control immigration

2 Jun – Boris Johnson auctions a cow, describing it as a 'beautiful milker'

3 Jun – Vote Leave vows to spend £100 million of the £350 million on the NHS instead of Brussels

5 Jun – John Major denounces Boris Johnson for a 'squalid', 'deceitful' and 'depressing' campaign

7 Jun – Deadline for voter registration crashes government website. Cameron calls out Leave's 'six lies' in an emergency press conference

9 Jun – On a visit to Northern Ireland, Tony Blair and John Major warn that Brexit could break up the UK. Amber Rudd attacks Boris Johnson in first three-way TV debate. Andrew Cooper's warning about falling Labour support for Remain prompts crisis meeting

12 Jun – In a Downing Street meeting, Cameron decides not to make a 'vow' on immigration

13 Jun – Stronger In clears the decks for 'Labour week', starting with a speech by Gordon Brown

14 Jun – Cameron thinks he should make an immigration pledge, but is again talked out of it. Ed Balls and Yvette Cooper also demand changes to freedom of movement

15 Jun – Cameron calls Angela Merkel but does not ask her for anything. George Osborne unveils an 'emergency budget' to plug a £30 billion black hole in the event of Brexit. Sixty-five Tory MPs vow to vote it down. Vote Leave unveils a 'Brexit Queen's Speech'. Flotillas led by Nigel Farage and Sir Bob Geldof clash on the Thames

16 Jun – Farage unveils 'Breaking Point' immigration poster. Labour MP Jo Cox murdered. Both campaigns suspended

19 Jun – A passionate Cameron tells *Question Time* audience Winston Churchill wouldn't have 'quit' on Europe

21 Jun – Final 'Great Debate' at Wembley Arena. Boris Johnson says 23 June can be Britain's 'Independence Day'

23 Jun – Referendum day

24 Jun – Broadcasters declare Leave victors at 4.39 a.m. Cameron resigns at 8.15 a.m. Johnson and Gove hold a press conference and discuss plans to run a 'Dream Team' leadership bid. Labour MPs say they will call a vote of no confidence in Jeremy Corbyn

25 Jun – Gove calls Johnson to say he will back him. Johnson plays cricket at Althorp House. Hilary Benn phones shadow cabinet to see if they will resign

26 Jun – Eleven members of the shadow cabinet quit after Benn is fired by Corbyn. Johnson and Gove meet at Thame, Oxfordshire, to discuss Johnson's campaign

27 Jun – Johnson's *Telegraph* article on Brexit is criticised for backing both the single market and free movement

28 Jun – Labour MPs vote by 172 to forty for Jeremy Corbyn to quit. He refuses. Breakfast meeting of Johnson, Gove and aides at Lynton Crosby's office to settle campaign tensions. Sarah Vine writes an email to Gove telling him to 'be your stubborn best'

29 Jun – Stephen Crabb launches leadership bid. Johnson pulls out of hustings, struggles to write his launch speech, and tries and fails to recruit Andrea Leadsom. Gove decides he cannot support Johnson

30 Jun – Gove issues statement saying Johnson is not ready to be prime minister and that he will run for the leadership. Theresa May and Liam Fox also launch their campaigns. Johnson withdraws

1 Jul – Gove launches his campaign

4 Jul – Nigel Farage resigns as Ukip leader for the third time

5 Jul – May tops the first Tory leadership ballot with 165 votes, with Leadsom on sixty-six, Gove on forty-eight, Crabb on thirty-four and Fox on sixteen

6 Jul – Chilcot report on Iraq War published. Nick Boles's text urging MPs to vote tactically against Leadsom leaks, damaging Gove

7 Jul – Leadsom supporters march on Parliament. In second ballot, May wins 199 votes, Leadsom eighty-four and Gove forty-six

9 Jul – In an interview with *The Times*, Leadsom implies she is better-qualified than May because she is a mother

11 Jul – Leadsom drops out of contest. May becomes Tory Party leader. Angela Eagle launches leadership challenge against Corbyn. Owen Smith says he will also run

12 Jul – After a seven-hour meeting, Labour's NEC rules that Corbyn is automatically on the ballot paper, ending the attempted coup

13 Jul – Cameron takes final cabinet and PMQs. May visits Buckingham Palace and becomes prime minister. She vows to create 'a country that works for everyone'

19 Jul – Eagle drops out, leaving Smith to take on Corbyn

24 Sep – Corbyn re-elected Labour leader with 62 per cent of the vote

Introduction

DEMONS UNLEASHED

Not long before David Cameron moved into Downing Street he spent some time with an old friend, a man very successful in his own field but who regarded the prospect of his old mate Dave becoming the head of government with some bewilderment. 'Isn't it odd,' he said, 'that by the next time I see you, you will be the prime minister?' The friend asked whether he was ready, whether Cameron felt up to the job. With the insouciance that became his trademark, Cameron replied, 'How hard can it be?'

By 10 o'clock on the evening of 23 June 2016, a little over six years later, Cameron knew the answer to that question. The polls had just closed on the third major constitutional referendum of his premiership, a vote in which he had placed Britain's membership of the European Union and his own career on the line. At that point Cameron was still expecting to win. His pollster and friend Andrew Cooper had published a poll that day putting the Remain campaign ten points ahead. Cooper's internal tracking poll had things closer than that, but most of the twenty-five aides and allies gathered on the first floor of 10 Downing Street, eating moussaka and drinking bottled beer, expected to scrape a win. David Cameron was a winner. He had been in trouble before, but he had emerged triumphant from the 2011 referendum on electoral reform and again in the Scottish independence plebiscite in September 2014. Just 413 days earlier friend and foe alike had doubted him, but at the 2015 general election he had won the first parliamentary majority by a Conservative leader in twenty-three years.

Nevertheless, as Cameron circulated in the Terracotta Room, aides could see he was nervous – the calmest man there, but nervous nonetheless. With several of them he found time to joke 'I've got both of my speeches ready!' One for victory, one for defeat.

Nerves in the room were eased somewhat at 10 o'clock as the BBC announced that YouGov's final poll had given Remain a 52–48 lead. Within three minutes the pound had risen on the currency markets and Nigel Farage, the leader of the UK Independence Party and the man who had done most to force Cameron into calling a referendum, had all but conceded defeat.

At around midnight, as the first results approached, Cameron and a smaller group of friends and aides moved to the Thatcher Room, a book-lined study where the former prime minister had liked to work. Cameron looked as if he was working too, peering down at a laptop. 'I'd never seen him on a computer before,' one friend said.

Cameron was poring over a list drawn up by Jim Messina, the US voter-targeting expert who had helped both Barack Obama and Cameron get re-elected. His model showed how well the Remain team would have to do in each area of the country to win. When Newcastle was first to declare at midnight, voters there backed Remain by the slenderest of margins: 50.7 per cent to 49.3 per cent. The Downing Street staff looked at Messina's model and saw that they needed a 52–48 win. A hoped-for four-point lead had evaporated into a margin of less than two points. Pulses quickened. Twenty minutes later, Sunderland delivered a stunning Leave victory, by 61 per cent to 39. Messina's model said Remain needed a 60–40 loss there to be on par. Two points short again.

Peering at the laptop like Downing Street's in-house psephologist, Cameron began commentating on his own downfall. 'He was comparing the results on Messina model,' an aide said. 'He'd say, "Well, that's three points short," or "That's two points short." He was incredibly calm.' And that was the story of the evening. At each turn, Remain was falling two to four points below expectations. Cameron's inner circle pinned their hopes on good results in Scotland and London. When they started to come in, Cameron said, 'We could still pull this back.'

But while Remain was winning big in its heartlands, turnout was lower than required. In Leave's strongholds, three million people who never usually voted had turned out. Gradually, and with a minimum of drama, hope began to fade. 'There was no panic,' one young adviser remarked, just a strange and creeping realisation that everything was going wrong, that the gamble had failed.

As Cameron sat at the laptop, others in the room thought back to the key moments that had brought them here – the rebellion of eighty-one

Tory MPs over a referendum in 2011; the announcement that Cameron would offer one in the Bloomberg speech of 2013; the pledges to deal with migrant benefits; the election victory in May 2015 that made it inevitable; the renegotiations with other EU countries which fell short of his previous pledges; the decisions by Michael Gove and Boris Johnson to put their principles and their ambitions before their loyalty to Cameron; the immigration figures; the debates; the posters; the murder of the Labour MP Jo Cox – a reminder that some political lives end much more tragically than in defeat at the ballot box.

For Craig Oliver, the director of communications, the memory that stuck in the mind was of a conversation with Cameron in the back of a car after the general election, when the prime minister had weighed up the pros and cons of the decision to hold a referendum. Cameron laid out the reasons in favour: the public's democratic right to decide, the need to placate his party, to lance the boil that had spread across British politics since the public were last asked their view on Europe in 1975. Asked for the case against, the prime minister said, 'You could unleash demons of which ye know not.'[1]

A Cameron confidant with whom Oliver discussed the moment said, 'I am sure he was thinking of the demons within the Tory universe, and whether they may take control and finish him off. The demons he'd been fighting hard to control all along. The demons that had played a huge role in making the Conservative Party unelectable for a generation.'

The demons were the forces of Euroscepticism that had been growing in the Conservative Party for three decades; they were the Eurosceptics who had forced Cameron to abandon his pledge to stop 'banging on about Europe'; they were the 'fruitcakes, loonies and closet racists' of Ukip he had once dismissed; perhaps also they were Michael Gove and Boris Johnson, whose decision to oppose him had put the result on a knife edge. Cameron also believed in the demons of economic disaster in the event of a Leave vote, the upsurge in nativist sentiment during the campaign, even the willingness of campaigners on both sides to stretch the truth to make their point during the campaign.

Draped across Cameron's knees, fast asleep, was his daughter Nancy. Numerous people remarked on her presence that night. Cameron was always a father as well as a politician. However hard he worked – and he worked much harder than his critics liked to pretend – he had always found time to go up to the flat and see the children. His ability to compartmentalise may have led people to label him a 'chillaxer', but it also meant that he was that rare species of prime minister not driven slightly mad in office.

Those searching for meaning and significance in the night's events might have looked down at the table they were sitting around, a beautiful circular piece of elm that was commissioned for the G8 summit in Lough Erne in 2013, a time when Cameron was top dog, playing host to Barack Obama, Angela Merkel and the rest. If he had paused to think of the German leader, did he thank her for the help she had proffered in securing a renegotiation of Britain's relationship with Brussels, or did he think – as several of those present that night did – that he had never asked her for enough, never put her on the spot, never forced her to choose between Britain's place in Europe and her precious free movement of people?

They might have considered the room they were in, the Thatcher Room, named after the prime minister who fell because her growing scepticism had offended the pro-Brussels establishment within her own cabinet. Cameron was on his way out because he had come to embody that establishment at a time when voters were never more inclined to thumb their noses at it.

For more than one of the people in the Thatcher Room in those small, dark hours, it was the figure who did not sit at the elm table that struck them most. George Osborne, the closest of the prime minister's allies, sat off to the left, alone and contemplating. Osborne had served Cameron, but he had hoped for a career that would outlive his friend's. Cameron at least had been prime minister. Still just forty-five, Osborne had every expectation of another decade at the top. Now he might soon be looking for work. Not only had he opposed the referendum as potentially disastrous for the country and the Conservative Party, he had to watch now as the career he had so meticulously constructed over the previous fifteen years turned to ashes. Osborne was usually talkative, quick with a joke, many of them with a razor-sharp edge. Not that night. He sat separately, his eyes fixed on a point ten yards beyond Maggie Thatcher's bookshelves. As the first result came in he said simply, 'This is going to be a very long night,' and returned to his meditations.

When hope, finally, was extinguished, just after 3 a.m., there was no moment of despair or rage. Cameron is nothing if not steady under fire. He had been the 'essay crisis' prime minister, never better than with his back to the wall and a short time in which to turn events around. But there would be no turning the referendum around, not five hours after the polls had closed. 'David Cameron takes good news the exact same way he takes bad news,' one aide present that night said. 'He just smiles. In his head he's made his mind up. But only when you've known him a while can you see the telltale signs.'

They all watched, and those of them who knew him well, who could read the eyes and the angle of the smile, knew the time had arrived. But because it had been done subtly, with little fanfare, they only slowly became aware that Cameron was no longer there. They looked around and registered the absences: Cameron, Osborne, Ed Llewellyn and Kate Fall. There was no sign of Samantha Cameron either. The prime minister, the chancellor, the chief of staff and his deputy. The 'Quad' which ran the coalition government had become well known. This was the real quad, which ran the Notting Hill set for fifteen years and had commanded a Conservative majority government for just one.

Those who noticed knew what it meant. 'At about 3 o'clock in the morning I went to the loo, and when I came back he'd gone downstairs just with George, Ed and Kate and we knew it was over,' one said.

Five hours later Cameron walked out into Downing Street with Samantha – for those who did not know what was coming, her presence was the clincher – and announced that he was resigning. Five days later he left Number 10 for the last time. At just forty-nine he was the youngest man to walk out of the famous black door as an ex-prime minister since the Earl of Rosebery in 1895.

What followed was the most remarkable moment in British politics since May 1940, when Neville Chamberlain was ousted at the point of the nation's greatest ever peril and replaced by Winston Churchill, its maverick saviour. For a moment it looked as if Churchill's biographer, the Brexit cheerleader Boris Johnson, would inherit the crown as his hero had done seventy-six years earlier. But in the fashion of previous revolutions the revolutionary leadership began to consume themselves. Driven by admirers who believed him the most significant Conservative thinker of his generation, and the dawning realisation in his own head that he could do the job himself, Michael Gove plunged the knife. He plunged it so hard and so deep that he wounded himself and left Johnson, once more, the recipient of a nation's good wishes. They were not the first victors in war who conspired to lose the peace.

* * *

It all now seems so inevitable. Britain had always been sceptical about Europe; it was now just expressing a historic feeling. Yet through it all, one fact screams loudest above all. Had just 600,000 people changed their vote, David Cameron would be hailed as the political escapologist of his generation. This book would be – even more than it is – about the mistakes and infighting of the Leave campaigns. Cameron would have been able to depart at a time and in the manner of his own choosing.

When the country voted Leave, the political class took it rather more literally than perhaps even some Brexiteers expected. Of the main parties' leaders who went into the 2015 election – Cameron, Miliband, Clegg and Farage – not one remains. Of the six cabinet-level supporters who signed the Vote Leave pledge the morning after Cameron's deal in Brussels, only Chris Grayling still has a cabinet job – and in January 2016 he looked the one least likely to keep his post. Of the four dominant modernising Tories of the last decade – Cameron, Osborne, Gove and Johnson – only one remains at the apex of politics, and even that was a close-run thing. Boris Johnson went from a popular campaign hero, to startled whipping-boy of the furious 48 per cent, to prime minister in waiting, to political oblivion, and then back to one of the four great offices of state, all in the space of a fortnight. Theresa May went from submariner during the campaign to the captain of the ship at its conclusion, then promptly consigned the ruling class of the Conservative Party to the backbenches, and the austerity economics that had dominated political discourse for six years to the dustbin of history.

These were events populated by a cast of characters who might have been created by Wodehouse or Trollope. In these pages you will find a championship-winning basketball player, an adventurer who smuggled himself into rebel-held Benghazi, a millionaire owner of assault weapons, a scholar of Bismarck who idolises James Carville – and more MPs and aides than is healthy who learned their trade from reading classic volumes of military strategy.

I'm not a sociologist or a political scientist. This is not a study of the decline of the post-industrial working class, 'post-truth' politics or the psychology of anger. You won't find a detailed psephological breakdown of which streets backed Brexit in Sunderland. It is not the story of the little guy, the canvassers and doorknockers who man a campaign. If this book in any way goes beyond journalism – and I make no such claims – it is unashamedly elitist history. It is a book about leaders and their closest aides, the decisions they make, how and why they make them, and how they feel when they turn out to be wrong. It is about dilemmas faced and confronted. It is about the battle between self and team. It is about principle and ambition, and how the two are sometimes so indivisible as to make divining motive pointless. It is about men who make decisions that are intellectually consistent and – by their own measure – morally sound, but which are simultaneously disastrous for themselves and those closest to them. It is about how doing what worked before doesn't always work again. Most of all it is about asking the question: how far are you prepared to go to win? Politics is a results business. There are no hung Parliaments in referendums, only victory or total, irreversible defeat.

There is a good case that four decades of Euroscepticism, coupled with the eurozone crisis and the mass migration from the Middle East, were more important than what happened during the campaign in determining the result. But this is a book that begins from the premise that the actions of key individuals, at hinge moments in history, are magnified out of all proportion. For the thirteen months between the general election and polling day, what David Cameron, George Osborne, Michael Gove, Boris Johnson, Nigel Farage, Arron Banks and Dominic Cummings thought and did decided the fate of the rest of us.

Two points of style and taste.

Anyone who has watched *The Thick of It* – the television comedy which is viewed by some in Westminster as an instruction manual rather than a satire – will know that British politics can be a profane business. Many MPs and their aides swear like troopers, and the rhythms of their speech often require expletival emphasis. I have censored these efforts where the profanity is simply used as punctuation – not least because the spin doctors from both main campaigns asked me to spare their mothers' blushes – but where it is essential to the emotion of the sentence I have left it in. Be warned.

Secondly, throughout the book I have ignored the prefix 'Lord' for political peers. This is not a pointed comment about the honours system, but I know of no one in Westminster who refers to Peter Mandelson, Rodney Leach or David Sainsbury as Lord This, That or the Other. So, if he will forgive me, outside the acknowledgements the Baron Mandelson of Foy in the County of Herefordshire and of Hartlepool in the County of Durham will be plain old Peter in these pages.

Those looking for a clear delineation of good guys and bad guys have come to the wrong place. I am not here to explore the rights and wrongs of Brexit, or to pass judgement on the questionable claims of the campaigns, but to explain why both sides used them. I hope that by the end, if you think it was moral to support Remain, perhaps you will appreciate that there was also a certain nobility on the Leave side, in doing everything possible to win a battle they regarded as existentially important. If you felt it was moral to vote to Leave, perhaps you will agree that the intensity with which David Cameron and George Osborne fought the campaign was proof of their passion and belief, not of the widespread view that all politicians are lying bastards who will say or do anything to hang on to power.

PART ONE

SKIRMISHES

FROM BLOOMBERG
TO BRUSSELS

October 2011 to February 2016

1

'MY LILY-LIVERED COLLEAGUES ...'

It says much about David Cameron's relationship with George Osborne that they kept a lid on it. The decision to hold a referendum on Britain's membership of the European Union was the most important Cameron made as prime minister – and his closest political ally, friend and adviser opposed it. Not just a little bit, but profoundly and wholeheartedly – and yet the disagreement did not leak.

It was late May 2012, and Cameron was just back from a NATO summit in Chicago. In a pizza restaurant at O'Hare Airport on the way home he had called a council of war with Ed Llewellyn and William Hague, his chief of staff and his foreign secretary, and decided he had no choice but to go into the 2015 general election with a pledge to hold a nationwide vote on the UK's relationship with the EU by the middle of the next Parliament.[1] Just before he became prime minister, Cameron had remarked, 'I don't want Europe to define my premiership.'[2] He had already discovered that was a forlorn hope.

'The biggest advocate of the referendum was William Hague,' a senior Downing Street official said. The foreign secretary told Cameron, 'You need to do this. I got killed by Europe. A Tory leader needs to nail this once and for all.'

George Osborne did not agree at all. The idea that the chancellor was concerned about the prospect of a referendum became known later, but few have appreciated quite how serious was his opposition. Osborne did not just think a referendum was a bad idea, he thought it was a disastrous idea. In successive meetings he was 'pretty hostile' to pressing ahead because he feared the vote would be lost. He warned Cameron he was taking a major risk that several uncontrollable forces would combine in a referendum campaign: 'anti-government sentiment, opportunism, genuine concern – and then you lose'. The picture Osborne painted was stark and prescient.

Strategically, Osborne saw three problems. The first was that the in/out question was an all-or-nothing proposition. This was not a referendum on integration or membership of the euro – Britain's membership was on the line. There was no way back if it was lost. The second, he told Cameron, was that the campaign would 'split the Conservative Party down the middle'. A senior Downing Street source recalled, 'George's view was that there's a good chance we'll lose, and it will destroy the Tory Party.' Thirdly, the chancellor had what now seems a more parochial political concern, that with Labour's Ed Balls and Ed Miliband making overtures to business, Tory support for a referendum would undermine business backing for the Conservatives in the run-up to the 2015 general election. A cabinet colleague said, 'George's view was, "Don't allow your entire premiership to be held hostage to this."'

Osborne's plan on Europe was to do what they had done for seven years since 2005, and avoid talking about it. When forced to give firm commitments they would say, 'No more integration, no bailouts,' and then hold out the idea of securing some extra powers for the UK as and when the eurozone needed a new treaty change. 'It's not perfect, but I reckon it's better than the alternative,' he argued.

Given the gravity of the decision and its implications, this was the most important political disagreement Cameron and Osborne had during their six years in power. It is a testament to the strength of their political partnership and their friendship that it never became front-page news, as even minor spats between Tony Blair and Gordon Brown did. Osborne told friends, 'My partnership with David Cameron has always been predicated on two things: one, he is the boss and I am number two. Second, that where we disagree, we disagree in private – I don't flounce off or resign or anything like that.' In the end Osborne could see the way the wind was blowing, and swallowed his doubts. A Downing Street aide said, 'George is essentially a real pragmatist, so he understood that that's where we'd end up.' But the decision would eventually send Osborne over the top in a fight that would define his career, but which he had opposed from the start.

Cameron was a pragmatist too. In opposition, the most prominent portrait on his wall was of Harold Macmillan, the one-nation Tory who had tried to take Britain into what was then the Common Market, until

France's President Charles de Gaulle – the first and most disputatious in a long line of Gallic protagonists – said 'Non!' Most Conservative leaders wanted to be Winston Churchill. Most Tory Eurosceptics wanted David Cameron to be Margaret Thatcher, whose best-known sentence on European integration was 'No, no, no.' But Cameron wanted to be Macmillan, a common-sense healer of divisions and manager of the nation's interests. Famously, when asked what was most dangerous for a politician, Macmillan had replied, 'Events, dear boy, events.' In his approach to Europe, David Cameron was never more like his hero. Temperamental incrementalism, a propensity to tactically manage rather than strategically plan, and a tendency to be driven by events would all define his response to the issue that now bookends his premiership.

At around ten minutes past eight on 23 January 2013 David Cameron took to the stage at the London head office of Bloomberg, the financial news service, and said to the expectant audience, 'This morning I want to talk about the future of Europe.' What followed was the most significant speech given by a British prime minister since Tony Blair made the case for the Iraq War. In its consequences for Britain, it was more far-reaching than that.

In bald, spare words, Cameron sought to confront the issue which more than any other had derailed the careers of Conservative leaders in his adult lifetime. In 1975, when the British public had last been asked its opinion about Europe, Cameron had been too young to vote, and the Tory Party had been broadly united in supporting membership of what was then the Common Market. Yet now, Cameron looked down the lens of the television-pool camera and said, 'The next Conservative Manifesto in 2015 will ask for a mandate from the British people for a Conservative government to negotiate a new settlement with our European partners … and when we have negotiated that new settlement, we will give the British people a referendum with a very simple in or out choice. To stay in the EU on these new terms; or come out altogether.' Cameron made clear that he personally wanted an outcome 'that keeps us in'. He concluded by saying, 'It is time to settle this European question in British politics.'

The speech marked the end of a long, hard road for David Cameron which began with his speech to the 2006 party conference, less than a year after he won the Tory leadership, when he urged his parliamentary colleagues to stop 'banging on about Europe'. Even at the time this was naïvely optimistic, since Cameron had already given ground to the Eurosceptics during the leadership election, matching a pledge from his Eurosceptic rival Liam Fox to take the Conservatives out of the European People's Party (EPP), the main centre-right (but devoutly federalist) grouping in the European Parliament. The promise helped him beat both Fox and David Davis, the former Europe minister known to colleagues as 'the Old Knuckleduster'. But in the capitals of Europe, leaving the EPP was Cameron's 'original sin', proof that he was another British leader unwilling to play by the rules of the club. Eleven years later it would be a factor, albeit a minor one, in hampering his renegotiation of Britain's relationship with Brussels. At home it was evidence for the Eurosceptics that, if they pushed him hard enough, he would retreat.

Cameron was no EU enthusiast. When seeking selection as the Tory candidate for Whitney, the Oxfordshire seat he was to win in 2001, he characterised his views as 'no to the single currency, no to further transfer of powers from Westminster to Brussels, and yes to renegotiation of areas like Fish where the EU has been a disaster for the UK', before adding for good measure, 'If that is being a Europhile, then I'm a banana.'[3] But for the Eurosceptics his heart was not in it. To Cameron, Europe was 'the E word'. In 2006 he described members of the UK Independence Party as 'a bunch of fruitcakes and loonies and closet racists'. That not only made a mortal enemy of Ukip's leader Nigel Farage, but contributed to a belief among the Palaeosceptic – a term I hope describes their longevity without implying that they were old-fashioned – old guard (not unfounded) that he viewed them the same way. Daniel Hannan, the Conservative MEP who was the intellectual godfather of what would become the Leave campaign, first met Cameron when he was running the Conservative Research Department in the early 1990s. 'I think his view then was that Eurosceptics were like the ancient mariner,' Hannan said. 'They were disagreeable bores who would hold you with their skinny hand. I think he approached the European issue through the prism of party management. I don't think he ever sat down and did a cost–benefit analysis of EU membership. He began from the position, probably true in the 1990s, that a lot of the Eurosceptics were quite difficult and obsessive people.' Whatever concessions were extracted, the Palaeosceptics came back for more. This was the era when, as the columnist Danny Finkelstein so memorably put it, the Eurosceptics 'wouldn't take "Yes" for an answer'.

The issue that calcified Eurosceptic suspicion of Cameron was his 'cast-iron guarantee' in September 2007 that he would hold a referendum on the Lisbon Treaty, which greatly deepened EU integration. Once the treaty was ratified in every EU country, including by Gordon Brown's Labour government, Cameron ditched the pledge, arguing that a referendum was pointless. He sought to placate the Eurosceptics with a speech in November 2009 announcing a 'referendum lock', ensuring a vote on any future European treaty 'that transferred areas of power or competences' from Britain to Brussels. It was a poor substitute for the in/out vote the sceptics craved. More importantly, as the then Tory MP Douglas Carswell observed, Cameron's original promise, 'although we reneged on it, established the legitimacy of a referendum'.

Even pro-Europeans look back on Cameron's decision with regret, since it meant that if there was to be a referendum in future, it would be an all-or-nothing proposition. Tory MP Alistair Burt said, 'I argued that the first chance the British people were going to get to vote on the EU they'd vote "No", no matter what the question was. I would far rather have had a question on a constitutional issue than "In" or "Out".'

With hindsight, the moment a referendum became inevitable occurred in October 2011. When more than 100,000 members of the public signed a petition demanding a nationwide vote, Conservative backbencher David Nuttall – whose name was regarded by Downing Street as eloquently descriptive – proposed a Commons motion calling for a referendum. Instead of letting the sceptics sound off in a vote that was not binding, Cameron unwisely turned the showdown into a trial of strength, ordering his backbenchers to vote it down. 'We cannot lie down on this,' he told his closest aides.[4] It is understandable that he felt like imposing some order. By that point, seventeen months into the coalition government, Cameron had already endured twenty-two backbench rebellions on Europe, involving a total of sixty MPs.[5] He ordered an 'industrial-scale operation' to rein in the sceptics.[6] Word spread that anyone voting for the motion would be barred from ministerial office for four years, or even face deselection. Despite the threats, and to Cameron's consternation, eighty-one Conservatives backed the motion, the biggest rebellion on Europe since the Second World War. At John Major's worst moment during the passage of the Maastricht Bill in 1993 only forty-one

Tory MPs had defied the whip. Without the heavy-handed whipping the rebel leaders could have mustered 150 votes against their own government. As young MPs, Cameron and Osborne had seen loyalty as the currency of promotion; now they were confronted by people who put principle first.

One of Cameron's closest aides said, 'For me the pivotal moment was the eighty-one rebellion. It was clear after that that the parliamentary party would not stand for anything but a referendum by the next election. I think the PM knew instinctively that was where he was going to end up.' It would be another nine months before Cameron accepted that logic, and fifteen before he did anything about it.

Cameron may not have wished to focus on Europe, but the eurozone crisis ensured that he had no choice. The Greek economy plunged into chaos shortly after the 'referendum lock' speech, and attempts to prevent an 'Acropolis Now' collapse preoccupied the EU into 2012.

Two months after the Tories' Commons rebellion, in December 2011, the nations in the eurozone demanded a Fiscal Compact Treaty to prop up their ailing currency. Cameron and Osborne sought protections for the City of London. In a strategy which he was to test to destruction, Cameron focused his negotiating efforts on Angela Merkel. They had a good relationship. The German chancellor had been to Chequers in 2010, when they kicked back watching episodes of *Midsomer Murders*. 'Just think, all this could have been yours,' Cameron had joked.[7] After a lunch in Berlin, Cameron thought she was on-side, but she then went behind his back to do a deal with the French. Cameron, realising he had been ambushed, called to warn her, 'I'll have to veto.' She replied, 'In that case I'll have to do it without you.'[8] On the evening of 8 December Cameron went alone into the summit room with twenty-six other leaders and found himself in a minority of one. At 4 a.m. he walked out.[9]

'We renamed it a veto to claim it was a veto,' one Downing Street aide recalled. Cameron's refusal vetoed nothing. The other twenty-six nations simply signed a separate treaty outside the EU apparatus. But Cameron was lauded at home as a latterday Thatcher, standing magnificently alone against the tide of integration. A Number 10 source recalled, 'Firstly, he never thought he was going to veto it. It was initially, "Oh fuck, what have we done?" Then the polls went up. It was a completely accidental triumph. The Foreign Office thought it was the end of the world.' The veto affair showed all too clearly that, despite her warm words, Merkel would not deliver for Cameron if she thought Germany's national interest and the good of the EU lay elsewhere. It was a lesson Cameron would have done well to learn there and then.

Cameron's honeymoon with the sceptics was brief. In June 2012, with Downing Street on the back foot over George Osborne's so-called 'omnishambles' budget, one hundred Tory MPs signed a letter, penned by Basildon MP John Baron, calling for legislation guaranteeing a referendum in the next Parliament. Two days later, at a summit in Brussels, Cameron rejected that plan. The Eurosceptics went into meltdown. 'The PM and the chancellor looked like they were seriously losing authority over the party,' a Downing Street source remembered.

In a bid to clean up the mess, Cameron wrote an article for the *Daily Telegraph* saying he was 'not against referendums on Europe', but that the time would not be right for an 'in/out' vote until Britain had 'define[d] with more clarity where we would like to get to'.[10] It was the first public expression of his desire for a new deal. Once again he had edged closer to a destination he did not desire, in order to placate people whose support he did not really want. Once again he had neither settled the issue to the satisfaction of his critics, nor properly confronted them. When Cameron told Nick Clegg about the article, the deputy prime minister told him he was 'crazy' to think he could buy off his critics. 'I have to do this,' Cameron insisted. 'It is a party management issue.'[11] Viewed after the political bloodbath that followed, the notion that holding a referendum might calm Tory divisions was farcically naïve.

It was the rise of the UK Independence Party (Ukip), and growing concern about immigration, that finally forced Cameron's hand. The eurozone crisis sent unemployment soaring, inspiring hundreds of thousands of people to flock to Britain to find work. Cameron's pledge to reduce net annual immigration to the 'tens of thousands' a year became untenable. The pressure this brought to bear on public services, coupled with the growing public view that yet another politician's promise was worthless, was deftly exploited by the blokeish but charismatic Ukip leader Nigel Farage, whose 'people's army' combined traditional EU constitutionalist pub bores with an anti-establishment grassroots movement that tapped into broader discontent with the Westminster elite. With the Liberal Democrats as partners in the coalition government,

Farage was able to hoover up protest votes which traditionally went to the third party. By the autumn of 2012 Ukip *were* the third party, consistently above the Lib Dems in the polls. In November Ukip grabbed second place in two by-elections in Rotherham and Middlesbrough. Cameron decided he had to act. He would have to enter the 2015 general election campaign with a pledge to hold a referendum.

Andrew Cooper, the pollster who was a key figure in driving Tory modernisation, said, 'Ukip, who nearly won the European elections in 2009, were very likely to win the European elections in 2014. We'd have been in meltdown and ended up being forced into a referendum commitment.' He told Cameron, 'Since it is a question of when, not if, let's do it now, let's do it calmly and set out a proper argument.' The prime minister saw the logic in this. As another member of his inner circle put it, 'There is an element where David thinks when the big judgement call needs to be made, "Put your balls on the line, let's do it."'

Once again, George Osborne was the most outspoken opponent of the idea. His father-in-law David Howell – a cabinet minister under Margaret Thatcher – told a Conservative activist that the chancellor 'implored' Cameron not to hold a referendum. Once again his objections were dismissed. In secret, Ed Llewellyn, the chief of staff in Downing Street, began work on the most important speech of Cameron's career.

By now some of Cameron's closest allies, including Steve Hilton and Oliver Letwin, were flirting with leaving the EU altogether. Most significantly, at the party conference in October, education secretary Michael Gove told journalists from the *Mail on Sunday* that on the current terms of membership he would vote to leave. Despite his resolute Euroscepticism, Gove, like Osborne, was a firm opponent of a referendum. He had two concerns. Even at this early stage he was worried that he 'would have to stand on a different side to the prime minister', which would be 'painful'. He also felt that Cameron had not worked out what his strategy was, and what Britain wanted out of Europe. Gove saw a pattern where the prime minister sought confrontation with the sceptics, told them 'You're all lunatics,' refused their demands, and then 'caved in'. A source close to Gove said, 'Throughout the time, Michael thought this whole thing was a recipe for disaster. What we're not doing is thinking through what Britain will be outside the EU, we're adopting a bunch of tactical strategies to stave off either Ukip's growth or our backbench problems.'

Gove went so far as to put these concerns in writing, emailing Cameron before the speech to tell him, 'You don't need to do this, you don't need to offer a referendum.'

'Don't worry, I know what I'm doing,' came the breezy reply.

Angela Merkel's views were assiduously sought before the big speech. A Downing Street aide recalled, 'We were paranoid about this thing going off completely half-cocked, with Merkel and [French President François] Hollande going out the next day to say, "This is a pile of absolute shit, Britain is going to get nothing from this." A lot of work was going into at least making sure they didn't blow the idea of negotiations out of the water.'

The prime minister gave Merkel dinner in Downing Street on 7 November, at which he explained, 'I've supported our membership of the EU all my political life, but I am worried that if I don't get the reform objectives I'm setting out, I won't be able to keep Britain in.'[12] Merkel called Britain Europe's 'problem child',[13] and urged him to 'couch the speech in an argument about Europe having to change' – in other words, a better deal for everyone. A Number 10 official recalled, 'The strategy was always: schmooze the pants off Merkel, get that locked down and then everyone else will fall in behind. It was damage limitation with the French. You got the sense that she was never wholeheartedly embracing it. The best you could hope for was that she could accept the political argument for him doing it and not stand in the way.'

After several delays, the speech finally went ahead on 23 January. Cameron actually struck a notably pro-European tone, praising the EU for helping to raise Europe from the grip of 'war and tyranny'. But it was an argument couched in Macmillanite practicalities: 'For us, the European Union is a means to an end – prosperity, stability, the anchor of freedom and democracy both within Europe and beyond her shores – not an end in itself.' He warned, 'democratic consent for the EU in Britain is now wafer-thin'.

Cameron spelt out his demands: more competitiveness and the completion of the single market, an end to 'one size fits all' integration. He said this would mean Britain abandoning the goal of 'ever closer union' written into the Treaty of Rome. He added, 'Power must be able to flow back to member states, not just away from them,' and called for 'a bigger and more significant role for national parliaments'. Finally, he demanded new rules that 'work fairly for those inside [the euro] and out'.

Heeding Merkel's advice on how to pitch his call for reform, he said, 'I am not a British isolationist. I don't just want a better deal for Britain, I want a better deal for Europe too.'

Largely forgotten afterwards, Cameron predicted that 'in the next few years the EU will need to agree on Treaty change', gifting him an occasion when Britain could get its new grand bargain. But when Germany cooled to that idea, his leverage was removed. Also forgotten, given how central it became to his deal, the speech included not one reference to immigration or migration.

Coming to the crux of the matter, he declared, 'I am in favour of a referendum. I believe in confronting this issue – shaping it, leading the debate, not simply hoping a difficult situation will go away.' Those looking back at the speech after the referendum would have been amused to find this entreaty: 'It will be a decision we will have to take with cool heads. Proponents of both sides of the argument will need to avoid exaggerating their claims.' Nevertheless, Cameron vowed that if he got the deal he wanted, 'I will campaign for it with all my heart and soul'.

The speech was met with a rapturous reception at home, where the sceptics seized on one key phrase: 'We need fundamental, far-reaching change.' When he entered the Commons chamber for PMQs later that morning he was met with a barrage of cheers. The Eurosceptics had got what they wanted.

Speaking in 2016, a Cameron aide said his main error was to lay out 'red lines', but not to use the speech to level with voters and his MPs that it was a starting point for discussion with Brussels, rather than an inviolable text. 'The problem was that we didn't make arguments like "We're going to have to compromise,"' a senior figure in Number 10 said. 'It was a huge error.' The Palaeosceptics who rejoiced at the speech were like Biblical or Koranic literalists – they planned to hold Cameron to every word of it. Bernard Jenkin seized on the comment that national parliaments were 'the true source of real democratic legitimacy and accountability in the EU', and warned Cameron, 'You've really got to deliver on this otherwise the Conservative Party will tear itself to pieces.' Cameron's response was to wave his hand dismissively and say, 'When the referendum comes the party will split, and that'll just have to be that.' To Jenkin the prime minister had the air of a man who had made the promise of a referendum that he never thought he would actually have to deliver, since by now few thought the Conservatives could win an overall majority at the 2015 general election and govern without the Lib Dems, who may have sought to veto any referendum. Iain Duncan Smith, the work and pensions secretary, said, 'I have no doubt that the thinking in Downing Street ... was that the outcome was likely to be a coalition government and ... that this referendum would be traded away.'[14]

For once, though, Cameron had gone far enough to satisfy the bulk of backbench opinion. He had adopted a position sufficiently robust to prevent the party disintegrating before the general election. For almost two years the Tory troublemakers, to adopt the classic dictum, would direct most of their piss outside the tent, and when they seemed in danger of misplacing the urinal – introducing a Private Member's Bill to hold a referendum – Cameron ended up adopting the Bill. But he was soon to discover the accuracy of one minister's theory of parliamentary urinators: 'Westminster is not divided into people inside the tent pissing out and people outside the tent pissing in, it is divided into people who piss and people who don't. It doesn't matter where the pissers stand, the piss always gets into the tent eventually.' As a description of what Cameron's Bloomberg speech set in train, it was hard to top.

The key question from this period is: could the referendum have been avoided, and if it could not, did Cameron have to offer an in/out vote by the end of 2017? When the cabinet was informed of the decision it horrified the veteran Europhile Ken Clarke: 'I was not consulted. I read about it in the newspaper. We had a row about it, but it was a done deal. I think it was the most reckless and irresponsible decision.'[15] Yet even a dyed-in-the-wool Europhile like Alistair Burt gave Cameron the benefit of the doubt: 'I don't blame the prime minister for calling the referendum, because you can't keep the people hostage, and it was important, not just for party management but important for the country, that the people had this vote.' There were practical concerns too. David Lidington, Cameron's Europe minister, said, 'Had he not promised the referendum, I think it would have been hugely difficult to win the 2015 general election at all.'

Cameron's aides believed failure to announce a referendum would have led to a leadership challenge when Ukip won the European elections in 2014. 'The idea that the PM was going to survive and face down his party is for the birds. We would have had a new leader coming in saying "I'm going to call a referendum," and probably saying they were going to back Brexit,' one said. The pollster Andrew Cooper agreed: 'If he'd taken the party on, I think he would have lost. Ukip was on the rise, the party was in revolt.'

Yet one of Cameron's closest aides believed that he may have stepped back from the brink if the Bloomberg speech had come after the Scottish referendum in September 2014, which uncorked the uncontrollable passions about which George Osborne had warned: 'After the Scottish referendum experience we realised you're unleashing things you can't control. That's the one thing I'd say would have changed our mind.' By the time Tory high command collectively came to recognise the risks, it was too late.

If Cameron had to offer a referendum, he did not have to offer an in/out referendum. A group of Eurosceptics – Bill Cash, Bernard Jenkin and John Redwood – went to see the prime minister before the Bloomberg speech to suggest he lance the boil by holding a 'mandate referendum' with the question 'Do you agree that the United Kingdom should establish a new relationship with our European partners based on trade and cooperation?' Cameron was at first interested in the idea, but later asked, 'Who's going to oppose that?' Jenkin replied, 'Exactly!' But Cameron saw the plan as potentially dangerous. He did not believe Britain's links to the EU should be confined to trade. Jenkin said, 'That referendum question, if approved, would have been completely incompatible with our present terms of membership. So he shied away from that and went for the in/out referendum.'

There were other options. Cameron could have devised his own mandate referendum, giving him licence to secure a deal when a treaty was next agreed. He could have defied the Liberal Democrats and begun a process of renegotiation with Merkel over a number of years, blaming his coalition partners for the lack of an immediate vote. He certainly did not have to say that there would be a referendum before the end of 2017. He could even have attempted to face down his party and confront their arguments. But in truth he had set himself on the path of tactical retreat from the moment he agreed to pull the Tories out of the EPP during his leadership campaign.

In calling for 'fundamental, far-reaching change' of Britain's relationship with the EU, the Bloomberg speech raised expectations that would be very difficult to meet. To get what he wanted from the other member states and keep Britain in Europe, Cameron had to persuade them that he was prepared to leave, a posture that was regarded as incredible by the sceptics at home, who demanded that he threaten to lead the UK out, while telling the world that he was only bluffing. As Tony Blair was to remark, 'David Cameron's strategy is a bit like the guy in *Blazing Saddles* who says, "Put your hands up or I'll blow my brains out!"'[16]

Rising immigration, fuelling the rise of Ukip, had led to Cameron's referendum pledge. By mid-2014 it was clear that measures to curb immigration would also have to be the centrepiece of his new deal with Brussels. According to the official statistics, net migration to the UK was 177,000 in 2012, rose to 209,000 in 2013, before soaring to 318,000 in 2014. Those figures would have been politically damaging in their own right, but juxtaposed with Cameron's long-standing pledge to limit net migration to the 'tens of thousands' they were explosive. As the figures rose, so too did support for Ukip. 'The thing which turbocharged Europe was the massive jump in EU migration,' a Cameron confidant said. 'That's what turned it from a niche Tory issue into a massive popular issue. The biggest problem with renegotiation was that it was absolutely clear we needed to control migration.'

The prime minister recognised the dangers, and used his speech to the Conservative Party conference in October 2014 to deliver a bold pledge: 'Britain, I know you want this sorted so I will go to Brussels, I will not take no for an answer and – when it comes to free movement – I will get what Britain needs.' The pledge was more than ambitious; as expectation-management went it was reckless, as Cameron would discover. Will Straw, who was to end up running the Remain campaign, said, 'He promised his grassroots more than he was ever able to achieve.'

The first effort to tackle the issue came a month later, in November 2014, when Cameron made a speech at JCB, the construction-vehicle manufacturer owned by his friend Anthony Bamford. The preparations for that speech led to another psychodrama with Merkel, serious clashes between Cameron's political aides and the civil service, a showdown with two of his most senior ministers, and did more to shape the final rene-gotiation deal even than the Bloomberg speech.

At heart, Cameron had two options: limit the number of EU migrants coming to Britain, or reduce the pull factors by cutting the benefits to which they were entitled. Iain Duncan Smith, the work and pensions secretary, and Michael Gove, by now the chief whip, pushed for quotas on the number of EU arrivals. The problem was that this flew in the face of the fundamental EU principle of the free movement of people. On 19 October the *Sunday Times* revealed that Cameron was considering 'an annual cap on the number of National Insurance numbers given to low-skilled immigrants from Europe'. Cameron blamed Gove for the leak. But at an EU summit later the same week, Merkel told the paper's Brussels correspondent Bojan Pancevski, 'Germany will not tamper with the fundamental principles of free movement in the EU,' words that killed the idea stone dead when they were splashed on the front page.[17] In a confrontation with Cameron in the British delegation's room, Merkel told the prime minister, 'You will not get support.'[18] Merkel had grown up under communism in East Germany. She was not prepared to compromise on the freedom to cross borders, which she had been denied for the first thirty-five years of her life.

The leak torpedoed a secret plan Oliver Letwin and a small number of Cameron's political advisers had been working on since July without the knowledge of civil servants. A Cameron adviser said the civil servants 'went nuts when they found out – but they never understood the view that we would struggle to win a referendum without a very serious immigration answer'. Cameron's policy staff then devised a time-limited 'emergency brake' which Britain could pull in extreme circumstances to halt EU arrivals. But the plan sparked some of the most heated rows between the politicos and the career diplomats and civil servants led by Ivan Rogers, Britain's ambassador to the EU, Cameron's civil service EU adviser Tom Scholar, and William Hague's special adviser Denzil Davidson. 'There was opposition from the civil service,' said a Downing Street aide. 'The FCO's approach was that this was completely unobtainable: "You'll get outright rejection."'

Another political aide said, 'The PM always wanted an emergency brake, he wanted to announce that in his immigration speech, but he couldn't because EU law wouldn't allow it. We'd go round endlessly in circles and come back to emergency brake. He'd go, "We must be able to do something about it!" We'd always come back to "It's not possible, free movement is a fundamental part of the EU." It was frustrating for the PM. He knew what he wanted to do, he knew what the British people wanted.' For their part the officials felt they were being asked to approve ideas with little or no chance of success, and that their job was to advise caution.

Ed Llewellyn had kept lines of communication open with the Germans, who wanted to be helpful but consistently made clear that freedom of movement reform – and treaty change – were not doable. But Cameron believed that he might be successful if he said a brake on numbers was the price of Britain staying in the EU. One of those involved in the deliberations said, 'A number of people in Number 10 – including the PM – suspected deep down that, when it came to it, in the early hours of a European Council meeting, the EU wouldn't let the UK leave on the basis of a temporary emergency brake. It would be high-risk, so the trick would be to keep any announced plan high-level – one of the reasons why the Gove leak, with all its detail, was so damaging.'

Two days before the speech, the emergency brake was still in the text and the civil servants mutinied. 'We asked them how it worked, because you can't just stop people coming into the country. How do you enforce it?' an official said. 'It's not something we can negotiate, and it doesn't work in practice. Why the hell are we about to put this in the speech?'

At the last moment, Cameron decided to switch to a proposal that had been drawn up by the Eurosceptic think tank Open Europe to ban EU migrants from claiming in-work benefits such as tax credits and social housing until they had been working in Britain and paying into the system for several years. Ivan Rogers' team in Brussels and Tom Scholar in London said that would not be tolerated by other EU nations either, but Cameron had to offer something on migration. A ban on migrants claiming child benefit for dependants living outside the UK and a pledge to remove those who had not found work after six months were also added. The changes happened so fast that Iain Duncan Smith, who had been sent drafts of the speech for his comments, had no idea the emergency brake had been removed until he turned on the television to watch Cameron speak. As man-management of one of the most influential Eurosceptics went, it left much to be desired. 'Up until two days before the speech, the emergency brake was there in the speech,' an aide involved in the deliberations said. 'The removal was so last-minute that the argument for the brake was still essentially running through the speech he delivered.'

Afterwards, rumours abounded that Merkel and her staff had read the speech and excised the migration cap. But a Downing Street source said, 'It wasn't blocked by Merkel, it was blocked by us, because we knew we would never get it. She had not seen the speech.' The Germans did have some input, however. 'Ed [Llewellyn] got the message from Merkel's chief of staff that she couldn't support it,' a Number 10 source said.

In fact the decisive intervention that killed off an emergency brake on migrant numbers, a policy which many Cameroons later believed might have been enough for them to win the referendum, was made by Theresa May, the home secretary, and Philip Hammond, the foreign secretary. Both were invited to see Cameron after the regular 8.30 a.m. meeting in Downing Street the day before the speech, along with a small number of officials. A week earlier, May had written Cameron a letter urging him to back an emergency brake. Cameron had made it clear that, despite Merkel's opposition, he was considering demanding the emergency brake on numbers anyway. 'The PM told them what the Germans had said, and asked for their view on whether we should go ahead and announce in any case,' a Downing Street source said. 'Hammond spoke first, and argued that we just couldn't announce something that would receive an immediate raspberry in Europe. It wouldn't be seen as credible domestically, and it would set us on the path towards Brexit. Theresa said very, very little, and simply said that we just couldn't go against Merkel.'

An eyewitness said, 'The PM was visibly deflated as they left.' Cameron turned to one of his officials and said, 'Look, we tried, but I can't do it without their support. We'll just have to go with the benefits plan. If it wasn't for my lily-livered cabinet colleagues …'

This position might seem reasonable, but given that May and Hammond would later be responsible for negotiating Brexit, it was also instructive of their approach. May was to write a second letter to Cameron on 21 May 2015 urging him to adopt tough immigration measures, but the Cameron aide said, 'It's true she obviously wanted as good an immigration deal as she could get. It's true that she wrote a letter. But when the crunch moment came – do we take a risk, do we go for something that is going to be tougher and that Merkel is not going to back, and that will be tougher to negotiate post the election? – her instinct was that if the Germans don't support it, we can't do it.'

A senior Downing Street source says, 'David Cameron was going for the welfare brake, and he said, "I need an emergency brake. I need to sort this out, because I think that's what will help." Who were the two people who told him not to do that because it's undeliverable? Your new prime minister and chancellor of the exchequer: Theresa May and Philip

Hammond. So when Theresa talks about "I will not take no for an answer," she was the one who folded then. Theresa May and Philip Hammond were the ones to say "You won't get the emergency brake."'

The benefits plan was toughened from a two-year ban on claims to three years, and then again to four years in the final draft. When Cameron finally gave the speech on 28 November, he said, 'Immigration benefits Britain, but it needs to be controlled. It needs to be fair.' He then used language that was to be adopted wholesale by the Leave campaign: 'People want government to have control over the numbers of people coming here ... they want control over who has the right to receive benefits.'

From that point onwards, David Cameron's renegotiation hung primarily on the success of a deal on migrant benefits, which was a pale imitation of the one he really wanted. But without the support of Merkel, May or Hammond he did not feel able to proceed. One close aide thinks this was a 'fundamental misjudgement': 'We genuinely thought at the time of that immigration speech we could get some significant movement on immigration. It evolved into controls on benefits because those are more achievable.' One of the civil servants saw the episode as all too typical of Team Cameron's general approach to Europe: 'That was the moment he gave up on controlling numbers, and it was almost by accident.'

Others think he should have been prepared to ignore the officials, and was too quickly frightened off by Merkel. She had rejected quotas, but she was never put on the spot in the small hours of a summit about an emergency brake on numbers. Ultimately the renegotiation was a political, not a legal, enterprise, and Cameron could have challenged Merkel to help find a solution. 'What I genuinely don't know is whether Merkel in her comments about emergency brakes had really given it any thought as a separate issue,' a senior minister said, 'or whether she treated it as the same issue: "quotas and emergency brakes together".' The whole focus of the JCB speech was to shift the debate to benefits. I wonder up to this day whether, if we'd pushed the emergency brake – in terms of numbers, not on benefits – we could have got that. My gut instinct was that the emergency brake was the outer reaches of negotiability.'

After the general election, the Syrian civil war created a fresh migration crisis which put the issue back at the top of the political agenda. In September 2015 Merkel made the rashest decision of her time in power,

announcing that refugees were welcome in Germany. The British reaction to Merkel's extraordinary offer was 'astonishment', according to a
source who was in touch with the Germans: 'She would defend it by
saying, "What do you expect us to do? We're not going to shoot people."'
The result was a vast human tide that prompted several EU countries to
reinstate border controls, including Germany. The International
Organisation of Migration estimated that one million migrants arrived
in Europe in 2015, three to four times as many as the year before, while
approaching 4,000 lost their lives while attempting to cross the
Mediterranean. Throughout the summer there were almost daily reports
from across the Channel in Calais, where migrants gathered seeking
passage to Britain. Gradually, but detectably, support for Brexit rose.
Andrew Cooper told Cameron the migrant crisis had cost Remain five
percentage points.

Merkel was not the only strong woman giving Cameron grief that
summer. On 30 August, a week after immigration figures were released
showing net migration had hit 330,000, Theresa May wrote a newspaper article announcing that migrants should be banned from entering
Britain unless they had a job to go to. She called for EU leaders to tear
up the rules on freedom of movement, and even questioned the existence of the Schengen Agreement, saying it had led to the deaths of
migrants and placed people at the mercy of people-traffickers. Going
much further than Cameron's renegotiation, she said, 'When it was first
enshrined, free movement meant the freedom to move to a job, not the
freedom to cross borders to look for work or claim benefits.' Five weeks
later May put down another marker with an uncompromising speech
at the Conservative Party conference which left parts of Downing
Street aghast. The speech, written by Nick Timothy, said asylum seek-
ers who entered Britain illegally would be barred from settling permanently in the UK. It led one MP to describe May as 'Enoch Powell in a
dress'.[19]

May's intervention was unwelcome, because it was becoming clear
that the four-year benefits ban was not going to fly with Britain's allies
(who wanted benefits phasing in much quicker). Europe minister David
Lidington approached Llewellyn at the Conservative conference and
said, 'We're not going to get four years.' But he added, 'I am starting to
pick up that people are talking about emergency brakes again.' The nego-
tiators put out feelers. 'The problem was, at that stage, because we'd

spoken so much about migrant benefits, the emergency brake proposal we'd heard from the others and the European Commission was of an emergency brake on welfare, rather than on numbers,' said Lidington. This new idea sounded good, but it meant watering down the plans outlined in the JCB speech, which were already a poor substitute for a proper limit on the number of new arrivals.

Just before party conference Sajid Javid, the business secretary, also floated an idea in conversation with George Osborne. He suggested free movement should be linked to a country's GDP, so migrants from richer countries in the EU could travel freely, but those from poorer nations could not. Javid believed something more on immigration was needed, but he was told the idea was 'not a flier', and not to put anything in writing to Downing Street in case it leaked. Number 10 banned him from addressing a Eurosceptic fringe meeting at the conference.

The realisation that the offering at the referendum would do nothing meaningful to limit immigrant numbers led to another bout of infighting over the scale of Cameron's demands. His younger aides – Mats Persson, Ameet Gill, Daniel Korski and Max Chambers – all wanted a bolder gesture than Ivan Rogers and Tom Scholar were prepared to endorse. 'I can promise you the PM kept coming back to the idea of an emergency brake. That's what he wanted all the way through,' one aide said.

Another member of the inner circle said Cameron and Llewellyn later regretted their caution: 'I know certainly Ed and indeed the PM do look back and think, "We should have probably gone hard and more publicly on the migration."' Cameron's opponents agreed. Daniel Hannan said, 'I think the huge mistake that he made, tactically and strategically, was to put all his eggs in the baskets of migration and benefits.'

Andrew Cooper, who was constantly polling and focus-grouping each iteration of the migrant plan, warned Cameron, as he was drawing up his formal proposals at the start of November 2015, that the benefits brake would not be enough to neutralise immigration as a referendum issue: 'It became clear very early on that it was obviously going to be a massive problem. We tested multiple different versions. The conclusion was: all the things that look achievable don't remotely pass the credibility test with the electorate.'

As Cameron began to finalise his renegotiation demands towards the end of 2015, he was preparing for a referendum that his closest ally George Osborne did not want, by working on a plan to reduce migrant benefits that his chief pollster thought was inadequate because a tougher plan had been rejected as unworkable by Angela Merkel and consequently by Theresa May. And all the while the migration crisis filled television screens, demonstrating the impact of Macmillan's 'events' on politics.

A member of Cameron's team said, 'Perhaps the biggest regret of David's premiership will be not going for the brake back in that speech. In the end, we actually got far-reaching changes to benefits to the surprise of many, even though it contravened every facet of EU law on non-discrimination. The Commission just found a way to bend the rules. But Tom [Scholar] had advised us that any substantial reform on free movement was simply not achievable and that free movement was a holy, inviolable principle. I regret that we trusted Tom too much. Who knows – if we'd gone with our gut, the boss could still be in Number 10 today.'

David Cameron had not yet lost the referendum, but his failure to demand a cap or an emergency brake on migrant numbers left him with a mountain to climb before he had even started. It was a situation the Eurosceptics were straining at the leash to exploit.

2

FOR BRITAIN

Bellamy's restaurant in Westminster is a pretty unglamorous place for a revolution to start. Located in 1 Parliament Street, at the slightly decaying end of the parliamentary estate, it is primarily a haunt for MPs' researchers flirting with their colleagues rather than an arena for discussing the great issues of the time. Yet it was in Bellamy's that a meeting occurred in 1993 which would help propel Britain from the European Union twenty-three years later.

Douglas Carswell was twenty-two, and had just finished a history degree at the University of East Anglia before taking a job 'stuffing envelopes in an MP's office'. If Carswell was typical of other young men educated at Charterhouse in taking the first steps up the political ladder at a tender age, it is tempting to think that he attracted the attention of Daniel Hannan because there was also something exotic about him. Beyond the intensity of his gaze and the lopsided jawline, so sharp it could slice ham, Carswell spent most of his formative years in Uganda, where his father – a Scottish doctor called Wilson Carswell – had diagnosed some of the first cases of HIV. Wilson's experiences under the dictatorship of Idi Amin were the inspiration for the character Dr Nicholas Garrigan in Giles Foden's 1998 novel *The Last King of Scotland*. Carswell later admitted that his libertarianism owed much to his experiences under Amin's 'arbitrary rule'. It also made him susceptible to Daniel Hannan's views about the European Union.

Born in the Peruvian capital Lima, Hannan also spent part of his childhood abroad and escaped to a top public school, in his case Marlborough, before he arrived at Oxford, where he beat Nicky Morgan, the future education secretary and Remain campaigner, to the presidency of the Oxford Union debating society. Hannan was in his first term at university when the Maastricht Treaty 'radicalised' him about leaving the EU: 'I can date exactly the moment of my activism on this issue which has consumed the last twenty-six years of my life. It was during a very short window between the overthrow of Margaret Thatcher and John Major putting his initials to the first draft of the Maastricht Treaty.' In that three-week period Hannan and the future Tory MP Mark Reckless founded the Oxford Campaign for an Independent Britain. 'Maastricht was the moment that the EU extended its jurisdiction into foreign affairs, criminal justice, citizenship, the environment, and also the moment where it adopted all the trappings and symbols of nationhood: the flag, the national anthem,' Hannan said. 'You couldn't con yourself any longer that this was a voluntary association of independent states, or a free-trade area.'

Hannan was also inspired by an interview he had seen with the Latvian foreign minister Ģirts Valdis Kristovskis, whose country was newly free from the Soviet yoke. Asked, on a trip to Britain, if Latvia was a properly sovereign country, he said, 'Yes, Latvia is now more independent than the United Kingdom.' 'That really hit home, that remark,' Hannan recalled. 'I suddenly thought, "My God, he's right." That was when I swore – the old storybooks would call it a terrible oath – that we were going to get out of the European Union, at whatever cost.'

Hannan was one of the most eloquent products of a Eurosceptic movement in the Conservative Party which grew slowly after the 1975 referendum on membership of the Common Market, and found full voice when Margaret Thatcher slammed her handbag on the table and demanded her money back when securing the British rebate in 1984. She would later become the first of three Conservative prime ministers in succession to lose the highest office as a result of the European issue.

The party was bitterly divided by the time John Major took over from Thatcher in November 1990. By the 1997 general election, when Sir James Goldsmith's single-issue Referendum Party grabbed more than 800,000 votes, the Conservative Party was verging on civil war. If Thatcher's fall, after the incision of the knife by her former chancellor and foreign secretary Sir Geoffrey Howe, was the last gasp of the Conservative Europhiles, so John Major's six and a half years in Downing Street were disfigured by the emergence of a group of committed and uncompromising Eurosceptics whom he dismissed as 'bastards' – a term that implies fringe relevance as well as unpalatable behaviour – but whose views (and briefly under Iain Duncan Smith, the sceptics themselves) came to dominate the party.

These Palaeosceptics earned their spurs during the battles over the Maastricht Treaty in 1992, and fought on, limpet-like but in vain, against the subsequent Treaties of Amsterdam (1997) and Lisbon (2007). It is interesting to speculate now about what might have happened if they had been more successful then. Bernard Jenkin said, 'If John Major had not forced through the Maastricht Treaty, and had not opposed a referendum on the Maastricht Treaty, the Maastricht Treaty would never have become ratified. There would have been no euro, no eurozone, no eurozone crisis, no bailout, no European citizenship, no migration crisis, and we would probably still be happily a member of the European Communities.'

When he bumped into Douglas Carswell in Bellamy's in 1993, Daniel Hannan was director of the European Research Group, a support service for Eurosceptic MPs who had agreed to pay him a salary. ERG held regular breakfast meetings in the Attlee Room in the House of Lords under the chairmanship of Malcolm Pearson, a Tory peer who would later defect to Ukip. Regular attendees included the Palaeosceptics, members of the Bruges Group, the Freedom Association and a certain *Times* writer called Michael Gove. At this stage most wanted to return to the pre-Maastricht deal, rather than questioning the result of the 1975 referendum. But when Hannan sat down to lunch with Carswell he immediately told him, 'We need to leave the European Union, and we need a referendum in order to do so.'

Carswell remembered, 'I said, "No, we need to reform the EU from within, we've got to use our influence, we've got to make it come our way." I said absolutely everything that the Cameroonians were saying later. Literally by the time we're having coffee, I think: "Yeah, we need to leave the EU, and this is the way to do it, this guy is talking sense." After forty-five minutes, I'm convinced. Dan spends the next twenty-five years trying to persuade the rest of the party. I wish everyone else in the Tory Party had been around that table. It would have meant a lot less grief.'

While the Palaeosceptics waged constitutional war in the Commons, for two decades Hannan became an intellectual driver of the push for a referendum, with Carswell at his side. When Cameron reneged on his 'cast-iron' pledge of a referendum over the Lisbon Treaty, Hannan resigned his 'admittedly very paltry' frontbench post in the European Parliament. When he called Tory high command in November 2009 to tell them of his decision, Hannan spoke to 'a very senior aide' to Cameron, who bears all the characteristics of Ed Llewellyn, and said, 'Just so you know, this was your last chance to have a referendum on something other than leaving. I'm now devoting myself, full-time, to getting a referendum on "In" or "Out". The response was laughter and a jaunty 'Good luck with that.'

Just over four years later it was party policy.

In 2011 Hannan wrote a blog suggesting the prime minister hold a renegotiation with Brussels and then a referendum afterwards. Now he was only two years ahead of his time. By then he had helped set up 'the People's Pledge'. In 2012 the organisation got the Electoral Reform Society to conduct a complete ballot of every registered voter in the marginal constituencies of Thurrock in Essex, and Cheadle and Hazel Grove in south Manchester, asking whether voters wanted a referendum. On turnouts higher than those seen in local elections, all three voted overwhelmingly in favour. 'It started becoming obvious to people that a referendum was coming,' Hannan said. Another of those involved was a young Eurosceptic called Chris Bruni-Lowe, who was to play a pivotal role in future events.

'Dan put in place many of the key ingredients that would go on to create the Vote Leave team,' Carswell said. 'He was one of the guys who put the machine together, and realised what the machine had to look like. He played an absolutely key role.'

Throughout 2011 and 2012 Hannan, Carswell, Reckless and other Eurosceptics met secretly to plot a guerrilla campaign to secure a referendum. They had gone up in the world from Bellamy's. The clandestine meetings, which included members of the government, met at Tate Britain, half a mile upriver from the Commons. 'Dan suggested it on the grounds that no MP or journalist would have the aesthetic inclination to ever pop into an art gallery in the afternoon,' Carswell said. 'Not once were we ever disturbed.'

The campaign began to bear fruit with the rebellion of the eighty-one. 'That's when actually we won the argument within the party,' Carswell said. 'From then on they stopped arguing against it from first principles, and it became about practicalities.'

Carswell also held talks in his Commons office with Lynton Crosby, the

Australian strategist who masterminded Boris Johnson's two London mayoral election victories; but no agreement was reached to work together.

When Cameron conceded a referendum in the Bloomberg speech, Hannan told the group, 'We've got it, now let's win it.' He had already begun to prepare. Knowing they would be facing the might of the Downing Street machine, he wanted a nascent 'Out' campaign in place in good time. In the summer of 2012 he approached Matthew Elliott and said, 'You are going to need to be the guy to run this thing.' The conversation took place in a summerhouse in the Norfolk garden of Rodney Leach, a Eurosceptic businessman who funded Open Europe.

Elliott, then thirty-four, had begun his career a dozen years earlier as a press officer for the European Foundation, a Eurosceptic campaign group, but made his name in Westminster as the co-founder in 2004 of the Taxpayers' Alliance, which hounded successive governments about wasting public money. In 2009 he also set up Big Brother Watch, a libertarian outfit that campaigned against state intrusion into citizens' lives. Both organisations were run out of 55 Tufton Street in Westminster, home to a network of conservative campaigns which acted as incubators for thrusting young Tories and wannabe spin doctors to learn their craft.

Elliott might have gone to work in Downing Street in 2011, but his appointment was blocked by Nick Clegg. The reason he was *persona non grata* with the Liberal Democrats – and the reason Hannan wanted to hire him – was that Elliott had run the NOtoAV campaign in May that year which crushed Clegg's hopes of electoral reform. Elliott's campaign helped to secure nearly 68 per cent of the vote in the first nationwide referendum for a generation.

Hannan had been impressed by Elliott, even though he thought his campaign – making a case that a 'Yes' vote would be costly because new voting machines would have to be bought – was 'a pile of crap': 'I knew it had to be Matt, not just in the obvious sense that he won it resoundingly, but he had shown huge sense of character in withstanding friendly fire. The anti-AV press were blaming him personally for what they thought was going to be a defeat. He had the strength of character to stick with what his polls were telling him, to disregard all of that. I thought this was the stupidest campaign ever, but he knew that it was working. He stuck to his guns.' Elliott's composure under fire would be seriously tested in the EU referendum campaign as well.

When Hannan approached him, Elliott already 'saw the EU as the next big thing', and had an idea about how he would run a campaign. He was a keen follower of American politics, and during Barack Obama's two election campaigns he had been impressed by the gaggle of groups backing the Democrat candidate which all had the title '… for Obama'. Elliott devised a referendum campaign that would feature different groups branded '… for Britain', and began registering dozens of websites, of which businessforbritain.org would be the centrepiece.

Around Christmas 2012, Elliott found himself on a plane to the US with Chris Bruni-Lowe, then at the People's Pledge. Bruni-Lowe recalled, 'He said he was thinking of a business campaign. He said he was fascinated by things like "Hispanics for Obama", "Latinos for Obama". He said business will be the big one, but we'll have "Bikers for Britain", "Women for Britain" and "Muslims for Britain".' Bruni-Lowe believed Elliott saw these campaigns as paper tigers, with only the business group as a serious campaigning organisation: 'He viewed everything as a front campaign.'

Elliott's other insight was that the best way to mobilise business voices in favour of leaving was to work initially with the grain of Cameron's renegotiation, rather than declaring immediately for Brexit. In April 2013, three months after the Bloomberg speech, Elliott set up Business for Britain, with the slogan 'Change or go': 'I realised business was the way into it. We did not do it as a hard Brexit campaign but went along the lines of the renegotiation, albeit pushing further what the PM would be thinking.'

The early backers included Eurosceptic stalwarts like Peter Cruddas, the former Conservative Party chairman, and Daniel Hodson, founder of the People's Pledge, but also more moderate sceptics like Stuart Rose, the former boss of Marks & Spencer. Some of those invited were also pro-Europeans, like Iain Anderson, the chairman of Cicero Group and a former spokesman for Ken Clarke. He said, 'I was invited along to talk to Business for Britain just in advance of it launching. It was put to me in that meeting with the BfB team that this was about strengthening the prime minister's hand in his renegotiation.' One businessman invited said the pitch was that BfB would 'put lead in Cameron's pencil'.

Having a broad base of support gave Business for Britain credibility with the media, and it quickly eclipsed Open Europe as the primary voice on EU matters in Westminster, in part thanks to its campaign director Rob Oxley, who Elliott had plucked from the Taxpayers'

Alliance. Oxley, the product of a Lincolnshire grammar school and family in Zimbabwe, was young, smart, hard-working, and understood the media. He was the perfect front man for Elliott.

Business for Britain's non-committal stance on Brexit did alienate some, including Bruni-Lowe, who wanted to see a full-bore campaign to leave the EU. Nigel Farage doubted that Elliott himself was committed to Brexit. 'When I was there, the majority of people were broadly Eurosceptic but not all Leavers,' said Bruni-Lowe.

The divisions between the Conservative and Ukip wings of Euroscepticism which blew up so spectacularly in the referendum campaign were sown in that period between 2012 and the general election. On the Tory side they were driven by an insight Douglas Carswell had about the role Nigel Farage should play in a referendum campaign, which emerged from polling data in 2012 and 2013. It was neatly captured by Sunder Katwala in a piece for the *New Statesman* in April 2014, 'the Farage Paradox'. Stated simply, the more media exposure Farage had, the higher Ukip's national vote share went – but at the same time the lower national support for leaving the EU fell. 'The most fervent advocates for leaving the EU were some of Remain's best chances for winning the referendum,' Carswell said. When Brussels was bailing out debt-ridden Greece, disapproval of EU membership rose to around 60 per cent. 'We thought, "We are going to win this." Then Ukip started to take off in the polls ...'

In 2013 YouGov's tracking poll on support for Brexit showed a sixteen-point lead for 'Out'. But by April 2014, with Ukip on the march, the two sides were tied, and YouGov's first poll after Farage trounced Nick Clegg in televised debates on Europe ahead of the EU elections that spring gave 'In' a six-point lead.[1] 'You see Ukip taking off, disapproval of the EU going down,' said Carswell. 'It's a direct correlation. This is what really obsesses us. We start to think we're going to lose [the referendum].' Carswell could see that to win, Ukip and its army of ground campaigners would be important, but he was worried that the party's image with the wider public was hurting the chances of Brexit. He could also see that Downing Street would do all they could to promote Farage and Ukip as the face of the 'Out' campaign: 'We understood that there was going to become a symbiotic alliance between the Remainers in Downing Street, and the purple Faragists.'

In the summer of 2014 he decided to do something about it. In great secrecy, and with Hannan's knowledge, Carswell began secret talks with Farage about defecting from the Conservative Party to Ukip. What Carswell now admits is that he jumped ship with the express goal of changing the image of Ukip and ensuring that it was an asset rather than a liability in the referendum campaign. A desire to 'do something about' the Farage paradox, he said, 'explains my behaviour subsequently': 'We wanted to put men in their trench, and to do that, we had to go over the top. And on 28 August 2014, some of us started going over the top, and we talked about a very different type of Ukip. We tried to decontaminate the brand.'

That was the day Carswell walked into 1 Great George Street, a stone's throw from the House of Commons, and stunned the waiting media, who had been expecting Ukip to unveil a new celebrity donor, by announcing that he was defecting from the Conservatives and calling an immediate by-election. Chris Bruni-Lowe crossed to Ukip with him, and would help run his campaign. In his defection speech, Carswell immediately struck a different tone from his new leader, hailing Britain as 'open and tolerant', praising political correctness as 'straightforward good manners' and declaring, 'I am not against immigration.' He condemned 'angry nativism' and said, 'We must welcome those who come here to contribute.' The detox was under way.

In the by-election on 9 October, David Cameron's forty-eighth birthday, Carswell slightly increased his majority to 12,404, with a 44 per cent swing from the Tories. In his acceptance speech he told Ukip, 'We must be a party for all Britain and all Britons, first and second generation as much as every other.'

He admits now that this was all part of the secret plan to win the referendum: 'Nigel did a superb job in making sure we got the referendum. One of the two reasons I joined Ukip was because I thought I could give an additional heave. But the other was all about trying to detoxify this brand that was ruining our chances of winning the referendum. I could see where this was going. If it became a choice between being rude about Romanian immigrants versus the economy, we would lose 60–40.' In April 2014 Farage had said he would be 'concerned' if Romanian men moved in next door.

If David Cameron was bewildered by Carswell's defection, he was incandescent four weeks later when Mark Reckless overshadowed the start of the Tory conference by jumping ship as well. The prime minister openly denounced Reckless for betraying the Tory activists who had helped 'get his fat arse' on the Commons benches. Reckless held his Rochester and Strood seat in the subsequent by-election on 20 November, but was to lose it to the Tories at the general election six months later.

The hunt was on for more defectors. Daniel Hannan had considered changing parties during the Tate Gallery talks, but ruled it out after the Bloomberg speech. Carswell said, 'Two [other MPs] were prepared to do it, but the circumstances slightly changed.' Shortly after the Rochester and Strood by-election, with panic rife in Downing Street, Cameron announced that he would legislate to hold a referendum within the first hundred days of a Tory government being elected. 'That closed off the possibility of anyone else coming over,' Carswell said.

That winter the Tate conspirators' plan appeared to be working. The huge excitement of the defections and the two by-election wins appeared to have solved the Farage paradox. Ukip were on just under 20 per cent in the polls, but there was no discernible downward shift in Euroscepticism. 'We looked like winners,' said Carswell. 'We thought at that point the Tate strategy had worked. Given what transpired, the battle had barely begun.'

During the 2015 general election campaign, Nigel Farage reasserted himself in the battle for the soul of Ukip. He sought to maximise the party's core support with his trademark provocative comments. In a radio interview he said breastfeeding mothers should 'sit in the corner'. During the main televised leaders' debate he complained about foreigners with HIV coming to Britain for treatment, at a cost to the NHS of £25,000 per year each. Carswell despaired. Despite predictions that Ukip might win between six and ten seats, only Carswell was successful, holding on to Clacton. Farage himself fell nearly 3,000 votes short in South Thanet, the seventh time he had tried and failed to be elected to Parliament.

Carswell breathed a sigh of relief when Farage stood down as leader after the election, fulfilling a promise he had made during the campaign, and handing the reins to Suzanne Evans, the media-savvy author of the party's manifesto. But there was despair among Ukippers who wanted a new direction when Farage un-resigned just three days later, sparking a coup to force him out again. Patrick O'Flynn, Ukip's economic spokesman, broke cover to brand Farage a 'snarling, thin-skinned, aggressive' figure who made the party look like a 'personality cult'. But the attempted putsch failed, and O'Flynn resigned. The result was a simmering civil war which played out for months as Farage loyalists went to war with his internal critics, with Carswell at the top of the list.

Chris Bruni-Lowe, who had switched his allegiance from Carswell to Farage, said it was Carswell's disdain for the leader that encouraged him to return: 'Nigel *had* decided he was going to leave, but Douglas Carswell called him that morning and said to him, "Are you planning on coming back?" Nigel said, "Well, I've not really given it much thought, but I probably will now there's going to be a referendum." And Carswell says, "You cannot do that, you're toxic. You'll damage the cause." And Nigel thought, "Well, fuck this."'

But Carswell was adamant that the election campaign had undone the good work of the previous autumn: 'During the campaign we talked about breastfeeding on LBC, we talked about HIV, we ran a general election designed to appeal to the base rather than attract support from beyond the base. It was a disastrous election strategy. After the general election, I thought to myself, "You can't detoxify the Ukip brand under the current leadership."' He resolved to 'switch my efforts to detoxify the Leave brand' instead, aligning with Matthew Elliott's operation to ensure that it became the official 'Out' campaign and to prevent Farage being a prominent part of it.

Carswell's first move was to write an article for *The Times* urging Farage to 'take a break', and arguing that the referendum campaign ahead should focus on the costs of EU membership 'instead of feeding the idea that EU membership is synonymous with immigration'.[2]

Farage was baffled: 'I read that and thought, "Fucking hell! I've spent ten years trying to do that!"'

The degree to which immigration should be front and centre of the referendum was a faultline that was to bitterly divide Ukip from Carswell and the Tory campaigners for the next thirteen months.

With the general election approaching, Matthew Elliott was under pressure to step up his campaigning and make explicit that Business for Britain would lead the 'No' or 'Out' campaign. In February 2015 he was approached by Richard Tice, a millionaire property financier who was a BfB signatory. 'He was saying, "Come on, why isn't BfB for Leave?"' Elliott recalled. 'I explained "change or go" had to be our position. It was a way we could keep as many business people engaged as possible. And there was always the possibility the PM would go for a more substantial deal than people thought he would, and we should therefore be urging him to push the boundaries of what renegotiation meant, rather than assuming it was a completely lame exercise.' Tice went away dissatisfied, but would soon find someone willing to run a more aggressive campaign.

In April, the month before the general election, another important meeting took place at the Caistor Hall Hotel in Norwich. David Campbell Bannerman, a Tory MEP who had previously been the chairman and deputy leader of Ukip, was determined to ensure that different branches of the Eurosceptic family worked together if there was a referendum campaign. 'I knew it was a bit like herding cats, and the real problem we were going to have was going to be fighting amongst ourselves,' he said.

Campbell Bannerman set up a 'Contact Group', and invited Elliott and other prominent sceptics like the businesswoman Ruth Lea and Rory Broomfield of the Freedom Association. The gathering would later be described by the Electoral Commission as a 'pivotal moment', and a key reason why Vote Leave was designated as the official 'Out' campaign.

Campbell Bannerman was also involved in another development that spring, the creation of Conservatives for Britain, the parliamentary wing of Elliott's operation. When Cameron won his majority in May, Elliott was shocked: 'I realised, "Crikey, I've actually got to set up this referendum campaign."'

At a lunch the following day Elliott met Campbell Bannerman, plus Nick Wood from the Westminster PR firm Media Intelligence Partners, a grizzled, chain-smoking former *Times* and *Express* political journalist who became Iain Duncan Smith's communications director when he was Tory leader. Campbell Bannerman recalled Elliott's shock: 'Matthew looked horrified at winning his own election. I don't think he expected it.' The discussion quickly turned to how to put pressure on the newly elected government. The strategy agreed was to form a group of Eurosceptic Conservative MPs, MEPs and peers to turn the screws on Cameron during the negotiations. Campbell Bannerman agreed to become co-chairman and run the operation in Brussels.

For the key post of co-chairman in the Commons, Elliott and Daniel Hannan approached Steve Baker, the MP for Wycombe. At forty-four, Baker had only been an MP since 2010 – but he was liked and trusted by all factions on the Conservative benches. An RAF engineer who retrained as a chartered surveyor and then a software engineer, Baker was devoutly religious – he was baptised during a full-body immersion in the sea – and had been gifted with the innocent face of a chorister. Behind the smile, Hannan and Elliott also saw a man prepared to take risks: Baker was a keen skydiver, with more than two hundred jumps to his name.

When Hannan approached him, he had just one pitch: 'There's no one else to do it.' Baker himself joked later that he got the job because he was a 'cleanskin', untainted by the battles of the past. Hannan remembered, 'I thought, everyone likes Steve Baker, everyone trusts him, he's a born-again Christian, he is just incapable of dishonesty.'

Baker was also a resolute Eurosceptic, who like Hannan had come into politics to get Britain out of the EU. Unlike Hannan, his inspiration was not a Latvian foreign minister, but David Cameron himself. Baker had flirted with the idea of joining Ukip, but decided the Tory Party was the vessel that would bring about Brexit: 'One of the principal reasons I knew the Conservative Party could be relied upon on the EU is that in 2007 David Cameron went to the Czech Republic and made a speech in which he said the EU was the "last gasp of an outdated ideology, a philosophy which has no place in our new world of freedom". David Cameron inspired me to join the Conservative Party.'

Cameron soon had cause to regret his own powers of persuasion. Friday, 5 June 2015 was the fortieth anniversary of the 1975 EU referendum, and Baker, Campbell Bannerman, Wood and Walsh decided it would be the perfect moment to launch Conservatives for Britain. Elliott was out of the country, and was nearly as blindsided as the prime minister when the story announcing the creation of the organisation appeared on the front page of the *Sunday Telegraph* on 7 June. By that point CfB had been meeting in secret for a month, and had already recruited fifty Tory MPs. Cameron admitted to Baker later that he was 'spooked' that no intelligence on the operation had reached him. Campbell Bannerman recalled, 'It wasn't expected, and we hit the Remain campaign very early and very hard. Steve did an excellent job of getting people on board.'

A week later, Baker had recruited 110 Tory MPs, thirteen peers and twelve MEPs. Sympathetic cabinet ministers privately signed up to the mailing list. Later that week Labour MPs launched a sister group, Labour for Britain, to escalate hostilities. Kate Hoey, Graham Stringer, Kelvin Hopkins and Gisela Stuart were all on board, along with the leading Labour donor John Mills, a veteran of the 1975 referendum campaign.

But there was a more seismic announcement to come. Elliott flew home and resolved to exercise greater control over the MPs. He had already secretly recruited just the man to do that. On 14 June the *Sunday Times* revealed that Dominic Cummings had been charged with setting up the 'Out' campaign. For Eurosceptics their hour had come. And so, now, had their man.

3

DOM AND ARRON

Few people would have given the scruffily-dressed man on the bicycle a second glance as he pedalled between offices and coffee shops in Westminster during May 2015. Dominic Cummings never wore a tie, preferred Converse trainers to work shoes, and with his high forehead and wire-rimmed spectacles had the air of a middle-ranking civil servant on an awayday – if your idea of a civil servant is of a hedge dragged through a man backwards. The impression of dishevelled provincial mediocrity was hardly dispelled by the flat vowels of his native Durham or his preference for conducting business meetings in Pret a Manger. Only his penetrating eyes hinted that this was one of Britain's most shrewd – and feared – political operators.

A former special adviser to Michael Gove, Cummings left the government in early 2014 after waging war on the educational establishment, the Liberal Democrats and the Downing Street machine in equal measure. He sat out the general election, not even bothering to watch the leaders' debates on television. But as Parliament reconvened ten days after the election, his phone began to ring. He received a series of calls from Matthew Elliott, Bernard Jenkin and Stuart Wheeler, the former Tory donor who had defected to Ukip, asking him to set up the 'Out' campaign.

Cummings had form where Europe and referendums were concerned. He was campaign director at Business for Sterling, which helped to keep Britain out of the euro. In November 2004 he led the 'No' campaign in a referendum on whether to set up a north-east regional assembly, winning a crushing 78 per cent of the vote, a result so emphatic it persuaded John Prescott to abandon the idea altogether.

With Elliott's success running the NOtoAV campaign, he and Cummings could muster three major campaign victories between them, but Elliott's experience during the 2011 referendum had convinced him that he was not the right man to take day-to-day charge of the campaign: 'I know my skillset is raising funds, organisation-building, gladhanding – which are very useful; it's part of the campaign. But one of the things I learnt during NOtoAV is I didn't really like and I'm not very good at running a war room. We needed somebody in there who was fearless, who was a warrior, who had a great strategic mind, who frankly had the appetite to take something on at a time when no one else thought it could be done. And Dom was the man to do that.'

Cummings is a Marmite figure, viewed by his allies as one of the most talented public policy professionals of his generation, a thinker with a Stakhanovite work ethic and a ruthless desire to promote his ideas, someone equipped with a rare ability to see around corners. For his enemies – who are legion – he is a raging menace, a Tory bastard love-child of Damian McBride and Alastair Campbell, a practitioner of the dark arts. Like all caricatures, there is some truth in both these portraits.

Those Cummings had angered in the past included David Cameron, most of his aides and Iain Duncan Smith, to whom he was briefly direc-tor of strategy before quitting and labelling IDS 'incompetent' as the Tory leader. When the coalition government was formed in 2010 Andy Coulson, Cameron's director of communications, barred Cummings from any job in Whitehall. He continued to advise Michael Gove, for whom he had worked since 2007, from afar, but only became his special adviser once Coulson had fallen from grace as a result of the phone-hack-ing scandal. Craig Oliver, Coulson's successor, was frequently infuriated to learn of Gove's planned education reforms from the media, and devel-oped a heartfelt detestation of Cummings which dulled his judgement. When it emerged that Cummings would run the 'Out' campaign, Oliver texted a journalist, 'Quaking in our boots about Dominic Cummings. Not.' That hubris would lead to nemesis a year later. When he left the government, Cameron himself labelled Cummings 'a career psycho-path'.[1] Nick Clegg called him 'a loopy individual'.

But no other special adviser in the coalition years bent a department to their will like Cummings did; no other worked out their goals and drove through reforms as effectively in the face of widespread civil service opposition. No other special adviser wrote a 240-page thesis on their particular area of expertise ('some thoughts on education and polit-ical priorities') which offered learned observations about Thucydides and statistical modelling via *The Brothers Karamazov*. Cummings was a true Renaissance man, combining highbrow humanity with a taste for medieval Whitehall warfare. If no other special adviser sparked such loathing, none generated the same levels of loyalty either.

Cummings' fearlessness in the face of authority had been forged in dark corners of the world. How many others, after graduating from Oxford with a First in Ancient and Modern History in 1994, would move to Russia for three years to help set up a new airline flying from Samara, on the Volga, to Vienna? KGB threats were issued, the airline only got one passenger, and the pilot took off without him. How many others after winning the north-east referendum would have retreated for two years to a bunker he and his father had built under their farm in Durham to read science and history in an attempt to understand the world?[2]

One of Cummings' heroes was James Carville, Bill Clinton's legendary message man, who revelled in the sobriquet 'the Ragin' Cajun' on account of his fiery temper and Louisiana roots, a man immortalised on film in *The War Room*, a documentary on Clinton's come-from-behind win in 1992. 'Dom watched *The War Room*, I would guess, forty to fifty times,' a friend said. 'He would sing the theme music. The missing Dom years were basically spent in a bunker under the Pennines watching *The War Room* on repeat.'

There is much of Carville in Cummings' approach. When his involvement in the campaign was revealed under the headline 'Tory bovver boy leads "No" fight', a Conservative aide remarked admiringly, 'Dom knows how to win, and he doesn't care who he pisses off in the process.'[3]

Cummings had never stopped being Eurosceptic, but his three years in government had radicalised him. The EU was, he believed, like much of Whitehall 'programmed to fail': 'It's a crap 1950s idea, it cannot work.' It was also stifling his efforts to reform education. In a blog written in 2014, Cummings' rage at the impotence of British ministers was vividly demonstrated: 'In order to continue the pretence that cabinet government exists, all these EU papers are circulated in the red boxes. Nominally, these are "for approval". They have a little form attached for the secretary of state to tick. However, because they are EU papers, this "approval" process is pure Potemkin village. If a cabinet minister replies saying – "I do not approve, this EU rule is stupid and will cost a fortune" – then someone from the Cabinet Office calls their private office and says, "Did your minister get pissed last night, he appears to have withheld approval on this EU regulation." If the private office replies saying "No, the minister actually thinks this is barmy and he is withholding consent," then [Ed] Llewellyn calls them to say "Ahem, old boy, the PM would prefer it if you lie doggo on this one." In the very rare cases where a minister is so infuriated that he ignores Llewellyn, then [cabinet secretary Sir Jeremy] Heywood calls to explain to them that they have no choice but to approve, so please tick your box and send in your form, pronto. Game over."[4]

With Cummings' appointment, Elliott had picked someone with an almost unique combination of Euroscepticism, organisational nous and the rage to fight a winning campaign. Douglas Carswell believed the nascent 'Out' operation had now found the third of its 'three indispensables': 'There were three people who if they hadn't been born or didn't exist, or weren't central in the referendum campaign, it means we would have lost. Number one is Dominic Cummings, number two is Matthew Elliott, and number three is Daniel Hannan. Every single other person played an important role, but those three were vital.'

When he arrived, Cummings knew exactly what he wanted to do with the campaign. In May and June 2014 he had been hired by Elliott to do polling and focus groups on how an 'Out' campaign might position itself. The paper he wrote one friend called 'the *ur* document of the campaign'. Cummings realised that the people and the views that would hold the key to a referendum victory were very far removed from the sensibilities of the London elite. He himself went to a fee-paying school, and in December 2011 had married Mary Wakefield, the deputy editor of the *Spectator* and daughter of Sir Humphry Wakefield, of Chillingham Castle in Northumberland. They lived in some comfort in Islington, the north London borough synonymous with the metropolitan moneyed classes. But Cummings remembered his upbringing in the provinces, rooted in the Durham yeoman class, and constructed his campaign plan accordingly.

A close ally said, 'He found that people in market towns in the Midlands hate London, hate the elites, think more money should go to the NHS, hate bankers and are not very keen on foreigners. He found that Europe was deeply unpopular, but that if you wanted to reach people you had to talk about immigration and the NHS. This was a campaign that would be ruthlessly focused on people as they actually are. There are two sorts of political communications operators in this business. There are people who see the population as they would like them to be, and there are people who see the population, ruthlessly, as they actually are. There is the wishful-thinking element, and there is the winning element.'

When Cummings met Elliott in May 2015, 'There was a road map already done.' His campaign blueprint, chillingly prescient of what would come to pass two years later, was outlined in an article for *The Times* on 26 June 2014. He wrote: 'The combination of immigration, benefits, and human rights dominates all discussion of politics and Europe. People think that immigration is "out of control" [and] puts public services under intolerable strain.' Crucially, the 'biggest change' Cummings noticed from when he was fighting to keep Britain out of the euro was that 'people now spontaneously connect the issue of immigration and the EU. The policy that they raise and discuss most is "the Australian points system for immigration" and many realise that membership of the EU makes this impossible ... The second strongest argument for leaving is that "we can save a fortune and spend that money on the NHS or whatever we want" ... On issue after issue they side with "let's take back control" over "we gain more by sharing power".' Cummings concluded that the referendum choice would come down to 'Do you fear economic disaster?' against 'the prize of controlling immigration and saving all the cash'.[5] He saw the linkage between immigration and control as the key to a referendum victory.

And yet there are hints that he did not want to focus on migration to the detriment of other arguments. Four days later his blog appeared, in which the very first point he made was: 'The official OUT campaign does not need to focus on immigration. The main thing it needs to say on immigration is "if you are happy with the status quo on immigration, then vote to stay IN".' Instead, he said, 'The OUT campaign has one essential task – to neutralise the fear that leaving may be bad for jobs and living standards. This requires a grassroots movement based on small businesses.'

Cummings and Elliott were to work hard to enlist business support, but ultimately they failed to get the backing they hoped for. But Cummings did understand, even in 2014, that Cameron would struggle to neutralise immigration as an issue, and that outsiders like Nigel Farage might have a role to play alongside the formal campaign: 'Immigration is now such a powerful dynamic in public opinion that a) no existing political force can stop people being so worried about it and ... b) it is therefore not necessary for the main campaign to focus on it in a referendum (others will anyway) and focusing on it would alienate other crucial parts of the electorate.'[6]

Throughout 2015 Farage and Ukip complained that Cummings did not understand that immigration was the key to victory, and would not make it the centrepiece of his campaign. These writings show that he did understand the issue, particularly its linkage with strain on the NHS. But in 2015 his priority was to get a fair hearing from the media, and that involved downplaying immigration.

As Cummings moved to build a campaign team, he was quickly reminded of why he had stepped away from Planet Eurosceptic. He told Elliott that Business for Britain would have to become a full Brexit outfit, or he would leave. A source close to Cummings said he despaired at 'dealing with a whole bunch of Tory MPs who were totally and utterly clueless about organisation, strategy, management and a whole lot of donors who were very reluctant to do anything'. Others told him, 'There's no way we can win.'

However, Cummings did develop a good relationship with Steve Baker – whom he judged 'one of the very few honest MPs' – which would prove useful in the months ahead. Though the two had a series of run-ins, Cummings never resorted to his most objectionable behaviour with Baker. Early in their relationship he said his approach would follow Bismarck's 'With a gentleman, a gentleman and a half; with a pirate, a pirate and a half.'

While Baker was a gentleman, Cummings was very soon butting heads with a fellow pirate.

On first inspection, Arron Banks does not have much in common with the man who would become his mortal foe. Short where Cummings is tall, brash where Cummings is cerebral, a fervent critic of 'failed special advisers' where Cummings was a serial creature of Westminster, a devotee of Mammon where Cummings is driven by the values of an Odyssean education. But look closer and the two might be cousins. Both share a fervent Euroscepticism, a loathing of most MPs, an ability to put other people's backs up, an absolute conviction that they are right, and an utter refusal to back down.

Banks, who spent his early childhood in South Africa – where he owns part of a diamond mine – was a successful businessman who had made around £100 million from insurance firms like GoSkippy.com and

Southern Rock, but was largely unknown outside politics until October 2014, when he abandoned the Tory Party and offered £100,000 to Ukip instead. When William Hague declared that he was 'someone we have never heard of', Banks promptly raised the donation to £1 million. To complete the portrait of an eccentric political berserker, he boasted about his stash of assault weapons in South Africa and about being expelled from school for what he called an 'accumulation of offences', including selling stolen communion wine to other boys.[7] He married a Russian model, had five children and bought a mansion north of Bristol previously occupied by musician Mike Oldfield, of *Tubular Bells* fame.

After the general election, Banks went to Farage and Chris Bruni-Lowe and offered to make another major donation to turn Ukip into a more professional outfit. In the midst of the leadership coup, and convinced the party was unreformable, they sought to divert his enthusiasm and cash towards Europe instead. They were driven by a growing belief that Elliott and Business for Britain would not commit to campaign for Brexit. Bruni-Lowe said to Banks, 'Why don't you think about setting up a referendum campaign?'

Banks did not need much persuading. His views had been shaped by Maastricht – 'I couldn't believe John Major sold out the country in the way he did.' Now he came to regard the Elliott operation as a similar establishment stitch-up. 'We got started because Nigel asked us to,' Banks said. 'His opinion was that if the organisation didn't get started quickly, we wouldn't have the time to match what the Remain camp was going to do. It was apparent that Business for Britain had no intention of getting the campaign started until Cameron came back with his deal, and they had a lot of people who didn't even want to leave Europe. Didn't take us too long to work out!'

Divisions with Elliott hardened when Farage and Bruni-Lowe were invited on a cruise in June 2015 organised by the Midlands Industrial Council, a group of influential donors of whom the businessman David Wall was the prime mover. 'Matthew was there to talk about his strategy,' said Bruni-Lowe. He said, "I'm planning to do this big campaign, we don't know what we're going to name it yet, we don't know when we're going launch it yet."' Elliott's hands were tied because some of the businessmen on the cruise were Business for Britain signatories, so he had to be careful not to exceed the terms of the campaign they had signed up to.

Bruni-Lowe said to Elliott, 'If you're going to do this campaign, why don't you get Nigel and every other person in a room and divvy up what they can and can't do? If you don't do that and you let Nigel out into the wild, then you lose control.'

When the ship docked at Jersey Farage asked to see Elliott, and they went to a pub with Bruni-Lowe. Elliott talked about the people he was trying to hire, but the Ukip pair regarded his answers as 'ill-defined', and shared a concern that 'there was no strategy'. They disagreed with him about the role of immigration and Farage in the campaign. Afterwards Farage turned to Bruni-Lowe and said, 'Shit, we've got a problem. We need to get Banks going as quickly as possible.'

On 21 June Banks briefed a story to the *Sunday Telegraph* announcing that he was going to raise £20 million to fund a campaign to leave, provisionally called 'No thanks, we're going global', the first of several incarnations of his 'Out' campaign. 'He went before Elliott,' said Bruni-Lowe. 'Banks basically gatecrashed it.'

From the beginning Banks had a brash role model in mind for winning votes and antagonising his opponents. He told Bruni-Lowe: 'The only way I'm going to do this is by being slightly Trump-esque, which is attack everyone to the point where I can get parity with them – and then try and compete with them on quality. I've got call centres, I'm ten times better than them.'

The second 'No' campaign was up and running even before the first had got properly organised. Its goal was not, initially at least, to usurp the Elliott–Cummings effort, but to chivvy them along and give a platform for Farage. 'Nigel and I effectively got Banks to set this up in order to give Nigel a voice,' Bruni-Lowe remembered, 'because it became clear when we sat down with Elliott that he didn't want to touch Nigel with a barge pole.'

Once unleashed, however, Banks was not the sort of man to play second violin to anyone else. He quickly showed he was not messing about by offering Lynton Crosby £2 million to run the campaign. Banks had stood for election as a Conservative council candidate back in the early 1990s, and his first campaign had been run by Mark Fullbrook, now the 'F' in Crosby's CTF Partners. Now he called Fullbrook to dangle the cash. 'They thought about it for a week but then declined it,' Banks recalled. 'Said they couldn't do that to Dave.' Banks shopped around and hired Gerry Gunster, a US political consultant who had won more than thirty referendums across the pond.

In July the rival campaign chiefs held peace talks in Elliott's office at
55 Tufton Street. Banks brought along Richard Tice, the property investor who had tried to get Elliott to declare for 'Out' in February. It was not
a meeting of minds. As Cummings remembers the discussion, Banks
announced, 'Me and Richard have been thinking about this for a few
months and we are going to set up the campaign for the Leave side. The
MPs don't know what they're doing.'

With this, at least, Cummings could agree. But then Banks also
attacked the men sitting on the other side of the table, who he saw as
products of the SW1 establishment: 'You guys don't know what you're
doing, all these Westminster institutions are crap.' This was particularly
cutting for Elliott, since he ran several of the groups from the office in
which they were sitting.

Elliott says, 'Banks's approach to that meeting was very much "I'm
going to be doing this, I know what I'm doing, you guys are Tories in the
pocket of Number 10 who have no intention of setting up a campaign,
I'm going to get on and do this. Either come with me or you'll be blown
away."'

Cummings recalls Banks saying, 'I've got more money than any of you
and I'm much more clued-up than any of you, so it's really a question for
you guys of, do you want to be part of what we're doing or not?'

Banks looked at Cummings and Elliott, but all he could were the faces
of two Westminster lifers. 'They just looked at us across the table and
said "You don't understand politics,"' Banks recalled, 'We just said, "All
right, let's get going then. We'll show you what we can do." That kicked
off the whole thing. I think both sides thought the other were idiots. I've
made hundreds of millions of pounds in commerce, and from what I can
see they've done absolutely nothing with their lives. In life, you get
people who are so clever they're stupid. Dominic Cummings certainly
falls into that category.'

Cummings did not know Banks, but he knew the type – cleverer than
a lot of MPs but out of his depth in terms of politics, a man who 'didn't
understand what he didn't understand'. He had dealt with self-made men
before. They believed in 'my way or the highway'. Banks was the kind of
bullish character who would create division rather than bring people
together. He also made it clear at the meeting that he was a great admirer
of Nigel Farage, and believed he should be the front man for the
campaign. Cummings concluded that judgement was a 'massive strategic

error'. Thanks to the work he had done in 2014, he believed that no campaign run and fronted by Farage could win. Banks could be useful, but Cummings had no intention of working closely with him.

Following the meeting, Banks 'blew hot and cold'. First, he tried to peel Cummings away from Elliott to work for him instead: 'You should come with me, I'll pay you loads of money.' Over the summer Banks texted Cummings and offered him a salary of £200,000 and a win bonus of the same amount. He claimed later that this was 'psychological warfare': 'It was definitely intended to destabilise them and also to show power, to show we could buy whoever we wanted.'

Banks also looked at Business for Britain's 'reform or leave' stance, and tried to convince Cummings that Elliott was 'not really committed to Out'. His mistake, though, was to assume that Cummings and Elliott were two peas in a pod. On one occasion he said to Elliott, 'All you guys are doing is trying to stay close with Cameron and get a job at Number 10.' No one with any knowledge of Cummings' contemptuous view of Cameron could have made such a comment.

Initially, Cummings found Banks's activities helpful because he could use him as leverage to 'bounce' other people into helping For Britain. He would tell them, 'If you don't set something up, Ukip will do it and we'll lose the referendum 65–35.' Cummings said, 'The fact that Farage was trying to get control of it was definitely useful to me in the early stage up until the end of July.' Quite soon, though, Banks became a nuisance.

A second effort was made to patch up relations a month later when Banks hosted Elliott at his club, 5 Hertford Street. 'Nigel and I were plotting the revolution from Mayfair,' Banks laughed. The meeting was called to discuss funding for the campaign. Banks says Elliott had questioned where he was going to raise the £20 million he had promised. 'If I have to write the cheque myself, I'll do it,' he replied. The distrust remained.

Daniel Hannan kept hearing from senior Tories and donors who could not understand why Elliott was refusing to cooperate with the energetic Banks: 'I spent most of that summer explaining to people why it would end badly. Every single one of them came back soon afterwards, saying, "God this man is impossible."'

What Banks and Farage ignored about Business for Britain and Conservatives for Britain was that by initially backing the renegotiation, the campaign was able to help define what it ought to look like. Throughout the post-election period, BfB briefed stories to the newspapers setting the bar higher and higher, culminating in a colossal thousand-page report called 'Change or Go: How Britain would gain influence and prosper outside an unreformed EU', which was serialised by the *Telegraph* from 21 June, ahead of the key European summit at which Cameron was due to offer a broad outline of his demands. It called for the return of the British veto and the right of national parliaments to overturn EU laws, as well as the repatriation of all social and employment laws.[8]

Rob Oxley, Elliott's spin doctor, said, 'The government were desperately trying to bring down the bar; we were trying to put it up there. There were loads of people who were saying, "You're traitors, you're just going to back Cameron." But I have no doubt that the work we did there was hugely instrumental in how the negotiations were perceived in February.'

The 'Out' campaign got fresh impetus when Cameron gave an overview of his demands at the European Council in Brussels in June. Much of the content of the Bloomberg speech and some of Cameron's other public pledges was missing. Cummings saw it as an 'important' moment. He called donors to say, 'Even if he comes back with what he's asking for, it is less than what you guys wanted, so you have an excuse to jump ship before the process has finished.'

A story which the *Guardian* published just before Cameron's summit press conference helped to turn the tide. It revealed that Cameron's plan was to run a referendum campaign based on the risks of Brexit. The paper reported a leaked account of a private meeting between the prime minister and a fellow EU leader which stated, 'He believes that people will ultimately vote for the status quo if the alternatives can be made to appear risky.'[9] The Italian embassy was suspected of the leak. It was the first proof that Cameron would re-enact the 'Project Fear' approach he had deployed in the Scottish referendum.

Rob Oxley made sure the story was distributed to key MPs: 'All the Eurosceptics read it. After that point we were able to start moving the Tory backbenchers.'

The summit also persuaded Elliott to act: 'That's when we started the process of moving BfB from "change or go" to being Leave.' By the end of July the board of Business for Britain had agreed that they should switch their allegiance fully to the 'Out' camp. A friend of Cummings said, 'Although Elliott was nervy about going out so fast, he essentially realised that if he didn't, then Dom would go home and Arron would take over the thing.'

There were already tensions between the two campaign leaders. MPs warned Elliott, 'You're going to be airbrushed out. Cummings is going to get the credit.' The seeds were sown of divisions not just between For Britain and Ukip, but within the campaign itself, which would explode a few months later. The issue grew more pronounced as Cummings hired the two members of staff he most needed to win the referendum.

Cummings' top priority was finding a director of communications. Initially he had only one person in mind – his old colleague from the Department for Education, Henry de Zoete. 'Zoot', as he was known, had been Gove's media spad throughout the battles with the educational establishment of the coalition years, but had left government to start his own company. Tall with a wispy ginger beard, de Zoete was the *yang* to Cummings' *yin* – calm when he was aggressive, softly-spoken when he was raising his voice, polite when Cummings was blunt to the point of rudeness. But the gentlemanly manner concealed the same steel will as Cummings. De Zoete wanted to make a go of his company and declined the offer, but he provided the perfect alternative solution: 'I think Stephenson will be interested.'

Paul Stephenson was the communications director for the British Bankers Association, where he was highly thought of, highly effective and highly remunerated. He was also highly bored. He had previously been a special adviser to Philip Hammond at the Department of Transport and to Andrew Lansley at the Department of Health, where he was drafted in to sort out the communications mess of Lansley's reforms. A fast-talking lover of good stories and a good lunch, he was one of the most effective Conservative media operators, respected and liked by journalists, who delighted in the staccato burst of his machine-gun laugh. Stephenson had been a diehard Eurosceptic for years, having worked on numerous anti-Brussels campaigns.

As significant meetings in the history of Leave's referendum win go, few can top that when Dominic Cummings sat in Paul Stephenson's garden in north London in July 2015 and, over bottles of beer, offered him the job. In truth, Cummings had not found a new *yang* to replace de Zoete. Stephenson was another *yin*. Like Cummings, he was a brilliant strategist, and inclined to choose the more aggressive of any two options. They hit it off straight away.

Stephenson had recently married, but he signed up at once, starting work in early September. His new wife said, 'Let me get this straight: you've just got married, you're taking a huge pay cut and you're about to annoy the prime minister and every other senior Conservative.'

A somewhat bashful Stephenson replied, 'That's about the size of it.'

Together, Cummings and Stephenson would form the engine room of the Leave campaign. With guile and cunning they were to take on the might of the Tory establishment and the government machine, and win. Most people who were there say their double act was just as important as that of Boris Johnson and Michael Gove. Without all four of them it is likely that Remain would have won.

Cummings also approached Victoria Woodcock, a former private secretary to Michael Gove, and persuaded her to quit her job. Described as a 'secret weapon' in implementing school reform, she had most recently been working in the Cabinet Office, where she had overseen the government's planning of the VE-Day seventieth-anniversary commemorations in May, a three-day jamboree involving politicians, the royal family and thousands of veterans. On 23 August the *Sunday Times* revealed that she would become the 'No' campaign's director of operations. Georgiana Bristol, a fundraiser for Boris Johnson's 2008 London mayoral campaign, was also on board as development director. Even at this stage, Cummings was consciously creating an organisation in which both Gove and Johnson would feel comfortable. He regarded Stephenson and Woodcock as 'by far the most important people in the whole campaign in terms of the permanent staff'.

It would have been understandable if Matthew Elliott felt a bit surrounded. The two key posts were now filled by Cummings' hires, and the media was more interested in him than in Elliott. The only person Elliott had hired who Cummings rated was Rob Oxley, who was installed as head of media and quickly grew close to Stephenson.

In the late summer Stephenson had lunch with Nick Timothy, and sought to get him on board as research director. As the right-hand man to Theresa May, the home secretary, Timothy had been one of the best special advisers in the government – fiercely intelligent, with a subtle political brain and (like Cummings) the backbone to stand up to Downing Street and drive through his minister's policies. Along with Fiona Hill, May's right-hand woman, he had kept the flame of her leadership ambitions alive throughout the coalition years without ever doing anything overt that would have attracted the ire of his low-key boss. He was also a committed Eurosceptic who wanted to leave the EU. In early July he had left government to become the director of the New Schools Network, a charity that helped establish free schools, and for months he had been cultivating a vast, lustrous beard that made him resemble Alexander Solzhenitsyn. Timothy was a perfect fit for the team of Tory bad boys. He had been kicked off the list of Conservative parliamentary candidates in December 2014 after he and Stephen Parkinson, another of May's special advisers, refused to campaign in the Rochester by-election, believing they were being asked to break the civil service code of conduct. Coming five months after Fiona Hill had been forced to resign by Downing Street, this had had the air of a vendetta by the Cameroons against May's team. Nonetheless, Timothy had led the crack team in South Thanet at the general election who prevented Nigel Farage winning a seat in Parliament.

Timothy was interested in a role, but he had just taken his new job. Over lunch he also expressed reservations about becoming too closely associated with some of the hardline Eurosceptics. For Britain assumed that May herself was 'nervous about it being a totally Eurosceptic clusterfuck'. Team May did seem to want a foothold in the campaign, though, and it quickly became apparent that Stephen Parkinson was willing to join as head of the ground campaign. He was a natural fit. 'Parky' had worked for years alongside Stephen Gilbert, the Conservative Party's ground-game expert on by-elections, and knew the ropes. 'They pushed Parky quite hard,' a campaign source said. Fate had another big job in line for Nick Timothy.

When Cummings met Paul Stephenson in his garden he had outlined a stealth plan for the campaign – to downplay issues like immigration until the 'Out' gang had won the right to be heard by polite society, and then get more aggressive in the run-up to polling day: 'Until February, we will only be talking to the bubble.' With that in mind, he wrote lengthy blog posts on reasons why Europe was bad for democracy, scientific endeavour and the way the civil service operated. For Banks and Farage this was proof that Cummings was a dilettante. But there was method in his intellectual verbosity: 'That was deliberately done; we were fighting for the right to be heard at the BBC,' Stephenson remembered. 'We went into the BBC and Dom went and did exactly that pitch to a load of execs, and I know from the feedback that people thought, "If that's what he's about, we quite like that." They'd have probably voted Remain, but they recognised we were not Nigel Farage or a bunch of racists. That was quite important to us.'

Cummings also wrote a blog suggesting that there could be a second referendum after an 'Out' vote, in which the public could give their views on any subsequent deal with Brussels: 'If you want to say "stop", vote no and you will get another chance to vote on the new deal.' The suggestion that Britain might vote 'No' to Brussels and then get a better deal and stay was catnip to the Westminster commentariat. To Cummings it was just another way of drumming up support from those who disliked Brussels but were not hardline Brexiteers. Once again, this reinforced the belief of Banks and Farage that Cummings and Elliott were not real outers, and that they would not set up a proper Brexit campaign until Cameron had his deal.

Steve Baker, the head of Conservatives for Britain, said, 'It was very clear that the government strategy was to create the tallest, steepest cliff-edge possible around the referendum. What Cummings was doing was reducing the height of the cliff. He's saying, "You can vote to leave now, and then they'll have to come back and check if you really meant it." That's why the PM hated it so much.' Baker added, 'Because Ukip didn't get the political sophistication, we had to drop it. That lack of trust and failure to understand that not everything's a conspiracy against them meant we couldn't use that strategy.'

Cummings was shrewd enough to talk about the idea to Boris Johnson, and the London mayor publicly endorsed the plan at the end of June. Johnson believed Cameron was not playing 'hardball' with the Europeans, and that floating the double-referendum idea would show them Britain was 'serious'.[10]

Cummings was delighted when Craig Oliver's first major intervention in the Europe debate, at the end of October, was to brief a speech by David Cameron declaring, 'Leave means leave ... That option of "Let's have another go" is not on the ballot paper.' Cummings told friends, 'You could tell from Number 10's reaction they hated it.'

But by then relations with Banks and Farage had completely ruptured over four issues: the double referendum, who would run the main campaign, who would represent 'Out' in the television debates, and immigration.

In July Farage met Cummings and Elliott in the latter's office in Tufton Street. The Ukip leader called for healthy competition: 'Look, Arron says you want a go at this, I want a go at this, I believe in competition, we guys have got to have a clean fight.'

Following this olive branch, Cummings was amused and a little horrified as the meeting went on and it became clear that Farage was 'obsessed' with being the face of the 'No' campaign in the debates. Cummings said, 'I don't know who is going to represent the official Leave campaign yet, but what I'm going to do is go through a rigorous process of testing everyone in a scientific way, and I will figure out who the people are who are the most persuasive to the people we need to vote for.

Farage queried this: 'Does that mean you're against me?'

'No. It just means I'm not against you or for you. This is an empirical business, Nigel, and I care about winning. You're a hero and you'll play a big part, but can we agree now to have you as our spokesman? No.'

After the meeting, Bruni-Lowe said, 'We went away realising we had to push Banks even more.'

Cummings' impression was that Farage and Banks did not believe they could win the referendum, but were already looking ahead to the world beyond, where they hoped to capitalise politically on the number of people voting 'Out', just as the SNP had done in Scotland after the independence referendum, where 45 per cent of the vote in 2014 translated into a near clean sweep for the Nationalists at the 2015 election. 'You run a campaign, raise a lot of money, get of lot of data, you then lose and then do an SNP,' was how he saw the Ukip strategy.

Another meeting followed in August with Banks, who got Cummings in to meet some advertising people. Cummings regarded their proposals, which were not based on market research, as 'garbage', and said so. His view of advertising agencies was simple: 'They all think they're geniuses and they all think the clients are morons.' His view of Banks now was that he did not understand public communication. In this campaign, Cummings would be driven by the data.

Towards the end of August, relations with Banks broke down again. On the 23rd the *Sunday Times* reported that Elliott would be chief executive of a new 'No' campaign and would re-use the striking logo that had been employed in the battle against the single currency, a white 'No' on a circular red background. The story also revealed that he had acquired office space in Westminster for fifty staff. Banks 'went mental' at the news that Elliott and Cummings had begun without consulting him. He protested to Cummings, 'I can't believe you've done this,' and complained about the 'air of entitlement' of the men from Westminster. Cummings replied, 'Arron, you've spent the last three months saying we're not committed to being outers and you're going to do this, and I kept telling you I was going to do it, and now we've done it, so why are you surprised?'

In early September, as a means of corralling more MPs from across the political spectrum, Bernard Jenkin set up 'ExCom', an exploratory committee that would form the parliamentary wing of the nascent Leave campaign. Dreamt up over dinner at the Jenkin family home in Kennington, south London, it subsequently met once a week on Wednesday after PMQs at 12.45 p.m., often in Owen Paterson's room. Regular attendees included Jenkin, Steve Baker and Paterson for the Tories, Kelvin Hopkins, Graham Stringer and Kate Hoey from Labour, Nigel Dodds from the DUP, and Ukip's sole MP Douglas Carswell. Hoey remembered 'a useful meeting with very, very nice coffee'.

Yet it remained a struggle to get those beyond the hardcore Eurosceptics to join up. Jenkin said, 'It was quite difficult to get people to engage with us at that stage because most people not unreasonably insisted, "I want to wait and see until the prime minister comes back from his renegotiation."' He told them, 'If we wait until he's done the renegotiation, and then try and set up a Leave campaign, there won't be much of a campaign.'

Elliott and Cummings had no more success when they asked Kate Hoey to join the board: 'They were very keen for me to go on that, mainly because "We must have a woman." I don't really go along with that kind of crap.' Graham Stringer represented Labour instead. Hoey also pushed for Daniel Hannan to join the board: 'I felt Dan was our most credible Tory. He was just so brilliant at speaking, but for some reason they didn't want him on the board.' These tensions would resurface with a bang in the New Year.

Farage and Bruni-Lowe waited in vain for Elliott to formally launch his campaign. Throughout August and into September nothing happened. Part of the delay was because on 1 September the Electoral Commission announced that the wording of the referendum question would be changed, so that instead of a 'Yes/No' answer people would vote 'Remain' or 'Leave' instead. The change necessitated costly and time-consuming rebranding. Banks, who had launched his campaign in July as 'the KNOW', renamed it 'Leave.EU'.

Elliott also needed to rethink: 'We were going to be called the "No" campaign. Then we had to rapidly book new websites and get a new logo, so that was a practical reason for delaying.' He also wanted to hold off because Steve Baker was drumming up support in the House of Commons for amendments to the Referendum Bill: 'They were doing very good work to make sure it was a more level referendum. Had CfB been a Leave organisation at that point, they wouldn't have got so many supporters as they did.'

None of these reasons washed with Farage, Bruni-Lowe and Banks, who saw only Conservative foot-dragging. They resolved to act as the provisional wing of Euroscepticism and force Elliott's hand. Chris Bruni-Lowe said: 'Our view was that Business for Britain would still be going about a week before the referendum if it hadn't been for Banks. We needed to smoke them out. Our view was that Banks wasn't going to get designation [as the official Leave campaign], but we wanted to get them off the fence. Banks liked the idea of making Elliott competitive. We decided to fully endorse Banks, as a party, knowing that it would piss off Carswell. And then force Carswell to go back to Elliott and say, "Look, you're leaving me in an impossible position."'

On 25 September Farage took to the stage at Ukip's annual conference in Doncaster and said the party would back Banks and Leave.EU. 'I basically held his hand up on the platform and said, "This is the team I'm backing,"' Farage said. When journalists asked why he was not supporting Elliott, who most of the media expected to run the official campaign, Farage said, 'Well, they haven't declared. This is the only game in town.' In his speech, Farage condemned Elliott and Cummings as 'soft Eurosceptics', and dismissed the 'For Britain' campaign as a 'talking shop in Tufton Street'.

The desired row with Carswell was immediate and explosive. Banks briefed the media that Ukip's only MP would also have to back Leave.EU or face deselection; when Carswell confronted him in a corridor, Banks dismissed him as 'borderline autistic with mental illness wrapped in'.

The comments were to damage Banks's chances of running the lead 'Out' campaign, but Farage's *coup de théâtre* had put Elliott and Cummings on the back foot. If they had assumed they were on course to win designation as the main Leave campaign, they had a fight on their hands. Fortunately, they did now have a name.

* * *

The first suggestion was not a success. Cummings and Stephenson went drinking and came up with the idea of 'Democrats'. They liked its American political overtones. But what had looked clever late at night did not look so smart the next morning. Stephenson recalled, 'We both went back to our wives that night and told them and they said, "We don't understand it." We came back the next morning and realised we agreed with them.'

In mid-September Cummings held a team meeting in what would become their office in the Westminster Tower by Lambeth Bridge, across the river from the House of Commons. 'It was still a building site,' Stephenson said. Cummings invited everyone to put possible campaign names into the middle of the table. Flicking through them later he suddenly said, '"Vote Leave", because it's an action.'

The pair then worked on a slogan, and came up with 'Get change'. They called in Elliott, who said, 'That's genius!' Cummings took a picture of the three of them to mark the historic moment that 'Vote Leave. Get Change' was established.

The following morning Cummings came into work and announced it was actually going to be 'Vote Leave. Take Control' instead. He said, 'I thought about it last night. I've done focus groups on this for years. I know this works.' Indeed, his *Times* article from June 2014 had identified 'Let's take back control' as a killer argument. The phrase had also been used on Ukip adverts.

'It goes back to the euro campaign,' he explained later, 'because we focus-grouped all sorts of different things for the euro and we never came up with something which beat "keep control". So I thought, let's play with that idea.' Stephenson led a rebellion in the office for an hour in favour of 'Get change', but Cummings was insistent: 'No, this is right.'

Vote Leave finally launched a couple of days after the Conservative Party conference. Both Stephenson and Rob Oxley wanted to make the announcement in a Sunday paper on the day David Cameron was due to do his conference interview with Andrew Marr, but it was decided that disrupting the prime minister's big moment would be seen by MPs and potential donors as 'too aggressive'. 'That was an underlying tension throughout the campaign: how aggressive can we be to Cameron without everything kicking off?' Stephenson said. It would not be long before Vote Leave was kicking very hard at the prime minister.

The launch was a low-key moment. Cummings had decreed that there would be no event or press conference. He knew Vote Leave could not compete with the 'In' campaign for major political and business endorsements. Many donors and MPs were not yet ready to commit, and a room full of Palaeosceptics was not the image he wanted to convey.

Instead of an event, an online video was posted which told viewers, 'Every week, the United Kingdom sends £350 million of taxpayers' money to the EU. That's the cost of a fully staffed, brand-new hospital, or looked at another way, that's £20 billion per year.' It concluded with the slogan, 'Vote Leave, let's take control.' The tone of the campaign was set.

The launch made Vote Leave resemble a tech startup, which in a sense they were. Their offices still had 'temporary carpet, with wires hanging out', Oxley remembered. One day Steve Baker walked in and wrote on a bare wall, 'You're all heroes.' There never was a big event. Banks thought the video was terrible. In an email to Elliott two days later he wrote: 'The website is awful, the Facebook page worse … You may know politics but have ABSOLUTELY no clue how to reach out to a wider audience … If this is your best shot you should be shot.'[11] Cummings' vindication came a week later when the In campaign launched. Their live event was derailed by gaffes, and slammed by the media as a shambles.

At Ukip headquarters, Farage and Bruni-Lowe were delighted their endorsement of Banks had borne fruit so quickly. 'Within a fortnight, Vote Leave was launched,' Farage said. 'So we were forcing the agenda. We were actually quite proud of ourselves, to be honest with you.' Rob Oxley admitted that there was something in this: 'One thing which they did was they effectively forced our hand.'

Having given Elliott and Cummings a shove, Farage and co. now decided they would pressure them to run the kind of campaign they believed would win. They had three demands: that Farage be prominent in the campaign, that immigration be its key message, and that Vote Leave set up a proper ground campaign to harness the Ukip people's army.

Bruni-Lowe was sceptical about Elliott's campaign model. The Taxpayers' Alliance and Big Brother Watch were media-driven organisations: 'They say to donors, "Look, we've got five hundred quotes in the media this week, give us money." It's not a real grassroots campaign. Our view was, if we can create competition, it will basically make Elliott do what he's never done before, which is set up a ground campaign.'

In October, Elliott and Cummings said they would engage with Ukip and Farage. Bruni-Lowe claims this led to an agreement that Ukip would be less aggressive. 'We said, "OK, we'll back off. And we'll let you do it."'

But the prospect of cooperation was soon dashed, when a damaging rift opened up over immigration. At the start of December Bruni-Lowe commissioned a poll of 10,000 people who were undecided how they would vote. It found that controlling the UK's border and setting 'our own immigration policy' was the number-one reason people gave that might persuade them to back Leave. Just under 38 per cent put it top, more than twenty points clear of saving money, which was second. By a margin of 59 per cent to 18 per cent these swing voters said Cameron and other leaders were wrong to sign an agreement allowing Turkish citizens visa-free travel in Europe.

Bruni-Lowe and Farage went to see Cummings to show him the polling. 'Immigration is the number-one issue for undecideds, even for the people who want to vote Remain,' Bruni-Lowe explained. 'Controlling the borders is the one issue that would make them vote Leave. We can produce literature in January on Turkey and immigration.'

Cummings declined the advice, saying that a focus on immigration would turn off undecided voters. He and others insist he always intended to use the issue nearer polling day. But he did not confide in the Kippers that day. They left in despair. 'Our view was that most undecided voters don't vote, and what we were going to need to do was motivate our base in the northern heartlands in order to get the turnout much higher,' said Bruni-Lowe. 'It was the number-one issue, and they just wouldn't acknowledge it. It was a class-based thing. They thought it was unpalatable at dinner parties. They wouldn't touch it. That was always the problem with Vote Leave.' Farage vowed to go it alone again. As they left, he said, 'Fuck that, we've got to just go for it.'

Vote Leave and Leave.EU were now effectively at war. It meant Cummings and Elliott were fighting on two fronts, because while the Eurosceptics were battling among themselves, their real enemy – the Remain campaign – had launched with a loud fanfare.

4

STRONGER IN

Andrew Cooper listened to the answers, made careful notes, and tried to remain positive. It was difficult. A thickset, balding man with hunched shoulders, it was said even by friends that he often appeared 'the most lugubrious man in the room'. In more than two decades as a pollster, and as one of the chief architects of David Cameron's modernisation of the Conservative Party, Cooper had overseen some pretty difficult focus groups – but these were not giving great grounds for hope to the embryonic EU 'In' campaign Cooper had been hired to help.

It was April 2015, just before the general election, and Cooper had seen the same warning signs in his polls. Sitting down with Peter Mandelson, the leading public relations executive Roland Rudd, Rudd's chief sidekick Lucy Thomas, and Susan Hitch, who worked with David Sainsbury, the millionaire former Labour donor, he took them through the evidence. His message was simple: Britain was much more Eurosceptic than they had feared.

'What we found was this very hard set view about why our hearts say we don't like the EU and why we should leave it,' Cooper said. 'One, it costs a bloody fortune. Two, immigration: migrants coming here and taking our jobs and our benefits, putting pressure on our services. Three, it meddles in our lives in ways which we didn't have before. The first two were much more important than the third.' But here was the kicker, the real punch in the guts for a pro-European like Cooper: 'Then you say, "OK, that's what you don't like. What are the positives?" And you'd usually get silence.' The focus-group members would look at each other sheepishly, and someone would say, 'Well, there's the trade …' But Cooper could tell their hearts were not in it.

After a month of work he outlined the headline voting figures. The raw statistics showed 'Yes' to Europe beating 'No' by 53 per cent to 47 per cent. But when he factored in differential turnout – the effect of passionate Eurosceptics being more likely to vote – the result was a virtual dead heat: 50.2 per cent for 'Yes', 49.8 per cent for 'No'.

Lucy Thomas was usually a cheerful soul. A former BBC reporter in Brussels, she was campaign director of Roland Rudd's pro-EU outfit Business for New Europe when the small team began putting together a prototype 'In' campaign. But even she struggled on the day she watched Cooper's presentation. She thought to herself, 'Oh God, this is going to be a lot harder than we thought. There was no sense of what the positives were.'

'They all thought it was a more challenging picture than they had hoped for,' Cooper said. 'Underlying attitudes were very sceptical.'

Cooper had been approached in February by Susan Hitch, who remembered his role on Better Together, the cross-party campaign that had helped to win the Scottish independence referendum the year before. In March 2015 Thomas hired Cooper's company, Populus. His first task was a 'segmentation analysis', dividing up the country into different groups of voters based on their attitudes to Europe. 'You're really trying to dig into people's deeper feelings,' he says. 'So rather than just asking about a referendum directly, you're trying to get a sense of their worldview and their feelings about multiculturalism, globalisation, engagement with other countries, their sense of optimism/pessimism. What the segmentation poll does is trying to get beyond the headline poll position to a deeper understanding of the country's attitude.'

By 15 April Cooper had found six attitudinally similar groups, given them names and constructed a profile of each one, complete with a picture of a typical member. He found that two groups – 'Ardent Internationalists' and 'Comfortable Europhiles' – accounting for 29 per cent of the population, were almost certain to vote to stay. A third, much smaller group, 'Engaged Metropolitans', was also overwhelmingly for Remain, and was very active on social media.

Cooper identified two resolutely 'Out' groups. 'Strong Sceptics' were almost entirely white, likely to be aged over fifty-five, from the C2DE social bracket and with only a secondary education. They were often Labour voters flirting with Ukip, and made up 21 per cent of the population. The 'EU Hostiles' were typically retired, living mortgage-free on a private pension, and supporters of Ukip who got their news from the *Daily Mail*. They made up 11 per cent.

For Cooper, the battleground would be over the other two groups. The 'Disengaged Middle' were typically in their thirties, relatively well-educated, middle-class, but not at all interested in politics. They knew almost nothing about the EU, and did not feel it had much to do with their lives. Seven out of ten in this group got their news from Facebook. The final group, who encapsulated the rhetorical challenge the campaign faced, were christened 'Hearts v Heads'. They were two-thirds female, more likely to be in late middle-age, married or divorced with children, working in a low-paid job or part-time. They were disproportionately likely to have left school aged sixteen, and to be struggling to make ends meet. They read newspapers and were interested in the issue of Europe, but found it very confusing, and felt conflicted. Over 80 per cent of them agreed with the statement 'My heart says we should leave the EU, but my head says it's not a good idea.' In the Scottish referendum, Cooper had had an identical segment which had helped Better Together to victory. In his April 2015 survey, 'Yes' led 'No' 55–45 among the two groups of key target voters. From that point on 'we only did focus groups among those two groups,' Cooper explained. Success depended on holding on to that lead.

The Remain campaign had no name, no strategy and no message, but when David Cameron secured his surprise majority at the general election the handful of people involved did know their target voters, and had enough data to begin constructing a plan. On election night Rudd threw a party at Villandry, a restaurant in London's clubland. When it became clear that the Tories were on course for victory, Lucy Thomas approached him and said, 'It's on. It's happening.' They both had another drink. All they needed now was a leader, a headquarters, and a proper organisation.

The outfit Cooper had signed up to was the third effort at creating a Remain campaign. The three driving forces were Peter Mandelson, the former EU Trade Commissioner and one of the founding fathers of New Labour; David Sainsbury, the Blairite peer and former Labour Party donor; and Roland Rudd, a debonair fifty-four-year-old who had founded Finsbury, one of London's powerhouse PR outfits. He had argued for years that Britain 'should lead not leave' the EU.

First Mandelson and Rudd had sought to empower an umbrella group called British Influence, run by Peter Wilding, a veteran of the EU battles of the 1990s. They then shifted resources to the European Movement, run by the former Tory MP Laura Sandys. Mandelson recalled, 'We had two false starts on the pro-European side funded by David Sainsbury. One was British Influence, of which I was joint president with Ken Clarke and Danny Alexander, which was established long before the 2015 election and was hopelessly run. The other initiative, after the election, was led by the former Tory MP Laura Sandys, which didn't come together. David then asked me to convene a viable campaign, which I did along with Damian Green and Danny Alexander during the summer of 2015. David paid all the startup costs. It would not have happened without him.'

Green, a Conservative former immigration minister, said the British Influence effort 'didn't work because it was basically run by elderly grandees who weren't going to get their hands dirty. David Sainsbury said, "We need people who'll actually do things."' Mandelson and Rudd recruited Will Straw, the thirty-five-year-old son of the former Labour foreign secretary Jack Straw, to run the operation. He had just fought the Lancashire seat of Rossendale and Darwen at the general election, but lost to Jake Berry, the sitting Conservative MP, by more than 5,000 votes. But Mandelson saw a bright and organised young man with politics in his blood, who was good with people and pleasantly devoid of the ego that afflicts so many in politics. He correctly judged that Straw could build a team. Straw's experience in Lancashire was also useful, because Ukip had won almost 7,000 votes in the constituency, and he was familiar with the issues that motivated Eurosceptic voters.

Shortly after the election Lucy Thomas recruited David Chaplin, an adviser to Douglas Alexander, the former Labour frontbencher, to help with the media operation. Softly-spoken but fiercely intelligent, Chaplin was one of the sharpest of a group of Labour aides who were now looking for work. With his sardonic sense of humour, he became the campaign's weary voice of reason when others indulged in flights of fancy.

Mandelson also emailed Ryan Coetzee, a nuggety forty-two-year-old South African political strategist with a closely trimmed goatee beard who had run the Liberal Democrat election campaign. The Lib Dems had been virtually wiped out in May, losing all but eight of their fifty-seven seats, but Coetzee was a tough pro who understood strategy, polling and message development. He was also used to adversity, having masterminded three election campaigns for the liberal South African party the Democratic Alliance, in an even more hostile electoral environment. In early July Coetzee went to Mandelson's Marylebone offices, where the peer 'interviewed me and I interviewed him'. After the wounding experience of the general election Coetzee 'wasn't particularly sure I wanted to do it'. But by the end of the conversation, he said, 'We both concluded it would be quite a good idea.' Mandelson said, 'Great! Come into the room and meet all the others.' They walked next door, to find Will Straw, Lucy Thomas and Andrew Cooper waiting.

On Friday, 3 July 2015 Straw organised a meeting at Mandelson's office with the three politicians – Mandelson, Green and Alexander – plus Rudd, Cooper, Lucy Thomas and Greg Nugent, the marketing expert who had won plaudits for his work on the branding of the London 2012 Olympics, and had also assisted the Better Together campaign in Scotland. The advertising agency Adam and Eve had done some work on what to call the campaign, and some ideas for logos, but Straw did not regard these as 'up to scratch', and as a result of the meeting North, another ad agency, was recruited. They devised the iconic red, white and blue Britain Stronger In Europe logo.

'You'd have these long meetings where you over-intellectualise a small number of words and colours,' Straw said. The idea had been that they would abbreviate the title to 'Stronger In', but the full name was the product of market research. They wanted to appeal to the patriotic vote, so 'Britain' was important, along with the red, white and blue colour scheme. 'Stronger', the most important word in the name, tested well in Cooper's focus groups. They considered just calling the campaign 'Britain Stronger In', but as Straw explained, 'If you didn't mention Europe at all then people might have thought you were for the Leave side, people wouldn't know what we were for.'

Straw insists he was aware that their opponents would shorten the name to 'BSE', the acronym associated with 'mad cow disease' in the 1990s, one of the most difficult periods of UK–EU relations: 'We did discuss the BSE acronym. We went in with our eyes open.' Cummings, Stephenson and Oxley would regularly refer to Stronger In as 'the BSE campaign', but Straw is adamant that the problem was not the acronym, but that 'in the end control rather than strength was what people wanted'.

In July, conscious he was running a Labour-heavy team, Straw approached Tom Edmonds and Craig Elder, who had run the

Conservatives' digital team during the general election, and asked them to join Stronger In. Another recruit was Stuart Hand, the Tory head of field operations. He was the man who had trained up Tory organisers to fight the so-called 40–40 marginal seats on which the Conservative majority was built. One of those constituencies was Rossendale and Darwen, where Hand's efforts had helped to stop Straw himself becoming an MP. When Straw interviewed Hands they shared a 'wry joke' about his Conservative opponent Jake Berry.

To run the campaign's outreach work with businesses and celebrities Straw brought in Gabe Winn, an executive from the energy giant Centrica. Winn was a personable and shrewd operator who was well plugged in to the Westminster world through his work and his brother Giles, a political producer with *Sky News*. The two had long joked about forming a public-affairs agency called 'Winn Winn'. Gabe hoped his move into politics would be just as successful.

Having got the nucleus of a campaign team together, the former political rivals gathered for an awayday at the Village Hotel in Farnborough. It went well. A sense of camaraderie developed. The only fly in the ointment was that David Cameron and George Osborne did not want the campaign set up at all. Mandelson had seen Osborne at the Treasury after the general election, and had reassured the chancellor that the campaign would be created in ways that were friendly to the government, allowing Cameron to take over its political leadership when the time came. At that stage Osborne had seemed relaxed. He even joked that he expected the campaign to be a full-on 'New Labour-style operation'.

Things changed towards the end of July, when Mandelson met Cameron at a leaving party for a Number 10 official. The prime minister was distinctly cooler, and complained that Mandelson's actions were premature, that the creation of the campaign would annoy the Tory Party, appear to pre-empt his negotiations in Europe, and even undermine them. He made clear his concern that a campaign run by all the pro-European 'usual suspects' would be counterproductive. In September he sent the same message to Mandelson via a mutual friend, urging him and the others to 'back off'.

In further conversations Osborne explained that the government, which was holding open the at least theoretical possibility that it might campaign to leave, couldn't just sign up to a pro-European campaign.

Privately he thought Mandelson and co. were 'unrealistic' because they wanted 'full government involvement' even at this early stage.

Mandelson stuck to his guns, explaining to both the prime minister and the chancellor, 'I have directed or chaired three general election campaigns, '87, '97 and 2010, and I know what's involved. You cannot create a national campaign from a standing start a couple of months before polling day, especially when you are having to counter twenty years of relentless anti-European propaganda in Britain.'

Damian Green also went to see Cameron after the election, but told colleagues 'it wasn't a meeting of minds'. Green argued that there would be a need for a 'pro-European Conservative voice in this debate', but felt the prime minister had only seen him 'out of politeness', and nothing came of the meeting.

Straw tried to smooth things over, going for a pint with Daniel Korski, the deputy head of the Number 10 policy unit, who advised Cameron on EU affairs. 'They felt that it wasn't inevitable that we would become the designated campaign,' Straw recalled. Indeed, Korski was arguing internally that the Tories should set up their own, separate, campaign. As late as November 2015 he and Mats Persson, the former head of the Open Europe think tank who had been recruited by Number 10, offered to leave and set one up. They suggested that Open Europe itself might be converted into a campaign vehicle.

'The problem was that Cameron did not accept that an all-party campaign was needed,' said Mandelson. 'Early on he let it be known to people like Ken Clarke that he didn't intend to run it that way. But Cameron had not thought this through. He was thinking in Tory Party terms, assuming that the voters would follow him as prime minister and party leader when the time came. He also didn't appear to understand his own legislation, which required a designated campaign on the Remain side to reflect cross-party opinion.'

The prime minister's attitude would shape his approach to Stronger In throughout the short campaign, when key decisions continued to be made in Downing Street, rather than at the campaign's headquarters in Cannon Street. The most serious immediate impact of Cameron's disapproval was that donors and businesses were deterred from signing up. A senior figure in the campaign said, 'They very actively told businesses not to cooperate, saying it would be regarded as a hostile act inside Number 10, so the campaign didn't have the ability to get people lined up.'

In accounts of this period in the press, the finger of blame has been pointed at Korski, the point man in Number 10 for many businesses. Korski says this claim is 'a total fantasy', and denies that he was proactively calling anyone. Instead, businesses called him after Sajid Javid, the business secretary, addressed the CBI on 29 June 2015 and rebuked the organisation for its pro-EU stance. Korski told those who rang him, 'It's not for me to tell you what to do. You've got responsibilities to shareholders, to staff.' He did not tell business leaders to say nothing. But he did advise some of them, 'If you're a very rich oil company with most operations outside the UK, or a tax base that's structured in a way that means you're not domiciled, think carefully about whether you have a legitimate voice in this debate.' To those who wanted to help Cameron he suggested, 'It's obviously better to say that you want to reform Europe, because if you say you want to stay in, then you're going to expose yourself to people who say, "You don't have a legitimate voice because you're a billionaire."' It is easy to see how this friendly advice might have deterred some from putting their heads above the parapet.

Roland Rudd, who ran the initial fundraising operation, achieved a breakthrough when he began approaching investment banks. He managed to get donations from Goldman Sachs, and that opened doors at JP Morgan, Morgan Stanley and Citibank. Rudd raised £1.5 million that way, and another half a million from 'big chunky donors' like Ian Taylor, Lloyd Dorfman and Andrew Law. Andrew Feldman, the Conservative Party chairman, got David Harding, a billionaire financier, on board. He became the treasurer. In the end, most of the financial support came from Conservative donors.

Over the summer and into the autumn, Ryan Coetzee worked with Andrew Cooper to draw up Stronger In's strategy. By the end of November he had completed the campaign 'war book' and 'messaging bible'. 'If you've not written it down, it's not a strategy,' Cooper said. 'The war book is everything we know: the segmentation, our strongest messages, "This is our message in a sentence", "This is our message in a paragraph", "This is our message in a page", media strategy, campaign grid. That's the Bible.'

The goal was to target the two persuadable groups, the 'Hearts v Heads' and the 'Disengaged Middle'. Cooper conducted regression analysis, a statistical device to estimate the relationship between variables, and discovered that both groups were susceptible to arguments about economic risk. Coetzee said, 'The two in-play segments in the middle believed it was riskier to leave than it was to stay. And when you look to the regressions, you found that the risk question was really driving the voting intention responses.' That appeared to be proof that Remain's target voters were not just concerned about economic risk, they were prepared to change their vote as a result.

Coetzee also accurately predicted what they would be up against. Even before Vote Leave had published its 'Take Back Control' slogan, Straw said, 'Ryan put together what he thought their script would be, and control was right at the heart of it.' Coetzee also spotted where Cummings would hit them hardest: 'Immigration, sovereignty and cost – those were the three we identified as our biggest weaknesses,' said Straw.

To help draw up responses, Cooper and Coetzee conducted big 'deliberative' focus-group sessions, with six tables of ten people being quizzed simultaneously on every aspect of the campaign. The sessions, effectively six focus groups at once, lasted seven hours. 'We did that in October and again in February,' said Cooper. 'You take them through: we say "this", they say "that". Say what our rebuttal of that point is. "What do you say now?" We're playing clips of people, to test precise messages. We're giving them new material, campaigning literature, graphics. That hugely enriched the campaign planning.'

The campaign had also acquired a base, though not an ideal one. Straw rented offices at 14 Dowgate Hill, fifty yards from Cannon Street station. The rather poky suite featured a main meeting room so small that only eight people could sit comfortably around the table, and a spill-over basement room known as 'the bunker', situated incongruously between an agency for film extras and a Botox clinic, whose facilities were used by at least one campaign staffer.

Before Stronger In could launch, it needed a board and a chairman to front the campaign. Mandelson and Rudd wanted someone with a business background – ideally a Tory woman. Damian Green recalled, 'The fear was it would look like a New Labour rump, and we were very keen that shouldn't happen.' Karren Brady, the West Ham United vice-chairman and star of *The Apprentice*, was approached, but she declined. Carolyn McCall, the boss of EasyJet, also turned the job down. 'Serving CEOs found it much harder to take on an additional task,' Straw recalled. The leading contenders were Richard Reed, the founder of Innocent smoothies, and Stuart Rose, the former chairman of Marks & Spencer, who Cameron had let it be known was his preferred option. The main attraction of Rose was that he had previously been a supporter of Matthew Elliott's Business for Britain, and that meant his recruitment could be presented as a defection.

Lucy Thomas said, 'Stuart was exactly what we needed as chair to make the pragmatic, reasonable and patriotic case. He'd run one of the best-loved British brands, and had a reputation for being a highly successful businessman as well as a nice, decent bloke. He was also a Eurosceptic who was rightly critical of the way the EU worked and in favour of significant reform.'

The only problem was that Rose, while happy to join the board, did not want to be chairman. Straw and Coetzee visited him in late September, and he said 'definitely, categorically' that he would not do it. Rudd received the same message. But Rose was finally persuaded by a barrage of calls virtually on the eve of the launch in early October, including one from George Osborne. Rose said, 'My first judgement was no, my second judgement was no, my third judgement was no – and then I failed to listen to my judgement. I was a square peg in a round hole.' 'On the Friday before the Monday launch, they didn't have a chairman,' a senior Tory said. 'George got him to do it. But that was very late in the day, and it meant he had almost no time to prepare or be briefed, which is why he didn't perform brilliantly at the launch.'

That was putting things mildly. Even before he spoke, Vote Leave's researchers had dug up comments Rose had made in April dismissing fears that leaving the EU would cause companies to quit the UK as 'scaremongering'. The night before the launch, the campaign briefed Westminster journalists that Rose would use his speech to dismiss those backing Leave as 'the Quitters'. But when he spoke on Monday, 12 October he refused to use the phrase, rendering every morning newspaper's story inaccurate. Rose recalls: 'I let myself down. I'm not used to being given a very closely drafted brief. I'm used to interpreting things in my own way.' If the press pack was unimpressed by that, their ire was greatly increased when Rose refused to take any media questions. The location of the launch, a former east London brewery, made the job of the parliamentary sketch writers too easy. References to Stronger In's failure to organise a piss-up in such an establishment abounded in the following day's papers.

To compound the problem, Rose then gave an interview to Rachel Sylvester and Alice Thomson of *The Times* in which he admitted,

'Nothing is going to happen if we come out of Europe in the first five years, probably. There will be absolutely no change.' His reputation as a gaffemeister supreme was set, and he enhanced it in January 2016 when he did a pre-interview soundcheck for *Sky News* and forgot the name of the campaign. Footage emerged of him saying, 'I'm chairman of Stay in Britain … Better in Britain campaign … Right, start again. I'm Stuart Rose and I'm the chairman of the Better in Britain campaign … the Better Stay in Britain campaign.' During the campaign he would tell a Commons Select Committee that Brexit would cause wages to rise. Afterwards, he felt 'battered and bruised' by the experience.

Lucy Thomas did not feel the Stronger In team could criticise Rose, who had had no yearning for the limelight, and was only doing the job 'as a favour': 'As with any successful business person doing political campaigning, it's really hard. You're used to answering factual questions about your business, not tricky political issues. So you answer what you've been asked directly, but don't realise that how it is interpreted might trip you up.' A politician involved with the campaign was less understanding: 'You hear business people say things like, "Why aren't politicians like us?" Well, business people discover that politicians have craft skills as well, like not saying stupid things while on public platforms.' Rose was a good chairman, however – 'consensual and encouraging', according to Mandelson.

Nevertheless, to have the front man neutralised so quickly made it difficult for Stronger In to build public momentum.

Lining up Tory board members was no simpler than locating a chairman. In the summer Mandelson called Ruth Davidson, the Tory leader in Scotland and one of the party's brightest hopes, to see if she would join. As someone who wanted to be as good at politics as she could be, Davidson saw the opportunity to learn from Mandelson as great 'career development'. But after the Better Together campaign, she realised she could not both campaign for Stronger In and fight the Scottish elections in May. She told Mandelson, 'I'm really sorry, mate. I've got a really big election coming up. This could be a breakthrough election for the Conservatives in Scotland.' She said later, 'Having been part of Better Together, having seen how much it saps out of you, I just didn't have the capacity for it.' In the event, Davidson would secure a breakthrough, beating Labour into third place. Her chance to play a role in the referendum would come later.

The full membership of the Stronger In board was designed to show breadth and experience, bringing together the political, business, education, culture and military establishments. At its furthest extremes it included General Sir Peter Wall, the former chief of the General Staff, and June Sarpong, the former MTV and T4 presenter who is now a panellist on ITV's *Loose Women*. Both Karren Brady and Richard Reed agreed to serve. In addition it was announced that the three living former prime ministers – Sir John Major, Tony Blair and Gordon Brown – plus Sir Richard Branson, Britain's best-known businessman, were also supporting the campaign.

The Rose débâcle suggested a need for a stronger media operation. In the autumn David Chaplin, who had been handling most of the story briefing with the lobby journalists, wrote a memo recommending that Straw bring in a heavy hitter to be the campaign's mouthpiece, allowing Chaplin himself to step back and do what he was best at, planning coverage over a longer period. From the beginning the campaign had one person in mind who was battle-ready to take on Vote Leave's Paul Stephenson.

James McGrory was educated at an independent school, but you would never know it. A rake-thin, ginger-haired mockney bruiser, he loved playing football and deploying sporting analogies in his attack quotes. He combined acute news judgement with an irrepressible thirst for placing stories (and not a little ability at the bar), plus the respect of Westminster journalists. For five years as Nick Clegg's spokesman he had ably fought the Liberal Democrat corner against newspapers which preferred to ridicule his boss. He never took anything personally, despite caring more than most about his cause. While others dealt with the Lib Dem wipeout at the election with alcohol and new careers in public affairs, McGrory disappeared to lick his wounds. Lucy Thomas first tried to sign him up in May. 'I was not in a frame of mind to get back into a campaign,' he said. But when Will Straw called later that summer he realised, 'This is the fight of your life – it was quite an easy decision in the end.'

McGrory's return to SW1 was greeted with mouthwatering expectation by those who had dealt with him before. The referendum would pitch two of the best spin doctors of their generation against each other. Both McGrory and Stephenson went into the tackle with their studs showing. To use an analogy about the Premier League's two greatest hardmen, which McGrory himself had sometimes deployed when discussing alpha-male journalists, it was 'a case of Keane against Vieira'.

McGrory joined at the start of December 2015. 'James added a huge amount of professionalism and energy,' says Chaplin. 'He was not willing to let anything go, he had fire in his belly for the smallest story, and was exactly what the campaign needed. For James it was personal and professional. He wanted to win, and he believed in it.' Lucy Thomas called him a man 'with the mouth of a football fan and the heart of a true sandal-wearing liberal'. McGrory saw his brief as to 'dial it up a couple of notches'. He soon did. They noticed at Vote Leave: 'We thought their press operation improved dramatically,' said Rob Oxley. 'Suddenly we started taking a bit of fire.'

McGrory's appointment meant Stronger In were ready to go into battle. Downing Street now had to decide whether they wanted to share a trench with them.

During the autumn Cameron remained 'very nervous about any contact with the campaign', Straw recalled, but clandestine meetings had begun with senior figures from Downing Street. The most important came on 26 October 2015, since it decided whether there would be a campaign at all. Straw, Coetzee, Thomas and Mandelson met Stephen Gilbert at Mandelson's offices in Marylebone. Gilbert was joined after a while by Craig Oliver, Cameron's spin doctor. 'They were coming to check us out,' says Coetzee.

Straw took the Tories through the organisational structure of the campaign and the relationship with the board. Coetzee gave a presentation on strategy, messaging and the progress made with building a predictive model for targeting voters. Thomas ran through the media plans. Straw said, 'We brought them up to speed with where we were with the organisation, how we were building a nationwide campaign, all the recruitment we'd done, where we'd had some blockages, where we needed their help recruiting Conservatives.'

Top of the list of Stronger In 'asks' was help in hiring Jim Messina, the wizard of target-voter modelling in both Barack Obama and David Cameron's re-election efforts. Roland Rudd had been briefing journalists since June that he wanted to recruit the American, but Messina had played hard to get. Coetzee had approached another set of US strategists, Civis Analytics, a New York firm founded by Dan Wagner, a Messina protégé from Obama's 2012 campaign. The talks had got as far as a draft contract.

Coetzee had spoken to Cooper and said, 'Andrew, the clock is ticking, because it takes time to put this stuff together.' To get maximum value from voter-targeting data the campaign wanted to use it to send out leaflets and emails before the regulated spending period kicked in on 15 April. After that they would only be allowed to spend £7 million on their campaign. The trigger for the meeting was a warning from Cooper to Downing Street that the campaign had been 'freaked out' by Messina's refusal to engage. Straw said, 'We basically got to the stage where if Messina wasn't going to work with us, then we needed to crack on with someone else.'

Gilbert and Oliver both began the meeting sceptical about joining forces with Stronger In. They both left believing they could do business together. Crucial to winning over the Conservatives was Coetzee's description of the target voter as someone who was a persuadable Eurosceptic, rather than an enthusiast for Brussels. 'I think their anxiety was, "Are these guys a bunch of Euronuts?"' Coetzee said. 'We understood that the marginal voter was concerned about the economy and immigration, and needed a "hardheaded case". It was immediately apparent to everybody that we were all speaking the same language.'

Gilbert told Coetzee months later, 'Our default position was "No". Our default was "Yes" after the meeting.' Craig Oliver's view was that there were benefits to the cross-party effort. 'Serious consideration was given to setting up another campaign,' a senior Downing Street source said. 'The danger would be that we would lose any contact with the other political groups that wanted to remain – and it would be seen as a Tory-only Remain vehicle.'

Straw recalled, 'I think what they realised from those meetings was that we were serious, professional, we had a proper plan in place and we were in a position to fight a referendum.' Crucially, the Tories were prepared to put the call in to Messina. Coetzee said, 'We got the Messina show on the road, but frankly months later than it should have been.'

Relations were cemented shortly afterwards when Gilbert joined Populus, Cooper's polling company, as a consultant so he could work more overtly for the campaign. In December and January there were also clandestine meetings between Straw, Gilbert, Oliver and Ameet Gill in the basement of the Conrad Hotel, next to St James's Park tube station.

Despite some hiccups, Stronger In had put together a talented team, and had won the trust of Downing Street. Now they needed the third leg of the Remain stool to step up – the Labour Party.

5

CORNERING CORBYN

The moment Jeremy Corbyn revealed what he really thought about the European Union came at a hustings during the Labour leadership contest in Warrington – the final such event organised by the party. It was Saturday, 25 July 2015, and the battle to succeed Ed Miliband was entering a crucial phase. The Blairite Liz Kendall, after an early flurry of media attention, had faded. Andy Burnham and Yvette Cooper were locked in an ever more bitter battle to be the flagwaver of the party moderates, the volume increasing as the contested ideological space narrowed. To the incredulity of the party's power-brokers, Corbyn, a sixty-six-year-old veteran from the hard left who had spent his career in exile on the backbenches, had emerged as the favourite to win.

Corbyn was a very unlikely leader. A rebellious backbencher, to the point of parody, for thirty years, he had only run because other members of the hard left like John McDonnell and Diane Abbott had already tried and failed. He only made the ballot paper because grandees like Margaret Beckett and Sadiq Khan had loaned him their nominations in order to 'widen the debate'. Now he was barrelling to victory on a wave of support from enthusiastic young leftists who admired his plain speaking and apparent personal decency – a sort of ageing Forrest Gump – backed up by Bennites who learned how to fight procedural battles in the 1980s and entryists from Trotskyite fringe groups. Having found no candidate they thought could win a general election, Labour activists resolved to elect the one who made them feel best about themselves in defeat.

Much ink has been spilled about Corbyn's true views on Europe, but no one seriously disputes that for much of his career he was a dedicated and consistent opponent of British membership of the European Union. In the 1975 referendum Corbyn voted to leave. Labour's attitude to

Europe changed when Jacques Delors, then president of the European Commission, made a keynote speech at the 1998 Trades Union Congress and outlined plans for 'social Europe', where workers' rights were enshrined in international law and social benefits were provided across the Continent. But Corbyn remained a Eurosceptic. Indeed, he became a close friend of the Tory Palaeosceptics campaigning against the Maastricht Treaty. 'Jeremy is a rigidly stuck in the seventies politician,' says the then shadow lord chancellor Charlie Falconer. 'That had made him – and he was quite proud of this – quite a pal of the Maastricht rebels. They had always counted Jeremy in as part of their calculations. Jeremy is somebody who almost prides himself on his good relations with obstreperous right-wing Tory rebels.'

At the Warrington hustings, Burnham, Cooper, Kendall and Corbyn were all asked directly if they would 'rule out voting "No" or campaigning for "No"' ahead of the referendum. The first three all ruled it out; Corbyn did not: 'No I wouldn't rule it out … Because Cameron quite clearly follows an agenda which is about trading away workers' rights, is about trading away environmental protection, is about trading away much of what is in the social chapter.'

If that part of his answer was at least sympathetic to notions of a social Europe, he went on to make clear that his objection to the EU stemmed from a belief that it was too friendly to big companies, the 'capitalist club' that other left-wingers had criticised before Delors came along: 'The EU also knowingly, deliberately maintains a number of tax havens and tax-evasion posts around the Continent – Luxembourg, Monaco and a number of others. I think we should be making demands: universal workers' rights, universal environmental protection, end the race to the bottom on corporate taxation, end the race to the bottom in working wage protection.' He concluded, 'We should be negotiating on those demands rather than saying blanketly we're going to support whatever Cameron comes out with in one, two years' time, whenever he finally decides to hold this referendum.'

Corbyn's views caused a crisis at the top of the party because they were at odds with Labour policy, confirmed by the acting leader Harriet Harman after the general election, in two key regards. Harman, backed up by Hilary Benn, the shadow foreign secretary, and Charlie Falconer, had ditched Labour's opposition to holding a referendum, which some saw as a contributory factor in Ed Miliband's defeat. She had also confirmed that the party supported Cameron's plan to renegotiate Britain's relationship with Brussels and the Referendum Bill to set up the process. Most importantly, she had confirmed that in all circumstances Labour would campaign to stay in.

'We did that on the basis that we'd lost a general election, and the Tories had got an overall majority,' said Falconer. 'Therefore the right thing to do was to accept that. But we did it explicitly on the basis that we were very pro-Europe.' There was no opposition in the shadow cabinet.

Harman's other key decision was that she wanted to set up a Labour campaign separate from the umbrella Remain effort which became Stronger In. Many Labour politicians believed it had been a mistake to campaign alongside the Conservatives during the Scottish independence referendum. Labour's involvement in Better Together had led to them being branded 'tartan Tories' by Nationalists, and was blamed for the party losing all but one of its Scottish seats in the 2015 general election. 'Her view was that Better Together and Scotland had been such a disaster that no cross-party thing could ever work again,' a Labour official said.

Interestingly, even before he was recruited by Stronger In, Will Straw had written to Harman on 10 June saying this was a mistake. He pointed out that while association with the Conservatives in Scotland had been counterproductive, 'Labour has the need to show economic credibility in England to gain votes from Conservatives. Part of our rehabilitation with the electorate could take place if our leadership shared a platform with respected centrist voices from other parties.' He also warned, with some prescience, that 'an isolated and underfunded "Labour Yes" campaign could potentially undermine efforts to keep Britain in the EU', since failure to canvass and encourage 'Labour voters in low-turnout areas' could mean many would 'not see the case for voting and stay at home'.

Straw was ignored, and Alan Johnson was put in charge of a totally separate 'Labour In for Britain' campaign. Johnson, the mild-mannered former home secretary, had been happily writing critically acclaimed memoirs and periodically resisting requests to lead a coup against Ed Miliband when he was asked to become the campaign's chairman: 'Hilary Benn and Harriet Harman nabbed me in the voting lobby and asked if I'd lead the campaign. I said I'll lead it if it's an unequivocal Remain campaign.' Johnson asked Harman, 'Do you want to wait until we have a new leader?' and she replied, 'No, let's get going.'

Working with Johnson were Brian Duggan, a personable, ginger-haired Labour official who had worked with Labour MEPs, and Sam Bacon, who cut his teeth with Chris Bryant, one of the most pro-European members of the shadow cabinet.

When Johnson saw Corbyn's equivocal comments at Warrington, he knew immediately that they could be a major problem, and was quick to demand clarity. He told the *Observer* that weekend: 'The Labour Party ditched its anti-European stance in the mid-eighties, at the beginning of our long march back to electability. The membership has a right to know if any leadership candidate wants to take the party (and the country) back to its isolationist past.'[1] Labour's Europe spokesman, Pat McFadden, went further, suggesting that Corbyn was lining up 'with Nigel Farage on a nationalist nostalgia trip.'[2]

After his appointment, Johnson saw three tasks ahead of him: 'Our job in the campaign was to unite the party, to make the argument, to get the vote out. Johnson believed Corbyn was still an Outer: 'I watched the leadership campaign with great interest. We all knew Jeremy was against [the EU]. He's not changed his mind about anything since he was fifteen; why would he change his mind on that?'

When Corbyn won a landslide victory on 12 September, one of the priorities of his new frontbench colleagues was to get him to come clean about his views, and to use Labour's annual conference to confirm the party's pro-EU stance. 'Jeremy had said, over the course of his leadership campaign, that he was unsure as to whether he would campaign to remain or leave,' a Labour official said. 'There was a mood from different sections in the party that he had to be clear about what his own personal position was.'

Corbyn was not just under pressure from the party establishment. His closest ally John McDonnell, who he was to appoint shadow chancellor, wanted him to keep Labour out of the referendum debate altogether until Cameron returned with his deal in February. A source who worked closely with Corbyn said, 'John McDonnell was most hostile to the EU, and he would have been pleased if we'd been campaigning to leave. John argued forcefully that we should say nothing until February.' Corbyn would have to choose. But despite his big win in the leadership election, the appointment of his first shadow cabinet was a shambles.

On Sunday, 13 September, amid farcical scenes, journalists were able to listen at the door of Corbyn's office for news of the latest moves as one moderate frontbencher after another – including the leadership candidates Cooper and Kendall – announced that they would not serve in his shadow cabinet. Those who were prepared to stay on vowed to extract concessions on Europe.

Charlie Falconer, who met the new leader in the Commons office of Rosie Winterton, Labour's chief whip, on the Sunday afternoon, was the first up. He said afterwards, 'A very important part of the shadow cabinet formation, which Rosie orchestrated, was that a term of a lot of us joining was that Jeremy would support Remain in the European referendum. It was very well known that Jeremy's attitude towards the European Union had always been that it was a capitalist club, which he opposed. When Corbyn asked him to be shadow justice secretary, Falconer said, 'That's ridiculous, because we disagree on Trident, we disagree on the European Union, we disagree on economic policy, we disagree on everything.'

Corbyn had run his campaign offering to paper over profound differences of approach with a 'new politics' in which debate would be encouraged and dissent allowed. 'Don't worry about that,' he told Falconer. 'We're going to be in a new era where you can all express your views.' Still unconvinced, Falconer made it clear that on the EU, things had to go beyond free expression – the policy had to be adhered to: 'The European Union issue is going to be a totally different issue. I can't be in the shadow cabinet if the position is that we're opposing or you're opposing remaining in the European Union. It's absolutely key.' Corbyn's answer was vague, but apparently affirmative: 'That would be no problem.' He suggested that he was prepared to support the Remain cause as a way of resisting right-wing policies.

Hilary Benn told Corbyn he would only serve as shadow foreign secretary in the same circumstances Falconer had outlined. Vernon Coaker and Luciana Berger took the same view, and secured Corbyn's agreement that Alan Johnson would continue as the campaign chief.

Even after the arm-twisting, Corbyn still sounded unsure when he addressed a meeting of the Parliamentary Labour Party the following Monday evening, telling MPs, 'We can't just give Cameron a blank cheque.' Fearing that the agreed position was already being eroded, Pat McFadden, the shadow Europe minister, made it clear that he would resign unless there was an unambiguous commitment to campaign to stay. The pressure resulted in Corbyn agreeing to a joint statement with

Hilary Benn that 'Labour will be campaigning in the referendum for the UK to stay in the European Union.' Cynics noticed that Corbyn stopped short of saying he would personally campaign in that way.

In an attempt to make things more secure, the frontbenchers ensured that a line was written into a document called the 'PLP briefing', which gives statements some constitutional force, stating that Labour would campaign for Remain. Alan Johnson called the document 'sacred, like the Dead Sea Scrolls of the party'.

Johnson believed that as the leadership contest went on, Corbyn had been surprised at the vehemence of the response to equivocating on Europe: 'I think Jeremy on the campaign trail picked up that actually he was on a hiding to nothing trying to persuade the Labour Party to leave. So the question in my mind wasn't whether Jeremy would eventually have to go along with the party on this, it was whether he'd keep me in place, and how much effort he'd put into it.'

First, Johnson wanted a reassurance that he would still be leading the campaign. He met Corbyn the Thursday after his election. Johnson found him vague, unfocused and keen to talk about almost anything other than the matter in hand: 'We had a conversation more about books. He was very interested in my books, he's tried to write five or six himself. He never actually said, "I want you to carry on with this job," or anything about Europe at all really. We just had a natter, and I was happy coming out that he hadn't sacked me! I wasn't really trying to get anything from it, I was trying to get a feel for getting him into a position where he'd come out and say "I'm for remaining in the EU."'

If Johnson had known how difficult it would be to get Corbyn to say that – or even to get another meeting with him, he might have tried a little harder to pin the leader down.

One reason why Corbyn had been prepared to bow to the overwhelming pressure in the party to approve official support for Remain was that the trade unions were firm supporters of the EU. Over the summer Brian Duggan put Alan Johnson, a former postman who rose to be general secretary of the Communication Workers Union, in front of as many union bosses as he could. Since he was running an independent campaign, Johnson was able to reassure them that they would not have to 'hold hands with David Cameron and George Osborne'. A campaign source said, 'We needed to get as many of the unions as possible on the side of Remain, both from a political point of view, because they could talk to their members, but also from a financial point of view, so they could make active financial contributions and donations to the campaign.'

Johnson's key phone call was to Len McCluskey, the boss of Unite, Britain's biggest union and Labour's biggest donor. Unite would eventually contribute around a quarter of the campaign's £4 million budget.

One reason why most unions got on board is that a secret operation had been under way over the summer to ensure that David Cameron dropped from his renegotiation any attempt to repatriate control of social and employment legislation. In January there had been reports that the prime minister intended to demand an opt-out from EU employment social protection laws such as the working-time directive and the agency workers' directive. By August the idea was dead. Senior figures in Labour and the trade union movement, including Frances O'Grady, the general secretary of the TUC, made private representations to Downing Street making it clear that they would not support the campaign if social and employment legislation was thrown into doubt. Eventually Ivan Rogers, the UK's permanent representative in Brussels, sent word that 'they weren't going to be part of the renegotiation'. A Labour source confirmed, 'We said, "We cannot guarantee Labour's political support for a remain campaign or for a remain vote if you do this." Cameron wasn't going to go near it, because we put sufficient pressure on him. That allowed us to go back to the trade unions and say, "You need to front up for Remain."'

The final piece in the Labour jigsaw was to reaffirm Labour's policy at Corbyn's first party conference in charge, to bind his hands going into the campaign. First they had to kill off a motion tabled by the GMB union that would have delayed Labour from making any decision until after Cameron had his deal – the same argument John McDonnell had been making. That would have been followed by a special conference to determine Labour's position. 'That would have been an absolute disaster,' says Alan Johnson. 'That would have meant the Labour Party had nothing to say on this issue on a timetable determined by the PM until he came back in February, then we'd have had to scramble around just as the campaign was beginning. It was a nonsense.'

Johnson spoke to Paul Kenny, the outgoing general secretary of the GMB, who said, 'Don't worry, Alan, we'll sort it out.' Kenny went to work with Pat McFadden and agreed that the GMB would work to pass a differently-worded motion which summarised Labour's existing pro-EU policy. It ended up passing without a vote, and established two important principles. The key section read: 'Conference supports the membership of the EU as a strategic as well as an economic asset to Britain and the Labour Party approves of UK membership of the EU.' Secondly, it made clear that Labour would not share a platform with the Tories, and reinforced the support for EU employment rights: 'Conference opposes working with any campaign or faction in the forthcoming Referendum which supports or advocates cutting employment or social rights for people working in the United Kingdom.'

The Europhile faction was amazed that they had got the motion through without meddling from Corbyn's advisers, particularly Seumas Milne, his director of communications, and Andrew Fisher, his director of policy. 'It pulled one over on his advisers,' said Johnson, 'because Jeremy's advisers – Seumas Milne, Andy Fisher – absolutely wanted to leave. They might be leaders of the Labour Party, but they've got the hammer and sickle tattooed somewhere.'

Another source said Corbyn's office was too busy enjoying his leadership lap of honour to understand the significance of what had happened: 'They hadn't realised that we had locked in Labour to a pro-European remain position.'

Labour In for Britain finally launched at the start of December. Alan Johnson was satisfied with where he had got to: 'We've got the leader – who's not in favour of the EU – saying he'll campaign for it. And we've got a unanimous decision on a very good motion.' When the launch occurred, though, 'Jeremy didn't come anywhere near it.'

That was only the start of Johnson's problems, but as David Cameron watched from afar that autumn he had every hope of having the Labour Party on-side when he completed his renegotiation. The prime minister's bigger problem was that he was facing a well-coordinated campaign of attacks from his own benches to water down the Referendum Bill.

6

GUERRILLA WARFARE

Steve Baker does not look like a military commander. In a decade as a Royal Air Force aerospace engineer he had never fired a shot in anger. As a devout Christian he hated war, and helped set up an educational charity called the Cobden Centre to 'promote social progress through honest money, free trade and peace'.

Yet when he was appointed commanding officer of the Conservative Eurosceptics in June 2015, it was as if Baker had been waiting for the opportunity to lead men into battle all his life. Politics is one of those arenas of conflict where armchair generals are just as effective as the physically brave, but no one could doubt Baker's bravery either. One of the reasons for his success at Conservatives for Britain (CfB) was his willingness, politically, to put himself in harm's way. Like all the best infantry officers he realised he should never ask anyone to do anything he was not prepared to do himself. Initially at least, it was a lonely business. 'When I launched myself out early over the top of the parapet, in a government with quite a slim majority, my colleagues were actually quite happy to hold my coat,' he observed later.

On assuming control of CfB, Baker did what any general worth their salt has done for the last millennium – he read Sun Tzu's *The Art of War*. He then picked up a book called *The Thirty-Three Strategies of War*, by Robert Greene, which explains how to adapt the strategies of Napoleon Bonaparte, Alexander the Great, Carl von Clausewitz, Erwin Rommel and Hannibal to life and politics. From Sun Tzu, Baker digested the insight that all wars are won in the preparation: 'I basically read the book and applied the book as bloody hard as I could. In particular you need guerrilla strategies. The whole of the launch phase of Conservatives for Britain was a very deliberated guerrilla operation. You have to keep people frightened. That's the guerrilla strategy: frighten them, use overwhelming force, disguise purpose.'

The launch of Conservatives for Britain was a piece of ambush marketing which left Downing Street and the Tory whips' office in a spin. Baker gathered support in secret, and on Sunday, 7 June 2015 he announced that Conservatives for Britain was in business and already had fifty MPs backing it. A week later the number had more than doubled. The victims of his 'frighten them' strategy were his own party leadership. 'They had to know they really were going to deliver fundamental change,' he said.

Like any guerrilla commander, Baker set out to harry the enemy, beginning a daily drip-feed of information to the media as more and more MPs signed up: 'How many have you got?' 'Oh, sixty-five, seventy-five, eighty … I'm not doing any more numbers until I hit a big number … now it's a hundred!' Baker was careful never to lie. Only that first weekend did he take a chance, telling journalists, 'We've got fifty and I'm confident that next week it will be one hundred.' He recalled, 'It bloody well was as well. I took a gamble that I'd get another fifty, and I did.'

When news of Conservatives for Britain broke, the whips, under their new chief Mark Harper, launched a frantic effort to assess the scale of the problem. 'To be honest, I think they're a bit frightened,' one MP said that weekend.

Baker realised that he could not employ a totally scorched-earth strategy. The referendum was a civil war within the Conservative Party. Baker wanted to win, but he also wanted there to be a Tory Party left standing at the end of the process. He resolved to act with politeness and decency throughout the battles ahead. 'The central point was to not break the Conservative Party,' he said. Baker led by example. When he launched Conservatives for Britain he had not told his whip, George Hollingbery, who was away: 'I bought him a bottle of whisky to say sorry.' He continued to shower the whips with gifts: 'I bought them flowers and chocolates, and I've tried to be nice to the whips whilst making their lives miserable.'

Downing Street initially dismissed the group as a mere talking shop, and pointed out that many of those signing up would probably not back Brexit. Like Business for Britain, Baker's outfit was ostensibly trying to stiffen Cameron's spine in the renegotiation rather than oppose him outright. But having built his army, the general intended to use it. He believed time was tight: 'We kept hearing the government's intention was to move to a referendum extremely fast, before we had any chance to organise.'

The Referendum Bill had been published in May, and the Eurosceptics were concerned that it stacked the campaign against them. Baker planned his military campaign. 'There were five early battles we had to win,' he said. The first battle seemed esoteric at the time, but may have been crucial. Following the Scottish referendum, Cameron's team believed that the SNP had derived a great deal of benefit from owning the 'Yes' side of the question on the ballot paper. Voting positively for independence seemed a more attractive thing to do than voting 'No' for the status quo. They resolved not to make the same mistake again. When the Referendum Bill was published at the end of May the EU question read: 'Should the United Kingdom remain a member of the European Union?' David Cameron would own the 'Yes' vote this time.

The sceptics protested. It would ultimately be for the Electoral Commission, the watchdog that oversees such issues, to decide the wording. There was precedent for the approach the government had taken. In 1975 the public had been asked, 'Do you think the United Kingdom should stay in the European Community?' That had delivered a 67 per cent share of the vote for 'Yes'.

The importance of the question was highlighted by polling from ICM, published in early June. It found that if voters were asked, 'Should the UK remain a member of the EU?' 59 per cent said yes. But if the question was, 'Should the United Kingdom remain a member of the European Union or leave the European Union?' only 55 per cent opted to remain. The Eurosceptics seized on this evidence. 'It seemed to reveal there was 4 per cent in what the question was, whether it was a "yes/no" question or a "remain/leave" question,' said Baker. 'We put forward a number of colleagues together to write to the Commission saying we strongly believe it should be "remain/leave", not "yes/no".'

On 1 September the Electoral Commission announced that it was changing the question to 'Should the United Kingdom remain a member of the European Union or leave the European Union?' The watchdog had commissioned its own research, and found that while the original question was 'not significantly leading' it was doubly unbalanced, since only the 'Remain' option was explained in the question, and the 'Yes' response was for the status quo. Baker's guerrillas had won an important victory, the significance of which was only understood nine months later. 'Bearing in mind ICM thought there was 4 per cent in that question, that battle alone could have won the campaign,' Baker said.

The second battle concerned the timing of the referendum. Cameron was expected to call it for spring 2016, and ministers saw the advantages of holding it on the same day as the local elections in England on 5 May. Elections to the Scottish Parliament and Welsh Assembly were also due on the same day. Prior to the publication of the Bill, the Electoral Commission had recommended that the referendum not be held on that date. But the wording of the Bill allowed the government to combine the vote with 'any election'. In early June Cameron said, 'I think the British public are quite capable of going to a polling booth and making two important decisions rather than just one.'

The Eurosceptics envisaged Conservative activists being asked to deliver double-sided campaign literature, urging a Tory vote in council elections and a Remain vote in the other. On this, crucially, they had the support of the Labour Party, which feared the referendum would boost turnout in Tory areas and damage their local election effort. In a bid to avoid a rebellion and a Commons defeat, the government performed a U-turn, and ruled out a referendum on 5 May. It was another morale-boosting win for Baker's team, setting them up nicely for the first real Commons showdown on the second reading of the Bill.

Baker's third battle, and perhaps the most important, was over the issue of purdah. 'Purdah' is the civil service term for the time between the formal start of an election campaign and the announcement of the results. During that period, government officials are forbidden from doing anything that might influence the vote one way or another. In pretty well all British elections there is a purdah period, usually of twenty-eight days. But buried in the small print of the Bill was a plan to scrap purdah altogether. When this was spotted by the Eurosceptics they immediately smelt a rat. They believed there was nothing to stop Cameron enlisting the Whitehall machine to pump out Remain propaganda until polling day. Owen Paterson accused the government of 'seeking to bend the rules to leave it free to fix the vote in its favour, right up until polling day'.[1]

Ministers argued that applying strict purdah rules during the EU referendum campaign would make government dealings with Brussels 'unworkable', and would open the door to legal action if a minister so much as made a statement on the EU. But the sceptics were unmoved, and when the Bill had its second reading in the Commons on the evening of 16 June they decided the time had come for a show of strength. They met in Baker's office in Portcullis House and agreed that they would mount the first major rebellion against a majority Tory government in twenty-three years.

'I will never forget the night of the first purdah rebellion,' says Baker. He walked with John Redwood, Owen Paterson, Bernard Jenkin and Bill Cash to the office of David Lidington, a 'little cell underneath the House of Commons'. It was a big moment for Baker. Lidington had helped get his name onto the Conservative candidates list, and Baker considered him 'my neighbour and friend'. Now he was there to tell him the Eurosceptics planned to defeat the government. 'We got into a lift and I thought, "God, what am I doing walking down this corridor with these guys?" We went to see David Lidington. It was a real *Reservoir Dogs* moment, because there weren't enough chairs. I can still vividly picture it in my mind. John Redwood got comfortable by crouching, I was leaning against a door sideways, Bernard was leaning against the door frame. And we were just scattered around the room talking about the way it was and the way we wanted it to be, and then telling him we were going to be rebels. It was like a horror film. All our game faces came out, and all of a sudden it was war. It was horrible.'

During the debate in the Commons that followed, Lidington said the government would amend the Bill in the autumn to prevent ministers paying for campaigning activity in the last four weeks before the poll. But the rebels rejected this as inadequate. In the end the government defeated Cash's amendment by 288 votes to ninety-seven, a majority of nearly two hundred, because Labour abstained, preferring to let the issue run and run. But Baker had shown his strength. In total, twenty-seven Tories defied the whip, including Liam Fox. The former defence secretary voted against his party for the first time in twenty-three years. 'I had no choice,' he said. Baker suddenly understood the power he now exerted as the shop steward of the Eurosceptics: 'We could have won if Labour hadn't peeled off.'

Baker, who was a teller for the rebels, made sure he was standing nearest the despatch box when the result was announced. Ostentatiously, he reached over and offered his hand to Lidington. Guerrilla war, but not a scorched-earth policy. 'The reason I did it was to show we weren't going to make it personal and nasty. Everyone was afraid we'd go back to a caricature of the Maastricht days. The point of these rebellions was always to win the referendum, it wasn't to be difficult.'

He made this point when he asked to see Cameron in July. They had a cordial meeting, during which Baker explained, 'I don't intend to destroy the Conservative Party. I intend to do this in a civilised way.' He said later, 'I'm quite sure he thought I was going to be bravely losing, that he was patting me on the head and that I'd be leading twenty-five Conservatives to a brave defeat.'

Bernard Jenkin led the next stage of the battle. Using his position as chairman of the Public Administration and Constitutional Affairs Committee, Jenkin first set up hearings on the purdah issue, summoning the cabinet secretary Sir Jeremy Heywood to explain his position, and then got unanimous backing from the other committee members to write a letter to Lidington at the start of July warning that the change to the rules made it 'appear that the government is seeking to circumvent proper processes to enable it to use the machinery of government for campaigning activity'.

When the Bill returned to the Commons on 7 September there was a head of steam for action. Vote Leave had spotted another potential minefield. Richard Howell, a cerebral-looking red-headed young man in his early twenties, was known in the office as 'Ricardo'. A key figure in the research team, Howell was an expert on EU law, and would be called 'a genius' by both Cummings and Michael Gove. He spotted that the government were trying to push through plans for a very short campaign. The Bill called for a designation process to choose the official Leave and Remain campaigns. Everyone had assumed that would take place in February, if that was when Cameron got his deal, with a referendum in June or July. But Howell noticed that the government had given themselves wriggle room to delay the designation process until just four weeks before polling day. It was already clear that Vote Leave might face competition for the designation from Arron Banks. The Bill would allow the government to campaign for several months before the official Leave campaign had even been selected, giving Dominic Cummings just four weeks to take the fight to Cameron. Rob Oxley said, 'We knew purdah would be a fight, but the four-week thing we were significantly worried about. The one member of staff that no one knows about who was most instrumental in us winning was Ricardo. He was the guy who was reading the parliamentary procedure. He understood it even more than Bill Cash.'

Jenkin tabled an amendment that would force the government to set out the rules four months before polling day, to prevent ministers 'bouncing' opponents into a quick referendum. This time, Labour lined up with the rebels and the SNP. Jenkin's amendment was conceded without a vote. Lidington sought to buy off the Tory backbenches by agreeing to amend the Bill, reinstating purdah to ensure a 'fair fight', but allowing ministers and officials to talk about the EU as long as it was not directly related to the referendum. But in the main vote the government lost by 312 votes to 285. It was Cameron's first Commons defeat since the general election. Thirty-seven Tories defied the whip.

Baker was conflicted but euphoric. 'We won it, because Labour was with us. That was one of the hideous parts of this process, we had to work with Labour and the SNP. But purdah was a big thing. It might have been enough to win the referendum.'

It is tempting to regard the purdah issue as just the kind of obscure constitutional humbug that the Palaeosceptics had specialised in for decades, but it had a material effect on the campaign. The start of purdah on 27 May 2016 coincided almost exactly with the moment the Leave campaign gained the advantage. It prevented Cameron from using the power of government to grab headlines. Paul Stephenson said: 'If there was no purdah, we'd have been screwed.'

Graham Brady, the chairman of the 1922 Committee, said, 'There were battles that were fought which ended up immensely important, and the point when the campaign turned was the point when purdah kicked in, and that thing – which seemed like a slightly dry little tussle in the Commons months before – actually might have been the thing that made the difference by ensuring that at least for part of the campaign it was fair.'

Brady himself was a pivotal figure in the fourth battle.

David Campbell Bannerman, the co-chairman of Conservatives for Britain, wrote a strategy paper before the general election, which he showed to Matthew Elliott, laying out some of the lessons of the Scottish referendum: 'My main concern was always that we weren't caught with our pants down. The key lesson was, you've got to neutralise the party machine. In Aberdeen, where I was, Labour got their vote out from the Better Together office. I thought, "We are in trouble if we are up against these type of machines." So part of Conservatives for Britain's role was to neutralise the Conservative Party.'

Steve Baker recruited Steve Bell, the president of the National Convention of the Conservative Party, as a vice-president of Conservatives for Britain, and urged him to use his influence. Brady, as chairman of the backbench 1922 Committee, also went to work on Cameron and the party board, making the case that the party would 'tear itself apart' if its activists, two-thirds of whom backed Brexit, were told to side with Remain.

On 21 September the Conservative Party board unanimously agreed that the party and its staff would remain neutral. Cameron himself proposed the solution. The decision had two practical consequences. It meant that the Remain campaign had effectively lost £7 million to spend, the amount the Conservative Party would have been permitted by the Electoral Commission. 'The equivalent of the entire budget of Vote Leave was taken out of the Remain campaign by keeping the Conservative Party neutral,' says Baker.

The second consequence of the decision was that Tory MPs would be barred from using their own canvassing data to target voters during the referendum: 'CCHQ will not supply funds or voter information to either campaign,' the party said. The decision upset pro-Europeans like Alistair Burt: 'I felt disappointed that the Conservative Party, the great European party over the years, had to fight this with its hands tied behind its back. I felt ashamed that we weren't able to say, "We are the Conservative Party, in favour of the European Union." But I've no doubt that had we done so there would have been mass resignations. For the long-term interests of the party those voices were right and I was wrong.'

Conservatives for Britain were not the only ones mounting ambushes in the Commons. On 19 November a combination of Labour and the Liberal Democrats passed an amendment to the Bill in the House of Lords to give sixteen- and seventeen-year-olds the vote, as they had had during the Scottish referendum. The government, this time with the backing of Baker and his supporters, killed off the plan, which Cameron saw as a precedent that would only help Labour in general elections. The sceptics saw it as a chance to prevent an influx of young voters likely to back Remain.

Stronger In campaign chiefs believe the decision was one in which the interests of the Conservative Party were put before those of the Remain campaign. 'The votes-at-sixteen decision in retrospect was a big mistake,' Will Straw said after the referendum, when Stronger In had lost by 1.2 million votes. Had there been a 75 per cent turnout among sixteen- and seventeen-year-olds, which would have been consistent with what happened during the Scottish independence referendum, and had three-quarters of them voted Remain, which would be consistent with what eighteen-to-twenty-four-year-olds did in the EU referendum, it would have represented a net gain of 650,000 votes for Stronger In. That would not, in itself, have been enough to get them over the finish line, but Straw believed 'it would have changed the atmospherics of the campaign'. If one in four of those young people had persuaded their parents to vote a different way, Remain would have won.

The fifth and final battle which Baker had mapped out months before came to a head in January 2016. Throughout 2015 David Cameron had insisted that ministers were bound by collective responsibility, and would have to resign if they wanted to campaign against him in the referendum. This position provoked fury among the Eurosceptics, and Graham Brady repeatedly raised the issue. Cameron knew it would be a problem. When he appointed John Whittingdale culture secretary just after the general election, Whittingdale told him, 'You do know I would probably campaign for Brexit.' The same message was conveyed by Iain Duncan Smith.

Chris Grayling, the leader of the Commons, and Theresa Villiers, the Northern Ireland secretary, forced a change of heart. Grayling said, 'I decided a long time ago that once we'd won the election and knew we were going to get the referendum I was never in any doubt I was going to campaign to leave.' At party conference in October he deliberately 'sailed close to the wind' when addressing a Business for Britain and Conservatives for Britain event. In the summer he had sat down with Daniel Hannan at a bar in Brussels to discuss how they were going to get involved in the campaign. 'I expected to have to resign to do it,' said Grayling. He also met Dominic Cummings and Matthew Elliott in November to let them know he would be on board. He had a further discussion with Elliott in December about his intention to tell Cameron after Christmas that he was going to declare for the Leave campaign. Rumours swept the lobby that Grayling was going to quit as leader of the Commons in January, and he discussed the prospect of an exit interview with at least one journalist. Downing Street briefed that he might be fired before he had the chance to jump ship. Paradoxically, that strengthened his position.

Grayling went to see Cameron in early November and said, 'My worry about where we are is that we are powerless to resist a decision that will cost jobs in the United Kingdom, that we have no ability to set limits on how many people come and work here, and we have little to do with the decisions of the EU.' Cameron replied that he hoped to keep his ministerial team together, and vowed to 'do my best' to get what he wanted. Grayling said he would support him as prime minister even if he failed, and they parted on cordial terms.

When the details of Cameron's preliminary deal were published Grayling decided the prime minister clearly had no chance of satisfying him, and that it was 'only a question of when' he would have to pay Cameron another visit. Grayling had been told by a ministerial colleague that Theresa Villiers was also considering her position. They talked over the Christmas break: 'I told her what I was going to do, and she agreed that she was going to put in a call to the prime minister on the same day.'

Shortly after the regular 8.30 a.m. planning meeting in Number 10 on Monday, 4 January 2016, Grayling saw Cameron and Ed Llewellyn in the prime minister's study and told them, 'I'm going to declare for Leave, and campaign for Leave. If you want me to resign I will.' He was expecting to have to go: 'David Cameron had always said up until that point that ministers will be expected to toe the line. So I expected to have to resign to do it.' But Cameron replied, 'Please don't. I'm going to let you campaign anyway, but in a few weeks' time.' Grayling pressed him: 'I'm really keen to get involved now, because I want to add a bit of weight to the campaign, there are things that I want to get going and doing.'

After two meetings they reached an accommodation. Cameron agreed to make a statement the following day that cabinet collective responsibility would be suspended for the duration of the campaign, in exchange for which Grayling agreed that he would not formally declare for Leave until after the Brussels summit more than six weeks later, at which Cameron hoped to finalise his renegotiation. Instead, Grayling would signal his intent by writing a piece for the *Telegraph*, and would be able to get involved informally in campaign preparations. Later the same day Villiers spoke to the prime minister, who told her she would be free to campaign after the summit. She said she was content to comply as well. Announcing the change to the Commons, Cameron said, 'There will be a clear government position, but it will be open to individual ministers to take a different personal position while remaining part of the government.'

Steve Baker, who had been a confidant for Grayling through the autumn, saw this commitment as key, because it liberated ministers, particularly those outside the cabinet, to back Brexit. Priti Patel, Dominic Raab, Penny Mordaunt and Andrea Leadsom were all relieved when they no longer had to choose between their beliefs and their careers. A Leadsom aide said, 'Those ministers wouldn't have been available to the campaign if Chris Grayling hadn't worked to do it.'

Daniel Hannan sees Villiers as an unsung heroine of Brexit: 'She doesn't get a scintilla of the credit she deserves. Her first act as transport secretary was to take down the EU flag from all of the buildings that she was responsible for. I only know this because a civil servant told me. Can you imagine any male politician making that decision then not telling anybody?'

A friend of Grayling believes Cameron should have called his bluff: 'The PM could have been completely bloody-minded. The gambler in me would have said, "Take a chance, see what happens, sack him, and if in two weeks on from this, if nobody else has gone, you get an even freer run."' Cameron at that stage believed that Boris Johnson and Michael Gove would support him, and that the only cabinet ministers who would back Brexit would be easy to dismiss as right-wingers with little public profile. Cameron felt the risks of giving ministers freedom were lower than the cost of enraging the party if he stuck to his guns. Once again the prime minister had done what was best for the Tory Party, rather than for the Remain cause. Ryan Coetzee, the head of strategy for Stronger In, believed Cameron was too ready to give ground to the rebels: 'If a stray dog comes to your campsite, you don't make it go away by giving it some food.'

In just six months, Conservatives for Britain had ruthlessly executed Steve Baker's guerrilla war plan. They had helped change the referendum question, the date and the campaign lead time, saved purdah, and ensured the Conservative Party was neutral and cabinet ministers could take sides. None of those things was sufficient to win the referendum on its own, but each of them was necessary, and together they may have been decisive. 'The war really was won in many ways in the preparation,' said Baker. 'The question might have been worth 4 per cent. The Conservative Party's neutrality took the entire Leave budget out of the Remain campaign. Neutrality made the superstars available. The principal purpose of CfB was making it possible to win the referendum and marshalling the MPs to do that.' By remaining polite, Baker also maximised the number of Tory MPs who joined the Leave campaign. As one MP put it, 'Steve's an aerospace engineer who doesn't much like conflict, but he held the government by the bollocks on this journey.'

It was just as well that Baker was blooded. As the New Year dawned his powers of negotiation would be put to the ultimate test as MPs, donors and his colleagues turned on Dominic Cummings, the man who held the entire Leave campaign by the bollocks.

7

THE COUP

Rob Oxley thought he had done pretty well. He'd been in a television debate with Lucy Thomas, and he knew he'd wiped the floor with her. Oxley had teased Thomas by referring to Stronger In as 'the BSE campaign'. The two were friends, but the taunt was as effective as it was childish. Normally highly composed, Thomas lost her temper, and a video of their exchange was quickly posted on the Guido Fawkes website. Oxley returned to the Vote Leave office pleased with himself – only to be told off by Dominic Cummings. Oxley thought he had done everything that had been asked of him. He had got across Vote Leave's favourite message, that EU membership cost taxpayers £350 million a week, he had called Stronger In 'EU-funded', and he had hurled the 'BSE' jibe.

But Cummings admonished him. When Thomas lost her rag, he told Oxley, 'What you should have said was, "And as I was saying, the BSE campaign …." Just double down.' That was Cummings all over. 'Double down' became Vote Leave's internal motto. 'If we'd started a row, you didn't withdraw, you doubled down,' says Oxley.

This uncompromising approach by Cummings was to spark an attempt to oust him which, had it succeeded, could have killed Leave's chances of victory stone dead.

Cummings' other instruction to Oxley that day was more obscure, but even more revealing of the kind of campaign he wanted to run. It was not just Steve Baker who had read classics of military theory. When Oxley returned to the office, Cummings told him, 'You've got to get in their OODA loop.'

'OODA loop' is a term from American military strategy that stands for 'observe, orient, decide, and act'. It was the brainchild of US Air Force Colonel John Boyd, a fighter pilot in the Korean War. Boyd believed that everyone makes decisions by following the four stages of OODA. He wrote: 'In order to win, we should operate at a faster tempo or rhythm than our adversaries – or, better yet, get inside [the] adversary's Observation-Orientation-Decision-Action loop. Such activity will make us appear ambiguous (unpredictable) thereby generate confusion and disorder among our adversaries.' Cummings describes Boyd as 'a brilliant guy, a modern-day Sun Tzu'.

In Cummings' view, with Thomas disorientated and on the run, Oxley should have made her more so. Vote Leave's strategy throughout the campaign was to disrupt and disorientate the enemy. Cummings' grounding in strategic theory did not stop there: 'If you're serious about these things, the classics speak truth,' he said. 'Thucydides, Clausewitz, Sun Tzu, Mao on guerrilla warfare.' Cummings had studied Otto von Bismarck at university under the historian Norman Stone, and had later read 'a whole bunch of biographies and original sources' on the nineteenth-century statesman after he stopped working for Michael Gove. He vowed to run the Leave campaign on the same principles as the man who unified Germany by means of war and exploiting the weakness of his enemies: 'Of the people we've got good sources for, he's undoubtedly the most extraordinary and most able political operator. He approached things with extreme flexibility. Always avoid being boxed in, always have two irons in the fire, wherever you can. Try to avoid dead ends, because you never know what's going to come and bite you in the arse.' Critics of Vote Leave's campaign messaging might also recall Bismarck's insight that 'People never lie so much as after a hunt, during a war or before an election.'

Since Cummings knew many of the Downing Street and Remain chiefs well, he also knew their weak points. 'Dom knew which lines would annoy the other side,' a campaign source said. 'He knew the pressure points of people.' When Downing Street's Daniel Korski was accused of bullying businesses, a dossier on Korski's pro-European background found its way to the media. When Kate Rock, a Tory peer who worked for Cameron, found herself in the news, one paper was encouraged to use an unflattering photograph that she was known to hate – both examples of getting in the enemy's OODA loop. 'The Labour press office did not know how to hit the Tories like we did,' the source said.

The happiest Paul Stephenson ever saw Cummings was on the morning he told the team to put the NHS logo on the side of Vote Leave's bus:

'He was literally jumping around saying, "We're going to use the NHS logo and they're going to hate it."' Health secretary Jeremy Hunt's team had already sent a legal letter threatening to sue Vote Leave for putting the logo on their leaflets. Stephenson responded that if they wished to impound the bus he would be happy to arrange a media call for Hunt to come down and do it personally.

Cummings' psychological warfare was good strategy, but it also caused a rift with MPs that was almost his undoing. From the moment he began briefing journalists in May 2015 about his approach to the campaign, he was clear that he wanted to take the Confederation of British Industry off the battlefield. He saw the CBI as irredeemably pro-EU, and as it was one of the most influential business voices in the country, he wanted it neutralised. Protests from Nationalists in the lead-up to the Scottish referendum had meant the CBI was forced to largely sit out that campaign. Cummings decided to stage a protest at the CBI's annual conference in November. Stephenson suggested they should infiltrate the conference hall and get people to hold up something. Cummings embraced the idea, and told the team, 'If there are not calls for me to be sacked after the CBI conference, then you haven't done your job.'

The team found two students – Phil Sheppard and Peter Lyons – from Students for Britain, Vote Leave's 'militant wing'. They created a fake company and gained access to the event. When David Cameron got up to speak on 9 November they held up banners reading 'CBI = Voice of Brussels'. The protest might have been even more dramatic. The usually cautious Matthew Elliott reminded people that Countryside Alliance campaigners had set off rape alarms during a protest at a Labour conference, though he denies suggesting their use at the CBI.

The stunt got huge publicity, but Eurosceptic MPs 'hated it' because they had been kept in the dark by Cummings. Steve Baker, by his own account, 'went bananas' and the two fell out 'very badly'. Baker says, 'I didn't like that it breached the PM's security. I didn't like that it involved lying to the CBI. I didn't like that it put those two young lads in a position where they'll always be remembered as the lads who did the CBI stunt.' Paul Stephenson rejects this argument: 'They weren't duped into anything. They were up for it. They knew exactly what they were getting into.' Both Sheppard and Lyons worked for the campaign until the end.

Baker's main beef was that the MPs had been frozen out. 'What I really hated is that my permission was not asked and I was not trusted with that knowledge. It really hurt that my reputation had been played with.' Peter Bone, the MP for Wellingborough, shared Baker's concern that the students would 'have a mark against them', while Bernard Jenkin was also 'very annoyed about it': 'Dominic became very much the focus of attention because he kept saying or doing very controversial things.' Jenkin believed the stunt might imperil Vote Leave's chances of winning designation as the official 'Out' campaign and put off voters: 'The reputation of the Leave campaign would be intrinsic to its effectiveness. Unlike a plain "No" campaign, in this referendum we were the people making the proposition, to leave the EU, and people would need to be able to trust our campaign.' When Baker refused to join Vote Leave's board because he did not feel Cummings was prepared to be held accountable, Jenkin, 'with some foreboding', agreed to take his place. 'The first thing I did was to ask the Compliance Committee to investigate the CBI stunt,' says Jenkin. 'It turned out there was nothing untoward, but the board needed to know that.'

The CBI protest might have upset the MPs, but it helped internal bonding in the campaign headquarters: 'It was blooding everyone for the campaign to come,' says Stephenson. 'The office got into its warlike mentality that day.' They would soon need it.

The event that sparked the anti-Cummings insurrection was the decision of Richard Murphy, Vote Leave's head of field operations, to resign at the end of November. Murphy had been brought in by Matthew Elliott from Conservative campaign headquarters, where he had been director of field operations, but he quickly clashed with Cummings. Murphy objected to the campaign director wanting to focus on digital rather than 'on the ground' campaigning in the initial stages. Cummings believed Murphy was too set in his ways. Stephenson describes him as 'old school': 'We created our own software for canvass returns and Murphy wanted to use this thing he'd been using for thirty years. It was a clash of cultures. He kept on threatening to walk out, and in the end he did.'

Cummings saw a man who was experienced but unwilling to adapt, and who 'hated' the questioning, data-driven campaign he was creating. At one point he told Murphy, 'Just saying it's what you've done for thirty years isn't good enough. Haven't you learnt that from Obama's campaign?' Murphy, he could see, found that 'insulting'. According to one witness, he replied, 'Why don't we use stuff that British people know about rather than Americans?'

Murphy's departure further unsettled the MPs at a time when they were already concerned about Cummings' attitude. Their mood darkened further when Murphy was tapped up by Arron Banks two weeks later as director of field campaigning for Leave.EU.

Shortly after Murphy left, MPs began getting calls from people spreading rumours that 'Cummings is a psychopath who bullies people in the office, threatens to beat people up.' Cummings was initially dismissive of this smear campaign. He had been the subject of false rumours before, when he was upsetting people in Whitehall, that he was 'a heroin addict or gay'. He assumed the MPs would not believe that he was actually threatening to kill people. Afterwards he realised this insouciance was 'an error'. Murphy's view that Vote Leave had no ground game caught hold with MPs. While Cummings had no background in field campaigning, Nick Varley, who was brought in by Murphy to be head of ground operations, said this was unfair: 'Dom never ignored the ground campaign, and knew it was vitally important.'

Murphy's departure enraged Peter Bone and Tom Pursglove, two Brexit-backing MPs from the Midlands who were experts in running field operations and believed that Cummings was not doing enough to prioritise the ground war. Bone was sixty-three, and a dead ringer for Sven-Göran Eriksson, the former England football manager. He often raised a smile at PMQs by asking Cameron questions from his wife, 'Mrs Bone'. If he was in the mood, Cameron would reply that he was doing his best to 'satisfy her'. Pursglove, who had just turned twenty-seven, was the youngest MP in the Commons. Known as 'Mini-Bone' at Westminster because the two were virtually inseparable, he had begun his political career working on Bone's election taskforce.

'The Bones' believed they had the blueprint for success because they had got Pursglove elected in the marginal seat of Corby, overturning a Labour majority of nearly 8,000. They knocked on every door in the constituency twice and campaigned hard on immigration, encouraging Tory voters tempted by Ukip to back the resolutely sceptic Pursglove while urging tribally Labour voters who would never vote Tory to support Ukip. In this successful endeavour the pair got no help from Tory HQ. 'They cut us off completely,' Bone said. 'We had a huge bloody row with them; they told us banging on about Europe won't win us the seat.'

Baker asked Bone and Pursglove to go to Vote Leave in October and give advice on the ground war. Bone believed in 'endless amounts of canvassing', since he had found knocking on doors was three times as effective in turning out votes as delivering literature. But he did not believe he got a commitment from Vote Leave to a proper get-out-the-vote effort. His mood darkened when Vote Leave sent him 130,000 leaflets suggesting that some of the £350 million-a-week cost of the EU could be spent on the NHS. He refused to deliver them, because he saw them as an attack on the government. Then Richard Murphy resigned.

If the MPs were angry about the CBI stunt and the Murphy defection, they were incandescent when a week later Vote Leave made its first overt attack on David Cameron. On Saturday, 5 December the *Daily Telegraph* splashed on claims that the prime minister had 'made clear to his close allies that he will lead the "Out" campaign if he considers the result of his renegotiation with Brussels to be unsuccessful'.

At Vote Leave the story was interpreted as an attempt by Craig Oliver to encourage Eurosceptic MPs who might have backed Leave to remain loyal to the prime minister. He told Cummings, 'We need to get him off this pedestal. It's not true. Let's provoke him.' Stephenson texted a couple of Sunday newspaper journalists, including Glen Owen of the *Mail on Sunday*. The following day the paper carried a quote from a senior source at Vote Leave saying, 'If Cameron thinks we'd want him leading the "Leave" campaign he's deluded. He's toxic on this issue. If there was a choice between who to put up in a television debate between Cameron and Boris, you'd want Boris every time.'

The quote caused uproar among Tory MPs, many of whom had pledged to avoid attacking the PM until the renegotiation was concluded. Cummings was blamed for the briefing, but in Westminster Tower it was Stephenson who was nicknamed 'Toxic' for the rest of the campaign. Explaining the rationale for the attack later, he said, 'The PM never again tried to lead the Leave campaign. And it was also a signal that "We're not scared. We're in for a fight."'

But the first people to pick a fight were Vote Leave's own MPs. Cummings had established a Monday-morning meeting at which they could sound off. That Monday, Bone and Pursglove joined the usual cast of Steve Baker, Bernard Jenkin and co. Baker complained about the *Mail on Sunday* story: 'While we're briefing that Cameron's toxic, it's going to be very hard to sign up colleagues.'

Tempers frayed further when Bone got into an argument with Cummings. First, he took issue with the campaign's messaging, saying,

'You're doing all this NHS stuff, £350 million, we don't think it's a winner.' Cummings explained that he had data showing that the messages worked, but that if MPs wanted to use different messages in their patch they were free to do so: 'With respect, this is an empirical question and I've got an empirical answer, and if you say your local area's different, fine. Do something different.'

Bone then raised Richard Murphy's complaints about the lack of a ground campaign. Cummings felt Bone had a point about the slow speed of the ground campaign, but blamed Murphy. Then Bone said Vote Leave should be trying to encourage Cameron to lead the campaign rather than alienating him: 'You can't say he's toxic, this is outrageous. The PM could have led the campaign!' Bone believed that if Cameron supported Leave they would 'win by a mile', and did not like the fact that their potential saviour had been 'insulted'. He saw Cummings and Stephenson's approach as '*West Wing* behaviour', after the grandstanding aides in the US television series. He told a friend, 'They really slagged the PM off, and that was clearly silly.'

Cummings regarded Bone as absurdly naïve about Cameron's intentions. Biting his tongue, he was relatively gracious at first, but eventually said, 'We think you're wrong, and if you don't like it, you don't need to be involved in the campaign.'

One observer described the putdown as 'brutal'. Bone stormed out of the meeting. After it broke up, Pursglove complained that Stephenson's briefing was 'very short-sighted'. But even Baker, who was annoyed by the 'toxic' quote, sided with Stephenson, saying, 'Tom, if the PM's going to lead the Out campaign, he's not going to decide against it because someone briefed against him.'

The upshot of the Bone–Cummings bust-up was that Bone and Pursglove, with the support of the Labour donor John Mills, set up a new organisation called Grassroots Out to help MPs create a ground game in their constituencies. The group's name was abbreviated to 'GO', and Bone had livid lime-green ties made up sporting the logo. GO quickly became a place where MPs annoyed by Cummings could find a home. Arron Banks targeted Kate Hoey and John Mills, urging them to help bring the two wings of the Eurosceptic movement together. By Christmas, Mills was openly calling for a merger with Banks.

Turning the screw, Banks began writing to Matthew Elliott suggesting a merger. Chris Bruni-Lowe remembers, 'We said to Banks, "You must write to Elliott as many times as possible because he's looking for the designation." So Banks said, "We're replicating each other on so many things, we're spending so much money, millions. Why don't we just spend it all on the same campaign?" Elliott would tell people, "We're not doing that. We don't trust this madman Banks.'"

Cummings' biggest problem, though, was a growing view among Conservative MPs that he was not the right man to run the campaign – they were. 'People like Bernard [Jenkin] and Bill [Cash], who didn't like what we were doing, didn't like the fact they weren't on the news every day, were causing trouble for us,' said one Vote Leave official. Jenkin says it is 'absolute rubbish' that they wanted more media attention, and that he was 'very happy to take more of a back seat'.

Cash, the MP for the Staffordshire seat of Stone, was respected as an authority on the minutiae of EU procedure, but was regarded by many colleagues as the last man with whom they would wish to be trapped in a lift. Even his friends admit that he had to be kept away from the public: 'Although he's absolutely right, he wasn't the face of Brexit we wanted to put on TV all the time,' another Eurosceptic MP said. 'Bill took it a bit hard. You can't put Bill out to sell Brexit to the people.'

Cash also clashed with Cummings over his contract and his pay. He had been fed rumours that Cummings was on a huge salary. In fact Cummings, Elliott, Stephenson and Victoria Woodcock, the most senior figures in the campaign, were all paid £96,000 per year. The standoff resembled a spat between two sets of groupies for a band called Euroscepticism. The Palaeosceptics had identified the act when it was just playing gigs in local pubs, always preferred their early stuff and resented the producer who had turned their minority pursuit into a stadium act even if that meant playing some different tunes.

Cummings' main beef, according to one of his closest collaborators, was that 'Conservative MPs have been in charge of Euroscepticism for the last twenty years, and it's been defeat after defeat for the period. I turn up and the group of MPs who are responsible for all those defeats tell me that they know how to win. I know if I let them run this campaign we'll lose. I don't have time to be diplomatic to them, I just have to get on with it and run it.'

That was certainly how Bernard Jenkin felt: 'Dominic was very down on anyone who'd been a Maastricht rebel. His narrative was that the Eurosceptics were completely incompetent and their image was hopeless. John Redwood, Peter Lilley, Bernard Jenkin, Iain Duncan Smith, Owen Paterson, all these people were toxic and therefore not the face of the campaign.' But Jenkin added, 'Sometimes, I did feel that people rather green on the subject weren't answering the questions as capably as some of us who'd been doing it for thirty years.'

Daniel Hannan could see faults on both sides: 'Although Dom was very brilliant, did the job for which he was contracted and carried it out superbly, he doesn't see the point of MPs. He's not a patient man if he thinks people are being foolish. A lot of MPs have big egos. They think they are terribly important, expect deference, and get huffy when they don't get it. A lot of MPs are thin-skinned creatures, and felt that they should have been in control, and I think they took it badly that the campaign was being run by someone who didn't pretend to defer to them. Leave.EU scented the opportunity of targeting Dom as the weak point, so they were constantly briefing against him.'

When MPs and donors complained that Arron Banks was bad-mouthing the campaign to other Tories in order to peel them off into GO, Cummings would reply, 'If you stop having meetings and talking about it, it will stop being a problem.'

But for Bernard Jenkin it was Cummings' manner, not his arguments, that was at fault: 'Some people think he made the situation worse, other people think he was a genius, and the fact is it probably was a combination of the two. Dominic was right in principle about not merging, it was just the tone with which it was being done which was so destructive.'

The MPs were right to think they had no power. Paul Stephenson said, 'Where did power sit in the campaign? Not really anywhere other than wandering in to have a chat with Dom.'

Everything acquired greater urgency in December, when it became clear that Cameron intended to do his deal in February. The day the Referendum Bill got royal assent, Cummings' favourite researcher, 'Ricardo' Howell, correctly predicted that the referendum would be held on 23 June. A countdown clock was put up on Vote Leave's wall. At the board meeting before Christmas Cummings said, 'I think these guys are going to go early. We have to start spending money and planning on this basis.'

Eurosceptic donors were also on the warpath. David Wall, the influential secretary of the Midlands Industrial Council, was concerned by Richard Murphy's departure. The two had worked together during the general election, when Murphy was responsible for checking that MIC money donated to Tory marginal seats was well spent. Chris Bruni-Lowe said, 'David Wall and lots of other donors who'd given a lot of money were just really unhappy – Patrick Barbour, Richard Smith, who owned Tufton Street.' The declared donors were unimpressed that Vote Leave was struggling to land new big-name backers and their cash. Conservative donors were under huge pressure from Downing Street to keep their wallets zipped. Rodney Leach of Open Europe phoned Tory donors to say, 'Give the PM a chance, he'll come back with more than people think, trust me. This will be a deal worth having.' This charm offensive frustrated Elliott: 'I had some quite senior Eurosceptic party people and donors who were quite convinced until the PM came back with his deal that it was going to be much more radical than it was. They literally thought the PM would come back with a trade-based relationship, and said we were being much too hasty in coming out for Leave.'

In early January 2016 a group of Leave donors gathered at Stuart Wheeler's home, Chilham Castle in Kent, to discuss merging Vote Leave and Leave.EU. Patrick Barbour and others were keen on the two groups coming together. Arron Banks was pushing the idea too, though he was not at the meeting. Paul Stephenson believed Banks deliberately 'started trying to make Dom public enemy number one with donors because Dom was the only thing stopping the merger'. Chris Bruni-Lowe, a Banks ally, said, 'The donors weren't giving any money because of Cummings. He is portrayed as some sort of genius, but most people saw him as completely mad.' During the meeting Cummings emailed Stephenson to tell him that some of the donors were discussing getting rid of him. 'It's a bit touch and go,' he said. Stephenson replied that if it would help he could tell people there, 'If you're off, I'm off,' and sent him a resignation statement that he could show them if necessary: 'If you need this, have it in your locker.' Cummings did not need the pledge on that occasion, but it was to come in useful soon.

Cummings also had his ear bent at the retreat by Daniel Hannan about who would represent the Out camp in the television debates. According to a Vote Leave official Hannan said, 'We don't just need the people who are the biggest personalities. We need the best debaters. People have been debating this for twenty years.' No one was in any doubt that he considered himself the pick of the bunch. In the Vote Leave offices Hannan was quickly dubbed 'the world's greatest debater'.

Hannan was in fact a very gifted speaker, and was deployed all around the country during the campaign in local debates. Stronger In officials regarded him as their most formidable foe in these encounters. But Cummings did not want Hannan fronting the campaign on television, and said to him what he had said to Nigel Farage, that he would test all the possible debate spokesmen and put up the one most likely to win over target voters. 'Dan, who basically helped get the thing off the ground, was then pushed out, because they were waiting for Gove,' said Bruni-Lowe.

The final straw for Cummings' critics came on 21 January, when *The Economist* published a cover interview with him. Bursting with his eclectic knowledge of everything from the EU to Soviet propaganda, it seemed calculated to offend the Palaeosceptics. Cummings argued for a simple campaign message about cost and control that could be digested by ordinary voters, rather than constitutional abstractions: 'The Eurosceptic world has thousands of books and zillions of pamphlets and has been talking about this for many decades. The challenge is not to say more things. The challenge is to focus, to simplify things.'

It may seem odd that an article in a low-circulation publication aimed at high minds could cause uproar, but it did. Cummings was not just running the campaign: a respectable part of the media had now made him the face of it too – and for many who had been campaigning on the issue for decades that was too much to bear. According to one senior figure at Vote Leave, Bernard Jenkin phoned him and said, 'We're going to lose the campaign because of Dom.' Hannan was also 'in a tailspin' about it. Another campaign official is clear that the article directly gave rise to an attempt to remove Cummings: 'The trigger for the coup was the interview Dom gave with *The Economist*, which caused various MPs to think, "Why aren't I on the front cover of *The Economist*?"'

In this toxic environment, tensions between Cummings and Elliott were amplified. Everyone at Vote Leave praised Elliott for creating the organisation and getting Cummings on board, but they also felt he was status-conscious. Cummings believed Elliott was 'discombobulated' by media rumours that Michael Gove would back Brexit, a development that would make him immovable and immeasurably more powerful. Looking back, Cummings said, 'Everyone's thinking at this point, "How do I get into controlling position?" And a lot of them, unfortunately for me, are thinking, "The clock's ticking and if Gove comes in then

Cummings is locked in. He's going to run it for good or evil. So you've got to get rid of Cummings before Gove moves." Elliott says his fear was that Gove would *not* join the campaign, not that he would.

In the final week of January, things came to a head. Bernard Jenkin, who as chairman of ExCom had borne the brunt of complaints from MPs, said he got a phone call. 'It was Matthew Elliott who rang me up after some kind of summit which was held in Chilham Castle in January and said to me, "Everybody agrees that Dominic's got to be moved to an advisory position." Dominic was never going to be removed totally. We wanted access to his expertise but we didn't feel he was right to be in a leadership role, running the entire organisation. He had a very autocratic management style. Some people hero-worshipped him, other people were terrified of him. And anyway, he had initially said to ExCom that he only wanted to set up the campaign, and had not wanted to run it.' Elliot flatly denied that this conversation took place: 'What Bernard says is complete rubbish, and he's obviously trying to displace the blame and throw the bloody knives in my direction.'

As chairman of the Commons Public Administration and Constitutional Affairs Committee, Jenkin had presided over a report into mismanagement at the children's charity Kids Company, run by the colourful and controversial Camila Batmanghelidjh, which was critical of the trustees. He worried that if the campaign disintegrated there would be similar questions for Vote Leave's board. 'My concern, shared with the other directors, was that Dominic represented a considerable risk to designation because you know you have to be a fit and proper person, you have to be pukka to get designation. Some of the things he did and wanted to do were not things that respectable companies did. Business people who were thinking about where to place their money could see that the way Vote Leave carried on was a bit of a risk, so they wanted to hedge their bets.'

The trouble with this approach is that political campaigns are not democracies. Nothing presages defeat like decision-making by committee. Campaigns are best operated as dictatorships.

Matthew Elliott vehemently denies that he orchestrated what became known as the coup. Friends say he recruited Cummings because he thought he was the best man for the job. But they admit that Cummings' rivalry with Arron Banks drove donors and MPs to approach Elliott to express concern about the way the campaign was being run. 'Vote Leave's

USP was that they were the nice cross-party campaign, positive, forward-looking, internationalist, more based on the economics than immigration, competent campaigners,' a source close to Elliott said. 'Banks was the nasty campaign, Ukip-based and unprofessional. That was the narrative between the two groups. But you got to a situation in January where it was quite difficult to sustain that. People were saying, "Hang on, you're saying these guys are unprofessional, but they've got six-figure numbers on their Facebook likes. You say they play dirty, but what about the CBI stunt?"'

Elliott's advocates say that MPs like Jenkin and Chris Grayling, newly liberated by David Cameron, began to question how the campaign was being run and why more money had not been raised. 'Matthew listened to them rather than shouting at them,' a friend said pointedly. 'He engaged with them, but he did not want to have anything to do with Ukip or Arron Banks.' Grayling said, 'I met two of the board members, including John Mills the chairman, and I simply expressed a worry that the rift between the different camps was actually putting people off at Westminster. The decision to go after Dominic Cummings and to remove him from his position was one taken by the board, and could only be taken by the board. I don't think they ever intended to remove Dominic altogether, they just intended to try and take him out of the front line. I think the board were generally worried the whole thing was going to fall apart.'

Banks sought to persuade Mills and other members of the Vote Leave board that the best solution was to sideline Cummings and have Elliott take charge of a merged campaign. 'The idea was that Elliott would be the chair of the combined organisation with Mills and Banks,' says Chris Bruni-Lowe. 'That was the plan, but it never happened.' Matthew Elliott remembers, 'I think in around November I was the nasty one, the one that Banks couldn't have anything to do with. Then it changed to being "They're both as bad as each other." Then it became Dom who was the one in his bad books.'

Banks also worked on Kate Hoey and other members of the Labour Leave organisation, who had also tired of Cummings. Banks said, 'Labour Leave were very discontented with Cummings. There was a Hertford Street lunch I had with Peter Bone, Tom Pursglove, Kate Hoey, John Mills and Matthew Elliott, where Kate Hoey just said to Matthew Elliott's face, "You've got to get rid of Dominic Cummings or we'll be walking." The feelings were very high. We tried to merge four times with them. It was always a different thing. First "Our donors won't allow this." Then "Our MPs won't allow it." Then "The cabinet ministers won't allow it." There was always an excuse why it couldn't be done.'

If the Vote Leave board remained divided about a merger with Banks, they did now agree that they wanted shot of Cummings. Daniel Hodson, the campaign's head of compliance, called a meeting with Cummings at 9 o'clock on the morning of Monday, 25 January to discuss Bill Cash's concerns about his contract. Cummings duly turned up at Westminster Tower, but there was no sign of Hodson. Then his phone rang and an 'agitated' Hodson said, 'You're not here for the meeting.' He was at 55 Tufton Street. Cummings explained that he was at the Vote Leave offices. Minutes later Hodson called back and said the meeting was definitely supposed to be at Tufton Street. Cummings, who was as usual rushed off his feet, said, 'I've got umpteen different problems going on. The meeting was meant to be twenty minutes ago. If you want to have this meeting, it's a trivial issue, come over here or let's do it another time.' Hodson blurted out, 'No, no, no, Dominic, I've sacrificed a lot for this campaign and I want to do this today.' Cummings thought, 'Fine, I don't want another argument, let's pop on a bike and go over there.'

While he headed off, Paul Stephenson and the other senior staff were waiting for a meeting with the leading Vote Leave politicians. Douglas Carswell and Dan Hannan were present, but no one else was. Stephenson thought, 'That's weird.' A short while later, Stephenson took calls from Laura Kuenssberg of the BBC and Chris Hope of the *Telegraph*, who had fresh intelligence. Kuenssberg told him, 'I've got this from someone who's never been wrong before – Dom's going to resign today.' Stephenson said, 'I haven't heard anything of that.' But he was seriously worried. Both journalists were well connected in the Eurosceptic world. At around the same time, Nigel Farage took a call from 'someone very senior on the board of Vote Leave', who told him, 'Cummings will be gone by half past ten.'

After a cycle ride of five minutes, Cummings sat down with Hodson, described by one Vote Leave source as 'a very sweet, old guy, an English gentleman eccentric'. Cummings could tell at once that something was wrong. Hodson said, 'I'm very sorry Dominic, but I'm afraid to tell you this meeting is not exactly what you thought it was.'

Immediately suspicious, Cummings remembered his time in Moscow and thought to himself, 'Where's the plastic sheeting?'

Hodson went on, 'The board's lost confidence in you, Matthew's lost confidence in you. You've got to go. But we don't want you to go completely. You've got many skills, Dominic. But Matthew's the manager, and Matthew's the one who should be running the campaign, and you've annoyed too many people.'

Cummings, his mind racing, played for time. 'OK,' he replied.

Hodson went on, 'There's some other people here who want to talk to you about this. And we have a suggestion of the way forward.'

At that point the key Vote Leave directors filed into the room, including Bernard Jenkin. They repeated Hodson's message: 'You can't manage this, Matthew's got to manage it, we want you to be an adviser, but you are no longer running anything here.' They offered Cummings a deal: 'You can have it the easy way or the hard way. If you do it the easy way, we'll pay you a bunch of money to be a consultant and you just tell everyone your wife's pregnant and that's the reason why you're heading off.'

Cummings looked around the room, read the faces of his opponents and made a judgement that they could be beaten. He couldn't help recalling several unpleasant experiences in Moscow: 'I've dealt with a lot, lot worse things than a bunch of clowns in a building in SW1.' He outlined the reasons why he thought the plotters were wrong, and then played what he hoped was his trump card: 'Have you thought through about what's going to happen in the office when you announce this?'

'What do you mean?' someone asked.

'Well, I don't think the senior people there will accept what's going on, and if they all walk out, then you haven't got a campaign organisation.'

This created consternation. 'Well, what do you suggest we do about that?' came a voice.

Cummings smiled and said, 'That just about sums you guys up, that you ask me for advice on how to do your own coup! Typical, especially of you, Bernard.' He then asked, 'What does Matthew think about this?'

'He completely agrees with all this.'

'Where is he?'

'Back in the office.'

'You're asking what's going to happen to the staff. Why don't you get the chief executive here to see what he's going to say about the staff?'

Someone phoned Elliott, and he arrived a short while later with Dan

Hannan. Hannan said Elliott asked him to accompany him to see if they could 'calm things down'.

What happened next is hotly disputed. A member of the board who was present that day is adamant that when 'Matthew joined the meeting, he initially supported the board line'. This supports the version of events Cummings recounted to colleagues afterwards. According to Cummings' account Hannan told him, 'Dominic, it's your patriotic duty to step aside for Elliott and tell the other staff it was a good idea.'

'Dan, I don't think you understand,' said Cummings. 'I don't think you understand that Paul Stephenson and Victoria Woodcock are much more capable than Matthew. And much more capable than you. And much more capable than the people around this table. I'm not going to go along and tell them what to do and they're going to do it, because they're not idiots. They know that you can't run this and they know that Matthew can't do this, so that's not going to work.'

'Well my God, if that happens and they all walk out, that's going to be a complete disaster,' came a voice.

'You should have thought about that before you started this stupid business,' said Cummings. 'You don't know what you're doing.'

Hannan admits that he was aware of the coup plans 'the night before', but insists his 'immediate reaction was we shouldn't lose Dominic'. He says that his role that day, along with Elliott, was to act as honest brokers between Cummings and the board: 'The two of us went in together, and suggested a compromise solution, which effectively both sides ended up rejecting at the time but ended up happening. I put on the table what I thought would be a compromise where Dom would focus on being the campaign director, but not do any tweeting and the things that were annoying people, which basically is what happened in the end.'

Hannan claims that Cummings said, 'No, no, I insist on having no conditions put on me,' while the hardliners on the board said, 'No, he's got to go.' Hannan explains, 'I was fairly disappointed to see people on both sides making it personal. It seemed to me that the obvious compromise was that Dom could focus on doing the strategy, and not do any of the MP interactions.'

Either way, there was now concern among the board members that the plans were unravelling. Jenkin says he discussed the implications of moving Cummings with Elliott, who had been of the view that two or three other members of staff might quit in protest, but that there would not be a mass exodus. He now believed that Cummings had got wind of the move against him and lined up support in the office to face it down.

Daniel Hodson then intervened, telling Cummings, 'We've got this contract. I want you to look at this contract.'

Cummings replied, 'You want me to look at this contract and you want me to talk with the staff. I'll go away and look at this contract.'

The plotters tried to stop him: 'You can't do that. The lawyers are all standing next door, and you can't leave until you've signed this contract.'

Cummings laughed again. 'I don't think you guys understand anything. The idea that you could hold me hostage in a room and get me to sign a contract. Who do you think you're dealing with? I'm going to go to the Pret down the road, I'm going to get myself a coffee and I'm going to read this contract. I'm going to suggest that you go to Vote Leave and talk to the staff there.'

He left the Tufton Street office and immediately called his PA Cleo Watson at Westminster Tower, who doubled as the head of outreach, to explain what was happening. She quickly gathered Paul Stephenson, Victoria Woodcock and Stephen Parkinson in Cummings' office and told them, 'A bunch of people are coming here now to tell us Dom is going on paternity leave. What are we going to do about that?'

Stephenson said, 'This sounds like a coup to me. I'll leave.' In what became the Leave campaign's 'Spartacus moment', Woodcock said, 'I'm off as well' and Parkinson agreed, 'Me too.'

They put Cummings on speakerphone. Agitated but not panicking, he said, 'There's a fucking coup going on. It's fucking Elliott. And all this lot are trying to get rid of me. You lot have said to me, you'll go. If that's what you're saying, excellent. This will kill the thing now.' At Cummings' request Watson moved his personal possessions into her desk drawers.

Matthew Elliott, accompanied by board member Alan Halsall, who even Cummings' supporters still see as 'a good guy', walked over Lambeth Bridge to Vote Leave and sat down with the three senior figures. Halsall asked them if they would quit. Stephenson said, 'We'll be gone within ten minutes.'

'So how many of your team would resign?'

'Most of them.'

'We're talking about half, two-thirds of the team going,' Halsall said reflectively, realising that the board's intelligence had been bad. In the classic outline of a failed coup, the plotters had sought to oust the president without first securing the support of the military and the civil service, and without seizing the headquarters of the state broadcaster.

Elliott, apparently nervous and seeing the way the wind was blowing, told his colleagues, 'I didn't want this to happen. Dom's very stressed. This is bad for the campaign.'

While that was going on there was another crucial encounter. Rob Oxley, the head of media who had worked for Elliott at Business for Britain and the Taxpayers' Alliance, bumped into Bernard Jenkin in Smith Square. Jenkin told him that Cummings was being moved to an advisory role, and that he needed to help settle down the campaign. Oxley let rip, saying, 'Dom's not the problem, it's Matthew.'

Oxley had twigged that some of the MPs thought he could replace Stephenson. He said to Jenkin, 'I reckon you guys think I can take Paul's job.' But he made it clear that despite his successful career, he did not yet feel capable of doing such a big job, and that he would never betray Stephenson: 'My loyalty is with Dom and Paul, and if they leave I would go too.' He predicted, 'The entire media team and research team would probably walk out at that point.' Jenkin seemed taken aback. Oxley recognised that without Elliott's patronage and advice he 'wouldn't be much' at such a young age, but when he had to nail his colours to the mast he chose Cummings. He raced back to the office and said to Stephenson, 'If I have to go and find a job, I will do.' It was partly that Cummings and Stephenson had taken him on and trusted him, it was partly that 'These were the only guys who'd shown me they were willing to win the campaign.'

'The Ox is a very loyal and great man,' says Stephenson, 'and was very important in stopping the whole thing from happening.'

When Cummings returned to Westminster Tower, he rallied his troops. Channelling the spirit of *Zulu*, he said, 'Gentlemen, we are surrounded. The good news is that we can shoot in any direction and we'll have a direct hit.'

Michael Gove first heard about the attempted coup when he received a text from the *Daily Mail* journalist Andrew Pierce saying Cummings was going to be sacked. He rang Cummings to offer assistance. 'Dom is rarely agitated, and even though he wasn't agitated, he was clearly in the middle of a drama,' Gove recalled. He then made a series of calls, to Peter Cruddas, the Tory treasurer who was funding Vote Leave, to Steve Baker and to Bernard Jenkin. To each of them he delivered the same message:

'Look, I haven't declared yet, but you won't have a chance of winning if you get rid of Dom.' The subtext, unstated, was that if Cummings was to go they would have little chance of securing Gove's support.

Jenkin said later that Gove was 'completely unexplicit' about joining the campaign, but 'the implication was, hang in there until cavalry arrive'. During the call he sought to placate Gove, telling him, 'Michael, if you come over you'll have a good campaign to join.'

Gove replied, 'Bernard, it won't be a good campaign unless Dom Cummings is running it.' He acknowledged the anger about the CBI stunt and the 'abrasive and undiplomatic' nature of Cummings' interactions with MPs, but backed him up on the central proposition that the campaign could not be won by the Palaeosceptics. To Cummings, he offered a little advice: 'The brutal candour of your analysis is correct, but you're leaving other people to sweep up after you. So you should restrain yourself.'

Chris Bruni-Lowe believed Cummings also played the Gove card to save himself: 'Cummings said, "I can get you Gove." And then that stopped it.'

Through it all, Cummings had one simple thought: in less than a month David Cameron would go to Brussels and finalise his deal. At that point, he believed, 'Michael will be on my side and then I'll be able to wrap all this shit up.'

While Gove was putting in calls, further soundings were taken in the Vote Leave office. 'Ricardo' Howell, the whizzkid of the research department, and his boss Oliver Lewis said that they would also walk. It became clear to Halsall and the other board members that Elliott had lost the office. As one Vote Leave staffer explained later, 'Being generous to him, most people didn't see what Matthew did, whereas they saw what Dom and Paul did. Being less generous, it was that they thought he wasn't actually doing anything.' Elliott was struggling to get donors to hand over money, but he had delegated the task of signing up business supporters to Lewis.

In the end, the key staff sided with Cummings because they thought he was their best hope of a referendum victory, and they believed he was a meritocrat. 'People wonder why so many staff are loyal to Dom and all the rest of it given his abrasive nature,' one said. 'It's because he doesn't choose phoneys, he only chooses people who are capable, and he's incredibly loyal to people who are talented and he goes to bat for them.'

Another staff member, reflecting at the end of the campaign, said, 'There's a number of reasons why we won. Cummings was responsible for more than half of why we were good and effective.'

As the situation became clear, Cummings took a call from a member of the board: 'We've reconsidered the situation. The staff won't agree to your going, therefore we think that maybe you should stay. But if you are going to stay ...' Thus commenced a negotiation about the future governance structure of the campaign that was to last a fortnight.

Vote Leave staff say that by the end of the day Elliott, having gambled and failed, was 'sucking up' to Cummings, telling him, 'Oh, Dom, all your training in Moscow must have really helped you with being able to get off that. Hats off to you.'

Elliott is adamant that he did not conspire against Cummings, that he believed their double act was the way to win the referendum, and that going it alone, or in tandem with Arron Banks, would have condemned Leave to defeat: 'Lots of donors and MPs came to me. They were trying to tempt me to ditch Dom and do it myself. I knew I'd be forced to join up with the other lot, it would be an embarrassing failure, and we'd lose. Even from a selfish point of view, there was no point in me wielding the dagger. I wanted to win the referendum, and I knew I couldn't do that without Dom at my side.'

Cummings' allies believe Elliott saw the opportunity to emerge as top dog and – at the very least – did not talk the board out of it. Gove's view was more generous than some. A friend said, 'Michael thought Matthew was not particularly brave on behalf of his comrades, but nor was he plotting against them. He was passive.'

The events of 25 January irreparably harmed some relations in the office. When Elliott found out that Oxley had sided with Cummings they had to have a reconciliation breakfast. Elliott's relationship with Victoria Woodcock never recovered. With Cummings it was hugely awkward. A Cummings loyalist said, 'Imagine: you're sat next to the person who tried to sack you, who's then said, "Nothing to do with me, it was the MPs."'

As a result of the peace talks it was agreed that a campaign committee would be established, giving a forum in which MPs could challenge Cummings. The make-up of the board changed, with John Mills stepping down. Jenkin persuaded Nigel Lawson to take over as chairman. Lawson agreed, on the condition that Cummings and Elliott left the board. Jenkin said, 'It was Dominic's difficulty in accepting that there

had to be proper governance which led to the row. He was determined
to be unaccountable, and what occurred is he basically agreed to be
accountable.' In truth, the changes were merely cosmetic. Cummings did
agree to moderate his public utterances, but nothing changed the fact
that he – with Paul Stephenson and Victoria Woodcock – continued to
make every major campaign decision without consulting the MPs.

A deal was also agreed to present the attempted coup to the media as
having intended to oust both Cummings and Elliott, in order to mini-
mise coverage of the rupture between them. Ten members of staff were
summoned to a 'farcical meeting' at which they were told that 'this was
a joint attempt to remove Elliott and Cummings together'. 'It was self-
evidently bullshit, and everyone in the room with two brain cells knew
it was bullshit,' said one of those present. 'The outcome was no quotes
would go out in Dom's name, Dom would remove himself from Twitter
and just tweet random things about science. The idea was to have Elliott
front and centre of the campaign, which is what he wanted, unsurpris-
ingly. After that, every quote from the campaign was in his name – other
than a couple from Rob when they were really, really outrageous.'

The fallout continued for days. Stories were briefed to the papers
blaming Jenkin and Grayling for the abortive coup. Jenkin was furious,
and Daniel Hannan visited Vote Leave and 'gave them a proper bollocking'. On the Wednesday evening, with the atmosphere still tense, Oxley
took it upon himself to call Steve Baker and say, 'We have to get this
sorted.' There were rumours that Conservatives for Britain were threatening to withdraw support from Vote Leave. Some of the staff at
Westminster Tower were threatening not to work for the MPs. Oxley
extended an olive branch to Baker, who was frank in return, admitting
that the MPs had had discussions about gutting Vote Leave and bringing
'our own people' in to run the campaign. Oxley said, 'If you do that,
you'll lose the designation process and you'll lose the race.' He felt as if
he was in 'nuclear disarmament talks'. When the meeting was over, Oxley
called Stephenson and told him to go to see Baker. Stephenson took
Stephen Parkinson with him, and they talked for more than an hour,
clearing the air about everything since the CBI stunt and coming to 'a
good understanding'. Baker said, 'I wore the UN blue helmet that week.
It's me who patched it up.'

Jenkin was 'very scarred' by the experience: 'For me, it was one of the
most horrid weeks in politics. I agonised about it and I am convinced I

had to do what I did, and then I was rather appalled when the rest of the board just backed down.' He objects to Cummings' depiction of the events as a coup: '"Coup" is the wrong word. The board was completely united that he should be moved but he browbeat the board into submission by threatening to blow up the whole campaign.'

The battle hardened the core team at Westminster Tower. Stephenson often thought back to that moment at difficult moments during the campaign: 'When things were bad, we'd be like, "Hang on a minute, we've been within a minute of walking out this office." When you're taking a shellacking from your government, at least you're not taking it from your own side. It helped road-test us.'

What occurred in that last week of January was pivotal to the success of the Leave campaign. Even if you believe that Cummings was out of control, ousting him would have created further chaos and rendered the Leave cause a public laughing stock. It may have deterred some ministers from signing up, or handed control of the campaign to Arron Banks, who most neutral observers believe would have repelled more voters than he attracted.

Steve Baker sums up what happened best: 'Dominic Cummings is like political special forces. If you don't care about what collateral damage you sustain, he's the weapon of choice. He operates with the minimum of civilised restraint. He is a barbarian. Dominic has undoubted mastery of leadership and strategy and political warfare. But he will not let himself be held to account by anybody. And that is basically what that attempt to sack him was about.'

Cummings may not have been the perfect campaign manager, but he was the best available to Vote Leave. The surest proof of this is that when his colleagues were asked to choose between him and the alternatives, every campaign official of note backed him. The failure of the coup meant that when David Cameron finally went to Brussels to sign his deal, Vote Leave were ready to eviscerate the prime minister rather than each other.

8

THE DEAL

David Cameron was twenty-seven hours into negotiating a new deal for Britain within the European Union when he snapped. It was late afternoon on Friday, 19 February, and Andrew Cooper, back in Britain, was surprised to receive an email from the PM in Brussels asking for some information. Cooper replied, not expecting to get a response, as he knew Cameron was up to his neck in a diplomatic negotiation that would define his premiership. What came back was a *cri de coeur*: 'Frankly, after a day and a half of talks with these people, even I want to leave the EU. I'm getting nowhere, I might have to walk away.'

Cameron had arrived in Brussels at lunchtime the previous day hopeful of securing agreement on the deal he had spent nine months negotiating with the other twenty-seven member states. Ever since early November, he and his officials had spent weeks discussing the small print with their partners and Commission officials. The summit was supposed to set a final seal on everything Cameron had set in motion with the Bloomberg speech three years earlier. But, after more than a day of negotiating, things had not turned out that way. The French, of course, had found fault with proposals that they believed would unfairly advantage the City of London. Britain's Eastern European allies were fighting a fearsome rearguard action against benefit cuts which would affect their citizens.

Cameron sat disconsolately in the Justus Lipsius Building where the European Council meets. At the best of times it was an unlovely pile of pink granite and glass, where politicians and journalists felt whole days of their lives slip away. On that damp and chill Friday the drab British delegation room was brightened only by the piles of Haribo sweets Cameron's team were chain-chewing. This raised their blood-sugar levels, but nothing seemed to raise their spirits. It was time to call on the big guns to sort out the mess. He said, 'I'd better make one last suggestion to Juncker and Tusk, but if that doesn't work the Poles won't accept this, then I'm going home and we'll come back to this in November.' After three years of building up to this moment, Cameron's gamble was close to failure.

The two EU officials charged with solving the British problem were Jean-Claude Juncker, the arch-federalist former prime minister of Luxembourg who had become Commission president in June 2014 despite Cameron's outspoken opposition, and Donald Tusk, the former prime minister of Poland who became president of the European Council – the shop steward for the twenty-eight heads of government – in December 2014, with Britain's backing. A senior figure at the summit concluded that Cameron had made a 'strategic error' with both appointments which made his renegotiation all the harder.

When he had decided to block Juncker's appointment Cameron had sought Angela Merkel's backing, thought he had it, only to see her bow to domestic political pressure to back down. Juncker was in pole position because he had been chosen by the EPP, the centre-right grouping in the European Parliament, from which Cameron had withdrawn the Tories. Downing Street had failed to understand the attraction in Germany of the new *spitzenkandidaten* system, whereby the main blocs in the Parliament nominated their preferred candidates on the understanding that whichever grouping got most votes in the European elections that year would get the presidency. While Downing Street spin doctors briefed stories about Juncker drinking whisky for breakfast, Peter Altmaier, Merkel's chief of staff at the German Chancellery, was doing a deal with Martin Selmayr, the German Commission insider who would become Juncker's all-powerful chief of staff, to ensure that Juncker got the job. When Cameron demanded a show of hands at the summit, just one rose alongside his own: that of the Hungarian prime minister, Viktor Orban.

One of Cameron's aides thinks it would have been better for his referendum prospects if he had accepted Juncker, rather than drawn attention to Britain's isolation: 'We introduced Juncker to the nation in a way that people saw the EU as a place which would go against British wishes. I don't think we suffered because he was in that role. I think we suffered because we were seen to fail to prevent him from taking that role.'

The same aide believes Cameron should not have backed Tusk, who was given Downing Street's support in an attempt to woo the Poles, who were crucial to any deal on migrant benefits. The alternative front-runner was Helle Thorning-Schmidt, the Danish prime minister and model for the main character in *Borgen*, the Scandi political drama series which was popular on British television, and who is married to Labour MP Stephen Kinnock. 'We vastly overestimated Tusk's capabilities,' the aide said. 'Helle Thorning-Schmidt has lots of flaws but she is very telegenic and articulate. She'd have been a persuasive, congenial, attractive spokesperson for a proposition that Brits generally tend not to like. Instead, we got a stuttering Polish prime minister whose command of the English language was not great and who struggled with the job.' The final problem was that Tusk's appointment led to a general election in Poland, which his Civic Platform party lost. 'That meant that we had a Pole in the job, but he had less traction in Poland than we did.'

The story of Cameron's renegotiation is one of piecemeal manoeuvres rather than a long-planned strategy. As one civil servant who watched it up close observed, 'My big criticism is they only ever worked from point to point to point. They never started with winning a referendum and working back from that. It was always tactical. It became driven by, "We've got to give a speech on this day."' The polls showed that voters were equally divided between Leave and Remain, but when they were asked 'Do you want to be in a reformed Europe' there was a large majority in favour. Cameron's mistake was believing the public would be happy to accept his definition of 'reformed'.

The one big strategic decision, made by Cameron and Osborne immediately after the general election, may have been the root of their defeat. They decided to ask only for what they thought the European Commission and the other member states would give them, rather than press them into uncomfortable demands to rewrite the fundamentals of EU law. One of Cameron's team said, 'We decided to go for what we can get and get it. That was George and Dave's decision. That was our first big error.' Osborne, the ultimate pragmatist, thought there was 'a gulf' between what was realistically achievable whilst retaining EU membership and what others thought could be achieved. The chancellor's position, communicated to his team, was, 'Britain holds very few of the cards.' He said privately, 'We wanted to be in a position where we recommended that we remained in. So you couldn't set out a list of demands which we had no prospect of achieving.'

Cameron was certainly not short of advice on what to ask for. In September 2011 a group of more than a hundred MPs led by George Eustice, Chris Heaton-Harris and Andrea Leadsom set up the Fresh Start project to draw up proposals for a new relationship with the EU. In July 2012 they released a paper called 'Options for Change' which called for a reduction in the EU budget, an overhaul of the Common Agricultural Policy and repatriation of European structural funds. In April 2013, after the Bloomberg speech had fired the starting shot, Fresh Start published a 'Manifesto for Change' calling for five changes to EU treaties, including powers to halt new legislation affecting financial services, the repatriation of all social and employment legislation, and the abolition of the Strasbourg seat of the European Parliament. William Hague, who wrote the foreword to both documents, privately told Leadsom, 'If I wasn't foreign secretary, I could sign up to virtually all of it. As foreign secretary I could probably sign up to 85 per cent of it.' Cameron had told Leadsom she was doing 'good work'. Yet by the time he started drawing up his own wish list it fell well short of Fresh Start's.

In 2015 Cameron did not seem inclined to ask even for what he had already publicly suggested he would demand. In the Bloomberg speech he had promised 'fundamental' reform. In March 2014 he wrote a piece for the *Sunday Telegraph* in which he said that the police should be free of 'unnecessary interference from the European institutions', including the European Court of Human Rights, and made two additional demands relating to immigration: new countries joining the EU should face initial controls 'to prevent vast migrations across the Continent', and the EU's principle of free movement should only apply 'to take up work, not free benefits'. Once again, Cameron had raised rather than moderated Eurosceptic expectations of what was possible.

Daniel Hannan went to see the prime minister before the general election to make an offer. He told Cameron, 'We should try and behave patriotically, and get the best deal possible. I don't want you to come back with a crap deal just because it makes it easier for us to win the referendum.' Hannan outlined a Eurosceptic wish list for the renegotiation, including repatriation of powers in non-economic areas and more defence of parliamentary supremacy. In short, what he wanted was a trading relationship and little else. By Hannan's account, Cameron said, 'Well that is doable, but that's not the direction I want to go in. I think we get a greatly amplified voice through having a common foreign policy. I think we get more security through common criminal justice policies. I don't want to do what you are suggesting, which is to opt out.' The prime minister had a deal of his own to offer: 'Help me get a Conservative majority, then get a referendum, and then you and I will go on opposite sides.' Hannan now says, 'In terms of understanding what is feasible today, the myth shouldn't be allowed to take root that these things were not on offer; it's that we didn't want to ask for them.'

After the general election, Cameron began a diplomatic offensive to secure support from the rest of the EU to include the migration proposals from the JCB speech in the renegotiation package. Cameron, Osborne, David Lidington and the new foreign secretary, Philip Hammond, went on a whistlestop tour of Europe. Craig Oliver recalls, 'The prime minister visited countries that no British prime minister has visited in a century.'[1] The challenge on immigration was that it was Britain's natural allies in Eastern Europe who were most antagonistic to reform of benefits and migration rules, since it was their citizens living in Britain who would be affected.

Part of the problem was that there was now no prospect of a new treaty which would have given Britain the leverage to demand sweeping change. When Lidington met his EU counterparts after the general election, 'The others were not buying into the idea that this was some opportunity for major European reform,' he said. 'When the decision to go ahead with Bloomberg was taken, that had just followed a state of the union speech by [then Commission president José Manuel] Barroso, in which he called for a new treaty. It looked as though eurozone dynamics were going to push France and Germany to some sort of deal straight away. The bandwagon was moving, and if we didn't latch our ideas for reform onto it, we were in danger of this other negotiation gathering speed without us. During 2013 and 2014, the impetus dropped away. All of a sudden, not because of anything we'd done or not done, this was just a British problem.'

Meanwhile the EU published its so-called 'Five Presidents Report', signed in June by Juncker, Tusk, European Parliament president Martin

Schulz, Mario Draghi of the European Central Bank, and Jeroen Dijsselbloem of the Eurogroup, which mapped out a blueprint for the future of the EU. Envisaging deeper economic, financial, fiscal and political union in the euro area by 2017, and full union by 2025, it was hardly helpful to Cameron. At the exact moment he wanted a hearing for a less centralised EU, the institutions were mapping out what Eurosceptics saw as a United States of the Eurozone.

Cameron and Osborne's cautious approach was endorsed by senior figures like chief of staff Ed Llewellyn and the senior diplomats on European affairs, Ivan Rogers and Tom Scholar. That put the civil servants on a collision course with Daniel Korksi and Mats Persson, the leads on EU affairs, Ameet Gill, the director of strategy, and Max Chambers, a special adviser and speechwriter, who all wanted Cameron to 'go big and not get all of it – get eight out of ten'. Mats Persson says: 'The biggest mistake we made was that we treated it as an exercise in political management, and a communication exercise, rather than going for proper and fundamental change.'

Korski was bright but passionate; in centuries past he would have been an imperial governor or a great duellist. He had arrived in Number 10 the previous April after an unhappy period working for Cathy Ashton, Britain's Commissioner in Brussels. His swashbuckling style was honed alongside Paddy Ashdown in Bosnia and in Kabul at the height of the war in Afghanistan, where he was private secretary to a minister in Hamid Karzai's government. He had also had a spell on secondment to the US State Department, helped set up the *Spectator*'s Coffee House website, and found himself, Zelig-like, in Tahrir Square during Egypt's version of the Arab Spring. Convinced Britain should be helping the Libyans to liberate themselves from Colonel Gaddafi, he took a car across the desert and smuggled himself into Benghazi to talk to the rebels. His time in Downing Street featured similar outbursts of impulsive activity.

Ivan Rogers and Tom Scholar clashed repeatedly with Korski and Mats Persson. A Swede by birth, at six feet seven inches Persson towered over everyone else in Downing Street – height he had put to good use as a member of the 2004 Liberty Flames basketball team at Liberty University in Virginia, where he studied on an athletics scholarship: the team won the Big South Conference that year. Persson was temperamentally ice to Korski's fire, but he believed from his time at Open Europe that Britain should push the limits of EU law to get change. 'Mats felt we could go a lot further,' a minister said.

'We were too beholden to Tom Scholar and Ivan Rogers,' one Cameron adviser said. 'They were status quo. They were happy to take "No" for an answer, happy to believe things weren't possible when they could be possible. I've lost count of the number of times Ivan threatened to resign.' The politicos say Rogers was aggressive in dismissing their arguments, and went over their heads to Cameron: 'He would send emails that were the stuff of legend, saying why didn't we know anything? We were just politicos, we didn't understand.' Another aide said Rogers' emails were 'notorious'.

Rogers also clashed with the special advisers over their desire to include reforms of the European Court of Justice in the renegotiation. 'Korski had a long-running battle with officials saying that we needed to do something, and he kept getting told that it was impossible to do something,' a Number 10 source said. A range of proposals were put forward, ranging from new rules on the selection of judges to proposals for the ECJ to get out of lower-level decisions. Their advocates believe the plan would have allowed Britain to get a serious review of the court on the agenda. It was rejected by officials over the summer.

Proposals for business reform, which would have demanded exemptions from EU regulation for small businesses which did not sell into the single market, were also abandoned. 'We had lots of other stuff on competitiveness, but we got browbeaten by officials into not doing anything on it,' an aide said. 'Mats and Dan would talk to their contacts across Europe and come back and say we have got political counterparts who are saying "There might be something here." And then they'd be met with officials going round their backs, persuading the PM they were being naïve.' The blame must rest, ultimately, with Cameron. 'Ivan and Tom got their direction from the top,' said one aide. 'They needed to be told to operate outside the tramlines of existing EU rules. But the PM never did that.'

None of these ideas in and of themselves would have salvaged the renegotiation, but they would have helped to make it more substantial. Collectively they ensured that George Osborne's battle to safeguard the rights of non-eurozone nations became the only significant element left on the economy, and magnified migration as the issue on which the deal would stand or fall. By the autumn one aide had concluded, 'If the referendum campaign is fought around what is actually renegotiated, we are fucked.'

Given how limited Cameron's demands were, some of his team believed he would have been better striking a quick and dirty deal and holding a referendum in the autumn of 2015, before Cummings had Vote Leave properly organised. 'The assumption was always that you want people to watch you sweat and fail and get up again and fight,' says a senior Downing Street source. 'The irony of the whole situation was it was really, really hard, and still people said it was worthless and a stitch-up. What David saw as a great diplomatic overture came to be seen as a diplomatic begging tour around Europe, unbecoming of a great nation. We should have accepted no one was going to believe it anyway, and do it sharp and short.'

Korski also tried and failed to get Cameron to talk more positively about Europe in the eighteen months before the deal. All Conservatives were familiar with Lynton Crosby's first rule for election success: 'You can't fatten a pig on market day.' Successful politicians lay the groundwork for the arguments they will make in a campaign long before polling day. Korski argued, 'We've got to speak differently about Europe if we're ever going to speak positively about Europe.' He devised initiatives to show that Cameron was getting his way in Brussels, taking business leaders there to cut red tape and putting the UK at the heart of plans for a 'digital single market'. But invariably Cameron would emerge at the end of EU summits to stress his frustrations rather than his achievements to the waiting media. A Downing Street official who sympathised with Korski said, 'We never pitch-rolled our proposition. I don't think it was in David's nature. He was temperamentally Eurosceptic.'

The business end of the deal-making came in four stages. On 10 November Cameron wrote a public letter to Donald Tusk, president of the European Council, spelling out the broad thrust of his demands. He fleshed it out in a speech at Chatham House, the international affairs think tank, on the same day. On 17 December he talked his fellow leaders through his proposals at an EU summit in Brussels. After six further weeks of negotiations, Tusk published a full draft deal on 2 February, laying out the precise details for the first time. The final showdown came two weeks after that.

After nine months of seeing Britain's wish list whittled down, Craig Oliver briefed the Sunday papers the weekend before the letter to Tusk that Cameron would be prepared to campaign to leave the EU if his demands were met with a 'deaf ear': 'If we can't reach such an agreement … we will have to think again about whether this European Union is right for us.'[2] The rhetoric was hardened to disguise the fact that Cameron's demands had softened. The 'Dear Donald' letter that followed outlined 'four baskets' of demands familiar to those who had followed the negotiation since June.

On 'economic governance', Cameron said changes in the eurozone must 'respect the legitimate interests of non-euro members'. He asked for a recognition that 'the EU has more than one currency', and that 'taxpayers in non-Euro countries should never be financially liable for operations to support the eurozone as a currency'. On 'competitiveness' he said 'the United Kingdom would like to see a target to cut the total burden on business'. He told Tusk that 'questions of sovereignty' were 'central' to the British debate, and demanded to 'end Britain's obligation to work towards an "ever closer union"' and a 'new arrangement where groups of national Parliaments, acting together, can stop unwanted legislative proposals'.

He argued that net migration to Britain of over 300,000 a year 'is not sustainable', and demanded assurances that 'free movement will not apply to new members until their economies have converged much more closely with existing Member States'. In a section inserted at the instigation of Theresa May, the home secretary, he called for a 'crackdown on the abuse of free movement', with 'longer re-entry bans for fraudsters and people who collude in sham marriages'. He went on, 'It means addressing the fact that it is easier for an EU citizen to bring a non-EU spouse to Britain than it is for a British citizen to do the same.'

Finally, arriving at the most controversial part of the letter, Cameron turned to the 'pull factors': 'We have proposed that people coming to Britain from the EU must live here and contribute for four years before they qualify for in-work benefits or social housing. And that we should end the practice of sending child benefit overseas.'

The only real surprise came not in the letter to Tusk, but in Cameron's Chatham House speech. There he proposed new arrangements to emulate Germany's constitutional court, which can 'review legal acts by European institutions and courts to check that they remain within the scope of the EU's powers. We will consider how this could be done in the

UK.' In this obscure paragraph Cameron had planted a colourful lure to land the biggest fish in the Tory Party. The week before, he had discussed the need to devise a means of asserting British sovereignty with none other than Boris Johnson, the mayor of London.

Cameron knew he needed reinforcements. When MPs debated the Tusk letter in the Commons later that day, Bernard Jenkin got to his feet and asked, 'Is that it?' The following morning the *Sun*'s splash headline was 'ARE EU KIDDING?' The *Mail* went with 'IS THAT IT, MR CAMERON?', describing the prime minister as 'in retreat over plans to strip benefits from EU migrant workers'.[3]

In Brussels, Nigel Farage met officials who were perplexed that Cameron's demands were so modest: 'There was general surprise, laughter in the Hack, which is the boozer I go to. A lot of very senior Commission figures drink there after work, and really they thought it was laughable he'd asked for so little.'

Cameron had ditched many of the ideas he himself had floated in the preceding three years. Conspicuous by their absence were any attempt to repatriate social and employment legislation – ditched at the behest of Labour and the unions – or to demand smaller EU budgets or assert UK judicial control over justice and home-affairs laws. Korski's efforts to put reform of the European Court of Justice on the table had been rejected, along with proposals to demand a 'one in, three out' rule for EU regulations, advanced by Sajid Javid, the business secretary.

During this period there had been no effort to talk to the Eurosceptics to get their ideas. Daniel Hannan says, 'When Philip Hammond was in Brussels, I went to speak to the guys who were with him and said, "Just out of interest, why have you not come to us, and found out what our bottom line is? It might have helped you get something that will be more sellable." The answer was, "Nothing would be good enough for you guys."' For Hannan that was certainly true, but his ideas would have improved the deal, and that could have helped Cameron to win over wavering MPs. One of his proposals was to ditch EU passports and return to the iconic navy-blue documents of the past. Hannan said, 'It would have been a visible symbol that we were outside the political union. I'm not saying that would have swung the issue, but I'm giving that as an example of the easiest imaginable thing that wasn't asked for.'

When the European Council opened on 17 December, Tusk declared it a 'make-or-break summit'. Cameron laid out his plans in a passionate forty-minute address to his fellow leaders over dinner. The benefits plans were the most controversial. Beata Szydło, the new Polish prime minister, said that stripping migrants of welfare would not be 'acceptable' because her citizens were 'building the GDP of Great Britain'. It was clear that the flat four-year ban on in-work benefits was a non-starter. Juncker proposed a compromise, combining the old idea of an 'emergency brake' with the benefits ban so payments could be temporarily halted. After the meeting concluded Cameron said 'We are well on our way to a deal,' and confirmed for the first time that the referendum would take place in 2016. But having not 'gone big' with his renegotiation, the measures to tackle immigration were growing both thinner and more difficult to explain to voters.

On 2 February Donald Tusk published the detailed draft plans for the renegotiation, and tweeted a little Shakespeare: 'To be, or not to be together, that is the question.'

Then all hell broke loose.

The publication of the Tusk draft was seen in Downing Street as simply a step on the path to the February European Council, at which the final deal would be done. In fact it was the first major media showdown between Number 10 and the Leave campaign. This confrontation shaped public views of the deal for good, and it was one that Cummings, Baker, Stephenson and Banks won hands down.

Tusk's sixteen-page paper confirmed that in the six weeks since the December council, Cameron's benefits plans had been watered down in two ways. Gone was the standing four-year ban for new arrivals, replaced with a proposal for a temporary restriction activated by an emergency brake. Instead of a total ban on welfare handouts for the four years, benefits would be slowly 'tapered' in. For a month media coverage had focused on what rabbit Cameron might pull from his hat to boost the deal. In the event, it emerged sick with myxomatosis.

Downing Street could not have stopped Tusk from writing the document, since it was usual practice for the Council president to circulate papers for discussion ahead of a summit, but they could have tried to prevent it being formally published. Tusk assumed the draft would leak, and decided it was better to put it in the public domain himself. Yet that gave it an official status that left Cameron less room for manoeuvre. As a minister said, 'When Tusk took the decision to formally publish we couldn't say, "We don't comment on leaked drafts, it's an ongoing nego-tiation."' Number 10 could also have pointed out where the document was lacking, if nothing else to show that they were fighting for more. 'We didn't give it such a warm reception,' one Downing Street official said.

The reception in the House of Commons was far from warm. Steve Baker, the head of Conservatives for Britain, saw an opportunity for another act of guerrilla warfare, even if it involved putting his reputation as one of Parliament's gentlemen at risk: 'The deal came out and we immediately rubbished it successfully. That was a purposeful strategy.' That morning Baker sat down with Paul Stephenson and said, 'I've got this idea, and it's a bit coarse, but what if I was to say, "It's like the prime minister's polishing poo"?' Stephenson, less delicate by nature, suggested a refinement: 'It's not good enough – you need to say something like "It's shiny on the outside and soft in the middle."' Baker recalled, 'It was breathtakingly crude, but also not out of order. I sat there in the chamber of the Commons that day, thinking, "Do I want to win this referendum or not?" I realised that if I stood up and made yet another tedious point of EU law it would be completely forgotten.'

Around 1 p.m. Baker got to his feet in the Commons and said to David Lidington, 'This in-at-all-costs deal looks and smells funny. It might be superficially shiny on the outside, but poke it and it is soft in the middle. Will my right hon. friend admit to the House that he has been reduced to polishing poo?' To his credit Lidington came back, quick as a flash, to say, 'I rather suspect … my hon. friend was polishing that particular question many days ago.' But Baker's gambit worked: 'It got me coverage everywhere. It was coarse, it was crude, my members didn't like me doing it, I'll probably never do anything like it again. But we had to make sure people knew it was poo. I had to swallow my pride and be a bit crude in order to be effective.' First blood to the Leavers.

Cameron's team knew the deal would be a big media moment. Craig Oliver asked the Stronger In digital team of Tom Edmonds and Craig Elder to map out a plan for a 'Twitter war room' to leap into action when it was signed, with MPs, business leaders and other influential supporters declaring that Cameron had got a good deal. 'Craig was very focused on how social media played out in the Westminster bubble,' said David Chaplin. 'This was about creating a tidal wave of sentiment on social media, from people that politicians and journalists would recognise.'

The paper prepared by Oliver goes into meticulous detail: 'Twitter Warroom to be set up in Nick Herbert's Conservatives for Reform in Europe Office ... Many supportive MPs are out of the country, so we will give those a set time to tweet remotely.' It detailed how Edmonds was 'working on paid push' for Cameron's Facebook page and an email to supporters on the day of the deal. Oliver himself planned to lead the tweeting from the prime minister's @David_Cameron account. In the Cabinet Office, a new unit was set up under Matthew Gould, returning to London after a spell as ambassador to Israel. Gould would run the civil service team who would prepare official government documents on the referendum. They would also have responsibility for rapid rebuttal to the media.

The only problem with all this planning was that it was built around the weekend of 20–21 February. On 2 February Gould's unit had not got off the ground, and Oliver's Twitter war room was no more than an idea on a piece of paper. Stronger In's David Chaplin says, 'In all the conversations that we'd had with [Number 10] I don't remember that Tusk paper or that moment ever really being signposted. Everything's easier in hindsight, but that was the moment the world reacted to the deal, because that was when they saw the parameters of what the EU was willing to offer us. We had not been asked to prepare any kind of reaction to that.' Will Straw is blunter still: 'We'd been told by Number 10 it wasn't going to be a big deal. The leave side just piled in at that point.'

By the time Cameron got to Brussels and Oliver's media plan cranked into action, the deal he had spent nine months negotiating was already a dead duck. A member of his team admitted later that the lack of preparedness was one of the signal strategic mistakes of the entire referendum campaign: 'The opportunity was lost in those two weeks, between the publication of the draft and the council meetings. And by then, the public's mind had been set.'

The following day's newspapers were merciless, with even sym- pathetic publications focusing on what had been traded away. The most damaging attack was the splash in the *Sun*, whose graphics department had done up Cameron and his team as the hapless platoon from *Dad's Army* with the headline 'Who do EU think you are kidding Mr Cameron?' The paper branded the deal a 'steaming pile of manure'. Cameron and the *Sun*'s editor, Tony Gallagher, had a 'face-to-face row' in Downing Street.

A poll by ComRes shortly afterwards found that only 21 per cent of voters thought the deal was a good one; 58 per cent thought it was bad. One minister said, 'What genuinely surprised Number 10 was not that the *Mail*, the *Sun*, the *Express* were supporting Leave, but that the tone of the criticism was so venomous.'

The media response to the Tusk document revealed one of the greatest strategic problems for the Remain campaign. The Tories at the top of Stronger In were about to run a referendum campaign based on a play-book devised by Lynton Crosby for winning general elections in an environment where the print media was sympathetic. But this time their natural allies were hostile. The *Sun* and the *Daily Mail* campaigned aggressively for Brexit from the off. Rupert Murdoch, the *Sun's* proprietor, was a Brexit sympathiser, and pushing 70 per cent of the paper's readers agreed. Sources at the *Mail* say the editor, Paul Dacre, believed passionately in leaving the EU, and felt that Cameron had never acknowledged the assistance the paper had given in propelling him to his majority the year before. The *Daily Telegraph* gave Cameron a fair hearing, but its proprietors, the Barclay brothers, had links to Ukip, and it too backed Brexit. The *Times* and the *Sunday Times* took a neutral approach and eventually split, *The Times* for Remain, while the *Sunday Times* called for a Leave vote as a way of getting a better deal from Brussels. Oliver could expect good shows in the *Guardian* and the *Independent*, but both were papers with dwindling circulation which did not speak to the kind of voters the 'In' campaign would need to convert. Only the *Mirror* papers and the *Mail on Sunday* went into what Oliver called 'campaign mode' on behalf of Remain. 'It pains me to say it,' a member of Cameron's team said, 'but if the *Mail*, *Sun* and the *Telegraph* had been for "In" we would have romped home.'

For Oliver a hostile press was unfamiliar terrain, both because he was used to supportive newspapers and because his core skillset since he moved to Downing Street from the BBC in 2011 was shaping broadcast coverage. Oliver, forty-seven at the time of the campaign, had been a reporter with a small Scottish TV station before rising through the ranks to become a senior executive at *ITV News*, from which he was poached by the BBC in 2006. There he boosted the ratings of *The Ten O'Clock News* and met his (now ex-) wife, the news presenter Joanna Gosling, with whom he had three daughters. John Simpson, the BBC's world affairs editor, judged him 'undoubtedly the best editor I ever worked for.'[4] It is little wonder that Oliver's view during the campaign was that what mattered was what led 'the six and the ten', the two main evening BBC television bulletins at 6 and 10 p.m. In this he was hugely successful. No one in government knew the BBC better, and a well-timed call to the right editor or correspondent could alter the tone of the coverage or the running order, winning him plaudits in Number 10.

Relations with the print press did not begin well, when Oliver initially refused to hand out his mobile phone number. The papers retaliated by ridiculing him for wearing a pair of Beats headphones by the American rapper Dr. Dre as he made his way up Downing Street for the first time – Dominic Cummings, for years an antagonist, referred to Oliver dismissively as 'Dre' ever after. In time Oliver came to understand the value of the papers in shaping the broadcast coverage, and he developed strong relationships with several newspaper political editors, his reputation growing in tandem with his influence in Downing Street. But he remained suspicious of print journalists, who he saw as a different species. They, in turn, swapped stories about his regular texts of complaint when their tweets did not meet with his approval. 'Craig was obsessed with what's happening now on social media, what's happening on the six and ten and who is going on the *Today* programme,' says a campaign source. 'Those are the four parts of Craig's brain.' By the time of the referendum Oliver's teething troubles with the newspapers were long in the past, but for the first time he was confronted with a campaign that was an away fixture. As a non-Tory working for Stronger In said, 'It turned out the emperor has no clothes. When the press are not supporting Cameron, the Tories didn't quite know what to do.'

Oliver did not believe there was anything he could have done to make the coverage of the Tusk draft more congenial. A Downing Street source familiar with his thinking says, 'You have to ask yourself about the fairness of the coverage of what Tusk was doing. It was part of a Brexit campaign – and very noisy. Would anything have been good enough?' Oliver would have plenty of good moments during the campaign, when his broadcasting expertise was invaluable to Stronger In. But the weekend of Donald Tusk's draft was not one of them – and it was to cost Cameron.

The one bit of good news for the prime minister that week was the emergence of Theresa May as a supporter of the Remain campaign. The home secretary had helped shape Cameron's letter to Tusk in November, but

Downing Street's worst fear was that she would announce that she had concluded, as the minister in charge of immigration, that it could not be controlled within the EU – a move that could have swung public opinion decisively against them. But May had also made a series of interventions making clear that she believed national security was bolstered when countries teamed up to combat cross-border terrorism and organised crime. In that vein, she had been willing to frustrate Eurosceptics by pushing through moves to opt back in to the European Arrest Warrant and thirty-four other EU-wide justice measures in 2014. Coupled with her innate caution and concerns about the economy, her security instincts were enough to keep May in Cameron's camp. 'She weighed the decision quite broadly,' a close aide said. 'For economic reasons she thought the risk was too great.'

May did not sell herself cheap. She insisted to Cameron that any deal included measures cracking down on 'sham marriages' which enabled non-EU nationals to stay in member states. She also demanded that residency restrictions imposed on the non-EU spouses and other family members of Britons should also apply to European citizens seeking to settle their families in the UK. May's importance was clear to Donald Tusk. As those elements made their way from proposals into the Council president's draft document, he repeatedly asked Cameron's aides, 'Will this be enough for Theresa May?' When the draft was published, Cameron, frustrated by weeks of evasions from May about her intentions, called to pin her down and she announced, 'This is a basis for a deal.' In Number 10, where May was seen as an at times truculent enigma, there was relief. One Downing Street official said, 'She said what she wanted, she helped us get it, and then she stuck to her side of the bargain.' Another Number 10 aide said, 'I think we overdelivered on what she wanted. Although I don't know how she could have ever credibly gone "Out", having read everything she'd said on Europe and security. She'd basically said, "If we leave the EU, paedophiles roam free."'

May's decision did disappoint some of her closest associates, who did not know which way she would go until the last minute, and would have preferred her to campaign to leave. Stephen Parkinson was already working for Vote Leave, and Nick Timothy was also a Brexiteer. 'Nick and Parky hoped she'd be for Out,' a senior Vote Leave source said. It is possible that if May had been inclined to back Vote Leave, she would have been put off by the chaos of the coup against Dominic Cummings just a week earlier. As it unfolded, Parkinson remarked to a colleague, 'She's not going to join this kind of organisation.'

Timothy was 'depressed' about May's decision when he saw Paul Stephenson later that day, believing she could have been the key to victory for Vote Leave. Stephenson said, 'Don't worry, the cavalry's on its way.' Vote Leave were growing in confidence that Michael Gove, and possibly even Boris Johnson, would be joining them.

With May on board, Cameron turned his attention to the preparations for the final summit and a last-minute burst of diplomacy. Of his four baskets, two were straightforward. British demands for the EU to become more 'competitive' were largely agreed. Belgium's objections to the rejection of 'ever closer union' were also easily resolved – the UK would get an opt-out while others continued down the path of centralisation. That left just two baskets in play. The first was the need to secure protections for non-euro countries, which George Osborne had made his responsibility.

Osborne told aides that sorting out rules that would allow the single-currency bloc to integrate further without letting them run roughshod over the nine countries outside the eurozone were 'the most important part of the deal in terms of Britain's actual position in the EU', even if the immigration measures were the 'most politically important'. Without action, every other country was expected to eventually adopt the euro, leaving Britain in ever less splendid isolation. The chancellor made a series of trips to European capitals – Berlin, Paris, Rome – and gave a speech to the German equivalent of the CBI, the BDI, calling for a set of principles which would be written into the European treaty ensuring that Britain would not be liable for future eurozone bailouts.

Two relationships were key to Osborne securing support for his proposals. He became close to the German finance minister, Wolfgang Schäuble, and also wooed Emmanuel Macron, the young French minister of the economy, like Osborne a reformer and a risk-taker. When the summit began, just one sentence in the draft remained in dispute. It would prove to be quite a sticking point.

Cameron prepared for the summit in the usual way, by lobbying Angela Merkel. On 12 February the two leaders talked tactics over dinner in Hamburg at the city's annual St Matthew's Feast. Merkel publicly declared Cameron's reforms 'justified and necessary', and said it was in Germany's 'national interest' for the UK to remain in the EU. His next stop, on the Monday of summit week, was in Paris, where he lobbied François Hollande. Their relationship, initially frosty, had improved after Cameron was quick to offer support when France was subjected to a series of terrorist attacks, first on the offices of the satirical magazine *Charlie Hebdo* in January 2015, and then at the Bataclan theatre in Paris that November. Nonetheless, the French continued to point out that free movement was one of the founding principles of the single market, and criticised anything that smacked of an '*à la carte*' EU.

Cameron also tried to curry favour with the Belgian prime minister Charles Michel, the leader most implacably opposed to greater powers for national parliaments, by sending him a collection of Beatrix Potter books for his newborn daughter, and with the Poles by backing an increase in NATO forces in Poland.

On Tuesday, Cameron met Martin Schulz, the president of the European Parliament, an institution for which the prime minister had made little effort to hide his contempt over the years. The previous June, Cameron had put aside his distaste for Schulz's federalist views and invited him to Downing Street, taking him to the service at St Paul's Cathedral commemorating the two hundredth anniversary of the Battle of Waterloo. Unfortunately, this meeting did not go as well as hoped. Cameron arrived half an hour late. 'Hi Martin,' he beamed. 'Good morning. All well?' With acid irritation Schulz replied, 'Technical problems?' The substance of the meeting with senior MEPs was not much better, as Schulz said there was 'no guarantee' they would not seek to amend any deal agreed by the Council after the fact – a gift to Eurosceptics, who did not believe the renegotiation would be legally binding.

Cameron was not the only one comparing notes. The so-called 'Visegrad Four' – Poland, Hungary, the Czech Republic and Slovakia – met together to discuss how they would thwart his benefits reforms. In one-on-ones, British officials were confident that the four countries were prepared to do business. But collectively the 'V4' gave each other the confidence to take a tougher line.

Shortly before the summit Cameron and Osborne had a sobering conversation with Lynton Crosby. The strategist had been using the back door of 10 Downing Street for several weeks to slip in for weekly meetings with the prime minister and chancellor. The three had been close since the 2005 general election, when Crosby had run Michael Howard's campaign and identified Cameron and Osborne as the party's stars of the future. Having overseen that gruelling campaign, Crosby had no interest in running Cameron's referendum war room, but 'he was providing weekly advice and his own polling', said a senior Tory. 'He was actually contracted to the Conservative Party, so he couldn't take sides.'

Crosby was attributed with near-mythical status after the general election, which makes it stranger that Cameron and Osborne chose, in February 2016, to ignore his very firm view that they should not rush into a deal or a referendum until the end of 2017. 'Don't go so soon,' he told them, and repeated that view to cabinet ministers. One of those who discussed the referendum with Crosby said, 'His argument was to play the referendum late, to run it into 2017, on the grounds that the more people were exposed to the argument, the more they'd likely want to remain in.' Another source said Crosby envisaged an even more dramatic gesture: 'One thing he did advise was to rip up the deal live on the steps of Downing Street. I'm not convinced that would have worked. It would have bought ourselves another year. We'd have got a bit more on immigration. But not enough.'

Crosby did not tell Cameron he would lose if his advice was not heeded. 'His judgement right up to – and including – the week of the referendum was that we were going to win,' says a Cameron confidant. Crosby's position was complicated by his close friendship with Johnson. 'We all knew he was talking to Boris too,' a Downing Street aide says. 'He treated us both with respect and equal distance. He must have been in a difficult position, actually.'

Cameron and Osborne decided to ignore Crosby's advice. Osborne strongly believed they would not get a better deal by waiting, telling Cameron, 'The EU is never – in my view – going to give Britain the benefits of membership without the costs.' He regarded the idea of 'banging the desk' and a staging a walkout as 'huff and fury without any substance to it'. For his part, Cameron wanted to get the referendum out of the way, fearing his chances a year later would be impaired by mid-term unpopularity, protest votes and a fresh wave of migrants. Andrew Cooper remembers, 'The big fear was another summer of migration issues dominating the news. The polls said that the previous summer had brought a 5 per cent swing from Remain to Leave, and we couldn't afford another 5 per cent swing.' He adds, 'The problem was, they had exhaustively established that this was as good as they were going to get.'

* * *

David Cameron began the final battle for his deal at 2.20 p.m. on Thursday, 18 February when he arrived on the red carpet outside the Justus Lipsius Building, telling reporters he was there to 'battle for Britain'. At 5.10 p.m., armed only with a red ring-binder of notes, he strode into the summit room on the eighth floor and faced his fellow leaders. After half an hour of small talk they posed for the traditional group photograph, and then had two hours of 'tense' talks. It was immediately obvious that it was going to be harder going than Cameron had hoped. He stressed that what he was after were just 'modest' requests which had already 'been badly received' at home and could not be 'watered down any further'. 'This is already a compromise on a compromise,' he said. 'I am not asking for anything impossible.'[5]

François Hollande was having none of it. With a vehemence that shocked Downing Street, the French premier went to war over the protections for non-eurozone countries, saying there could be no 'British veto' on eurozone policies. French officials had given no indication of the scale of their objections in preliminary talks. In the privacy of their delegation room, Cameron's aides made pointed remarks about the 'French resistance'. 'With Hollande it has been a debate about three words, for four days,' one official complained later.[6]

Cameron was soon fighting on two fronts. The Visegrad Four attacked *en masse* against the benefit cuts, particularly those to child benefit being sent back home. Cameron's opening demand on benefits was for a 'temporary' emergency brake that would let him slash in-work benefits for up to thirteen years – an initial period of seven years which could twice be extended by three years at a time. The Czech Europe minister Tomáš Prouza declared, 'It's about as temporary as the stationing of Soviet troops in Czechoslovakia.'[7] Cameron's bottom line was a brake lasting seven years.[8] The Poles were insisting that there was no way any emergency brake could last for more than five years. To cap it all, Charles Michel of Belgium demanded an extra clause making it clear that any deal would be a final offer that could not be improved if Britain voted to leave. 'There's no second chances,' he said.[9] Enda Kenny, the Irish prime minister, was a rare voice in support. He urged the other leaders to give Cameron a break: 'His party is divided, his cabinet as well. He faces a hostile media. Let's give him the tools for this fight.' Then, quoting from *Macbeth*, Kenny concluded, 'If it were done when 'tis done, then 'twere well it were done quickly.'[10] Angela Merkel also made warm noises, but others present felt she was 'detached' and preoccupied with the migrant crisis.

At 7 p.m. the meeting broke up with no agreement. Cameron, growing increasingly anxious, warned that he could not go home with a dodgy deal: 'It would be suicide. I would not have the support of my cabinet. And I would not be able to win the referendum.' He had expected pushback, perhaps even a few confected rows, but this was much worse than that. As one aide put it, 'Everyone was playing bad cop.'[11]

No army can fight on an empty stomach, and no EU leader should be expected to negotiate in the same condition. Over a dinner of avocado and shrimp 'imparfait', cod loin with wheat-beer emulsion and duo of potato, light mango mousse with caramelised pineapple and coffee, the leaders discussed the migrant crisis. After dinner, Tusk emerged at 1.20 a.m. and said, 'A lot remains to be done.' An hour later Cameron held an emergency meeting with Tusk and Juncker, the two presidents sitting across a table from him in a fifth-floor room resembling a police interrogation cell. The Council president agreed to press on with face-to-face talks with the three biggest troublemakers: the French, Czechs and Belgians. Cameron returned to the British delegation room, as soulless as it was airless, tired and depressed. There he wolfed Haribo sweets – one of twenty-three bags consumed by the delegation in the thirty-three hours of negotiations – and drank coffee while his aides swigged Diet Coke.[12] Then he tried to sleep. At 4 a.m. he was summoned to see Tusk. They were still nowhere near a deal. Tusk sent the leaders to bed and asked them to return for a discussion over an 'English breakfast'. Cameron left, pale and drawn, at 5.40 a.m., for the British ambassador's residence. Dispirited but determined, he told his team, 'I'm ready to stay here and work, but I am not going to take a deal that's not right.'[13]

After just three hours' sleep, and fortified by a breakast of scrambled eggs, Cameron was back at the Justus Lipsius Building at 10 a.m. on Friday for another meeting with Tusk, who was sustaining himself with croissants. Announcing this controversial Continental breakfast news, an aide addressed British reporters: 'I hope that doesn't offend you.' Cameron told Tusk, 'I'm happy to stay until Sunday. I've told the wife and children.'[14] They agreed that there was no point summoning the national leaders to their 'English breakfast' – even the prospect of a fry-up had not been enough to satisfy the French or the Visegrad Four.

As the day went on Tusk held a series of one-on-one encounters with the holdouts, and the failure to convene for a meal became the subject of a running joke on the flatscreen televisions in the vast atrium of the Justus Lipsius Building which becomes the press room during summit weeks. 'Breakfast' became an 'English brunch' at 11 a.m., which was then delayed until 'lunch', then a 'late lunch', then 'high tea' at 4 p.m. Even the apparent prospect of scones and cucumber sandwiches did not do the trick. At 5.30 p.m. the screens in the press room announced that there would be an 'English dinner' at 8 p.m. Tired of waiting for the authorities to feed him, the PM and his team ordered pepperoni pizzas from a nearby takeaway. In the meantime he had held bilateral meetings with Matteo Renzi, the Italian prime minister, Hollande and Merkel. Also peckish, the German leader popped out for a bag of Belgian *frites* drenched in andalouse sauce, mayonnaise spiced with pepper and tomato at a nearby fast-food joint.[15] Those not involved in the crisis talks watched with wry amusement. Lithuanian president Dalia Grybauskaitė commented, 'The timing all depends on the deepness of the drama some countries would like to perform.'

For Cameron's staff the summit dissolved into long periods of boredom punctuated by panic. 'It's a very odd environment up there on that floor,' one said. 'The leaders withdraw to their national offices while envoys shuffle between them trying to gain agreement about a text. Suddenly you have these moments of great rush, and "Oh my god, there's a text," then, "The text's not the right language," and "Who do we need to manoeuvre around?" Then suddenly you've got two hours when fuck-all happens because everyone's negotiating without you.' Richard Holbrooke, the legendary American diplomat, once remarked that 'Diplomacy is like jazz: endless variations on a theme.' A Downing Street source said, 'I think EU negotiations are a bit like that. You're constantly open to how you're going to play it.'

Cameron's meeting with Hollande eventually resolved the eurozone issue, with the PM reassuring the French premier that Britain was not trying to opt out of all EU financial-services legislation. 'There were some tweaks of wording,' a delegation member said. Cameron's crucial encounters were with Beata Szydło. It was the Polish premier's first European Council after winning a general election for the conservative Law and Justice Party, led by Jarosław 'Jerry' Kaczyński. Szydło refused to give any ground at all on the length of the emergency brake or the level of child benefit paid to children living overseas.

For years the Palaeosceptics had fought for a referendum so they could reclaim sovereignty and battle over whether the UK could avoid the jurisdiction of the European Court or repatriate entire areas of competence from Brussels. Now, as one report later put it, 'Britain's place in Europe was resting on whether or not 34,000 children of East European migrants could carry on receiving full child benefit, at a cost of £25 million a year to the taxpayer – about 0.2 per cent of Britain's £11 billion annual payment to the EU.'[16] David Lidington said, 'It really boiled down to stuff which cost nothing at all in the grand scheme of things.' But Downing Street knew Szydło 'could not be seen to cave', and 'probably had quite restrictive riding instructions from Kaczyński back in Warsaw'.

While Tom Scholar and Ivan Rogers worked on the Polish officials in Brussels, Daniel Korski, whose parents were both refugees from Poland, began talking to contacts in Warsaw around Kaczyński, urging them to remind Szydło that 'Cameron is our friend and we need to help him.'

By 5 p.m. there was still no agreement, and Cameron lost heart, sending his text to Andrew Cooper about wanting to leave the EU and announcing that he would give Juncker and Tusk one last chance to sort out the benefits issue: 'The Council now needs to act this out, I'm not doing any more.' A source in the room said, 'We were very close to saying, "There's no deal now, we'll come back to it in November and see what happens then." It wasn't done in any sort of grandstanding fashion.' Would Cameron ever have walked away? Another delegation source said, 'It's hard to tell with David. It was quite fluid at times. I think in the wrong circumstances he would have walked away from it.' Another official who was present disagrees: 'I think the PM said it knowing enough that it would drive them to sort it out.'

Rogers and Scholar sent Martin Selmayr, Juncker's right-hand man, a message: 'We're pretty much at our limit now, we need you to help if there's going to be a deal.' Selmayr was regarded as a slippery customer about whom the best that could be said was that he hated the French as much as the English. He was also the most formidable official in the Commission, a man who loved making deals. The big guns wanted the issue resolved – a Number 10 source said, 'Tusk and Juncker were being helpful, saying, "For God's sake, we don't want this hanging over us for the next six months." Merkel wasn't fired up, but she said, "Let's do this."'

Suddenly word came via the Czechs that the V4 were shifting. The threat of Cameron walking away was sobering for those in Eastern Europe. 'They were thinking about Putin the whole time,' one of Cameron's team said. 'The Law and Justice government knew we had supported a very tough line on sanctions on Ukraine, that we'd been supporting NATO's persistent presence in the Baltic region. They were also pretty scared about the interests of the remaining non-euro countries in the EU in the absence of the UK.'

But they still needed a ladder to climb down on benefits. Around 6 p.m. Tusk proposed a compromise. There would be one seven-year-long emergency brake, two years longer than the Poles wanted. Britain wanted the payments cut to the same level at which they were paid in the immigrants' home country. To the V4 this was unacceptable. The Poles then agreed to the principle of indexing child benefit based on each country's living standards. The situation was complicated by the fact that the Polish government had won the election on a pledge to raise rates of child benefit at home. Which rate would apply, and how would it be indexed? Ivan Rogers saw that the negotiations were descending into the weeds, and advised Cameron not to engage on the micro detail. The Poles' final issue was that they were not prepared to allow a cut for anyone already getting the payment. Cameron said 'No.' That would mean full child benefit still being sent abroad in 2031. Tusk suggested another compromise: a 'transitional period' during which migrant workers could carry on claiming child benefit until 2020. Cameron agreed. In the end, there was a fudge that allowed both sides to claim victory. A Number 10 source said, 'It allowed them to show you'd have some kind of rate that was proportionate to income without us committing to the rate of actual benefit.'

Around 8.30 p.m. the leaders finally sat down to an 'English dinner' of artichoke with goat's cheese and rocket, fillet of veal with tarragon *jus* and passionfruit *bavarois* for pudding. The V4 finally agreed terms. But there was a final crisis. As the dessert was served, the Greek prime minister Alexis Tsipras spoke up. His country was still suffering from the debt crisis; now it was on the front line of the migration crisis, its islands overwhelmed in places with refugees, he said, and here was the British prime minister having his concerns dealt with by Brussels with more urgency than Greece's. Cameron thought Tsipras was about to veto the whole deal. Emboldened by this intervention, the Portuguese prime minister António Costa also spoke up. He demanded to see the full text of the agreement before even considering giving his approval. Then Stefan Löfven, the Swedish premier, announced that he would have to consult with his coalition partners at home. The deal required the unanimous support of all twenty-eight member states. One of Cameron's aides described it as a 'cliffhanger moment'.

In the event, the darkest hour was just before the dawn. After another half an hour of horse-trading the deal was done. The doughty Dalia Grybauskaitė of Lithuania was the first to announce, 'Drama over.' Tusk then tweeted, 'Deal. Unanimous support for new settlement for #UKinEU.' Jonathan Faull, the British director general of the European Commission – Jean-Claude Juncker's chief negotiator – and other EU officials met in the press bar and clinked glasses. 'It shows Europe listened and responded,' he said. 'I hope people in Britain understand that.'[17]

At 11.10 p.m. in Brussels, just into the evening news at home as Craig Oliver had wanted, a tired but triumphant Cameron emerged to announce that he had his deal: 'I believe we are stronger, safer and better off inside a reformed EU, and that is why I will be campaigning with all my heart and soul to persuade the British people to remain.' For Labour's David Chaplin, watching the 10 o'clock news in London, it was 'the most surreal moment' to see a Conservative leader taking this step. Chaplin had worked with Coetzee, Straw and Cooper on the 'Stronger, Safer, Better Off' slogan. 'Suddenly the prime minister stood up and read out our script almost word for word. My jaw dropped. It was like watching the prime minister read out your homework on national television.'

But did Cameron's own homework deserve a good grade? To this day, Cameron's closest aides say he and Ed Llewellyn believed he had got substantive reforms that would have made a material difference to Britain's EU membership. 'They put everything into it,' Andrew Cooper said. 'Endless sleepless nights and difficult conversations. David and Ed genuinely feel that if one is dealing with the realities of the European Union, they got something quite significant – and many other EU countries would agree. But to any observer with a little more distance from the process, it looks much less substantive. And from the considerable distance of a voter, even if you had the chance to explain it to them, it was totally inadequate, given what we knew they hoped for.'

The problem, as Cooper's polling showed, was that 'What most voters clearly wanted was a big reduction in the numbers of people coming here – rather than a time-limit on benefit entitlement.'

Cameron deserves credit for getting his fellow leaders to accept reforms they initially opposed. 'That's the thing that frustrates me in all of this: even to get what the PM got was really hard work,' one official said. 'They salami-sliced us the whole way.' But it was Cameron's own public pronouncements that had helped create expectations he could not meet. As Cooper puts it, 'The problem was not that David Cameron wasn't tough enough or shrewd enough in his negotiating stance, but that it was a mistake to suggest in the first place that very significant control over free movement was achievable. It created a massive expectation problem, which turned out to be a hole below the waterline of the campaign to staying in the EU.' Cameron's most reckless pledge was the one he made at the 2014 party conference, when he said he would 'get what you need' on immigration. One close friend said, 'I was astonished during the campaign that Leave didn't play that over and over again, because basically he did take no for an answer. We could not credibly present this as a reformed EU.'

The Eurosceptics certainly agreed, and had done their best to set benchmarks Cameron could not reach. The Fresh Start Group issued an analysis of the deal which concluded, 'The changes on offer fall far short of the opportunities that we identified, with the vast majority of key underperforming EU policy areas unaddressed.' The prime minister had 'partially achieved' ten of their objectives, but had 'not attempted' another eleven. Business for Britain, before it morphed into Vote Leave, had also fenced Cameron in. Matthew Elliott said, 'We were very confident by the time he came back with his deal that we could win that expectations game.' The Eurosceptics unleashed an effective media barrage.' On the day, Richard Tice, the co-chairman of Leave.EU, said, 'The prime minister promised half a loaf, begged for a crust and came home with crumbs.' Daniel Hannan tweeted, 'Britain banged the table and aggressively demanded the status quo. The EU, after some mandatory faux-agonising, agreed.'

Hannan believes the limited nature of the deal dramatically increased the number of Tory MPs and MEPs prepared to defy Cameron and back Leave. In the end more than 140 MPs did so – three times the number of hardcore sceptics. 'I cannot overestimate the impact of the deal,' says Hannan. 'The view was: if this is how they treat us now, when we are about to vote on leaving, imagine how they will treat us the day after we vote to remain. That pushed so many people.' Nigel Farage agreed the deal was a crucial moment: 'If it had been something real on migration, I think it would have been much harder for us to win. Much harder.'

Given the deal's reception, could Cameron ever have grasped the nettle and – as he had obliquely threatened – lead the Out campaign? No one close to him thinks so. 'There were little moments where his heart said, "You know what, fuck it, it would be great to do this,"' one confidant explained. 'But he saw how much Britain's influence was magnified by "being in the room". He's an innate conservative in the small "c", not wanting to change stuff sense.'

The poor media and public reception for the deal persuaded Britain Stronger In Europe to ditch their plans to promote it, and to focus instead on their core messages. In Downing Street Craig Oliver and Ameet Gill were both keen to move on. 'Maybe if in the first week we'd absolutely sold the welfare brake we wouldn't have got into such a mess over immigration later, but I don't think that would have happened really,' a campaign source said. 'Number 10 shat themselves when the right-wing press turned against it, and they decided, "Right, we'll never mention this ever again."' Ryan Coetzee, Stronger In's head of strategy, agreed that there was no point in lingering on the outcome of the renegotiation: 'The deal that was done on benefits didn't address the fundamental concern which people had. Therefore the decision was "Let's move the hell out of this negotiation as soon as possible and let's make the core case." Despite not having something to offer on immigration, we did have a lead on the economy. We did have a lead on risk.'

The problem with the core case was that its lead advocate was Cameron, who until that very day had been claiming he could back Leave if the deal was sub-par. This troubled Coetzee: 'I think the most legitimately potent argument of the leave campaign, was "If it's such a catastrophe to leave, why were you prepared to do it in February?"' David Chaplin regarded the renegotiation as one of Remain's 'biggest strategic weaknesses' for this reason: 'You have this landmark policy, Euroscepticism, for decades, then you do a massive U-turn and say, "Actually, we have to stay." You lose people's trust. Cameron did a hand-brake turn on Europe.'

The deal was banished from Stronger In's script. Two months later, when Joe Carberry suggested in a planning meeting that they refer to the renegotiation, one of those present says, 'Craig Oliver laughed out loud and said, "No, no, no, we never mention that."'

Even if they had wanted to talk about the deal that weekend, it's doubtful the campaign would have been successful, because at 5 p.m. on Sunday, 21 February Boris Johnson followed Michael Gove and declared that he would back Brexit. David Cameron had been to Brussels and – within the narrow parameters he had set himself – got largely what he wanted. Yet in the moment of this qualified success he had also suffered his most grievous blow as prime minister, the one that would ultimately bring him down.

BORIS AND MICHAEL

Oliver Letwin was determined to give his mission one more go, even if it was beginning to resemble *Mission: Impossible*. Cerebral but absent-minded, the Cabinet Office minister was someone who could not be let out in public, but he was David Cameron's most adept policy fixer.

His task this time was to convince Boris Johnson to back the Remain campaign by producing a new Sovereignty Bill that would enshrine in law the idea that the British Parliament, not the European Court of Justice, was the master of the UK's destiny. There was just one problem with the plan: every senior government lawyer from the Attorney General downwards believed that each form of words Letwin had come up with was either irrelevant or illegal. Johnson was also coming to that conclusion. The mayor of London had floated the idea himself in early November 2015, and persuaded Cameron to include it in his speech to Chatham House on the day of his 'Dear Donald' letter to Tusk. The experience of running up against the limits of what was possible in reforming the EU was pushing Johnson towards the exit door. Michael Gove had not been convinced either, which is why David Cameron had taken responsibility for sorting out the 'sovereignty lock' away from the justice secretary and passed it to Letwin.

It was after 9 p.m. on Tuesday, 16 February – two days before Cameron began his summit marathon in Brussels – when Letwin dialled Johnson's mobile. When the phone went, the mayor of London was sitting at the dinner table in his Islington home, several glasses of wine to the good. Letwin launched into his best case for the sovereignty plan, but had barely opened his mouth when Johnson said, 'Oliver, how good to hear from you. Do you mind if I put you on speakerphone? I've got the lord chancellor here.' Johnson pushed a plate aside and placed his iPhone between himself and Gove and said, 'Michael, what would you like to ask?'

Letwin had called to try to circumvent Gove's growing influence over Johnson, only to find them dining together. His shock can be imagined, but he remained the model of cordiality. He and his officials ran through the latest iteration of the plan as Johnson added Martin Howe, a QC who was the son of Thatcher's foreign secretary Geoffrey Howe, to the call. 'He was being patched through from Barbados, where he was on holiday,' says Johnson. 'Oliver was on the line with his civil servants. We discussed the latest draft. It was obvious listening to Martin Howe that it wasn't really going to fly.' Letwin realised he had failed: Johnson would not be persuaded. He reported back to Cameron, who invited Johnson to 10 Downing Street the following day for a final reckoning.

Dinner that night at Johnson's home in Islington was the most important culinary confab in British politics since Tony Blair and Gordon Brown sealed a pact that would clear the way for Blair to run for the Labour leadership in 1994. The Granita restaurant in which Brown agreed to stand aside, in return for promises still disputed to this day, is long since defunct. But it is noteworthy that its location, 127 Upper Street, was just four hundred yards from Johnson's home. In its impact on the country, the BoGo Concordat has every right to be considered the more significant event.

Johnson and Gove met at Oxford, where Boris was two years ahead of Michael. An adopted child raised by a Scottish fishmonger and his wife who won a scholarship to an independent school, Gove recalled meeting his more obviously illustrious colleague (Eton and Balliol) on his very first day at university at the bar of the Oxford Union, where both were to prove themselves gifted debaters. 'He was a striking figure with sheepdog hair and penny loafers,' Gove told Johnson's first biographer, Andrew Gimson. 'He seemed like a kindly, Oxford character, but he was really there like a great basking shark waiting for freshers to swim towards him.' Johnson, having failed once to become president of the Union as a Tory, ran again, and won by presenting himself as the candidate in tune with the sensibilities of the SDP, a chameleon quality that was to remain a feature of his politics. In this effort, Gove admitted, 'I was Boris's stooge. I became a votary of the Boris cult.'[1]

For the next two decades Johnson remained the senior man. Both had successful careers in journalism, Boris at the *Telegraph*, Gove at *The*

Times. Johnson invented the 'straight bananas' school of reporting from Brussels, where he highlighted idiocies – real or imagined – of the system and became Margaret Thatcher's favourite journalist. Both used their columns to point out what was wrong with the European Union. Johnson got into Parliament with Cameron and Osborne in 2001, while Gove arrived four years later. Yet by 2007 Gove was in the shadow cabinet and a key member of the 'Notting Hill set', the group of socially liberal, upwardly mobile Tories who took over the party in 2005. Johnson was in the wilderness after lying to his party leader, Michael Howard, about an infidelity. He got his second chance the following year when he was elected mayor of London, but when the Tories returned to government in 2010 it was Gove who became the transformational reformer as education secretary. Johnson presided over London's revival after the financial crash, and cemented his position as the most popular and recognisable politician in the country during the 2012 London Olympics. Gove was one of the few people Johnson regarded as an intellectual equal – 'Boris rates Michael's brain in a way he doesn't rate Cameron's,' says a friend. As 2015 drew to a close it was to Gove that he looked for help in making his decision on Brexit.

David Cameron made several mistakes in the final year of his premiership, but none was as disastrous, or as curious, as his confident belief that both Gove and Johnson would support the Remain campaign, in essence because he had asked them to. All of those who worked closely with Gove over the previous six years believed he would back Brexit when he was forced to make a decision, though the man himself wrestled with his loyalty to Cameron. Dominic Cummings is blunt: 'I thought he'd be for Leave all along.'

Yet David Cameron, his wife Samantha and some of his closest Downing Street aides all drew a different conclusion, believing that Gove would put personal loyalty before principle. Their miscalculation spread a degree of complacency about the outcome of the referendum that affected the strategic planning for the campaign, and their disappointment, even fury, at Gove's decision greatly poisoned the well in the Conservative Party at the key moment when Number 10 was trying to keep MPs on the prime minister's side. Understanding why Gove made the decision he did – and why Cameron misread him so catastrophically – is the key to understanding why Britain backed Brexit. It is a complex story of personal belief, the nature of political friendships, decisions that had previously stretched the bonds of loyalty, the influence of key advisers, the murky depths of human psychology, and even that hoary old English staple, class. Little that happened in the campaign and the leadership election that followed was not coloured by Gove's choice.

Throughout the coalition years Gove took a vow of silence on Europe, since he knew his stance was unhelpful to Cameron and he did not want to distract media attention from his own school reforms. This Trappist positioning probably lulled the prime minister into a false sense of security. Cameron's view, as Gove saw it, was 'You, Michael, have said we should stop banging on about Europe, therefore I assume your dutifulness towards me will trump your views on this issue.'

However, Gove believes there was a consistency to his position that made it clear where he would stand on Brexit. He was a regular intervener – meddler, some other ministers would say – in Whitehall 'write arounds', the letters circulated to the relevant ministers on each government decision. Gove offered his views on other people's policies, and was never slow to point out what he perceived to be the idiocy of EU rules. Gove says, 'There were plenty of episodes and moments when people would have seen I was more difficult on this issue than the average bear.'

Gove and Cameron did have a substantive conversation on Europe in November 2015, in which the justice secretary sought to outline what the PM would need to make a success of the renegotiation. He told Cameron, 'Everyone's telling you what you must get out of the renegotiation in order to please them. For me, the big problem is that, fundamentally, laws are made which we cannot change. But speaking as your friend and your adviser, not just Michael Gove, you will lose unless you get a good deal on migration. That's the critical thing.' It was to be sound advice.

During the conversation, Cameron appeared to acknowledge that Gove and Johnson harboured a more ideological Euroscepticism than his own. He said, 'There's a spectrum. George is more pro-European than me, so is Theresa, then there's me, then there's you and Boris.'

He was not taking any chances, though, and despatched a succession of ministers and Gove's friends in an attempt to persuade him to support the Remain campaign. They included Nick Boles, a close friend of twenty years' standing, and Ed Vaizey, who had languished for six years as arts minister, where he was effective but overlooked for promotion. Cameron dangled the ultimate carrot, telling Vaizey, 'I'll put you in the cabinet if

Gove votes the right way.' He was probably joking. Nick Herbert, who was running the Conservative In campaign, and Charlie Taylor, one of the most innovative head teachers liberated by Gove's school reforms, also made representations.

There were also private drinks with Osborne either side of Christmas 2015. Gove and Osborne were even closer than Gove and Cameron. Gove fully expected to back the chancellor in any future leadership election. Such was their friendship that in October 2014 *The Times* reported that George Osborne's dog had married Gove's dog in 'a ceremony with flowers'. In March 2014 the *Mail on Sunday* reported comments Gove made over dinner at Rupert Murdoch's Mayfair home in which he declared, 'There are only two people fit to be prime minister: George Osborne and William Hague.' He also said, 'Boris is incapable of focusing on serious issues and has no gravitas. The whole Boris routine will wear thin with the electorate very quickly if he became PM. And he can't make tough decisions.' Given what happened later, these comments reverberate with significance.[2]

When they talked, the chancellor told Gove, 'All DC wants to do is make sure you'll do what we say on Europe.' Osborne, whose future depended on holding the warring factions together, also warned Gove that if he did choose to back Brexit, however hard he tried he would end up campaigning on immigration and being fully embroiled in the campaign: 'The conveyor belt will take you further and further away from us.' But Gove was unable to commit, telling Osborne, 'Don't ask me my view, because if you ask me, I'm out.' It is notable that Osborne, unlike Cameron, was never convinced that Gove would be with them, telling the prime minister, 'I have my doubts.' Unlike Cameron, Osborne did not feel aggrieved about his friend's views. Both had opposed a referendum to start with, Osborne for precisely the reason that if you hold a referendum 'you can't control what people do'. One friend even advised Gove that if he wished to help Osborne's leadership hopes he should back Brexit, since he could join forces with Gove to unite the party afterwards.

On 18 December, just after Cameron had laid out his four baskets at the Brussels summit, the prime minister asked Gove to do *The World at One* on Radio 4. It was a 'straight-bat, Geoffrey Boycott-ish interview', in which Gove avoided committing himself. He said: 'The European Union is not working,' but hailed the 'progress' made at the summit. Asked point-blank if the cabinet minister who was rumoured to be coming out for Brexit was him, he said, 'No … I'm confident he can secure a deal … where our interests are safeguarded.'[3] That was true, as far as it went – Chris Grayling was in fact the minister pondering resignation. Gove had always resolved to declare his hand only once Cameron had secured his deal. But Gove now believes Craig Oliver heard that interview and concluded, 'Well, if he's prepared to defend this, then he'll be OK.' Early in January, Downing Street spin doctors began briefing that Gove would be on-side.

The moment that best explains the Cameroon misreading of Gove's position – and the one that sparked the deepest rancour afterwards – came when Gove and his wife, the journalist Sarah Vine, spent New Year with David and Samantha Cameron and some of their closest aides at Chequers. Both Camerons left the party with the impression that Gove would back Remain.

Gove is adamant that Cameron himself never asked him outright if he would support him on Europe. He did tell the prime minister to his face, 'If you lose you mustn't resign.' If this looks in retrospect like an attempt to salve his conscience and dodge the consequences of his actions, he is insistent that at this stage he had not yet reached his final decision. At the party he was questioned about his intentions by Christopher Lockwood, an Old Etonian who had worked at *The Economist* before Cameron recruited him to Downing Street. In response he gave an answer that left room for manoeuvre in both directions: 'If it was anyone but DC as prime minister then there would be no question [that I would back Brexit], but I would find it very difficult to vote against him.' If that suggested Gove might put loyalty first, it certainly did not guarantee it, and in essence it made it clear that he was fundamentally supportive of Brexit.

The more important conversations, though, were between Sarah Vine and the Camerons. Friends of David and Samantha Cameron are adamant that Vine said she expected her husband to remain loyal. 'There was a conversation at Chequers at New Year,' says one friend of Samantha, 'which left Sam with a very strong impression that Michael would back Remain.' This pledge would have had the quality of a blood oath to Samantha Cameron. Vine was the godmother of her younger daughter, Florence, and the two couples had holidayed together. They sent their children to the same primary school, and their daughters, Nancy

Cameron and Beatrice Gove, went to the same secondary school. Vine herself has confessed that she misled her friend. When Gove's decision to back Brexit was finally revealed she wrote an article for the *Daily Mail*, admitting, 'I blame myself in part for any misunderstanding. In earlier, albeit informal, conversations in which Mr Cameron had asked me about Michael's intentions, I had not been entirely transparent – mostly because I genuinely wasn't sure which way Michael was going to go, but also because, being frightfully middle-class about it all, I didn't want to start a row.' Describing her husband's decision as 'torture', she added, 'Michael has been like a cat on a hot tin roof, locked in an internal struggle of agonising proportions.'[4]

Gove has also acknowledged privately that his wife had given the wrong impression 'in her desire not to create a problem'. But he also admitted that some of the fault was his: 'My great sin was that I didn't say at an earlier stage, "I'm probably going to campaign for Out."'

Immediately after the New Year, Gove went to stay for a couple of days with Sir Theodore Agnew, a patron of the academy schools Gove had championed as education secretary who now served as an executive director at the Ministry of Justice. He told Gove, 'Don't do it,' and offered two explanations. As a member of the MoJ board, Agnew was keen to see Gove continue with the prison reforms he had already begun to map out: 'It's more important that you carry on with your domestic reforms.' He also questioned whether the Foreign Office and the rest of the civil service were 'up to' the task of capitalising on the opportunities presented by Brexit. Gove heard the same argument about the capacity of the government to make the most of leaving Europe from Rodney Leach, the veteran Eurosceptic who funded Open Europe and was now urging fellow Tory donors to get behind Cameron.

The week before Cameron's deal negotiations, Gove went to Scotland to see his adoptive parents. Gove's father had lost his fish business as a result of the Common Fisheries Policy, and one friend said he believed Gove felt it would have been a betrayal of his parents to back Remain. On his return to London he met his three special advisers, Henry Cook, Henry Newman and Beth Armstrong, to run through the pros and cons. They all agreed that he should follow his conscience. The argument they collectively made went like this: 'Everyone knows what you believe. If you support the PM, everyone will know why you're doing it. But your currency in politics, your capacity to achieve things, will be diminished.

Rather than being an independent figure who followed through on principle, you will forever be seen as a Jeeves figure, a stooge, someone who is a wholly owned subsidiary of Cameron Inc., not an independent political act.' To Gove, who had been someone else's sidekick ever since being Johnson's 'stooge' at Oxford, this was telling.

There had also been several conversations with Dominic Cummings, who was sufficiently confident of Gove's position by late January to confide in Matthew Elliott that he thought his old friend 'would be on board'.

Yet Gove remained uneasy, and – contrary to the view that later developed of her as a Lady Macbeth figure urging her husband to acts of greater political destruction – Sarah Vine was also torn. 'Sarah and I realised there was no happy outcome,' Gove said. 'Either I'd not be true to my friends, or not be true to my beliefs. That's a stark version, but there was no way out. Other people could duck the choice, but if you're a cabinet minister it's a bit difficult.'

The first alarm bells sounded in Downing Street after Donald Tusk had spelled out the details of Cameron's deal on 2 February 2016. Two days later Sam Coates wrote a story for *The Times* revealing that Gove was 'intellectually convinced of the case for leaving but worried about contributing to a campaign that would wreck Mr Cameron's legacy'. Gove had confided his dilemma over lunch a few days earlier to a 'surprised' Danny Finkelstein, the *Times* columnist. He did not believe Finkelstein was Coates's source, but he knew he had said the same to others who might have been. The following Monday, 8 February, the prime minister was due to give a flagship speech on Gove's plans for prison reform, and Ed Llewellyn did not want the issue of the justice secretary's position on the EU to distract attention. The Number 10 chief of staff phoned Gove on the 5th and said, 'We need you to go out and do an interview saying you'll back the prime minister either way, because he's going to be asked about it.' Gove replied, 'Well, I can't really do that.'

On the day after Cameron's prisons speech, Shrove Tuesday, Gove met the prime minister and George Osborne in Cameron's flat above 11 Downing Street. There he finally made it clear that he was inclined to back Brexit. Cameron appealed directly to Gove's loyalty: 'You know if I lose, then it will destroy me. You can't do this.' If the words sound pleading, the prime minister's tone was not. He spoke evenly and purposefully at what can now be seen as one of the turning points of his premiership.

It is a feature of every single account of those around Cameron during the period of this book that he kept his calm while the crisis raged around him.

Osborne then made a broader case that Britain was always going to have a relationship with Europe, it was just a matter of geopolitics how that relationship was defined: 'Yes, we can get irritated with this particular form, but ultimately we have to be realists about it.' He then appealed again to Gove's sense of loyalty, warning that he risked destroying the Cameroon modernisation project they had all worked on together for a decade: 'If Dave loses, then the party will be in the hands of the people we've been trying to argue out of their traditional prejudices.'

Gove explained that he had felt obliged to suppress his feelings on Europe, but the referendum meant he had no choice but to express them: 'I'd put my feelings in a box, and now the box has been opened. My feelings on this have been unleashed. And it's just incredibly difficult for me. If I take a particular view to row in behind you, then everyone will know it's insincere.'

If this was the clinching argument for Gove, it does not fully explain his decision to put his beliefs before his friendship with Cameron. The fascinating thing about the choice he made is that his colleagues, friends and aides all believe that Cameron had made it very much easier for him by breaking the bond of loyalty between them in July 2014, when he sacked Gove as education secretary and demoted him to chief whip. Lynton Crosby, the Tory election strategist, had detected in polling and focus groups that Gove's radical school reforms and uncompromising approach to the educational establishment – which Cummings termed 'the blob' – were wildly unpopular with public-sector voters the Tories wished not to antagonise ahead of the general election. Crosby ordered non-core noises off silenced, a process he termed 'stripping the barnacles off the boat'. For Cameron, moving Gove was a pragmatic move to win an election. To many Tory MPs it was a betrayal of one of the few ministers, along with Iain Duncan Smith, who had given reforming shape to Cameron's premiership.

The move also cost Gove more than £30,000 in salary, no small matter for the couple, who as one friend puts it 'have made no secret of their injudicious handling of overdrafts'. Perhaps this inspired the venom with which Sarah Vine greeted the decision. She tweeted, without comment, a column by her *Daily Mail* colleague Max Hastings with the title 'A shabby day's work which Cameron will live to regret', which described the move as 'worse than a crime'. That was the first splinter in her relationship with Samantha Cameron. Sarah certainly took the move worse than Gove himself. 'It really did affect him, but Sarah was kind of snarling,' says a friend who recalls an outburst by Vine at their home near Ladbroke Grove in west London.

Those who know both Gove and Cameron say the prime minister never realised how hurtful the move was to his old friend. 'David just kept smiling and assumed if they didn't talk about it that everything would be fine,' says one mutual friend. 'And for a long time, because he's a jammy sod and because he and Michael don't like causing a scene, it appeared to be fine. But it wasn't fine.'

Gove 'can entirely understand why it happened', but described his demotion as 'a wrench'. He said, 'I would like to think that I would have, if I'd been in the PM's shoes, said to Lynton, "I'm not going to make calculations like that, and these are things I believe in and we're going to go into the general election fighting full-throatedly for them."' But Gove accepts that that may have meant that Conservatives wouldn't have won the election: 'In crude terms, I cannot blame anyone for giving Cameron advice or for his taking it. I wasn't badly treated.'

Gove took the decision on the chin and concealed how painful it was, but Cameron should have realised when it came to Gove's Brexit decision that loyalty is a two-way street. Reflecting now, someone who has worked closely with Gove over the past six years concludes, 'I don't think Michael was ever in play for Cameron. Possibly he might have been if education hadn't ended badly. I think the sacking from education is the pivotal moment.'

Any friendship with a prime minister is by its nature unbalanced, but Gove's with Cameron was unusually so. To the commentariat, Gove was a glittering jewel in the Notting Hill set, an erudite, witty and intellectual presence who deferred to Cameron and Osborne but explained them better to the world at large than they explained themselves. To Gove's closest associates, Cummings included, he was still the adopted child who made his way to a fee-paying school on brains and a scholarship, shone at Oxford without ever troubling the membership secretary of the Bullingdon Club, and was then indulged and patronised by Cameron's gang of public schoolboys. They say the best way to understand Gove and Cameron is to read *Brideshead Revisited*, Evelyn Waugh's novel which was adapted for television to great acclaim in 1981, four years before Gove arrived at Oxford. Imagining Gove in the role of Charles Ryder, who is enthralled by the aristocratic Flyte family, provides one explanation of his motivation.

As one close ally sees it, 'Michael was a spoddy, unfashionable geek, who turned up at LMH [Lady Margaret Hall] – a spoddy, unfashionable Oxford college and basically went a bit Charles Ryder. He was slightly captivated by the gilded elite of bronzed tennis-playing types at Brasenose [Cameron's *alma mater*] and Christ Church. The Cameron circle's view is that Michael is funny, Michael is clever, but he's a little bit crazy and he's a little bit funny because he believes things.' This observer's view, one at least partially shared by Cummings, whose disdain for the Cameron circle is pronounced, is that Gove was 'basically a bit of a performing monkey at the dinner parties. He was funny and clever but he wasn't one of them – not even a day boy. Michael was a kind of psychic prisoner of the Cameron circle, and the education thing was what broke that particular spell, the spell that might have descended when Charles Ryder first saw Brideshead.'

In seeking, since the referendum, to analyse why Cameron read him incorrectly, Gove has privately voiced the view that the PM probably believed he was 'tamed by being made chief whip' and 'taken down a peg or two', and that his 'attentive and dutiful' stance led key people in Downing Street to assume that the stridency of his views on Europe had been curbed. In addition, Gove thinks Downing Street assumed that the loss of the education job would have taught him not to be unduly influenced by Cummings. Cameron's attitude was supposedly, 'You would have seen that naughty Dominic Cummings got you into trouble towards the end of your time in the Department for Education, therefore you won't fall for his blandishments again.' In the end it was Cummings who read Gove right. More than that, friends say that it is wrong to accuse Gove of disloyalty. He chose loyalty to his father and to Cummings over loyalty to Cameron.

In searching for motivational cues in popular culture it is impossible to avoid *Game of Thrones*, the bloodthirsty swords-and-sex television drama series. Gove is not only (like Cameron) a fan of the series, he is also a keen wargamer who plays the *Game of Thrones* board game (and a Wars of the Roses game called Kingmaker) with an eclectic group of Westminster politicos, historians and journalists. 'I like *Game of Thrones* because it is escapist fantasy and utterly unlike daily political reality,' he has said. But it is hard not to draw parallels between this enthusiasm and what later ensued. In Kingmaker, fellow players have revealed, Gove prefers to represent the underdog Yorkist forces. In *Game of Thrones* he is an enthusiast for the feuding Lannister clan. In a bizarre but highly revealing video, recorded in the writer James Delingpole's garden in October 2014, Gove said, 'My favourite character in *Game of Thrones* is undoubtedly Tyrion Lannister. And the moment I loved the most is when he leads what's apparently a hopeless charge of his troops in defence of King's Landing against the forces of Stannis Baratheon. And you see there this misshapen dwarf, reviled throughout his life, thought in the eyes of some to be a toxic figure, can at last rally a small band of loyal followers.' It is hard to think of a better metaphor for the referendum campaign and how Gove saw his role in it. David Cameron might also have considered that Tyrion Lannister killed the father who had never respected him with a crossbow bolt to the guts.

In his final meeting with Cameron and Osborne, Gove sought to express his reluctance to campaign against the prime minister. 'I don't have any relish for it,' he said. This attempt at conciliation created greater problems, by convincing Cameron that Gove had promised not to campaign hard. But Gove and his friends are adamant that he never pledged to maintain a low profile. An MP who is close to both men says, 'Michael never gave that promise! The assumption was that he was such an ally and he'd go through all this hand-wringing, but in the end good old Michael would come round, when that was never the case.'

One of Cameron's closest aides declares this 'absolute bullshit': 'It was the lies that hurt. If he had been straightforward and said, "I want this with all my heart and I'm going to fight this campaign," that would have been one thing, but he didn't do that, he said, "I'm going to take a back seat. I'll be on their side but I won't be involved." David always thought that was the deal.'

Having been, at best, opaque in his intentions about Brexit, Gove seems to have been disastrously unclear about his intentions in the campaign, to the detriment of himself. 'Michael's so very polite that when he says "Yes" he means "No", but he thinks the manner in which he says it indicates the underlying intent,' says one ally. Another observes, 'It wouldn't be the first conversation with George and Dave where Michael's committed to X and he's thought, "I haven't committed to X."'

Dominic Cummings summed up the confusion with an old Russian aphorism: 'They say in Moscow everyone's right and everyone's unhappy.'

Gove's decision was wounding for Cameron. One minister who discussed it with the PM said, 'He believes that people owe him allegiance and that he is doing them a favour by having them in his cabinet. He saw this as an issue of loyalty.' One of Cameron's closest aides said he dealt with the decision better than many of his staff, who developed an instant and unshakeable loathing of Gove: 'They just hated him. He was like the devil to some of them. They spoke about him with such wrath and venom. When it got to the leadership contest they wanted literally anyone but Michael to win.' Another long-standing Cameron adviser believes Gove had set out to deceive: 'Michael made the whole thing into a bit of theatre. He put on a good show of being a tortured soul and not knowing which way to go. The anger was with Boris, but Michael was much cleverer about it all. Boris was worried he was going to win this and ruin Britain. He wanted to be a heroic loser. But Michael knew what he was doing. He plotted it like a chess game.' The source says that 'it took a while' for Cameron to share this anger. The 'proper fury' only came once the referendum had been lost.

Even after he had outlined his position, Cameron and Osborne tried to persuade Gove to change his mind. The prime minister and chancellor revealed that they were having a hard time turning the screws on other members of the cabinet. Called in to see them, the first question many of them asked was 'What's Michael doing?' This was a clever way of flattering Gove, but it also had a basis in fact. Two of Osborne's closest allies, Sajid Javid and Liz Truss, were both wavering, temperamentally disposed to back Brexit but receiving intense briefings from the chancellor on the economic risks of leaving. Truss, who was close to Gove, was a recipient of 'death by PowerPoint', according to one cabinet source. 'We think if we can get you on board, then we can get everyone else on board,' Cameron told Gove. 'If you don't then all hell might break loose.'

Gove agreed then, and in a subsequent conversation with Osborne, not to lobby his fellow ministers. When he had finally made up his mind and his position became public on Friday, 19 February, Osborne told him, 'At the cabinet on Saturday, don't trash the deal. We need to get other people on board.' Gove agreed: 'I'm not going to make a broadcast, I'm just going to release a statement afterwards.' He concluded later, 'In the end the only person who I influenced by my decision was Boris.'

Gove's allies believe he would have jumped alone, but Johnson admits Gove's decision made it 'much easier' for him. When they met for dinner at Johnson's home on 16 February they had an implicit understanding that their fates were linked. What transpired that week not only gave the Leave campaign a head and a face, it changed the future path of British history.

Boris Johnson had been dreaming about being prime minister since he was a young man and put aside his first stated political ambition to be 'World King'. The events of 2012, when he embodied the get-up-and-go spirit of a nation inspired by the London Olympics and defied political gravity to scrape a second term as mayor, made his future the single most intriguing question in British politics. Having handled riots, terrorist attacks and strikes in the capital, Johnson had done a lot of growing up. The prospect of him running for the leadership was live and, to a grow-ing number of Tories, no longer ludicrous. His own jokes about there being 'more chance of me being reincarnated as an olive' had given way to proper campaign planning.

As soon as he was re-elected as mayor, Johnson began building a campaign team. He remained in regular contact with Lynton Crosby, who had masterminded both of his mayoral victories. In May 2012 he recruited Will Walden, a former BBC producer, to be his spin doctor. Walden is an affable bear of a man who remains calm in the midst of chaos and had a shrewd understanding of how to get the best from his boss. In early 2014 Johnson also acquired a campaign manager.

Ben Wallace, then a member of the Tory whips' office, approached Johnson and asked to help him become leader. Wallace is a former Scots Guardsman who was mentioned in dispatches in Northern Ireland and had a spell as a member of the Scottish Parliament before becoming MP for Lancaster and Wyre in 2005 (and for the newly formed Wyre and Preston North from 2010). Wallace is an entertaining and clever opera-tor who likes the company of journalists, something which may have contributed to Cameron's decision to overlook him for promotion for four years. He was a committed pro-European and had a spell as parlia-mentary private secretary to the arch-Europhile Ken Clarke. When that came to an end he thought about the qualities he admired in Clarke – intellect, an interest in people, real character and a commitment to reform – and sought another to champion. After asking himself, 'Boris has the character, but is he a leader?' Wallace visited Johnson at City Hall, and quite early in the meeting said, 'I think you should be the next leader of the party. I'd like to help you.' He then recruited his constituency neighbour Jake Berry to help out in the Commons.

Fearing that the Tories would lose the 2015 general election, from the autumn of 2014 Johnson quietly prepared for power, getting selected for the safe seat of Uxbridge and South Ruislip that September, although he continued in his role as London's mayor. Cameron and Osborne concluded that defeat would mean the prime minister would have to resign as leader of the Conservative Party, and Osborne's leadership prospects would also be sunk. After a period of trying to promote Sajid Javid as an alternative to Johnson, they reluctantly concluded that they would not stand in his way if the situation arose. Osborne visited Johnson at his country home in Thame, Oxfordshire, that autumn and delivered a message of conciliation. However, as soon as Cameron won his majority in May 2015, Johnson was out in the cold again and preferred to concentrate on his City Hall duties rather than accept the junior post of culture secretary in Cameron's post-election reshuffle.

In Parliament, Wallace's strategy was for Johnson to remain 'low-key and loyal', and he encouraged Johnson (who is more shy than is publicly apparent) to get to know his parliamentary colleagues after seven years out of Westminster, particularly the new intake of MPs. At Wallace's instigation he began hosting curry dinners at his home in Islington for half a dozen MPs at a time. In the autumn of 2015 Wallace and Berry were joined by Nigel Adams, a *bon viveur* from the Yorkshire seat of Selby and Ainsty, and Amanda Milling, the MP for Cannock Chase who had once been Berry's constituency chairman and was the main point of contact for the 2015 intake. Berry began to keep 'the book' of supportive MPs.

Together they piloted Johnson through an attempt to torpedo his credibility at the 2015 party conference. The *Spectator*, which Johnson had formerly edited, ran a cover story under the headline 'Boris in the Wilderness' which contained none-too-subtle briefing from the Cameron and Osborne camps about the 'momentum' behind Osborne, contrasting his networking with MPs with the more laid-back approach of the Wallace operation.[5] Requiring the speech of his life to get back in contention, Wallace and Berry forced Johnson to rewrite and rewrite until he was ready. The media judged it his best piece of oratory to date.

Cameron, perhaps enjoying the rivalry, then used his own speech to heap praise on Osborne ('our Iron Chancellor'), almost ignored Theresa May, and then got a standing ovation for Johnson by saying, 'I want to single someone out. He's served this country. He's served this party. And there's a huge amount more to come. So let's hear it for the man who for two terms has been mayor of the greatest capital city on earth: Boris Johnson.' The PM told journalists he would give Johnson 'a big job' once his mayoral term was complete. He told Johnson, 'I will make sure you are competitive' with Osborne in any future leadership race. Word began to spread that Johnson might be made foreign secretary, though a Downing Street source said later, 'It would have been defence secretary. That was the PM's idea.'

When Johnson came to make his decision about whether or not to support Cameron in the referendum he was back in the prime minister's good books, with every prospect of getting one of the top jobs in government. If he looked at backing Brexit with one eye on the leadership, there was also an alternative path – one which Wallace and most of the rest of his campaign team wanted him to follow – of taking a good job, showing he could run a department, building parliamentary support and then taking on Osborne in 2018 or 2019.

Johnson's involvement in the referendum issue began straight after the Bloomberg speech, which was immediately before the World Economic Forum in Davos. Throughout the annual get-together of world leaders and tycoons Johnson found himself doing media defending Cameron. At Zürich airport, as he was about to fly home, he spoke to Cameron on his mobile phone. Wedged in a corner, just before going through the metal detectors, Johnson told Cameron: 'You have to drive the hardest bargain and you have to be prepared to say that you'll walk away in order to do that.' He repeated the same view on and off when they spoke over the following two years. An aide says, 'That's why he hoped the renegotiation would be stronger, because he felt that Dave understood that. You start wide, you don't start narrow. If you're not prepared to walk away, you're going to get fucked.'

In the early part of 2015, before the general election, Johnson approached Cameron and Osborne and asked them to let him be the lead negotiator for the prime minister's new deal. Taking the view that the job could not be combined with running City Hall, and fearing the bold scope of demands Johnson had in mind, they declined. 'My offer to

Dave was, put me in charge of everything,' Johnson says. 'I said it to George, I said it to Dave. There was no particular enthusiasm whatever for that. I would've loved to have done it.' Cameron and Osborne were right to think Johnson would have pushed them to demand far more from the renegotiation, including sweeping reforms of the Common Agricultural Policy, repatriation of social and employment laws and a veto over EU laws: 'I spoke to [Cameron] about it: wholesale CAP, wholesale Social Chapter would have been the reform I wanted. Stop the legislation.'

Johnson was abroad, visiting Israel and the Palestinian territories in November 2015, when he made another play to beef up Cameron's blueprint for reform. On the flight home he summoned the author to his flatbed seat and outlined a demand for Parliament to be granted an emergency veto over EU law: 'You could amend the Act which says that all EU directives, regulations and other obligations have supremacy over British law to say that it has supremacy unless expressly overturned by Parliament.' Best of all, 'You don't need Angela Merkel's permission at all. All you need is to get it through the House of Commons.' Johnson revealed that his lobbying had persuaded Cameron to put the idea of a sovereignty lock in his Chatham House speech the week before. He thought the plan would be 'an absolute game-changer'.

'I became depressed about the direction of the negotiations; it was clear that nothing was happening,' he said later. 'And I got a rush of light to the head and thought maybe we could give Parliament the power to block stuff it doesn't want. And so you could have a sovereignty clause with some real meaning and bite. It would assert the ultimate sovereignty of Parliament in such a way as to stop the individual bits of the EU's legislation. I persuaded myself that it could be made to work.'

By this stage Johnson was already contemplating backing Brexit. As early as June 2015, to the intense irritation of Downing Street, he had endorsed Dominic Cummings' idea of two referendums – the first intended to shock Brussels into conceding more. From the autumn Cummings met Johnson several times to lobby him to back Leave. Cummings' wife, Mary Wakefield, had worked with Boris at the *Spectator* and was a friend. These were informal conversations over a drink. But of the two wives it was Marina Wheeler, Johnson's wife of twenty-two years, who was to prove the more influential. A highly respected barrister who had just taken silk, she had read a lot about the European Court of

Justice, and had begun to form the view that it had gone rogue and could not be reined in.

By the New Year, Wheeler, along with Michael Gove, was reinforcing Johnson's view that the logic of his position would be to back Brexit. In a blog published by the *Spectator* the week before Cameron's final deal, Wheeler condemned the renegotiation for failing to tackle the 'Court of Justice of the European Union, whose reach has extended to a point where the status quo is untenable'. She accused the ECJ of 'eroding national sovereignty' by imposing the EU's Charter of Fundamental Rights – fifty 'rights, freedoms and principles' – on member states. Britain was given an exemption from the Charter in 2007, but since then, Wheeler pointed out, the ECJ had ruled that the opt-out had no legal force. 'Here is an opportunity to restore a measure of constitutional coherence,' she wrote. 'Let us not pass it by.'

Johnson denies that he put his wife up to her stance: 'She was just saying what she thought. Some of the conversations with Marina about the European Court of Justice were quite illuminating. She fortified me in thinking that I wasn't insane to want to get out. Marina is very, very centrist, reasonable. I'm much more right-wing. I was very struck by the level of her indignation about what was happening. It was a feeling that my instincts were right.' To one of his inner circle he confessed, 'She was the one who persuaded me in the end.'

Following Johnson's November intervention, Cameron had a clever idea. If Boris wanted reassurance on sovereignty, who better than Gove to deliver it? Adapting the old adage about thieves, he 'set a Eurosceptic to catch a Eurosceptic', and asked the justice secretary to get to work. Since the European Union Act 2011, which instituted the 'referendum lock', it was written into statute that EU law only had supremacy over British law because Parliament had chosen to decide that it should. Now sceptics wanted a statement that whenever it liked Parliament could simply overrule Brussels, and vote down regulations of which it disapproved. Government lawyers made it clear that that would be tantamount to leaving the EU, but Cameron and his aides asked Gove to devise something subtler. With help from Dominic Raab, a former international lawyer and now a junior minister at the Ministry of Justice, he studied whether they could strengthen the provisions of the clause, or draw up an entirely new Sovereignty Bill. They consulted four constitutional lawyers, and quickly concluded that the plan would not work, and

that any move to amend the 1972 European Communities Act would see
the European Court of Justice launch legal action against Britain. Gove
reported back to Downing Street: 'Two objects can't occupy the same
space at the same time. The European supreme court is either the
European Court of Justice in Luxembourg or you're not in the European
Union, in essence.'

Oliver Letwin took over the responsibility for finding a solution, but
he had no more success. As with much of Cameron's renegotiation in
Brussels, civil servants and government lawyers studied the legal detail
and proclaimed idea after idea illegal under EU law. To the distress of
some of Cameron's aides, there was no political decision to overrule
them. Mats Persson remembers that Cameron had also been told that his
benefits demands were 'impossible' when he first made them, but he had
still won concessions. But at the top of Downing Street there was a willingness to operate within the tramlines of existing law, rather than to
challenge its basis. Persson wanted a Sovereignty Bill which ruled that 'if
there is a conflict between EU law and UK law in areas where we consider
the EU not to have special competence or where it has overstepped the
mark, then UK law takes precedence'. He says, 'Instead we considered a
largely watered-down version of it which didn't really change anything,
just restated the existing position. The problem we had was that the Bill
was either seen as irrelevant by key Tories or illegal by lawyers. The
version we considered was largely irrelevant. But perhaps what we
should have done is simply to say, "We're doing this. It's happening elsewhere in Europe. We are a sovereign country."'

A Number 10 source elaborated: 'A Bill is not illegal until it is tested.
You could put it on the statute book. It only becomes illegal when the
ECJ rules it's illegal. In that standoff, I think if you stand up to the ECJ
or Brussels. If the country is big enough they always back down. I think
that would have happened here. Maybe Gove wouldn't have bought it,
but I think Boris would have.'

On Thursday, 11 February Johnson went to see Letwin in 9 Downing
Street to hear his plans, which included an instruction to the courts on
how to interpret the balance between EU and British law. It was their
third meeting; Ed Llewellyn had sat in on a previous one. Johnson was
not impressed. 'I saw various drafts of it but in the end it was a chimera.
What became clear in the conversations with the lawyers was it was just
a Professor Brainstawm contraption, like making cucumbers out of

moonshine. It was a strange device. Did it change the price of fish? Did it change the ability of the EU to regulate the price of fish? Did it change the ability of the Court of Justice to issue judgements overturning legislation, thereby changing the ability of Britain to regulate the price of fish? No.' He left depressed that the plans were not going to satisfy him or answer the challenge laid down by his wife, and told Walden, 'I don't think there's much there.'

'I was really hoping that it would work,' he says. 'And it didn't work. I suppose I was trying to persuade myself that it could work. But it ultimately was untenable. You could publish such a Bill, but it was pretty clear that the government lawyers thought themselves that it wouldn't work. And then there was no chance of getting it through the House of Lords. It would be difficult to get it through the House of Commons. Even if you used language that really did bite, it wasn't going to deliver.' Johnson also consulted a pro-European professor called Alan Dashwood, a friend of Marina's who helped write the Maastricht Treaty. 'We had him over for dinner and we talked about it for hours, and it was obvious that he saw through it straight away. He said, "This is either illegal or it's nothing. There's no way of making it work."'

Throughout this period, Johnson had tried to persuade Cameron to beef up a renegotiation he regarded as lame, and sought a mechanism that would have given him the cover to support the Remain campaign. He was now confronted by the realisation that none of these efforts had worked, and the logic of his position was that he should vote to leave.

On Sunday, 14 February, Johnson dropped a hint that he was considering backing Brexit, telling the London edition of the BBC's *Sunday Politics* that Britain had 'nothing to fear' outside the EU. He promised to 'wait until the prime minister does his deal' before, with a typically Johnsonian flourish, vowing to 'come off the fence with deafening *éclat*'. He added, 'Whatever happens, you will hear a lot from me.'

Before he went to dinner at Johnson's home in Islington the following Tuesday, Gove had another drink with Osborne and told him he was now 'almost certain' to back Brexit. Earlier in the day Cameron had had an ominous phone conversation with Johnson, who had indicated that he was leaning that way too. He was invited to a meeting at Number 10 the following morning.

Despite the weighty matters under discussion, the dinner was not without its farcical elements. Gove could not understand why Johnson had invited Evgeny Lebedev, the proprietor of the London *Evening Standard*, to join them at such a sensitive gathering. Lebedev, who had been a staunch media ally of Johnson as London mayor, was expected to be accompanied by the actress Elizabeth Hurley. 'Liz Hurley didn't show up,' says Johnson, perhaps because a press photographer was positioned outside his house. Johnson could not understand why grainy pictures of Gove arriving at the dinner appeared on the front page of the *Mail on Sunday* the following weekend, and was mildly put out that Sarah Vine wrote an account of the evening for the *Daily Mail*. Long before Gove and Johnson fell out, Johnson's aides confided their suspicion that Vine had tipped off the photographers.

When Oliver Letwin called, dinner had only just been served. Vine recalled, 'Michael and Boris leaned into the iPhone, Boris firing questions at it, Michael making listening noises. I, too, listened dutifully for a few minutes, but it really was a very lawyerly conversation, and the aroma rising from the slow-roasted shoulder of lamb was getting to me. I tucked in. Marina and Evgeny followed suit, and we spent the next twenty minutes attempting to make polite conversation in stage whispers, Boris shushing us every time we got too loud.'[6]

As the evening drew on, Johnson and Gove 'compared agonies'. Both had the same dilemma: settle for the quiet life of Remain, or risk their careers on Brexit. Boris, Vine remembered, was 'very agitated, genuinely tortured as to which way to go, although not for quite the same reasons as Michael'.[7] In a version of events that later reached George Osborne's ears via Lebedev, Gove put the arguments for loyalty: 'We've got to stick with David and we've got to be loyal,' while Johnson mused aloud, 'I don't see why. It's all right for you, Michael – but what's he ever done for me?' On hearing this later, Osborne is said to have remarked, 'Apart from making him mayor of London, I can't think of anything!'

'The dinner was great fun,' Johnson recalls. 'Gove and Sarah were on good form. And we talked a lot about the issue, though not exclusively. We were both in the same position. The truth of the thing is we were both tiptoeing round it – "This is going to cause such problems." We were talking it over from that point of view: the issue and the downsides. We both agreed at that dinner that we were leaning towards Out, but that neither of us had made a final decision. We got out the cigars and had a drink. At the end, everyone else buggered off and Michael and I sat at the bar and talked. We drank a prodigious amount, I can tell you that much.'

Gove's impression of Johnson was that he was a sincere Brexiteer, but that he could not wholly divorce the decision from its impact on his own future. 'Boris in his heart I think believed in and believes in Brexit,' Gove said, 'but he wanted to know what I was going to do. I didn't show my full hand at that point. I wasn't absolutely certain.' Gove's read on Johnson's mental gymnastics was this: 'I'd quite like to do this, I'm a romantic opponent of what the EU stands for. And it certainly won't do my leadership ambitions any harm.'

At times Johnson was almost wistful about what a decision to back Brexit might mean, knowing full well that, win or lose, it would make him the darling of the Conservative grassroots, and the prohibitive favourite to be the next prime minister. But, far from a man salivating at the prospect of obtaining the keys to Downing Street, Gove detected 'genuine oscillation' in Johnson's mind, and believed he was 'wrestling with the consequences'. He saw across the table a man who was 'highly competitive and very ambitious', but who also had 'a bit of him which is nervous, scared about what taking on the big prize would mean'.

Gove, whose house is lined with thousands of books on history and politics, also saw parallels between Johnson and Winston Churchill, whose biography Boris had written to considerable acclaim sixteen months earlier. Gove said, 'I think he recognised it would be a bigger gamble [to back Brexit] but one with potentially bigger consequences – a bigger place in history, a noble cause to fight for. One of the things that Churchill always did was he wanted to put himself at the centre of events. There's a self-dramatising quality, and I think it's the same with Boris.'

As the dinner broke up neither man had fully committed to Brexit, but both had a clear understanding that if they did so they would not be alone. Gove said, 'I'm probably going to back Leave, but I am not certain.' Johnson said that was his view as well.

The following morning, looking somewhat under-refreshed, Johnson cycled to Downing Street and strolled up the street wearing a tube driver's beanie hat and with a rucksack hanging open over his shoulder. After forty minutes he emerged to declare that there was 'no deal'. What happened in the meantime is shrouded in mystery, as he and the prime minister met alone, but enough has been gleaned from conversations with their aides to reveal that the meeting was extremely heated. By one account Cameron was 'puce-faced' at Johnson's refusal to fall into line, and behaved in a 'rude and rather pompous' fashion. Boris had written a column for the *Telegraph* a week earlier in which he said Britain could prosper outside the EU, and Cameron handed him a typed response to the points he had made. Afterwards Johnson told an ally, 'He looked down his nose at me. He handed me an essay reply to my article. It was utter rubbish, bunkum. We ended up having a row. He got all pinch-cheeked.'

When interviewed for this book during the referendum campaign, Johnson was a little more diplomatic: 'I was summoned in. I think they were expecting me to say, "Fantastic, it's all looking good." And so it was a bit of a tense meeting. We didn't have a physical fight. We stuck well away from violence, I would say. We had an argument about the issue, the whole thing. I'm a very old friend and admirer of the prime minister, so it was a free exchange of views. I remember it as being a discussion of the substance. I remember a discussion about sovereignty and getting quite heated about it.'

Cameron later recounted details of his showdown with Johnson in Number 10 to a minister. It irritated him that Boris regarded him as a rival, when in fact it was Osborne, not Cameron, who was Johnson's rival. 'I'm not competing with you. We're not competing together. I'm the prime minister,' said Cameron. It is easy to see how Cameron might have found Johnson infuriating, possible too to see how Johnson might have found Cameron's tone patronising. The PM also took Johnson to task for his support for a second referendum, which would give the Brexit-supporting ministers a mandate to try to get a better deal: 'What you're saying is that you can negotiate better than me, and I don't think you can.'

For all the talk of substance, Johnson's team are adamant that Cameron tried to tempt him into line with the promise of advancement. 'He was offered any job in the cabinet except chancellor,' a close ally said.

Those who spoke to Johnson afterwards say he was furious at Cameron's tone. 'He changed after the meal with Gove and the meeting with Dave,' recalls one of his team. 'That really got his goat. It clearly angered him. Gove and Boris egged each other on on sovereignty. Gove promised to be in the playground with him and said he wouldn't hang him out to dry. Then Dave pushed him over the top.'

*　*　*

Gove finally made up his mind to back Brexit on Thursday, 18 February, after calling Paul Marshall, a hedge-fund manager he had got to know through his chairmanship of the Ark chain of academy schools, and Steve Hilton, the former Downing Street blue-skies thinker and Notting Hill set stalwart who had emigrated to the United States. Gove wanted Marshall's perspective as a non-Tory, and Hilton's input because of his knowledge of the Cameron 'friendship group'.

'Am I mad in doing this?' he asked Hilton. 'Will everyone think, "What a bastard, this is indefensible. Principle, schminciple"?'

Hilton replied, 'No, I'm so glad you said that's what you're going to do. I think that's what you should do, and I completely agree with you.'

Marshall also said, 'It's the right thing to do.'

Emboldened by the support of people he trusted, Gove then spent most of Thursday and Friday writing a 1,500-word statement on why he was backing Brexit. On the Friday, his decision leaked out. Gove says he was not responsible for this, and that his intention was to speak to Cameron on the Saturday before the cabinet met. Gove's allies accuse Craig Oliver of being behind the leak, on the grounds that Downing Street did not want his decision to back Brexit overshadowing their PR offensive into the following week. Oliver denies this. Some of Johnson's aides accuse Gove's aides of prematurely putting out his decision in order to bounce Boris into Brexit.

When he gave his press conference in Brussels on Friday evening, Cameron sought to make light of Gove's decision: 'Michael is one of my oldest and closest friends, but he has wanted to get Britain to pull out of the EU for about thirty years. I am disappointed but I am not surprised.'

Cameron returned to London late on Friday night, and called a cabinet meeting for 10 o'clock the following morning. It was the first time the cabinet had met on a Saturday since the Falklands War. The gathering was a respectful and light-hearted affair in which Cameron and his ministers stressed their desire to pull together as a united party after the referendum. In a twenty-minute opening statement the PM issued a plea for unity, telling his colleagues 'I believe in this team,' and saying it was important to him that everybody 'disagreed honestly'. Ministers then spoke in descending order of importance. George Osborne and Theresa May backed Cameron before Michael Gove spoke for the Brexit cause, explaining why, with a 'heavy heart', he wanted to be 'true to my convictions and my country'.

There was even time for sexual badinage. After the senior ministers, Cameron called on his minister of state at the Foreign Office to speak: 'Joyce Anelay.' The surname is pronounced 'anally'. Greg Hands, the chief secretary to the Treasury, piped up: 'Ooh, Prime Minister!' Cameron replied, 'Well, Greg, is there anything else you would like to tell us about your position?' This was greeted with 'gales of laughter'.

The meeting broke up at 12.17 p.m., and Cameron announced on Twitter that the cabinet – minus the six Brexiteers – had agreed to recommend staying in the EU. In the street outside he announced that the referendum would be on 23 June.

The five expected Brexiteers – Chris Grayling, the leader of the Commons; Iain Duncan Smith, the work and pensions secretary; John Whittingdale, the culture secretary; Priti Patel, the employment minister; and Theresa Villiers, the Northern Ireland secretary, had met in Duncan Smith's room at the start of the week, and again on Friday, to coordinate the next steps. They collectively agreed that they wanted to support Vote Leave for the official designation. There was discussion of staggering their public appearances, but Paul Stephenson persuaded them it would be a more powerful image to have them arrive together at Westminster Tower after the cabinet meeting. 'We wanted a big show of strength,' said Matthew Elliott.

As they filed out of the Cabinet Room, Grayling turned to Michael Gove and asked, 'Are you going to come over with us?' He said, 'Yes.'

Keen to observe propriety, Grayling, Whittingdale and Patel abandoned their ministerial cars at the Commons and got into Steve Baker's waiting BMW for the short trip across Lambeth Bridge. Gove cadged a lift with Theresa Villiers, who kept her official vehicle since as Northern Ireland secretary she required protection officers.

At Vote Leave's headquarters the gang of six were greeted with applause. Grayling made a short speech, and then they all signed a giant placard saying 'Let's take back control'. Rob Oxley credits Paul Stephenson with stealing the news that day: 'Having all of them there with that big pledge wall was so effective. Rather than the story being the PM recommending this deal, it very quickly became Tory Party politics. That footage still got used as stock footage six months later. A campaign which gave more media access was able on that day, one of the biggest days, to win the six and ten.' Matthew Elliott was also euphoric: 'I basically knew at that point that it was almost certain we'd get the designation and it would be far easier to recruit business leaders and raise money.' He spent the afternoon on the telephone to donors, telling them, 'I told you we'd be getting these guys, now we're fully up and running.'

After a round of media interviews, Grayling joined the team in a pub around the corner on Black Prince Road. It was there that 'somebody took a phone call after which there was a bit of a buzz because we thought we were going to get Boris'.

It has become a given in some quarters that Boris Johnson was a dedicated supporter of EU membership who decided to back Leave for the simple and cynical motive of advancing his career. Certainly it is true that in the millions of words he had written up until February 2016 he had never once advocated withdrawal in speech or print. But for the previous seven years he had been advancing ever closer to a position where Brexit was the natural conclusion. As a journalist, Johnson had produced scare stories on Brussels' overreach while Project Fear was still two decades in the future. He had also repeatedly irritated Downing Street by speaking out on Europe, most notably at the Conservative Party conference in 2009, when he called for an in/out referendum more than three years before it became Cameron's policy.

Johnson quite consciously positioned himself as the most stridently Eurosceptic of the senior Tories while Michael Gove was keeping his views shrouded from the public. In August 2014 he backed a report by his own economic adviser Gerard Lyons that leaving the EU would be better for Britain than remaining on the existing terms. He argued that the country should 'not be frightened' of quitting, and warned Cameron, 'The UK can only achieve serious reform if it is serious about leaving.'

That same month, Ben Wallace visited Johnson in Thame for lunch. They cooked a couple of steaks and drank a memorable bottle of 1970 claret. Johnson chose the moment to take his pro-EU campaign manager into his confidence. 'I must warn you,' he said, 'that I could always recommend that we leave Europe.'

If Johnson had not made the binary choice about membership before 2016, that was in part because he had not had to; but he had begun to feel an inexorable pressure building. Far from rushing towards Brexit, he appears to have sought reasons to back Remain, but to have concluded that they were not good enough:. 'I'd obviously had a huge interest in it over the years, but I kept shelving it as a decision I knew I was going to have to make. I could see it coming down the track. I was thinking, "Oh God, I'm going to have to work out how can I spend almost twenty-five years as a Eurosceptic and then when it finally comes to it, just meekly fold my tent and not give battle."'

Over the Christmas break Johnson read several books, as well as Business for Britain's mammoth 'Change or Go' document. He went back to first principles: 'In an argument you need to set out a problem, then look at the downside and risks of getting out, and then you need to come and decide what your conclusion is. And that's what I tried to do. The truth is there was a certain amount of yo-yoing around in my head.'

Johnson's view, from first principles, was that 'the whole European Union project has changed so dramatically from what it was. It's so anti-democratic that it will eventually bust apart. I just think it's wrong for this country. We're becoming invisibly captured by a new system of government. And I think it's profoundly unhealthy because no one knows who these people [in Brussels] are, and they're taking a huge number of decisions. There's a moral laziness about relying on the EU to take all these big decisions for us.'

In a column for the *Telegraph* on 7 February he set out the balance of risks: 'Britain in the EU good, in so far as that means helping to shape the destiny of a troubled continent in uncertain times, while trading freely with our partner. Britain in the EU bad, in so far as it is a political project whose destiny of ever closer union we don't accept and whose lust to regulate we can't stop.' Those seeking to read the runes could take anything they wanted from that. 'For the last couple of years I have argued that we would be – on the whole – better off in a reformed EU, but that Britain could have a great future outside.' He questioned whether Cameron's renegotiation was a 'bazooka or popgun', asked why the PM did not 'try harder' to regain control of the UK's borders, and concluded, 'In deciding how to vote I (and I expect a few others) will want to know whether we have genuinely achieved any reform, and whether there is the prospect of any more.'

Throughout 2015 the author saw Johnson half a dozen times, including accompanying him on two week-long foreign trips. On each occasion he expressed the view that Cameron's renegotiation was hopelessly limited: 'I was amazed they didn't ask for more. That really pushed me over the edge. They thought all they needed was to have a rigmarole of reform.'

If the deal was pushing him out, there were also heavy pressures in the other direction. 'What I really didn't want was unnecessarily to cause grief for Dave and for the government. I really didn't. I didn't see any point in that. What was there to gain by that? Nothing at all. I didn't want to be at variance with my party.' There were also the social and family aspects. Johnson had spent two lengthy spells of his life in Brussels. He genuinely believed that Europe 'needs us'. His father Stanley was a former Commission official. In Islington, his wife's friends were Remainers: 'There are lots of people I know well who are Europhiles, and I didn't know what it would do to my family, for heaven's sake. Those were my hesitations.' Odd as it may sound, Johnson also told friends in this period that backing Brexit and playing a prominent role in the campaign would mean missing a pre-booked family holiday, which he was reluctant to do.

Pressed by MPs on both sides to declare – including Bernard Jenkin and Sir Nicholas Soames – Johnson sought to avoid committing himself by saying, 'I'm not an Outer.' He said later, 'That was my holding line.' As holding lines go it was pretty poor, since it contributed to the notion that he had reversed his true position by declaring for Brexit. His aides and friends say the reverse is true: he was trying to persuade himself he was not an Outer – and failing.

The sum of these factors was that supporting 'In' was much the easier option. Yet that may be, perversely, precisely the reason he resisted it. As Gove observed over dinner in Islington, Johnson appeared to crave a role at the centre of political drama. 'I thought it would be just lazy of me not to stand up and be counted,' he said. 'I basically think that I'm constructed for combat.'

The man whose political advice Johnson valued above all others, Lynton Crosby, also supported him once Cameron had ignored his advice to delay the deal. A source close to Johnson is clear that Crosby effectively gave his blessing if that was the course Johnson wished to pursue. 'Lynton basically said to Dave, "You need to wait." And Dave said, "I can't." On the basis of him not doing that, I think Lynton's view [to Boris] was, "You've just got to go for it, mate." I don't think there was anything in Lynton's view which suggested he thought Boris was doing this for political reasons. He thought it was what Boris believed in.'

Yet on the Friday of Cameron's deal, when news of Gove's decision emerged, Johnson had still not definitively decided what to do. MPs say he told someone, 'I'm veering all over the place like a shopping trolley.'

Johnson sought to clarify his thoughts by writing not one but three newspaper articles, two for Brexit and one backing Remain.

Johnson's plan, as a £275,000-a-year columnist for the *Telegraph*, was to make his formal announcement at 10 o'clock on Sunday evening with a piece for Monday's newspaper. He sent the first article, for 'Out' (see Appendix 1) to Marina, Walden and Wallace at 6.32 on the Friday evening. As a distillation of his thoughts about the great issue of the time it is a curiosity, the first quarter of its 2,500 words being about lorries. It opens by trying to explain the importance of sovereignty to an imaginary eighteen-year-old. Johnson draws on his experiences as mayor dealing with a spate of cyclist deaths caused by the blind spots on trucks. He proposed that London become a 'Safer Lorry Zone', but his efforts to get better-designed lorries were deterred by the Department for Transport due to EU regulations. 'Here I was, mayor of a city clamouring for measures to protect cyclists; here was the British government, with all their plenipotentiary authority. There was nothing they or I could do, not with any speed. That was because this thing called sovereignty – the power given to them by the British people to take decisions on their behalf – was no longer in Westminster.'

Johnson goes on to rehearse Marina's observations about the European Court of Justice and the Charter of Fundamental Rights. He praises Cameron for having 'achieved a great deal in a short time' in Brussels, and Letwin's 'heroic intellectual labour' on the Sovereignty Bill, but concludes, 'It cannot stop the machine; at best it can put a temporary and occasional spoke in the ratchet.' He dismisses the economic risks of Brexit as 'exaggerated', and finishes by saying, 'The choice belongs to those who are really sovereign – the people of the UK. And in the matter of their own sovereignty they, by definition, will get it right.'

Having completed the Out article, Johnson was on a roll, and tried an experiment, a contradictory piece backing 'In'. He says, 'You know how it is when you've written something and it's much easier then to write something else. In half an hour I wrote one thousand words. The article was basically "It's crap, but ..."'

When the *Sunday Times* revealed the existence of this Remain article (see Appendix 2) a week later it sparked a frenzy of speculation. People have claimed since that it was far more persuasive than the original. The truth is that it was a slipshod piece of work, apparently written by Boris to convince himself that the argument for remaining was weak. Indeed,

in excusing and dismissing criticisms of Cameron's renegotiation it actually attacks the deal more aggressively than his first piece. It was written
in such a stream of consciousness that it does not even include paragraph breaks. Yet had sections of it emerged during the referendum
campaign it would have seriously embarrassed Johnson, since it shows
how felicitously he is able to embrace contradictory positions, and how
conscious he was of the risks of leaving the EU, which he publicly
downplayed.

It begins by damning Cameron's deal with faint praise: 'We were
hoping that he was going to get really deep down and dirty, in the way
that the Bloomberg speech seemed to indicate. He was going to probe
the belly of the beast and bring back British sovereignty, like Hercules
bringing Eurydice back from the Underworld. I had the impression that
this was going to be the beginning of a wholesale repatriation of powers
– over fisheries, farming, the social chapter, border controls, you name
it: all those political hostages joyfully returning home like the end of
Raid on Entebbe. It was going to be a moment for the ringing of church
bells and bonfires on beacons, and union flags flying from every steeple,
and peasants blind drunk on non-EU-approved scrumpy and beating
the hedgerows with staves while singing patriotic songs about Dave the
hero. I don't think we can really pretend that this is how things have
turned out. This is not a fundamental reform of Britain's position in the
EU, and no one could credibly claim it is.' He concludes that the EU
'elephant in the room' is 'still trampling happily on British parliamentary
sovereignty, and British democracy'.

Attempting to find reasons to vote Remain, he urges readers to 'Shut
your eyes. Hold your breath. Think of Britain. Think of the rest of the EU.
Think of the future. Think of the desire of your children and your grandchildren to live and work in other European countries; to sell things
there, to make friends and perhaps to find partners there. Ask yourself:
in spite of all the defects and disappointments of this exercise – do you
really, truly, definitely want Britain to pull out of the European Union?
Now?'

He then goes on to acknowledge many of the risks of Brexit which he
would spend much of the campaign rubbishing. 'There are some big
questions that the Out side need to answer. Almost everyone expects
there to be some sort of economic shock as a result of a Brexit. How big
would it be? I am sure that the doomsters are exaggerating the fall-out

– but are they completely wrong? And how can we know? And then there is the worry about Scotland, and the possibility that an English-only Leave vote could lead to the break-up of the union. There is the Putin factor: we don't want to do anything to encourage more shirtless swaggering from the Russian leader – not in the Middle East, not anywhere. And then there is the whole geo-strategic anxiety. Britain is a great nation, a global force for good. It is surely a boon for the world and for Europe that she should be intimately engaged in the EU. This is a market on our doorstep, ready for further exploitation by British firms: the membership fee seems rather small for all that access. Why are we so determined to turn our back on it? Shouldn't our policy be like our policy on cake – pro-having it and pro-eating it? Pro-Europe and pro-the rest of the world?' If any of that had emerged before polling day, Johnson would have been the object of ridicule.

He goes on to say that the deal is not as bad as he first painted it, pointing out that Cameron is 'the first PM to get us out of ever closer union' and the deal 'has some good stuff on competition, and repealing legislation, and on protecting Britain from further integration of the euro group'. He writes: 'Now if this were baked into a real EU Treaty, it would be very powerful. Taken together with the sovereignty clauses – which are not wholly platitudinous – you can see the outlines of a new role for Britain: friendly, involved, but not part of the federalist project.' He concludes, 'Yes, folks, the deal's a bit of a dud, but it contains the germ of something really good. I am going to muffle my disappointment and back the PM.'

Johnson sent the 'Stay' article in an email to his wife at 9.04 p.m. The following day he shared it with Walden and Wallace. But he quickly decided it 'was not worth the paper it was written on', saying to Walden, 'This is going to make me vomit. I just don't think this is good enough. It's a crap argument. It just isn't there.' A friend says, 'Did he want it to be? Possibly in his heart. But he never had any intention of using it, he just had to weigh up the arguments. He wanted to see if it added up to a hill of beans. He very quickly became clear in his own mind that it didn't.'

Walden, as Johnson's gatekeeper, had told members of the campaign team that they were not to try to influence his decision. But having read the first article and slept on it, Ben Wallace emailed Johnson to criticise it, pointing out on the cycle-safety issue that government departments often hide behind Brussels as an excuse for inaction: 'When it comes to the Lorry example you use DforT may have been slightly doing the same.' With his close links to Scotland, Wallace also warned that Johnson was 'quite wrong' to dismiss the risks to the union. 'I strongly believe that BRITExit would lead to break up Britain,' he wrote. Johnson took some of Wallace's criticisms on board, and the third and final piece he wrote for the *Telegraph* made less of the lorry issue and attempted to answer some of his better lines from the 'In' piece.

The following morning, Saturday, 20 February, Johnson emailed Cameron to tell him he was leaning towards 'Leave'. A source who discussed the message's contents with Boris said, 'It was hand on heart, "This is an incredibly difficult decision for me as you know. We've worked together, we're friends." The gist of it was, "Having looked at the stuff I've written over the years, I've reached the conclusion that we should be pressing hard. My heart says it has to be Out. I don't want you to see this as anything other than a sincerely held belief."' Cameron did not reply. Downing Street claimed later that Johnson did not tell Cameron his intentions until minutes before he announced them to the world, but he insists, 'I gave pretty good notice saying which way I was going.'

Seeing the way the wind was blowing, Cameron phoned one newspaper editor in a rage and said, 'I can't understand why Boris, as leader of the great financial capital, won't support the City.' At around 1 p.m., four hours after he received the email, Cameron got a text message from Boris suggesting he was wavering. In the intervening four hours Johnson had faced an 'absolute barrage' of messages from friends like Sir Nicholas Soames urging him to remain loyal to the PM. 'They were absolutely ruthless,' said Johnson. 'They got every friend of mine they could think of to ring me and badger me.'

The PM told a minister the message said, 'Cancel that, I'm dithering.' On the day, Cameron told Craig Oliver that Johnson had used the phrase, 'depression is setting in'.[8] In the message Johnson quoted from a poem by Rudyard Kipling, saying he would probably 'be crushed like the toad beneath the harrow'.[9] He also predicted that he would become the target of a 'hate machine' by his rivals – part of the message Cameron did not reveal to Oliver. Johnson denies that the toad quote meant he thought Brexit would lose: 'What the text was really saying was that I was depressed. My anxiety was about the misery of being at odds with Dave and George. I felt this was going to be a nightmare.'

Johnson spent the weekend at his cottage in Thame with his sister Rachel, 'hammering away at his hot laptop, frying sausages'. He told her, 'My mind's flashing like a traffic light.' They played tennis in the rain. Rachel asked if he really wanted to be on the same team as George Galloway and Nigel Farage. Boris said he was concerned with the issues, not personalities. Rachel warned that he would be accused of betrayal and opportunism, and 'outlined four scenarios that sketched out his political future whether he came down for "In" or "Out"'. Boris replied, 'I don't give a stuff about that, or the leadership.' When she realised his mind was made up, Rachel texted Marina to say, 'I will support him whatever he does, but he'll need balls of steel.'[10]

When Johnson phoned Wallace to say 'I've made my decision,' his leadership campaign manager told him, 'Then you'd better fucking win.'

Cameron and several allies made final appeals to Johnson that weekend not to follow Gove, exerting an 'enormous amount of pressure' by phone and text message. Cummings, Gove and others also tried to contact him: 'I had to turn my phone off,' Johnson said. 'I was being texted the whole time. I think you can probably safely say there was no one who was relevant to the whole thing who didn't try. I couldn't get back to everybody. It was just too much.'

On the Sunday morning the prime minister was put on the spot by the BBC's Andrew Marr and asked what his message to Johnson would be. Tackling his concerns about sovereignty head-on, he said leaving the EU would actually reduce Britain's ability to do things: 'You have an illusion of sovereignty but you don't have power, you don't have control, you can't get things done.'

By then, Johnson's plan to wait until 10 p.m. to declare his intentions in the *Daily Telegraph* was looking impossible. With Boris on his way back from Oxfordshire, Walden arrived in Islington at midday to find thirty journalists already besieging the house. He called Johnson and said, 'This isn't going to happen, you're not going to be able to hold off. You're going to have to say something.'

Boris called the paper and broke the news. At around 4.45 p.m. Walden reminded him to contact Cameron. Johnson sent a brief text to the prime minister announcing that he would shortly be making a statement. Downing Street briefed that they were only given nine minutes' warning before Johnson stepped out of his front door to address the waiting media. Craig Oliver says, 'I know that the prime minister felt that he was only finally clear within the last quarter of an hour of it happening.'[11] Walden briefed the press in turn about the email sent to Cameron the morning of the day before.

At 5 p.m. Johnson emerged to the shouts of reporters and an explosion of flashbulbs. Jostled by the media scrum, he said, 'The last thing I wanted was to go against David Cameron or the government. But after a great deal of heartache, I don't think there's anything else I can do. I will be advocating Vote Leave. Because I want a better deal for the people of this country.'

Later he said, 'I felt greatly relieved when it was done. Everyone said I was completely incoherent! There were literally hundreds of people there. It was insane. It was an imperial goatfuck.'

Across the political spectrum there was an immediate recognition that Johnson's decision had changed the game. Nigel Farage recalls, 'When Boris announced on that Sunday that he was joining the Leave campaign, I jumped for joy.' By contrast, Anna Soubry, a pro-EU business minister, said, 'Boris was critical, that was a killer blow for Remain. I think we could have just about coped with Michael Gove, but to have Boris join Leave was devastating.'[12] Lucy Thomas from Stronger In did an interview on Sky News ten minutes after the declaration. 'I remember saying, "This campaign's bigger than just one person." Inside I was not happy. Suddenly the task just became much bigger.'

In Downing Street and at Stronger In Andrew Cooper's polling had shown that if Cameron came back with a deal, supported by Johnson and other senior Tories, a big bloc of Conservative voters would take the party line, but if Johnson opposed such a deal they would not. 'The key variable was Boris,' says Cooper. 'We knew that Boris being opposed to the deal meant we weren't going to get a bounce. One of the big potential pillars of the campaign had been removed. It meant all we really had was the economy.'

Cooper took a very uncharitable view of Johnson's decision. 'Boris didn't have a strong view either way, and no one ever knew what he was going to do. He wrote the two different articles. He was almost by self-definition wavering in the middle. So his eventual decision to campaign in the way that he did is hard to see as anything other than a cynical and entirely self-serving act.'

Cooper's view was quick to gain currency. The *Independent* splashed the following day with the headline 'OUT for himself'. Sir Nicholas Soames, an arch-Europhile, tweeted, 'Whatever my great friend Boris decides to do I know that he is NOT an outer.' George Osborne took the same view, telling friends that Boris had repeatedly told him he supported Britain's membership of the EU. Since he shared the same ambition, Osborne did not see it as dishonourable of Johnson to want to be prime minister, but he believed that he saw the referendum as 'a vehicle' for that ambition. Osborne also believed that Johnson did not want to find himself on the wrong side of his *Telegraph* readers. But the chancellor was sanguine. Johnson's choice was just the kind of unpredictable event that he had warned Cameron was possible in a referendum.

That was not Michael Gove's view: 'Boris's personality and political views are entirely congruent with wanting "Out". The point has been made by lots of people that he is great fun to be around; the point that is often underestimated is that he's someone who is driven by passion and conviction.'

It was not Boris Johnson but David Cameron who ensured that the referendum campaign would have unavoidable consequences for the leadership of the Tory Party. By telling the BBC at the start of the general election campaign that he would not serve a third term, Cameron had guaranteed that the decisions others made would inevitably be seen through the prism of the looming contest to succeed him. By backing Brexit, Johnson knew he would enjoy the good wishes of the Tory membership, who would pick the next leader. But if there was a leadership element to the decision – and it is impossible to conceive that there was none – backing Brexit was not his only option.

It is easily forgotten that Johnson, like most people, did not expect Vote Leave to win the referendum. In a conversation with Walden that weekend he said, 'How could it be seen as a career move, given that I've been offered every possible job other than chancellor or prime minister?' Such a job would, as Cameron once promised, have made him 'competitive'. He also had reason to think Cameron might withdraw the offer if he backed Brexit. On *The Andrew Marr Show* that Sunday the PM suggested he would show forgiveness to those, like Gove and Duncan Smith, who had believed for years in going it alone. He did not include Boris on that list.

'The easy life, easy option, was to take one of those jobs and carry on,' a friend who spoke to Johnson that weekend says. 'Place him in one of the great offices of state, allow him to prove himself. Seeing the turmoil he went through that weekend, I had absolutely no doubt – and I was prepared to put on my most cynical hat – that he was doing this out of conviction, and actually he thought, "This could well be the undoing of me." I believe he thought he'd never serve in government.'

Walden, like Rachel Johnson, 'war-gamed' the implications for Boris's leadership prospects of the four possible outcomes (winning and losing as either a Brexiteer or a Remainer), but to both Boris was dismissive. Walden told a friend that week, 'Did I warn him of the likely scenarios of all these things? Absolutely. Did he care? Yes. He thought about it. Was that the primary motivation in his thinking? Absolutely not. The reality is that there are inherent dangers on both sides.'

Much of what has been written about Johnson's choice is speculation. It is a fact that Ben Wallace, his leadership campaign manager, advised him not to campaign for Leave. In his email sent at lunchtime on Saturday, 20 February he warned Boris that he would find it more difficult to get the support of MPs if he associated with the Brexiteers: 'Rapidly this campaign will be about "In" and "Out". It will not be about courts or negotiating papers. On the Out will be Farage, Galloway, Cash, Jenkin, Ukip and all the anti-free traders.' Wallace dismissed Gove as 'impulsive', but warned Johnson, 'He, however, has a patron in the form of George. You do not.' He concluded, 'Colleagues have always wanted to support you but the question they all ask is "can Boris do serious and statesmanlike?" Ask yourself if you are on the side of the cast of clowns listed above what might they say?' He rounded off, 'If however you wish to disagree … I will still support you to be leader. It will be a harder fight but still doable. The upside is that if the Outers win then you will be master of all.' At that time Johnson thought the Brexiteers would lose.

Perhaps the prospect of becoming 'master of all' was too much to resist, but it meant tearing up the 'low-key and loyal' approach Johnson had pursued for two years. Another well-connected Tory doesn't think there was any calculation at all: 'Boris, the guy's so feral, he just follows his instinct. His instincts were "Out".'

Whatever the ultimate motivation, Johnson was never more the embodiment of the nation than at that moment. For many voters the decision was finely balanced between the desire for sovereign control and the risks of economic downturn. Every voter weighed self-interest and the national interest. By plumping for Brexit after personal agonies, Johnson mirrored the decision of the country. Unlike most voters, his decision had a material effect on the outcome. The result was close enough that it is possible that whichever side he chose would have emerged victorious.

The retribution from David Cameron was swift. Addressing MPs in the Commons on the Monday, the prime minister outlined his deal and asked them to back him. In comments that his aides acknowledged were aimed squarely at Johnson, he said, 'I have no other agenda than what's best for the country.' Watching in Boris's office, Walden said aloud, 'Wow, that's pretty strong.' Cameron also took aim at the double-referendum idea: 'I have known a number of couples who have begun divorce proceedings, but I do not know any who have begun divorce proceedings in order to renew their marriage vows.' There were gasps from MPs, who saw this as a dig at Johnson's occasional marital woes.

The man himself did not see it that way. Johnson said later, 'I genuinely didn't feel it in the way that some people did. Genuinely not.'

When he got to his feet to ask a question, one hand fumbling down the back of his trousers, Johnson looked nervous. Running his hand through the platinum bird's nest on his head, he asked Cameron to explain in what way the deal returned sovereignty to the Commons. Unsatisfied with the answer, he yelled 'Rubbish!' as Cameron finished.

When Johnson returned to his office, Walden explained how Cameron's attacks were being interpreted on social media: 'Christ, he had about three pops at you.' Johnson quickly took umbrage. In a phone call with another ally that evening he said, 'These fuckers. They think the whole thing is run by intimidation and fear.'

Cameron's attack quickly backfired. Johnson resolved that he would fight hard to win the referendum. One Brexit minister said the Eurosceptics were reminded of the British and Irish Lions rugby tour of South Africa in 1974. During that ill-tempered series Willie John McBride, the Lions captain, hit upon a coded cry to alert his men to an impending punch-up. 'The Lions had a call, "99", which meant everybody piled in,' the minister said. 'That was our "99" moment. We agreed from then on there would be collective self-defence.'

Wallace texted Johnson to say, 'It's simple really, Boris. I think your choice will either make you PM by October or in the final two in 2019.

Either way, you need to show and be the future PM. Therefore in the campaign you need to act it. Be above things and lead.'

If the implications for Johnson of his decision were political, for Michael Gove they were social. On the Saturday evening he and Sarah attended the fiftieth birthday party of fellow Notting Hillite Andrew Feldman, the Conservative Party chairman. Gove offered not to go but was assured he was still welcome. While he sat at one end of the table talking to former Tory treasurer Howard Leigh and his wife Jennifer, at the other end Sarah was having 'an upsetting conversation with Sam' Cameron. It would be two months before details of the bust-up became public. An eyewitness was to tell the *Sun*'s Tom Newton Dunn that a 'blazing row' ensued in which the prime minister's wife accused Vine of 'betrayal' and Gove of abandoning her husband. Voices were raised. There was 'effing and blinding'.[13]

Friends say Samantha Cameron was also furious that Vine had chosen to write about her husband's agonising decision the following week in the *Daily Mail*, revealing details of her discussions with the Camerons. 'In Sam's world you just don't behave like that,' one confidante said. 'She has made clear she doesn't ever want to see Sarah and Michael darkening their door again.' A Downing Street aide added, 'You can chart her fury by each of Sarah's articles. She thought it was ludicrous.'

The Goves had a long-standing engagement with George Osborne at the chancellor's grace-and-favour Buckinghamshire home, Dorneywood, on the Sunday. Again Gove offered to cancel, but Osborne said, 'Look, just come.' He saw the dangers in long-established friendships fracturing, and said he would fight to keep lines of communication open. Osborne calculated that Gove would be the key to reunifying the party – and consequently to his own leadership hopes – after the referendum, and resolved to hug him close.

In a conversation with Nick Boles, which was relayed to Gove, Cameron voiced the hope that their friendship would survive. But at that point he was expecting to play the role of magnanimous victor. 'I'm sure everything will be all right in the end – provided we win,' he said.

Of all the things that ensured Cameron did not win, Gove and Johnson's decisions to campaign for Leave were among the most important. Without them, most people involved think Stronger In would have won easily. Nick Wood says, 'If Boris and Gove had not backed Leave we would have lost. They gave people "dinner party cover" to vote "Out". The fact that two intelligent, thoughtful men kicked against the prevailing metropolitan tide created space for others to come in behind them.'

At that point it was not inevitable that Brexit would happen, but the pieces were in place that meant it could. What happened next during the campaign would define whether that weekend marked the end of the beginning, or – as it turned out – the beginning of the end, for Cameron's premiership.

PART TWO

BATTLE IS JOINED

THE CAMPAIGN

February to June 2016

10

PROJECT FEAR

It was just a few days after he returned from Brussels when David Cameron understood that his gamble to use the referendum to draw a line under the Conservative Party's divisions on Europe had failed. Having lost Boris Johnson and Michael Gove, the whips fought to get other MPs to fall into line. Those in play received calls from Cameron and George Osborne. The hardest to get were asked to Downing Street to see the prime minister personally. Cameron deployed a winning blend of charm and steel. 'I think everyone who went into Number 10 emerged backing Remain,' said one adviser. The only problem for the prime minister was that, in growing numbers, backbenchers and ministers were refusing to see him.

When the call went out to Rishi Sunak, Cameron's aides were confident of success. To Cameron and Osborne, Sunak was the future of the Conservative Party, a slight but bright thirty-five-year-old with a degree from Oxford and an MBA from Stanford who graduated from helping in his mother's chemist shop to founding an investment firm that did business from Berkeley to Bangalore. William Hague, who regarded him as 'an exceptional individual', had helped him land his old seat of Richmond in Yorkshire at the 2015 general election. Sunak was the child of immigrants, a man with an international outlook. But when the call came in saying 'We'd like you to come to see the prime minister,' Sunak politely declined. 'It will only make it worse,' he said. Sunak was backing Brexit, and did not want to be talked out of it. 'That was the moment when Dave and George had their head in their hands,' a Number 10 source says. 'If we couldn't get a guy like Rishi we knew we were in trouble.'

Downing Street had expected up to seventy Brexiteers, but with Steve Baker and the Gang of Six putting in calls for Vote Leave, the number of

Tory MPs backing Leave crept inexorably over a hundred, eventually topping 140. The prime minister secured a majority of his MPs, but only just. The shock was profound. For months Cameron's confidence had relied on three assumptions: that the deal would sway waverers, that loyalty to him would count for something, and that even hardcore rebels could be bought off with either sticks or carrots. All three proved fallacious.

At Vote Leave, Rob Oxley believed Cameron's poor deal had made it much easier to win over wavering MPs: 'With key people like Anne-Marie Trevelyan and James Cleverly, who wanted to remain loyal, Cameron didn't give them the lifeboat they needed to back Remain.' Tory MPs say one female MP burst into tears in the Commons chamber when she realised how little Cameron had come back with, because she was caught between the pressures of her very Brexity constituency association and her loyalty to the PM.

Liam Fox, the former defence secretary, spoke for many that week when he told a friend, 'Dave and George are furious at the lack of deference from the 2010 or, even more, the 2015 intake. They were unprepared for the level of ideology. For them Euroscepticism has always been a tool to use, not a position they actually believe in. They thought everyone behaved like that. They miscalculated.'

The level of optimism about who would back Cameron out of personal loyalty was breathtakingly naïve. Craig Oliver's media plan for the weekend of the deal envisaged a supportive broadcast interview by George Eustice, the farming minister. Eustice was Cameron's communications director when he first became leader, but he was also a hardline Eurosceptic who had once been a member of Ukip and had founded the Fresh Start Group. Eustice duly declared for Leave.

The mutinous atmosphere on the backbenches was laid bare at a meeting of the 1922 Committee on the Monday night after the deal. Andrew Feldman, the party chairman, sought to 'focus minds' by giving a presentation on boundary changes in which fifty MPs would lose their seats, a far from subtle hint about the fate that awaited those who displeased Cameron. But when he announced that the party was scrapping separate candidate lists for future MPs and MEPs, the Eurosceptic Andrew Bridgen piped up, 'I'm glad you're doing that, because a large number of us in this room are rather hoping we won't need any MEPs in a few months' time.' There was loud cheering as Feldman stood mute.

Bridgen was one of many MPs approached by Cameron's parliamentary private secretary Gavin Williamson with the promise of future advancement. He says, 'I was offered a job before Christmas. But it would have required me to campaign for Remain, so I refused it. I was offered immigration minister with no power to control it.' Bridgen smelled a rat, and believed the offer was only dangled to keep him quiet. He considered it 'for a millisecond', then said, 'I can see where this is going. I'm going to be campaigning for Leave. I'll see you after the referendum.' Williamson did not give up. In April, just before the local elections, Bridgen claims that Williamson even offered him his own job if he changed sides to back Remain: 'I could have been Cameron's PPS, but I wouldn't switch.' Either Williamson had a highly developed sense of humour, or Downing Street was getting desperate.

In fact Williamson, along with Oliver Dowden, a key link between Number 10 and the parliamentary party until he became an MP in 2015, had long warned Cameron that up to half his MPs would back Brexit. 'The strategy was to make the likes of IDS and Grayling look like isolated fools,' says a Downing Street aide. 'The PM had thought at most about a third would support it. He always thought Gavin and Oliver were expectation-managing him so that when they got just thirty against us it would look like a triumph.'

Just two weeks after the deal, Cameron confessed that 'the game was up' for his strategy. He told one adviser, 'I'd hoped I'd fix the economy, fix Scotland and fix Europe, and we'd have this referendum, we'd win it and the party would be overwhelmingly in favour of staying in.' He had dreamed of saying to Bill Cash and Bernard Jenkin, 'It's all over.' The source says, 'It became clear when we got the numbers that that would not be the case. At that point the project had already failed. The issue was not off the table for a generation.'

Cameron may have lost much of his party, but as the campaign got going he had acquired new friends at Stronger In, and together they embarked on an operation to maximise the campaigning advantages of government. After the deal there followed a month in which, Will Straw argued, 'By anybody's reckoning we blitzed it,' characterised by good teamwork between Number 10 and the campaign as Stronger In built up 'our credentials on the economy and security and on our place in the world'.

Stronger In tried to sell voters on two themes. One was a positive message, a case for the benefits of EU membership: 'Stronger, Safer, Better Off.' The other was negative: 'Don't risk it. Leaving the EU would be a leap in the dark.' Across Whitehall, Cameron's aides activated their address books and called in favours from contacts. The first product of their labours appeared in *The Times* on Tuesday, 23 February, the morning after Cameron's statement to the Commons, when two hundred business leaders, thirty-six of them from FTSE 100 companies, put their names to a letter arguing that 'leaving the EU would deter investment and threaten jobs. It would put the economy at risk'.[1] The signatories included the bosses of Asda, British Telecom, Marks & Spencer, Kingfisher and Vodafone. First blood to the Remain campaign. The letter was a joint effort between Gabby Bertin, Cameron's director of external relations, Daniel Korski, who had also been working with businesses, and Gabe Winn's team at Stronger In.

It was followed a day later by a letter organised by Korski from thirteen retired military commanders, who warned that Britain should stay in the EU to protect itself from 'grave security threats' posed by Islamic State and Russia. The signatories included the former chiefs of the defence staff, Field Marshal Lord Bramall, who took part in the Normandy landings in the Second World War, Field Marshal Lord Guthrie, Marshal of the RAF Jock Stirrup, Admiral of the Fleet Lord Boyce, plus General Sir Michael Rose, former director of special forces. To the Labour staff at Cannon Street the show of force was impressive. 'They had, frankly, the kind of external muscle you would kill for, coming from a Labour Party background,' said David Chaplin.

On the Thursday the three-day onslaught was completed with a letter to the *Guardian* from NGO luminaries from Oxfam, Action Aid, the World Wildlife Fund, Save the Children and Christian Aid, arguing that EU membership helped fund efforts to tackle the 'humanitarian emergency in Syria' and poverty in Africa. Straw regarded this as important to tie in support from 'soft lefties'. The letter was coordinated with help from Brendan Cox, a former aide to Gordon Brown who had worked at Save the Children and whose wife was Jo Cox, the Labour MP for Batley and Spen, a rising star on the opposition benches.

The PR offensive seemed to have an immediate effect on the polls. Surveys conducted on 28 January and 3 February had both put 'Leave' ahead by margins of up to nine points. But new surveys from 1, 2 and 3

March put 'Remain' in front by two, five and three points respectively. The main problem with the letters is that they did little to reshape public distrust of the deal, set a fortnight earlier when Donald Tusk published his draft. 'We had planned these three big interventions,' Chaplin says. 'They were great stories, but by the time we got to them the envelope had been sealed.'

A secondary issue arose when General Rose announced that he had only asked to see the letter, and had not endorsed it. 'Has the world gone mad?' he said. The letter had been sent to him by Cameron's military adviser Colonel Nick Perry, but the papers blamed Korski, who also faced accusations of bullying Bramall, who nonetheless went on to make several pro-Remain interventions. The idea of an overbearing government behaving like a playground bully entered public consciousness.

Letters and articles were to follow from entrepreneurs, former UN secretaries general, former US secretaries of state and national security advisers, former NHS chiefs, former intelligence chiefs, and on the eve of the referendum itself Korski and co. drummed up 1,280 business leaders to back Remain. On that list, the number of directors of FTSE 100 companies had risen to fifty-one. Most notoriously, towards the end of May the campaign issued a 'luvvies' letter' featuring entreaties from nearly three hundred actors, directors, writers and musicians, as well as terrible puns about Britain's 'role on the world stage' and the risk of 'shouting from the wings' in the event of Brexit. Both campaigns had promised heavyweight celebrity backing, but when Gabe Winn started calling round seeking support for Remain he found most were not interested, after having seen celebrities who spoke out during the Scottish referendum get trolled on social media.

These establishment endorsements frustrated Vote Leave, which could not compete in enlisting the great and the good, since they got huge broadcast coverage. But they also helped the Leave campaign paint itself as an insurgency taking on the establishment. Daniel Hannan says, 'They campaigned, as far as I could see, chiefly through letters by hoary-headed grandees in *The Times* saying we are ordering you little people to vote Remain, to support our income. You had to be an actor, or an academic, not to understand that the rest of the world just sees a privileged group trying to cling on to its subsidies.' As Robert Oxley put it, 'The whole "It's the establishment versus the real people" thing was slightly born of the fact that none of the establishment wanted to back us.'

Some in the Remain camp agreed with this analysis. David Mundell, the Scottish secretary, warned both Cameron and Straw early on about one of the lessons from Scotland: 'There was far far too much emphasis on business. Ordinary people do not care what businesses think. They care what their own employer thinks. They don't care what the CBI thinks. The wider public are generally anti-business these days.' To Mundell's chagrin, 'I do not think that was taken on board.'

The Eurosceptics had also taken a leaf from the Scottish Nationalists during the previous referendum. Very early in the campaign they labelled any and every intervention by Stronger In as an example of 'Project Fear'. Their rage – and their taste for guerrilla warfare in the media – would achieve full expression in early March when John Longworth, director general of the British Chambers of Commerce, was suspended after speaking in favour of leaving the EU. A recent survey had found that six out of ten BCC members wanted to stay in Europe, and Longworth's allies said he was ousted after the BCC board was contacted by Downing Street. Boris Johnson was quick to issue a statement denouncing the move: 'It cannot be right that when someone has the guts to dissent from the establishment line, he or she is immediately crushed by the agents of Project Fear.' Liam Fox accused the government of behaving like a 'mafia protection racket', and declared, 'Project Fear is turning into Project Intimidation.' Once again Korski was the man in the firing line.

The truth was more complicated. A senior figure in the BCC had met Cameron a couple of months before, and pledged that the organisation would not take sides in the referendum. Yet when the BCC held its annual conference Longworth did an interview with *Sky News*, and then a platform speech to the conference, making it clear that he was a personal supporter of Brexit. Korski tried to call him, but could not get through. He later spoke to a member of the BCC board, and asked how Longworth's speech was compatible with the position of neutrality: 'I don't understand, you've got a survey which says most of your members are for remain, you have an avowedly neutral position, and your secretary general is on the podium of your national conference saying he's arguing to leave ... how on earth are all these things compatible?' The reply came, 'It's a big problem for me and my board, leave it with me.'

Korski remained angry for months about claims that he got Longworth fired: 'At no point did I ask for his resignation. At no point. It is not for me, in a democracy, to sit in the PM's office and to ask for the dismissal of a person in a private organisation such as the BCC. It is absurd.' He believes the way he was depicted by the media as the puppeteer of 'dark forces' against Brexiteers was anti-Semitic, a claim also made by the *Jewish Chronicle*: 'The smear I was subjected to was extraordinary. I thought it was all very, very suspect.'

Cameron also deployed the government civil service machine to maximise Remain's early campaign advantages. Bernard Jenkin and Steve Baker felt they had ensured government neutrality during the purdah votes. They had not reckoned with the ingenuity of Sir Jeremy Heywood, the owlish cabinet secretary who had made himself indispensable to four successive prime ministers. No sooner had the six Brexiteers departed the Cabinet Room than Heywood issued advice to civil servants across Whitehall that officials should not show papers relating to the EU to ministers campaigning to leave: 'It will not be appropriate or permissible for the Civil Service to support ministers who oppose the Government's official position by providing briefing or speech material on this matter.'

The ban was supposed to be limited to documents relating directly to the referendum, but in some departments civil servants also stopped ministers seeing letters addressed to them if they mentioned the EU at all. Iain Duncan Smith discovered that officials in the Department of Work and Pensions had been ordered to send government statistics bolstering the case for staying in the EU to the Cabinet Office without getting them signed off by him first. Michael Gove and John Whittingdale also hit the roof, since legal responsibility for the work of their department resides with ministers. Amid claims from one special adviser that Heywood was mounting 'a coup', Britain's top mandarin was summoned to explain himself before Bernard Jenkin's Select Committee. Heywood smoothed the troubled waters, and issued a clarification that placated the Brexiteers.

Claims that the government was abusing its position erupted again on 6 April, when Downing Street announced that £9.3 million of taxpayers' money would be spent on producing and distributing a pro-Remain leaflet to be sent to every home in the country. The Eurosceptics quickly denounced it as 'Project Fear propaganda', but this time the government did not back down. When James Wharton, whose Private Member's Bill on a referendum had helped get the whole ball rolling, said voters were complaining that the leaflet was not 'sufficiently absorbent for the use to which they wanted to put it', Craig Oliver was happy to stoke the public-ity. 'If they're going to have a row about this leaflet then great, people are more likely to pick it up off the doorstep and read it or ask questions about what it says,' he told campaign staff.

Against the weight of the establishment, Gove, Johnson and Vote Leave's only offensive weapons were their own words, crying 'Project Fear' at every turn or poking at David Cameron to get attention. On the Wednesday after Cameron's deal was finalised Gove gave an interview to the BBC's Laura Kuenssberg, questioning whether it was legally binding. Number 10 hit back, wheeling out the Attorney General Jeremy Wright, his predecessor Dominic Grieve, and Donald Tusk, president of the European Council, to contradict him. A minister then briefed the *Daily Telegraph* that Gove would be sacked after the referendum. The gloves were off. In his first print interview after his announcement that he would be backing Leave, Gove deployed rhetoric that would have been alien to him in normal circumstances, accusing the EU of fuelling the rise of 'Hitler worshippers' in Europe. It was Gove, not Johnson, who first used the Nazi dictator as a rhetorical device.

Pointed comments from Leave's two big guns would always have media currency, but in truth they were a minor irritant to Stronger In, the equivalent of Palestinian schoolboys throwing rocks at an Israeli tank. When Boris Johnson broke off from a speech to silence Channel 4's Michael Crick, who was doing a piece to camera at the back of the room, the media compared Britain's most popular politician to Donald Trump. Neither of Vote Leave's men had hit their stride. Leavers felt on the back foot, inundated by the full weight of the government PR machine while their biggest assets endured a level of scrutiny they had never previously experienced. Bernard Jenkin remembers 'all that deluge of propaganda' drowning out Vote Leave's own efforts: 'It wasn't that their messaging was very good, it was just that you couldn't get anything else over. It crowded everything out.'

It was in this context that there arose what appeared to be an attempt by Michael Gove to take on the political establishment by deploying the one figure who could trump every one of Stronger In's independent advocates – Her Majesty the Queen.

* * *

The affair broke like a tidal wave across the campaign on the morning of 8 March, when the *Sun*'s front page screamed, 'Revealed: Queen backs Brexit'. The paper detailed an 'alleged bust-up between her and Nick Clegg over Europe', in which the monarch 'let rip at the then deputy PM during a lunch at Windsor Castle', telling him the EU was heading in the wrong direction. It quoted a senior source saying, 'People who heard their conversation were left in no doubt at all about the queen's views on European integration.' The paper also revealed another occasion on which she supposedly told a group of parliamentarians, 'I don't understand Europe.'[2]

Clegg initially issued a non-denial denial, saying he had 'absolutely no recollection' of the incident, though his line was to harden as the week went on. The claims caused uproar, and Westminster sleuths soon identified the lunch, in April 2011, from the Court Circular. The finger of blame pointed at Gove, who was present along with Cheryl Gillan, then Welsh secretary, Lord McNally, a Lib Dem justice minister, and Judith Simpson, a clerk. Buckingham Palace denied the story and complained to the new press watchdog, Ipso, which eventually ruled that the headline was misleading, since the term 'Brexit' was not coined until after the event. Gove denied that he was the source, but some courtiers confirmed that the queen, a devotee of the Commonwealth, was no fan of the EU. Credible Westminster figures now say Gove had labelled the queen 'a Eurosceptic' at a private social function several months before the *Sun*'s story broke.

After the referendum, Clegg said he was certain Gove had briefed the story, but insisted the event described by the *Sun* 'just didn't happen': 'Michael Gove obviously gave this to the *Sun*. I know he did. He leaked that, and I can see why he might think that's an interesting thing to do, to try and drag the queen into it, but it didn't happen. It was not true, it was a very mendacious thing to say. I think it was very, very disrespectful of Michael Gove to have done that.'[3]

The pressure of having journalists on his doorstep every day caused Gove to slip up. When he emerged from his home on the morning of Saturday, 12 March he said, 'I don't know how the *Sun* got *all* its information.' Pressed again, he repeated the same form of words. Westminster journalists, who knew Gove always spoke precisely and had a strong aversion to lying, were convinced this was tantamount to an admission of guilt that he was responsible for some of the *Sun*'s story. They were not alone in that. Shortly after Gove's statement, Sir Nicholas Soames, a close friend of Prince Charles, took to Twitter to write, 'Is the Gover now owning up to an inexcusable mistake in breaching an oath and a confidence? If so, now very serious consequences.' He later issued a coded call for Gove to resign: 'If he has made a terrible misjudgement, I am sure he will know the right thing to do.'

Later that afternoon Gove took a call from Simon Walters, the political editor of the *Mail on Sunday*, who said he was planning to print a story detailing how Gove had dined with Rupert Murdoch, the *Sun*'s proprietor, shortly before the original story appeared. Gove did not dispute the account. He assumed the story would be on the front page the following day, and that he would be sacked from the cabinet. Heart in mouth, he thought, 'Right, that's my career gone.' He was at a friend's birthday party in Oxford when he saw that the *MoS* front page was actually a serialisation of David Laws's book on the coalition government. The headline 'Gove is nuts, Boris is after my job', detailing David Cameron's private thoughts, would usually have been alarming, but Gove was relieved. The 'Queengate' story was inside, and focused on his comments the previous morning. His lunch with Murdoch was only mentioned in the eighth paragraph.[4]

The furore had two effects. It helped Vote Leave wipe out Stronger In's media domination for a week. It also closed off what could have been the government's trump card. During the Scottish referendum, the Palace and Downing Street had conspired in a plan to have the queen signal that she was concerned about Scottish independence. If there had ever been a similar plan to have her express concerns about Brexit, it was now dead in the water.

In the same week that Gove was enraging the Palace, he also terminated Downing Street's last hopes that he would keep a low profile. On 9 March it was announced that he and the Labour MP Gisela Stuart would become joint chairs of Vote Leave. Gove would chair the Campaign Committee, while Stuart would anchor the board. Cameron's reaction was one of shock. Craig Oliver says, 'He felt that Michael had given him the impression that he would not play a very significant role in Vote Leave, and when it was announced that he was in fact the chairman of Vote Leave, that was a moment of surprise.'[5] It was a natural step as far as Matthew Elliott was concerned. Since he had declared his position Gove had taken on 'a natural leadership role' at Vote Leave. Elliott characterised the relationship between Gove and Boris Johnson as 'the manager and the star player'.

Gisela Stuart appears to have been the team psychologist. Elliott knew her from the NOtoAV campaign, and wooed her to join Vote Leave over two dinners at Grumbles restaurant in London's Churton Street. Paul Stephenson helped seal the deal, as he had worked closely with Stuart's husband Derek Scott, Tony Blair's former economics adviser, on the 'I want a referendum' campaign which attempted unsuccessfully to get a vote on the Lisbon Treaty. Stephenson says, 'I don't think I can overstate the importance of Gisela to the whole operation. She brought stability where there had only been chaos on the Labour side. She helped temper some of the stuff so that it would play better with Labour voters. Also, she worked really well with Michael and Boris. She was the calm one who helped guide the three of them through.'

In the first phase of the campaign, though, it was the Tory, Labour and Lib Dem staff at Stronger In who really showed how to do cross-party politics, while the two Leave campaigns waged war on each other. 'They were tearing themselves apart,' says Will Straw. 'We looked united and they looked divided.' Had Remain won, most of those involved believe the creation of a non-dysfunctional cross-party campaign would have been one of the referendum's more notable achievements. Tories who could remember the disastrous divisions of the 2010 election campaign on the Conservative side agreed that it was far easier to work with the likes of Straw and James McGrory than it had been with some of their own. The two sides bonded in what was a fairly poky war room on the ground floor of 14 Dowgate Hill. 'There were a lot of sweaty Pret lunches,' recalls Joe Carberry.

Ameet Gill and David Chaplin worked closely together, holding a joint grid meeting every day at noon, meticulously planning the next seventy-two hours – which stories were to be briefed, the events that were planned to dramatise them, which politicians were due to appear on broadcast media, and who would be responsible for delivering each aspect of the plan. Gill led on Conservative events, Chaplin on Labour, Lib Dem, Green Party and trade union interventions. Chaplin says, 'Ameet was one of the smartest people I've ever worked with. He had a very clear idea about what he wanted to get out of each day. He had been through the sausage-making machine. He knew how to make stories, he knew how to get politicians to say things, and he knew how to grid a campaign. He knew how to make magic things happen in campaigns, and magic things did happen. We got Tony Blair and John Major to walk over the Peace Bridge in Derry. That was my best day of the campaign.'

The two great research brains, Adam Atashzai from Downing Street and Labour's Joe Carberry, also formed an effective double act. 'They were a quite phenomenal team,' says Straw. Carberry concentrated on running the research operation and the day-to-day rebuttal of Vote Leave stories. Atashzai led on briefing Conservative politicians and debate prep. Both are among the brightest talents in their respective parties. At the media end, Craig Oliver and James McGrory put their coalition differences behind them to telling effect. In another example of the curious cross-party connections that thrived during the campaign, Stronger In's regional director in Yorkshire was Oliver Coppard, who had been the Labour candidate in Sheffield Hallam at the general election. Then he had been trying to oust Nick Clegg; now he was working hand in glove with Ryan Coetzee, Clegg's strategist, and McGrory, his spin doctor.

No two people better embodied the willingness to get along than Craig Oliver and Lucy Thomas. Campaigns are intense experiences, and romance is not uncommon. It flourished here. The relationship was an open secret at Stronger In following two slips by Oliver, who separated from his wife in 2014. On one occasion the director of communications bought a book and left it on his desk in Downing Street, inscribed with a romantic message. Later the same day, an eagle-eyed Number 10 staffer spotted the same volume on Thomas's desk at Stronger In. Their relationship became more widely known one evening when Thomas rushed into a meeting and sat down looking flustered. Oliver texted her a message: 'You look shattered xxx'. Immediately everyone's phones started vibrating. Oliver had inadvertently sent his private missive, complete with three little kisses, to the campaign WhatsApp group. Craig Elder of the digital operation responded, 'You don't look too good yourself, mate. But we keep it to ourselves.'

If some of the Labour and Lib Dem staff occasionally saw Oliver and his fellow Tories as arrogant and overconfident, having seen the Conservatives beat the odds in Scotland and then beat them in the general election, they were happy to acknowledge that they were dealing with proven winners who were highly professional. McGrory says, 'I found them extremely good to work with, and much easier than during the coalition government. It was a really fun place to work – up until the last four hours.'

Nonetheless, the structure of the Remain campaign was somewhat unwieldy, particularly when compared with the small war room operated by Vote Leave, where Cummings, Stephenson and Woodcock were able to make most decisions quickly, with little input from others. The need to keep a broad coalition together meant Cummings' periodically benevolent despotism was not a viable management style for Stronger In.

A second complication was that not all decisions were made in Cannon Street. While Straw was in titular control, and is acknowledged to have been an effective and fair manager, the power rested with Craig Oliver, the most senior link man with Cameron and Osborne, whose views were disseminated – it seemed at times – on tablets of stone. Many major decisions were made in private meetings at Downing Street which would typically include Cameron, Osborne, Oliver, Gill, Stephen Gilbert and Andrew Cooper, but not often Straw or Coetzee, still less McGrory, Chaplin or Carberry. This meant it was difficult to challenge the underlying assumptions of the campaign. 'It is difficult for a campaign to have control of what they are doing when big decisions are taken elsewhere and then decreed to staff, even senior ones,' says a Labour source who had run other campaigns. On paper Ryan Coetzee was director of strategy, but his main role was handling Cooper's polling and running the focus groups. As one non-Tory puts it, 'The real director of strategy was George Osborne. In the short campaign, the Cannon Street team were basically the delivery function for the strategy which was set in Number 10.' When someone wanted to rethink strategy it was common for Ameet Gill to say, 'Look, we've discussed this. And we've just got to carry on doing what we're doing.'

Peter Mandelson says, 'We had created the campaign vehicle but waited for the prime minister to jump into the driving seat and take us off. What became clear was that he didn't want any back-seat drivers, he didn't want anyone grabbing the steering wheel. I think many of us didn't realise that would actually mean that we would be left at the roadside as he drove off hard in the campaign, but that's effectively what happened.'[6]

Coordination would have been easier if Oliver, as he originally planned, had moved to Cannon Street at the end of February. The campaign had got as far as writing a press release announcing that he was joining full-time, but Oliver changed his mind on learning that he would have to surrender his Downing Street pass and work BlackBerry. 'He couldn't resign entirely, because then he wouldn't get access to Number 10,' says Straw. 'It was frustrating.' The team did get a boost on 1 March when Charlotte Todman, who had worked with Liz Sugg on Cameron's events for the previous six years at Number 10, resigned from the civil service and joined the campaign. She quickly became a trusted link between Downing Street and Cannon Street, explaining her two sets of colleagues to each other and forging a harmonious cross-party team with strategic infusions of Malbec, ensuring that even Labour staff helped to make Cameron look good on the road.

In the first phase of the campaign the government maximised their ability to grid carefully coordinated announcements, but they knew most random events would assist Vote Leave. At the end of March a series of surprise events illustrated how quickly even a well-executed campaign can be blown off course. The coordinated suicide bombings in Brussels on 22 March, and the Tata steel crisis which engulfed the government eight days later, not only left little space in the news agenda for Stronger In's message, but both also put aspects of EU regulation in a negative light. The ISIS terror cell behind the Brussels bombings, which was linked to the perpetrators of the Paris terror attacks the previous November, highlighted the difficulty of preventing radicals returning from Syria from moving freely in the EU's no-borders Schengen Zone – three of the Brussels cell are believed to have fought there. The Tata crisis highlighted the difficulty of the bloc imposing high tariffs on Chinese steel when the interests of countries producing and consuming steel across the EU diverged. State-aid rules also made it more difficult for the British government to intervene to help.

Tory dominance of the campaign also affected the amount of time devoted to particular issues, the angle from which they were approached, and the main spokesmen employed to convey them to voters. Straw said he had to 'fight hard to make sure Labour and indeed the Lib Dems, the Greens and the trade union movement were given space in the grid'. David Cameron and George Osborne assumed a lion's share of the responsibility. But Labour staff were concerned that the senior Tories did not understand how to pitch their messages at Labour voters, since

Lynton Crosby's campaign blueprint had never had to appeal to them. 'The refusal to listen to and understand Labour and Lib Dem voters was a major strategic error,' says one campaign official. 'Our message-carriers were not the right ones to win in the areas we needed to. The Number 10 grid had three PM-led days a week. Number 10 genuinely didn't seem to understand that he doesn't have universal appeal, and his credibility had been impacted by his decision to call this referendum and his inability to keep his party together.'

The situation became more acute when Downing Street was hit by two unforeseen crises that dramatically undermined public trust in both Cameron and Osborne, hobbling their main message-carriers for the rest of the campaign.

THE IDS OF MARCH

No one had seen David Cameron this angry in a long time. 'You have behaved dishonourably,' he spat. Some claim the words 'You shit!' also passed his lips. It was just before 9 p.m. on Friday, 18 March and Iain Duncan Smith, the secretary of state for work and pensions, had just informed the prime minister that he was resigning from the cabinet. It was a month into the referendum campaign, and two days after George Osborne delivered a crucial budget that Cameron hoped would give the Remain side a boost. Yet now a former party leader was quitting in disgust at that same budget, with a parting shot that seemed designed to destroy the credibility of the chancellor. Cameron was furious and did not hold back, launching into an expletive-laden rant. 'It was a proper eruption,' said a Number 10 source later. 'The full Malcolm Tucker.'

The explosive conversation was the culmination of a week of arguments between Duncan Smith, the Treasury and 10 Downing Street over cuts to disability benefit. Twice that day Cameron had spoken at length to Duncan Smith to try to talk him out of resigning, but he was determined to go, and to wound Osborne as he left. Duncan Smith's allies saw it as the natural dénouement to a terrible relationship which had simmered throughout the coalition years. Osborne believed afterwards that it was a premeditated attempt to damage him so that his warnings about the economic dangers of Brexit would not be heeded. When the story broke, the papers took one look at the calendar and pronounced it 'the IDS of March'.

Duncan Smith's was a career bookended by battles over Europe, but which had found meaning when he developed an agenda for social reform out of the dying embers of his leadership. One of the most resolute of the Maastricht rebels, he had shocked the country by winning the

Conservative crown in 2001, principally because he was not the Europhile Ken Clarke. But Tory MPs had long memories, and failed to see why they should show personal loyalty to a man who had defied the whip under John Major. As the dissent grew, MPs joked that IDS stood for 'In Deep Shit'. Duncan Smith managed just two years in the hot seat before the plotters brought him down. He might have been best remembered for a party conference speech in which he vowed, 'The quiet man is turning up the volume,' had he not visited the Easterhouse estate in Glasgow, where the deprivation and family breakdown shocked him into developing ideas for welfare reform which Cameron asked him to continue in government in 2010.

Duncan Smith's feud with Osborne dated back to the emergency budget after the 2010 election, when IDS refused to countenance cuts in his department until he had been guaranteed £2.5 billion to fund Universal Credit, his ambitious scheme to replace a raft of state handouts with one benefit payment. Duncan Smith believed Osborne did not care about the poor. Osborne believed Duncan Smith was engaged in a quasi-religious mission to save them from themselves. At every budget and Autumn Statement negotiation thereafter, 'Osborne turned up with a loaded revolver and demanded more cuts,' a friend of IDS remarked. The two men could not have been more different. Duncan Smith was a rural social Conservative wedded to his principles, Osborne a metropolitan liberal who loved the game of politics. Duncan Smith had never forgiven Osborne for a passage in Matthew d'Ancona's book on the coalition which quoted the chancellor as saying, 'You see Iain giving presentations and realise he's just not clever enough.'[1]

IDS had a tempestuous relationship with Cameron, who asked him to move to the Ministry of Justice in the 2012 reshuffle. But after Danny Finkelstein, a friend of Osborne's, went on *Newsnight* to speculate about him changing jobs, Duncan Smith detected an Osborne plot and refused to budge. He then threatened to resign in November 2015 to stop Osborne raiding the Universal Credit budget.

All of which meant that when the chancellor demanded more welfare cuts ahead of the budget, Duncan Smith's hackles were quickly raised. The genesis of the crisis was a pledge to cut £12 billion from the welfare budget in the Tory election manifesto. Osborne had expected that amount to be slashed in a new coalition agreement with the Liberal Democrats, but when the Conservatives won a majority he had to find the full amount. The election had also removed a set of key allies of Duncan Smith, who had worked effectively with Steve Webb, his Lib Dem deputy. His special adviser Philippa Stroud also departed for a seat in the Lords. 'Philippa was always able to calm things down,' says a source. 'The absence of the Lib Dems has also been hard for Iain because on a lot of issues they backed him up against the Treasury.'

In the run-up to the budget, attention fell on overspending by the Department for Work and Pensions (DWP) on Personal Independence Payments (PIPs) for 600,000 people with long-term health problems. Duncan Smith's department had to respond to a court ruling that anyone who needed to sit down to put on their shoes, or required a handrail in the bathroom, was entitled to disability benefits in perpetuity. DWP officials tweaked the wording of the regulations so they were more clearly related to need, but wanted that announcement to stand alone. The Treasury, wishing to bank the savings, presented the changes as a fiscal rather than a fairness measure. Osborne insisted the disability benefit cuts, £1.3 billion a year, be 'scored' in the budget red book to help his numbers add up. 'That meant even if we ditched the plan, we would still have to find the £1.3 billion of in-year cuts from somewhere,' an ally said. A Tory frontbencher says, 'I blame George entirely. George was disrespectful, rude and outrageous in the way he handled it. They both agreed to change the descriptions that were ratcheting up the cost of disabled, but what he wanted to do was slam it in the red book and embarrass Iain, which was just a crass and stupid way to handle it. He deserved what he got from Iain.'

The following Wednesday, Osborne announced in the budget that he was raising the tax-free allowance for income tax to £11,500 and the 40p tax threshold to £45,000, a move designed to be a feel-good policy for middle-England voters, who Cameron and Osborne wanted to woo ahead of the referendum. But Duncan Smith was irate that benefit cuts for the vulnerable were 'juxtaposed' with tax cuts for the middle classes. 'This is the pits,' he told aides. Eight Tory MPs went public to complain about the cuts to disability benefit, and another twenty put their names to a private letter urging Osborne to think again. They were also threatening to join forces with Labour and the SNP to inflict the first defeat of a Finance Bill since 1994, over VAT on women's sanitary products.

The 'tampon tax' rebellion was the brainchild of Paul Stephenson and Steve Baker. 'We knew that if we picked the right topic, we could basically defeat the government on confidence motions,' says Stephenson, who did a secret deal with Labour to force Osborne's hand. He approached an old friend with links to the Unite union who worked for several hard-left Labour MPs. Crucially, his contact was someone who was in regular touch with the Labour leadership – 'He could get through to McDonnell and Corbyn's office quickly.' It is one of the great ironies of the campaign that a Tory working for Vote Leave found it easier to get cooperation from Jeremy Corbyn than Alan Johnson, the leader of the Labour In campaign. With the SNP and Baker's rebels on board, they were guaranteed to win. Baker sat in the Commons chamber with two text messages on his phone, one saying 'Don't rebel' and the other saying 'Over the top'. Staring at a Commons defeat, Osborne accepted the amendment.

The row was perilous for the chancellor. The previous autumn he had been forced to back down over plans to cut £4.4 billion a year from tax credits, in the face of a backbench rebellion. Osborne's critics wondered if he was heading for another omnishambles.

Downing Street demanded that the DWP defend the cuts. Camilla Cavendish, Cameron's head of policy, visited the department on the day after the budget, and insisted that they fall into line. 'You have got to go out and sell this policy,' IDS was told.[2] Justin Tomlinson, a junior DWP minister, was sent out to defend the cuts, and Duncan Smith himself issued a letter to MPs urging them to back the plans. But by the Friday the screeching brakes of an impending U-turn were audible across Whitehall.

With opposition mounting throughout the day, Osborne took soundings and began a climbdown. At 7 p.m. the Treasury announced it was rethinking a series of measures from the budget. In a statement released at 8 p.m., a government source said of the cuts to disability benefits: 'This is going to be kicked into the long grass. We need to take time and get reforms right, and that will mean looking again at these proposals.' The Treasury sought to claim that they were only peripherally involved: 'It's not an integral part of the budget – it's a DWP package that came out beforehand. We are not wedded to specific sums.'

The U-turn came too late. By then Duncan Smith was already on the telephone to David Cameron trying to resign. Believing the changes were 'toxic' and feeling exposed by the growing public backlash, he 'woke up on Friday morning resolved to resign', says one ally.[3] He discussed the idea with Philippa Stroud and Tim Montgomerie, the Conservative activist who had worked for him as leader. After lunch, Duncan Smith finalised a resignation letter at his home in Buckinghamshire and sent it in his ministerial car to Downing Street. The letter did not arrive until around 5 p.m. Duncan Smith had tossed around threats to resign in the past as others discuss the weather, so David Cameron did not immediately think all was lost. Travelling back to Number 10 from the airport, the prime minister picked up the phone and began a conversation which, with a half-time break, went on for much of the next four hours.

Cameron was so desperate to keep Duncan Smith on board that he criticised George Osborne, his own closest ally. 'He just threw George under the bus,' says a source close to Duncan Smith. 'He said, "George has totally fucked this up, it's completely his fault. I'll make sure he sorts it out. I won't let him do anything like this ever again."' Cameron promised that Craig Oliver would brief the media that Duncan Smith had halted the disability cuts. He even offered to change the way Osborne prepared for budgets in future, so as to avoid last-minute surprises for other cabinet ministers. Time and again he asked IDS to 'come in' to Downing Street to discuss the issue face to face. A Number 10 source says: 'The prime minister felt strongly that if he had concerns or was thinking of resigning, there should have been a conversation or a proper meeting with the PM first.'

Friends of IDS say there were job offers too, most prominent of them the suggestion that Duncan Smith, a former lieutenant in the Scots Guards, might become defence secretary. 'The kitchen sink was thrown at Iain,' says one friend. 'Cameron asked him what he wanted to stay. He said he could have anything.' When Duncan Smith remained unmoved, Cameron asked him, 'Can you please reconsider? Please do me the courtesy of thinking about it.' Duncan Smith told Cameron he was 'entirely resolved', but agreed to the request to delay.

When he called back, with the clock approaching 9 p.m., he said, 'I came into politics to make reforms and defend the poor, and I can't defend the poor any more.' He began to tell Cameron that he had released a resignation statement to the media, but as he did so the news flashed up on *Sky News*. The letter had arrived in journalists' email inboxes at 8.56 p.m. Sick of Duncan Smith's dawdling, one of his confidants had persuaded him to authorise its release before he picked up the phone to Cameron, so he could not be talked round.

Furious at being blindsided, Cameron launched into his expletive-laden rant. An IDS ally says, 'Every third word was an expletive. Iain described it as a "Soames-type outburst".'[4] (Sir Nicholas Soames is a fan of profanity.) Duncan Smith responded, 'You have gone too far this time. You cannot expect me to put up with being undermined any longer.'[5] He accused the prime minister of failing to support his welfare reforms and allowing the Treasury to 'salami-slice' cash from the benefits system. A friend says, 'It was quite an explosive conversation. Iain was pretty shocked.' Downing Street denied that Cameron called IDS a 'shit', but they don't deny that he went 'absolutely ballistic'. He was particularly angry not to have had a hand in shaping Duncan Smith's resignation letter, such documents often being crafted in tandem in these circumstances.

The letter was the most devastating since Sir Geoffrey Howe quit Margaret Thatcher's cabinet twenty-six years earlier. It suggested that the government was breaking Osborne's promise to the British people that 'We are all in this together,' and took aim at the chancellor's Achilles heel, the notion that he was more interested in numbers than people. 'I have for some time and rather reluctantly come to believe the latest changes to benefits to the disabled, and the context in which they've been made, are a compromise too far,' wrote Duncan Smith. 'While they are defensible in narrow terms, given the continuing deficit, they are not defensible in the way they were placed within a budget that benefits higher-earning taxpayers.' He concluded, 'I hope as the government goes forward you can look again at the balance of the cuts you have insisted upon and wonder if enough has been done to ensure "we are all in this together".'

Just after 11.30 p.m. Cameron responded, expressing bemusement at Duncan Smith's decision: 'We collectively agreed – you, Number 10 and the Treasury – proposals which you and your department … announced a week ago. Today we agreed not to proceed with the policies in their current form … In the light of this, I am puzzled and disappointed that you have chosen to resign.' Duncan Smith was replaced by Stephen Crabb, the Welsh secretary, who was raised by a single mother on a council estate.

The following day, Duncan Smith went on *The Andrew Marr Show* (bumping Sir John Major, who had been due to make the case for the Remain campaign) and gave an impassioned defence of his conduct and his concern for the disabled, in an appearance more fluent and persuasive than he had ever managed as party leader. Turning the heat on Cameron, he accused the prime minister of 'drifting in a direction that divides society rather than unites it', and making it look as if the Conservative Party had stopped caring about those 'who may never vote for it'. He declared, 'Europe has nothing to do with this.'

Nevertheless, there was profound suspicion in both 10 and 11 Downing Street that the resignation was a stunt intended to damage them, because Duncan Smith wanted Britain to leave the EU. A senior government source said: 'Word reached us that he regards Europe as far more important than welfare, and that he didn't care whether he kept his job. We knew a month ago that a cabinet minister was planning to resign. He's quit over a policy that was being reversed. It's not logical.' Ros Altmann, the pensions minister, was sent out by Downing Street to attack her old boss, accusing Duncan Smith of trying to inflict 'maximum damage to the party leadership in order to further his campaign to try to get Britain to leave the EU'. A minister familiar with Cameron's views said: 'Dave is utterly furious with him. He feels IDS has clearly been looking for an excuse to resign.'

Duncan Smith had certainly been close to resigning over the referendum campaign. He had a blazing row with Cameron in February, before the deal, because he perceived that the prime minister was already overtly campaigning for 'In', while the Brexiteers were forced to stick to the non-aggression pact negotiated by Chris Grayling until the deal was finalised. A source said, 'He told the PM he had broken his word and it was outrageous for him and other ministers to promote the deal openly when dissidents like him had kept quiet as agreed.'[6]

Duncan Smith's allies insist it was his long-standing feud with Osborne that was decisive. A former frontbencher said that week, 'Why the fuck would he resign over Europe when he can say anything he wants about the European question? What would be the point in that? It's completely ludicrous.' Yet it is also true that Duncan Smith was feeling constrained over Europe. At a cabinet meeting just before his resignation, Cameron had taken him to task for public comments he had made on the EU's deal to grant visas to Turks, an issue he regarded as a security risk. Cameron regarded it not as a referendum issue but as a matter of government foreign policy. In what was seen by one colleague as 'a direct rebuke to Iain', the PM told his ministers, 'You can't publicly oppose government policy. Collective responsibility has not been lifted on the Turkey deal.'

Whatever its initial motivation, Duncan Smith's attack had a damaging effect on Osborne. A poll by YouGov a week after his resignation found the chancellor's personal ratings lower than at any time since the 'omnishambles' budget. Only 17 per cent believed that he was doing a good job, half the level at the general election, when he had last asked voters to trust him. Seeing Osborne wounded, his enemies in the parliamentary party came out in force. One minister compared him to the hapless 1970s sitcom character Frank Spencer. 'It was a brilliant budget,' he said mockingly. 'You have to admire the sheer genius of George. Very few people would be able to damage the Tory brand, upset the public, cause the resignation of a senior member of the cabinet and miss your self-imposed targets all in a single week.' Another minister was crueller still, comparing Osborne to the sinister Child Catcher in *Chitty Chitty Bang Bang*, an *ad hominem* attack that infuriated the chancellor's aides.

The Remain campaign had staked its success on convincing voters to trust their economic arguments. Now the chief salesman of that strategy was damaged goods. Less than three weeks later, David Cameron suffered the same fate.

When the so-called Panama Papers were made public on 3 April, Cameron's team in Downing Street breathed a cautious sigh of relief. The mass WikiLeaks-style data drop of files from the Central American law firm Mossack Fonseca looked at first sight like a problem on a scale not seen since the expenses scandal of 2009, when the financial self-indulgences of MPs and ministers at taxpayers' expense destroyed public trust in the political class. To the pleasant surprise of Tory high command, not one serving member of the cabinet featured in the eleven million documents. But then the BBC's *Panorama* detailed how Blairmore Holdings, a company owned by the prime minister's late father, the investment banker Ian Cameron, used Mossack Fonseca.

A week later, after relentless public pressure to disclose the small print of his finances, Cameron became the first prime minister to publish extensive details of his tax return. What took place in the intervening period – a masterclass in how not to handle a sensitive issue – combined an enraged son's fury at posthumous slurs against the father he regarded as a hero and the age-old political truth that the cover-up (or the appearance of one) is worse than the crime.

The subject of offshore funds and the whiff of tax avoidance was dangerous terrain for Cameron, who had been robust in condemning companies like Amazon and Google for arranging their affairs to the detriment of the Revenue. He had also gone out on a limb to condemn the comedian Jimmy Carr for using an accountancy scheme to avoid tax. But when Westminster journalists asked whether Cameron had benefited from Blairmore Holdings, his official spokesman said it was 'a private matter'. There would be four more different lines from Downing Street before the week was out.

When a set of hostile newspaper front pages dropped the same evening, Cameron's spin doctors went a step further, saying he had no shares in the company. That did not clarify whether he had once done so, or had profited in the past. The following day Cameron said, 'I have no shares, no offshore trusts, no offshore funds, nothing like that.' Journalists noted his use of 'have' rather than 'had'. That afternoon Downing Street provided yet another statement saying, 'To be clear, the prime minister, his wife and their children do not benefit from any offshore funds. The prime minister owns no shares.' They challenged his critics to 'put up or shut up'. On the Wednesday a fourth statement was forthcoming: 'There are no offshore funds/trusts which the prime minister, Mrs Cameron or their children will benefit from in future.' That dealt with the present and the future, but there was still no mention of the past. Cameron sought to draw a line under the affair, giving an interview to ITV's Robert Peston in which he admitted that he and Samantha had sold shares in Blairmore worth more than £30,000 in January 2010. The profit was 'subject to all the UK taxes in the normal way', Cameron said, but it fell just below the threshold at which capital gains tax would have applied. The prime minister expressed distress that his late father was 'being dragged through the mud'.

Finally, on 10 April, with the media clamour refusing to abate, Cameron published a summary of his tax return. It showed that he had earned over £1 million since 2009, and was pocketing £93,000 from renting out his family home in Notting Hill. Most interestingly, Downing Street also revealed that he had received £200,000 in cash from his mother, who felt the £300,000 inheritance he received from his father was not large enough, because his brother had received the family home.

The papers pointed out that that sum would not be liable to inheritance tax if his mother lived for seven years from the time of the gift – and speculated that the money may have come from Blairmore. A chastened Cameron said, 'I know that I should have handled this better, I could have handled this better. Don't blame Number 10 Downing Street or nameless advisers, blame me.' In a pointed intervention, a source close to Boris Johnson said, 'Boris has never had any trusts, shares, offshore investments or any gifts from his parents.'

Cameron had been furious at the suggestion that his father had done anything wrong. There was nothing illegal in any of the arrangements. Yet the manner in which the information had to be dragged from him left the impression of something shifty, and reinforced the notion that he was a very wealthy man whose concerns were quite different from those of ordinary voters. A minister said, 'He doesn't think £30k is a lot of money, so in his mind what he did was completely different to Jimmy Carr.' Adapting *1066 and All That*, a former minister said the tax affair would make it more difficult for Cameron to win the EU referendum: 'The Inners are right but revolting, the Outers are wrong but romantic. That makes the result more dicey.'

Anna Soubry, a Remainer, defended Cameron robustly on *Question Time*, saying he had been right to speak up for his father. 'I felt very strongly that it was dreadful what had happened,' she said later, 'because his father had been trashed outrageously and wrongly. And he was hurt, desperately hurt.' Two days later Soubry was having her nails painted when she got a text from Cameron thanking her. 'It took my breath away, the generosity of what he'd said. He's a real person.'

Real or not, Cameron's personal-trust ratings took a hit. Stronger In's best asset would have to fight harder to get a hearing from now on. George Osborne thought that what had happened to them both was worse than unfortunate. The chancellor is not a believer in conspiracy theories, but he did think it 'pretty shocking' when he saw Cameron's face on the news during the tax controversy next to that of Vladimir Putin, whose henchmen had used Mossack Fonseca's services. A source close to Osborne said, 'Generally in life George thinks it's cock-up not conspiracy, but on the Iain Duncan Smith attack on him after the budget, he errs more on the conspiracy side of the argument. It meant that both of them were reputationally damaged going into the campaign.'

DESIGNATION'S WHAT YOU NEED

The smoking terrace of the Boisdale was a good place to look a man in the eye and read his intentions. The Scottish restaurant near Victoria station fortified its guests with specially reared meats and offered a choice of more than a hundred single-malt whiskies and a fine array of Cuban cigars. It was a Nigel Farage sort of place. The Ukip leader dined there in mid-October 2015 with David Wall, the industrialist who arranged political donations from a group of wealthy businessmen behind the Midlands Industrial Council. For four hours Farage and Wall held court, and in that time they tried to matchmake an alliance between the titular heads of the rival 'Out' campaigns, Arron Banks and Matthew Elliott.

The Electoral Commission would have to designate just one outfit to run the official Leave campaign. Farage had encouraged Banks to set up Leave.EU to force Vote Leave out of the starting blocks. A short while before the meeting, Vote Leave had finally launched. Now Farage and Wall wanted to see if the two sides could come together to form a united organisation. Neither Banks nor Elliott liked the idea.

Banks says, 'The way that Nigel saw it was we caused them to get started, because they were so paranoid about us winning the designation that they then started to pull their finger out and started to do stuff. What happens of course is that all of Elliott's donors start to write to me saying, "Elliott is a wonder boy, you must work with him, you must stop this conflict between the two parties."' But the omens were not particularly good. 'There'd been lots of exchanges of emails where I basically told just about everyone in Vote Leave what I thought about them, what I thought about their organisation,' Banks remembers.

When Elliott joined Farage and Wall they asked him bluntly, 'Is there any way you can work with Arron Banks?' He replied, 'There's no way under any circumstances.' Farage tried another tack: 'If God Himself came from heaven and smote down the British people and said, "I will deliver Leave if you work with Arron Banks," would you work with Arron Banks?' Elliott said, 'No.'

Farage recalled, 'We had a couple hours of Banks and we had a couple hours of Elliott. And it was absolutely clear from that minute that Elliott and Cummings were not prepared to work with anybody. This was going to be their show and their game.' Farage had hoped that he and Chris Bruni-Lowe could join forces with Vote Leave: 'I tried like hell to get a unified front. I thought it would have been far more intelligent to get a lot more business leaders, to get Mick Cash from the RMT union involved. How could you rationally have a Leave campaign and not at least have some cooperation of Chris and I in what they were doing? It's madness.' If Farage and Banks could not join Vote Leave, they would have to beat them.

What followed was like a US primary election as the two teams fought it out to represent the Leave team in the final showdown against Stronger In. Just as in most American elections, the primary was uglier and more heated than the main event. Observers mocked the *Life of Brian*-style battle between the Eurosceptics as 'the Judean People's Front v the People's Front of Judea'. From that point on, only one could win.

Banks's durability was a surprise to Cummings and Elliott. 'Dom and I felt that Arron would probably fade away fairly quickly, and that once we had our launch in October, it would cease to be a big issue,' says Elliott. 'But then there was this epic struggle between the two sides.'

At its heart was a clash of truculent egomaniacs who were convinced they knew best how to run a campaign and seize victory. The right to be top dog combined with radically different philosophies about how to appeal to voters created a combustible mix. 'Our vision was to be a non-Ukip, cross-party campaign, targeting swing voters,' says Elliott. On the other side was Banks, with his bottomless bank account, his Bristol call centre staffed by two hundred workers ready to hit the phones for Brexit, and a formidable social media operation. 'They were flush with cash, building up a huge supporter base on Facebook,' Elliott recalls.

Arron Banks did not need any more inspiration to take on Vote Leave and beat them than his innate competitiveness, but he also believed

victory for Leave.EU in the designation battle was vital because that
would mean immigration could be put at the heart of the campaign
message: 'We saw it as critical to winning the campaign. If we didn't win
the designation there was going to be trouble, because Vote Leave weren't
going to talk about immigration.' Banks had hired US political consultant Gerry Gunster to conduct huge sample polls to divine the key issues:
'We knew that if we were on immigration we were winning, and if they
were on the economy they were winning. Gerry also realised cleverly
that even though the headline polling – Ipsos MORI and the like – didn't
show immigration as the only issue, if you started to take into account
things like education, schools, that sort of thing – it added up to immigration being the only issue that people cared about. Vote Leave's premise was that immigration was toxic, and they had to win over the centre
voters. What we realised was that the centre voters were not important,
and they were going to back Remain. What was important was winning
Labour voters, people who had never voted before, and people who were
on the right of the Conservative Party.'

Banks is an intriguing combination of shrewdness and showmanship,
and he deployed both with gusto in the battle for designation. To get
noticed by the newspapers, to garner himself air time on television and
to bamboozle his rivals he decided as a deliberate strategy to be louder,
more aggressive and more controversial than anyone else. In this he had
a clear role model across the Atlantic – Donald Trump: 'I think we were
running a Trump-style campaign of getting our own publicity. And I
think it worked very well. We would do something that was controversial and then not apologise for it. That was the usual method.'

In these offbeat endeavours Banks had an able collaborator in Andy
Wigmore, Leave.EU's spokesman. A native of Belize, Wigmore was a
junior staffer to Michael Portillo in the 1990s. He worked part-time as a
diplomat for Belize and was an Olympic-standard shooter – 'ranked 274
out of 274 in the world', according to one report.[1] Journalists were soon
amused by his haphazard interventions. On 11 March he complained to
one political editor, 'IGNORED AGAIN. Not being funny but yet again
we are being ignored for quotes – today's paper a perfect example. What
do we have to do to ask for a fair hearing?' The journalist responded to
this angst-ridden missive: 'You're the main quote in the main EU story
of the day on p.6!' Wigmore replied: 'I'm sorry you are correct and I am
a massive twat.' But Banks loved Wigmore's devil-may-care approach to

dealing with the media: 'Andy was a lot more talented than people give him credit for.'

Wigmore was not just aping Trump, he had taken advice from Trump's advisers. In August 2015 he flew to the US. 'We went to see some of Trump's people. His way of doing things was to create as much noise by being as outrageous as he possibly could. We took that strategy and employed it. At the time, Farage was considered a has-been, not to be taken seriously. Because the media wanted to airbrush Nigel out, the only way we could do it was to be as outrageous as possible. That was our strategy. We had to play the press like Trump has, like the string of a lute.'

Banks and Farage would deliberately say something outrageous, and Wigmore would highlight the comments on social media: 'If people are outraged, you can do one of two things. You can ignore it and then it dies, or you can react and take it down, not apologise, but then see what the reaction is. When you take it down it's like an admission of guilt, so you get the double hit with the press. Then you put it back up and get the treble hit with the press. In some cases, within an hour, we would change a headline on Facebook or Twitter maybe five or six times, just to gauge the reaction. We were monitoring how many people looked and shared it, where it went, and reacted accordingly.'

After the Paris and Brussels terror attacks, and assaults by migrants on women in Cologne on New Year's Eve, Farage said free movement 'has meant the free movement of Kalashnikov rifles'. Wigmore did up an advert: 'We knew it would be outrageous – it was. The vitriol that we got from the press worked. We took it down, they responded. We put it back up, they responded. You've spent no money whatsoever getting Nigel headlines.'

One of Banks's other publicity wheezes was to arrange a huge pop concert at the Birmingham NEC. He talked about the event from the summer of 2015 all the way through to June 2016, when it was finally canned. On three occasions he announced a line-up of artists, only to have the plans collapse. *Britain's Got Talent* presenter Alesha Dixon, boybands 5ive and East 17, dance act Sigma and veteran American pop group Sister Sledge all pulled out when they realised it was a political rally. The final line-up for 'the Last Night of the Brexit Proms' included three of the original members of Bucks Fizz and an Elvis impersonator. The idea was finally killed off by the Electoral Commission, which ruled that the cost would cause Banks to breach campaign spending rules. But the event had served its purpose. 'We got maximum publicity with that without having the concert,' Banks said. 'The press got it into their heads they were going to bring this concert down whatever happened. They would call up the agents and say, "You know this is a racist campaign." So we had to get a new line-up and start all over again.' Unbowed, Banks booked the American singer Alexander O'Neal for his Brexit night party instead.

One of Banks's favourite gambits was to threaten to sue at the drop of a hat. Newspapers and Vote Leave officials both felt the hot breath of his lawyers on their necks. Following an article in *The Times* which quoted sources at Vote Leave accusing Leave.EU of being racist and homophobic and making elliptical accusations of data theft, Banks got the high-profile law firm Mischon de Reya to serve papers on Matthew Elliott himself outside Westminster Tower – and had the event filmed for his own amusement. 'They called us racist, homophobes and data thieves, which we obviously took massive exception to. We got a wonderful video of the Mischon de Reya service agent coming and saying, "Are you Matthew Elliott?" and he says, "Who's asking?" and the bloke says, "Mischon de Reya," and he says, "I'm not Matthew Elliott." It's priceless. The person says, "We know you're Matthew Elliott." He just looks at the guy with a disgusted look. We weren't afraid to be aggressive. It let them know we weren't going to be steamrollered. We imprinted ourselves into the campaign in a way that they never thought we would.' Bruni-Lowe agreed: 'Banks's controversy actually helped him, because he was suing everyone. He'd tell the BBC, "You better put me on." And they did.' In the autumn, Banks sent Cummings and Elliott a bizarre email: 'I'm aware that I have a personal investigator on my tail. The heat is obviously rising in the kitchen!! You might want to watch out – I have a business that specialises in personal security and counter intelligence and if [you] need any help shout … It's almost certainly going to be a very dirty war.'[2]

Douglas Carswell, the Ukip MP backing Vote Leave, did not see the funny side: 'I am absolutely convinced that we would have won by a considerably larger margin if Matthew Elliott and Dominic Cummings had not spent weeks being harangued, threatened, bullied by people who were never actually on our side.' Daniel Hannan felt Banks was so aggressive he was prepared to put success in the referendum at risk: 'There were lots and lots of ways in which we were damaged by Arron Banks and Ukip. They sent us lawyers' letters, they hired private investigators, they were giving out Dom and Matt's phone numbers and telling people to spam them; it's not the behaviour of someone who actually wanted to win. Behavioural psychologists teach us to infer motive from behaviour, not the other way around. I put together everything that Banks was doing, and I cannot believe that he was primarily interested in winning this referendum. He wanted to be the guy who won. If he couldn't be that guy, I think winning was not particularly high on his agenda.'

Even Steve Baker, the great conciliator within Vote Leave, was unable to bridge the gap between the Cummings and Banks operations. In the tempestuous days after the attempted coup he talked to Andy Wigmore and suggested a week's truce between the two sides. He said, 'I will come to you to talk about how we can fix this thing, but only if you show it's possible that we can work together. If we can't have a week's truce, then I can't work with you.' On 3 February Baker went on *Newsnight* to denounce Donald Tusk's draft deal, and was asked about relations with Leave.EU. He indicated that he was supportive of Cummings, and that there had been 'genuine disagreements over strategy and tactics' with Banks. 'Then all hell broke lose,' Baker recalled. 'They exploded at me down the phone and redoubled their efforts to destroy Vote Leave. Dominic did tell me they didn't want to have a constructive relationship, they wanted to destroy us. That was the point I realised Dom was right'.

Despite the increasingly toxic relations, Vote Leave wanted to maintain their reputation as the good guys in the fight. Cummings banned the press team from attacking Banks and Farage. When Rob Oxley produced a dossier on Leave.EU's gaffes, with screen grabs of late-night tweets by Banks and Wigmore, he was told he could not release it. 'For all the arguments about these sides warring, for the majority of the time it wasn't initiated by us and we rarely responded,' he says. 'If we did respond, we then got dragged down to their level, and everyone would go, "Oh, why can't you guys stop fighting?"' When journalists phoned Oxley or Paul Stephenson seeking a comment on the latest Banks provocation, they would say, 'We wish them well.' A campaign source said, 'That was internal code at Vote Leave for "Fuck you." Now when I hear people say "We wish him well," I can't quite decide whether they do!'

One of the criteria the Electoral Commission would use for deciding who to grant the designation to was evidence of effective cross-party cooperation. With that in mind, Banks sought to coax the leading Labour politicians attached to Vote Leave away. In the first week of February, Kate Hoey announced that she was quitting. John Mills, who was then still chairman of Vote Leave, emailed Cummings and Elliott: 'We have lost Kate. The bottom line is that Labour Leave are fed up with the way they have been treated by Vote Leave.'[3]

Hoey said Cummings 'continually irritated me with his arrogance', but that the reason she left Vote Leave was that it was 'a Tory body': 'Dominic wasn't interested in Labour, he wasn't interested in Labour areas. I don't think he could accept that there were people with different views about how to best run a campaign.' She also claimed that Brendan Chilton, the driving force behind Labour Leave, was told he could not produce his own leaflets without approval from Vote Leave. 'It was ridiculous,' she said. Hoey believed after the referendum that she was right to quit, because it allowed her to concentrate on turning out the Brexit vote in Labour areas: 'If there had been no Leave.EU and there had been no Labour Leave, Vote Leave could not have done as well.' The Labour Leave operation decamped from Westminster Tower to 30 Millbank, just across the river, where Banks's London operation was based.

The designation battle pitched Banks and Leave.EU against Cummings and Vote Leave, but there was a third player in town – Grassroots Out, set up by Peter Bone and Tom Pursglove in December 2015. The aim of this organisation was to take the Brexit argument to the country through small-scale campaign events in town squares, village halls and street stalls. The two Tory MPs were also keen to see one united front. Another peace summit was set up, this time at 5 Hertford Street in Mayfair, Banks's club, attended by Bone, Pursglove, Hoey, Banks, the donor Richard Tice and Matthew Elliott. Bone told them all, 'Come on, it's not in our interests to be divided, let's work together. That also means Ukip.' A source said, 'We all agreed to step back. Leave.EU were willing to compromise, but Vote Leave wasn't.'

Despite the failure of this overture – by some counts the fifth attempt at a merger – Farage decided he wanted to get involved with Bone and Pursglove's grassroots effort, and hold a series of rallies to drum up support. Chris Bruni-Lowe said, 'There was just no real ground campaign by the Leave side. So they came to Nigel, realising they needed a figurehead. Nigel said we also needed Kate Hoey.'

By the time Hoey left Vote Leave she had been hearing for months that Farage was 'toxic'. When she finally met the Ukip leader, she says, 'I almost expected him to have horns on his head, I had heard so many horrible things about him.' Instead, they hit it off. 'He represented four million voters, who we had to get active. Without the Ukip people on the ground, we would not have won it.' Hoey's new friends persuaded Banks to finance a series of big rallies under the GO banner addressed by the likes of Farage, Pursglove and Bone, Bill Cash, David Davis and Liam Fox.

The first, in front of a crowd in excess of two and a half thousand, was held in Kettering on 23 January. Banks says it was 'a highlight' of the entire campaign. The local Tory MP Philip Hollobone, Sammy Wilson of the DUP, Bone, Pursglove, Hoey, Farage and Fox all appeared. 'It was the first time he'd shared a platform with Conservatives, Labour and other parties,' says Banks. 'He was very emotional about it, because he's been on the outside for twenty years. Vast numbers turned up on the day. There was a queue all the way back to the railway station, the roads were chock-a-block. The hall filled up and there was a massive crowd of people outside.' Banks was 'amazed' at how nervous the politicians were. 'They were not used to speaking to crowds that big. Liam Fox was pacing up and down in the green room with his notes. When Nigel came on, the crowd just erupted. He got a standing ovation. This was from Conservative voters, not Ukip. It became apparent he was very popular among certain sections of the Tory Party.'

Afterwards Farage and Banks went for a curry with the Conservative MPs. 'He got quite drunk afterwards,' said Banks. 'He entertained all the people in the restaurant.'

Farage was struck by how much he had in common with the Tories and with Hoey: 'The astonishing thing was the level of agreement on so many issues. In 1975 Enoch Powell and Michael Foot shared platforms on this issue, but they had almost no commonality at all. And yet here you could see something really remarkable was happening.'

On 5 February another rally followed in Manchester, where the bonding continued. After it was over David Davis, Hoey, Bone, Pursglove and Chris Bruni-Lowe found themselves sharing a McDonald's in the small hours of the morning. A photograph exists of Hoey swigging red wine from a plastic cup, like a scene from the film *Sideways*. Bruni-Lowe wondered if the common approach could lead to a political alignment after the referendum.

That night Peter Bone decided it was time for a realignment of the campaign. Grassroots Out would become just one pillar in a more ambitious grouping called GO Movement Ltd. Banks immediately saw the advantages of the new umbrella group. He agreed to fold Leave.EU into it, alongside Ukip and groups representing Labour and trade union supporters of Brexit. On 6 February Pursglove said GO Movement Ltd would apply for designation by the Electoral Commission as the official Leave campaign. Vote Leave had a new opponent, and one that was not yet tainted by Banks's predilection for controversy.

Farage said, 'Leave.EU was a battering ram. The conception of Grassroots Out was brilliant. Untainted. It came from nowhere. It had not been involved in this trench war with Cummings. There were eighteen separate political organisations supporting it – everyone from Ukip to the New Communist Party of Great Britain. It was a remarkable, incredible cross-party alliance. I think it spurred the other side on, doing things on the ground campaign they would never have done.'

'Banks was more clever than we gave him credit for,' acknowledges Rob Oxley. 'He saw his opportunity with GO. They wanted to create as much of a fight between Vote Leave and Leave.EU so that GO came through the middle as a unity candidate – in spite of the fact that it was just another puppet for Banks.'

Peter Bone believes it was far more than that. The need to consult others also helped, briefly, to tame Farage. Bone, Pursglove, Farage and Hoey formed a campaign 'quad', signing off all advertising and campaign messages together, forcing each one to take account of the views of their political opponents. 'Basically Nigel became a team player,' said one of those involved. 'He didn't attack the PM, he kept much much more to script.'

The other, more significant effect, was that the battle between GO and Vote Leave led to an upsurge in ground campaigning activity. GO did rallies and task-force canvassing on the model created by Bone and Pursglove. Vote Leave responded with street stalls. 'We did ten times more campaigning than if we'd been one organisation,' Bone said. 'It was hugely beneficial to the overall cause, and I don't think that's ever really been recognised.'

In the aftermath of the Vote Leave coup attempt, Cummings and Elliott were seriously worried. GO seemed to have all the momentum. They looked like a broad-based organisation, Vote Leave like the party poopers who wouldn't join the team. But their decision to keep their distance from Banks was vindicated when he gave an interview to Lucy Fisher of *The Times* in which he made two costly mistakes. Turning his guns on Vote Leave, he boldly declared, 'The enemy for us is not the "In" campaign – they're laughable – the enemy is our own side. Our job is to defeat the enemy and move on.' He also took aim at David Cameron, whose son Ivan had died in 2009: 'Anyone who can use their disabled child as a prop to show that they're human is in my mind a dreadful person.'[4]

When Chris Grayling saw the interview he texted Cameron to say, 'If Banks gets the nomination, I won't work with him.' Many other Tory MPs felt the same way. Banks admitted, 'According to Peter Bone that lost half the Conservative support we had for GO, lost thirty Conservative MPs. Elliott had copied it all and sent it to every MP.' Oxley confirmed that Vote Leave saw the 'real enemy' line as 'great ammunition for us'. Elliott and co. hit the phones to say, 'Why do you want to involve yourselves with people saying we're the real enemy?'

Further controversy attached itself to GO on Friday, 19 February, the night when Cameron was toiling to conclude the deal in Brussels. Another large audience gathered at the QEII Centre in Westminster. Special guest speakers were billed. One was originally meant to be Chris Grayling, but as the summit dragged on he was not released from cabinet collective responsibility in time. Much speculation surrounded the second speaker, who had been secured by Nigel Farage alone. Nick Wood, whose firm Media Intelligence Partners (MIP) was providing comms support for GO, was shocked to arrive in the green room to find an instantly recognisable black hat sitting on a sofa. It belonged to George Galloway, the professional controversialist who had been an MP for Labour and then for the anti-war Respect Party. Farage had set Galloway up a few nights before when he had appeared on Galloway's *Sputnik* programme on Russia Today, the television channel funded by the Putin regime.

Farage explained, 'I watched him on the *Sunday Politics* and Andrew Neil said, "Give me one reason, George Galloway, why we should leave the EU." And he said, "Cathy Ashton." I nearly spat my coffee down my shirt laughing. It was brilliant. I was aware that one of the big difficulties we had was there were whole segments of the community we couldn't scratch. But George could. His speech at the QEII rally was terrific.'

Galloway is one of the finest public speakers of his generation, but when he appeared that night there was uproar. Dozens of people walked out in disgust. Arron Banks, standing at the back of the hall, said, 'Bearing in mind that was a hugely Ukip crowd, about a third of the crowd I thought were getting up to lynch him. The atmosphere was red-hot.'

But Galloway was a big draw in Labour areas, and Bruni-Lowe judged that having Respect on board gave GO another string to its bow in convincing the Electoral Commission they had cross-party support. 'We polled Remain voters. Especially in the north, he is the most well-known Labour figure. It pissed a few people off, but actually it was the right thing. In order to win, you've got to work with everyone. That Westminster event was extraordinary. There was just an electric atmosphere.'

After the referendum, Farage still thought it was worth involving Galloway. 'People got the message that "This is not just posh Conservatives. There are people across the spectrum who feel this way." His appeal may not be as big as it used to be, but Bradford [where Galloway was an MP between 2012 and 2015] voted Out. He did meetings all over the country. He did black Christian meetings, he did Muslim meetings, he worked his blooming socks off. Having someone who could talk to a community who Labour ought to have had in the bag as Remain was a very good thing to do. I've got no regrets about that at all.'

The reaction among the Tories was very different, and played a significant role in denying GO the designation. Nick Wood said, 'Other speakers in the room shared a platform with Galloway without knowing he was going to be a speaker. David Campbell Bannerman and Bill Cash both withdrew their support for the GO Movement's bid for designation as a result. A fantastic event with 2,500 people and powerful speeches from David Davis, Farage, Hoey, Cash and Campbell Bannerman was ruined by Galloway's appearance – which led the 10 p.m. bulletins – and ultimately undermined GO's chances from there on in. Government ministers were reluctant to campaign with GO after that episode.'

Just as it had been the previous autumn, Douglas Carswell's decision to support Vote Leave also created complications for Farage as Designation Day approached. With Ukip's only MP on one side and its leader on the other, the party needed to set up an internal process to decide which campaign it would support for designation. Bruni-Lowe recalls, 'The only way we could deal with this problem was actually to get our national executive, MEPs, myself and Nigel to endorse one of the campaigns by going to see both of them. So we went to Bristol and stayed in Banks's castle for two days. The MEPs loved it. And we then went to see Elliott.'

Banks hosted the MEPs at Old Down Manor, a country house in Gloucestershire that he hires out as a wedding venue. 'It's quite amusing how they were having their meetings at Stuart Wheeler's place, Chilham Manor and we used that place,' he says. 'It was like a Jilly Cooper novel. We had a country-house-off! The highlight of the evening was [Ukip MEP] Margot Parker fell in the swimming pool and had to be rescued. It was a classic Ukip night out. The wine flowed pretty heavily, but she fell in before we had dinner. I had to pull her out.'

Banks and Farage gave a presentation, and then Peter Bone and Tom Pursglove appeared from London to speak. Bone talked about putting aside party differences and not attacking the prime minister. This message went down no better with Ukip than it had done during his argument with Cummings. Banks explained, 'Some of the Ukip MEPs go almost viscerally mad when they see a Tory. I was at the back with a couple of the lady MEPs from the north-west and I had to hold them back. They weren't impressed. It went down like a bag of sick.'

If the Banks event was awkward, it was as nothing compared to the appearance of the Ukip MEPs at Vote Leave's offices. Bruni-Lowe remembers Cummings appearing 'unshaven, shirt hanging out', and still talking about the double-referendum idea and his theory that 'Ukip were toxic'. 'He said they didn't have a problem using Nigel, but then said it will probably turn off all the cabinet ministers. We had furious arguments in that meeting. Elliott stood up and couldn't control the meeting. Our MEPs were just going for him, saying, "Why aren't you using Ukip?"' Some of the female MEPs resented the fact that Suzanne Evans, who had been sidelined by Ukip because of her opposition to Farage, was on the Vote Leave board.

According to Bruni-Lowe's account, Farage said, 'I don't want to be the face of this at all. I just want there to be a number of different voices involved.' Rob Oxley remembers things differently: 'Farage turned up late. He missed the whole part of the presentation where we were talking about us wanting to be consensual. We said, "You have appeal in certain places, we want to use it. No one's going to sideline Nigel." But he was not the person we wanted leading the campaign. He then started ticking us off: "Why aren't you putting us forward? Why don't you follow me on Twitter? Why don't you re-tweet me?" He arrived to kick off a row and a stink.'

Whoever was to blame, the meeting was a disaster, and with the full backing of his MEPs and Ukip's NEC (but not his sole MP), Farage went on television and formally endorsed GO. 'We had no option, because Vote Leave was so unpalatable to us,' said Bruni-Lowe. 'They hated Ukip, hated Nigel, wanted a double referendum at that time. And we were still unconvinced that many of them actually wanted to leave the EU. That was the end of any real negotiations between us and them.'

While Vote Leave and the GO Movement feuded, there was now a new civil war – between Leave.EU and Grassroots Out within the GO movement. It was as if the Front of Judean Peoples had broken off from the Judean People's Front while it battled the People's Front of Judea.

In late February Nick Wood's MIP, handling GO's comms requirements, moved into offices paid for by Banks in 30 Millbank, next to the Leave.EU comms team led by Andy Wigmore. There were no TVs, no grids, no stationery – and when a TV did arrive it was leant against a box on the floor for weeks, as the handyman was too busy to put it on the wall. Not the ideal set-up for a national referendum campaign. There were immediate tensions. Banks was highly suspicious of people with connections to the Tory Party. He told Wood to 'butt out' of the George Galloway rally because of his previous links to Elliott, dismissing him as 'another failed Tory spad (aged 106)'. Wood was infuriated by Banks's anti-politics sentiment when he was up to his neck in the biggest political campaign for a generation. Wood was friends with Eurosceptic right-wingers like Iain Duncan Smith, Owen Paterson, David Davis and Liam Fox, who were all *persona non grata* under Cameron, and objected to being seen by Banks as a member of the Westminster establishment: 'To him we're all elitist co-conspirators determined to subvert the will of the people. My friends in politics are people who tried to burst the bubble, not live in it.'

One day an abrasive young Leave.EU staffer dumped thirty boxes in the GO office, oozing with lurid green Grassroots Out ties, mouse mats and keyrings. When Wood returned to find the office resembling the warehouse of an extreme faction of the Green Party, he marched purposefully next-door. The air turned momentarily blue, and shortly afterwards a troop of his young neighbours returned, barely concealing their loathing, to shuffle the boxes back. 'He's a fucking cunt, your boss,' one of the Leave.EU people told a member of Wood's staff.

MIP had far more cordial relations, despite their generally opposing views, with Labour Leave, thanks in no small part to the ebullient character of its general secretary, Brendan Chilton. Wood recalled, 'He took meeting the stereotype of a champagne socialist very seriously, and for dinner after the rally in Glasgow, chomped through fillet steak garnished with scallops, slurped Bolly ("What's the point in drinking anything else?"), all the while explaining with genuine sincerity that Cuba and Venezuela were bastions of social success, and Castro and Chávez the political idols all other leaders should emulate.'

The final breach between Grassroots Out and Leave.EU came in April, when financial declarations made to the Electoral Commission showed that Peter Bone and Tom Pursglove, as directors of Grassroots Out, had paid themselves a total of nearly £40,000 over a three-month period – Pursglove as chief executive and Bone for accountancy services. They had not told the comms team, Farage, Hoey, Banks or Richard Tice about these arrangements. Banks erupted and told Buzzfeed, which broke the story, 'We are extremely shocked and disappointed to discover that two elected individuals have treated the GO BREXIT campaign as a business not a cause, and would urge them to do the honourable thing and donate the sum directly to a smaller BREXIT group.'[5] Later that afternoon, at a meeting in Bone's office, it emerged that they had in fact donated the money back to GO already. Bruni-Lowe said the incident 'soured' things for Farage: 'He thought these were good guys. Nigel didn't take any money, Hoey didn't take any money. It was quite a bizarre thing for them to have done.'

After the attack by Leave.EU on GO, Wood pulled his team out of Millbank. They left instantly on a Friday night, with their office belongings in ghastly green GO carrier bags. From then until polling day Grassroots Out concentrated on their ground campaign.

Money was still a problem over at the People's Front of Judea. With the declarations of Boris Johnson and Michael Gove, Matthew Elliott found it easier to raise money, but many donors held back, not convinced Vote Leave would win the designation. Elliott said, 'You started hearing more and more, "If you guys get designation, I'll give you some money, but at the moment it all seems very messy." Having

Michael and Boris around to attend fundraising dinners helped enormously. But we certainly didn't get floods of cash until we got the designation.'

A key factor in Vote Leave's favour was the Contact Group, which had been set up the year before by David Campbell Bannerman and met every Monday at 11 a.m. at Westminster Tower. Campbell Bannerman had been a special adviser to Patrick Mayhew when he was Northern Ireland secretary under John Major, and played a role in the early stages of the peace process. He saw the same objectives for the Contact Group: 'To bring people together who are at war'.

To give it extra clout, Chris Grayling began to chair the group once he had publicly declared: 'I was very concerned that one of the five criteria for the Electoral Commission was that you had to demonstrate that you can represent the views of other groups who are also campaigning for the same objective. That actually was one of the things that got Vote Leave the designation ahead of Grassroots Out.'

The Contact Group was an eccentrically eclectic talking shop. On one occasion left-winger John Boyd (the elderly leader of Campaign Against Euro Federalism) challenged Grayling's authority to chair the meeting. 'Who are you?' he asked. 'I am the leader of the House of Commons,' Grayling replied.

As head of outreach, Grayling decided that he should talk to Nigel Farage and Arron Banks. On the Friday before the designation announcement, Farage travelled to Grayling's home in Epsom, and they had a 'quiet cup of coffee in the RAC club'. 'We talked about how we made sure that after the designation his team Ukip, Grassroots Out and Vote Leave could essentially fire in the same direction,' Grayling explained. A few days later, Farage phoned and asked Grayling to appear on a platform with him at Stoke-on-Trent the Monday after the designation. Grayling agreed, and spoke alongside the Ukip leader, Kate Hoey, Peter Bone and Tom Pursglove. He was greeted with tumultuous applause in what is a rock-solid Labour town. 'It was a very surreal experience,' he said. 'I will never get a standing ovation in Stoke-upon-Trent again in my life.' He got a lift home with Farage.

Grayling's meeting with Arron Banks, at his Bristol office on 15 April, was less successful. Grayling's adviser Bill Clare was insistent that Banks and his publicity-hungry sidekick Wigmore guaranteed that details of the meeting would not leak. Grayling urged Banks, 'One thing you could do is ensure that nothing comes out of Ukip on a par with the Aids comments during the general election [when Farage had suggested that immigrants with Aids should not be treated by the NHS], because that would seriously undermine the campaign.' Banks got 'very shirty'. The meeting ended abruptly. Grayling says he left, while allies of Banks claim he was 'thrown out'.

The designation documents were due in at midnight on Thursday, 31 March. The decision would be announced two weeks later. Peter Bone said afterwards that he had never worked so hard as he did preparing GO's submission along with Tom Pursglove and Richard Murphy, the exiled field operations man. They sent the document off on the final afternoon. Bone expected to win, believing GO had a broader reach into Eurosceptic groups and across the country.

At Vote Leave there was chaos. While GO had focused on winning the designation, the senior staff in Westminster Tower spent their time and mental energies combating the initial onslaught by Downing Street and Stronger In. Preparation of the designation document was allowed to drift. The winning campaign would have to demonstrate the levels of support it enjoyed, its campaigning ability, its organisational ability, and outline how it planned to represent and engage other campaigners seeking the same outcome.

At 10.30 p.m. on the day before the deadline 'Ricardo' Howell was writing the section on engagement with other campaigns when Victoria Woodcock said, 'Wouldn't it be worth working out what the actual criteria are?' Howell read them all and, horrified, announced to the room, 'We haven't answered any of them, and all our material in this section's irrelevant, and it's worth twelve out of fifty points.' They stayed up until 3.30 a.m. rewriting the whole section. 'It was quite literally an essay crisis,' a Vote Leave source said. 'It was down to Vicks that we got it in.'

They finally sent the document in at 11.40 the following night, twenty minutes before the deadline. As key moments in the referendum campaign go, this ranks highly. But for Woodcock's intervention, or with a delay of twenty minutes, Arron Banks would have been running the Leave campaign and Nigel Farage would in all likelihood have been the central figure in the televised debates.

*   *   *

On Wednesday, 13 April the Electoral Commission announced that Vote Leave would be the official 'Out' campaign, because it had 'better demonstrated that it has the structures in place to ensure the views of other campaigners are represented in the delivery of its campaign'. It singled out the Contact Group as a decisive factor. In effect while offering a voice to GO people in their campaign, but refusing to join GO themselves, Cummings and Elliott's refusal to work with Banks had paid off. Out of fifty points, Vote Leave scored forty-nine and GO forty-five.

Nigel Farage was relieved: 'In terms of the criteria we should have got it, but in terms of administration, quite what we would have done if we had got it I'm not really sure!'

But Banks smelled a rat. The day before the announcement, Steve Bell, president of the National Conservative Convention, tweeted his congratulations to Vote Leave for winning the designation. It reinforced Banks's belief that he was the victim of an establishment stitch-up. Banks claimed, 'It was rigged, no amount of good work would have got us designation. We filed a 2,000-page designation document and Vote Leave hustled theirs together at the last minute. When Steve Bell, three days before the designation was due to be announced, said they had won, we knew we might be in trouble. We wrote to the Electoral Commission saying, "What the hell's going on? You're not meant to have made the decision yet." They brought forward the decision and announced it the following day.' Three of the commissioners had recused themselves from the decision because of conflicts of interest, and Banks later told the Treasury Select Committee that a fourth should also have done so, which would have meant the Electoral Commission had no quorum to make the decision. He told the MPs, 'In the business world, that would be out of the question and pretty reprehensible.' In fact Bell sent his tweet because a Vote Leave computer man sent out a test message to key figures without including the vital heading 'THIS IS A TEST'.

True to form, Banks threatened to seek a judicial review of the decision: 'We would have won. The problem we had was, we were told if we went for a judicial review, it could knock the whole referendum timetable off its course.' Farage and Bruni-Lowe went to see him, and the Ukip leader made the case, 'We can probably do as much damage not being the designated campaign as being it.' When Banks backed down, Farage and Bruni-Lowe headed to Shepherd's restaurant in Westminster and had a good bottle of red.

Victorious, Vote Leave put on a rally to launch the formal campaign, and unveiled a new poster. Perhaps it was tiredness, perhaps it was over-confidence, but the poster promised to spend the UK's entire £350 million weekly contribution to the EU on the NHS – the only time they ever said the whole sum would go to the Health Service. 'That was one of our campaign fuck-ups,' a campaign source admitted. 'We'd had an argument about the wording internally. But as ever the ruling was, "It's a row we want to have."' At a rally in Manchester that night, Boris Johnson finally showed what an engaging campaigner he could be. Of EU membership he said, 'We are passengers locked in the back of a mini-cab with a wonky satnav driven by a driver who doesn't have perfect command of English and going in a direction, frankly, we don't want to go.' He compared David Cameron and the other Remainers to 'the prophets of doom who said the Millennium Bug would cause planes to fall from the sky.'

The prime minister was privately relieved that Vote Leave had won, as he believed it would be easier to put the Conservative Party back together again after the referendum if Ukip was not running the campaign. The Conservative Leavers also wanted to preserve the party, because they believed that was the only way of delivering Brexit if the people voted to leave. Steve Baker said, 'It had been obvious since the general election, and certainly the election of Jeremy Corbyn, that only the Conservative Party can govern the UK. That means if you want to leave the EU the first thing you need is to get a referendum, the second is to win the referendum. The final step is to form a Conservative government willing to take you out. Therefore don't destroy the Conservative Party.' Baker felt Farage and Banks never grasped this point. They complained that the campaign was arranged for the convenience of the Tories, and sought to take it over. But without a stable government to deliver Brexit, it would never happen.

Senior figures in Vote Leave are adamant that the designation battle was crucial to the final result. 'If we had lost the designation we would have lost, no question,' says Daniel Hannan. By winning the day, Vote Leave ensured that Douglas Carswell became a key figure on broadcast media as the Ukip representative from the official campaign, which meant he got air time that would otherwise have gone to Nigel Farage. 'Had Douglas not been there to take his share of it, I'm not sure we would have won,' Hannan added. 'Everything he said was aimed at people who hadn't yet made up their minds. The same cannot be said of every other Ukip leader.' Without Carswell, Vote Leave would also have struggled to show the breadth of support they needed to get the Electoral Commission endorsement. 'The only thing of significance that I helped do was to make sure Vote Leave got designation,' Carswell said.

On the losing side, Farage and Bruni-Lowe were sanguine. They did not believe the battle had been in vain. The challenge of GO ensured that Vote Leave had raised its game in the ground war. 'The designation fight made it more likely that we won,' Bruni-Lowe said, 'because Elliott had no street stalls in December, but then there were a thousand street stalls in March. Because Banks and him were going at each other it was competitive. It really helped.'

The Ukip pair also think losing the designation gave them a freer hand than if they had been the official campaign. Farage says, 'The campaign not being united left me completely free to go off and do my stuff around the country.' For good or ill, that is exactly what he did.

While Farage fired up the engines of his purple open-topped bus, Vote Leave had another charismatic outsider to deal with. Barack Obama was coming to town.

13

'BACK OF THE QUEUE'

When the leader of the free world told the British public they would get no special favours from him there were audible intakes of breath. Journalists who had been expecting Barack Obama merely to issue a warm endorsement for David Cameron's campaign to keep Britain in the European Union felt their pulses quicken and their hands scribble faster. At the rear of the grand Foreign Office room an American diplomat let out a gasp as the words passed his boss's lips.

Obama blinked slowly, regarded the roomful of eager scribes like a professor addressing a group of dim undergraduates, and shook his head in a 'You guys!' manner before delivering his line: 'The UK is going to be in the back of the queue.'

It felt like a sentence crafted somewhere over the mid-Atlantic, an orphan utterance resulting from the hasty coupling of two people divided by a common language. 'In' the back of the queue, not 'at' the back, gifted to the soundbite by an American mother; 'queue' the product of an English father. Even the dumbest observer knew an American would instinctively have used 'line' instead.

Standing at his own podium next to Obama, David Cameron studied his guest with all the intensity of a lover on a first date who thinks he has met 'the one', not wanting to give anything away while rejoicing inside that his wildest expectations have just been exceeded, the smallest hint of a smile playing around his lips.

It was Friday, 22 April, and the president of the United States had just torpedoed a month of claims by the Brexiteers that Britain would be at the top of the list for a free-trade deal from its closest ally if it left the EU. The Special Relationship would ensure that Britain was looked after, Vote Leave claimed. Yet here was the man himself saying it was not so.

For immediate impact and a clear-cut public relations victory the Remain camp had no better moment at any time in the campaign. Obama had done what was asked of him, and much more. To use an American phrase, the president of the United States had brought a gun to a knife-fight.

As the press conference finished, the journalist Paul Waugh turned to a senior aide from Number 10 and showed him a tweet which read, 'This is the best day of Cameron's life so far. Sorry, Sam, but you can see it in his face.' The aide laughed loudly. The purveyors of conventional wisdom decreed that it could be a knockout blow for the Leave campaign. And yet it was not.

Obama had addressed the British press in the Locarno Suite at the Foreign Office. The barrel-vaulted grand reception room was among the finest Whitehall had to offer. Designed by George Gilbert Scott in the 1850s, it was named after the treaties signed there in 1925 that attempted to stabilise Europe after the turmoil of the First World War. Doubtless Obama's intention was the same: to help bind Britain into the future of the Continent. The truth of his intervention, though, is that it ended up being as successful at supporting the existing order as the Locarno Suite's namesake deal.

From the moment Cameron called the referendum, a visit from Obama was on the cards. The queen's ninetieth birthday celebrations would be the perfect cover for a visit to Britain by America's first family. Soon Ameet Gill was building his campaign grid around the final week of April.

The Obama administration did not need any encouragement to make the case for Britain to remain in the EU. As early as August 2012 the US ambassador in London, Louis Susman, had warned Nick Clegg that if Britain left, 'You guys may soon not count in Europe any more.'[1] On 17 January 2013, less than a week before the Bloomberg speech, Obama called Cameron and advised him against increasing Britain's distance from the EU.[2]

Downing Street's rollout of the Obama narrative began on the morning of Thursday, 21 April with a letter to *The Times* from eight former US Treasury secretaries warning that withdrawal from the EU would be a 'risky bet'. They wrote: 'If Britain exits, it should not take for granted its global primacy when it is no longer the gateway to Europe.' The letter was another Daniel Korski production. The following morning Larry

Summers, who served under Bill Clinton, went on the *Today* programme on Radio 4 to reinforce the message.

It was another article in that morning's papers that caused Obama to pull out the six-shooter. Boris Johnson had written a piece on the president's visit for the *Sun*. Brexiteers like Chris Grayling and Liam Fox had previously urged Obama to keep out of the EU debate. Fox had organised a letter a month earlier to the new US ambassador, Matthew Barzun, signed by a hundred MPs, warning that any intervention from the president would undermine the 'validity' of the referendum's result. To get attention, Johnson needed to say something more eye-catching. His article seized on reports from 2009 that one of Obama's first actions as president was to return a bust of Winston Churchill, which had sat in the Oval Office under George W. Bush, to the British embassy in Washington. The story had become iconic in the US, where it was seen as symbolic of Obama's foreign-policy pivot away from Europe. 'It was a fine goggle-eyed object, done by the brilliant sculptor Jacob Epstein, and it had sat there for almost ten years,' Johnson wrote with his usual brio. 'Some said it was a snub to Britain. Some said it was a symbol of the part-Kenyan president's ancestral dislike of the British Empire – of which Churchill had been such a fervent defender.' When Obama was first elected much was indeed written about his anger at the treatment his grandfather had received from the British in Kenya. But Johnson's intervention immediately sparked accusations of racism.

As the *Sun* hit the streets Obama was flying to the UK from Saudi Arabia, and he spent the flight reading up on referendum issues. Craig Oliver and Helen Bower, Cameron's official spokeswoman – a civil service appointee – had been liaising for weeks with Josh Earnest, the White House press secretary, and Ben Rhodes, a deputy national security adviser who was the main point man for the trip, about the 'underlying arguments'. But when Obama landed, the Americans requested more information. 'They were keen to know what the IMF and Mark Carney had said, the arguments we had been making and the arguments some of those on the other side have been making,' a Downing Street source said.

After lunch at Windsor Castle with the queen and the Duke of Edinburgh, Obama arrived at Downing Street and went into a short *tête-à-tête* with Cameron, Ed Llewellyn and Mark Lyall Grant, Cameron's national security adviser. The president had Rhodes and Susan Rice, his

national security adviser, in tow. It was here that the British team showed
Obama Boris Johnson's article. 'They largely talked through the policy
issues, but they also talked about the politics around the referendum,
including the Boris article,' says a source. Obama was 'animated' about
his desire for Britain to stay in the EU, citing the UK's central role in
encouraging the rest of the EU to impose economic sanctions on Russia
over its aggression in Ukraine.

A second meeting then took place involving senior ministers, including George Osborne, Philip Hammond and Theresa May. There are
conflicting accounts of how the words 'back of the queue' found their
way into Obama's mouth. A senior Downing Street source says, 'There
was a discussion about trade deals. No words were suggested. Obama
had spotted that the economy and trade was a key part of the argument,
and wanted to make an intervention.' But had he? Another senior figure
in Downing Street interviewed for this book has a different version of
events: 'My understanding is that it was George Osborne who came up
with it. He needed it, and he came up with the line "back of the queue".
I've heard that from someone who was in the room at the time it was
suggested.' Craig Oliver says Osborne pointed out that Vote Leave's
claims that Britain would get a trade deal were flawed, but denies that
Osborne fed Obama the line. Osborne has told friends that it was
Obama's idea. 'He suggested it in the meeting,' a source close to Osborne
said. '[Obama] said, "Of course Britain would be at the back." And he
asked whether it would be helpful to say that, and we said it would. But
it wasn't George's phrase.' The chancellor dismisses the idea that he got
Obama to use 'queue' rather than 'line'. The Osborne confidant said, 'I
know he used the word "queue", but George would use "line" if he was in
America.'

Obama and Cameron emerged just after 5 p.m. for the press conference, deliberately timed so the highlights would be fresh for *The Six
O'Clock News*. The president was clear: 'This is a decision for the people
of the United Kingdom to make. I'm not coming here to fix any votes.
I'm not casting a vote myself.' But he rejected Johnson, Fox and Grayling's
view that he should mind his own business: 'I am offering my opinion,
and in democracies everybody should want more information, not less,
and you shouldn't be afraid to hear an argument being made.' Moving on
to the trade deal, he took aim squarely at Vote Leave's forehead and, in
his languid style, pulled the rhetorical trigger: 'My understanding is that

some of the folks on the other side have been ascribing to the United States certain actions we will take if the UK does leave the EU – they say for example that "We will just cut our own trade deals with the United States." I figured you might want to hear from the president of the United States what I think the United States is going to do ... Maybe some point down the line there might be a UK–US trade agreement, but it's not going to happen any time soon because our focus is in negotiating with a big bloc, the European Union, to get a trade agreement done. The UK is going to be in the back of the queue.'

Then he trained his fire on Boris Johnson. He confirmed that he had moved the Churchill bust from the Oval Office because he wanted to replace it with one of Martin Luther King: 'I thought it was appropriate – and I think most people in the United Kingdom might agree – as the first African-American president.' But he revealed that he had another Churchill bust outside his private study in the White House residence – 'I see it every day.'

In the offices of Britain Stronger In Europe, near Cannon Street station, thirty senior staff watched in awe. 'It's not often you get complete silence in an office like that,' said one of those who was present. But when Obama delivered his rapier thrust at Johnson 'there was an eruption'. James McGrory joked, 'That couldn't have gone much better if I had been playing the role of Barack Obama myself.' In the Locarno Suite a member of the White House staff turned to one of Cameron's press handlers and said, 'I haven't seen him so on the argument for a while.'

But the president's performance enraged Eurosceptics, who pointed out that Obama would no longer be president when a trade deal was negotiated. Justice minister Dominic Raab said, 'I don't think the British people will be blackmailed by anyone, let alone a lame-duck US president.' Ukip MEP Patrick O'Flynn tweeted: 'What has Dave got lined up next? Invite Angela Merkel over to say she will invade us if we vote "Leave"?'

Knowing the media would seize on the queue/line aspect, Craig Oliver was quick to downplay any suggestion of collusion, telling journalists, 'This is the leader of the free world. He is not some puppet we can get parroting what we want. He said what he said because he believes it.'

Obama's trip continued for another day. He and Michelle had dinner with the Duke and Duchess of Cambridge, and the president did a town-hall meeting with students the following day, at which he met Jeremy

Corbyn backstage. The Labour leader pronounced their meeting 'excellent', although it remains a closely guarded diplomatic mystery what Obama made of Corbyn's talking points on 'post-industrial societies and the power of global corporations'. Obama's reward was a round of golf with Cameron on the Saturday at The Grove in Hertfordshire. The PM managed a par on the first hole, and 'only lost one ball!'

The PR push was rounded off when Obama's former secretary of state Hillary Clinton also called for Britain to stay in the EU. Her senior policy adviser Jake Sullivan told the *Observer*, 'Hillary Clinton believes that transatlantic cooperation is essential, and that cooperation is strongest when Europe is united.'

Some Stronger In officials had concerns about the visit. But, as Will Straw reasoned, 'If Obama was going to come here, let's try and make it as impactful as possible. What it did do was knock out from under them the argument that they could easily negotiate free trade deals with the US.'

Cameron, Osborne, Oliver and the rest of the leadership team put their feet up, patted themselves on the backs on a trip almost perfectly executed, and waited for the polls to shift in their direction. One man already knew they would not – Dominic Cummings.

When Obama delivered the 'back of the queue' threat, one Vote Leave staff member said the initial reaction at Westminster Tower was 'a real sense of panic'. The fear subsided when, with the entire office watching the television, Cummings walked into the main campaign war room and announced, 'This will have no effect,' then walked straight back into his office. Later he said, 'Do not worry about this. SW1 hysteria is not the same as the real world. We would have been worried about Obama if it had been done in a gentle, subtle, cautious, careful, intelligent way. But as soon as he said "back of the queue" ...'

Cummings' instincts were very quickly confirmed by Vote Leave's focus groups. Under the radar, he had managed to hire Henry de Zoete to run them and oversee the campaign's digital operation. 'He said straight away Obama is not good for them,' Cummings recalled. The phrase de Zoete kept hearing from voters was 'None of your business'. The reaction to 'back of the queue' was 'really bad'.

The old Gove gang was now properly back together. As one of the few people on earth Cummings is prepared to take advice from, 'Zoot' acted as a guru to the senior staff. 'Zoot instituted a real message discipline which Lynton [Crosby] would have done and which we didn't have before,' says Stephenson. He could also be a wise judge when the others disagreed. Oxley recalls, 'In the team, Paul and Dom were the ultra-aggressive ones, whereas me and Parky were the more measured ones. And Zoot was sometimes the impartial arbitrator.'

Matthew Elliott says, 'We knew from our activists talking to people on the doorstep and also from our focus groups that people really hated that moment. How dare the president of the US say that to Britain, when we'd been the first in the queue when it came to military action in Iraq and Afghanistan? We've got a special relationship with the US, so how dare the president of the US come over here and insult us like that and inter-vene in our referendum? That backfired.'[3] In Downing Street, even one of Cameron's closest aides believed Obama's intervention would be counterproductive: 'I think Obama was fucking awful. As someone who believes in remaining in the EU, as someone who's incredibly loyal and thinks David Cameron was a brilliant prime minister, it jarred with me.' He also said that the 'back of the queue' line was 'just not true'. Cummings' confidence was confirmed by polls published later that week showing no Obama bounce for Stronger In. If anything, they had shifted slightly in Vote Leave's favour. Before Obama's visit, six out of the previous seven polls had given Remain the lead. After it, three of the next five put Leave ahead.

Remain had thrown their two hardest punches so far. The week before Obama arrived, the Treasury had published its first major dossier on the economic risks of Brexit. They had then wheeled out the leader of the free world. The media had declared them the big victors of the week. Yet far from lying face-down on the canvas seeing stars, Cummings was still aiming for them.

Boris Johnson did not watch the Obama press conference because he was holding a surgery in his Uxbridge and South Ruislip constituency, but aides were quick to draw the president's comments to his attention. Privately he was somewhat chastened by the furore over his 'part-Kenyan' comments. Will Walden and Ben Wallace both warned him the article was not helpful, either to the campaign or to himself. Wallace regarded the suggestion that Johnson was racist as a 'disaster' for his leadership hopes, and became irritated that the necessities of fighting the referendum campaign were hurting his chances of recruiting MPs from across the ideological spectrum of the Conservative Party. When he read the *Sun* piece he emailed Johnson to say, 'You'll forgive me if I think it's utterly crap.' Johnson sent him a text: 'I understand if you want to bail. Not easy at the moment.' The two soon patched up their differences, but Wallace confided to a friend that week, 'It has created a proper Stop Boris movement where one didn't exist before.' Cabinet ministers were now privately encouraging Cameron not to give Johnson any cabinet job after the referendum. One said that week, 'Boris has behaved appallingly. When this is over, a large number of us will be saying that we need team players.' Churchill's grandson Sir Nicholas Soames, an old friend, said, 'Boris Johnson has really bogged it and showed himself up as an ocean-going clot.'

Within Vote Leave there was also irritation with Johnson for causing the backlash. 'Obama coming here and telling us what to think is insulting, but Boris issues a borderline racist insult and it all rebounds on us,' said one campaign official at the time.

The failure of the Obama visit to turn the referendum decisively in Stronger In's favour highlighted several problems with the Remain campaign. Their reliance on third-party endorsements from the great and the good was seen by voters as patronising. The esoteric discussions about trade relationships, however comprehensively Remain won them, never cut through to voters concerned about immigration and the pound in their pocket. Finally, attempts to make a pitch about Britain's place in the world, in which well-known foreign figures could have been particularly of use, never really took off, despite repeated attempts by Cameron to make the case that the UK was safer in an interconnected world. Of the campaign's 'Stronger, Safer, Better Off' mantra, 'safer' never really flew. The one time it did register in the public consciousness it was a disaster which further undermined trust in the prime minister.

On 8 May the *Sunday Times* splashed on a warning from Jonathan Evans and Sir John Sawers, the former heads of MI5 and MI6, that leaving the EU might undermine Britain's ability to protect itself from terrorists because it could damage intelligence sharing: 'When a father walks out of a family,' Sawers said, 'rarely is there a happy relationship afterwards between the two.' It was the beginning of a three-day offensive to finally win the 'safety' argument.

Things went wrong on the Sunday evening, when Downing Street sent out a briefing for the newspapers with extracts from a speech Cameron was due to make the following day reflecting on how the EU had helped preserve the peace in Europe since 1945. In Britain, Conservative politicians have traditionally credited NATO with this achievement. Cameron's speech was a nuanced argument about the need to work together. It was accompanied by a Tom Edmonds video of four veterans of the Second World War speaking movingly about why they did not want to see the unity they had fought for unpicked. Several Stronger In staff regard it as the best ad they created throughout the entire campaign. It brought tears to the eyes of some. And yet hardly anyone noticed it, because Cameron's speech implied that failure to vote Remain might lead to war.

The briefing, which contained the spiciest elements of the prime minister's speech, shorn of their context, created a newspaper frenzy. The *Sun*'s intro the next morning read: 'BREXIT could see Europe descend into World War Three, David Cameron will say today.' The *Daily Mail* splashed on 'EU VOTE: NOW PM WARNS OF WAR AND GENOCIDE'. Even the *Times* front page announced, 'Brexit will raise risk of world war, PM claims'. The lobby seized on Cameron's references to World Wars I and II, the Battles of Blenheim and Waterloo and the Spanish Armada as proof of what happens when we do not hold 'our neighbours' close. He said, 'Can we be so sure that peace and stability on our continent are assured beyond any shadow of doubt? Is that a risk worth taking? I would never be so rash as to make that assumption.'

One of those involved in crafting the speech said, 'It was a briefing, not a speech problem. We never said "World War III". We said, "Can you guarantee peace on the Continent?" I think the press totally distorted it.' Andrew Cooper, for one, believed the speech made a legitimate argument: 'It's easy to take for granted the fact that not a long time ago there was war in Europe, when you look at razor wire going up in Eastern Europe.'

But the 'World War III speech', as it became known, was quickly seen as the apogee of Project Fear absurdity, and – in some quarters – as evidence that Cameron was prepared to say almost anything to put the wind up voters. A reference to the serried ranks of gravestones on the Continent went down badly with Arron Banks, who said, 'His remarks about the men lying in the Commonwealth war graves are frankly insult-

ing. They fought to defend democracy and the right to self-determina-
tion, not to pave the way for the UK to chuck them overboard for an
anti-democratic European customs union.'

Unlike in 1975, the Second World War was a distant memory, and
most voters had no personal recollection of the dangers Cameron was
seeking to evoke. Michael McManus, a Conservative activist who
worked with Ted Heath, a key figure in the first referendum, said, 'Part
of the problem is generational change. In 1975, Willie Whitelaw was not
only a popular figure, but his reasons for being pro-European came
straight from the battlefields of Western Europe. That argument was not
an embarrassing argument in 1975. Ted Heath was involved in protecting Liverpool during the Blitz, and then leading his men across Europe.
Heath was mentioned in dispatches. Whitelaw and Peter Carrington
won the Military Cross. These are people who'd fought for their country,
and they'd seen the destruction of Europe, and we just have a younger
generation who don't carry the same credibility on this argument. David
Cameron made one speech on that basis and was widely ridiculed for
it.'

The newspaper reception to the speech was so negative that Adam
Atashzai suggested the campaign stop pre-briefing the papers altogether
and give the stories instead to the BBC and ITV, who could be expected
to cover them without the same slant. A Number 10 source says, 'Adam's
view was, "Fuck the lobby. Just ignore them. They are our enemy, they
want to kill us." We knew this is what it must feel like to be the Labour
Party during the general election.' If Craig Oliver was tempted by that
course of action, he did not say so, and the attempt to engage with the
newspapers continued.

The 'World War III' speech not only damaged trust in Cameron, it
also overshadowed the rest of the security push. The day after the speech
– the seventy-first anniversary of VE-Day – the *Daily Telegraph* carried
a letter from five former NATO secretaries general, including Peter
Carrington, saying Brexit would 'give succour to the West's enemies'.[4] *The
Times* ran a letter from thirteen former US secretaries of state and
defense and national security advisers warning that Britain's 'place and
influence in the world would be diminished and Europe would be
dangerously weakened' by a vote to leave.[5] Daniel Korski had also
arranged a piece by US General David Petraeus, alongside whom he had
worked in Afghanistan, at the end of March.

The public may have ignored the arguments, but Vote Leave found these letters an annoyance. Chris Grayling travelled to Washington and made a speech on Capitol Hill about Brexit, wrote a piece for the *Wall Street Journal*, and spoke to the Atlantic Council, which he believed was involved in helping Downing Street to organise the letters from American dignitaries. He tried to make American politicians look differently at Brexit: 'Just imagine in 2008 a young Senator from Illinois had turned up in New Hampshire wanting to be a presidential candidate, arguing that the United States could no longer function as a separate independent nation, that it needed to sign up to a union of the Americas.' As a result of his visit a letter, orchestrated by George Holding, a Republican Congressman from North Carolina, saying the president should not have got involved was signed by ten members of Congress. Released a week before polling day, it said: 'Regardless of the outcome of the referendum, citizens of the United Kingdom should know that we will continue to regard our relations with the United Kingdom as a central factor in the foreign, security, and trading policies of the United States.'

Despite Grayling's effort, Downing Street won the tactical campaign battle on security hands down, but they never persuaded voters that Brexit would endanger their security. Korski might have been well advised to heed the advice of eighty-five-year-old Frank Carlucci, who served as both national security adviser and defense secretary under Ronald Reagan. When Korski phoned and asked him to sign a letter, Carlucci told him how Reagan had approached him during the 1987 British general election, when it looked briefly as if Margaret Thatcher might not win. Reagan said, 'Frank! I've decided I'm going to make an intervention in the British debate.' Carlucci replied, 'Mr President, that's a great idea. However, you may just want to think about some of the consequences here.' He told Korski that he persuaded Reagan against making a full-throttled intervention in the campaign, adding, 'I'm telling you this story, are you sure the right course of action is to now make our voice known?' Korski said, 'I think people want to hear what our allies and friends think.'

Ultimately they did not.

Andrew Cooper says he 'struggled' to sell the security argument in focus groups. When he raised the issue he found voters saying, 'If that means security from terrorism, I quite like the idea of shutting my borders, thanks.' Worse, when participants had decided they did not believe the proposition, they resented it even being used: 'That's actually a really gross thing to say.'

Cameron believed it was true that cooperation on terrorism was enhanced by EU membership. 'David felt so strongly that it's true that he was very reluctant to leave it alone,' says Cooper of his February super focus group. During the lunch break he phoned Ameet Gill and said, 'They're just not buying this. Can you explain to me why David said he believes it so strongly?' In the afternoon he repeated Cameron's argument that the EU helped countries share data quickly and get access to terrorist watchlists. The voters simply did not believe him. A typical response was, 'What do you think, they're going to take our password away from a secret database after we left the EU? Of course they're not.'

By mid-May it was clear the security argument was not working. On the upside for Stronger In, they seemed to be close to total victory on the economic case for staying.

THE ECONOMY, STUPID

Somewhere in Downing Street two phones pinged at the same time. One of them belonged to Ameet Gill, the director of strategy and master of the campaign news grid. Opening the group messaging service WhatsApp, to his surprise he saw a picture of a scantily clad woman in a bikini staring back at him. The image was labelled 'the Albanian model'. Gill laughed. Giles Kenningham, one of Cameron's spin doctors, received the same picture. The message was from Paul Stephenson, the director of communications at Vote Leave, and it was a jokey admission of defeat.

The one thing worse than being insulted in politics was being ridiculed, and as soon as David Cameron returned from Brussels he and his team began a process of trying to mock the Leave campaign for refusing to tell voters what 'Out' would look like. In a political version of the seaside arcade game Whac-A-Mole, Stronger In stalked the Brexiteers from one country to another, bashing each suggestion about which country's trade relationship with the European Union Britain's would most closely resemble after Brexit. First there was Norway, which was a member of the single market without being a member of the EU. That European Economic Area (EEA) status involved complying with EU rules without being able to help set them, paying into the EU budget and accepting the free movement of people. Then there was Switzerland, which was a member of the European Free Trade Area (EFTA) and had signed a series of bilateral treaties with the EU – but that would mean negotiating more than a hundred separate agreements with the EU for different goods and services. Others talked about the 'WTO model', where common tariffs agreed by the World Trade Organisation would be imposed on traded goods like food.

Stronger In's researchers went to town, digging out comments by a range of Eurosceptics from Boris Johnson to Nigel Farage. On 28 February, the weekend after Cameron's deal, they published a pamphlet detailing how those backing Brexit had proposed an alphabet soup of twenty-five countries the UK could emulate, all the way down to the tiny Pacific island of Vanuatu. 'They have had more positions than the *Kama Sutra*,' said a senior government source.

Two weeks later, Boris Johnson seemed to have found the answer. On 11 March he used a speech in Dartford to say that Britain 'can strike a deal, as the Canadians have done, based on trade and getting rid of tariffs'. Canada's free-trade deal with the EU was due to sweep away 97 per cent of trade tariffs. However, it took five years to negotiate, from 2009 to 2014, and it still had not come into effect two years later, when Johnson hailed it as a blueprint for Britain. David Cameron responded directly, tweeting the same day that the plan would 'mean seven or more years of uncertainty'. Four days later Johnson was offering another option, 'associate membership' of the European Union, like Turkey, which is in a customs union with the EU. On the same day the prime minister used a speech in Felixstowe marking one hundred days until the referendum, to go on the attack: 'Those people who want us to leave cannot tell us what alternative they would put in place. To start with they said "We are not going to tell you what the alternative would be," then they said they wanted full access to the single market ... Then they said they want a Canada-style free-trade deal ... Today, the leaders of the Leave campaign are saying they don't really want a Canada deal at all. They are literally making it up as they go along.' In the great game of Brexit trade Whac-A-Mole, Canada got a firm bonk on the head.

This slow unravelling was infuriating to Dominic Cummings, who had decreed from the beginning that Vote Leave should never be pinned down to one trade model, because no two Eurosceptics could agree on the issue, and the public did not understand it. He had told Vote Leave staff: 'No one knows what the single market is. The MPs don't know what the single market is! No one knows! No one will know what it is by the end of this campaign. Period.'

The week Barack Obama came to town, Michael Gove was supposed to draw a line under this bruising opening period for Vote Leave. In what was billed as the definitive speech of the 'Out' campaign so far, he gave a passionate oration claiming Brexit would trigger a 'democratic liberation of a whole continent'. He then veered into the trade issue, and created a hostage to fortune that would dog the campaign for weeks: 'There is a free-trade zone stretching from Iceland to Turkey that all European nations have access to, regardless of whether they are in or out of the euro or EU. After we vote to leave we will remain in the zone. The suggestion that Bosnia, Serbia, Albania and Ukraine would remain part of this free-trade area – and Britain would be on the outside with just Belarus – is as credible as Jean-Claude Juncker joining Ukip.'

Gove's suggestion that Britain should emulate Albania, a small, impoverished country, caused great excitement at Stronger In, where Craig Oliver began texting and calling journalists in an attempt to turn Gove's argument into a gaffe. 'They hoisted the white flag on the economy,' he said. Critics pointed out that although countries such as Albania enjoyed liberalised trade with the EU in goods, services, which are a key part of the UK economy, were excluded. 'The Albanian model' quickly became a byword for Leave confusion on the economy, reaching its apogee when Edi Rama, the Albanian prime minister himself, weighed in to declare that Gove's suggestion was 'a bit weird'. He said, 'The Albanian–EU relationship is not a model for Britain to emulate.'[1]

On 28 April George Osborne gave a speech at the annual Westminster Correspondents' Dinner in the House of Commons, a black-tie bash that is the Lilliputian cousin of the White House Correspondents' Dinner in Washington. It came just after media reports that John Whittingdale, the Brexit-backing culture secretary, had unknowingly been in a relationship with a dominatrix sex worker from Eastern Europe. Osborne could not resist saying of the evening's event, 'Putting together the seating plan must have been a real nightmare. The referendum means we're all arguing amongst ourselves. The Canadian model. The Albanian model. The Ukrainian model. And that's just John Whittingdale's table.' Whittingdale had the good grace to laugh. The more serious aspect of the joke was that Vote Leave's position was a laughing stock. It was in this context that Paul Stephenson sent his WhatsApp message.

On 8 May, Craig Oliver declared victory in the great Brexit trade debate. Gove, in an interview with the BBC's Andrew Marr, declared explicitly, 'We should be out of the single market.' This position had been implicit in his Albanian comments, but for Stronger In, having Vote Leave's chairman state clearly that he did not want to be part of the free-trade area of five hundred million people in which the UK did more than

40 per cent of its business was the first goal of their economic strategy. Oliver texted journalists: 'Big moment – Gove says out of single market. Leave will never hear the end of it.' George Osborne, on Robert Peston's ITV show immediately afterwards, said that leaving 'the largest free-trade area in the world … would be catastrophic for people's jobs and their incomes and their livelihoods'.

If Remain had won the referendum, there are many who believe this would have been the clincher. 'I think that was a really, really decisive moment,' Will Straw said later. The reasons why it was significant, though, were not those originally thought. At the time it looked in Westminster as if Remain had successfully kicked Leave from position to position until they got what they wanted. The game of Whac-A-Mole was over, and Vote Leave looked defensive and indecisive – Stronger In were also well under way with the second part of their economic strategy: raising the sense of economic risk around leaving.

George Osborne was totally open about his plan: it was to follow exactly the same playbook during the EU referendum that had led to victory in the Scottish referendum and given the Conservatives their surprise majority in the general election the year before. The first leg of the strategy was to publish reports by the Treasury on the risks of leaving the EU. Before the Scottish referendum Osborne had joined forces with Labour and the Liberal Democrats to make clear that an independent Scotland would not be entitled to join a currency union with the rest of the UK if it voted to quit the Union, a move which put the SNP on the spot about whether they would keep the pound. Government estimates of the black hole in Nationalist finances if the oil price fell had also hurt the SNP. This time Osborne planned two major documents, one on the short-term implications of leaving the EU and another on the long-term risks.

'George was using the formula of the Scottish referendum, where the production of Treasury documents had really anchored the No to Independence campaign,' a source familiar with the chancellor's thinking says. 'He had driven those documents internally and gone up to Scotland a couple of times to make speeches. That was the model. After the general election, once it was clear the referendum was going to happen in the next couple of years, the Treasury diverted civil servants and resources to the European section of the international division.

Some of the brightest Treasury civil servants were then put on producing and preparing the documents.'

The second strand was to deploy third-party endorsements to bolster Osborne's case about the dangers of Brexit. Having been at the top table of international finance events for six years, the chancellor was well connected with the key players. At a G20 finance ministers' meeting in China on 27 February, a week after the deal, he succeeded in having 'the shock of a potential UK exit from the European Union' inserted into the communiqué as one of the main risks to the world economy in 2016. Osborne had been the first Western leader to propose Christine Lagarde as head of the International Monetary Fund (IMF) before she took the job in 2011. Now she repaid the favour. On 12 April the IMF listed Brexit as a key risk in its latest World Economic Outlook, which downgraded its growth forecasts for Britain. Maurice Obstfeld, the IMF's chief economist, said 'a Brexit could do severe regional and global damage'.

David Cameron was quick to tweet, 'The IMF is right – leaving the EU would pose major risks for the UK economy.' Osborne called it the 'clearest independent warning of the taste of bad things to come'. Doubtless they both believe this, but Vote Leave were quick to seize on this apparent enthusiasm for bad news as evidence that the prime minister and the chancellor were intent on 'talking down Britain', a theme that would cut through with voters.

On 18 April, Osborne produced his first document. Judging the short-term impact of Brexit the more politically effective of the two papers, he decided to save that for closer to the referendum. Instead, he released the paper detailing the long-term economic risks. The two-hundred-page document's most eye-catching statistic was that Britain would be poorer to the tune of £4,300 per household by 2030 if the public chose to leave the EU. The Treasury's main calculation was that if Britain managed to negotiate a trade deal like Canada's, GDP – the measure of total economic output – would be 6.2 per cent lower by 2030 than it would otherwise have been. That would leave a £36 billion-a-year black hole in the public finances, necessitating cuts to the public services or adding 8p to the basic rate of income tax. If Britain was left with a WTO-style trade deal with tariffs, the shortfall would be £45 billion by 2030, or 10p on the basic tax rate. Osborne said leaving the EU would be 'the most extraordinary self-inflicted wound', which would leave Britain 'permanently poorer', and claimed Gove and Johnson were 'economically illiterate' to suggest the UK could retain 'all the benefits' of EU membership with 'none of the costs'.

Osborne's two papers were highly detailed, and were endorsed as serious pieces of work by independent observers like the Institute for Fiscal Studies and the LSE. The leading role in putting them together belonged to Sir Dave Ramsden, the Treasury's chief economic adviser, who had devised the five economic tests used by Gordon Brown's Treasury which determined that the Blair government would not join the single currency. 'Dave Ramsden was very important and lent credibility to the whole thing,' says a Treasury source. 'People give Ed Balls credit for keeping us out of the euro – it was actually Dave Ramsden.'

But the headline figure of £4,300 per household was problematic. Since it had been arrived at by dividing the total loss of GDP by the number of households, it in no way described what would happen to actual family incomes. The sum was also based on the number of households in 2015, not how many the Treasury expected there to be in 2030. This was for a very good reason: as the Brexiteers were quick to brief to the Eurosceptic papers, the number of households in 2030 was projected to grow from twenty-seven million in 2015 to more than thirty-one million, much of it fuelled by immigration.

The following morning Stronger In tried to keep the economy theme ticking over with a letter from two hundred entrepreneurs, published in the *Financial Times*, expressing the fear that a vote to leave would 'undermine the ability of Britain's entrepreneurs to start-up, innovate and grow'. The signatories included the government's technology adviser Martha Lane Fox, fashion designer Anya Hindmarch, and Jacqueline Gold of underwear retailer Ann Summers.

But by then the backlash to the Osborne document was drowning out everything else. The papers led on the three million new immigrants. Michael Gove accused Cameron and Osborne of treating voters like 'children capable of being frightened into obedience by conjuring up new bogeymen.' The Tory MP Andrew Percy said 'Project Fear' had 'turned into Project Utter Crap'. Peter Bone branded it 'George's dodgy dossier'.

Nevertheless, coming three days before Barack Obama's visit, the first Treasury paper, which got wall-to-wall broadcast coverage, helped to give Stronger In their most dominant week of the entire campaign. Will Straw saw the documents as important headline-generators: 'I think we should have done more to join the dots on why there were risks of leaving, but if you wanted to get coverage then numbers were the most compelling way to do that. We absolutely dominated both broadcast and the papers the following day with that announcement.'

Eurosceptic MPs certainly thought they were losing. Paul Stephenson said later, 'That week most of the MPs were meeting, saying, "We need to hire someone else, it's a disaster."' On Wednesday that week the BBC's Andrew Neil asked Labour Leave's Kate Hoey if she could 'name any reputable independent study that shows us better off if we leave?' She replied, 'Not better off as such.' At the same time a Tory close to Boris Johnson revealed, 'He thinks they're getting murdered on the economy.'

Even Vote Leave's supporters thought they were losing on the economy. Eight economists, headed by Professor Patrick Minford, an ally of Margaret Thatcher, decided to launch their own Brexit campaign. Minford said the Treasury's claims were 'dishonest', and claimed that Brexit would boost GDP by 4 per cent a year: 'The campaign to leave is doing well politically, but I think that the economic argument that has been put by the other side, if it is not rebutted, will cause them to lose because people are concerned by the economics.'

On the back foot over the economy, Vote Leave was also finding it more difficult than expected to raise cash, with potential donors coming under huge pressure from allies of Cameron not to give money. One Brexit donor even claimed that month that he had been the subject of a witch-hunt by HM Revenue and Customs: 'I have had twenty-five years of unquestioned tax returns, and just as I became a higher-profile figure I've had the nastiest, most aggressive tax investigation my accountant has ever seen. I don't think that's a coincidence.'

At Vote Leave HQ they tried to keep their cool. Paul Stephenson, who had spent much of January setting up a regional business network with at least two business voices in every region, said, 'They whooped us on the national stage. But when you've got every acronym under the sun and every economist backing you that's easy. But we didn't need to win on the economy, we needed to neutralise the economy.'

The other key third-party advocate, from Osborne's point of view, was Mark Carney, the governor of the Bank of England. Andrew Cooper's focus groups found that the Canadian was one of the three most trusted voices on the economy: 'When you ask, "Who would you believe?" the three answers were always Martin Lewis, the Money Saving Expert guy, Mark Carney and Richard Branson,' said Cooper. On 19 April, the day after the first Treasury document was published, Carney appeared in front of a House of Lords Select Committee and warned that Brexit could result in lower growth, higher inflation, and cause the City of London to lose its place as one of the world's 'pre-eminent' financial centres.

On 12 May Carney gave a press conference to discuss the Bank's regular monthly inflation report. In it he warned that the consequences of a Brexit vote 'could possibly include a technical recession' – defined as two consecutive quarters of shrinking GDP. He also predicted higher unemployment and high inflation. The IMF stepped up to provide a one–two punch. The following day Christine Lagarde, who was in London to present the IMF's annual health check on the UK economy, endorsed Carney's warning: 'We have looked at all the scenarios. We have done our homework and we haven't found anything positive to say about a Brexit vote,' she said.

But some in the Remain campaign were concerned about these interventions. 'It was just the elites talking to elites, saying it's in your best interest to do this, and people weren't listening,' said Phil Wilson, the Labour MP who chaired the Labour In for Britain parliamentary group. 'Many voters thought, "What's the IMF? What's that got to do with my life? What's the OECD? What's that got to do with me?" It wasn't something that was real for them in their communities.'[2]

Some Labour staff at Cannon Street believed the switch from the game of trade Whac-A-Mole to ramming home a noisy assessment of economic risk in which Osborne took the lead was proof that the Tories did not know how to appeal to Labour voters. For the Conservative target voter warnings about the state of the economy were normally paramount in confirming voting intention, but they had far less of an effect on Labour voters.

'The campaign set a trap for the Leave campaign early on by creating a dividing line on access to the single market,' a Labour campaign source said. 'They were bounced into all these different models. All of our focus groups suggest people were worried about them not having an answer. This approach was dropped by Ameet, Craig and Stephen, who took the campaign onto an economic-risk message during the short campaign. When we started just saying "The economy will be fucked," it showed what a profound misunderstanding they had of Labour motives. Across the north-east and the north-west people already felt like the economy was pretty fucked and not working for them. It was just a Tory voter strategy. That was a massive mistake.' Those who had not worked on a Crosby-style campaign before also found the relentless focus hard to deal with: 'It was such a boring campaign to work on, because we just did the same story in the short campaign day in and day out.'

The failure to understand Labour voters was a factor in one of Osborne's least successful interventions. On 21 May the chancellor, in Japan for a meeting of G7 finance ministers, trailed the headlines of his second Treasury document on the short-term risks of leaving the EU. The big announcement was on house prices. A Brexit vote would cause an 'immediate economic shock' said the chancellor, unveiling analysis showing that two years after a vote to leave, house prices could be between 10 per cent and 18 per cent lower than after a Remain vote.

Osborne's announcement from halfway around the world infuriated Ryan Coetzee and Will Straw, who believed the chancellor's pitch, while perfectly tailored to the aspirational Tories, was not a suitable message for Stronger In's less-affluent target voters. 'Will and I said, "You're confusing the Tory market with our market,"' Coetzee recalled. 'Half of our voters think that's a very good idea. And then Osborne went to Japan and said it anyway.' Watching at home, Coetzee said to Straw, 'What the fuck was that?'

When Osborne said he was planning to make the argument again, Coetzee said, 'That just cannot happen.' The problem, swiftly revealed in focus groups, was that young people – a key part of Remain's voter base – wanted to see house prices fall, because they could not afford to get on the housing ladder. 'The Tories don't usually have to worry about eighteen-to-twenty-fours, but we did,' says Coetzee. The BBC also found that Osborne's house-price announcement had backfired. Jonathan Munro, the Corporation's head of news-gathering, said, 'What our audiences told us in feedback, in phone-in programmes and online, was, "House prices are going to fall? Great! I can afford a house, or my kid can afford a house." They took it in a completely different way from the way that it was meant as it was delivered by the chancellor.'

Downing Street's relentless focus on economic risk led to clashes over whether Stronger In should make more nuanced or more positive arguments. Early on in the campaign Peter Mandelson sent emails to the Number 10 team warning that voters were feeling bulldozed by Cameron and Osborne. He said voters would not be 'carpet bombed into voting remain'. Mandelson was careful not to criticise Osborne, since he agreed with his basic strategy, respected his thoroughness and wanted to make him an ally. But in an email to senior campaign staff on 20 May he warned, 'At the moment we are making claims about risk/leap in the dark without backing it up sufficiently, explaining why and using the firepower we have at our disposal. Leaving the EU will be like taking a wrecking ball to our economy that will get worse with time. We have to support our argument in a graphic, granular way through the words of major brand-named manufacturing employers. If we fail to do this, we will lose the argument.' It is a 'great regret' to Mandelson that he failed to engage Osborne with his argument.

Throughout the campaign, Straw and the others were also under pressure from Roland Rudd to make a more positive case for the EU. Rudd says, 'We needed a really good, positive agenda about how Europe was really good for Britain, why we shared similar values and why we had to be for our own, why it was good for Britain to be at the heart of Europe, and we never sold that as a package at any stage really during the campaign.'

The issue came to a head on the evening of Wednesday, 20 April, when Cameron gave a speech to a Stronger In fundraising dinner at the Berkeley Hotel in London. The event raked in around £500,000 from just 120 guests – one bidder paid £14,000 for Mandelson and Alastair Campbell to come to his home for a 'dinner with the kings of spin'. The promotional material even promised, 'If you find them on a good day, Alastair may even act out scenes from *The Thick of It*, while Peter may try to perform scenes from *Yes, Minister*.' Chris Hope, the *Telegraph*'s chief mischief-maker, got himself invited. But when Craig Oliver saw the table plan he tried to have Hope banned. The journalist had to agree the evening was off the record. That night Cameron gave what Rudd thought 'the most positive speech on Europe I had ever heard': 'It really was a rallying call, and that was the first time I thought, "Wow, I've got Cameron completely wrong. His real view of Europe is exactly like mine."' When Hope asked if he could write up the speech, Craig Oliver said, 'No, absolutely not.' 'That was a mistake,' Rudd said later. 'It was a great speech.'

There were Tories, too, who wanted to run a more positive Remain campaign. Alistair Burt said he was worried that 'the case for Europe was not being made'. Neil Carmichael, another of the endangered Tory Europhile species, gave up waiting to be asked to help with the campaign and set off around the country on his own, inviting himself to universities. His adviser Lewis Robinson says, 'We understood that if you're going to ask people to support this proposition, you've actually got to go and sell the message in a relatively positive way. Everyone was waiting, saying, "Once the prime minister weighs in, it's all going to be OK, because everyone loves the prime minister." He was only one guy at the end of the day.'

The main Tory campaign organisation, Conservatives In, run by Charlotte Vere and Nick Herbert, made a virtue of being a Eurosceptic group that was a pragmatic rather than enthusiastic supporter of EU membership. They forged the Tory MPs into a campaign unit but kept a low media profile. Watching from outside, Ryan Coetzee believed that for such a group to make a positive case was difficult after three decades of relentless Euroscepticism from the Tory hierarchy: 'The Conservative establishment – with the exception of people like Ken Clarke and Damian Green – have been slagging off the EU year in year out. It's like the opposite of rolling a pitch. It's like scuffing up the pitch before the game.'

Nigel Farage had spotted Cameron and Osborne wheeling out their favourite playbook: 'We'd seen a Scottish referendum fought on negativity. We'd seen a general election fought wholly on negativity. This was the third election in a row we'd seen fought on negativity. There was not a single good reason anyone gave to stay in the EU. There was nothing. We got criticised for some of the areas we touched on, but actually we were saying "Britain's going to be stronger, safer, better, more global." It was a much more uplifting message.'

Concerns about the failure to deliver a positive message were also raised at three 'Remain cabinets' chaired by Cameron for the ministers supporting Stronger In. At the third meeting in the Pillared Room on the first floor of 10 Downing Street, Nicky Morgan, the education secretary, questioned Cameron's approach. 'Why are we running such a negative campaign?' she asked. 'We seem to be appealing to our own Eurosceptic supporters, not appealing to people in the centre, who are there to be persuaded.' Morgan was backed up by Anna Soubry and Justine Greening, who wanted more focus on translating the economic warnings into people's everyday lives. 'The PM wasn't having any of it,' says one of those present. 'During the whole Remain campaign we never said what we were for. It was always what doom and gloom is going to happen, not "This is what the EU does for us."'

It is telling that it is female cabinet ministers who were so vocal. They believed a more positive campaign might appeal to women voters. At one of the Remain cabinets Andrew Cooper gave a presentation pointing out that a typical Leave voter believed 'gender equality has gone too far'. Morgan and Amber Rudd, the energy secretary, exchanged looks. Rudd would play a prominent part in the TV debates, but Morgan's campaign project to appeal directly to women had been sidelined. The education secretary had asked other female ministers to contribute essays to a booklet on the importance of the EU, under the title 'Women for Remain'. Now she wanted a slot in the campaign grid to promote it and get media coverage. A source close to Morgan says, 'We just couldn't get it gridded. We had twenty different female ministers ready to do a photocall and hit the television studios, but we could not get a slot.' The project got off the ground in April, and the booklet was finally launched on 16 June, three hours before Jo Cox was murdered. It disappeared without trace.

Despite these internal disagreements, by the final week in May, Stronger In believed they had won the economic argument hands down. They had shown that the Brexiteers wanted to quit the single market. They had gained the support of nearly every major international economic watchdog. They had injected a memorable figure about the scale of economic risk into the political bloodstream. They had convinced the media that they were trouncing Vote Leave on the economy. The plan mapped out by Osborne and Cameron may have been boring, but it was working. Ever since he had drawn up the message bible in November, Ryan Coetzee had been working on the basis 'that if the merits of the argument are entirely on your side, that if every credible institution known to humankind will back you up, that if the bulk of economists and business leaders, nationally and internationally, will back you up, then the average voter out there will go "I should probably listen to this," right?'

Wrong.

On 25 May, Coetzee presented evidence from two focus groups that, in fact, Stronger In's messages were failing to cut through at all. The following day, Cooper's tracking poll put Remain behind for the first time. They were not winning on the economy at all.

In an email sent to senior campaign staff at fifteen minutes past midnight on 25 May, Coetzee summed up the crisis facing the campaign:

'Voters are very sceptical about our warnings on the economy. They don't trust these reports. They don't trust the numbers. They don't trust the Treasury. And many don't like the messengers (though obviously Tories like them more). Therefore the upshot of all of our comms around these warnings is to reinforce uncertainty, not persuade people that leaving would be bad ... So we need to understand that we haven't actually "won the argument" on the economy. What we have succeeded in doing is reinforce risk. They are not the same thing.'

Coetzee explained that the reason they had not won the argument 'outside Westminster is because we have [not] managed to explain to people WHY the economy would be hit'. He said the voters he was meeting in focus groups 'literally have no idea why our claims are true. They have zero grasp of the economy.' Among a male group of voters in Ipswich, he said, 'not a single person thought jobs would be lost if we left'. He concluded: 'We must not assume (as we do far too often) that people share our assumptions ... It is obvious to us that action X causes reaction Y. It is not at all obvious to them ... They make no connection between lower growth and less money for public services. You actually have to say, "If the economy slows down it means businesses and people make less money, and less money means less tax revenue for the government, which means less money for the NHS." We need to join the dots for people much, much more than we do ... We have generated a lot of smoke and therefore kept them worrying about the prospect of fire without actually convincing them that there is in fact a fire.'

In a follow-up email at 9.10 a.m. he said, 'In every group now, people immediately and spontaneously bring up "scare mongering".' He also expressed concerns that the original campaign message was being drowned out: 'I think we have wandered off half of our core message. Our interventions have been heavily focused on risk – IMF, Carney, Treasury, prices, etc. – but we have not been making the "Stronger, safer and better off" part of the argument that precedes the risk warning. Our approach was always meant to be benefits plus risk. We've become too risk heavy and have lost benefits. We need to rebalance.'

The first problem Coetzee's work identified was that jubilation at Gove ditching the single market – believed to be Stronger In's great early success – was entirely misplaced because voters had no idea what it meant: 'People had absolutely no idea what the EU was or how it worked at all, to a point that it beggars belief. No one had ever heard of the single market or knew about what it did. Politicians, journalists and the campaign would say "Leaving the single market's bad." Try saying that to some in-play person in Doncaster, they'll have literally no idea what you're on about. *Literally* no idea.' It was not until David Cameron's second television debate appearance on *Question Time* towards the end of the campaign that the prime minister comprehensively explained in simple terms the way a hit to the economy would mean less money for the NHS and other public services.

The second problem was that voters did not believe anything they were told by the Treasury, including the £4,300 per household figure. Will Straw explains, 'Most people thought there was a cost from being in the EU, so it left people a bit incredulous. They thought there would be a saving from leaving.' The polling and focus groups showed the number had a 'spurious specificity' about it. Andrew Cooper says, 'The £4,300 a year sounded much too high to be believable. It sounded too specific to be believable.' Straw says, 'If you're earning £16,000, then it just feels like an enormous amount of money.' Coetzee 'banned' the use of the £4,300 figure. 'We're never using that term again,' he said.

James McGrory, who learned what it was like dealing with a hostile press while working for Nick Clegg, believed the problem was that the Conservative papers, which were willing to accept Osborne's questionable calculations during a general election campaign, now chose instead to unpick them: 'You cannot run the kind of campaign that focuses on economic risk and is fronted by Conservatives unless you have the echo chamber of the right-wing press. Having tried it out, I actually think it is impossible. Not only do they not echo you, they actively seek to undermine you.'

The worst problem with the figure was that by making bold claims about the future, the campaign undermined one of its strongest accusations against the Brexiteers: that a vote to leave was a vote for uncertainty. And yet here was the Treasury saying it knew what the specific costs would be.

After the referendum, George Osborne still believed the exercise of publishing the documents had been legitimate, telling friends the forecasts in the papers would 'stand the test of time' because post-Brexit calculations by the IMF, the World Bank and commercial banks after the vote drew similar conclusions. He acknowledged privately that putting such emphasis on one number 'clearly didn't work as well as it should have done', but he believed the problem was not with the number itself, but with the campaign. 'It was more a symptom than a cause,' a source close to Osborne said. The problem was that these dry documents did not speak to voters. As Alan Johnson, head of the Labour In campaign, put it, 'We thought jobs and the economy were going to be dominant, and that would appeal to the head. What we couldn't find was an appeal to the heart.'[3]

The third problem, linked to the second, was that the economic-risk strategy depended on Osborne and Cameron delivering and winning the argument. Both had credibility problems – Cameron following the deal, the tax affair and the World War III speech, and Osborne since the budget débâcle. In Peter Mandelson's phrase, both 'lost altitude' during the campaign. On the same day Coetzee sent his emails, YouGov found the number of voters who trusted Cameron on Europe was down to 18 per cent, compared with 31 per cent for Boris Johnson. Coetzee saw the same trust problem for Cameron that had dogged Nick Clegg. As he told campaign colleagues, 'Our message was very good with the Lib Dems, but the problem is no one fucking believed us. It's the same with this. No one fucking believes us.'

The fourth issue was the belief that the Tory fear strategy – successful in 2014 and 2015 – would work again. That meant there was huge resistance to changing it in the final month of the campaign. When Coetzee's emails dropped on the morning of 25 May, Will Straw replied, 'I think this is a timely warning against premature jubilation.' But the senior Tories insisted they stick to the plan of hammering economic risk. Andrew Cooper wrote, 'People always complain about negative campaigning, but we know that when done consistently and effectively it works.' Ameet Gill agreed: 'Before we recalibrate, are any of the fundamentals changing? I do worry we won't get cut through b/cast stories if we don't lead on risk.' When Craig Oliver became full-time communications director of the campaign two days later, on Friday, 27 May, he was insistent that all Stronger In needed was greater clarity and persistence, telling staff, 'We shouldn't be deflected.' A long-standing aide to Cameron says, 'Craig was adamant throughout that we stick to the plan. If he tries to rewrite history he is a liar.'

The final problem was that even if Stronger In had tried to change course, the media were losing interest in the economic arguments. At the end of May they began focusing heavily on immigration. 'There was a view that we'd won the economic argument, and immigration was a more interesting topic,' says Will Straw.

There was also a more interesting number than £4,300.

From the very first video with which they launched their campaign in October to polling day, Vote Leave stuck to their claim that Britain sent £350 million a week to Brussels, and that the money would be better spent at home. Dominic Cummings had the number emblazoned on the campaign bus. The claim was appended to nearly every email the campaign sent. And it was parroted by voters at every turn. It became a focus of claims that Vote Leave were fighting their campaign on lies. But to Cummings it was the key to undermining Osborne's economic-risk onslaught. He summed up Remain's fatal fallacy to colleagues: 'They never saw £350 million as the economy.'

Essentially there are three figures for Britain's contribution to the EU budget: £19 billion is the gross figure, provided by the Office for National Statistics; £15 billion is the gross figure minus Britain's rebate, first negotiated by Margaret Thatcher; £11 billion is the net figure, which also takes into account money spent in Britain by the European Commission, including regional funds and farming subsidies. Rob Oxley, through his work at Business for Britain, tended to use the £15 billion figure – £250 million a week – but Cummings wanted to use the gross figure. Doing so meant that Vote Leave could make an important point about the money. 'The Remain side tried to claim that money that we got back was somehow EU money, when in fact it was British taxpayers' money,' says Oxley. The weakness in Vote Leave's argument was that the rebate money never left the country, so it was incorrect to say that the UK "sends" £350 million a week to Brussels. The counter-argument was that when a worker talked about their pay packet, they would use the gross figure, not their income net of tax.' The sum had a basis in reality and in the official figures, but Andrew Dilnot, chairman of the UK Statistics Authority, twice said he was disappointed that Vote Leave stuck to the figure, as it was 'misleading and undermines trust in official statistics'.

Alastair Campbell, who advised Stronger In, gained a reputation for playing political hardball when he worked as Tony Blair's spin doctor, but he believes the use of the figure went beyond anything he ever authorised: 'The £350 million a week was actually a straightforward lie.

I can't remember campaigns where you mount the campaign based on a lie, and then when it's exposed, you just keep going, as Johnson and co. did.'

Cummings did not mind one bit about the controversy the figure generated. Every time there was a row about the size of the cost to taxpayers of EU membership, it simply reinforced in voters' minds that there was a high cost. 'It was a row we wanted to have,' says Oxley. '"It's a row we wanted to have" sums up our campaign.' Henry de Zoete's focus groups proved that the number cut through to ordinary voters. Bernard Jenkin added, 'It was deliberately controversial.'

Cummings repeatedly impressed upon Vote Leave staff what he had learned from the North-East Says No campaign and the original battle against the euro: 'You win campaigns like this through message discipline and consistency.' When the number came under attack and jittery MPs phoned him, Cummings told them, 'Stick to your guns.' Daniel Hannan saw the same determination as Matthew Elliott had shown when peddling a cost argument to win the NOtoAV campaign: 'They had the character and the presence of mind to say, "We know what's working,"' says Hannan. 'And it did work.'

Oxley believes Stronger In were no saints themselves: 'Some of their press releases suggested that every bit of trade which the UK did with the rest of the world was down to EU membership. Both campaigns had some pretty tenuous numbers. The difference was that we used our tenuous numbers more effectively than they did.' Or as Alan Johnson put it, 'I felt we had the lyrics, but they had the best tunes.'

Michael Gove was surprised that Cameron and Osborne did not make more of their own headline-grabbing figure, and had then abandoned it. In exchanges with other ministers, Gove teased them about the Conservative Party's own efforts in previous campaigns, arguing that the £350 million figure was more honest and reliable than the 1992 general election claims that Labour was plotting a 'tax bombshell'. 'Having spoken to people in Number 10, they knew it was no more rubbish than some of the figures on which they've won campaigns and elections,' a Gove ally said.

While Remain campaigners were congratulating themselves on winning the economic argument, and debating the difficulty of campaigning against a bunch of liars in an environment of 'post-truth politics', Cummings was getting on with telling voters the EU was wasting their money. Paul Stephenson said, 'If you go to the pub now and talk to someone about the EU, what they will tell you is it costs three hundred million quid a week, and yes, we get some of it back, but it all goes on roads in Greece. To normal people that is the economy.' One of Cameron's aides admitted after the referendum, 'They won on the economic argument; it was just a different economic argument to the one we thought we were having.'

At the start of the campaign George Osborne knew what he wanted to achieve, and he had followed the plan to the letter. 'We played an absolutely textbook campaign,' a pro-Osborne source says. 'You secure economic advantage so people think the economic risks lie with the other side. You run a disciplined campaign with dossiers, leaflets and well-crafted soundbites. Everyone's on-message, no one screws up, you pull apart the other side's figures. That is how all my adult life you've won general elections. Not just Tony Blair and Bill Clinton, but also John Major, and David Cameron a year ago.'

This time it did not work.

Having been neutralised on their strongest suit, if the Remain campaign was to win they would need to neutralise their opponents' biggest asset, Boris Johnson, without destroying the Conservative Party.

BLUE ON BLUE

Those who were there compare it to the Christmas truce of 1914, when British Tommies and their German counterparts climbed out of their trenches and played football together in no man's land before returning to their positions. It was 25 May, a month before the referendum, and relations at the top of the Conservative Party had been shredded. David Cameron was away, and George Osborne was due to take Prime Minister's Questions in the Commons. The chancellor had been on the defensive since the budget and Iain Duncan Smith's resignation. A good performance would be an opportunity to stabilise his position, to get back in the leadership game. Osborne knew now that there was a chance Remain might lose the referendum. The man perhaps most responsible for that situation was Michael Gove. But in Osborne's hour of need it was Gove he called on to help with his PMQ prep.

Gove had been coming to the Wednesday-morning sessions off and on even after he had, in the eyes of many around Cameron, betrayed the prime minister. He attended six or seven sessions after the deal, but his appearances had tailed off as the campaign got uglier. 'Michael is terrible at interpersonal conflict. Much, much worse than the PM,' a friendly minister said. 'It was completely surreal,' says a Number 10 aide. 'You'd see David and Michael joking about how to have a go at Jeremy Corbyn, and inside the PM was very hurt by Michael's disloyalty.' But Gove returned for Osborne. Re-embracing his role as the resident court jester he suggested some jokes, polished some others. What everyone remembers is his advice on how best to take on the Brexiteers.

A minister close to both Osborne and Gove says, 'He provided answers to tricky questions from Eurosceptic backbenchers. He would deliberately say with a *faux* accent, "Well, the European Union safeguards our security. Access to the market gives us our prosperity."' A Downing Street aide compared Gove at these sessions to the guest expert on the television quiz show *Countdown* who chips in with an amusing contribution from time to time: 'Michael would offer a couple of gags and then be left with his pen and his paper. Then halfway through, someone will say, "Michael what have you got?" It was cordial but ever so slightly awkward.'

Osborne survived a withering onslaught from his opposite number Angela Eagle. But the chancellor's efforts to keep the ruling clique of the Conservative Party, the Notting Hill set, together were less successful. The referendum was a Conservative tragicomedy to match the Blair–Brown years, albeit one played out with the forced gentility of a social psychodrama like *Abigail's Party* rather than the boiling rage of an *EastEnders* Christmas special. Throughout, Cameron and particularly Osborne sought to keep up appearances. 'George was trying to save the relationship in order to rebuild the party afterwards,' says a mutual friend. 'Underneath, Gove and Johnson's decision to contest the referendum and threaten the future of Cameron's government stirred great passions. There are people in David Cameron's team who will never speak to Michael Gove again. There are others, like George Osborne, Oliver Dowden and Ameet Gill, who think what is done is done, and will attempt to keep friendships intact.'

What is not in doubt is that, in their prosecution of the referendum, Tory high command placed the preservation of some semblance of Conservative Party unity after polling day ahead of doing everything possible to win the vote. Believing they would win, Cameron and Osborne's worst fear was so-called 'blue-on-blue' attacks, a military phrase for friendly-fire incidents in wartime that happily gels with the Conservative Party colours. For all their disappointment and anger with the leading Brexiteers, Cameron and Osborne refused to attack Gove and Johnson head-on throughout the campaign, and ordered Stronger In to handle both of the leading Brexiteers with kid gloves.

Cameron maintained a back channel to Johnson throughout the campaign, and made soothing overtures about his future in the cabinet. This created tensions within the Remain campaign, with Labour and Liberal Democrat officials believing they were forced to fight with one hand tied behind their backs. When Cameron and Osborne did finally allow the cabinet and party grandees to lay into Johnson, it was too late.

He had already established his credentials as the most trusted and most popular political voice of the campaign.

Cameron's wariness about sanctioning blue-on-blue attacks was conditioned by the response to his own statement in the Commons on the Monday after the deal was done. He issued instructions to ministers and his own staff in Number 10 – some of whom would have happily punched Gove and Johnson – that there was to be 'no slagging off of Boris'. Yet Cameron himself was personally seething, at Gove's lack of loyalty, and at what he saw as Johnson's inconsistency and ulterior motives for backing Brexit. When he got to his feet in the Commons, he could not resist a dig at Johnson's ambitions. When Gove questioned the legality of the deal, Cameron wondered aloud to a minister whether the justice secretary could keep his job after the referendum. That conversation found its way to the *Telegraph*, which revealed that Gove faced the sack. Cameron felt Gove had misled him about the prominence of his role in the campaign, but the reaction looked like overkill. 'You don't brief the papers that you're going to sack Michael if you want to encourage ministers to campaign quietly,' said a Vote Leave source. 'It made people realise they had got to win to survive.'

The reaction from Conservative backbenchers was fury. The Brexiteers felt bullied, and briefed the *Sunday Times* the following weekend that there would be a leadership challenge against Cameron even if he were to win the referendum. It was already a given amongst many that if he lost the referendum, as Ken Clarke was to put it, Cameron 'wouldn't last thirty seconds' as prime minister. Under Tory rules a leadership election would be called if 15 per cent of the parliamentary party demanded one. With more than 140 MPs committed to leaving the EU, just a third of Brexit backers could have forced a showdown. A normally mild-mannered Eurosceptic said, 'He looks like he doesn't give a shit about party unity. He's trying to pick a fight with us. It will bite him in the arse.' Andrew Bridgen, the most usual of all the usual suspects when it came to challenging Cameron, compared him to the outgoing US president: 'Obama and Cameron are both lame ducks.' There must have been something in the water that week, because Philip Hammond, the dry-as-dust foreign secretary, called Bill Cash 'a total shit' in a confrontation over an EU legal report which Hammond had not wanted Cash to make public.[1]

After that, Tory high command backed off. For the next three months there would be a period of awkward co-existence, punctuated by minor crises. When the 'Queen Backs Brexit' story appeared, Cameron resisted calls for a leak inquiry. He did not want to be in the position of having to fire Gove mid-campaign, a move that would have led to mutiny on the backbenches.

Cameron tried to keep lines of communication with Johnson's camp open. Craig Oliver briefed journalists that there would be a 'reconciliation reshuffle' after the referendum, and the prime minister spoke on several occasions during the campaign to Ben Wallace, Johnson's campaign manager. Now minister of state in the Northern Ireland Office, Wallace was an outspoken supporter of the Remain cause, which put him in a position to liaise between the two teams. They first talked when Cameron visited Northern Ireland over a weekend at the end of February, and again when the PM campaigned in Lancashire. They discovered, to their mutual amusement, that they had both been giving Johnson the same advice before he made up his mind. Cameron thanked Wallace for helping to dissuade Johnson from declaring his hand on the Friday night or the Saturday, when it would have overshadowed coverage of the deal, and made it clear that despite Johnson's backing for Brexit there would still be 'a big job' for him once the campaign was over. In an exchange that was clearly intended to get back to Johnson, the prime minister said, 'I've told Boris I'm going to make him competitive and he'll get a big job in the cabinet. It's up to him to do the job. Of course I'm a massive fan of George, but if it gets to the membership Boris will be the PM.' Cameron also made clear his irritation with Gove for failing to take a low profile, saying, 'Michael had one of his flummoxes.'

On 9 April Cameron and Johnson were both supposed to address the Conservative Spring Forum, which had the potential to be a blue-on-blue disaster unless it was properly managed. The week before, there was a clandestine meeting between Cameron and Johnson's spin doctors. Craig Oliver and Will Walden went for a drink in the bar above Roux Parliament Square. The wood-panelled room, littered with sofas and leather armchairs, was the closest thing to a gentleman's club within a stone's throw of the Houses of Parliament. Oliver and Walden agreed that the event would be a Europe-free zone, and that Johnson and Cameron would turn their guns on Labour and Jeremy Corbyn, rather than sniping at each other. Walden received reassurances that if Johnson joined the cabinet he would be allowed a properly staffed private office.

This would be the first of several occasions on which agreements made in social settings proved difficult to deliver in the heat of battle.

At the Spring Forum, while a mob of protesters outside denounced Cameron's personal tax arrangements, he and Johnson both attacked Labour – but Boris could not resist cracking a couple of Europe-related jokes and describing the 23 June referendum date as 'Independence Day'. Having previously compared himself to James Bond battling the EU, he referred to the new Bond movie, *Spectre*, as a 'very important study in what happens to an unelected bureaucratic cabal'. Johnson successfully grabbed the headlines, but Team Cameron reflected, not for the first time, that he could not be trusted. Confronted about reneging on the deal, he said, 'I made a joke, an elliptical joke.'

On 14 April Tory MPs had an awayday in Oxfordshire which proceeded more smoothly than in years past, because the usual raucous after-dinner speeches poking fun at colleagues were scrapped to avoid ill-feeling between Brexiteers and Remainers. Instead Andrew Feldman put £2,000 behind the bar, and Cameron told a joke about a farmer inviting a new neighbour to come to his house for a party where there might be dancing, drinking and 'rough sex'. When the neighbour asks what to wear, the farmer says, 'It doesn't matter, it's only going to be you and me.' Some 308 MPs turned up, a much higher number than normal. 'It was very successful,' Johnson said. 'Nobody talked about Europe.'

Cameron used the occasion to corner Wallace to complain about a viral video Vote Leave had produced that implied he was a liar about his tax arrangements, and consequently could not be trusted on Europe. They were soon joined by Johnson. Cameron said, 'Can we please cut out the personal attacks?'

Johnson agreed, 'No, no, we shouldn't do anything like that.' Cameron and Wallace then teased him about the company he was keeping.

'Are you going to see your mate George Galloway?' Cameron asked.

The following day, Johnson took a train to Manchester for a major Vote Leave rally. On the way he did an interview for the *Sunday Times* and the *Sun on Sunday*, personally attacking Cameron, Theresa May and George Osborne for failing to secure a promise in the deal with Brussels that only EU migrants with a job could automatically come to the UK. 'We were just told to "bog off",' he said. He then rehearsed a line he was to use at the rally, branding the Remainers 'the Gerald Ratners of politics' – a reference to the jewellery retailer who infamously described one of his products as 'total crap': 'All they can ever say is "Yes, I know it's crap, but we've got no choice. Yes, it's crap, but getting out would be worse." It's the Ratnerisation of British politics.' He complained that the Remain camp wanted 'to take me out'. If they did not wish to before the Ratner comments, many did so afterwards. Coming just twenty-four hours after he had pledged to Cameron not to sanction personal attacks, Johnson's line created fury in Downing Street. Cameron allies briefed that he would get his 'revenge' after the referendum, and ministers told Number 10 they did not want Boris to get any job if Remain won. 'If we win I'll want retribution,' said one.

Wallace was increasingly concerned that the vicissitudes of the referendum campaign were causing Johnson to get carried away and damage his long-term prospects of the leadership. 'You can't call the prime minister Gerald Ratner and sit in his cabinet,' he told Boris. As a Remain supporter, Wallace thought Johnson's own arguments were sometimes 'crap' as well. He teased him, 'Brexit isn't going to be perfect either, you know. If we're Ratners, you're H. Samuel.'

Not only was Sunshine Boris turning into a campaign attack dog, he had also cancelled a curry with Conservative MPs in order to attend a dinner of Brexit ministers instead. He refused to apologise for the Ratner comments, not least because he had captured in his usual ear-catching way a truth about the weakness of Cameron's pitch to voters. He had also not forgotten Cameron's attack on the Monday after the deal. 'It's all very well but the prime minister insults me at the start of this campaign and said I did it all for political calculation,' he texted Wallace.

It was not just Johnson who was attracting Cameron's ire over blue-on-blue attacks. His biggest concern was ministers denouncing government policy to score points in the referendum. As far as the prime minister was concerned, cabinet collective responsibility had only been suspended on issues directly relating to the EU; but the Brexiteers pointed out that that could include almost all aspects of government policy. Before Iain Duncan Smith's resignation, Cameron had reprimanded him in cabinet for criticising the government's position on Turkey. Once he had walked out Duncan Smith became the provisional wing of Vote Leave, prepared to attack with both barrels. 'It is helpful that IDS walked,' a Cameron confidant said, 'or we would have had to sack him.' Cameron confided to one cabinet minister that he was keeping 'very good notes' on his colleagues: 'He knows exactly who has said what, who has breached the spirit of collective responsibility,' the minister said. Chris Grayling and Dominic Raab were generally seen to have behaved within the bounds of propriety. Uniquely among the Brexiteers, Grayling texted Craig Oliver to warn him when he was due to make a major broadcast appearance. But Downing Street became increasingly annoyed at aggressive quotes given by Penny Mordaunt, the armed forces minister, and particularly Priti Patel, the employment minister, who attended cabinet.

Patel crossed Cameron's invisible line on 18 April when she blamed migration for a shortage of school places on National Offer Day, when the parents of five-year-olds found out if they had got the primary school of their choice. Lucy Powell, the shadow education secretary, did her job by denouncing the government's 'broken school places system'. But then Patel issued a press release of her own, taking aim at her own government: 'The shortage of primary school places is yet another example of how uncontrolled migration is putting unsustainable pressures on our public services. It's deeply regrettable that so many families with young children are set to be disappointed today.'

When she read the statement, the education secretary Nicky Morgan was furious. She texted Patel, accusing her of doing Labour's bidding: 'Very disappointed to see you've decided to reinforce Labour's attack on primary paid provision in aid of your Brexit campaign.' Patel defended herself, texting back: 'Labour's attack is on government policy and approach, including funding. My point is one we and party have made on migration and pressures on public services.' Morgan wasn't finished: 'I'm afraid the press and commentariat aren't making that distinction.' Patel replied: 'I understand. That was not the intention.' Morgan was still angry, as she was facing the prospect of being hauled into the Commons to make a statement in response to an Urgent Question: 'Now triggered a UQ from Labour. Thanks so much.' She texted Ed Llewellyn in Downing Street asking, 'How does this sit with collective responsibility?' The chief of staff responded that Patel was 'totally out of order', and said he would raise the issue with Cameron. A short while later 'Priti was hauled in and bollocked,' a Vote Leave source said. Number 10 briefed that she had 'behaved appallingly'.

David Chaplin admitted that Stronger In were caught flat-footed by the attacks on the government by its own ministers: 'What we hadn't appreciated is that there was nothing more newsworthy than a senior

Conservative attacking the government and their own prime minister. It was box office, and the BBC lapped it up every night on the news.'

As ever, the minister Downing Street was most concerned about was Theresa May. On 25 April the home secretary made her only major speech of the campaign. Since backing Remain she had kept her head down, and details of what she was going to say were a closely guarded secret. Number 10 staff claim to have seen her full speech only at 11.30 the night before, after parts of it had been briefed to the morning papers and the BBC. The headline was that May announced that Britain should withdraw from the European Convention on Human Rights, a position that cut across Tory policy. Michael Gove had worked up plans for a British Bill of Rights to replace the Human Rights Act, but that envisaged remaining signatories to the ECHR. In a rebuke to Cameron, May unhelpfully suggested that Britain had 'forgotten how to lead' in Europe. She used the full authority of her office to argue that EU membership made the UK 'more secure from crime and terrorism', but inevitably her speech touched on immigration, the issue on which Downing Street feared to tread. With Gove warning that Macedonia, Montenegro, Serbia, Albania and Turkey were due to join the EU, May stoked the fire, warning that Albania, Serbia and Turkey had 'serious problems with organised crime, corruption, and sometimes even terrorism', and suggesting that they should not be allowed to enjoy 'all the rights of membership'. In the question-and-answer session afterwards, she admitted that EU membership made it harder to control the 'volume of immigration'. She said she did not believe 'the sky will fall in if we vote to leave', but added that as a 'result of a hard-headed analysis of what is in our national interest' she had concluded, 'I believe the case to remain a member of the European Union is strong.'

When the Downing Street communications team saw the proposed advance briefing for the papers, they asked for the line on the sky not falling in to be removed. 'They thought that was a really good line,' says a Number 10 source, 'but it was too easily misinterpreted. They didn't brief it in the end. But her team had their own way of doing it. They refused to use any campaign language. There was no core messaging in the speech.'

The speech was so balanced that it was seen in Westminster as an attempt to position May for a potential leadership bid. She had done just enough to placate the Remain camp without alienating the Brexiteers.

Indeed, in the case of Iain Duncan Smith, she had thrilled them. The former leader called it a 'remarkable intervention' which had 'utterly undermined' the government's position on the ECHR and immigration.

In Downing Street and Stronger In, the speech was regarded as unhelpful. A Number 10 source said that when Craig Oliver saw it and digested the statement on the ECHR, he erupted, 'For fuck's sake, it's a fucking disaster.' While some Tories thought May deliberately kept her head down during the campaign, in fact that suited Cameron and Osborne just fine. A Stronger In source said, 'I think the universal view was that it had been pretty awful, and that she basically conceded that immigration was a massive problem and there was not much you could do about it inside the EU. The view from Number 10 was that she shouldn't really be used. The view was that it had been so hopeless that it was best not to go there again.'

George Osborne was hugely irritated by May's performance, and her failure to step up and be helpful to the campaign. Downing Street sources say he continually criticised May's absence from the fight. A source close to Osborne says, 'George thought it was more important to Britain to remain in the EU than to position himself for the Conservative leadership.' Alastair Campbell also thought May should have done more: 'Jeremy Corbyn did not campaign well or effectively, but he did campaign. Theresa May was barely out there at all. Corbyn ends up taking a lot of the blame. May becomes PM.'

But Ameet Gill, who knew May better than most people in Downing Street, disagreed with this assessment. When he watched political speeches he tried to take a step back and imagine what his sister would think. He told Craig Oliver, 'My sister is going to watch May on the six o'clock news tonight and think, "This is a woman I respect, who's kept us safe, and she looks sensible."' After the referendum Gill told a friend that he thought May's performance was 'the best speech given in the whole referendum campaign', because it was cerebral and not hysterical. It wasn't 'Eighty million Turks are coming to Britain.' It wasn't 'Prepare for World War III.' It was a balanced judgement that Britain should stay in from a credible figure. Another Downing Street aide says, 'To be honest, we were just grateful the home secretary was on the Remain side, not the Out side. There's a general narrative that she kept out of it, and that's true. But I think also we kept her out of it. I think it's unfair to paint her as some deeply calculating person. We were equally guilty as her in that respect.'

The day after May's speech, the growing tensions in the Remain campaign over what to do about Boris Johnson and the other leading Conservative Leave campaigners came to a head. The non-Tory staff in Cannon Street were growing increasingly irritated that their hands were tied. In one incident, the communications team were prevented from including a line in a press release condemning Lord Lawson, the former chancellor who was an advocate of the WTO trade model, for dismissing the threat of tariffs as trivial. 'It was ridiculous,' said one staffer. 'You need to direct your fire to your target.'

Tensions flared on 26 April, when a group of senior figures met in George Osborne's Commons office for a discussion on the state of the race. In addition to the chancellor, those present included his special adviser Thea Rogers, Peter Mandelson, Will Straw, Craig Oliver, Ameet Gill, Stephen Gilbert, Nick Herbert and Joe Carberry.

Carberry complained that not being able to carry out blue-on-blue attacks was hampering day-to-day communications because even when a junior Tory backbencher did something on behalf of Vote Leave, the Stronger In press team was unable to hit back properly. The blue-on-blue ban meant they had to waste time finding someone from Labour to deliver the riposte. To make matters more complicated, the broadcasters were beginning to tire of the same faces. 'The BBC are turning down bids from us trying to send them Chuka Umunna because he's been doing far too much,' Carberry explained.

Craig Oliver could see where this was going, and he was not prepared to let the idea gain traction. Looking 'quite defensive', Oliver argued that the campaign should not take the gloves off: 'Doing blue on blue just leads to psychodrama.'

George Osborne could see both sides of the argument, and intervened to offer a compromise. 'Look, you can do blue on blue, but you can't do any on Gove or Johnson.'

One of those present recalls, 'That was the first time that rule – which stayed throughout the entire campaign – was enforced.'

Some view it now as a major strategic error not to do more to take the shine off Johnson's campaign bonhomie. 'When Boris Johnson's waving around asparagus saying "Take back control," they're running a campaign based on his force of character. And if you're not allowed to take on that character, you're weakened,' says one senior figure.

Those initially pressing for more personalised attacks on Leave's main spokesmen included Peter Mandelson. His fear was that Gove and Johnson were building up too much authority and credibility. In failing to take them on, he believed, Stronger In missed an opportunity to define their most dangerous opponents in the eyes of voters. On one occasion Mandelson told George Osborne, 'We feel like sometimes we're taking a spoon to a knife-fight.'[2] Mandelson said later, 'All the time we were being held back because the prime minister just simply didn't want – and I completely understand why – to deepen the chasm that had broken out in his own party. He thought that at the end of the day after he'd won the referendum he would have to bring everyone together, and he didn't want to poison the atmosphere any more.'[3] Roland Rudd, who had been at Oxford with Johnson, also wanted the gloves off: 'He's undermining us, we should be much tougher with him,' he told the campaign.

The issue came up again a month later when Oliver, Gill and Gilbert visited Cameron at his constituency home in Dean, Oxfordshire, over a weekend. On the Monday morning, 23 May, Oliver told the senior staff in the Cannon Street office that the issue of blue on blue had been raised with the prime minister. A lengthy discussion had ensued. Cameron was furious that his aides were questioning the ban. 'He went mad and just shouted,' said one source. Cameron yelled, 'It's a fucking trap, can't you see? It's a fucking trap, that's exactly what they want me to do.' Oliver not only recounted the prime ministerial eruption, but also sought to explain Cameron's logic: 'It will be harder for him afterwards to get the party together. The rebels will have licence to say he took them on personally, he didn't behave prime ministerially, he took on his colleagues.'

A Downing Street aide said after the referendum that Cameron should have gone after Gove and Johnson: 'Our opponents were running a vicious guerrilla campaign, willing to stoop to anything, to say anything. David always thought, "I've built this great election-winning machine, and we mustn't drop that on the floor." I think in hindsight he should have gone much more aggressively after these people.'

Protecting party unity was a persuasive argument if you believed Remain were on course for victory, and the greater peril was the prospect of a Tory civil war or even a split after the referendum. But for some, this attitude revealed one of the systemic problems with the campaign. One said, 'I remember thinking, number one: we're totally dominated by Tory internal party management here. This whole campaign is run by Conservative concerns, which has got to be a bad thing. But number two: they're already planning victory! The PM had basically decided he'd won, and I think that attitude bred a complacency which ultimately was a bit disastrous.' Despite the doubts, the non-Tories did not fight the decision. Even the Labour and Lib Dems present were prepared to defer to Cameron, because he had a proven track record. What it meant, as James McGrory recalls, is that 'lines were just being edited out of press releases that are too personal', and 'social media graphics were produced and knocked back'.

One of those images was an advert showing a tiny Boris Johnson sitting in Nigel Farage's breast pocket. A similar picture of Ed Miliband in Alex Salmond's pocket had been used to devastating effect during the general election. The Boris–Farage advert did not perform particularly well in the focus groups, but it was seen as a useful weapon in the media war. In an email to staff after one focus group, Ryan Coetzee wrote, 'Boris/Gove in Farage's pocket didn't really work. People didn't seem to buy the idea that Farage is really in charge. I think it would be a winner in Westminster, however. As a PR stunt, it works because a lot of journos have already reached this conclusion and they would write it up if we briefed it properly.'

When, in early June, John Major warned that the NHS would be as safe with Johnson and Gove as 'a pet hamster would be with a hungry python', Oliver would not sanction a viral advert of a snake sporting the heads of the two Brexiteers. 'Everyone said it. Tom Edmonds said it. Will Straw said it. "We need a graphic now with a snake with Boris and Gove's head on it. Or one of the two,"' someone on the call remembers. But instead of agreeing, 'Craig went ballistic. He really shouted.' 'Can we stop having this fucking conversation?' he yelled. 'It's not going to happen. We're not having this conversation again.' Those who were present say it was the angriest they saw the director of communications during the entire campaign. 'That killed it,' a Stronger In source says. 'They saw that Johnson and Gove were cutting through and running away with this thing. They knew they had to be attacked, but they wouldn't do it themselves because they were convinced they were going to win, and that it would make it harder for Cameron to put the party together afterwards.'

The strategy of attacking Johnson using other grandees created further frustrations on 7 June, a day on which Peter Mandelson and Sajid Javid – business secretaries past and present – made a key intervention in the attempt to convince voters that leaving the single market would be a risk. Carberry and his team had spent hours working up a research and story package, the top line of which was that businesses would face an extra £34.4 billion in export tariffs and additional charges if Britain voted to leave, an annual burden approaching £80,000 per company. Since Coetzee's focus groups had shown that many voters had no idea what the single market was, Carberry hoped the story would lead the news. To attract more publicity he suggested that Mandelson should use the launch of the report to attack Johnson by name, knowing that it would make the media more likely to cover the event. At 5.49 p.m. on 4 June he emailed Ameet Gill with a script he had written for Mandelson. It said, 'The Leave campaigners are more interested in their futures within the Conservative Party than the future of our country. Theirs is not a project about giving power to the people, but a project to grab political power for themselves.' The script called for Mandelson to accuse Johnson and Gove of attempting 'political fraud of historic proportions', and to declare that they 'must never' become prime minister: 'If you think you can approach the British people with an economic decision of this degree without a competing economic argument – you should be discounted from holding high office.' Carberry's text concluded with a dig at Johnson for a photo opportunity in which he sold a cow at market: 'The truth is, selling livestock is the closest Boris has come to a trade policy in this campaign.'

Mandelson never gave the speech. Three minutes after Carberry emailed it to Gill, the Downing Street grid master replied, 'This is good but sorry we can't put saj [sic] in position of standing on a stage listening to this. References to Boris and Michael need to be taken out; as do any references to people having th[e] ability to be pm.'

To make matters worse for the team behind the single-market intervention, it was totally overshadowed by Cameron's decision to hold an emergency press conference that day to denounce the Leave campaign's six 'complete untruths'. Craig Oliver explained, 'The prime minister had watched the *Ten O'Clock News* and he had felt that the programme had been full of Leave lies that hadn't been properly rebutted. People were saying there's going to be an EU Army and Britain is going to be a

member of it, that Turkey is going to join the EU and that millions of
people are going to come to this country.'[4] Cameron said the Leave
campaign was 'resorting to total untruths to con people into taking a
leap in the dark. It is irresponsible, it is wrong. And it's time that the
Leave campaign was called out on the nonsense that they're peddling.'
But, asked whether he was accusing Johnson and Gove directly of lying,
even then Cameron pulled his punches. It was a cop-out. For some of the
non-Tories on the team this was evidence that, whatever they claimed,
Conservative high command 'were actually quite obsessed by Boris and
Gove', to a degree that they were prepared to overshadow one of the
campaign's own economic interventions. 'I think that was disastrous,'
says one senior figure at Stronger In. 'The single market was the core of
our economic messaging. I think that day was really a day where we lost
our strategic focus and probably never recovered from it.'

The problem confronting Stronger In was that Johnson was a popular
personality, not judged by voters as other politicians were. 'Boris Johnson
is Mr Teflon,' Coetzee wrote in late May. 'Almost all respondents find him
funny and entertaining; some take him seriously, some don't; but all of
them discount his blunders and gaffs [sic] with "but that's Boris". He's
seen as quite fake, but cleverly so – someone who "knows exactly what
he's doing". They think his decision to join the Leave camp is definitely
aimed at winning the Tory leadership, but they don't hold that against
him. They see him as a celebrity, not a leader, but they don't hold that
against him either. Basically, people have their view of him and very little
seems to change it.'

These findings suggest that there was not much the Remain campaign
could have done to – as Boris worded it – take him out. The prevailing
view of the senior Tories was that attacking Johnson would not only fail,
but would distract attention from the economic arguments. 'I thought
blue on blue was a total disaster, because campaigning is about delivering a message,' said a Downing Street aide. 'The message was this: "We
have less money if we leave the EU. And your family will have less
money." That's all we needed to say. I don't see how "Boris is an arsehole
and makes you less well off" helps you.'

But the fact remains that relentlessly undermining Johnson's credibility was not tried, and that meant abandoning a key plank of the Crosby–
Cameron–Osborne winning strategy. A cabinet minister says, 'One of
the golden rules of the political campaigns which we had fought – which

were: one, get trust on the economy; two, sign up the media; three, make sure your opponent's reputation is trashed – was not followed.' Indeed, there is a case that the Remain campaign failed on all three of those points: 'Because of our concern for keeping the Conservative Party together and not making this campaign into a Conservative soap opera we did not go after Boris and Michael. It was partly a concern for party unity. And it was also a concern it would not work. It would create a great storm. Every time there was a blue-on-blue argument, it merely undermined the government's argument that sensible people were voting "In". It put off non-Conservative voters. But we did discuss it a lot.'

The PM was so reluctant to countenance blue-on-blue rows that he refused from the beginning to do a head-to-head debate with another Conservative. Cameron is a more precise and much more experienced debater than Johnson, and perhaps ought to have challenged his old frenemy. Joe Carberry is clear that, from his perspective, the failure to tackle Vote Leave's two main message-carriers was the biggest mistake of the campaign. 'We argued for more direct attack on Boris and Gove, but Number 10 always said no,' he recalls. 'In hindsight that definitely hurt the campaign. The other side had no such hesitation over blue on blue, didn't care about post-campaign consequences, and used it to pretty devastating effect.'

With Cameron unprepared to act, more effort could have been made to enlist the Labour Party's help. On occasion the shadow chancellor John McDonnell warned left-wing voters that a vote for Brexit would hand power to the right wing of the Conservative Party, but it was not a message he delivered consistently. A Number 10 aide says, 'I think Corbyn and McDonnell and the SNP could have done that message: "You think you're going to get rid of the Tories. You're not. You're going to get rid of all the nice Tories and get all the evil Tories." That might have worked. You didn't need blue people bashing blue people, you want the deep red smashing the deep blue.'

McGrory and Carberry were also 'desperate' to devote an entire campaigning day to attacking Johnson and Gove's arguments on sovereignty. They wanted Tony Blair to deliver the message, 'I know a thing or two about the exercise of power, about taking big decisions, about how our nation's destiny is shaped by those decisions.' The plan was 'utterly knocked back', on the grounds that it was not a core economic argument and that 'people don't want to hear from Tony Blair'. He and Nick Clegg were seen as 'too toxic' by the Tories. McGrory disagreed, pointing out that Michael Gove was also wildly unpopular with some sections of the public, 'but Vote Leave stuck him on the telly all over the campaign, aggressively appealing to non-Tory voters, to whom Michael Gove is nobody's idea of an un-fucking-baggaged individual'. The focus groups showed that David Cameron was more popular, but, as McGrory points out, 'He's not universally loved. He's not Donald Duck.'

Again, though, the non-Conservatives were not willing to die in a ditch to change the established strategy of appealing to Cooper's target voters with an economic-risk argument. 'It is quite difficult to argue against,' says McGrory. 'You're in politics with people who you respect, they run the country, and they just won an election victory that nobody expected, which you were on the sharp end of, a year earlier. When they say, "This is how we won it and this is how it's done," what evidence do you have for your alternatives? Answer: not much; gut instinct.'

There were two final 1914-style truces. On 6 May, the day after the local elections, in which the Tory vote held up remarkably well and Labour actually lost seats – a disastrous performance for an opposition mid-term – Lynton Crosby received the knighthood Cameron had arranged for him. To celebrate, Crosby lunched with Boris Johnson before heading to the Australian High Commissioner's residence, where a party was thrown in his honour. All the principals from both sides attended. Johnson and Osborne happily posed for pictures together.

Six days later there was another party, this time at the London Transport Museum, to mark Boris Johnson's eight years as London mayor. Cameron was in benevolent mode, making a 'funny and generous' ten-minute speech praising Johnson as 'a great partner' and retelling his favourite story about their rivalry. When one of their early meetings was deadlocked over money for London, Johnson sought to discover Cameron's bottom line. Spying the prime minister's briefing papers, he lunged and tried to grab them, but Cameron beat him to it, and the two grappled. Cameron told the crowd: 'That came as a great surprise to my PPS, who walked in to find two grown men wrestling on the floor.' In the past, Cameron and Johnson had both insisted that they got the document. This time Cameron said, 'I'm not quite sure who got the piece of paper.' From the wings, Johnson yelled, 'I did!'

Johnson's speech at the Transport Museum was also an olive branch of sorts. He joked that he had only been Cameron's 'third choice' as mayoral candidate, and acknowledged that he had not always been a dream ally. A former aide who was present says, 'It was Boris saying sorry that he hasn't always been easy. If you had just arrived on earth you wouldn't have realised there had been any friction between them.' Downing Street aides reported that the PM still felt a form of frustrated affection for Johnson. 'He is much more pissed off with Gove,' one said that week.

Cameron still thought he was going to win the referendum, but he had begun to realise that the Brexiteers would dominate the party whatever the result. He told one broadcast journalist his successor would be a Brexiteer, and said to a minister, 'Only three people can do my job: George, Boris and Theresa.' Taken together, that meant Cameron thought Johnson would succeed him – a belief that made him even more reluctant to sanction attacks on him. Meanwhile, his own backbenchers were plotting to humiliate him.

Cameron used the Queen's Speech on 18 May as an attempt to calm the tensions and unite the party around agreed policies. The end result was a fresh blue-on-blue incident, orchestrated by Paul Stephenson and Steve Baker, which led to one of the most symbolic government setbacks in the Commons in nearly a century. Having forced George Osborne into overturning the 'tampon tax' at the time of the budget by threatening to amend the Finance Bill, Stephenson called Baker in early May and said, 'We've got to do something on the Queen's Speech that will advance the cause. What do you think we could do that colleagues would vote for?'

The last time a Queen's Speech had been successfully defeated on its legislative programme was in 1924, when Labour tabled a motion of no confidence in Stanley Baldwin's Conservative government as an amendment to the speech, paving the way for Ramsay MacDonald to form the first Labour government. Since the passage of the Fixed Term Parliament Act in 2011, defeat on a Queen's Speech was no longer seen, constitutionally, as a confidence motion that would force a prime minister's resignation. But it still carried immense symbolism. In order to prove a point and embarrass Cameron the Eurosceptics set out to defeat their own government, simply because they could.

If they were to be successful, they would need Labour and SNP support. The issue they alighted on was the trade deal being negotiated between the EU and the United States called the Transatlantic Trade and Investment Partnership, or TTIP (pronounced 'tee tip'). Critics of the deal claimed it would give American healthcare companies the right to sue for access to the National Health Service, and could mean that the privatisation of elements of the NHS would become irreversible. The government said the NHS was not threatened by the deal. Baker joined forces with Labour MPs to put down an amendment saying that the Commons should 'respectfully regret that a Bill to protect the National Health Service from the Transatlantic Trade and Investment Partnership was not included in the Gracious Speech'.

Baker says, 'We reached a point where we could win what votes we wanted in the House of Commons. I sat in the tea room and sent a text message saying, "Please reply 'Y' if you're willing to vote for the amendment." I had a bulk SMS to 130 Tory MPs.' More than twenty-five Tory MPs agreed to side with Labour. Baker says, 'Colleagues piled in and the government had to accept an amendment on the Queen's Speech. David Owen tabled the same amendment in the House of Lords and it passed, and the result was a historic moment took place without comment. A government was defeated on the Queen's Speech in both Houses of Parliament. Without so much as a vote.'

Cameron had resisted calls to engage in blue-on-blue attacks in order to preserve a semblance of Tory unity, but whether he liked it or not, by the third week of May he was presiding over a party in meltdown. It is far from clear that savaging the leaders of the rebel forces would have saved the day. We know only that Cameron's relative passivity did not work. But by the end of May the increasingly fractious tone of the campaign meant that Cameron and Osborne no longer minded if others went on the attack. When Michael Heseltine and John Major said they wanted to hit Boris Johnson, far from discouraging them, the Downing Street team helped promote their appearances. Johnson, spooked by the attacks, gave the green light to Vote Leave to pursue its own blue-on-blue strategy, which turned the referendum campaign on its head.

16

TURNING POINTS

Michael Gove was troubled. He had taken the most difficult decision of his life, he had rejected and angered the man to whom he owed his political career, he had put his principles on the line – and he could not see how they were going to win. The justice secretary spoke up in a morning meeting at Vote Leave in mid-May: 'We've got to think of something. What can we do?' One of those present said the mood was 'grim'. Vote Leave was 'taking a heavy pounding'. Every time Paul Stephenson briefed a good story it would get trumped by the government pumping out the latest piece of official 'propaganda'. Gove was making speeches, eloquent but perhaps less nuanced than his usual fare. Boris Johnson had begun a bus tour that was catnip to the lobby correspondents. But every night, or so it seemed, George Osborne's economic arguments were leading the news bulletins – and the media had decided that Leave was losing on the economy. They knew Andrew Cooper was briefing journalists that Remain were winning by ten points.

The calmest man in the room was Dominic Cummings. A few days after the Obama visit he stood up in the middle of the office and said, 'Guys, we know that our messages beat their messages. Right, now let's crack on and win this thing.'

Cummings knew what was needed. From mid-March the campaign committee, chaired by Gove, had met every Thursday. At each and every meeting Cummings ran through the latest polling. At each and every meeting he said what needed to be done. He repeated himself again: 'If you want to win this campaign, you have to take a baseball bat to David Cameron on the combined subjects of money, the NHS and immigration. If you do that, you will win. If you do not do that, you will lose. It is very simple.'

For months the MPs would not listen. They would turn up and complain that Cummings was running the wrong campaign. At the end of each meeting he would say, 'We want to win, therefore whatever we just talked about now, what we're going to talk about in the campaign is 350 million quid, immigration, Turkey. And we'll win.' Those key messages were used in the parts of the campaign Cummings could control: the leaflets, viral videos and social media advertising. But from mid-March until mid-May the MPs would not play ball. Attempts to hit hard had been greeted with queasiness by Gove in particular. In early April the campaign made a viral video on the back of the Panama Papers, saying in effect, 'David Cameron's been fiddling his taxes for years, how can you trust him on Europe?' The video went on Facebook, but when Henry Cook, Gove's spad, showed it to Gove, he said, 'We have to pull this.' Cummings argued that it would be worse to remove it, since a journalist spotting that it had gone would write a story about self-censorship.

Vote Leave was also under pressure from its supporters. Paul Stephenson attended a meeting of PR professionals sympathetic to the Brexit cause who had been assembled under the banner of Communicators for Britain. They included Margaret Thatcher's favourite marketing man Tim Bell. The PR men had been complaining. Stephenson outlined the Vote Leave strategy, then listened politely while more than twenty people made a series of different and sometimes contradictory points. At the end of each contribution he courteously said, 'Yes, that's a good point,' or 'Yes, I'll get back to you on that.' When everyone had finished, Bell said, 'What are you actually going to do with all this feedback? You keep on agreeing with everyone, but you can't possibly use all these ideas – you need a simple message that you stick to, and it's not coming across.' Stephenson replied, 'We are! That's why we will keep on talking about taking back control.' Bell was unimpressed, and told others at the meeting that Vote Leave had run an 'awful' campaign and that they would not listen to advice from experienced campaigners such as himself.

One way of getting more aggressive would have been for Johnson and Gove to do some shared campaign events with Nigel Farage, an idea the Ukip leader began to push in May. Farage and Arron Banks had been in touch with senior Conservatives like David Davis and Liam Fox through their involvement in the GO Movement. At one point Nick Wood texted

Chris Grayling in exasperation to say Vote Leave was treating Farage like a 'pariah'. The problem, from their point of view, was many of the Tory big beasts had no more influence over Cummings than Farage. Indeed, they felt excluded. A regular 8.15 a.m. meeting Cummings hosted for the first couple of weeks after the deal, which enabled Iain Duncan Smith and Chris Grayling to feed their thoughts into the campaign, was cancelled. Duncan Smith was particularly aggrieved. 'Those carried on for two or three weeks,' said Grayling, 'then Dominic dropped them because so many people were out on the road, after which IDS was very cross. After that there was very little interchange between the core team of the campaign and the rest of us.' Chris Bruni-Lowe also remembers Duncan Smith voicing concern that the campaign was being lost: 'IDS had massive issues with Cummings. He said, "They're fucking the whole thing up. It's a disaster. They've got no strategy. I just don't think they're very good these guys, they're really not very good."'

Farage had a meeting in May in the House of Lords with a group of donors including John Mills, Patrick Barbour, Richard Smith and Malcolm Pearson to discuss what to do about Vote Leave's problems. Kate Hoey and Bill Cash also attended. 'At that time we were in bad shape,' says Bruni-Lowe. 'We were tanking in the polls, they weren't talking about immigration.' Among the ideas floated to turn around the campaign were a huge event at the Royal Albert Hall or a five-city tour with Farage, Hoey, Johnson and Gove. Both Farage and Bruni-Lowe claim that Johnson and Gove refused to make decisions without clearing them with Cummings first – and the last thing he wanted was his two star performers on a platform with a man he regarded as toxic.

Farage and Johnson had long mobile-phone conversations. Farage recalled, 'With Boris, I was saying, "You're going around the country in a sleek coach. I'm going in a charabanc. What we ought to do is find a town to converge on." We had a laugh about it. We said, "It would be rather like the Russians and the Allies meeting on the Elbe. It would be a huge media circus. And it would allow us to dominate the agenda for twenty-four hours." But Boris had to ask the bosses. In the early conversations he said it was a good idea, but that was vetoed.' Farage was perplexed that Gove and Johnson were not masters of their own campaign: 'None of them could make decisions. I got the impression from senior political leaders that they were getting instructions from the apparatchiks. I couldn't work it out.'

Bruni-Lowe says one of the reasons Johnson gave for pulling out was 'I want to be prime minister, but if I lose this, I'm screwed.' Boris's view was, 'I can't be seen with you because I have been told by Cummings that it will damage my chances with the Tory grassroots.' At this, Farage replied, 'We're losing this really badly.' To which Johnson said, 'Yeah, I know.' Bruni-Lowe adds, 'Nigel and I realised he'd be *awful* as a prime minister. He's so indecisive it's unreal.' Nevertheless, so keen was Farage to pull off a joint appearance with Johnson, which would have been a huge media event, that Bruni-Lowe commissioned some polling to show that it actually made sense for Boris to cooperate.

Farage also bent Gove's ear when they had dinner one Monday evening at the home of a Ukip donor called Christopher Mills. Gove was accompanied by Stephen Parkinson. Farage and Mills's aim was to ensure that Ukip's views and those working closely with them, like Kate Hoey, were respected. Reporting back later, Gove said Farage was 'perfectly reasonable for about twenty minutes, but then he suddenly realised that he had to be angry about something'. The Ukip leader launched into a series of complaints: 'Why aren't you doing this? Why won't you appear on this platform with me?' Gove concluded that Farage wanted 'special status' as the leader of a party that had won four million votes at the general election, but also the opportunity to tell Vote Leave to do things differently, so that if they lost he would 'have an alibi for failure'.

Farage was frustrated that Gove would not listen to his views on the campaign: 'I was trying to tell all of them that their messaging was rubbish. I also urged Gove to drop the £350 million. I said, "Michael, you can't claim to give all this money to agricultural subsidies and £350 million to the NHS." It was a big mistake. Our polling showed people thought we gave the EU £1 million a day. If you tell them it's £34 million a day, that's fine. It didn't need to be £350 million a week.'

By the third week of May Cummings believed he had the right message, but his two main spokesmen would not weaponise it by attacking David Cameron. Farage and Bruni-Lowe believed Vote Leave were losing the referendum because they were not prepared to go hard enough on immigration. Bruni-Lowe recalls Johnson telling Farage, 'I don't want to touch immigration stuff.' The Ukip leader replied, 'If you don't touch it, you won't win.' In the final week of May, that all changed. And so, perhaps, did the result of the referendum.

On 15 May the *Sunday Telegraph* published an interview with Johnson in which he compared the European Commission's quest for a superstate to Hitler's Third Reich. Putting on his classical scholar's hat, Johnson said the 2,000 years since the Roman 'golden age' had been characterised by repeated attempts to unify Europe under a single government: 'Napoleon, Hitler, various people tried this out, and it ends tragically. The EU is an attempt to do this by different methods.' His words caused uproar.

On 17 May Michael Heseltine, a devout pro-European and John Major's deputy prime minister, went on television to denounce Boris's 'preposterous, obscene' campaign claims. He told *ITV News*, 'If you're going to be a prime minister, you have to be able to take the strain of campaigning. You have to be careful what you say. You have to think about whether you mean it, really mean it; and Boris is not passing that test.' In his memoir of the campaign, Craig Oliver admitted calling Heseltine to discuss Johnson's comment before he jumped in a cab to the TV studios. The highly personal nature of Heseltine's response, which seemed designed to damage him personally, brought home to Johnson what was at stake.

Around the same time Johnson claimed EU rules meant bananas could not be sold in bunches of more than two or three. Stronger In arranged for people dressed as gorillas brandishing inflatable bananas to follow Johnson. On 7 June John Major went on *The Andrew Marr Show* and dismissed Johnson as 'a court jester' who was guilty of 'deceit' on the £350 million-a-week claim and was running a campaign 'verging on the squalid' on immigration. Major concluded by warning Johnson that if he continued 'to divide the Conservative Party', and then became leader, 'he will not have the loyalty of the party he divided'. At the Stronger In offices in Cannon Street, this fusillade was greeted with glee. On the WhatsApp chain for the senior staff, Craig Oliver said, 'I think we can say he's delivering.' Will Straw replied, 'Brutal.'

That Craig Oliver was aware of both Heseltine and Major's attacks in advance is indisputable. He was overheard in the Stronger In office saying words to the effect of 'Just wait for Heseltine,' and told another colleague, 'Major's going to blow the doors off.' One campaign insider says, 'The two attacks on Boris and Gove, the Heseltine one and the Major one, they were arranged by Number 10.' A senior figure in Downing Street, of impeccable standing, has pointed the finger at George Osborne: 'He wanted to blow up Boris Johnson. That was his only goal.

Personally I love George Osborne, I massively admire him. But this whole referendum campaign for him was about Boris Johnson. George got into the mindset that you had to kill Boris Johnson's credibility, because he was the most effective thing for Vote Leave.' Having ruled out dirtying his own or Cameron's hands with blue-on-blue activities, it seems the chancellor was content to encourage others to get stuck in.

Heseltine's attack was also a big moment for Paul Stephenson. Vote Leave had had a good newspaper hit that same morning when the *Daily Mail* published a leaked letter showing that Cameron had discussed how big business could support the Remain campaign before he had agreed his final EU renegotiation. Rupert Soames, chief executive of Serco, wrote to Cameron on 8 February, ten days before the summit in Brussels, and pledged to contact FTSE 500 companies and urge them to mention the perils of Brexit in their annual reports. The letter had been copied to the Ministry of Justice because most of it concerned prisons, for which Serco has public-sector contracts. Craig Oliver immediately suspected that Gove had seen it and leaked it, something he denied. When Heseltine launched his attack, Oliver used all his broadcast contacts to ensure that it was more prominent on the bulletins than the Serco letter. Stephenson watched, frustrated, then called the BBC to complain that 'You're just taking their stuff every day.' He says, 'We had thought that was going to be a good day. What Craig did very well was focus on the 6 and 10 o'clock bulletins. He got Heseltine on. We had Boris on the bus talking about fat cats and corruption in Number 10. And instead the BBC ran on Heseltine saying Boris isn't fit to be PM. It was a really good move by Craig.'

The BBC stuck to their guns, but Stephenson received an assurance that Vote Leave would have their days leading the bulletins. That evening Stephenson and Cummings plotted over a few beers, discussing the obsession of lobby journalists with seeing the referendum through the prism of the Tory leadership. That was why Heseltine's comments had been so newsworthy. Cummings vowed to provide stories and angles that would emphasise the Tory civil war: 'They are playing into the leadership. Let's beat them at their own game,' he said. First he would have to persuade Johnson and Gove to play ball. That task became much simpler the following morning when the *Sun* splashed on a story that the Remain camp were spreading entirely false rumours that Boris Johnson's wife was involved in a sex scandal.

The paper revealed that MPs were peddling a rumour that Marina Wheeler was the female QC who had recently been caught with her knickers at half-mast with a fellow lawyer outside Waterloo station. The woman had originally accepted a police caution, but then claimed sexual assault in order to guarantee her anonymity. Johnson had known about the story for weeks. Katie Perrior, a leading political PR who helped run his first mayoral campaign, heard the rumours from a barrister friend and phoned Wheeler to warn her. Will Walden had previously killed the story when a Sunday newspaper attempted to write about it. Johnson believed the *Sun*'s splash was 'in some ways useful' because it killed off the rumours of his wife's involvement. But the fact that someone had peddled the story to Britain's best-selling newspaper shocked him to the core, and convinced him that his opponents would stop at nothing to destroy him personally. In the Vote Leave offices it was assumed that the story had been spread by supporters of George Osborne, though there is no suggestion that the chancellor himself knew anything about it.

Cummings, Gove, Johnson, Stephenson, Gisela Stuart and Matthew Elliott had an 8 p.m. conference call that evening. Gove said, 'They are going after you personally, Boris.' Another of those who was on the call says, 'All politicians are more sensitive than you think, and Boris particularly so. He has a soul and feelings like everyone. I think he felt wounded by it.' If Johnson had ever believed that losing the referendum honourably would still enhance his career, those who worked with him at that time saw a belief grow that he had to win. Gove said later, 'We both knew that in different ways, we were being lined up for punishment beatings, that the whole of *bien pensant* London regarded us as thought criminals. Win or lose, we were going to be blamed for all sorts of terrible things. And that inevitably created a sense of, "Well, we've got to do our very best to put our case across with vigour."'

Cummings believed the attacks on Johnson were 'a terrible, ironic self-inflicted move from Number 10. It was extremely stupid.' That week he had two conversations with Boris, one on the phone and another face-to-face. He told him, 'These guys are not just trying to win, they're trying to destroy you.' Johnson said, 'What do we have to do in order to win?' Cummings replied, 'This is what you've got to do,' and repeated his mantra: 'You've got to take your baseball bat to the government over cost, money, £350 million, immigration, new countries joining and the NHS.'

Until that point Rob Oxley, who had spent a large amount of time with him on the Vote Leave battlebus, said Johnson was determined not to get into a war of words with the prime minister: 'He was so clear that he wasn't going to attack Cameron.' After Downing Street amplified the Heseltine comments, Oxley says, 'I noticed on the bus how Boris's attitude hardened a little as Number 10 did brief against him.'

Not only was Johnson radicalised, Gove felt he had to back him. 'Michael felt sorry for Boris, and Michael felt that Number 10 had behaved disgracefully and that he had to support Boris on general principle,' says a close friend. 'First, they backed Boris into a corner. Second, Michael felt morally obliged to support Boris. That week definitely changed how Michael saw things. Until then, Michael had been holding back on all sorts of things, and then Michael definitely changed.'

There are some who worked in Downing Street who think the Heseltine attack was a mistake. A senior figure close to Cameron says, 'It was a huge miscalculation. It tipped Boris over the edge.' A source close to Johnson says: 'I think he was certainly hurt by the personalisation of it. He would pretend otherwise – "Water off a duck's back" – but I think it was personally galling for him to become the target.'

That same day, Wednesday, 18 May, Stephenson had gone into the office and made another inspired suggestion: 'Let's come up with some policies.' Cummings liked the idea, and hit on the key measure – 'an Australian points-based system' for immigrants. For months Stronger In had been telling voters the Brexiteers had no plan for the day after the referendum. It might have been sketched out on the back of the proverbial cigarette packet, but now they did have a blueprint for Brexit Britain. The following week, when the new immigration figures were due to be published, voters would be presented with the opportunity to wield the baseball bat – and Boris Johnson was now prepared to swing it hard.

If we have to pinpoint a day when Vote Leave gained the upper hand it is undoubtedly Thursday, 26 May, because that was the day the latest immigration figures were published. For Cameron they were disastrous. They revealed that net migration had reached 330,000 in 2015, around half of it from other EU countries. It was more than three times the government's 'tens of thousands' target.

The immigration figures got wall-to-wall broadcast coverage, in part because of a row the week before. The government had buried some

HMRC immigration statistics on the day of the Queen's Speech. The details made the front page of several national newspapers, but the BBC largely ignored them. Cummings had phoned senior management at the BBC to say, 'You get Craig Oliver on the phone morning, noon and night. This is the first time I'm complaining. I hope you listen.' The Corporation had an internal review, and vowed not to downplay the issue again. Stephenson said, 'When the ONS stats hit that Thursday, the BBC had basically committed to it being top of the news.'

In a rare move for the Leave campaign's leading show pony, Boris headed to 4 Millbank, home of the BBC and *Sky News*'s Westminster studios, and did a full round of television and radio interviews. That morning Stephenson had told him, 'You've got to go and smash it really hard.' He did. Johnson still said in every interview that he was pro-immigration, but his argument was about control and democracy. He said that it would be fine for Britain's population to rise to seventy or eighty million, but only if the public supported it: 'What we were saying was have a system whereby the UK government has to take responsibility and agree the numbers.'

Watching from the Labour In campaign, Alan Johnson was hugely frustrated that Cameron had stuck to his 'tens of thousands' pledge, which he thought was 'impossible to do'. Annual immigration had been 118,000 when Johnson was home secretary, and that was only 'because the economy tanked'. He says, 'Cameron repeated that pledge at the 2015 election and then got his comeuppance when those statistics were released. It became a referendum about immigration, and in particular his failure.'

In getting Boris into a position where he was prepared to attack on immigration, Cummings had an ally in Lynton Crosby. The Australian was in close contact with his former charge throughout the campaign. He had been contracted to write a weekly column for the *Daily Telegraph*, in which he analysed polling by ORB. Crosby's columns were rather Delphic, offering some hope to both sides. But Johnson knew in advance what he was going to write, and would occasionally refer to advice he had received from 'our friend Down Under'. Matthew Elliott said, 'Lynton was saying, "If you want to win this, you've got to do more immigration."'

Johnson and Gove spent a large part of the day the immigration figures came out together, discussing the upcoming television debates. As they digested the figures, Johnson turned to Gove and said, 'I think we should write a letter. They're really in trouble on this.' They went to see Cummings, who seized on the idea. He had resolved to feed the lobby stories that would dramatise the rivalry at the top of the Tory Party. Now he had the chance to do just that. Cummings and Stephenson wrote a draft of the letter, which argued that the government was wrong to pledge to cap immigration while remaining in the EU. The key section read: 'Voters were promised repeatedly at elections that net immigration could be cut to the tens of thousands. This promise is plainly not achievable as long as the UK is a member of the EU and the failure to keep it is corrosive of public trust in politics.' Gisela Stuart was asked to add her signature to the letter to give Johnson and Gove a tiny figleaf of cover for their blue-on-blue attack.

When he first saw it, Gove thought the letter was 'quite strong'. Stephenson sought to reassure him with a jokey 'Don't worry, Michael, it's a cross-party letter.' Gove replied, 'I know you think I'm being weak, but it is very important we get the language right. It's my name, I need to be comfortable.' Together, Stephenson and Gove toned the letter down, but it had deliberately been written so that it would be incendiary even after it was watered down. Matthew Elliott says, 'At times, getting them to do certain things took a bit of hand-holding. The letter was a bit of hand-holding.'

The letter was given to the *Sunday Times*, which splashed on it under the headline 'Boris and Gove lash Cameron on immigration', and framed the intervention as 'a direct challenge to David Cameron's authority'.

Those who were there say neither Johnson nor Gove expected the huge reaction the story generated, recasting the blue-on-blue battle for the rest of the campaign. 'They didn't mean it as personally as sometimes it was taken,' one source said. 'But Dom and Paul knew exactly what they were doing.'

Chris Grayling was uneasy about the letter: 'I never approved of it. I thought they could have done it without actually attacking the prime minister. Maybe it was only winnable going after the prime minister, but I was not comfortable about doing it.'

Gove later concluded, 'I don't think we committed any professional fouls, but I think there were a few times where we went in quite hard and the shoulder-charge was quite aggressive – but it's a campaign.'

The letter was the first shoulder-charge. It would not be the last. One of Cameron's aides says, 'That open letter was the turning point in the campaign, to be honest. I think we were all surprised at what they were doing and how they were doing it. That weekend we were all worrying about how we would ever put this back together again. From that moment on I felt like they had momentum. It felt like a steam tanker had just turned around.'

On the same day, Priti Patel wrote for the *Sunday Telegraph*, effectively accusing Cameron and Osborne of being too rich to understand public concern about immigration: 'If you have private wealth ... you'll be fine. But when public services are under pressure, it is those people who do not have the luxury of being able to afford the alternatives who are most vulnerable.'

The gloves were off, but the letter and Patel's coded insult were not even the most aggressive Brexit assaults on Cameron that weekend.

Early in the campaign, one member of Cameron's inner circle confessed to a Labour figure at Stronger In that Downing Street expected a leadership challenge: 'Win or lose, we think they'll get fifty backbenchers to challenge Cameron.' The first stirrings of a plot now emerged.

After Michael Heseltine's attack on Boris Johnson, Stephenson remembered a conversation he had had with Cummings weeks before about how some of the more hotheaded Eurosceptics would have their uses at points in the campaign. Cummings, with his usual delicacy where MPs were concerned, had said, 'We just need to kick the flying monkeys in the cage and release them at the right point.' Now Stephenson went in search of a flying monkey to turn up the pressure on Cameron. He called Steve Baker and said, 'They're playing a really rough game here, and basically taking on our main guy. They're talking about leadership. They're playing dirtier than us. We need to be thinking about people who can do similar stuff on our side.' Stephenson kept this conversation secret, not even telling Rob Oxley, in order to 'protect him'. Baker reported that many MPs were furious with Cameron's approach, but some were worried about launching *ad hominem* attacks.

What happened next is still the subject of controversy. Baker denies that he asked anyone to attack the prime minister. But when Andrew Bridgen, the MP for North-West Leicestershire, broke cover that weekend and declared that Cameron was 'finished', win or lose, he believed he was acting with Vote Leave's support: 'They asked for volunteers, and I said I'd do it.'

Bridgen is a self-made millionaire, who made his money from potato-farming. Diminutive in stature and a blunt speaker, he had disliked Cameron since he paid a visit to his constituency eight years earlier. 'There was always enmity between me and David Cameron,' he explained. 'In 2008, when I was a candidate and he was the leader of the opposition, in front of constituency workers he told me that my constituency was "a dump". I told him I didn't want him to come again.' Bridgen had picked Cameron up at the local railway station in a battered diesel VW Passat, and asked him to sign some bottles of whisky for a local party raffle. Two Tory activists were sitting in the front of the car. Cameron asked, 'Where are we? What's your major conurbation.'

'Coalville.'

'That's a right dump,' said the Conservative leader, who had visited it in 2005 with his predecessor Michael Howard. 'It was a right tip.' Bridgen was horrified. His own home is just north of Coalville. At the 2010 election, he says, 'I couldn't put David Cameron on any of my leaflets, because he had no regard for my people.'

It was an exchange that was to have far-reaching consequences for Cameron. In June 2013 Bridgen announced that he had submitted a letter of no confidence in the prime minister to Graham Brady, the chairman of the backbench 1922 Committee. He withdrew his letter in April 2014, and Cameron survived. Bridgen now changed his mind again, prompted in part by comments Cameron had made earlier that week, that Remain was the 'moral case' in the referendum. He approached several Sunday-newspaper journalists, and pre-recorded an interview for *Pienaar's Politics*, Radio 5 Live's flagship weekend political programme. He said Cameron was 'finished', that even a Remain win would make a leadership challenge 'highly likely' because 'the prime minister has put himself front and centre of a fairly outrageous "Remain" campaign', and that Brexit would lead to 'an orderly departure' for Cameron. In the *Sunday Times* an MP – named weeks later by another newspaper as Bridgen – went further, saying, 'I don't want to stab the prime minister in the back – I want to stab him in the front so I can see the expression on his face. You'd have to twist the knife, though, because we want it back for Osborne.' The MP said victory in the referendum depended on 'catching the prime minister with a live boy or a dead girl'.

On the Sunday, the Conservative MP Nadine Dorries – who had

talked tactics with Bridgen – told ITV's Robert Peston she was also backing a leadership challenge. 'My letter is already in,' she said.

Bridgen explains, 'We were five points behind in the polls. The government had set the whole agenda. Every day, no matter what Leave said, Remain had always got the story. They were willing to unleash the dogs on Boris. We just had to wrestle the initiative away from the government, and a kamikaze attack was the only way to do it. We didn't have much left to lose.'

Steve Baker denies that he asked Bridgen to wield the knife: 'Absolutely not! Andrew Bridgen is a great colleague, but I have never put anyone up to do something I would not do myself in public. I never approved anything which was personally nasty against the prime minister.'

It is not clear how many Tory MPs shared Bridgen and Dorries' views. 'I knew of one or two people who were seriously thinking of signing letters, and I tried to persuade them not to,' says Chris Grayling. 'I don't think there were nearly enough for there to be a threat to the PM. It might have got to twenty or thirty.'

On the Sunday Paul Stephenson was at a social event with some BBC executives where he learned that Craig Oliver had been calling in the small hours of the morning trying unsuccessfully to keep the 'corrosive of public trust' letter and Bridgen's attack off the top of the news bulletins. Stephenson was struck by one senior figure in BBC news who criticised the Remain campaign, saying, 'I'm just bored of all these economists and experts.' Vote Leave would be pushing at an open door with their plan to publish policies like an alternative government.

Between the immigration figures and the weekend attacks on Cameron, Vote Leave had engineered a perfect storm that allowed a media already weary with Stronger In's economic warnings to fashion a completely new narrative. Stephenson thinks Vote Leave got lucky that week, and that in a different climate the letter could have backfired: 'Because the prevailing narrative was "We're on the up," that was seen as strategic brilliance. If we'd had the wind against us, it would have been seen as the last roll of the dice, and stupid. That week we got very, very lucky, but you've got to take the rub of the green when you get it.'

On Monday, 30 May, the day after the bombshell letter on immigration, Vote Leave issued its first policy. Johnson, Gove and Gisela Stuart announced that a post-Brexit government would scrap the VAT paid on household energy bills, saving consumers £1.7 billion a year. The same day, an ICM poll put Leave six points ahead, and YouGov gave Leave a seven-point advantage. On Friday, 3 June, Johnson and Gove said £100 million a week of the £350 million saved would be ploughed into the Health Service budget, an annual cost of £5.2 billion. George Osborne described both announcements as 'fantasy economics', on the grounds that any savings would be eradicated by an economic downturn following a Leave vote. Stronger In put out a dossier detailing how Leave campaigners had made nearly £112 billion of unfunded spending pledges. Matthew Elliott says, 'We'd been constantly hit by both sides saying "Where's your plan?" What we did was to give a vision of "what Out looks like". The significance was not the sums, but the decision by Gove and Johnson to start acting like a government in waiting. Sandwiched between the two announcements was a third moment that would alter the course of British history.

On Wednesday, 1 June, Johnson and Gove announced that a post-Brexit government would adopt an Australian-style points-based system for immigration. In a joint statement, also signed by Priti Patel, they said migrants would be barred from entering the UK unless they could speak good English and had the right skills. Revisiting the argument that had enraged Nicky Morgan a month earlier, they warned that the scale of immigration had placed 'strain' on public services, and that 'class sizes will rise and waiting lists will lengthen' if Britain did not leave.

The Stronger In leadership recognised the dangers of Vote Leave embracing immigration, but initially felt it was an admission of failure by Cummings and his team. 'They ended up marching to Nigel Farage's tune,' Will Straw observed. However, Stronger In knew immediately that it would be a problem, because the points system had been Ukip policy for a while, and voters brought it up unprompted in focus groups. 'The points-based immigration thing really cuts through to people,' said Ryan Coetzee. 'Lots of voters would mention it.'

After the announcement appeared, the Remain camp held a conference call that night, including Craig Oliver, Adam Atashzai, James McGrory and Joe Carberry, to discuss how to respond. They decided to issue a very factual response, pointing out that the Australian points-based system actually admitted a higher number of people per head of the population than the current British system for non-EU migrants. Some now think that was an opportunity missed. One says, 'We ended up doing a factual "Why the points-based system is bad". In hindsight, if the PM had just come out and slapped it down and said, "This is ridiculous. This shows these people are not ready to run the country," that would have been far more powerful.'

A month later, one of those involved reflected that Dominic Cummings was more adept at making the blue-on-blue issue work for him: 'They used psychodrama to their advantage, we didn't. Our response was really weak. We were never as aggressive as them because we wouldn't do blue on blue.' A cabinet minister agrees: 'With hindsight maybe we should have done more, but it was not obvious that that would have worked by that late stage. If that was going to happen, it needed to have happened months earlier.'

Cameron probably had grounds to sack Gove for drawing up alternative government policies in defiance of the basis on which Cameron had suspended cabinet collective responsibility. But 'that's not David. It just wouldn't have been him,' said one of his closest aides. If Gove's abandonment of the single market looks, in retrospect, like the moment when Vote Leave publicly acknowledged that immigration was a more important issue than the economy, the week of alternative policies seems like the moment they acknowledged publicly that the result of the referendum would seal Cameron's fate. If Cameron had fired Gove at that time he might have provoked an attempt to oust him. By not doing so he only showed that his cabinet, as well as his backbenchers, had now become ungovernable.

Planting the idea of an 'alternative government' in journalists' thoughts was Paul Stephenson's explicit goal when he came up with the idea of policy proposals, but both Johnson and Gove took some coaxing. The following Saturday, Cummings and Stephenson went to Johnson's house in Islington to brief him for a rally that night in east London and his appearance on *The Andrew Marr Show* the following day. Gove, Will Walden and Henry Cook were also present. Stephenson explained that at the rally they would be unveiling Vote Leave's pledge card.

Johnson: 'Pledge card? What pledges?'

Stephenson: 'The pledges we've been making all week.'

Johnson: 'Pledges? We can't make pledges. We're not the government. Can I call them options? Policy options for the government.'

Walden: 'The press release has already gone out.'

Johnson: 'I don't think we can call them pledges. Pledges of options?'

Stephenson: 'That doesn't quite have the same ring. How I would describe it is a series of policies that the government is unable to bring in at the moment unless we vote Leave and take back control of these areas.'

Michael Gove (tongue firmly inserted in cheek): 'Exactly. We are being helpful to the prime minister by setting out policies he can bring in after we vote Leave.'

At this the room dissolved into laughter. When Johnson and Gove were absent, 'when the alternative government are in power' became an in-joke. If he saw a news bulletin he disliked, Cummings took to saying, 'When the alternative government is in power we'll nationalise ITV and privatise the BBC – then who'll be laughing?'

The alternative government reached its apogee on 15 June when Vote Leave published a 'roadmap' of six new laws that they would introduce in the event of Brexit. Everyone else called it a 'Brexit Queen's Speech'. The plan included legislation to repeal the 1972 European Communities Act; a special Finance Bill to scrap VAT on household fuel; an NHS Funding Bill to channel the extra cash to the NHS; a Free Trade Bill; an Asylum and Immigration Control Bill; and an Emergency Provisions Bill to end the judicial supremacy of the European Court of Justice and remove EU citizens 'whose presence is not conducive to the public good'.

So intoxicated was the media by this glut of announcements that Vote Leave broke every rule in the election playbook, holding visually unexciting press conferences at their headquarters by Lambeth Bridge. 'Normally that would be dull as dishwater,' said a despairing David Chaplin. 'You would strike that out of a campaign plan for looking pale, male and stale.' But Leave didn't need visuals when the words were so strong: 'These guys were willing to go to any length to make the news.'

Just at the time Johnson and Gove began to behave like a government in waiting, the Remain campaign lost the support of the real government apparatus. On the morning of Friday, 27 May, the day after the announcement of the immigration figures, the formal purdah period kicked in. From that point onwards the campaigns could only spend £7 million each, and the civil service was barred from doing anything that might affect the referendum result. Stronger In could no longer rely on government reports, or advice from officials. In the run-up to the midnight deadline, an effort was made to publish as much as possible on government websites. Reports, statistics and analyses that the Remain campaign could draw attention to later were dumped online in places where journalists would not look. Osborne had also laced key statistics in the footnotes and appendices of Treasury reports, which he would return to later.

From the Friday morning the Tory elements of Stronger In were fully integrated into the team in Cannon Street, with Craig Oliver and Ameet Gill soon running the show. Oliver, the most expensive employee, was paid a monthly salary of £9,333 for a four-day week.

From that point on, Oliver led an early-morning conference call for the media teams at 6.15 a.m. At 7.30 a.m. there was a second conference call, in which Stronger In would tell Labour In, Conservatives In and the Liberal Democrats about their plans for the day. Downing Street had regular internal briefings at 8.30 a.m. and again at 4 p.m. Gill and David Chaplin led the grid meeting at noon. There would be another conference call at lunchtime, another in the late afternoon to discuss the morning news agenda, and a final call at around 10.15 p.m. It was late in the campaign to go on a full war footing. 'I was really impressed with the Number 10 team,' says Chaplin. 'They worked incredibly hard, and when they turned their attention to something, shit happened in a good way. But until purdah, they themselves were doing other things. They had the Queen's Speech and then the budget. In hindsight it might have been better to send staff across earlier who weren't also responsible for government business.'

The Tories also came with a very clear agenda of how to win elections. McGrory summed up their approach as: 'We've won an election in 2014, we've won an election in 2015, and we're going to make damn sure we're going to win this one in 2016, and we did it the following way: set the parameters of the debate early, hammer that core message and stick to it.'

Message discipline meant not saying things, as well as saying them. One of the special advisers who stayed behind in Number 10 was Laura Trott, who ran the non-Europe grid. She would spend the next month trying to shut down all other news, so government announcements did not cut across Cameron's campaign messages. By polling day Trott's spreadsheet of blocked announcements had more than 150 items listed.

The start of purdah has become an almost mythical moment in the story for the Leave campaigners, who believe their victories in the

Commons the previous autumn effectively sidelined the government for the last four weeks before the vote. Bernard Jenkin says, 'The atmosphere was instantly transformed, and I hazard a guess that we would not have won the referendum if there had not been purdah, because as soon as the government was taken off the airwaves, we were in a different ball game.' Matthew Elliott agrees: 'The key turning point wasn't so much us talking about immigration, it was basically when purdah kicked in, which meant we were able to start dictating the broadcast agenda. Once you move into purdah period it became easier, because the BBC were giving more balanced coverage to both sides, so the good stuff we were putting out started getting the good coverage it deserved.'

But James McGrory believes it was a 'lazy assumption' of post-referendum coverage that losing the government machine was critical to Remain's loss: 'We did have a rough ten days at the start of purdah where they had the upper hand in the air war on both immigration and the alternative government stuff. They had a very good run. But other than that, most days we topped them on the news.'

Graham Brady, the chairman of the 1922 Committee, gives credit to Cummings for his timing: 'Vote Leave managed to get the immigration issue to be salient at exactly the right moment. The first point where I started to think these guys were actually living up to their reputation was at the point that purdah kicked in, immigration went to the top in the public debate and the postal votes were arriving on people's doormats. I suspect an awful lot of the votes were cast that week.'

When he saw that Vote Leave had announced the points system, Nigel Farage was overjoyed – though he could still not understand why no one had told him in advance: 'There should have been loose coordination, at a very minimum. We should have known because we could have been in there to bat with them.' But he believed a turning point had been reached. 'The day that the referendum campaign changed was the morning Boris and Gove started talking about an Australian-style points-based system. Within forty-eight hours I thought, "We're going to win this."'

Farage believed it was only the pressure he and Ukip had put on Vote Leave that caused them to change: 'The whole Vote Leave strategy was flawed from the start. The strategy was not to challenge the prime minister's renegotiation. Disaster. So we started challenging it, they started challenging it. The next strategy was not to discuss immigration at all, because that would put off swing voters. Again, that was wrong. My nightmare was that it would be me against the world. We'd have got 42 per cent and lost. We could not win it on our own. We needed some big hitters from across the political spectrum. Once we got them talking about immigration, we were off to the races.'

Craig Oliver also believed Cummings had been forced to run a campaign he had originally resisted. 'The truth is, Leave said they would not run a migration-only campaign,' says a Number 10 source. 'There's tons of evidence. In the end, they did. They moved off their strategy and onto something many of them felt decidedly squeamish about.'

That is not the whole story. Johnson, Gove, Iain Duncan Smith and Priti Patel had been talking about immigration for weeks, particularly in terms of how it impacted on public services. Gove made a speech about Turkey and four other countries with a combined population of eighty-eight million people joining the EU three weeks earlier. What changed was that the attacks on Johnson persuaded the two leading Brexiteers to accept Cummings' advice that the way to maximise coverage was to fuse their long-standing messages with blue-on-blue action that would excite the media. The immigration figures provided the perfect opportunity.

Cummings' original research in 2014 had shown that immigration was a key factor in shifting attitudes and votes on the European Union. When he and Stephenson met in the latter's garden in July 2015, the campaign director made clear that he would only move onto the issue in the final few weeks: 'It's there, it's a massive issue, we can go hard on it at the end – and we probably will go hard on it at the end – but we lose a whole bunch of people if we do it straight away.' Cummings and Stephenson had also been approving far more aggressive social media adverts focusing on immigration since the start of the campaign. In total, Vote Leave sent out a hundred million leaflets and half a billion adverts digitally. Cummings said, 'All of those tens of millions of leaflets dropping in June were all signed off on May 2nd. That was full of immigration stuff far before all of these discussions about Boris and Michael.'

Ryan Coetzee, Remain's chief strategist, believes that Cummings always intended to use immigration, because he had spotted the viral videos and social media advertising which were often ignored by Westminster journalists: 'The points-based thing is when they adopted the Farage position and became far more shameless about their xeno-phobia than they had been before. Before that they were doing it online, but they weren't doing it with the newspapers.'

Gove had warned Cameron in November that he needed a good deal on immigration, as it would be a central issue in the campaign. He believed the issue was the prime minister's weakest card, and that the volume of complaints from Downing Street and Stronger In were in direct proportion to the political damage it was causing them. As one senior figure in Vote Leave put it, 'If you hit the PM's Achilles heel with an arrow, then they're going to scream all the louder.'

A Downing Street insider with whom Cummings was in contact throughout the campaign also believes that he had always intended to end up where he did: 'I think Dom always knew he was going to go hard on immigration by the end of it. They opened up the campaign with NHS and sovereignty – shows they're not the race campaign, gives them credibility – and then they go with Turkey. I do think Vote Leave was very good.'

Stronger In and Downing Street's mistake, perhaps, was to see the economy, the cost of the EU, public services and immigration as separate campaigning issues. Cummings' goal was to fuse them into one issue. Bernard Jenkin says, 'We never campaigned on immigration, we campaigned on control. The two things towards the end of the campaign – £350 million and Turkey joining the EU – these had massive cut-through, and this was Dominic's finesse, to express things in as controversial a way as possible so that they were attacked by the other side, so that on the evening news your messages were being talked about.'

On this subject, as on so much else, there may never be agreement between the two sides, or within the two factions of the Leave campaign. Cummings says, 'The idea that we got forced by Ukip – in what form did we get forced by them? There's no forum for them to force us into anything. Ukip were irrelevant in any strategic decisions we made.' A cabinet minister involved in the campaign (not Gove) says Farage's belief that he was instrumental in the pivot is 'absolute bollocks': 'I think what Dominic did was look at what resonated and play to it.' Arron Banks does not accept this: 'For Cummings to say that was part of his plan is risible nonsense. They were losing until they got back onto immigration with three or four weeks to go.'

*   *   *

With the points-based system in the public mind, Vote Leave sought to ram home their advantage by relentlessly highlighting the prospect of Turkey joining the European Union. In his speech at the end of April, Gove had drawn attention to how Britain was due to pay almost £2 billion to Turkey, Albania, Macedonia, Montenegro and Serbia by 2020 to help them prepare to join the EU. Poking fun at his own slip-up over the Albanian model, he argued that the real 'Project Albania' was the one where eighty-eight million citizens from the five countries could 'soon' have 'the right to live and work here'. In the week of the points-based announcement he underwent a televised grilling by *Sky News* in which he stressed, 'The EU is already opening visa-free travel to Turkey. That would create a borderless travel zone from the frontiers of Syria and Iraq to the English Channel.'

The weekend before the 'corrosive of public trust' letter, 22 May, Vote Leave had published a new poster featuring footsteps walking through an open door shaped like a passport, and the slogan 'Turkey (Population Seventy-Six Million) is Joining the EU'. Penny Mordaunt raised the spectre of 'threats to UK security' because 'crime is far higher in Turkey than the UK' and 'gun ownership is also more widespread'. Mordaunt claimed, 'Because of the EU's free movement laws, the government will not be able to exclude Turkish criminals from entering the UK.' She made matters worse by going on television to deny – inaccurately – that Britain could veto Turkish accession.

This intervention was 'too much' for Boris Johnson, who has Turkish ancestry on his father's side. In one of the few major disagreements among Vote Leave's core team, Johnson erupted with rage and refused to peddle the same argument. On 15 March he had suggested that Turkey joining the EU was 'not going to happen in the foreseeable future', and the idea of Turks getting visa-free travel to the EU was 'simply not on the cards'. 'He felt the Penny thing was too much,' an ally said. 'He was pretty angry about that, and he made his views pretty clear to Dom. I remember him waving his arms and gesticulating quite wildly on the phone.'

Johnson was not the only one who was angry. Even more than Vote Leave's use of the £350 million figure, Gove's insistence that Turkey could join the EU provoked accusations of lying from Cameron's team. The prime minister attacked Mordaunt's claims as 'absolutely wrong', and told Robert Peston, 'It is not remotely on the cards that Turkey is going to join the EU any time soon. They applied in 1987. At the current rate of progress they will probably get round to joining in about the year 3000.'

The form of words risked a diplomatic incident, but did not go far enough for the PM's critics. Turkey was another issue where Stronger In staff were frustrated by Downing Street putting good government before winning the referendum. As prime minister, Cameron could not wholly abandon a long-established policy of support for Turkish entry to the EU. 'The Leave campaign exploited it ruthlessly,' says Will Straw. 'It seems to me that the hardest possible language was important.' In Number 10 there was serious discussion of announcing that Britain would veto Turkish membership; Craig Oliver privately pressed Cameron to do so. A Downing Street source says, 'Craig was always clear that we needed to be clear that Leave were lying when they said Turkey would be joining in a few years, with potentially millions coming. There wasn't a single credible person in the world who thought that was true.' Will Straw recalls, 'From a comms point of view Craig knew what needed to be said. The formulation I was hoping for was for [Cameron] to rule it out under his premiership.' Daniel Korski also wrote a memo recommending that the PM say explicitly that Turkey would not become a member of the EU while he was prime minister. But Ed Llewellyn told Cameron that would mean changing government policy on a whim, and said, 'You have to ride this out.'

Cameron's view was that he could not jeopardise counter-terrorism cooperation with the government in Ankara just to win a campaign argument with Michael Gove. A senior figure in Downing Street says, 'To David's great credit, although it arguably lost him the referendum, he said, "We've got serious equities in Turkey today on counter-terrorism, on countering ISIL. [Turkish president Recep] Erdoğan is not someone who's going to take lightly us throwing him overboard." His position was a very statesmanlike one. Unfortunately, the debate we were in didn't allow for that statesmanlike behaviour. When people say politicians are venal and supine, here's an example of somebody who took a principled decision for the security of the country.'

Despite the furore, Vote Leave kept pushing the Turkey line. In Westminster Tower Cummings would walk past Richard Howell most evenings and ask, 'What's in the grid for next week, Ricardo?' Howell would reply, 'Next week is Turkey week, boss.' The campaign director's response would always be, 'That's right. Every week is Turkey week.' 'Turkifying' stories became a key goal for the research team.

The issue became most acute for Cameron on the weekend of 11–12 June, eleven days before the referendum, when the *Sunday Times* splashed on a cache of five leaked Foreign Office documents, one of which showed that a diplomat in Turkey advised ministers that a proposed EU deal with Turkey on visa-free travel within the Schengen area could lead the UK to extend the same privilege to up to 1.5 million 'special passport holders' from Turkey. Janet Douglas, the deputy head of mission in Ankara, recognised that this 'would be a risk, but a significant and symbolic gesture to Turkey'. This plan was rejected by ministers, but the other documents suggested that the UK was encouraging the rest of the EU to grant visa-free travel to Turks in order to prevent a Turkish threat to 'open the floodgates' to Europe for migrants. Downing Street got Theresa May and Philip Hammond to denounce the 'selectively leaked quotes', but Iain Duncan Smith accused Cameron of being 'in cahoots' with the European Commission to perpetrate 'an appalling deceit' on the British public. People in Downing Street told a journalist at the *Sunday Times*, 'You have cost us the referendum.'

The Turkish issue certainly had traction with voters. On polling day, Will Straw was handing out Stronger In stickers in Lambeth, generally getting a highly positive response. But, he said, 'There was one bloke, a Leaver, who said if we vote for remain the Turks will be here in three months. That was his entire motivation for voting Leave.'

With immigration dominating the news agenda and Gove and Johnson hitting the government hard, the mood of the Gove campaign WhatsApp group of Conservative spads changed. The jokey tone of Paul Stephenson's Albanian model picture was gone. When they were on the back foot in the week of the first Treasury document and the Obama visit, one of the Downing Street officials had joked that Vote Leave would be easier to defeat than Labour: 'Last year felt more difficult than this. You're worse than Miliband. Don't you want to come and join us?' Now the same official messaged, 'I can't believe you're running this sort of campaign.'

Will Straw was disgusted by the way Gove and Johnson exploited the Turkish issue, comparing the footsteps poster to Nigel Farage's 'Breaking Point' image later in the campaign: 'I didn't think there was any difference at all between Nigel Farage's poster and the Vote Leave poster saying

Turkey is coming. Michael Gove said he shuddered when he saw the Ukip poster. Did he shudder when he first saw that Turkey poster and signed it off? It's exactly the same: that brown people are coming to this country. That's what both those posters are intended to say.' A minister supporting Remain said, 'It felt from our side that you now had politicians as intelligent as Gove and as attractive as Boris spouting Ukip policy. Britain is very lucky that we haven't had a populist politician as good as Marine Le Pen. Farage is neither as nasty nor as good as she is. Suddenly you had Farage's words and Boris's voice, and that is a very powerful combination.'

Ryan Coetzee accused Vote Leave of deliberately tapping into a culture of distrust that was fuelling populist movements across the West: 'They spent lots and lots of money online and in their literature telling people stuff that is not true. It was designed to make you fear foreigners. I don't know why people wring their hands about this stuff. It *was* mendacious and xenophobic. In the English language, those are the words that best describe what they did. And frankly I personally don't care what people think; that's the truth. They did it into an environment where there was so much paranoia and distrust that people were all too ready to believe this stuff.' Coetzee believes it is '100 per cent true' that people have been 'left behind' by globalisation. But, he says, 'What the Leave campaign offered them was an enemy, a bogeyman. What Britain needs to offer those people is a future.'

Several members of the Stronger In team believed they had to offer voters a concrete response on immigration as well. As early as November, Coetzee had worked up a 'message script' on what the campaign could say about immigration, which his polling and focus groups showed 'actually worked with the marginal voters – it absolutely didn't work with people who were definitely going to vote Leave, because only an end to free movement would satisfy those people'.

In one sentence, the slogan was 'We want fairness, not a free for all.' Addressing public concern about welfare, the one-paragraph version explained: 'Those coming here shouldn't be able to get something for nothing. People from other European countries should not be allowed to access benefits until they have paid into the system. But those who come here to work hard, pay their taxes, contribute to our economy and support our public services should be welcomed.' The full script also pointed out that '100,000 EU citizens work in our health and social care system,' and that 'EU citizens have contributed £20 billion more in taxes than they have taken out in benefits. The facts are clear: the overwhelming majority of EU citizens in Britain are contributors, not freeloaders.' It concluded with the line, 'So let's ensure fairness. But let's not throw the baby out with the bathwater.'

James McGrory said, 'It wasn't a silver bullet, but it had been tested to destruction both in focus groups and with polling, and it did appeal to people, but it needed to be constantly made by everybody.' However, for months and months the message script was ignored by senior politicians of all stripes. Will Straw recalls, 'We did know what we needed to say as a campaign, but we could never get the politicians to say it.' Coetzee explains, 'We had a government that was locked in and committed to a net immigration cap policy, which is indefensible. On the Labour side, once you finally got Labour to actually be involved in the campaign at all, they had anything between two and five policies.' It was only when Sadiq Khan, the new London mayor, and Ruth Davidson, the Tory leader in Scotland, used the script in the final debate of the campaign at Wembley Arena, two days before polling day, that it finally saw the light of day. By then it was too late.

Three days after the immigration figures came out, Straw was no longer prepared to tolerate the failure to tackle the subject. He wrote an email to the senior staff in which he warned, 'We've got a real issue here. They are going to focus relentlessly on this and as things stand they are going to pound us every day unless we either wrest it back onto the economy or can find a viable response.'

Straw had previously raised the issue in the meeting on 26 April in George Osborne's Commons office, the same meeting at which blue-on-blue attacks on Johnson and Gove were rejected. 'We are getting pummelled on immigration,' Straw said. 'We need to find a way to get on our script.'

He felt strongly that something needed to be done. When he had fought Rossendale and Darwen in 2015, 'I had more conversations with people about immigration than any other issue.' He believed that the campaign had to 'recognise that people have legitimate concerns about immigration, and particularly about the pace of change'. But he also knew from his doorstep chats that 'You can make common ground with people on some of the positive aspects of immigration.' He was struck by data showing that more than 80 per cent of voters agreed that 'If people come here and work hard and pay their taxes, contribute to society, they should be welcomed, that nobody should be entitled to get something for nothing from the welfare system.' Here, in fact, was the basis of an argument that Cameron's renegotiation had secured valuable new protections on welfare for EU migrants. 'You could also say that the NHS would grind to a halt without people from other countries, not least the EU. You could also talk about the benefits of free movement to Brits who wanted to study, travel, live, work, retire abroad – and then, having met people halfway, then you could set out the problems and consequences of the Vote Leave approach, and really tear apart their argument that the Australian points system was any kind of answer, because the conse- quence was that you would lose access to the single market and see the border move from Calais to Dover.'

In his email, Straw suggested that David Cameron make a major speech in Dover, just as Tony Blair did during the 2005 general election campaign, tackling the issue of immigration head-on. Max Chambers, one of Cameron's special advisers who was heavily involved in Europe, also suggested a Dover-style intervention. 'Probably our biggest strategic mistake in the campaign was to fail to challenge the idea that leaving the EU was the answer to the problem of immigration,' said Chambers. 'It will eventually become clear that it isn't, and the backlash won't be pretty. I was arguing from about eight weeks out that we should consider a speech like Blair's in the 2005 election, when the Tories were running a very similar campaign to Vote Leave. Blair used it to ridicule Tory immi- gration policy, but also to reassure, arguing that voters' concerns were being addressed and that, though important, this issue wasn't the basis on which to decide the future of the country. I thought it would be smart to build the defensive arguments for later on, and identify the holes – which were huge – in Leave's plans on immigration.'

Straw's second suggestion was that Stronger In should propose a package of measures to ease the impact of immigration on the most impoverished communities and their overstretched public services. If Johnson and Gove could behave 'like a political party in an election', so could Stronger In: 'It seemed to me to make sense for David Cameron to set out the kinds of things you could do to alleviate people's concerns. We certainly talked about a migration-impact fund. We talked about whether he could explicitly say that there will be no free movement for new countries joining the EU. Could you get more money for border controls?'

In the meeting on 26 April Osborne replied, 'I agree with what you're saying, but I don't think that will work. I think we just need to stick to the economy.' Others held their tongues. 'That's quite a hard thing to come back against,' a campaign source recalled afterwards. 'You've got the chancellor and the guy who's basically running the campaign saying "No." That's then set.'

Stephen Gilbert, as a veteran of the Major government, understood the position Straw adopted, that the campaign should confront its greatest weakness. Mandelson wrote 'a couple more notes' to Tory high command saying 'We need to do more on immigration.' He argued that the referendum would come down to a choice between the economic necessity of remaining in the single market and ending free movement, and that the campaign could not shy away from this choice. Mandelson believed that confronting the issue would allow Cameron to say, 'We are listening, we get it, but you don't have to vote to leave the EU in order to get some response on immigration.' But that approach was opposed by the Conservatives at campaign HQ, like Craig Oliver and Ameet Gill. Oliver, as master of message-control, was clear. Time and again he told campaign staff, 'If we're talking about the economy, we're winning. If we're talking about immigration, we're losing.'

Straw was frustrated: 'Those who had essentially grown up in the Crosby era were more wedded to this idea that you just focus on one thing.'

Max Chambers acknowledges the problems, but thinks it was a mistake to do nothing: 'We were caught in a catch-22, because we didn't want to raise the salience of immigration. In hindsight, this was the wrong call. It's easy to see why we made this mistake, but it left us horrendously exposed when Leave pivoted onto immigration late on. A single speech might not have made the difference, but silence definitely didn't help the cause.' James McGrory agrees: 'I think you can legitimately argue the greatest failing of our campaign was an inability to tackle in a meaningful way people's concerns about immigration.'

It was not just campaign ideas on immigration that were ignored. The Europhile Tory MP Neil Carmichael came up with an idea for a viral advert based around the 1980s hit TV show *Auf Wiedersehen, Pet*, which featured a group of Geordie labourers who go to work in Germany because they cannot find work at home. Carmichael thought the idea would appeal to Labour voters in the north-east, and help depict immigration as a two-way process. The idea was passed on to the Labour In campaign, since one of the show's stars, Kevin Whately, was a Labour supporter. But the idea 'ran into the sand'.

The main reason Cameron and Osborne refused to sanction a switch to confronting immigration was a simple one. Throughout the campaign Andrew Cooper's polling showed that the economy would trump immigration, and that immigration would not take Leave over the finishing line. The pollster had conducted 'regression analysis', where you examine the explanatory power of different policies, words and phrases. 'It consistently had the Leave campaign "owning" immigration, but it had very low explanatory power,' says a senior campaign source. 'People who had already made their minds up to vote Leave were voting Leave because of immigration. There was very little you could do to shift them, but it wasn't pushing other people.'

Politicians who had spent any time on the doorstep did not believe Cooper's analysis. Damian Green, the former immigration minister, raised the issue at 'more or less every board meeting': 'This doesn't accord with my experience or the experience of anyone else who is going out and knocking doors,' he said. Cooper responded, 'This is what the data is telling us.' Stuart Rose, the chairman of the board, said its members 'did want us to have more answers on immigration': 'Should I as chairman have pushed harder? I suppose I should. We relied heavily on Stephen Gilbert and Andrew Cooper. They had the answers, they had the plan. Possibly naïvely, I thought they had it sussed out.'

Jim Messina told colleagues Cooper was 'the worst pollster I have ever worked with'. When the American completed his first batch of data-modelling in March, he told Cameron that the race was closer than Cooper's polls were showing. Messina considered telling Cameron and Osborne that he should take over the polling work, and regretted later that he did not.

He was staggered by Cooper's habit of providing two sets of polling numbers to campaign chiefs. In early March, after discussion with Coetzee, Cooper started producing a second tracking poll with a different methodology. It tried to predict how undecided voters, and those who said they would definitely vote but did not yet know which way, would jump, based on their underlying attitudes. The effect of this was to improve Remain's standing by up to 2 per cent on some days. Cooper insists these weighting changes had the support of campaign chiefs, and that he had 'strong objections' to circulating both tracking polls. In order to prevent leaks or complacency the new, adjusted, more optimistic data was only shared with the most senior campaign officials. The consequence was that Cameron's false hope that he would win, and did not need to change strategy, was boosted, because the secret poll would prove to be even less accurate than the original. A senior figure in the campaign said, 'How is it possible that you email political leaders and say, "Here are our numbers but I don't believe them so I built a second set" – and not just once, repeatedly?'

Many at Stronger In believe Cooper's polling was one of the key reasons they lost. 'We were extremely data-led,' says one. 'The polling was consistently telling us we were ahead, up to and including the final day. You run a different campaign depending on whether you are ahead or you are behind. Secondly, we were told that immigration had a high-watermark, that public anger at immigration couldn't get them 50 per cent; and thirdly we were told that for the key in-play segments, economic risk trumped immigration every time. You run into a pretty big problem if you run a data-led campaign and all your data is fucking wrong.'

Will Straw's critics now say he should have been stronger in demanding his say. 'I'm afraid Will Straw capitulated completely to the dead hand of Downing Street,' says one Stronger In board member. 'He would take all of his orders from them. He thought, "That's where power is, Downing Street rules supreme."' Another campaign official says, 'Will did a good job in putting together the Stronger In campaign and bringing together people from different parties. But when there was a question of leadership either Craig or Ameet pulled rank over Will. They could always point to an election victory, whereas he couldn't.'

It is certainly unimaginable that a heavyweight campaign chief like Lynton Crosby would have allowed himself to be subordinated as Straw was. But even an experienced pro like Peter Mandelson also felt sidelined. Straw understood that stories about splits and division would have been damaging if the campaign did things the PM would not support: 'We certainly didn't want to do anything that David Cameron would distance himself from. It would have looked really bad, but also my approach is not to have big stand-up rows and to posture, it's to build trust with people.'

James McGrory believed Straw did the right thing in allying himself so closely with the Tories, because without a cooperative Labour leader, he had no political counterweight to deploy: 'Will would have had more strings to his bow if he could have turned round and said, "I have a highly motivated, highly mobilised Labour Party under a dynamic, progressive, in-favour-of-Europe leader, and I'm going to bring all of our firepower to the table." What Will was shrewd enough to understand was that our best political asset was the upper echelons of the Conservative Party. If your organisation is to be docked with theirs, you're going to have to acquiesce to a lot of what they want to do.'

The problem for the campaign was that the main lesson the Tories had learned from their other successes was that in a successful campaign you stick to Plan A. 'Our fundamental problem was that we didn't change,' says another Stronger In source. 'Compare that to Vote Leave. They pivoted on that first week of purdah into immigration. We didn't have anything on immigration, because that was Cooper's advice. We were told that we couldn't attack them personally, even though we tried. Therefore we were left, throughout the whole of June, with a strategy which in late May we had identified to be flawed. And that fundamentally is why we lost.'

Stronger In saw the economy and immigration as separate campaign battlegrounds. Cummings and Farage understood more clearly that they were the same issue. This is an analysis George Osborne accepted after the referendum. 'I have to accept that immigration people saw as an economic issue, not just an identity issue,' he told aides. 'They felt their economic circumstances were being undermined by immigration.'

'Project Fear does work, we were just out-project feared,' says one of Cameron's more astute aides. 'Immigration of itself won't beat economic risk. What they did is they made it a personal economic-risk argument, which they got across more effectively than we did.' When Stronger In tried to itemise the cost to families in pay and mortgage rates and the price of the weekly shop, they were not believed. Vote Leave 'linked immigration more effectively to the pound in your pocket and your family's future', the Number 10 official says. 'The wrong conclusion to draw from this is that personal economics doesn't matter and immigration is more important. Economic risk was and always will be the single most important thing that people care about. The question is: how do you get there? It's the same force that won us the general election which beat us this time.'

17

AUNTY BEEB

Craig Oliver was furious. He had just tuned in to his first BBC bulletin of the day, and his former employers were leading with a row orchestrated by Vote Leave. Four senior Tories had issued a statement accusing the Bank of England of 'peddling phoney forecasts'. Just as Stronger In promoted the views of experts to bolster their case that cutting ties with Brussels would damage the economy, so Vote Leave sought to rubbish them. But in twenty years around broadcasting, Oliver did not think he had seen anything like this. In a joint letter, Michael Howard, Nigel Lawson, Norman Lamont and Iain Duncan Smith – two former Tory leaders and two former chancellors – said the Bank and the Treasury were guilty of 'startling dishonesty' for claiming a Brexit vote would plunge Britain into a recession.

The day before, Mark Carney, the governor of the Bank, had issued a fresh warning that the pound would slide on the currency markets if Britain was to vote to leave. That had prompted an accusation from Boris Johnson that Carney was 'talking Britain down', and was effectively part of the Remain campaign. 'We're obviously going to be hearing Project Fear moving into its final fusillade,' said Johnson. The letter was now effectively accusing Carney of politicising the Bank. The four grandees accused the Bank of England and the Treasury of peddling phoney forecasts and scare stories to back up the attempts of David Cameron and George Osborne to frighten the electorate into voting Remain.

Oliver, as he did most mornings, picked up the phone, dialled a number he knew well and made his views known to a senior BBC executive. He expected a story like that to get big play in the Brexit-backing newspapers, but not on the BBC. No formal complaint was issued – Oliver preferred to do these things informally – but he believed the Corporation had misunderstood its role in the referendum campaign, and was all too often giving air time to stories from Vote Leave that were untrue or nonsensical, and rather than call them out, news bosses attempted instead to balance the volume of coverage. Bluntly, he told his contact that the BBC should not be giving credence to a claim that the Bank was taking sides, and called the decision to lead on the attack on the Bank 'the nadir' of BBC coverage. A Downing Street source said, 'When Craig woke up and heard they were accusing the Bank of England of peddling false information as part of a conspiracy to keep us in the EU, it seemed to him that was a patently ridiculous thing to say, and it was incumbent on an organisation that is supposed to be impartial to question the impact they were giving such a statement by leading on it.'

Oliver had held deep concerns about the BBC's coverage since the time of the deal, but it became a particularly acute problem once purdah kicked in and the 'short campaign' began. He believed the national broadcaster had confused its traditional responsibility to be impartial with the requirement during an election campaign to be balanced. The need for balance, he felt, was making it more difficult for the BBC to exercise impartial scrutiny of Vote Leave's claims. 'We have deep concerns about how they handled it, because it's fair to say that on a number of occasions they mistook balance and impartiality,' said a senior Number 10 source. 'Craig pointed out that there is a difference between balance and impartiality throughout the campaign.'

The BBC's decision to lead on the Bank of England story brought to a head an ongoing process of cajoling and pressurising the Corporation. Stronger In had three major gripes about balance. Once purdah kicked in on 27 May, they accused the BBC of handing out the same number of lead items in its broadcasts to both campaigns, meaning that a major intervention by a world leader or financial institution had only as much chance of leading the news as a stunt cooked up in the Vote Leave press office.

Will Straw said, 'They threw their story into the day, and we threw our story, and by and large both got covered, and sometimes we would lead and sometimes they would lead. I think the BBC made some pretty odd editorial decisions along the way, but that meant that come the evening they'd all be rolled into one story.' A Number 10 official added, 'They seemed, particularly on morning bulletins and on the internet, to be obsessed by providing a fifty–fifty balance, where Leave would lead off on one day and Remain on another.'

To make matters more awkward for the broadcasters, the two campaigns were not even engaging with each other. Stronger In would push a story on the economy, while Vote Leave would hammer immigration. A senior BBC source said, 'Those two arguments never really met. It was like parallel railway tracks, so you'd give one side a lot of exposure on a story on whichever of those tracks they were on. It wasn't necessarily balanced by someone on the same track, it was balanced by someone on the other side of the argument arguing something totally different.'

Secondly, the Remain campaign felt that within each news item, a spurious balance would be created between one of their experts and a Vote Leave mouthpiece simply contradicting them. A member of the Stronger In board says, 'I say this with great trepidation because I love the BBC and I hate people who criticise the BBC, but unfortunately the BBC was terrible for us. They got obsessed about having to have equal billing on every side of the argument. You'd have the IMF, then you'd have a crackpot economist, or you'd have a FTSE 100 CEO and then someone who makes a couple of prams in Sheffield. It was balanced in terms of the amount of coverage, but not balanced in terms of the quality of the people.' This view was widely shared among all sections of the Stronger In alliance. A senior Downing Street source gave another example: 'You'd have ten Nobel Prize-winning economists who were given equal weight to Penny Mordaunt.'

This situation ought not to have come as a surprise to David Cameron, who had been warned about how the broadcasting rules would play out in the final four weeks by the Scottish secretary David Mundell, who knew better than most what had happened north of the border in 2014. In a Remain cabinet meeting held after the deal was done, Mundell told his colleagues the contest would get difficult once the short campaign began. He says, 'There was a failure to understand that in the final part of the campaign, which is a regulated media part, you just get a quantitative balance on the television. George Osborne can pop up with a five-hundred-page document, and the other side just need someone else to turn up and say, "That's crap." And that counts as a debate. It's not a qualitative debate.' After the referendum Mundell said, 'That's what the Leave side did much better. They just had a number of simplistic slogans to use for their two-second clip. There's no point in saying "Here's a

5,000-page report saying everything's going to go belly-up" when some-body else rocks up and says "No it's not. We're taking back control.'"

Finally, Oliver and the others believed that the BBC was failing in its duty as an impartial arbiter of national debate to scrutinise what they saw as Vote Leave's lies. David Chaplin says, 'The BBC's approach to the campaign seemed to be: divide every news bulletin, give three minutes to Leave and three minutes to Remain, instead of using some editorial judgement and being able to call out both sides when they feel the story is either misleading or untrue. I think the BBC have some real questions to answer about whether they see themselves as an information-aggregation service or providing editorial analysis of news and content for their viewers.'

In such a fractious and binary contest as the referendum, it was inev-itable there would be complaints. Some at the BBC believe they did not get it right: 'It makes me feel queasy that we gave Vote Leave such a free ride,' says one political reporter. Others reflect that it is rare for the Corporation to be accused of being too balanced.

When Craig Oliver and others phoned to complain, BBC bosses made the argument that they always judged stories on their news value. As Vote Leave had spotted, blue-on-blue action or – in the case of the Bank of England story – attacks on a third party were inherently newsworthy. A Treasury source said, 'What Leave did effectively was attack the indi-viduals and the institutions. And that worked in some ways, because they would get a morning headline in the papers and by lunchtime the BBC were doing it. I don't think the BBC had a glorious campaign.'

The Bank row had begun a few days earlier when Bernard Jenkin, a director of Vote Leave, wrote to Mark Carney seeking to silence him by warning that he was 'prohibited from making any public comment, or doing anything, which could be construed as taking part in the referen-dum debate'. Carney responded that all his interventions had related to the Bank's 'statutory responsibilities', which included a duty to assess the implications of Brexit on the Bank's 'core objectives'. David Cameron gave the story fresh life by tweeting, 'It's deeply concerning that the Leave campaign is criticising the independent Bank of England. We should listen to experts when they warn us of the dangers to our economy of leaving the European Union.'

Stronger In had the backing of most economists, but the same news judgement applied when the group organised by Patrick Minford chose to back Vote Leave instead. Jonathan Munro, the BBC's head of news-gathering, explained, 'It is patently newsy if there's a huge weight of opinion from one sector of society such as business leaders and economists in one camp, and somebody from the same group defies that and goes counter-intuitively the other way. The Remain supporters seemed to lose sight of that. They got massively more air time on the economy issue, but the opposite was also true on the immigration issue. I've not had a single complaint from them about the balance on the immigration issue because it was playing the opposite way.'

Munro admitted that the BBC did try to balance its lead items, but did not set a fixed period over which the two campaigns would get equal time at the top of the bulletins, in order to allow news judgements to dominate – though more attention was paid to this closer to polling day, as an imbalance in the final days could not have been corrected: 'This wasn't an election, it was a binary choice, so we felt that achieving balance was important – but it's not just judged by who gets the first slot on a programme or how many guests are on from each side. Sometimes a campaign might be the lead story because it's in trouble on a claim. Being the lead might be the last thing they want. That's why impartiality is a better benchmark. We'd obviously be conscious of one campaign dominating for a day or two, but we never inflated a story from the opposite camp to get balance in. The fairness of coverage has to be judged over the length of the story – a number of days or weeks, not just hour by hour.'

After the campaign, the BBC's internal review found that their coverage was almost entirely balanced. The Corporation took their responsibilities seriously during the referendum. In classic bureaucratic style, they set up two steering groups three months before the campaign, one to handle news programmes, the other to deal with issues like guests with strong opinions appearing on other shows. Many of those on these panels had been involved in the Scottish referendum, and sought to follow what had worked before. Charlotte Moore, the Controller of the BBC's TV channels; David Jordan, the director of editorial policy and standards; Katie Searle, the head of political programmes; and Robbie Gibb, the editor of live political programmes, were all involved. All BBC reporters were put through an online training session run by the BBC Academy, which explained details like the difference between the European Court of Human Rights and the European Court of Justice, so those who had not covered EU issues in any depth would be comfortable

David Cameron makes his Bloomberg speech in January 2013, promising to hold an in/out referendum.

Boris Johnson announces that he is backing Brexit on Sunday, 21 February 2016. Remain campaign polls showed he made a Leave win much more likely.

Nigel Farage in the lurid green tie of Grassroots Out, the vehicle the Ukip leader sought to use to seize control of the Out campaign.

Let's take back control

The 'Six Brexiteers' from the Cabinet – John Whittingdale, Theresa Villiers, Michael Gove, Chris Grayling, Iain Duncan Smith and Priti Patel – after declaring their support for Vote Leave on 20 February 2016. Five months later only Grayling and Patel still had jobs.

Boris Johnson preparing to sell a cow ('a lovely milker') on the campaign trail. Johnson's campaign events attracted huge media interest.

Nigel Farage with the controversial 'Breaking Point' poster released on 16 June, just hours before Jo Cox was killed. Farage believed concerns about immigration were the key to victory.

Bob Geldof, accompanied by left-wing activists, expresses his admiration for Ukip's flotilla of fishermen on 15 June.

Farage (channelling Alan Partridge) with Kate Hoey, a leading light in the Labour Leave campaign.

Jeremy Corbyn mugging up on Labour's policy. The leader's reluctance to campaign for Remain was a handicap to the campaign.

George Osborne campaigning in a referendum he never wanted. The chancellor's warnings about the economic risks of Brexit were not believed, and damaged his personal standing.

Boris Johnson watching Michael Gove. The 'manager and the star player' of Vote Leave formed a Dream Team afterwards, but it fell apart after five days.

Boris Johnson celebrates another Leave victory.

Arron Banks awaiting the result. The Leave.EU boss copied Donald Trump's outrageous statements to get publicity.

Nigel Farage had lost seven national elections, but won the most important fight.

Dominic Cummings punches the ceiling as Vote Leave wins.

Daniel Hannan gave a *Henry V* speech to campaign staff as Leave won.

Boris Johnson watches David Cameron resign. His aide Will Walden is to the left.

Samantha Cameron tearing up as her husband throws in the towel.

Michael Gove and Boris Johnson's victory press conference. Ruth Davidson thought they looked like 'a couple of teenage arsonists'.

Boris Johnson's notes announcing that he will not run for leader.

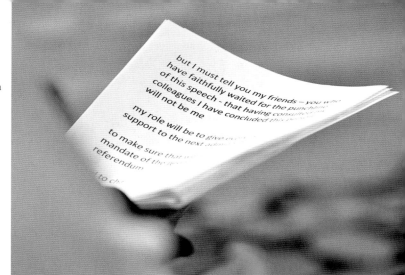

but I must tell you my friends — you who have faithfully waited for the punchline of this speech - that having consulted colleagues I have concluded this ... will not be me

my role will be to give my support to the next ...

to make sure that we ... mandate of the ... referendum

... to ch...

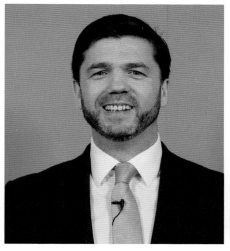

Stephen Crabb finished fourth in the leadership contest.

Liam Fox. MPs think he did a deal with Theresa May.

Tim Loughton leads the Leadsom for leader march on Parliament.

Andrea Leadsom tells her team she is giving up the fight.

A placard held aloft as thousands protest against the referendum decision on 2 July.

Theresa May, with her husband Philip, after becoming Conservative Party leader.

explaining them to viewers. 'That was an unprecedented scale of training just to avoid any pitfalls,' says Munro. There were also live sessions in Old Broadcasting House with some of the BBC's Europe correspondents, including Katya Adler, the Europe editor. Her perspective, as someone with British, German and Spanish family lines and grandparents all over Europe, was valued by colleagues.

The Corporation's critics say this planning was not enough, and the BBC's coverage of the referendum distorted the result. The most serious charge is that in aiming for balance they failed to challenge misleading claims. Central to Craig Oliver's 'frequent calls' to the BBC were complaints that the Corporation was reporting as news 'things that were clearly not true', with just a line of rebuttal from Stronger In. 'The power of big lies is the real concern,' a Downing Street source said. 'If you are going to run a campaign that is based on spurious nonsense and have it reported as acceptable, or even facts-based, there are some questions to answer.'

Oliver was particularly aggrieved by what he perceived to be a misleading statement on Vote Leave's campaign bus that the £350 million no longer sent to Brussels in the event of Brexit would be spent on the NHS: 'Look at what was on the side of the bus, look at what they said, and look at how those claims disappeared in a puff of smoke two or three days after the campaign. Why did they disappear in a puff of smoke? Because they are not true.'[1] Oliver was so irritated by the sight of the bus on the news that he encouraged the BBC to stop showing footage of it, even if it was just in the background. 'It was certainly the case that the Remain campaign were very keen for us to stop using the £350 million,' says a BBC source. 'We didn't stop using it, we did make a policy that every time it was shown we had to explain that this was a gross rather than net figure, and it was highly disputed. That had the effect that we were using it less often, because it's quite a cumbersome thing to explain every five minutes. It certainly wasn't banned, but we did feel we couldn't let it sit there in shot without explaining the dubious nature of the figure.'

Oliver was not the only one to complain about the coverage. Chris Patten, formerly both a Conservative Party chairman and director general of the BBC, always a Europhile, registered his concern in 'unimpressed notes', as did Gus O'Donnell, the former cabinet secretary. A senior figure in the Corporation's political coverage says, 'There were calls every day. It was a constant thing. There was no one great crisis about it. But the problem is that it is very easy to identify the problem, it's much more difficult to identify a solution when you are committed to impartiality. Chris Patten was very active, and made a lot of calls to [BBC director general] Tony Hall and [director of news] James Harding. Gus O'Donnell also thought it was a problem, but was more low-key about making his views known.'

Lucy Thomas, the deputy director of Stronger In and a former BBC journalist who had reported from Brussels, regretted that the BBC did not do more to adjudicate between the two campaigns: 'There was no independent arbiter of truth. Nobody was able to rule on whether what a campaign was saying was fact or fiction. Broadcasters usually do more of a job of that. It just became tit for tat, and nobody was really any the wiser.' George Osborne is not a BBC-basher by instinct, but he has told friends he does not think the BBC did their job particularly well because they were too content to cover stories as 'on the one hand, on the other', and did not 'pull apart' the claims made by Vote Leave. A Treasury source said, 'People wanted information, and they were confused about what decision to make. They trust the BBC. And yet they believed there was a genuine economic argument for leaving, so that didn't help.'

Jonathan Munro defends the BBC against this charge, pointing out that reporters repeatedly challenged claims by both sides: 'There's obviously a difference between balance and impartiality. They overlap a lot, but they're not the same thing. The answer to the question about how we'd intervene to correct things is that we did what we'd normally do. If someone makes a claim that is questionable, spurious, debatable, our job is to take it apart and put it back together again, in whatever order is factually right. Of the various claims that either side made which are debatable factually, a number of them became things we questioned regularly, for example the £350 million figure on the side of the bus, the claims about Turkey being fairly close to accession of the European Union.'

The problem for the broadcasters, as well as the Remain camp, was that Cummings' refusal to change his core message meant each of these claims was made day in and day out during the campaign. During the Wembley debate in the final week, the BBC prepared short explainer films on various issues. The one on Turkish accession concluded that the chances of Turkey joining the EU any time soon were incredibly small, verging on impossible. But a BBC source who was present says Vote

Leave did not complain: 'They were just delighted that Turkey was being mentioned in the debate. They didn't mind that we were taking apart their spurious claims, they were just delighted to get that agenda discussed. The extent to which they were putting stuff out there, both sides, which was extremely questionable – and most people objectively would say they were on the verge of being completely untruthful on some issues – was not a concern to them.' That night a BBC staff member turned to an executive and said, 'They're just not playing by the Queensberry rules. We've never seen that before.'

This was a huge frustration to Craig Oliver, since his selling point as a spin doctor was to help shape broadcast coverage. To some degree he was successful. Will Straw says, 'There were a couple of moments in the campaign where I was really impressed with his ability to shape broadcast news.' On one occasion early in the short campaign, Vote Leave were set to dominate the day's news agenda with a major press conference, but rather than admit defeat and return to fight another day, Oliver was determined to get his pictures into the broadcast package. He came up with the idea of issuing a document with blank pages to denote what Vote Leave had to say about what the world would look like post-Brexit. A member of Stronger In's design team watermarked the document with an image of two fingers crossed, to signify that Vote Leave was merely hoping for the best. The document was printed overnight and a poster of the crossed fingers prepared, which Yvette Cooper unveiled the next day. That day's broadcast coverage was about how the Leave campaign didn't have an answer. 'It was incredibly effective,' recalls Straw. 'That brought home to me why he's held in such high regard.'

Despite his sometimes sarcastic humour, delivered in grating tones, even the Labour people liked the fact that Oliver ran a tight ship and gave clear direction – after the Ed Miliband regime, it was a novelty. On one occasion Joe Carberry said to Adam Atashzai, 'We're just not used to this – one person saying one thing and everyone saying, "Yep."' One of Cameron's aides says, 'The Labour Party guys were so impressed with the way he'd just ring up. They'd never seen anything like it. He was so effective. This is why Lynton rates Craig.'

Yet as the campaign went on, Oliver's competitive advantage was diminished as Vote Leave became savvier about their approach to the broadcasters. Once Stephenson and Oxley started to learn the tricks about who to call and when, they got better at promoting their stories.

'As the campaign went on, I learned how Craig Oliver did it,' says Oxley. 'We recognised somebody incredibly capable, and started replicating what he was doing. There is a trick to making something lead at the BBC.'

Oxley and Stephenson were helped by the fact that a campaign that is trying to overturn the existing order in a way that could bring down the government is inherently more interesting to journalists than one arguing for the status quo. A Downing Street aide said the broadcasters got bored with Remain's talking points: 'One BBC guy told Craig, "You've won the economic argument. We'll just do immigration, it's more interesting."'

It was not always plain sailing for Vote Leave. During the period when Stronger In was wheeling out its expert supporters, they were hamstrung by the lack of third-party support, particularly among national and multinational businesses. Stephenson could land stories easily in the *Mail* and the *Sun*, but they were sometimes ignored by the BBC. Controlling his main mouthpiece was not a cakewalk either. 'Our difficulty was getting splashes into broadcasts,' he says. 'Boris was the only guy who could get the whole media pack there.' When they got there, in the early stages of the campaign Vote Leave could not guarantee that Johnson's most interesting soundbite would be on the subject they were trying to promote that day. 'Getting Boris to say what we wanted him to say so it would link up with the grid wasn't easy,' says Stephenson. But as the campaign went on and Johnson came under attack from allies of Cameron his appreciation of the support of the Vote Leave team increased, and he was more inclined to stay on-message, particularly after he started receiving media training for the television debates, which also helped to focus his mind on the key messages.

No one at Vote Leave thought they would get many votes from BBC employees, but they believe the Corporation was aware that it had made mistakes before in covering EU issues, and was prepared to give the campaign a fair hearing. 'I think if we'd done this ten years ago we'd have been screwed,' said Stephenson. 'I think there was recognition they didn't get it on the euro.'

In trying to shape the headlines, Vote Leave were often quicker to respond. From January members of the press team were in the office from 7 a.m. It was not until purdah kicked in, and Craig Oliver instituted a 6.15 a.m. media conference call, that Stronger In had the edge. David

Chaplin says, 'I think that we definitely had a disadvantage in relation to how quickly we got going. It felt like they were basically up and running from the Tusk letter with a 24/7 political and media operation.' At Vote Leave Rob Oxley remembers, 'We went onto a campaign war footing very early on, much earlier than the other side. If there was a story which came out in the morning, we'd already done a detailed press release by 8 a.m. We could see their stuff was only coming out at 9.30 a.m.'

Vote Leave were very successful at injecting their campaign talking points into the broadcasts. Keeping the Tory wars simmering meant it was the BBC's political editor Laura Kuenssberg who tended to handle the coverage, rather than the economics editor Kamal Ahmed, which meant the soap opera tended to trump the economic arguments. When Ahmed did get on air, it did not always please the Remain camp. One interview he did with George Osborne, on the threat to house prices, was held up as proof of how the BBC adopted Vote Leave's tropes. Ahmed's first question was to ask the chancellor whether he was trying to scare people. 'He literally delivered Leave's line,' said Ryan Coetzee.

Another occasion which enraged the Remain strategist came when Steve Hilton, Cameron's former confidant, publicly backed Vote Leave, and got more publicity than George Soros, the investor who made billions betting against the pound on Black Wednesday, coming out in support of Remain. 'A lot of people lost the plot,' Coetzee says. 'It was capped for me by the day when Steve Hilton led George Soros on the news. Because Hilton is *who*? Seriously!' In news terms, however, it is far from clear that Soros was a bigger story than another of the prime minister's closest friends opposing him.

Vote Leave also maximised their broadcast headlines by putting Boris Johnson in campaigning events that achieved striking visuals. During the campaign he was seen clambering into a truck, doing doughnuts in a sports car, and, most notoriously, selling a cow. 'We felt on the six and the ten that we matched Craig Oliver in a way that he'd never been matched before,' says Oxley. 'We also started to beat them because we took more risks. We specifically exposed Boris to the public. I remember in January sitting in a meeting with a bunch of BBC execs saying, "We want the pictures to go with the stories." So we thought if we were going to talk about agricultural subsidies, let's go and sell a cow.' This was sometimes high-risk. Oxley literally had his head in his hands as Johnson clambered into the driver's seat of a truck in Dartford.

Told he couldn't drive it, he is said to have replied, 'I'm the mayor of London, of course I can drive it.' Oxley recalls, 'He could have stalled it or he could have crashed it – both very bad metaphors for a campaign. In the end, the result was him driving off. Great pictures, everyone loved it.'

Stronger In also had successful visuals, Tony Blair and John Major crossing the Peace Bridge in Northern Ireland among them, but the prime minister's security requirements made it more difficult for him to be spontaneous, and the need for cross-party cooperation sometimes got in the way. A plan for Cameron, Labour's Harriet Harman, Lib Dem leader Tim Farron and Natalie Bennett of the Green Party to do an event, each with a Mini in the colour of their party, was a logistical nightmare. The mother of one of the Stronger In events team drove her green car to London from Warwickshire, only to find that Bennett wanted to be filmed with a bicycle instead, meaning the visual of the four cars driving away together was lost.

One major difference between the referendum and the general election was that Leave had so much of the newspaper market cornered, which inevitably spilled over onto the broadcast bulletins. A Downing Street source complained that this meant the BBC was trying to maintain balance in a media environment that was unbalanced: 'In a normal situation the BBC can be in a situation where it does do balance, but in a general election you have the *Guardian* and the *Mirror* campaigning for the Labour Party, the *Telegraph* and the *Sun* campaigning for the Conservative Party, the *Mail* doing its own thing. But each side has its champions. In this there was no overt real champion for Remain, which meant you had an environment where whatever Leave said was given proper currency.'

This complaint comes quite close to suggesting that since the newspapers were biased towards Leave, the BBC should have sought to tip the balance back the other way, which is not how the executives there saw their role. Once the referendum was over, executives did a second, qualitative, review of the coverage, and concluded that the BBC had been unfair during the campaign – but not in the way Craig Oliver believed.

It found that because most BBC reporters live and work in London, which voted to remain, they did not reflect enough of the pro-Brexit feeling from the rest of England and Wales. A source familiar with the review said, 'There was some criticism, which I wouldn't shy away from, that some of the Leave people we interviewed were a bit shaven-headed, tattooed, they looked like they were slightly on the far wing of the campaign. We could have done more to give what I would call "ordinary decent Leave voters" a little bit more air time.'

That is not a finding that the Remain supporters embrace. They believe that the BBC let down the British viewing public by not doing more to hold Vote Leave to account. 'They failed the country, in my opinion,' said a Number 10 insider. In fact the more justified charge is that the BBC, like most other media outlets, simply got the story wrong. One of David Cameron's closest aides said, 'The BBC fucked up the 2015 election by predicting a Labour–SNP coalition. It worked for us, but it was totally shit journalism. They fucked up the referendum because of this weird obsession they had with misunderstanding what impartiality actually means. For two elections in a row they have had a demonstrable impact in a negative way. The solution is very clear: you don't report things that are palpably untrue.'

Some BBC staff shared these concerns. But Jonathan Munro says, 'It's very easy for the losing side to turn its fire on the BBC, because it's such a loud voice in the national conversation. We saw exactly the same with some extremist elements of the Nationalist supporters in the Scottish independence referendum. I think they would really struggle to pin a charge against us that we "failed the nation". We gave the issues of the EU referendum a monumental amount of air time across all different kinds of formats.' He concludes, 'There's a truism here about all election campaigns with a democracy in a free media: the failure belongs squarely on the shoulders of the people who lost the campaign.'

One of the reasons Leave were victorious is that their figureheads were able to shine in the most high-profile cauldron of all, the battle-ground of the televised debates.

18

DEBATING POINTS

When the pudgy American walked into the open space on the four-teenth floor of Westminster Tower in mid-May, no one was very impressed. He reminded one of those present of Baloo the Bear from *The Jungle Book*. And when he opened his mouth and started spouting clichés about political communication, his audience began to look nervously around the room hoping to catch the eye of a kindred spirit. Eyebrows were raised. Eyes were rolled. The consensus view that developed within seconds was, 'Who the hell is this guy?'

The man did not have an easy audience. Boris Johnson was someone who had turned himself into one of Britain's best political communicators by doing things his own way. His gift was born, not taught. Michael Gove had not got where he was by doing media training either. While Johnson relied on wit and bluster, working his way to a point in ever decreasing circles until he hit on the winning form of words, Gove had one of the most structured minds in Westminster. Words poured from his mouth and his pen in perfect sentences and paragraphs. If both men were idiosyncratic speakers they were instantly, recognisably themselves whenever they opened their mouths. Asked at the end of May whether he was going to try to speak more succinctly in the television debates, Johnson replied, 'It's pathetic, really, but I can't. I have to do it my way, otherwise the mental exhaustion will be intolerable, trying to remember what the bloody soundbite is. It will come out in the wrong order. It's hopeless – I'm fifty-one now, I'm going to do exactly what I do.'

But Dominic Cummings and Paul Stephenson realised this would not be enough, not when both men would be facing their first ever prime-time national political debates, on which might hang the fate of the entire campaign. So they went looking for help. Baloo the Bear's name was Brett O'Donnell, and he was to prove one of Vote Leave's secret weapons in the battle for Brexit.

When it comes to debate prep, the thing to have was an American. British politicians – Johnson and Gove included – are frequently obsessed with American politics, and like to get the same treatment as the candidates they watch every four years on their televisions in the small hours of the morning. Since 2010 David Cameron had used Bill Knapp and Anita Dunn, who helped Barack Obama get elected in 2008, to train him up for his debate appearances. Knapp helped Cameron again during the referendum.

O'Donnell, who was known as 'the candidate whisperer', had worked with George W. Bush in 2004 and prepared Mitt Romney for his 2012 debates with Obama, one of which was the president's worst ever night in a presidential debate. He was John McCain's director of messaging, and ran Michelle Bachmann's presidential campaign in 2012. He had also done a couple of Senate races for Tea Party candidates, whose demographic was similar to some Leave voters. O'Donnell was recommended to Gove by Dan Senor, a Republican political consultant who had advised Marco Rubio's recent campaign for the 2016 Republican presidential nomination. Yet when O'Donnell first opened his mouth that day in Westminster Tower, many Vote Leavers wondered what they were paying the big bucks for. He appeared to know very little about British politics. 'People were quite sceptical at the beginning,' a source said. 'He was this guy with his funny charts.'

But, slowly and emphatically, O'Donnell won them over. He explained that debates are 'messaging opportunities', a chance to hit the public with your campaign's best lines. 'My shtick is debates aren't really debates,' he explained. 'They're not about winning and losing. They're about message and moments. And so I had to coach those guys into understanding how to drive a message and then creating moments that will dominate the press coverage of the debate.'

O'Donnell showed a video of Evander Holyfield, the former world heavyweight champion, after he had won a fight. Holyfield was repeatedly asked about details of the bout: 'Why did you do this?', 'Why did you do that?' To each and every question he replied, 'I just want to praise the Lord and thank the Lord above for everything he's done for me.' O'Donnell said that was an example of using every question as a messaging opportunity. Then he played a tape of Bill Clinton's acceptance speech at the 1992 Democratic National Convention, in which he used the phrase 'build a bridge to the twenty-first century' around thirty times in his half-hour speech. When it was over, O'Donnell switched off the television, turned to his audience and said, 'That's boring, but what are people going to write about the next day? I want you to build a bridge out of the European Union. Find every opportunity.'

By now he had most of his audience eating out of his hand. Apart from one. In that first session O'Donnell created a messaging document and an attack grid, and explained to his audience how they should respond to attacks from Remain and how to get on the offensive with their own attacks. Andrea Leadsom and Gisela Stuart, who were due to feature in the first big three-way debate on ITV, were fully engaged, leaning forward. But while everyone else was listening eagerly, Boris Johnson whipped out a copy of *The Times* and started reading it. The message could not have been clearer. Johnson was not interested.

In the second prep session O'Donnell arranged a practice debate, with some of his staff and Michael Gove's special advisers, Henry Cook and Beth Armstrong, playing the Remain team. Their attacks were scripted. Johnson still appeared nonchalant. 'Don't worry, I've got this,' he said as O'Donnell tried to advise him. According to O'Donnell, the result was not pretty: 'We did a practice debate the next time I came over and my side, the Remain team that we'd coached up, unleashed fury on them.' Johnson, Leadsom and Stuart floundered. O'Donnell was not impressed with what he heard: 'Those guys were all talking as though they were lecturing the senior economics class at Cambridge, as opposed to talking to voters in England.'

Gove and Cummings were seriously worried. They had lined up the most popular politician in the country for the big showdown, and it looked as if Boris was going to blow it. Worse than that, for the first time in the campaign Cummings himself had been completely outmanoeuvred by his two enemies, Craig Oliver and Nigel Farage.

As coalitions go, it is not one likely to meet with favour from the members of either party, but the alliance that saw Nigel Farage take on David Cameron in ITV's solo leaders' debate was forged the previous summer. In the run-up to the general election, Craig Oliver had won plaudits for playing the broadcasters off against each other so that the prime minister only had to do one full debate with six other leaders, allowing him to rise above the squabbling fray. For the referendum, he had two goals – avoid going head to head with Johnson or Gove, and get onto the same programme as Nigel Farage, where Oliver believed the comparison would help Cameron. In this he had a willing ally in the Ukip leader, who was keen to play a prominent role as the campaign reached its climax.

In the summer of 2015, while Dominic Cummings was still constructing a campaign, Farage met ITV executives for lunch at the Betjeman Arms pub at St Pancras station. ITV said they were interested in featuring the Ukip leader in one of their debates. 'What if we don't get designation?' Farage asked. 'They didn't care,' he said later. 'They were interested in ratings.'

Craig Oliver was interested in playing ball with Farage, who he saw as a referendum vote-loser. 'Craig suggested to ITV that Farage should be part of the landscape,' says a Downing Street source. 'They said that was fair, but Nicola Sturgeon should be in the other debate they did. We agreed.' Another Number 10 official says, 'Craig basically did a deal with his old boss at ITV.' By April the fix was in, but ITV asked Ukip not to make any announcement about the plan, because Downing Street was concerned that it would give Ukip an electoral boost at the local elections. Douglas Carswell was not surprised: 'There was this weird symbiotic relationship between the Remain ultras and the Leave ultras. They all want to define it as Ukip nativism versus Cameroonian economic managerialism. That was a surefire way for us to lose the referendum.'

Paul Stephenson had been in sporadic discussions with Chris Ship, ITV's deputy political editor, and Michael Jermey, the network's director of news and current affairs – characterised by one Vote Leave source as 'a really obnoxious ITV suit'. But he got the impression that the ITV men did not want to talk to Vote Leave. Rather than wait for one of the groups to get the official designation, ITV had approached politicians directly about the debates, including Farage, Boris Johnson, Priti Patel and Iain Duncan Smith. When Stephenson explained that Vote Leave were likely to be the official campaign group, ITV held a meeting at which they made it clear that they weren't interested in talking to them about the one v one debate, as that would be Farage v Cameron. They then said Vote Leave could put up who they wanted in the three v three debate, but that they really wanted Johnson. Stephenson expressed displeasure at these arrangements, and pointed out that ITV were basically doing

Cameron's bidding. ITV agreed to regroup and discuss the matter again after designation. Ship and Stephenson then had a conversation in which the Vote Leave man threatened not to take part in the three-way debate if they were excluded from the head-to-head with Cameron.

On 6 May, the Friday after the local elections, Cummings met Farage and Chris Bruni-Lowe at Westminster Tower. Bruni-Lowe said Cummings began 'trying to feel us out about the debates', asking why Downing Street had 'gone cold'. 'It was clear he was fishing for us, because I was organising the thing and I knew that they didn't want to deal with Cummings. It was a triumph to get Nigel in. Cummings went totally mental, because we'd basically just outfoxed him.'

The following week Stephenson was supposed to be having a meeting with ITV on Thursday the 12th, but at 9.59 the evening before he received a call from Ship, who gave him 'a heads up' that they would be announcing a Cameron v Farage debate in their 10 p.m. bulletin. Having refused to talk to the broadcasters for weeks, Craig Oliver had phoned them all that morning to agree formats, and had encouraged them to make immediate announcements. *Sky News* revealed their plans the same day. Stephenson told Ship that ITV's actions would cause real issues, and that they should have discussed it with Vote Leave first. 'It was two fingers up to us,' a campaign source said. 'ITV had just done exactly what Craig had asked in order to secure the PM on their programme. It was a shabby stitch-up.'

The row erupted while Rob Oxley was on the road with the first Vote Leave bus tour. He was dining with lobby journalists in a pizza restaurant in Exeter when the news broke. He immediately called Stephenson to agree a response to give to the lobby. Both had been drinking. Stephenson wanted an aggressive stance, with accusations that ITV had lied and a suggestion that Vote Leave might consider court action. The initial response was robust, but then before midnight an email popped up in the journalists' inboxes taking the rhetoric up a notch. Dominic Cummings had intervened. The email accused ITV of having 'lied to us in private while secretly stitching up a deal with Cameron', and said the broadcaster had 'effectively joined the official In campaign and there will be consequences for its future'. Turning on the political editor, it continued, 'ITV is led by people like Robert Peston who campaigned for Britain to join the euro.' (Peston had reported years before that Britain would join the euro, but had not campaigned for it.) The email also predicted

Cameron's imminent demise, saying, 'The people in Number 10 won't be there for long.'

One ally said that Cummings, embarrassed that Vote Leave had been outmanoeuvred, had adopted Lynton Crosby's 'dead cat on the table' ploy – where a controversial statement is made to distract the media. 'Not so much a dead cat, more an entire abattoir,' the source added. The next morning, one of Stephenson's friends in Downing Street texted him, 'How's your hangover?' The statement had certainly been over the top, and Oxley had a tough time when he was sent onto the *Today* programme at 7 a.m., still somewhat fragile, to defend it. 'It's not how I wanted my debut on the *Today* programme to be,' he says.

The email outburst was seen in Westminster as proof that Cummings had finally lost his mind, but there was method in it as well. Cummings' real audience was not ITV executives but bosses at the BBC, which was considering holding a Farage v Cameron debate of its own on the Sunday before the vote. Cummings explains, 'Everyone thought we'd gone mad, but it was not to do with ITV. By chance, we had a guy who was in the BBC about other stuff the day that ITV announced the whole thing, and he overheard various conversations. He called up and said, "You guys are going to get totally screwed tomorrow morning because the BBC are going to do exactly what ITV have just done to you. And the meeting they're going to do that is tomorrow." Some powerful forces at the BBC wanted to announce that they were going to cancel six months of negotiations we were all agreed on, and do Farage versus Cameron instead. We wanted them to look at it and say, "We don't want to get dragged into a knife-fight with people who will do anything." And that's what seemed to happen.' BBC sources say Cummings had duff information, and that any chance of a Cameron–Farage contest died when Vote Leave got designation – but the campaign believed the rumour, and acted.

The Farage v Cameron affair soured relations between Vote Leave and ITV from then on. Senior campaign staff and ministers cut the broadcaster off, culminating in an attempt by Cummings to ban Robert Peston from the victory press conference the morning after the vote. 'Their coverage was an absolute disgrace, and didn't even attempt to achieve balance,' said a campaign official. 'They threw everything at trying to get a Remain vote.' These are claims that were strenuously denied by ITV.

Boris Johnson was 'fuming' at Cummings, and publicly dismissed the issue as 'microcosmographia': 'Boris didn't like the term "consequences".'

Cummings' behaviour that week contributed to Johnson and Will
Walden's later view that they did not want him involved with the Tory
leadership campaign that followed the referendum. At the Vote Leave
offices, where rows were there to be exploited, 'consequences' became a
new catchphrase – 'When someone did something that was annoying,
we would say, "There will be consequences!"'

David Cameron was advised to do no face-to-face debates. Instead,
Craig Oliver negotiated him three solo appearances. In addition to facing
the ITV audience back-to-back with Farage, he would also appear on a
Question Time special for the BBC. His first outing, and the most uncom-
fortable, would be an interview with Faisal Islam, the political editor of
Sky News, followed by an audience question-and-answer session on 3
June. Michael Gove would do the same the day after.

While Cameron was put through his paces by Bill Knapp, Islam had
also been prepping with Esme Wren, Sky's head of politics, for three full
weeks. Relatively new to Westminster, Islam was yet to make his mark,
but the preparation showed. To Cameron's evident surprise, the normally
mild-mannered Islam aggressively put him on the spot about his
campaign claims. 'What comes first? World War III, or the global Brexit
recession?' he asked, to wounding laughter from the audience. Cameron
was reduced to calling his interrogator 'glib'. Worse was to follow in the
Q&A session, during which student Soraya Bouazzaoui accused him of
'scaremongering', and when Cameron tried to answer, interrupted him
to say, 'I'm an English Literature student, I know waffling when I see it,
OK?' It was a bruising encounter which opened the eyes of campaign
spin doctors and some journalists to the depth of anti-EU feeling in the
country.

Michael Gove, watching at home, was decidedly nervous. It was his
turn in the bearpit the following evening. 'I've never done anything like
this before,' he said. Gove had been a frontline politician for a decade,
but he had never before been the main man. When he had last appeared
on *The Andrew Marr Show* it had not gone well. Popular with the
commentariat, he had lost his job as education secretary because he was
unpopular with the public. Now the hopes of the Brexiteers rested
squarely on his shoulders.

Brett O'Donnell helped Gove to prepare, testing him repeatedly with
every possible question, putting him under pressure, interrupting him

and persuading him that every question was an opportunity to get across his message. 'I don't think Michael had a question that we hadn't gone through,' he said later. O'Donnell knew exactly what he wanted Gove to say: 'When I got there, they had tested "Take back control", but they weren't really using it. Their message was "£350 million" on the side of the bus. That's not a message, that's a fact, so I said, "You guys need a message." I really drove the campaign to use that in virtually all their communications.' In his appearance on Sky, Gove, who had made himself a name for felicitous turns of phrase, trotted out 'take back control' with metronomic relentlessness. A Gove aide said, 'What Brett did was exercise some message discipline, something Michael had always resisted. He had always regarded media training as cheating and a little beneath him.' Tweeting from home, Boris Johnson cheered on 'the Gover'.

O'Donnell also set out to humanise the slightly geeky Gove, interviewing him about his life and family before the Sky grilling. Gove's Euroscepticism was grounded in his own history. His father's fish business, he said, had gone belly-up in his teenage years. O'Donnell seized on this, and urged Gove to deploy it in his Sky appearance. 'My father had a fishing business in Aberdeen destroyed by the European Union and the Common Fisheries Policy,' he told the audience. When Faisal Islam contested the existence of the free-trade zone Gove hoped Brexit Britain would join, saying, 'It doesn't have a website, so it doesn't exist,' Gove won laughter and applause when he replied, 'Most of the people in this audience don't have their own personal website. I don't doubt that they exist.'

Gove's toughest moment led to his most memorable line. Pressed on why more financial institutions and businesses were not backing Leave, he responded, 'I think the people of this country have had enough of experts … I'm afraid it's time to say, "You're fired!"' The line was the antithesis of Gove's career to date, which had been grounded on seeking out expert practice around the world, but it touched a chord with voters.

David Cameron could not believe what he was hearing. Michael Gove had been the intellectual beating heart of the Tory modernisation project, and he now sounded like a Luddite. 'The PM was raging about that for days,' a Number 10 aide said. 'He couldn't believe Michael, of all people, would say that. He was pretty contemptuous of him giving respectability to an argument like that.' Ryan Coetzee, Stronger In's head of strategy, said the comment helped him 'understand Michael Gove'.

Coetzee counted himself a fan of mavericks, and of expanding choice in education. But he found himself concluding, 'More than any specific ideological vision he has, Gove is an ideologue. You do get the whiff of burning witches. The thing about ideologues, whether they're left or right, none of them need experts because *they're* the expert; because the ideology has the answer. Ideologues force the world to conform to their theory instead of having their theory conform to the world. That, to my mind, explains Michael Gove.'

Despite the horror of London intellectuals, Gove's performance – unlike Cameron's – exceeded expectations, and even prompted leadership chatter. Gove ruled himself out, telling the audience, 'The one thing I can tell you is there are lots of talented people who could be prime minister after David Cameron, but count me out.' However, he left the studio knowing he had been tested at the top level and survived. His performance, eight days after the immigration figures, a week after purdah began, and five days after the 'corrosive of public trust' letter, was a key moment in the campaign.

Brett O'Donnell said, 'Michael really drove the message that night and really connected with the audience, whereas Cameron had been very standoffish with the audience, almost confrontational at times. I felt that was a high-watermark for us because I thought that coming out of that appearance, everyone started to believe we could win.'

Nigel Farage liked journalists to think he was the ultimate improviser, but he did not take any chances ahead of his televised showdown with Cameron on 7 June. He prepared for the contest with an all-day preparation session the day before. 'I always do a lot more than I make out,' he said. He had recruited an eclectic team of advisers to put him through his paces, most notably David Davis, the former Tory leadership candidate who would go on to become minister for Brexit. Chris Bruni-Lowe says, 'David helped craft Nigel's arguments and gave notes as well as speaking on the phone often. David also talked a lot about his debate with Cameron from the 2005 leadership contest, and gave his advice on how Nigel should approach it. David also did the spin room for us that evening.'

Farage and Cameron would never be on stage together, but their performances would be judged against each other. Farage's other helpers included Kate Hoey, Mark Reckless, his advisers Gawain Towler, Chris Bruni-Lowe and Michael Heaver, Jago Pearson from Nick Wood's firm

MIP, and Leave.EU's Jack Montgomery, who was seconded to Farage's team after the designation.

Before he went on stage Farage slipped out for a cigarette, and on the way back there was an awkward encounter as he walked straight into David Cameron's entourage coming the other way. One of Farage's team tweeted a picture of a startled Cameron with a horrified female aide by his side. 'Everything was choreographed so I wouldn't bump into him,' Farage said. 'It was a complete fluke.' The two contenders exchanged minimal pleasantries. 'He looked very unhappy to see me, but more comfortable than Osborne when I met him on the Peston show the Sunday before. Osborne was so odd. Poor chap.' Gawain Towler said the chancellor had his 'nose in the air – it was almost like a caricature of a child'.

Farage had a tough time from the ITV audience. The most heated encounter came when Imriel Morgan, a young black woman, told him, 'You are going to increase the fear and discrimination of black British people through your anti-immigration rhetoric. Are you encouraging racism?' The charge led to a furious back-and-forth exchange in which Farage defended himself as a supporter of the Commonwealth, but appeared snappy. Later he admitted, 'It was tough,' but refused to give ground: 'A lot of people didn't like it, but do you know what? It consolidated our support. The idea that if we'd sounded like social democrats and suddenly we'd have picked up more votes is absolute rubbish.' But by the standards of his incendiary claims about health tourists with HIV during the general election, Farage was subdued.

Had he not been, Downing Street officials later revealed that Cameron was prepared to leap on anything outrageous that Farage said, and hammer him. 'We thought Farage would totally go for the PM and say lots of horrible things. He was really prepared to lay into Farage,' says an aide. 'He was prepared to go on and say, "This guy's really unpleasant. I've listened to this guy for several years now, and I just want to get something off my chest: he calls Chinese people chinks, he calls gay people fags, and this is not British, it's not who we are and it's not right. It's divisive and it's wrong and we should have no part in it. It's not the Britain I love." He was going to totally go for it, but the moment never came.'

Cameron faced a tough time on his 'tens of thousands' immigration pledge, but unlike the *Sky News* showdown, he benefited from going second, and was less tetchy, even laughing when asked if he was 'finished' whatever the result of this referendum. An hour later he was on the terrace of the House of Commons having a pint and drawing reflectively on a cigarette, though it was notable that more Labour MPs than Tories went over to talk to him. Both Stronger In and Vote Leave thought Cameron had won the exchange. Rob Oxley despaired at Farage's testy attitude with the black audience member, fearing that it would cost them votes. 'That debate showed you more than anything why Cameron was a 45 per cent politician and Nigel Farage at best a 15 per cent politician. He was aggressive towards the audience. Our focus groups told us he was not going to help us.'

Vote Leave's bigger concern at that point was whether the first three-way debate would go ahead without their star performers. After Paul Stephenson played hardball with ITV, who wanted Boris Johnson on the stage, Chris Ship approached Jago Pearson at MIP to come up with an alternative threesome to the Vote Leave line-up. Pearson reported back that David Davis, Liam Fox and Kate Hoey were prepared to step in, and a meeting took place between Ship, Pearson and Nick Wood at the Slug and Lettuce pub in Victoria to go through the details. ITV gave Vote Leave a deadline of midday on the Monday before the debate. They signed the agreement at around 11 a.m. – propelling Boris Johnson into the limelight.

The first three-way debate, on Thursday, 9 June, marked a change of direction for the Remain campaign. After months of resisting blue-on-blue attacks, Craig Oliver decided that the story he wanted leading the news that evening was a series of punchy attacks on Boris Johnson. The former mayor, the Tories reasoned, was likely to be the story of the debate anyway, since the media would lap up his first major television test. Better that the headlines talked about Johnson being on the back foot than one of Vote Leave's attack lines. James McGrory says, 'They felt that if they hadn't done that, the field would have been left to Boris and whatever pronouncement he made would then be the main story that led on the news and in the papers the next day, whereas in fact the main story that ran was "Boris gets attacked." They felt that was the lesser of two evils.'

Oliver's first wheeze, undeniably clever, was to deploy an all-female line-up against Johnson. ITV had separately approached Nicola Sturgeon, the Scottish first minister, whose debate performances during the general election had been lauded by the media. Labour had put up Angela Eagle, the shadow leader of the Commons, who did a fine line in sarcastic put-downs during business questions at the despatch box every Thursday. To complete the set the very willing weapon Oliver deployed from Conservative ranks was Amber Rudd (the sister of Roland Rudd, the PR man who helped set up the campaign), who was seen as a rising star in the cabinet. In the preceding months Downing Street officials had begun to talk up the energy secretary as a possible leadership candidate if George Osborne was unable or unwilling to run. A quietly effective secretary of state, with a sharp mind, she was virtually unknown to the public. This was to be her coming-out party.

Oliver believed, rightly, that Johnson would find it less easy to bluster his way through a ninety-minute debate or deploy the full extent of his dismissive wit in the face of a three-way assault from female politicians. But Dominic Cummings had already decided he would surround Johnson with two female outriders of his own. The Labour MP Gisela Stuart and Andrea Leadsom, Rudd's deputy at the Department of Energy and Climate Change, would complete the Leave team.

In prep sessions for the debate the Remain team tested attack lines. Lucy Thomas, who had organised the sessions, played Andrea Leadsom, with Will Straw playing Gisela Stuart and Tory adviser Ed de Minckwitz universally praised as an uncannily accurate Boris Johnson, trotting out lines in a plummy voice about how Stronger In were 'talking down Britain', complete with bold gesticulations and a Johnsonian ruffle of the hair. 'Craig came up with some ideas, Amber came up with some of her own as well, as did Angela Eagle,' recalls Straw. Oliver primed Rudd with a witty and effective gag that seamlessly combined an assault on Vote Leave's cavalier use of figures with Johnson's leadership ambitions: 'The only number Boris is interested in is Number 10.' Rudd was 'very up for' her role as 'rebutter in chief', and was a fertile source of further lines. She arrived having already come up with lines to take on Vote Leave's dispar-aging of experts, including 'If you were building a bridge you'd get an engineer to do it.' Lucy Thomas said, 'She'd really done the homework. She was funny but also authoritative.'

Thomas had a harder time preparing Angela Eagle to accept the campaign's messaging, since she did not want to be heard parroting David Cameron's lines. 'I kept trying to say, "We've tested these messages endlessly, they're not Tory messages, they're the ones that we know work,"' says Thomas.

The main problem for the Remain team's preparation was that Nicola Sturgeon was unable to travel south to take part in the messaging sessions. Instead she sent Kevin Pringle, a seasoned SNP spin doctor who had been director of communications for the Better Together campaign in Scotland. Downing Street officials say it was a struggle to persuade the SNP to include their key messages in Sturgeon's opening and closing scripts.

They also had to face down an attempt by Sturgeon to deal in her opening statement with the apparent conundrum that she had argued for Scottish independence north of the border, but was now campaigning to remain in the European Union. Thomas says, 'People naturally thought, "Hang on a minute, how can you be for independence in Scotland and then pro-Union when it comes to the EU?" It's both confusing and, to many in our focus groups, hypocritical. Yet the SNP wanted to put this issue up front and to deal with it straight off. We said, "Are you sure that's wise? Let's just make the positive case."' Eventually Oliver convinced Pringle that this would distract from Stronger In's core messaging, and should be delayed until later in the debate. However, Sturgeon's absence meant that the three Remainians had not had a chance to interact or properly coordinate their lines of attack. It was a factor that was to dent their effectiveness.

Alastair Campbell, Tony Blair's old spin doctor, helped with the debate prep. He had been advising Craig Oliver on how to handle a hostile press, and told him the debates were 'moments where you could communicate your strategy unfiltered by the media'. Campbell was pleased the Tories had ditched their aversion to blue-on-blue attacks. When Johnson had written his article about the 'part-Kenyan' Barack Obama, Campbell had texted George Osborne to suggest, 'Why doesn't somebody come out and say if you say that about the president of America when the president of America is on our soil, you are unfit for high office?' Campbell understood Downing Street's reluctance, but felt it was a mistake not to challenge Johnson. He told Oliver, 'How can you play down blue on blue when what Boris is doing is driving a strategy which is probably going to end in Cameron having to go? What is more blue on blue than that?'

Campbell told the team, 'On every single answer, one of you must be thinking about rebuttal. They are coming out with a load of lies. We have to just keep pushing back at them, without it looking like just whingeing.'

He also gave a pep talk to Amber Rudd, telling her she could use her status as a relative unknown as an advantage: 'This can be a really, really big moment for you. Show that you've got fight. The TV debates made Nicola Sturgeon as a national figure. The same thing can happen to you. It's time to show Boris Johnson that he's in for a fight.'

The target of these thoughts slowly learned to take direction from Brett O'Donnell. Will Walden explained to the American consultant that to get Johnson to concentrate he needed to be a disciplinarian. 'Initially Boris wasn't as focused as he needed to be,' says O'Donnell. 'Then Boris realised he needed to get serious and start working. He turned it on. Boris went and did his homework and really flicked on the switch.' A Johnson ally says, 'As soon as he trusted Brett, everything changed. Boris fully admitted that it wasn't necessarily his greatest skill. It made him nervous. In Brett, he found somebody who was able to understand the importance of distilling messages. If they wandered off-message or got it wrong, he literally said, "Do it again and do it right." There was an element of respect for his directness and this Zen-like focus on the message. That work changed Boris as a public performer.'

In his debate prep, O'Donnell told Johnson, Leadsom and Stuart to zoom in on the important arguments they needed to make, and to use the questions as an opportunity 'not just to answer the person in front of you but to have a conversation with the audience'. He told his charges, 'Don't get involved in the back-and-forth, don't rise to the bait. Always go back to "Take back control".' O'Donnell offered to reward them with an expensive meal out if they used the phrase often enough on the big night.

He also worked with all three candidates, as he had with Gove, to sell them to the public as people as well as politicians, telling them, 'People have to get to know and like you. And if they like you, they'll vote for you.' He encouraged Leadsom to talk about her experience as a business-woman and a mother, while the German-born Stuart worked 'as a mother and a grandmother' into her answers, along with the line 'as an immigrant ...' which would prove highly effective.

Vote Leave's planning was made easier because the Remain camp had briefed that Stronger In's team of women would give Johnson a hard time. 'They telegraphed their attacks,' says O'Donnell. 'There was a story that the women were going to come after Boris. We practised exactly how to handle that. We literally did hours and hours of practice debates. And Boris bought into the notion that we had to be working with the other two. So we scripted out who would take the lead on which issues. Every one of them would tell you the practice debates were way harder than the actual debates, because I always want them to see the worst that can happen rather than go easy on them.'

Disastrously, the worst that could happen was on display on the day of the debate. O'Donnell had set up a mock debate, and his scripted Remain campaign stand-ins had wiped the floor with the Leave team. 'It was a total shitshow,' says one campaign source. 'They were all awful. Leadsom was worse than Sarah Palin when Brett had done her.'

Another source who was present says, 'Brett would go, "It was fine." And they'd go, "No, no it wasn't." It was a deliberate tactic. He'd say, "Well, it was OK." And they said, "You're not telling us the truth, are you?"' O'Donnell then delivered the verdict, 'It's fine, but if you want to deliver that tonight, you'll get yourselves crushed.' O'Donnell says, 'The morning of the ITV debate was a disaster for everyone, but especially Andrea. I gave them a pretty harsh critique and sent them to go work on their material. They returned a couple of hours later for another practice and things went much better.'

The trio 'prepped to death', a friend of Johnson said, with the two women intervening to cut off attacks on Johnson and pivot onto Vote Leave's talking points. 'We did talk about the idea of whether that would look bad – whether it would be too defensive to get these fantastic grandmother figures to defend him. It was an organic thing. They just became a better team.'

The ITV debate was arguably the most exciting ninety minutes of the campaign, and it was Vote Leave's teamwork and message discipline that meant they edged a win. But it was Remain that got the headlines. All three Remain women went for Johnson early and often, guaranteeing easy copy for the newspapers. Rudd, wearing stern but trendy plastic glasses, peered at her Tory colleague and said, 'I fear that the only number Boris is interested in is Number 10.' Attacking Leave's 'sneering' at experts, she said, 'If you wanted to build a bridge you would talk to expert engineers to make sure it didn't fall down. If I wanted expert advice on a good joke I might ask Boris.'

Sturgeon called the £350 million figure a 'whopper', while Eagle said 'Take that lie off your bus,' and warned voters that Johnson did not care about the risk of job losses in the event of Brexit because 'You only care about your job that you want to be your next one.' She added, 'Beware of the blond bombshell.' Throughout it all, Johnson kept his composure and delivered a couple of barbs of his own, pointing out that Sturgeon had denounced the negativity of the Remain campaign. 'I agree with Nicola,' he beamed. Leadsom showed a willingness to take on Rudd – her boss at the Department of Energy – and Stuart exuded calm. Paul Stephenson says, 'She was – in my view – the key person in the debates. They couldn't accuse us of being little Englanders when we had a German-born lady on the stage. Her "I am an immigrant" line worked perfectly.'

The Remain team was relieved with the outcome of the debate, not least because they had not had time to prepare together. They had succeeded in what they had set out to achieve. Will Straw recalls, 'The decision taken in the ITV debate was that if we weren't careful this would be Boris Johnson's moment. There was going to be huge raking over of everything that was said, and let's make sure that was an attack on his character, rather than whatever bullshit he was trying to get across. We succeeded on those terms.'

But the view in the press room was that Rudd's final attack on Johnson was a step too far, crossing the line from pointed political attack into something more personal. As she summed up, Rudd made a reference to Johnson's love life: 'Boris, he's the life and soul of the party. But he's not the man you want to drive you home at the end of the evening.' When Adam Atashzai heard the line, he was not expecting it. He said to himself, 'Ooh, hello!'

In the Leave camp there was euphoria that Johnson had not risen to the baiting. 'He didn't burn in the frying pan,' an aide said. Afterwards he swapped 'kisses and smiles' with his team-mates. A source close to Johnson said: 'They've made a big mistake. Boris is the most popular politician in the country, and all they've done is make this campaign all about Boris.'

Alastair Campbell said, 'I think Amber Rudd did really really well; she was tough, she was strong, she was really up for it as well, but it allowed Boris to play the victim. If you're doing an underdog campaign then that's actually quite helpful.' Craig Oliver could not understand the fuss. His view, summarised by a Number 10 source, was, 'The pro-Brexit press were going to sing the praises of Leave, or write another story. The other story was "Boris criticised". They wrote it, and our clips were better on the news. If you look at what was said, it really is quite pathetic how the Leave campaign started crying about it. There were a couple of good jokes – no more.' Rudd was publicly praised by Cameron, who tweeted that she was 'a star'.

The verdict of the public, though, was different. On 14 June Ryan Coetzee emailed the senior staff at Stronger In about a focus group in Durham. It made for grim reading: 'A few had watched the ITV debate but it hadn't enlightened them in any way. They really did not like the personal attacks. This is consistent with the attitude of undecided/ persuadable voters in all groups. Given we are talking to these people in the debates, we need to ban all personal attacks from the BBC debate. It really does just turn these voters off.' He also found that 'a few' English voters 'responded very badly to Sturgeon, as was the finding in Worcester last week. I hope her presence in that debate helped drive up SNP support levels because despite her good performance, I don't think she really did us much good.'

The Remain camp had to reluctantly admit that they had got it wrong. They would field an entirely different line-up for the final debate at Wembley. Vote Leave would stick to exactly the same team. But Stronger In had bigger problems than that. The following day they held a crisis meeting to discuss another big beast who was not doing them any good – Jeremy Corbyn.

19

LABOUR ISN'T WORKING

There were exactly two weeks until polling day when the Remain campaign went into crisis mode. The trigger was an email from Andrew Cooper on the evening of Thursday, 9 June. At around 4.30 that afternoon Will Straw, Craig Oliver, Stephen Gilbert, Ryan Coetzee and Ameet Gill went into private conclave in a cramped meeting room just off the main war room at the Cannon Street offices. Watching from outside, James McGrory, Joe Carberry and the others sensed immediately that something was seriously wrong. 'I'd been on enough campaigns to know there was a wobble going on,' says McGrory.

Andrew Cooper's latest tracking poll data showed a flat blue line which indicated that Tory support for Remain was holding up; but the Labour line was dipping considerably, and from a lower starting point than they would have liked. The Lib Dem and Green lines had also dropped. The data, which was presented to the Stronger In board on the Friday morning, showed that support for Remain among Labour voters had dropped from 70 per cent to 60 per cent. Overall they were now trailing Leave.

The diagnosis was clear: the campaign had become too Tory-focused. The senior staff briefly considered launching an entirely new campaign, Progressives for In, to get the media to report left-wing views. But when Straw contacted Patrick Heneghan, the Labour official overseeing the Labour In campaign, he said, 'The Labour Party will never share platforms with the SNP or even the Liberal Democrats. It's never going to happen.' The better solution was obvious: get Labour voices on television arguing for Europe. They decided to clear the grid. Emerging from the meeting, they told McGrory and Carberry, 'We're changing it up.' Straw and his fellow Labour campaign officials began calling senior Labour politicians to ascertain their availability, while Joe Carberry dug out Labour-friendly stories on the impact of Brexit on the NHS, public-sector funding and job losses. David Chaplin started planning a grid of announcements.

Craig Oliver and Ameet Gill reported back to Downing Street, where the prime minister agreed to take a back seat for a few days to give Labour voices the chance to dominate the airwaves. A senior campaign source said, 'Cameron supported this. Stephen and Ameet and Craig, they "got it" very quickly. Osborne was not persuaded that it would be preferable to continuing the economy assault.'

Cooper's warning came at a time when Tory high command was also hearing worrying anecdotal evidence from the ground. Labour MPs backing Remain reported back that they were not campaigning in their own seats, having been shocked at the Eurosceptic reception they received on the doorstep. Some felt that any form of organised canvass-ing activity would only boost the Leave vote. In a Remain cabinet meet-ing Anna Soubry, the business minister, whose Nottinghamshire seat was a Tory–Labour marginal, warned, 'I'm really worried about Labour voters. Their support is very soft, and the Labour Party are not doing anything.' Labour's own internal analysis of the postal votes that had already been counted was predicting a 53–47 victory for Leave. A focus group conducted by the party in Lewisham, south-east London, found Labour voters angry because they did not know their party's stance on Brexit. Alastair Campbell had emailed George Osborne to suggest that MPs with Midlands and northern seats – like William Hague, David Blunkett, Alan Johnson, Margaret Beckett and Nick Clegg – should all join the Remain battlebus to campaign together in the big northern towns. 'I was really worried it was slipping away,' he says.

As luck would have it, Yvette Cooper was already due to unveil a poster the following morning, Friday, 10 June. It featured an image of Boris Johnson, Nigel Farage and Michael Gove throwing dice and a slogan urging voters, 'Don't let them gamble with your future'. Cooper spiced up her rhetoric and appealed directly to Labour supporters, saying, 'The Leave campaign is made up of right-wing Tories who have never cared about Labour voters and working people. Right-wing Tories hand-in-hand with Nigel Farage are gambling with this country's future for their own political purposes.' It was the kind of 'red on dark-blue' attack that the campaign had sought for months.

Clearing a grid was one thing; getting Labour high command to do anything useful with the time set aside for them was another. Peter Mandelson rang Tom Watson and Iain McNicol, the general secretary of the party, to tell them of the dire situation and to ask them to pull out all the stops, promising that the campaign would fight to secure them air time and would provide any resources and back-up they needed. Both Watson and McNicol made it clear that the leader's office was the obstacle to anything happening, and that Seumas Milne, Corbyn's director of strategy and communications, and all-purpose panjandrum, was blocking effective campaigning by going over campaign materials and scripts with an unhelpful fine-tooth comb. They said they would do all they could, but without Corbyn's or shadow chancellor John McDonnell's support (which neither expected) there was a limit to what they could do. Straw says, 'All of us were absolutely clear about the need to get Labour into the debate. We had no trust in the leadership to deliver it, so we had to deliver it ourselves.' Cameron agreed to stand aside from an event at de Montfort University in Leicester, but all efforts to get Jeremy Corbyn to take his place failed. 'We spent the entire weekend trying to get Jeremy to go to that event, and he basically just refused hands-down,' says a Labour source. 'Tom Watson was ringing him, Ed Miliband was ringing him.' Eventually Gordon Brown was lined up instead.

The situation was all too familiar to the Labour people at Stronger In, senior officials in party headquarters and those around Alan Johnson, who was running the Labour In for Britain campaign. For months Corbyn, McDonnell and Milne had engaged in a policy of non-cooperation and obstructionism that convinced many leading Remain campaigners and Labour frontbenchers that, at best, they did not care if Stronger In won the referendum, or at worst – a sentiment that grew towards polling day – that they actively sought to sabotage the campaign.

The first sign that Jeremy Corbyn did not regard Europe as a priority came in the first week of January when he fired Pat McFadden, his shadow Europe minister. McFadden was one of the canniest MPs in the Commons. But he blotted his copybook with Corbyn by suggesting that the leader was soft on terrorism following the Islamic State attacks in Paris. At the instigation of Hilary Benn, the shadow foreign secretary, McFadden was replaced by another pro-European, Pat Glass. But the loss of McFadden from the front line robbed the Labour In campaign of a doughty warrior who would have been more prepared to go toe-to-toe with the leadership. 'We lost a very effective media communicator, a very effective campaign strategist in quite a brutal way,' says a member of Labour In.

After Cameron returned with his deal in February, Alan Johnson began drumming up support from senior Labour figures on the ruling National Executive Committee (NEC), but found it lacking in the leadership. 'I went to the NEC and spoke to them. And then I went to the shadow cabinet. And Jeremy made it so clear that this wasn't a priority.' In the shadow cabinet meeting Corbyn ignored Johnson and asked Pat Glass to speak instead. 'Jeremy referred to her all the time, and ignored me,' says Johnson. 'I'd been around long enough for it not to have caused any damaged feelings.' But when Glass said that Johnson, as the head of the campaign, should address the meeting, Corbyn said, 'Well, let's get this hurried up please, because John McDonnell's got an important statement to make about finance.' Johnson was astonished: 'For most people, Europe was the most important decision we'd ever made. More important than general elections. More important than the 1975 referendum, because then we weren't wrenching ourselves out of something after forty-odd years. Once I had said my bit, Jeremy said, "Right, I'll take some questions, but please can we hurry up?" That epitomised his approach to all this. He was not concerned about whether there was a Leave vote. In fact, people have said he might have voted Leave. It wouldn't surprise me if he did.' Corbyn has publicly said that he voted Remain, but many in his own party still doubt him.

Corbyn's, at best, tepid enthusiasm for the EU was mirrored by his key adviser Seumas Milne, a willowy Wykehamist and former comment editor of the *Guardian* whose columns had led to him being labelled a Stalin apologist who blamed the West for most of the world's ills. At the newspaper he was known as 'the Thin Controller' for his Svengali-like influence. Milne had written as recently as July 2015 that 'Many progressive people in Britain … are moving towards voting no in the planned in–out referendum in the face of its brutal authoritarianism towards Greece.' His closest ally was Andrew Fisher, a hard-left activist who had urged people to vote for Class War rather than the Labour Party in the general election. In an interview with Croydon Radio in 2015, Fisher said he was 'agnostic' about the EU. Only Corbyn's then chief of staff Simon Fletcher, a former aide to Ken Livingstone, was a significant pro-EU voice. John McDonnell's team were also divided. James Meadway, an economic adviser, wrote on the Counterfire website: 'In our own referendum, on British membership of the EU, the left must vote No.'[1]

Charlie Falconer, the shadow justice secretary at the time, said Milne was explicitly equivocal about the result of the referendum: 'Seumas made it clear to me: "If we stay in the European Union then Jeremy will get the credit for having contributed to staying, and if we lose, then the position will be that Jeremy will be known to have been lukewarm about it, will appear to be close to the public. That's how he sees it."' In a similar vein, a member of the shadow cabinet claimed Milne had called this scenario 'a win–win'.

Alan Johnson believes Milne was the major impediment to a proper working relationship between his campaign and the leadership: 'The people in his office made life as difficult as they could for people running our campaign. People like Brian Duggan, Patrick Heneghan and Sam Bacon were all frustrated by the leader's office. They'd tried to get dates in the grid and they didn't want to know.' Johnson says the campaign descended into a series of 'painful episodes', but throughout it all there was little engagement from Milne. 'Seumas Milne, he's head of strategy and he never turned up at a single meeting before the campaign began. I don't think he turned up to one afterwards either.' Johnson also wanted Corbyn to campaign on the EU before the local elections in May. 'Alan multiple times tried to set up a meeting with Jeremy's office,' says a source in a position to know the workings of Corbyn's office, 'but Seumas basically vetoed it multiple times. He wasn't interested.'

Early in the campaign Johnson's team, led by Brian Duggan, drew up a core script for use by Labour politicians which talked about the EU providing prosperity and protections on issues like workplace rights, consumer rights and the environment, and boosting Britain's role in the world. It was signed off by the campaign, party HQ and Corbyn's office in the autumn of 2015. A party official says, 'We'd tested it with focus groups, we'd tested it with Labour voters. The only problem was the leader of the Labour Party, having signed it off, never used it.'

Labour had an important role to play in the campaign, because they could make arguments that were distinct from those of the central Stronger In campaign. 'Cameron wasn't going to go heavy on workers' rights. We could,' says Alan Johnson. 'This agenda ought to have appealed to Corbyn; it was at the heart of the "social Europe" agenda mapped out by Jacques Delors which the leader had cited as his reason for supporting Remain.'

But Corbyn, who had no experience of top-level politics until he won the Labour leadership in September 2015, was unable to make this argument compelling or accessible to voters. He talked about the 'Posted Workers Directive', which governs workplace rights for those sent abroad within the EU. 'We did the workers' rights stuff but we didn't do it in the right way,' says Johnson. 'We didn't spend enough time talking about the bits in that social dimension that did matter to people, like paid holidays.'

Corbyn's idiosyncratic approach to leadership, and the apparent hold Milne had over him, were on display when Alan Johnson and Brian Duggan went to see him in February, just before Cameron's deal, with the shadow home secretary Andy Burnham, to develop a handling plan for the referendum campaign. Hilary Benn's adviser Imran Ahmed and Seumas Milne were also there. Corbyn opened the meeting by thanking everyone for coming, and then, to the consternation of his visitors, promptly said, 'Let me go and make some tea.' One of those present said, 'He basically spent about ten minutes talking about making tea for us all, and then said, "Alan, talk us through the chronology of what's about to happen."' Johnson ran through the phases of the campaign – the deal, designation, the short campaign – suggesting areas where Corbyn would need to make decisions. At that point Corbyn finished making the tea, looked up and said, 'Seumas, what do we think?' The source said, 'Then Seumas basically gave the leader of the Labour Party's view back to the room. It was bizarre.'

After the meeting, Brian Duggan sent an email to Milne and the others saying, 'This is the core script, we're agreed and signed off,' and inviting anyone who wished to make comments or changes to do so. He never heard anything more about it.

Instead of following the agreed core script Corbyn, under the influence of John McDonnell, pursued a different agenda, entitled 'Remain and Reform', which focused on things they wished to change about the EU. The issue first came to a head in December 2015, when Corbyn visited Brussels to address the Party of European Socialists. Attempts to draw up a section of his speech on Brexit proved divisive. Johnson and Duggan sent over the script, whereupon 'Seumas got into a huff because his view was that the leader's office hadn't had any input and that it didn't reflect Corbyn's values,' according to a source familiar with the discussions. When Corbyn arrived in Brussels he used three slides, the second of which listed all the things that were wrong with the EU, while the third detailed what needed to change. Someone who saw it said, 'It was a bucket list of shit you don't like, not an argument for remaining in.'

Alan Johnson asked for the 'Remain and Reform' idea to be tested by Labour's polling experts, and found that it did not work. A Labour official says, 'We were doing focus groups twice a week, and people would say to us, "We don't know what that means."' Johnson says, 'The phrase did not resonate at all. If you tell people "Here are all the things that are wrong with the European Union" in the run-up to 23 June, you're going to get people saying, "Well, if there's that much wrong with it, I'm going to vote to leave." My mantra was, "We don't need to say what's wrong with the EU, we've got the *Daily Mail* to say that, they do it every day, they've been doing it for years." Yes, you can say the EU isn't perfect. But you then go on to say what's right about it.'

Corbyn's office showed no interest in the research. Johnson concluded that Corbyn and McDonnell deliberately took a different stance because they regarded him, a man who had held five cabinet posts under Tony Blair and Gordon Brown, as ideologically unsound: 'They insisted on Remain and Reform because they don't like unity. Unity with terrible class traitors like me sullies them. It reduces their intellectual self-esteem. So they have to devise another thing so they're differentiated from us. That's the way I rationalise it.' At the Scottish Labour Party conference in Perth in October 2015, McDonnell is said to have approached Nigel Griffiths, a former MP who was a leading light in Labour Leave, and said, 'Keep up the good work, mate.'[2]

Another Labour insider said Corbyn was manipulated by McDonnell and Milne: 'He's an appalling leader. McDonnell and Seumas have got him by the ears. He doesn't have any interest in power at all, whereas Seumas and McDonnell do understand power. Therefore any decision to do with power is made by McDonnell and Seumas.' He added, 'Seumas took great pleasure from pissing off Alan and stopping Jeremy getting sucked into the campaign. John on the other hand is a conscious Trot, so he understands the mentality of keeping silent on one's objectives and doing things along the way in order to obtain those.'

For months, Corbyn and his office resisted calls by Johnson and the Labour In campaign to declare his personal support for staying in

Europe. 'We kept trying to get him to say, "That's why I am campaigning to remain in the EU,"' recalls Johnson. 'It's a simple sentence. It kept going into speeches, and it kept coming out. It would be taken out by Seumas Milne, it would be taken out by Andrew Fisher.' This account is supported by a source close to Corbyn's office: 'The EU bits in his speeches would just be deleted when they came across John or Seumas's desks.'

Corbyn would film fortnightly Facebook videos telling his supporters what he was doing. It would have been natural, in the midst of a historic election campaign, to devote one to the EU. He refused. 'You can always tell what he doesn't care about if he refuses to do a video on it,' says a source close to the leadership. 'Over the course of six weeks, we repeatedly tried to get Corbyn to do a video on the EU, to just tell a story about why he went the way he did in the EEC referendum and what has changed. He absolutely refused to do it.'

When David Cameron returned from Brussels with his deal it unleashed a tempestuous row at the top of the Labour Party about how Corbyn should respond. The campaign did not want Corbyn to trash the deal, but some of his closest allies were determined that he reject it. 'Andrew Fisher and others desperately wanted Corbyn to come out against the emergency brake,' a Labour source said. Opposing Cameron's plan to limit welfare payments to EU migrants might have seemed just to the far left, but the shadow cabinet, led by Hilary Benn, regarded it as electoral suicide, since it was Labour's voters who were most affected by wage pressures from immigration. 'You had Alan saying that we should pretty much unequivocally welcome the whole deal, including the benefits brake,' a senior Labour source said. 'You had Hilary saying there are bits of the deal we can criticise, but it doesn't make any tactical sense to be too critical. And you had Jeremy's office arguing that we should oppose the whole thing.'

Insiders say Milne also opposed the agreement Cameron had secured to cut red tape, regarding it as 'a figleaf for privatisation', and even the protections negotiated by George Osborne to protect non-eurozone countries from being discriminated against, 'because it's promoting our financial sector, which he hates'. Milne ordered a member of Corbyn's staff to go through the deal and find things Labour could oppose: 'You've got to find something wrong with each of these things,' he said.

A first draft of Corbyn's statement to the Commons was written by Josh Simons, a young staffer in the leader's office. It was critical of some of Cameron's rhetoric about immigration but welcomed the rest of the deal, including the benefits brake. But when the speech was sent to Milne and Fisher they were 'horrified', and began a thirty-six-hour process to change the text. After rewriting it they sent it to Hilary Benn and Andy Burnham. By now it said Labour actively opposed the benefits brake. The two shadow cabinet members said there was no way they could support the new position. The speech was finalised by committee until all that was left was a hotchpotch that was neither wholly critical nor remotely positive. It still found time to disparage the benefits brake: 'We are discussing the future of a continent and one English Tory has reduced it to the issue of taking away benefits from workers and children,' said Corbyn. Journalists regarded it as one of the most incoherent statements by a party leader on a major occasion that they could remember. Josh Simons left Corbyn's office soon afterwards to work for the Labour In campaign.

Peter Mandelson says, 'It was very difficult to know what Jeremy Corbyn's motives were. Did he just get out of bed the wrong side every day and not want to help us, or was there something deeper? Did he simply not want to find himself on the same side as the prime minister and the government, or perhaps he deep-down actually doesn't think we should remain in the European Union? Who knows?'[3]

Labour's referendum campaign was slow to get going in part because the party was focused on the local elections on 5 May. Campaign staff believe they should have been more proactive at getting party activists canvassing across the country to ask, 'How are you going to vote in the EU referendum?' – a question which had been added to activists' doorstep scripts in January. Some felt that even asking the question would stir up Ukip support in the council elections. But it meant that the party was less able to pinpoint sympathetic voters during the referendum campaign. 'There were some abysmal returns in some areas of the country, and that's when we needed the information,' says a Labour official. 'We could have been much more forceful.' There was certainly no pressure from Corbyn or his team: 'They were not bothered which way this went. The party was bothered. They let the party down.'

Alan Johnson says, 'The party made it absolutely plain, once the local elections were out of the way everyone in the party would be focused on

Europe.' On 8 April Iain McNicol, the general secretary, issued a memo telling all party staff, 'Labour's campaign to stay in the EU is a national Labour campaign of historic importance and as such all staff should, once the May elections are complete, consider the campaign as their top priority.' Once again, the problem was that 'the leader's office didn't really participate'.

Patrick Heneghan, the executive director of the party, spent two weeks negotiating with Simon Fletcher from Corbyn's office to agree a regular fixed schedule of planning meetings, grid meetings, media sessions and meetings on polling to bring together the leadership of the campaign and Corbyn's team. 'By and large the leader's office never turned up to the meetings,' says a campaign source. Those working with Alan Johnson could not decide if this was sabotage or incompetence. 'I think it was a mixture of the two,' one said. 'With Seumas and Andrew, it was sabotage. The rest of the office and the rest of the operations, it was incompetence. The sensible people lost all authority and Seumas took it all. In the middle of the campaign, Simon Fletcher was completely sidelined.'

Duggan and Heneghan would join Stronger In's morning call at 7.30, then hold Labour In's morning meeting at 8.30 for the party to run through the main news and events of the day. Eleven members of the campaign were invited to the meeting or to phone in, along with ten members of Corbyn's circle, including Milne, Fisher, Fletcher, Corbyn's spokesman Kevin Slocombe, deputy chief of staff Annelise Midgely and Katy Clark, Corbyn's political secretary. Corbyn's team not only hardly ever turned up or dialled in, they actually complained that the meeting was too early. Two Labour officials have revealed that Katy Clark was enraged by what she considered an early start. By this stage of proceedings Stronger In were holding their first conference call at 6.15 a.m.

'The feedback from the leader's office was it was too early,' a campaign official said. 'We then moved the meetings back to 9 a.m., and that was also considered too early. It then transpired that Katy thought that we were having these meetings at such an ungodly hour of the day because it was a conspiracy to freeze the office of the leader of the Labour Party out of meetings, even though everyone else managed to turn up to work at 9 o'clock in the morning.'

Another furious campaign official said, 'It got to the point that it was a running joke – "Is there anyone from the leader's office on the call?" Either through incompetence or sabotage, they just couldn't manage to make it to work to attend a campaign meeting to keep us in the European Union.' The meetings went ahead without Corbyn's team, and 'every now and then you'd have to call a crisis meeting' at which the campaign would ask why Corbyn's staff were not turning up to other meetings. 'Seumas and Andrew would just never turn up, and they were the people who had ultimate authority. Everyone would agree there was a problem, and then you'd go away and the problem would surface that afternoon because you were trying to get a sign-off or a quote for tomorrow morning's papers and Seumas would block it.'

Despite the obstructionism, there were plenty of Labour figures prepared to step up and work with Alan Johnson, and with Will Straw at Britain Stronger In Europe. They included Gordon Brown, Ed Miliband, Harriet Harman, Alistair Darling, Stephen Kinnock, Chuka Umunna, Yvette Cooper, Pat McFadden and Emma Reynolds. Straw and Johnson spoke regularly, but Straw had no relationship at all with Corbyn's team: 'I emailed his office during the Labour leadership contest, before it was obvious he was going to win, to say, "We'd love to make contact with you. I recognise you're busy but let's get in touch."' After Corbyn's win, Straw bumped into John McDonnell at the studios of *Sky News*, and he offered Straw a cup of tea. 'That never happened. Then it took six months for me to get a single meeting with Jeremy Corbyn's team, and that was the only meeting. In March. It was basically hopeless. He didn't want to engage.' Ryan Coetzee adds, 'Jeremy Corbyn was an absolute disaster. We came to the conclusion they didn't want to win.' Straw still believes it was a mistake for Harriet Harman to set up a separate Labour In campaign, because it robbed the party of a seat at the table at Cannon Street: 'That was one of the main reasons Labour got such little exposure. That was a massive mistake that Labour made.'

Not having support from the leader's office was debilitating for Labour In, since it meant there was a limit to how much they could lean on members of the shadow cabinet or the Parliamentary Labour Party (PLP) to help out, as Alan Johnson was on the road a lot of the time and could not perform that function himself. Johnson's team asked Corbyn's office to provide a single individual with clout to be the political campaign coordinator, a job that Douglas Alexander had performed during the general election campaign. 'We put some names to the leader's office,' a campaign official said. These included pro-Europeans like Chris Bryant and members of the soft left like Lisa Nandy. 'They wouldn't accept any politician. They literally vetoed every name, and we asked them to suggest their own and they couldn't or wouldn't.'

Eventually a compromise was reached. Simon Fletcher, Corbyn's chief of staff, who supported remaining in the EU, would cross over to the campaign to perform the role full-time. On the face of it this was an elegant solution that ought to have led to greater cooperation. The reality was that in leaving Corbyn's office, Fletcher lost all authority, and eventually his chief of staff title. A prominent pro-European, who cared about the Labour Party, Fletcher was no longer anywhere near the leader. One source who worked closely with Fletcher said he was keen to escape precisely because he was losing the power struggle for Corbyn's ear with Seumas Milne: 'He and Seumas were clashing. Seumas was winning.' The rivalry ran deep. Milne had aligned himself with John McDonnell, who had been a bitter enemy of Ken Livingstone and Fletcher when they were on the Greater London Council together in the 1980s, the last time the far left had any meaningful role in British public life. The distance between Milne and Fletcher was vividly illustrated on the night of the referendum itself, when Milne arrived at Labour HQ around 11 p.m. He saw Fletcher and said, 'Long time no see.' A witness said, 'They hadn't spoken for three weeks.'

Despite Fletcher's presence, Labour In could not get members of the shadow cabinet to campaign. A member of the Stronger In media team says, 'The shadow cabinet was banned from doing anything for us by Seumas. Even when people like Heidi Alexander or Seema Malhotra would approach us they'd then get slightly threatening calls from the leader's office, and their offers would quite quickly be retracted. They couldn't even do quotes for us.'

Alan Johnson phoned Corbyn and said, 'Look, the risk is that we might lose this. If Leave wins this, you're going to take the blame. You've got to start doing more. You've got to make it clear to the shadow cabinet, they've got to give at least two dates for doing things between now and the end of the campaign. You've got to make sure John McDonnell is doing stuff that's actually going with the grain of the campaign, not going against it.' Johnson recalled, 'To all of this he says "Yes" – we have these very pleasant conversations – but I doubt he did a single thing about it.'

It was not just shadow cabinet members who were absent. Other prominent figures who might have been expected to put their shoulder to the wheel were already looking beyond the referendum at how they would move to oust Corbyn. One campaign staffer said, 'Labour was just consumed by what to do about Jeremy. I don't think the moderates were thinking, "Let's lose the referendum, then we can unseat him." But they were distracted by "Who is the unity candidate?", "What's the process?", "How do we trigger a contest?", "Should we trigger a contest?" They couldn't bring themselves to focus on the campaign.'

By April, Corbyn's lacklustre performance was driving the pro-Europeans among his shadow ministers over the edge. Charlie Falconer threatened again to resign unless Corbyn raised his game. Chris Bryant would also erupt, telling Corbyn to his face that membership of the EU was 'absolutely in my life's blood, and I can't stay around if we don't do more about it'. Falconer recalled, 'There were occasional shadow cabinet meetings in which, particularly, Chris Bryant would be absolutely explosively rude about it. And we'd all agree. Hilary was good at it as well.'

Corbyn's behaviour stoked bemused irritation among his colleagues on 13 April, when his spokesman criticised the government pamphlet sent to every home at a cost of more than £9 million. Corbyn said ministers should be taking 'an even-handed approach' to informing the public, implying that the same amount should be given to Vote Leave. He appeared to be doing Dominic Cummings' bidding.

The following day, Corbyn raised further suspicion about his motives when he gave his first big speech on Europe in the campaign. It was billed as an explanation of the journey he had been on since voting to leave the EU in the 1975 referendum. But its tone suggested that journey was far from complete, offering only half-hearted endorsement for Remain. Corbyn noted that he was delivering it at the Senate House building in central London which featured in George Orwell's *Nineteen Eighty-Four*: 'This building was the Ministry of Truth,' he said. 'Let us see.'

Alan Johnson says, 'When we finally got him to say something, which was the Senate House speech, there was a kind of knowing little wink. "Here I am supporting the EU, but this is the Ministry of Truth, so you know, maybe you ought to read between the lines." Because it certainly wasn't a wholehearted, full-throttle support.' Indeed, Corbyn spent as much time discussing his historic opposition to the EU. 'I remain very critical of its shortcomings, from its lack of democratic accountability to the institutional pressures to deregulate or privatise public services,' he said, before saying he would support the EU 'many warts and all'. He also attacked the Conservatives, making a united Remain front difficult, and offered unqualified support for unlimited immigration: 'There is nothing wrong with people migrating to work across the Continent.' Labour, he concluded, had decided to back EU membership, 'and that's the party I lead and that's the position I am putting forward'. But that tortuous form of words stopped short of saying loudly and clearly, 'I back Remain.' It was to be a running theme of his public appearances.

At Cannon Street there was irritation. 'That felt half-hearted,' says David Chaplin. 'We realised we could not rely on Jeremy Corbyn to make an unapologetic Remain case.' Kate Hoey, speaking for the Brexiteers, said Labour voters would 'see through' Corbyn's speech: 'We know first of all, that he doesn't really mean it.'

Corbyn mustered little more enthusiasm for the launch of Labour's campaign battlebus on 10 May. The party's press office prepared a news release the night before to run in the morning papers, but it contained no quotes from Corbyn himself, because his office had refused to clear them. Sarah Brown, a press officer, asked for approval to send the release at 3 p.m. It contained the quote, 'This campaign is vital to our country's future. Labour is for staying in because we believe the EU has brought investment, jobs and protection for workers, consumers and the environment.' But five minutes later Kevin Slocombe, Corbyn's spokesman, made it clear that Corbyn had no intention of saying those words, and said he would supply some more. At 3.34 p.m. Brown had to report to her colleagues, 'JC words won't be ready in time so Kevin has asked us to take them out.'

At the event, Corbyn appeared uncomfortable even with the new words with which he had been supplied. Will Straw, watching on television, was furious: 'He was reading notes off a piece of paper.' Labour's bus tour got nothing like the publicity of the Vote Leave battlebus, which was deliberately painted red to suggest to Labour voters that backing Brexit was their party's choice.

Labour's bus was the focal point of a regional media tour by Alan Johnson, which got to more than two hundred seats over the course of the campaign. 'It was an incredibly professionally-run operation to hit four or five constituencies in a given day,' a campaign source said. And yet Corbyn barely used the bus, and John McDonnell did not appear for a single day.

Labour's biggest problem was Corbyn's inability or unwillingness to brief and deliver news stories that could get broadcast coverage – the aim in any national campaign. Stronger In would agree days when Corbyn or McDonnell would have a clear run to create news, only to see them fail. Alan Johnson says, 'We agreed with Stronger In, on days when we have something important to say for the Labour Party, they won't put anything into the media. They'll keep the media day clear for us. And they did that a couple of times. And it cocked up completely, because it either wasn't used by Jeremy or it wasn't used in the way we were expecting.' Milne appeared to deliberately delay the release of quotes to the newspapers until it was too late to use them.

Corbyn's defenders say he did more campaign events than any other Labour politician. Emily Thornberry said, 'All leading members of the Labour Party were out actively campaigning, and Jeremy played his part in that collective effort by doing a lot of media appearances, by doing a lot of meetings up and down the country. He played his part. I don't think that it's appropriate for people to try to blame one individual.'[4]

But from Stronger In's perspective these were the wrong sort of events, because they were never designed to attract broadcast coverage. Alan Johnson says, 'You start the news cycle on the *Today* programme and then carry it through on a speech or a Laura Kuenssberg interview. That's what you do in a general election campaign. It keeps your message in focus. But they would do something at 6.30 p.m. at night in some union hall somewhere, and call that their contribution to the EU debate.' These events were characterised by a Labour official as 'three hundred Trots shouting "Jez we can!"'

Will Straw says, 'He and his team had this view that if you do a lot of evening rallies that is campaigning, and you talk to thousands of people. That can win you a Labour leadership contest with half a million voters. If you want to communicate with millions of people, you need to get on the evening news and in the morning papers, and as far as we could see he just did not have a coherent operation. I suspect there were some people within the campaign, in his office, who were actively opposed to the whole thing.' A senior Labour official adds, 'You need to do things in the morning, you need to place the stories the night before, all the things that most people accept are basic professionalism. They just don't get it.'

Worse than that, some members of Corbyn's frontbench team believed his operation actively abhorred basic political tactics honed over the past three decades. 'They regard anything that smacks of being organised and professional as New Labour witchcraft,' one said. At one point in the campaign John McDonnell refused to go on Labour's battlebus. 'The word we had back was that John wouldn't go on it because it's too "New Labourish" to be on a bus,' said a party official.

When Corbyn did go on television, his message was counterproductive. On 10 June, just as Stronger In were holding their crisis meetings to try to get more Labour coverage, Corbyn was a guest on the talkshow *The Last Leg*, on which he admitted, 'I'm not a huge fan of the European Union.' Asked how keen he was to stay in the EU on a scale of one to ten, he replied, 'Oh, I'd put myself in the upper half of the five to ten [range], so we're looking at seven, seven and a half, maybe seven.' Corbyn's supporters thought the appearance winning. Emily Thornberry said, 'The thing about Jeremy is that he is authentic, he's an honest guy and in giving the EU seven or seven and a half out of ten he was speaking on behalf of an awful lot of people. That real voice was an important one.'[5]

If many of Corbyn's critics tried to laugh along to *The Last Leg*, they had failed to see the funny side the weekend before, when he disappeared on a six-day holiday at the very time the Leave campaign was moving into the lead. By then polls were showing that Corbyn's Euro-agnosticism had left around half of Labour voters unclear where their party stood on Brexit.

David Chaplin, at Stronger In, said, 'Corbyn scuppered opportunities for Labour to lead the news, missed the chance to offer a clean and clear message to the Labour activists that they should be campaigning, and frankly showed a lack of patriotism about what he wanted our country to be like. He treated it like it was a third-tier issue at a constituency-office surgery. If the leader of the opposition doesn't have a clear view and isn't willing to express it, how can he claim to deserve that title? He actively undermined the campaign with the language he used.'

Corbyn's team did come up with one eye-catching idea for the leader during the campaign. In the midst of a dogfight over immigration and the possibility of Turkey joining the EU, it was proposed that Corbyn actually visit Turkey to meet some refugees. Alan Johnson says, 'He wanted to go in the middle of the campaign to Turkey to discuss open borders and the need for open borders.' Johnson regarded the idea as 'a disaster'. James McGrory, Stronger In's spin doctor, remembered, 'When I first heard that, I said, "If I'd been making up what is the worst possible thing that Jeremy Corbyn could do right now, I might not have been able to come up with something that shit."'

Yet the plan was embraced by Seumas Milne, who would have known that it would create huge difficulties for Remain campaigners. 'Seumas supported it,' says a Labour Party official. 'Do I think Seumas's support for campaigning on behalf of refugees was naïve? Absolutely not. Corbyn would have been hanging out with refugees and saying "We should welcome more" in among a campaign which had become about immigration. I don't think you can get any clearer evidence of Seumas's hostility towards the campaign. He's not a plonker; he knows how broadcast works, he knows how newspapers work, and he knows that would have been seriously damaging. And yet he fought hard to do it.'

Internal discussions about the Turkey visit started in mid-April and carried on for three weeks, into the second week of May. Eventually, 'both the Labour In campaign and some people internally in the leader's office realised it was fucking nuts and said, "You absolutely cannot go."' Hilary Benn also had 'quite a direct conversation' with Corbyn about the idea.

Milne was also instrumental in disrupting an attempt to highlight Labour unity on staying in the EU at the start of June, ironically insisting that the word 'united' be removed from a letter to the *Sunday Mirror* signed by Labour MPs in support of the Remain campaign. The episode is a classic example of the obstructionism of Corbyn's office to their own campaign. Alan Johnson called it a 'ludicrous farce': 'It was getting really serious. Labour supporters didn't know where Labour stood. Jeremy's Senate House speech led the news all day, but three weeks had gone by and there were no other contributions from the leader of the Labour Party. I was getting seriously worried.' Corbyn agreed to the publication of the letter, and the text was cleared by Simon Fletcher and sent to the newspaper. The key section read, 'The Labour Party is united in arguing that we are better off remaining in the European Union.'

Then, Johnson said, 'A phone call comes from Seumas Milne from his holiday home in Portugal saying "That letter needs to be changed." The word "united" had to come out, and something about immigration.'

Corbyn's office wanted to replace the 'united' sentence with 'The Labour Party overwhelmingly believes that we are better off remaining in the European Union.' With just a dozen Labour MPs backing Leave, either phrasing was reasonable, but the campaign had already spent three days getting the MPs to approve the letter. 'They all have to traipse into the PLP office to get the staff there to check it and sign it,' a campaign source says. 'It's logistically not that easy.'

What then ensued was a furious exchange of emails and calls in which Corbyn's inner circle dug in, demanding changes to the letter in the face of warnings that it would wreck the story. At 11.13 a.m. Andrew Fisher, the hard-left policy director who had previously stated his ambivalence towards the EU, sent an email to Sarah Mulholland, a Labour official, demanding that two sentences be added to the letter to soften any criticism of immigration. 'It is not migrants that undercut wages, but unscrupulous employers,' read one of them. She replied, 'If I recirculate the new text it will get leaked.' Fisher pushed back: 'These are agreed lines – and nothing new or controversial.'

At 12.54 p.m. Patrick Heneghan emailed: 'From the campaign's point of view this letter was signed off by Simon F for the leader's office and then Alan for the campaign. There is no way we can simply add words to text we have asked 200 plus Labour MPs to sign without causing a huge internal row and potential story. If we do ask them to sign a new version then a) it will leak and b) many won't agree to those words – specifically those that would like a harder line on immigration. Alan's view is that it goes in its current form.' Johnson explains, 'It would also mean some poor sod in the Labour Party having to contact 213 MPs to change a text they'd already agreed.'

Corbyn's office refused to accept the logic of this position, and at 2.04 p.m. Karie Murphy, Corbyn's gatekeeper, declared, 'Seumas will not sign this off.' Heneghan had now had enough, and warned of the damaging publicity that would ensue if Corbyn backed out: 'If we are saying JC is not agreeing to [put] his name to the letter then we need to fully understand what this could mean in terms of the campaign.'

Sick of the meddling, Johnson phoned Corbyn, who was in Cardiff for another of his evening rallies. 'I said to him, "Jeremy, this is a nonsense, it's not about the words now." The point wasn't changing the words, it was changing the letter. Jeremy said, "Oh, sounds very sensible, Alan, what you're saying. The letter should go." I was convinced it had all been sorted.'

It had not. After Johnson spoke to Corbyn, Seumas Milne phoned the leader and persuaded him to change his mind once more. At 9.20 p.m. Milne sent an email saying, 'Have just spoken to Jeremy in Cardiff, he fine to go ahead with compromise amendment to draft text for *Sunday Mirror*: i.e. with additional sentence about strengthening workers' rights and tweak about Labour overwhelmingly for Remain, but minus earlier draft line about migrants which some PLP signatories might have had a problem with.' The MPs had not, of course, had a problem with anything in the original letter, because they had already signed it off. At 10.12 p.m. Fisher circulated the new version of the letter.

Johnson intervened again to say, 'I spoke to Jeremy at 6.45 and he told me he understood the problem – which is that the wording is not the issue. The problem is getting over two hundred MPs to agree revised wording … on a Saturday … What is going on here? Why all this hassle to change the wording? A story about Labour unity will become the opposite if a) we can't get authority for the changed version from some MPs or b) some understandably ask why the perfectly adequate wording is being changed.' At 11.02 p.m. Milne again put his foot down: 'I spoke to Jeremy again at 9 p.m. and he confirmed he would like to go ahead with the modest amendments circulated.' The following morning Johnson sent another furious email: 'So we spend Saturday morning in a pointless exercise of trying to get approval to amend a perfectly adequate letter that had already been approved and sent – ludicrous!'

Not one word of the letter appeared in the *Sunday Mirror*. Instead its sister paper, the *People*, ran a story highlighting the chaos: 'Jeremy Corbyn was at odds with his own MPs last night – after hijacking an appeal for party unity over the EU,' the paper said, explaining how Corbyn 'signed up' to the letter, 'but then changed his mind before signing up again – and then changing his mind AGAIN.' Johnson says, 'What should have been "Here's Labour united" became "Here's Labour disunited." That was typical of the way that office operated.' A Labour official said, 'Seumas is not stupid, he knew where this was going, and that's what they wanted.'

John McDonnell created almost as much bad feeling as Milne. His only meaningful campaign events were regarded by Alan Johnson's team and Stronger In as counterproductive. On 17 May Will Straw and David Chaplin cleared a day in Stronger In's grid for Labour. 'We wanted Alan

Johnson to do it,' Straw recalled. Johnson said it would be John McDonnell, to which Straw agreed.

McDonnell would give a speech to union leaders at the TUC. On 10 May, six days before the speech, Simon Jackson, the party's director of policy and research, who was working for Labour In, emailed to say, the 'campaign is obviously keen to get as big a hit out of this as possible'. Maighread McCloskey, the head of research, suggested they work up a story idea showing that Brexit would add to economic pressure for more spending cuts, which Labour opposed, allowing them to bash the Tories and encourage their own voters to back Remain at the same time. On 16 May Jackson reported that Stronger In had 'more or less cleared their grid for tomorrow', and the campaign was keen to brief a story into the morning newspapers to give McDonnell 'a fair wind'. By 11.15 a.m. the campaign team had prepared a press release for the following day's papers saying, 'Labour's shadow chancellor John McDonnell MP will warn that leaving the European Union will mean the Tory government needs to implement even more spending cuts and tax rises in order to meet its inflexible and discredited surplus target.' It explained that Tory cuts would mean reductions equivalent to the loss of 2,900 police officers, 20,000 nurses, 18,000 midwives and 16,500 teachers.

But McDonnell did not want to make the announcement which his own party had been preparing for him for nearly a week. He also declined stories that were offered that morning by Stronger In. At 12.26 p.m. his spokesman James Mills announced, 'John wants to make some tweaks.' At 2.12 p.m., Mills circulated an entirely different press release that said, 'Labour will rescue the EU referendum debate from the fearmongers.' It quoted the shadow chancellor as saying, 'I want to rescue the debate from the negativity and Project Fear on all sides.' All the statistics that might have made Labour voters think twice about a Leave vote had been removed. In his speech the following day, McDonnell said, 'The debate has degenerated into the worst form of negativity and brought out the worst in Westminster politics.'

To make matters worse, McDonnell was also due to go on the *Today* programme on the morning of his speech. But, James McGrory recalled, mid-afternoon, 'McDonnell's people phoned back and said, "Oh no, John's not going to do it tomorrow." "What do you mean he's not going to do it any more?" "He hasn't got very much to say." "We asked you in the morning, 'Do you want a story?' This is the biggest referendum of our lifetimes. I think we can rustle together something for a ten-minute appearance on the radio. What about something on the economy?" "No, he's not doing it."' Without broadcast interest, McDonnell's speech got almost no pick-up. 'It was a damp squib, nothing happened,' Alan Johnson says. 'He didn't get any coverage at all. He always insisted on doing it his own way.'

McDonnell's refusal to do an interview on the BBC's flagship morning news programme, and his use of Vote Leave's 'Project Fear' attack line, left his own party staff in despair. David Chaplin said, 'We cleared the grid for John McDonnell, and when the opportunity was given he deliberately scuppered it. There's a huge sense of anger, confusion, betrayal.'

When the campaign then approached McDonnell's office asking for further dates when he was available his aides stalled for time, and then offered 23 June. 'We pointed out that he couldn't really be on the road on polling day,' a campaign source recalled.

The story McDonnell had rejected was revived on 10 June, when deputy leader Tom Watson, Angela Eagle, Owen Smith and Yvette Cooper gave a press conference warning that a vote to leave the EU could lead to a fresh wave of austerity, including £18 billion of benefit cuts and tax rises. Watson said a Leave vote would lead to a takeover of the government by 'extreme Brexiteers', and a 'Tory Brexit budget'. McDonnell refused to have anything to do with the press conference.

Following the crisis meeting in Cannon Street, three days of the grid were cleared for Labour, but McDonnell refused to cooperate with another flagship campaign moment. On 15 June Tom Watson made a speech outlining how enlarging the EU single market would create 1.3 million new jobs by 2030. The figure was based on analysis by the Centre for Economics and Business Research. Once again the details of the announcement were sent to Corbyn and McDonnell's offices. But when they studied the details, they noticed that some of the jobs were to be generated by the planned transatlantic trade deal with the EU, TTIP. Andrew Fisher in Corbyn's office replied, 'We don't politically support many of the underlying assumptions in the CEBR report ... We are not backing TTIP.' He said that neither Corbyn nor McDonnell was 'happy to support this'. Watson ignored them, and did the event with Alan Johnson the following day.

*   *   *

While Corbyn and McDonnell came in for most criticism over Labour's campaign, there were also concerns in the shadow cabinet and among the Stronger In team at Cannon Street about the performance of the Labour In campaign. While Alan Johnson was widely popular, his laid-back approach may not have been best suited to a campaign of such visceral aggression. A Labour source says, 'AJ was a really strong media performer, he was well liked by activists, he had the trust of MPs, but he had never run an election campaign before. It needed someone who had experience of running a national election campaign, particularly when he had one hand tied behind his back by Jeremy Corbyn. Brian Duggan did a great job, but he's not Alastair Campbell.' A Stronger In source said Johnson even refused to do broadcast interviews. The umbrella campaign had a letter from four former Labour health ministers – including Johnson – warning about the dangers of Brexit to the NHS. '*Good Morning Britain*, which is a great great audience for us, said they would drive a camera to his house in Hull. He just needed to pop outside at 6.50, done before 7 – and he refused to do it.' Charlie Falconer says, 'Alan is absolutely trusted by everybody. People trust his politics, he's always in the right place politically. He never lets you down, he never stabs you in the back. But any energy in the Labour Remain campaign couldn't come from Alan, it would have to come from the leader down, and it never came. So Alan was left revolving around the country in his bus, always well received but generating no political interest or energy because it was just his view, not the view of the Labour Party with some welly behind it.'

The incident which brought home the problems at Labour In to those at Stronger In occurred at 9 a.m. on Monday, 20 June, the first day of the final week. Labour had been assigned the following day in the grid, and Chaplin and Carberry held a conference call with Duggan, Simon Jackson, the party's popular press spokeswoman Sarah Brown, and Katy Dillon, the head of broadcasting. Asked what their plan was for the following day, the team at Labour HQ replied, 'We've got some Jeremy Corbyn words.'

Chaplin and Carberry asked what they would say, but the Labour staff did not know, because they had not seen the quotes. Carberry said, 'With the greatest of respect, unless he comes out as transgender or something, he's not going to splash a paper just with some words.' Given their previous experience with Corbyn's office, the Labour staff had to admit that any words would probably be late and next to useless. At Cannon Street they were unimpressed. They hung up and found research indicating that Brexit would add £580 annually to the cost of food, drink, petrol and clothing for the average family. It made the front page of the *Daily Mirror* the following day. Retail bosses hit the airwaves. Stronger In had saved the day, but the incident left a sour taste in the mouth. 'We ended up getting a really good show,' a campaign source said. 'They knew they were going to get rubbish from Corbyn's office, and they were going to allow that to happen. That to me epitomises their whole approach, which is they didn't do it professionally, they didn't do it with commitment, and they were prepared to allow just days to fall away in the grid. There's a lot been said about Corbyn and Seumas, and that is definitely true. But quite frankly, AJ and the Labour Party core machine did not come to the game either.'

In the final two weeks several efforts were made to stage campaign interventions by Labour's biggest names, but personal rivalries and Corbyn's distaste for his predecessors got in the way. Labour campaign officials wanted a day on which every living Labour leader, past and present, would campaign at the same time. Meanwhile, Stronger In were working on a plan to line up all four living prime ministers to stage what they hoped would be the crowning moment of the campaign. Both were derailed by clashes of egos.

Alan Johnson says, 'Even when it came to the final throes Jeremy wouldn't appear on a platform with Tony Blair, so we couldn't do a Labour leader thing. He was reluctant to appear on a platform with Gordon Brown. That was stymied. It was very important who he appeared on platforms with. Amazing, given the people he'd appeared on platforms with before.' Corbyn had previously spoken alongside the terrorists of Hamas, who he referred to as 'friends', as well as invited IRA men to the House of Commons, but he would not do an event with the man who won his party three general elections.

The Corbynista attempt to erase Blair from history went to extraordinary lengths. On 4 June all of Labour's living previous leaders had written a joint letter to the *Daily Mirror*, saying the party's 'founding purpose' was boosted by being a member of the EU. It was the first time Blair and Brown had done anything together since falling out in office. The other signatories were Ed Miliband and Neil Kinnock, and interim leaders Harriet Harman and Margaret Beckett. Corbyn did not sign the letter.

On the Tuesday of the final week of the campaign, Labour In sought to revive the idea for a series of events around the country. Corbyn, Brown, Miliband, Kinnock, Harman and Beckett were all due to make speeches. Blair was at his mother-in-law's funeral, so he could not do a campaign event, but he wrote an article for the *Daily Mirror*.

The campaign prepared a press release headlined 'Jeremy Corbyn and past Labour leaders launch last 48 hours call to action'. At 2.26 p.m. on the 20th, Sam Bacon sent it to Corbyn's office. It detailed all the campaign events featuring Corbyn, Miliband, Kinnock, Harman, Beckett and Brown, and added, 'Tom Watson will also be doing an event in Brighton, and Tony Blair has written exclusively for tomorrow's *Daily Mirror*.' At 3.59 p.m. Seumas Milne sent out a 'revamped' press release removing any reference to 'past Labour leaders', changing the wording to 'Jeremy Corbyn and other leading Labour figures'. He instructed the press office to highlight the roles played by Brown, Harman, Beckett and Kinnock. All mention of Blair had been removed. A Labour official says, 'Corbyn wasn't sharing a platform with Tony Blair, he wasn't in the same room as him, he didn't need to be in a photograph with him, it was an op-ed in the *Mirror*. They made us pull the press release, rewrite the whole thing, not brief it, and effectively disassociate ourselves from the Tony Blair op-ed. The press release then went out at five to six, which was far too late.'

There was one last Blair purge. At Labour's final rally in London on the night of Wednesday the 22nd, Alan Johnson says, 'There was a video film, and a bit in it where Tom Watson was saying "What a great contribution these people have made" happened to make the terrible cardinal sin of mentioning Tony Blair and Gordon Brown, and Jeremy's office insisted on that being cut.'

The attempt to get David Cameron, Gordon Brown, Tony Blair and John Major to a joint event was similarly doomed. The plan was to place them all behind podiums in Downing Street and have them give statements. At the time Gordon Brown's spokesman denied that he was responsible for the event not happening, citing 'diary clashes'. But four different figures with a reason to know say that Brown was to blame, because he did not want to share a stage with either Blair or Cameron. A senior figure in the Labour In campaign says, 'Gordon wouldn't share a stage with Tony. Tony was up for it. Gordon asked with a week to go, "What can we do to turn this around?" and we said Gordon could just suck it up and stand next to Tony. But he wouldn't do it.' James McGrory at Stronger In says, 'Gordon just didn't want to do it.' Alan Johnson says, 'Gordon's problem was appearing with David Cameron, because of what Cameron had done in Scotland.' Johnson says Brown was 'very bitter' that on the day after the Scottish referendum the PM had proposed a new system of 'English votes for English laws'. But Andrew Cooper claimed Brown's feud with Blair was more significant. 'Gordon Brown wouldn't do it with Tony Blair. Gordon Brown did come out and do things with Cameron. Gordon Brown was also sceptical that it would work, and he made the point that in Scotland it would be incredibly damaging to be in bed with the Tories. He offered that as another reason for not doing it.'

Brown was certainly keen not to be seen with Cameron. On the Thursday of 'Labour week' Brown give a barnstorming speech in Manchester, reprising the revivalist-preacher style of oratory he had deployed to good effect in the closing days of the Scottish referendum campaign. Cameron was on the same bill, and Brown had got it into his head that the prime minister would be on stage three hours after him. Incredulous Stronger In officials, including Labour staff on the campaign who had known Brown in Downing Street, explained that no campaign event would last that long. Brown was not to be placated, and began 'ranting and raving' that he had been 'lied to by the Tories'. In an exple- tive-laden screaming fit he accused one of his former aides of having 'become one of them', and shouted, 'You've betrayed me! You've betrayed me!' Another member of Stronger In staff said, 'He went completely mad. Shouting and screaming. He was vile.'

Nonetheless, Brown did contribute. His speech at de Montfort University in Leicester on the Monday helped kick off 'Labour week'. A video he produced, making the patriotic case for EU membership while walking through the ruins of the old Coventry Cathedral, was regarded even by aides to George Osborne as the most effective viral video of the campaign. Stronger In and Labour In succeeded in lining up a range of heavy hitters, with multiple appearances by Ed Miliband. London mayor Sadiq Khan agreed to campaign all week. 'I think it did help put Labour back on the map in the campaign,' said David Chaplin. 'It also took some pressure off David Cameron to carry the entire Remain side on his shoulders. But, arguably, it was too late in the day to start that conversa- tion with Labour activists, and the leader should have been having that conversation with them weeks, if not months, before.'

Corbyn's approach to the referendum baffled and enraged most of his party apparatus. Peter Mandelson says, 'We were greatly damaged by Jeremy Corbyn's stance, no doubt at all about that. Not only was he most of the time absent from the battle, but he was holding back the efforts of Alan Johnson and the Labour In campaign. At times they felt actually their efforts were being sabotaged by Jeremy Corbyn and the people around him.' A Labour In official says, 'He didn't actually make a Labour argument to Labour voters about why Labour voters should vote remain. I think they let the country down. I don't think they understand the significance of what they've done.'

It was made clear to Corbyn by members of the shadow cabinet and rebel MPs that if the referendum was lost, his lacklustre performance would trigger a leadership challenge against him. But it is hard not to conclude that everything Corbyn and his office did was designed to scuttle Labour's own Remain campaign. His allies say that he is a different sort of politician who campaigns in a different way, that he is not bound by the way politics is done by others. But even in these terms he failed to step up. Since his leadership win he had inspired hundreds of thousands of young people to join the Labour Party, swelling membership to more than half a million. Many of them were members of Momentum, the left-wing pressure group set up to turn support for Corbyn into a political movement. He could have asked them to hold rallies throughout the country in key Labour seats, he could have had a bus tour linking these events, and appeared on prime-time television to make the Labour case for remaining. He did none of those things.

Charlie Falconer says, 'When Jeremy came in for very substantial criticism within the Labour Party during the campaign for not doing enough he did what Jeremy always does, he became incredibly active. But he never got Momentum to have rally after rally. We urged him to get his mojo out there. He could've made it part of his crusade. But the problem was, it was never part of his crusade. I shouldn't criticise him for that, because his political views had been clear all along. His decision to agree to Remain was a purely tactical one to form a shadow cabinet. It was pressed upon him, at a point when he was unsure about what he was doing.'

By the penultimate weekend of the campaign, David Cameron and the other Stronger In leaders did decide to act to try to make up for Corbyn's inactivity. That same weekend they faced another, equally seismic, decision – whether to finally do something about immigration.

20

IMMIGRATION CRISIS

This was the inner core, the people who were really in charge. George Osborne, Ed Llewellyn and Kate Fall: the other members of the quad, the political family. The others were hired help, but the best of the best: Craig Oliver, Ameet Gill, Liz Sugg, Andrew Cooper, Stephen Gilbert, and George's sidekick Thea Rogers. No Will Straw. No Ryan Coetzee. They met on Sunday nights in David Cameron's study in Downing Street. They were the people the prime minister trusted, the people who made the decisions – and they had to decide. They were getting killed on immigration, trust, Turkey. Being a prime minister is about making decisions, hundreds of them every day. Some of them minor. Some of them can change a country. Some of them can decide your fate. Politics is also the art of the possible. What was possible? David Cameron had to decide.

Those who were there say it was not a crisis meeting. Thursday's, when the campaign decided to clear the grid for Labour, was a crisis meeting. This, they told themselves, was a weekly stocktake, but it was potentially the most important of the campaign. There were eleven days to go. The following weekend would be too late to make any meaningful changes. Andrew Cooper says, 'There wasn't panic, but deep concern, calmly addressed. It grew right through the final two weeks.' Panic had never been David Cameron's way – some thought that was part of his problem. But they were worried about the situation, of that there is no doubt. George Osborne had begun to wonder if they would lose the referendum.

Cameron asked Cooper to start with a review of the polls. 'What's the situation?' he asked. The picture was concerning. Since the beginning of June things had moved away from them. 'It's basically 50–50,' said

Cooper. They weren't losing. They weren't winning either. They had all fought referendums before; they knew that undecided voters tended to stick with what they knew. That had happened in Scotland. Cooper said, 'We still believe that in the end they will move back to the status quo because that's the pattern of referendums, and we expect undecideds – if they vote – to break for Remain. So neck-and-neck isn't the end of the world, but it's a very worrying situation.'

The Scottish referendum playbook had one last ploy in it. When the polls had showed the Nationalists ahead, Cameron and the other leaders had signed 'the Vow', a pledge to the Scottish people that they had listened to their concerns on the need for greater devolution. Should Cameron now deliver a new vow on immigration? Could he?

In the case of Scotland, the vow had summarised promises made during the campaign by Better Together. This time Cameron would have to go further than he had been prepared to during the campaign to turn around the narrative that was dominating coverage of the campaign. Senior Labour figures, including Will Straw and Peter Mandelson, who were getting worrying feedback from their MPs, particularly in the north of England, had been arguing for weeks that Stronger In should tackle the immigration argument head-on. Ever since the meeting in George Osborne's office on 26 April, Straw had been pushing for a migration-impact fund to help communities hit by high immigration. But as Cooper explained, 'We tested these ideas in focus groups and the voter reaction was, "Well, you could achieve that and more by voting to leave and taking total control."' The other question was whether Angela Merkel could be enlisted to get something more on free movement. It would have been a long shot, but that is what it might have taken.

When George Osborne did an event in May with Ed Balls he had indicated sympathy for a vow.[1] But by the time of the meeting in Downing Street, the chancellor had decided that offering more on immigration, or seeking to coopt the Germans, would not work. They had been round and round the houses with Merkel. He did not believe they could have got more at the summit in February. Osborne said, 'My concern is that it will make immigration front and centre when we are trying to wrest it back onto the economy. And ultimately, how credible will it be?' He thought voters would say, 'Hold on, we've just had a nego-tiation, and you've proved you can't achieve some opt-out from free movement, so why are we going to believe you now, with a couple of weeks to go?' Gill and Cooper agreed. Cooper's polling was still showing that immigration had 'low salience' in changing the votes of Stronger In's two groups of target voters. He says, 'From the perspective of how the last-minute "Vow" had played out in Scotland, those things look like what they are, which is panic. Most voters don't believe these last-minute rabbits out of hats anyway. We tested literally dozens of different arguments and rebuttals, but nothing really worked. My view was that, since we knew that what it was possible for us to say would not meet the concerns of voters, anything that we did say would simply draw attention to the fact that we had no substantive answer to the concerns about free movement.' Craig Oliver also wanted to stick to Plan A. His concern was that 'suddenly making a speech about immigration in the final days of the campaign' would 'essentially change your message'. He thought it would have 'looked like panic or looked like you were changing what you had said all along. Part of a campaign is deciding on your message and sticking to it.'[2]

'There was unanimity in the room,' says Cooper. 'We understand what's happening, we understand it's very tight, we understand the pull for their side of Turkey, immigration, borders, free movement. We do not have a message to take that on with, therefore all we can do is double down on the economy.' With that they turned to a discussion of the grid for the coming week.

The level of Conservative caution on immigration had already been revealed on the previous evening, Saturday, 11 June, during a conference call to plan the Labour fightback. Gordon Brown was to deliver a speech the following Monday in which he planned to issue a five-point plan to persuade Labour voters to back Remain. The fifth point of the plan was to introduce a migration fund along the lines of Straw's proposal. The Conservatives tried to veto the idea, because they feared the media would run away with it. 'Number 10 was terrified of us mentioning it, absolutely shitting themselves about any mention of immigration,' says one of those on the call. 'Ameet said we shouldn't do it. Craig said Gordon can't mention it. This is the fifth point in a five-point plan and the story's about Labour, so the migration fund was never going to be the big story of the day, but they were so concerned about immigration being the story at all that that was a major issue.' Oliver went to check with Cameron and came back to tell Straw and Mandelson, 'The PM's absolutely clear this mustn't be about immigration.'

When Brown made his speech, at de Montfort University in Leicester, he talked about a 'European solidarity fund' for areas hit by population increases, but the migration fund was not flagged in press releases, and Brown was criticised by the media for downplaying the impact of immigration.

The issue would not go away. On Monday the 13th, with ten days to go, Peter Mandelson sent a memo seeking to give life to the ideas Will Straw had been articulating. During the Saturday-night conference call he and Craig Oliver had clashed. Mandelson had been talking that morning to Leo Gillen, a friend who ran a pub in Hartlepool, the town he used to represent in Parliament, about how bad the local feeling was on immigration. Mandelson raised the idea of a migration fund. 'I think you need to listen to what hard-nosed Labour voters in Hartlepool are saying,' he said now.

Oliver snapped back, 'I don't need to listen to them. I watch the news and read the focus groups. I know what people think.'

Another campaign official listening in was amused by the spat between the alpha-male spin doctors: 'I can imagine how annoying Craig must have found that, as if Peter was up there knocking on doors ...'

Mandelson wrote two memos about immigration, one early on in the campaign, in which he argued that Stronger In needed to give some ground. He hoped that would mean voters would feel less inclined to use the referendum as the vehicle for registering a protest vote on immigration. He was told that Cameron was opposed to making any concession, and wanted to fight on economic territory.

The second memo, on 13 June, warned, 'The problem is that we – political mainstream/Remain – appear not to be listening on immigration. We have thought throughout that jobs will trump migration and for a lot of C2DE voters that has surprisingly turned out not (yet) to be the case.' Mandelson admitted that the campaign had 'not got a handle on the issue or the strength of feeling about it', and again questioned whether they should 'offer something on immigration' to 'dissuade people from using the referendum as the only means of forcing us to act'. He suggested, as Straw and Max Chambers had before, that Cameron should make 'a big speech' along the lines of the one Tony Blair made in Dover in 2005. He envisaged Cameron saying, 'We hear your anxiety and realise [we] have to respond,' and then making a series of pledges. He proposed:

- New funds to alleviate housing/school/NHS stress where there is higher concentration of EU migration
- A new law to protect against wage undercutting by EU nationals
- Initiation of discussion at EU level to consider further moves to restrict welfare migration/limit economic migration
- Agreement with Merkel and Hollande to set up EU examination of the management of free movement of labour and relevant legislation like posted workers directive
- An invitation by government to other parties to consider immigration issues on a cross-party basis and develop solutions to protect communities
- A new affordable housing programme that only people who have lived in UK for X years qualify for.

Mandelson said he understood the drawbacks of changing tack 'at this late stage', but said Cameron should 'consider very carefully the case for doing so.'

Mandelson heard nothing back from Downing Street, but in Number 10 they were having another serious wobble. On Monday evening Craig Oliver wrote an email to Cameron saying he needed to seriously consider an immigration pledge. On Tuesday morning Oliver met Ameet Gill and Graeme Wilson in his office to discuss the idea. Gill was always opposed, because he thought the options lacked credibility, and they should not spend the final week of the campaign talking about immigration. Wilson agreed. Oliver and Gill then went to see Cameron in his office, along with Ed Llewellyn and Kate Fall. The prime minister began the meeting thinking he needed to act. Llewellyn also seriously wondered if action was required. They discussed making a public statement on the Thursday, a week before polling day. 'The conversation followed DC waking up and saying, "I've got to do something on this now. It's now or never. I think I need to do this,"' says a Downing Street source.

The PM's aides knew they would not get anything substantive agreed by Merkel or the other leaders, but could they at least get an acknowledgement that more needed to be done? In this scenario Cameron would have said, 'Don't worry, I've listened. I've spoken to Merkel and Hollande and the rest. If you vote "In" they will give us something.' But they feared it would be a gift to Vote Leave if any EU leader came out before polling day and said it was not going to happen. As the conversation went on,

Cameron realised, 'God, this is potentially very messy.' A senior figure says, 'That's why we didn't do it, because we had nothing. The view was if we were going to do something it would be on the Thursday, but we quickly went off the idea.'

Craig Oliver, meanwhile, was again pressing the case for Cameron to say that he would veto Turkish membership of the EU, as a different way of tackling voters' concerns. The director of communications was seen going in to see Cameron on his own. His argument was, 'You don't need anyone else's agreement to say you'll use the veto, so why don't you just say you'll use it?' But Cameron was not persuaded. His view was still, 'It will massively inflame relations with Turkey, who are a vital CT [counter-terrorism] partner.' Another aide says, 'The Turkey veto was a seductive idea, and Craig was very keen on it, but it unravelled as soon as you thought about it. Were you going to veto Serbia, Albania, Montenegro and the rest as well? What would the response in Turkey be? They had just signed a migrant deal, would they welch on that? It was a bit ill-thought-through.'

Some colleagues believed that, having argued throughout the campaign that they should stick to the economy and avoid talking about immigration, Oliver was seeking an alibi in case the campaign was lost, putting himself in a position where he could claim that his warnings were ignored. Everyone knew he was working on a book. 'Maybe if he hadn't spent so much time writing down what other people said in meetings, he might have run a better campaign,' said one Cameron loyalist. 'Craig was always one of the people saying, "We've got a plan, we've got to stick to it." We all heard him say it.'

Ryan Coetzee was also concerned that the campaign had nothing to say on immigration. On the same day, Tuesday, 14 June, there was a discussion at Cannon Street about doing a vow on immigration. Coetzee asked Stephen Gilbert, 'Is there a solution on immigration? Because if there is one, let's find it now!' He had emailed the senior staff at Stronger In that morning about a focus group in Durham. The women he met there had been 'very hard to persuade that EU migration isn't as bad as the right-wing press makes out (they were mostly *Daily Mail* readers). They also believe public services are under severe strain. They don't believe facts about immigration that contradict their feelings, although they are impressed by the benefits deal the PM made.' His email concluded, though, 'The truth is there is little we can say to them on immigration, short of "We have closed the borders." His counsel now was that any action would have to be substantive: 'You've got to do something on immigration which solves the problem. The worst thing you can do is pour petrol on the fire. So you can't say let's talk about immigration but not in a way which doesn't solve people's problems. Because then you're really fucked.'

Coetzee continued throwing out ideas: 'Can you literally just close the border?'

'It's illegal.'

'Fair enough. Here's a brainstorm: can you people get Merkel to get a conference call together with other leaders in Europe and say, "Our choices are some sort of immigration emergency brake while we work on what to do about free movement, or we're going to lose Britain"?' Will Straw said Cameron should encourage Matteo Renzi, François Hollande, Angela Merkel and Jean-Claude Juncker to support an agenda for the UK's next presidency of the EU, due to start in July 2017, which would include cooperation on illegal migration. He again pressed his case for a migration-impact fund to address pressure on public services, more resources for border controls to police illegal migration, and a cross-party commission on immigration to develop common solutions. Coetzee backed him up. Adam Atashzai argued with Straw: 'It's too late. You can't just turn around after decades and decades of politicians saying "We promise to control immigration," and when they fail, right at the last moment say, "This time we mean it." It's for the birds.'

Nevertheless, Cameron and Angela Merkel spoke on Wednesday, 15 June. A Number 10 official says, 'They set up a call thinking they might say, "Do we need to look again at free movement?" By the time they'd decided not to, the call was happening, so the PM and Merkel had a bit of a chat. But he definitely didn't ask for anything, which is why it was weird.' A senior figure in Downing Street confirmed, 'David Cameron did not ask Merkel for more.'

It may well have been implausible to get any immediate movement from the German leader, but Straw's plan to persuade other countries to agree to do more on illegal migration was not necessarily pointless. An announcement along those lines would not have swayed most planning to vote Leave, but, presented in the right way, it might have persuaded some to change their vote. Once again Cameron did not put Berlin on the spot and warn that failure to help would see Britain leave the EU.

One of his circle now regrets that he did not try: 'The frustrating thing is if they'd agree on a cap on numbers, that would have been fine. We've put ourselves through all this shit, and all for the sake of an emergency brake.' Fundamentally, Cameron still thought he would win the referendum. Another chance was missed.

Straw's call for a financial package to help local authorities hit by high immigration was also rejected. 'They thought the package would just inflame the situation without solving people's problems,' says Coetzee. As an experienced strategist, he understood that you should not change tack with less than two weeks to go unless you are certain it will work: 'You don't run a campaign in retrospect. When you fundamentally change your strategy, you've got to be very careful because you don't know if it will work or not. There's a risk either way. It's legitimate to have that conversation, but it's legitimate to be cautious about not changing the strategy. Even if we'd had more to say on immigration, we wouldn't have been able to solve people's problems on free movement, which means we wouldn't have been able to help.'

The immigration debate took another twist when the Brownite faction in the Labour Party used their heightened prominence in 'Labour week' to begin arguing that their party should embrace a tougher line on the subject. Following Brown's speech on the Monday, Ed Balls gave an interview to the *Daily Mirror* on Tuesday the 14th in which he said, 'We've got to reform free movement. We're going to have to find a way in which to have managed migration, not free migration.'

At Cannon Street there was incredulity and fury. The grid had been cleared to give Labour figures air time, and Balls, a hugely experienced politician, had chosen to use his fifteen minutes of campaign fame to try to talk about the subject which two top-level meetings in the space of forty-eight hours had concluded should not be talked about. Balls' intervention contradicted Corbyn's free-for-all approach to migration, and was quickly supported by Tom Watson, the Labour deputy leader, who said, 'I think we have to reassure people that, if they vote Remain, that isn't the end of the reform package for Europe. A future Europe will have to look at things like the free movement of labour rules.' An article by Balls' wife Yvette Cooper on the same day also criticised Cameron for failing to talk about immigration, and said Britain should use its presidency of the EU in 2017 to call for border checks in the Schengen Zone and restrictions on migration from future accession countries. A source close to Cooper says her original plan had been to wait until after the referendum and use a close victory for Remain to seek to change Labour's policy. But the Brownites moved beforehand because of the silence from Corbyn and Cameron: 'They sought to try and fill that vacuum, but it probably wasn't as well thought through as it could have been.'

Coetzee says, 'They decided to hold a policy seminar on the subject at a critical moment in the campaign.' Straw phoned Balls to complain, but Balls refused to back down. A Labour source at Stronger In says, 'The floating of potential immigration reforms, days from polling day, was one of the most unhelpful steps that senior figures in the Labour Party could have taken at that stage. They should have known better. It's legitimate to make those kind of suggestions and promises when you are running for government, but when you are not even in a position where it's conceivable to enact them, I think it's irresponsible to force people on your own side to react to your blue-sky thinking on an unhelpful issue in the midst of a heated campaign.'

George Osborne finally closed down the prospects of a vow in a *Today* programme interview on Wednesday morning, ruling out any further immediate changes to freedom-of-movement rules. His appearance was supposed to kickstart a forty-eight-hour push on economic issues into the final weekend, with Mark Carney due to make his final intervention on the Thursday, and a set-piece speech by Osborne at the Mansion House the same evening. But the plan was undermined by an interview Theresa May gave to the BBC's Laura Kuenssberg on Wednesday afternoon which put immigration centre-stage again. May's second intervention of the campaign was even less helpful to Downing Street than the first. She contradicted Osborne, saying, 'There are some changes coming up in free-movement rules, to make it easier for us to deal with illegal immigrants, and I think again, as I've said, that we should look at further reform in the future.' A Downing Street official says, 'We were getting back to the economy, and it was the wrong moment to do that. I think she hadn't done media for a while. It was a cock-up.'

May was not the only one still thinking action was needed. Early on the morning of Thursday, 16 June, Coetzee and Straw were in a huddled and hushed conversation in the central pod in the Stronger In war room in Cannon Street. Coetzee was overheard saying, 'Why doesn't the government just say we would end free movement?' Straw, taken aback, looked at the Lib Dem and said, 'Well that would mean leaving the EU ...'

Coetzee responded in his broad South African accent, 'Oh yeah. Shit' – the key word pronounced 'sheet'. The eavesdropper was disturbed by the exchange: 'That was the moment I thought, "We really are fucked."'

21

GEORGE'S MONSTROUS MEDICINE

Before he had even made his pitch he knew it had backfired. George Osborne was on the *Today* programme to make his last bid to win the referendum. But what he had heard on the news ten minutes earlier made him realise his guns were spiked before he had even fired his first shell. He announced that if the country voted to leave the European Union he would have no alternative but to hold an emergency budget the week afterwards to plug a £30 billion black hole in the nation's finances. This time the chancellor had taken the precaution of enlisting the backing of his Labour predecessor Alistair Darling. But by the time he spoke, Tory rebel leader Steve Baker had pulled off his greatest commando coup of the campaign. Having got wind of the chancellor's plan the day before, Baker had worked in secret to line up a declaration from fifty-seven Tory MPs, announcing that they would vote down any such budget. Osborne's most audacious bid yet to raise economic risk exploded on the launchpad, and his personal reputation with it. From that point on the Stronger In campaign was struggling, and the chancellor's own leadership prospects were in freefall.

Again, Osborne was arguably too specific about the risks. Instead of issuing a general warning that there would be less money for public services, or higher taxes, he outlined plans to raise £15 billion from a 2p rise in the basic rate of income tax, a rise in the higher rate to 43p in the pound, a 5 per cent rise in the inheritance tax rate and a 5 per cent increase in alcohol and petrol duties. He also outlined spending cuts worth £15 billion, proposing to reduce health, defence and education spending by 2 per cent, and to slash 5 per cent from policing, transport and local government. 'The problem was that conceptually it was more of the same,' Andrew Cooper said later. 'It was a Tory government saying with slightly odd specificity that some terrible things will happen.' A close friend of Osborne says, 'David and George were both intensely focused on the fact that their careers might be about to end, so it was win at all costs. With George this often translates into going massively over the top on everything, going hyper-aggressive on everything – and in George's head, the bigger the number, the scarier it was.'

The non-Tories at Stronger In were concerned, but did not try to prevent the emergency budget announcement from going ahead. Ryan Coetzee says, 'I didn't throw my toys about the Brexit budget. You're in a campaign with a team of people. You hang together. You don't agree with every decision that's made. And you mustn't afterwards, when it goes wrong, go around falsely distancing yourself. We all sat in the room and signed off the grid.'

Part of the problem was that Osborne was widely distrusted by voters. The emergency budget now ensured he was widely distrusted by his colleagues too. 'George's numbers were awful,' says a senior Remain campaign figure. 'He was very obsessed with banging away at the economic-risks stuff in a way that was not really credible.'

Osborne's announcement had turned into an immediate disaster thanks to the foresight of Rob Oxley, Vote Leave's head of media. In the early stages of the campaign he noticed that Stronger In were using a company called MailChimp to send out their press releases. 'It's designed for mass email marketing, so it's designed to be quite easy to sign up to,' says Oxley. On one occasion Stronger In tweeted a link to a MailChimp online press release, rather than linking to their own campaign website. Since Stronger In had not added security to their lists, Oxley found the subscriber list and added an email address for a fake news agency he had created. He and others in the office added themselves to Stronger In's press list, broadcasting list, volunteer and activist lists, so they quickly started seeing press releases issued hours before publication to journalists 'under embargo', as well as some internal communications telling ground organisers when and how to dial in to conference calls.

Around 2 p.m. on Tuesday the 14th, one of Oxley's fake email addresses received the embargoed press release that had gone to a select group of newspapers detailing Osborne's big announcement on the emergency budget for the following morning. That gave Vote Leave an eight-hour head-start in preparing a response before the story appeared in the newspaper first editions. He and Dominic Cummings agreed that the time had come once again to 'release the flying monkeys'. Stephenson phoned Steve Baker, explained the situation, and said, 'We need an operation.'

Baker was just walking into a meeting of the Vote Leave Parliamentary Council, attended by sixty MPs and peers. Seeing an opportunity to cut short a laborious process, he filled them in. 'They universally agreed we were not having the threat of an emergency budget the next week to terrify the public.' Baker had forced an amendment on the Queen's Speech, but this, he said, was 'the most tense moment, the most difficult': 'Now we were asking colleagues to promise to vote down a budget. Traditionally it's a confidence measure. In extremis, colleagues might think they were being asked to surrender the whip, to properly die in a ditch.' He sent an email, and then a text message, to his mailing list of rebel Eurosceptics: 'CFB flash: please check email now and reply Y to support response to Brexit emergency budget.' Then, with help from his fellow Tory rebel Bill Wiggin, he hit the phones. 'In an hour we realised we had twenty. Then I started ringing around and realised, "My God, we're going to have over fifty."'

Cummings penned a press statement expressing surprise that the chancellor was 'threatening to renege on so many manifesto pledges'. It said: 'It is absurd to say that if people vote to take back control from the EU that he would want to punish them in this way. If he were to proceed with these proposals, the chancellor's position would become untenable.' Once again Cummings had made the referendum a leadership issue. Now all there was left to do was wait.

That afternoon Paul Stephenson briefed the newspapers with Vote Leave's latest alternative government wheeze, which would go head-to-head next morning with the punishment budget. It was Cummings' idea: 'We have to do a Queen's Speech.' Gove thought the name too provocative, so Stephenson renamed it 'Policy Framework for Government post Brexit'. The hacks called it a 'Brexit Queen's Speech' anyway.

The stage was set for a showdown between the two stunts, neither of which had any meaningful basis in political reality – a budget that the man announcing it did not intend to give if he won the referendum and would not be around to present if he lost, versus a fabricated manifesto by a cross-party group that by definition would never form a government. Stephenson said afterwards, 'I love the lobby, but you call them up and say some really important stuff and they're like, "No, no, no." You call them up with a made-up Queen's Speech and everyone's, "Brilliant! We're going to splash that." Some did. Some splashed the Brexit budget, which was also obviously a made-up thing too.'

Stephenson had one last trick up his sleeve. Knowing that Osborne was going on the *Today* programme to do the flagship 8.10 a.m. interview to promote his emergency budget, he phoned a contact at the BBC and briefed the details of the backbench mutiny. He embargoed the story until 8 a.m., so the first Osborne heard of it was as he was sitting down at the microphone for his own interview. Stephenson pulled Chris Grayling, who was supposed to do the Vote Leave response at 8.30, and replaced him with Baker, who was much keener to put the boot into the chancellor. 'We needed him to go in really hard, and he did, in his reasonable way,' recalls Stephenson. Baker said, 'It's not a budget, it's a campaigning device, and if it is proposed, we will bring it down.' He said afterwards, 'We completely spoiled their news story.' When he got off air Baker received complaints from Conservative MPs that they had not been included in the threat to vote down the emergency budget. The number of rebels rose to sixty-five.

Tory MPs quickly seized on the 'punishment budget' name. Not missing an opportunity to attack his old foe, Iain Duncan Smith told LBC Radio that Osborne was deliberately trying to panic the markets. 'Of all the things I think that the Remain camp has done, this one probably is the most bizarre and the most ridiculous,' he said, calling Osborne's behaviour 'more irresponsible than I've seen from any chancellor at any time'. As journalists sought the views of other parties, to those watching from Cannon Street it seemed that the world had gone mad. 'I saw senior people tweeting things like "The DUP won't support George's Brexit budget,"' says one Stronger In source. 'There *was* no fucking budget.' Nick Clegg said later, 'The moment where I really thought that things were going pear-shaped was when I woke up and I heard this to my mind ludicrous announcement from George Osborne to threaten the country with a punishment budget if they had the temerity to disagree with him.'

In Leicestershire, Andrew Bridgen believed the emergency budget gambit 'really backfired', to a degree that may have cost Remain the referendum. 'These brilliant politicians misjudged the British public,' he said afterwards. 'A large number of people in my constituency who were good Tories and planning to vote Remain were riled by that punishment budget. They came to me afterwards and said, "Actually, Andrew, I voted to leave. I'm not going to be bullied by George Osborne." That pushed a lot of soft Remainers into Leave. That's what happens if you are perceived to be out of touch with the people.'

The 'punishment budget' was immensely damaging to the chancellor, and would have given rise to calls to move him from the Treasury even if Remain had won the referendum. The focus Vote Leave placed on his position becoming 'untenable' meant that Alistair Darling's role was almost completely lost in the media coverage. An Osborne aide said, 'Darling was the man who took the call in the Treasury from RBS saying, "We've got three hours of money left and then this bank's going to collapse," and he was saying, "I'm more worried now than I was in 2008." That should have been the top story. But it was hard to break out of that prism of blue-on-blue arguments.'

Daniel Hannan believes the idea torpedoed any lingering trust voters had in Osborne's economic arguments. 'They made some incredible claims, like the emergency budget, which made everyone think, "If you are saying something that implausible, why should we believe anything else you have said?" That is really a bad place to be in politics.'

The problem for Osborne was that he made his move in an environment of mutinous rage on the backbenches. The prospect of Cameron's defeat and resignation was uppermost in people's minds. At PMQs the week before, Brexiteer Richard Drax had accused Cameron of 'losing the argument'. Loyalist Andrew Griffiths 'took a pop' at Drax from the green benches. Griffiths, a former aide to Eric Pickles, then came under fire from Eurosceptic Stewart Jackson, who told him, 'Your career high has been as Eric Pickles' toilet-warmer' – all while the television cameras rolled.

Robert Syms, a Brexiteer but a leadership loyalist, was circulating a letter to be produced if Cameron lost the referendum, urging him not to resign. The 'save Dave' operation was seen as a 'put-up job' by the whips, designed to give Cameron 'dignity in dying'. That week a gleeful Andrew Bridgen told colleagues, 'The careerists are shitting themselves. It's no fun when you've gone around kissing people's backsides for years to discover that you've been kissing the wrong backsides.' One of the arses people had been kissing was George Osborne's.

*   *   *

Knowing the mood of his parliamentary colleagues, Osborne was aware that he was killing his hopes of the leadership by announcing the emergency budget. Andrew Cooper said he had made the decision to do everything possible to win the referendum: 'We weren't going to leave anything in the locker room.' James McGrory watched the chancellor's self-immolation with admiration: 'To be fair to Osborne, he put his money where his mouth was, and I respect it. He gambled a lot – and lost. But he and his team put their back into it, and gave us some of the best media days in the campaign. He could have gone about this very differently due to personal political calculation.'

Prior to the emergency budget, Labour staff at Stronger In believed their Conservative counterparts in the campaign were trying to promote Osborne's leadership prospects. A Labour source says, 'The backdrop to the entire campaign in terms of staff relations was dominated by Project George and the leadership. I know Adam Atashzai was very pro-George, and it seemed to me like Ameet [Gill] was charged with elements of the succession.'

But when Osborne had to choose between his career and victory in the referendum, he put the referendum first. He told friends after polling day, 'I knew that was the choice I was making.' Osborne knew it was dividing the party, and he thought it was highly likely that David Cameron would have to resign almost immediately. But in the end, he believed the cause was important enough for him to spend every bit of political capital he had. An Osborne aide added, 'He could have done the minimum possible, let it be Cameron's referendum. But when there's a campaign going he wants to be involved in it, and George does think he can do it better than other people.'

But Osborne's enthusiasm proved an irritation to some in Downing Street, who felt they could not control the chancellor's media interventions. Events were planned without the knowledge of Number 10 or the campaign. 'They were a law unto themselves,' one Remain camp source said. But the emergency budget was not a case in point – it was fully signed off by Cameron's team. A minister who is close to Osborne said he felt he had to battle alongside Cameron. 'David felt quite lonely leading it. There was definitely a point where he called for help.'

While Osborne is popularly seen as an arch-Machiavelli, his biggest secret was that he was absolutely committed to membership of the European Union. An MP who has worked closely with him said, 'To him the idea that any half-serious person could look another finance minister or banker or anyone with any intelligence in the eye and say leaving was a good thing was mentally retarded.' Osborne came across as far more pro-European in private than he did in public. He gave a speech to a group of potential donors at the Mandarin Hotel in Knightsbridge during the campaign that struck one observer as revelatory: 'George was open and liberal and tolerant and diverse and outward-looking. I didn't hear a Conservative chancellor, I heard a man who shared the same values and positive agenda for Europe that I shared. But I never really heard him say it publicly.'

Osborne regarded himself as a Eurosceptic, an 'honourable position' he believed had become wrongly equated with wanting Brexit. He had been involved in the campaign to keep Britain out of the euro, and wrote William Hague's speeches on the subject. To Osborne being a Eurosceptic meant wanting a union of member states in which Britain was not part of ever closer integration, not part of a political project, not part of joining the euro – but not leaving the EU either, because of the risks to the economy and European security. To those who saw him as a schemer, he would say he used his political skills to deliver the socially and economically liberal country he wanted to see. A Cameron aide who admires Osborne said, 'Everyone thinks of George as a political politician. He's actually a conviction politician. He threw his leadership chances under the bus.'

As an example of Project Fear, of backbench guerrilla warfare and blue-on-blue brutality, the emergency budget was the biggest day of the campaign – but it wasn't even the most eye-catching event of that day.

Reporters in the House of Commons press gallery did not need any encouragement to flee when Twitter began to light up with news that Nigel Farage was leading an armada of boats up the Thames to Parliament. At 12.30 that Wednesday afternoon a lacklustre PMQs was drawing to a close, and the scribes raced to the terrace to witness one of the more bizarre encounters of the referendum. Farage was at the head of a pro-Brexit flotilla of fishing boats protesting against what the Commons Fisheries Policy had done to their industry. Riding alongside, leading the charge for the Remain campaign, was the seventies rock star and Live Aid founder Sir Bob Geldof, responding forcefully through a loudhailer.

What can now be revealed is that the encounter was the product of the Ukip leader's enthusiasm for cooking sea bass, and a secret deal between Downing Street and a group of far-left activists that would have made both sides blush if it had emerged during the campaign.

Farage has long been a fishing fanatic, both for relaxation and as a key strand of his irritation with the EU. 'He is a fisherman. That's what he does for fun,' said his spokesman Gawain Towler. 'Get a small boat, sod off into the Channel and find himself some bass. The new rules mean he can't land a bass – can't even take one bass home. He's quite a good cook. It really mattered to him. That is his joy. And sometimes we're driven by things other than high politics.' Farage's fishing forays were also popular with the staff at Ukip's offices. 'He goes sea fishing, which means he can sod off for six hours without anyone contacting him, which is brilliant!' Politically, Farage regarded the fishing industry, which had lost 80,000 jobs since the 1970s, as potentially a key beneficiary of Brexit, because Britain could reclaim control of its territorial waters. 'It matters to him, it is deeply symbolic, we are an island nation,' Towler said. 'A nation should control its own waters.'

All of which meant that when Bob Spink, who had become Ukip's first MP when he defected from the Tories in 2008, approached Farage saying that some Essex fishermen wanted to sail up the Thames, Farage embraced the idea and said, 'Let's think bigger.' He met some Scottish deep-sea fishermen, set up Fishing for Leave, and arranged for a fleet of thirty-five vessels to rendezvous off Southend pier at 6 a.m. on the big day. They met Farage and his team at Butler's Wharf, by Tower Bridge. Towler had deliberately chartered a boat owned by Sir Richard Branson, a prominent supporter of the Remain campaign. 'We were going to have a bit of fun, food and drink, trawl up the Thames, get some nice photos,' he recalled. 'There was going to be a small series of articles about it, just to get the fishing community a voice. And then Sir Bob happened.'

At 10 a.m. Towler was standing near City Hall when a large boat went past with loudspeakers blaring. 'I thought, "What the bloody hell is this?"' It was Geldof, accompanied by Rachel Johnson, Boris's sister, and a boatload of young people having a party. Stronger In had also arranged for pro-Remain signs to be hung over Tower Bridge. Spotting an opportunity for mischief, Towler wandered over and said, 'You do realise that's against bylaws, don't you?' The campaigners were cleared off Tower Bridge, but their banners disrupted Ukip's camera shots. The Port of

London Authority was forced to open the bridge for twenty minutes to let the larger vessels through, and a dozen of them were allowed to proceed to Parliament.

Geldof's boat, *Sarpedon*, blasted out songs including Dobie Gray's 'I'm in With the In Crowd' as a handful of dinghies bearing In flags sought to disrupt the Leave flotilla. The two armadas exchanged hose fire, before a police launch got between them. The creator of Live Aid, who knew a thing or two about publicity stunts, pulled alongside Farage's vessel and addressed him through a loudhailer: 'You are no fisherman's friend,' shouted Geldof, pointing out that when Farage was on the European Parliament Fisheries Committee he attended just one out of forty-three meetings. 'You are a fraud, Nigel. Go back down the river, because you are up one without a canoe or a paddle.' Geldof had read up for the occasion. When he met Alan Johnson on the *Question Time* set later that day, the Labour In campaign chief said, 'You'd better be clued up on the Common Fisheries Policy.' Geldof replied, 'Alan, I know every fucking dot and fucking comma of the fucking Common Fisheries Policy.'

Emboldened by the success of the ambush, Geldof and some of his young supporters turned the music back up, had a drink and began flicking V-signs at Farage's protesters. They looked like a bunch of Hooray Henrys on a pleasure cruise. Farage called their behaviour 'disgusting', but he was delighted by the publicity. 'We used to protest against the establishment, now the establishment protests against us,' he said.

That was precisely the image Daniel Korski had been trying to avoid. Geldof had approached Stronger In because he wanted to do an event, but had not been able to recruit volunteers. Korski first considered approaching Conservatives In, but realised 'it wasn't going to look good if people in suits and little buttons walked up on the boat'. So through several intermediaries he hatched an audacious plan and did a clandestine deal with groups including Momentum, the left-wing supporters of Jeremy Corbyn.

When Korski met one of the activists he decided to 'suspend the fact I think they're a dangerous, ludicrous, radicalised faction, endangering this nation, and they suspended the view I was a nasty imperialist capitalist pig'. Korski asked, 'Can we meet in Starbucks? I mean, that's unless you're going to ransack it while we're there.' Then he offered the scourge of austerity capitalism a chai latte. He arranged with Momentum and the other groups – UK Uncut, Another Europe is Possible, We Are Europe

and Students for Europe – that they would put volunteers on boats and
unfurl banners across the bridges. A Momentum source said, 'We were
looking for events which could get media attention. Our analysis was
that the main Stronger In was not doing a good job on exciting and
mobilising young people.'

Neither Korski nor Momentum had bargained on Geldof being so
aggressive – but Ukip could not have been happier. 'They turned what
was going to be a photo op and a nice few stories into a global news
sensation,' says Towler. 'Because Bob Geldof started being a berk. And
what did we do? We said, "Bloody brilliant!"' Farage recalls, 'It was
extraordinary. Had it not been for what happened the next day, then the
enduring image of the referendum would have been middle-class
millionaires and Bob Geldof flicking V-signs at me and the fishermen.
The Remain side came out very badly. It was in a way the high point of
the campaign.'

If the emergency budget was drama and the flotilla was farce, what
came next was tragedy.

22

BREAKING POINTS

For the majority of those on the front line of the referendum campaign it had been the most bitterly fought and intense political experience of their lives. Many thought the well-being of their country was at stake. They got up before dawn and went to bed in the smallest of hours. But at 12.53 p.m. on Thursday, 16 June, a week before polling day, it all came to a juddering halt. At that point none of it seemed to matter any more.

Jo Cox, the Labour MP for Batley and Spen, was on her way to a constituency advice surgery at a library on Market Street, Birstall, west Yorkshire when she was attacked by a man armed with a knife and a firearm. Eyewitnesses said the man stabbed her, and when she fell to the ground, he shot and stabbed her again. A witness, retired rescue miner Bernard Carter-Kenny, tried to intervene but was stabbed in the abdomen. Cox, who was just forty-one and had two young children aged five and three, was pronounced dead at the scene at 1.48 p.m. Soon media reports began circulating that the perpetrator had yelled 'Britain first' or 'Put Britain first' as he attacked her. While other MPs had suffered violence in the intervening years, Cox was the first to be killed in the line of duty since the IRA murdered Ian Gow in 1990. She was also an outspoken supporter of the Remain campaign – indeed, she and her family had been in one of the inflatable rubber dinghies that had been buzzing around Nigel Farage's Thames flotilla the previous day. Later that afternoon, as her death was made public, Cox's husband Brendan issued a statement urging people to 'fight against the hatred that killed her'.

Thomas Mair, aged fifty-two, a constituent of Cox who had links to the National Alliance, an American neo-Nazi group, was arrested shortly after the attack. On Saturday, 18 June he was charged with her murder.

When he appeared at Westminster Magistrates' Court and was asked to confirm his name he said, 'My name is death to traitors, freedom for Britain.' Asked again, he repeated the same phrase.

Those who knew Cox mourned a rising star, and someone who had spent her life doing good for others. In the days following her death, David Cameron and Jeremy Corbyn stood together for the first time during the campaign on a visit to her constituency. Parliament was recalled for a day of emotional tributes. For everyone involved in the referendum campaign, the questions that hung in the air were: was she attacked because of her views on Brexit? And would her death affect the outcome?

At Cannon Street, Stronger In staff were in a state of shock when they heard the news. David Chaplin stared at the television, unable to 'process what was happening'. He thought of his many friends who had become MPs the year before: 'It could have been any one of them.' He texted many of them to say he hoped they were OK. Will Straw's wife Claire had worked with Jo Cox over many years at the Gates Foundation, the charity run by Bill and Melinda Gates, and was also an intern for Cox on her campaign to decrease the incidence of maternal mortality. Straw was on a call when the news came through: 'I could see people quite visibly shocked. I got off the phone and felt like I'd been punched in the gut. We then made a decision very quickly that we would suspend the campaign.'

The attack on Cox was made public as David Cameron was in the air on his way to Gibraltar, where he was due to appear at the biggest Remain rally of the campaign, in front of 15,000 people. The inhabitants of the Rock were devotedly pro-EU, and feared Spanish meddling if they lost the protection of Brussels. Craig Oliver put an urgent call through to the aircraft, and Cameron made the snap decision to cancel the rally. Charlotte Todman's team had been on the ground for two days ensuring that the visuals from the event would look spectacular on the evening news – they had to cancel plans to project 'Stronger In' onto the Rock. People were already flooding into the square, their faces painted, as vendors sold 'David Cameron ice cream'. The prime minister paid a quick visit to the swish Rock Hotel to meet Fabian Picardo, Gibraltar's first minister, where he did a clip for the broadcasters. While he was there he learned of Cox's death, and flew straight home.

Vote Leave had been having another good day when news about the attack began to filter through. Rob Oxley was trying to control an immense press pack that was on the road with Boris Johnson. The journalists had great pictures of the former mayor with Steve Hilton, David Cameron's old friend who was now campaigning for Leave. When he heard what had happened, Oxley felt sick. After hearing the rumours about the shouts of 'Britain first', he feared the TV cameras would turn up at the suspect's house and find a Vote Leave poster in the window. Penny Mordaunt was also on the bus that day. As a defence minister she was patched into conversations about security for MPs. That was how the Leave campaign learned that Cox had died several hours before the news was made public.

Vote Leave also suspended their campaign, and cancelled a rally in Birmingham on the Saturday. Matthew Elliott was speaking on a panel at York University's Festival of Ideas when the campaign WhatsApp group started beeping incessantly with news of what had happened. 'I thought it was over basically,' he says. At Westminster Tower, Dominic Cummings was more confident that the public would make a different judgement. He told staff, 'We're suspending our campaign as a mark of respect, but my instinct is this will have no effect on the result. Most people are going to say this was a lone nutter, and he doesn't represent my views.' Nonetheless, the mood at Vote Leave headquarters was very downbeat. On their conference call that night Boris Johnson said, 'We're fucked, we're totally fucked.' Cummings and Paul Stephenson tried to convince him that the situation was salvageable, but they were uncomfortable themselves. Stephenson recalled, 'Suddenly we're these racists. It was nasty. It was a dicey moment.'

When an email from Stronger In appeared in one of Vote Leave's fake-account inboxes inviting volunteers to dial in to a conference call, two senior staff did so. They heard Will Straw say, 'We need to recognise that people have been pulled up short by Jo Cox's death. It is now time to make a very positive case for why we want to be in the European Union', and to 'call out the other side for what they have done to stir division and resentment in the UK'. A transcript was leaked to the *Daily Telegraph*. For Straw, it was the lowest moment of the campaign. Considering that his wife had known Jo Cox, his words were understandable, but they sparked claims that the Remain campaign was exploiting her death. David Chaplin is adamant that Straw did nothing wrong: 'Will was right to say "Of course it's going to change the way we think," but we initiated no new activity.'

When Rob Oxley, who had not been on the call, heard Straw's words he was enraged, and convinced the referendum was lost: 'It was difficult to understand where we could go from there. We could see them mercilessly exploiting it. It proved to me they thought people who backed leave were xenophobic. It almost gave them permission to run the campaign they'd wanted to run of painting us as the bad guys.'

Cameron had given an interview to the *Sunday Times* before setting off for Gibraltar, warning that Brexit was a one-way vote from which there was no return. It was supposed to be accompanied by a picture of a new campaign poster showing a hand grenade with the pin pulled out. This was one of the most striking images the campaign had produced, and made Cameron's point effectively. It had polled well in focus groups, but it now looked deeply inappropriate. An anxious Craig Oliver phoned the newspaper to pull the image.

Nigel Farage was also concerned: 'I worried greatly that an event like this could turn opinion, though I remembered Anna Lindh, a very prominent Swedish politician, was murdered in the street in a very similar way in the run-up to the Swedish vote on whether they should join the euro or not. She had been a very prominent supporter of joining the euro. The upshot was that in Sweden it made no difference at all.'[1]

But the Ukip leader immediately found himself in the eye of the growing storm. On Thursday morning, a few hours before Cox was killed, Farage had unveiled a provocative poster about immigration featuring a long stream of migrants at the Croatian–Slovenian border under the slogan 'Breaking Point'. The poster had attracted only minor interest when it was released on advertising vans. Now it became the focus of a public debate about whether Farage was stirring up racial hatred, and whether an atmosphere of 'fearing the other' had fuelled both Cox's killing and Leave's lead in the polls. Labour frontbencher Emily Thornberry said, 'I thought that Nigel Farage's poster was disgusting. We have a responsibility as politicians not to play the race card. Nigel Farage was attempting to divide people and get the debate about Europe to be just about immigration and about fear. I think that poster was unforgivable, it was irresponsible. He should be ashamed of himself.'[2]

The poster was intended to be the first of a series of hard-hitting adverts to be released by Ukip each day until polling day. It had first been offered to Vote Leave early in the New Year. Matthew Elliott had worked on the NOtoAV campaign with Family, the advertising agency behind the advert. Paul Sykes, the millionaire Ukip donor, had approached Elliott and said, 'Matthew, trust me, it's going to be great. It will be an ad campaign you'll be able to see from the moon.' But Cummings and Stephenson had vetoed the idea. They said they did not wish to work with Sykes.

Farage and Chris Bruni-Lowe saw the advertising campaign, which Sykes had vowed to pour up to £2 million into, as another means of pressuring Vote Leave to go harder on immigration, or if they would not, to push things further than Cummings was prepared to go. The Ukip men flew to Sykes's home in Jersey to discuss the details with him. 'We spent two days brainstorming ideas,' says Bruni-Lowe. 'This was around the time of the campaign when no one was talking about migration apart from us. We were about ten points behind. Our view is we needed to do some hard-hitting immigration stuff to maximise our vote, to give us a chance of winning.' Ukip insisted the poster was legitimate. The main image had appeared on the front pages of national newspapers, and the advert itself was placed in four nationals the morning Jo Cox was killed. Farage said, 'It was only because of the atrocity that happened ninety minutes afterwards. The Remain side decided to conflate the two things, and it was a pretty vicious weekend. I'd used a very similar poster for the London Assembly elections. A few people on Twitter said it was ghastly; we said it was true. The idea was to launch six separate posters in the last week, and this was the first.'

Bruni-Lowe is clear that he and Farage knew they were pushing the limits, but they were prepared to do so because they considered it the only way to win the referendum. They wanted to put the issues out there, in the hope that Vote Leave's big guns would at least endorse their substance, if not their style: 'Our view was that if we did this with a massive point, to kick the door open, others could say, "I wouldn't have done that, but there is a legitimate point to be made." But they bottled it. We were happy to be the bad people, as long as they said that stuff. But they didn't. They said it was a racist poster. They completely shot themselves in the foot.' Both Boris Johnson and Michael Gove condemned the poster. Gove said he 'shuddered' when he saw it.

Senior figures in Vote Leave spent the days after Jo Cox's death trying to rein in Farage. On Thursday evening Matthew Elliott phoned Ian Wright of the Family ad agency to ask, 'What else do you have coming out? Do you understand that more ads like this will blow up in your face personally as an ad company, and set us back?' He found Wright 'in complete shock' about Cox's death and the reaction to the advert.

At 8 a.m. on Friday, the day after Jo Cox's murder, Chris Grayling got a text from Cummings saying, 'Chris is there anything you can do to stop Farage publishing more of these posters?' Grayling went to see Farage at a pub near his home in Kent. Uncharacteristically, the Ukip leader drank coffee, while Grayling sipped a Diet Coke. 'He agreed to refocus his campaign on sovereignty, because we both agreed that the Jo Cox thing was tragic, and we wanted to make sure that the last few days ran smoothly. By the time I got to the pub he'd agreed to wait a day to publish the next one.' Boris Johnson and Iain Duncan Smith also spoke directly to the Ukip leader about the posters.

As a result of Jo Cox's death Farage had also cancelled a planned speech on Friday in which he intended to say that border controls and visas would be imposed as soon as Britain voted Brexit. He had heard that David Cameron was planning to say something on the Monday, warning that a vote to leave would actually lead to a flood of migrants flocking to Britain before the UK could pull out of the EU. In fact Downing Street had no such plan, but Ukip wanted to pre-empt it. Bruni-Lowe says, 'We were going to say we'd have an immediate halt on migration.'

Arron Banks regarded the fuss about the poster as another example of the delicate sensibilities of the metropolitan media, and encouraged Farage not to back down: 'That offended the Westminster bubble of jour-nalists, but it doesn't offend the rest of the country. Nigel was extremely concerned, he thought it meant the momentum had died. I said, "You're in this bubble as well."' Farage came under sustained pressure to apolo-gise. Andy Wigmore, Banks's campaign spokesman, came up with a solution: 'He didn't apologise for the poster, he apologised for the timing of the poster – and that set the whole news cycle going again.' Even this was just a tactic to keep the issue in the headlines: 'We wanted to keep immigration in people's minds as long as possible, so apologising for the timing kept the thing going for another day or two. You can argue about the sensitivities of it, but all the polling we had right from the beginning said "If you're talking about immigration, you're winning; if you're talk-ing about the economy, you're losing."'

Farage says, 'By Monday, the whole debate was on immigration again. Whatever miseries I'd had to withstand – and the media was the most aggressive I've ever seen in my life, as if I'd actually done it [killed Jo Cox] – but by the Monday morning, we realised the debate is back on migration.' He put out other posters paid for by Sykes, but they were unmemorable and relatively uncontroversial. Steve Hilton also got publicity on the subject of immigration on the final Monday of the campaign by revealing that he had been in a meeting with David Cameron in 2012 at which the prime minister was warned that his 'tens of thousands' net migration pledge was 'impossible' to deliver.

Ukip insisted the 'Breaking Point' advert, which ran in many northern regional newspapers, helped win the referendum. 'It went down extraordinarily well there,' said Bruni-Lowe. Farage saw Vote Leave as hypocritical: 'They used migrant boats as a fundraising email. They did an Abu Hamza poster. They did Turkey posters! Christ! I wouldn't have done those. There was total hypocrisy. The establishment were in full cry looking for someone to blame.' Gawain Towler says, 'There was a lot of "If we lose, we blame Farage" around that weekend.'

Daniel Hannan argued that the poster was more about Farage's ego than the referendum result. 'Can you imagine there being an undecided voter who is on the fence, who would be convinced by that poster? Was it actually ever going to switch anyone into the Leave column, or was it about grabbing back the spotlight? The people for whom migration was the top issue were a minority within the Leave voting population. And even among them' – Hannan pointed to an LSE study of the opinion polls conducted after the election which suggested Vote Leave were ahead throughout the campaign – 'we were well ahead on the morning that poster was unveiled. And then we collapsed. As a matter of observable fact, we collapsed when that poster came out.'

The immediate perception in both campaigns and the media was that Jo Cox's death would benefit Remain. Vote Leave had been on a roll for days, and the halt in campaigning had destroyed their momentum. The 'Breaking Point' poster had offended polite opinion. Even Leave campaigners who were disgusted by Farage believed they would be damaged by association. Their mood improved, however, when Henry de Zoete reported back on the focus group he had done on the Friday evening, the day after Cox's murder. He found that people did not blame Vote Leave for her death, and resented the suggestion that the campaign was somehow responsible: 'Normal people think this is just a crazy mad guy, it has nothing to do with the campaign – and if anyone tries to make it about the referendum, it's going to help us.'

Polls show that Remain got a three- or four-day bounce from Cox's death, but that it was already dissipating by the time polling day arrived. Stronger In campaign officials now believe, though, that this was not just down to swing voters repelled by Cox's murder. They think a bigger factor was 'shy' leave voters becoming more reluctant to tell pollsters they were backing 'Out', something which may have given false comfort to the Remain camp in the final days. Alan Johnson says, 'I feel all it did was make people more reluctant to admit that they were Leavers. They almost felt guilty about it because of Jo.'

Some Remain campaigners go as far as to say that halting Vote Leave in their tracks was actually counterproductive. During the Scottish referendum campaign the *Sunday Times*/YouGov poll that put the Nationalists ahead with eleven days to go not only galvanised the entire political class to go north and campaign for the union, many believe it also focused the minds of voters on the fact that the referendum was an all-or-nothing choice, in which a Yes vote would mean there was no way back. Adam Atashzai, who was monitoring the financial markets and the value of sterling in order to pounce on evidence of turmoil, believed the markets 'would have created flashing lights on the news'. Another senior figure in the campaign described Jo Cox's death as 'a disaster' for Stronger In: 'That weekend, I bet the papers would have splashed on a five-point Leave lead in the polls, and I think on Monday and Tuesday the markets would have crashed. We would have had a cycle which was much closer to Scotland. Actually it took the sting out of the campaign. It meant that the bounce back to the status quo never really happened. That was something we were banking on happening.'

Cox's death also meant Mark Carney's final intervention on the day of her killing received almost no publicity. 'He was just wiped off the news agenda, and that was devastating from our point of view,' a Tory source said. George Osborne was also forced to cancel his speech at the Mansion House, making only a few brief remarks. Stronger In had hoped that would kickstart a new economic push over the final weekend. The tragedy also made it more difficult for Labour politicians to campaign. 'It put the campaign in aspic for a few days,' says David Chaplin. 'We were in the midst of the Labour Party fightback, and the Labour Party, for completely obvious and correct reasons, felt the need to fully suspend campaigning for even longer than we did.'

The final insight is one that Lynton Crosby is fond of, the idea that 'polls are actors' and affect the behaviour of voters. Remain appeared to open up a lead early in the final week, and there was anecdotal evidence after the referendum that some voters who wanted to stay, believing the 'In' campaign was going to win, felt safe staying at home or registering a protest vote for 'Out'. Others believed David Cameron's claims that he would not resign if he lost.

But by the weekend before the vote, when the prime minister began his final campaign push, his closest ally had already concluded that the referendum was lost and he would have to go.

23

WEMBLEY

David Cameron felt the anger welling in him. He had been doing this for four months, and he had taken some hits. There were four days to go, and the polls were not where he wanted them to be. The party was on edge. Gove and Boris, the great betrayers, were looking confident. The great game plan was not working as it had before. At the end of the week he had had a conversation with George Osborne that had made him fear the worst. And now, on live television, he had just been compared to Neville Chamberlain.

It was the final Sunday of the campaign, and Cameron was on the BBC's *Question Time* special, his last big broadcast. The audience had been hitting him hard on immigration. He needed to do something. A questioner came at him on the deal, saying it was not legally binding: 'Mr Cameron, you say that your policy that you've negotiated with Europe cannot be overruled – it can. So are you really the twenty-first-century Neville Chamberlain, waving a piece of paper in the air, saying to the public, "This is what I have, I have this promise," where a dictatorship in Europe can overrule it?'

Cameron rolled his lower lip into his mouth, biting it gently. His tongue flicked briefly out, like a viper's – and then he went for it: 'At my office I sit two yards away from the cabinet room where Winston Churchill decided in May 1940 to fight on against Hitler. The best and greatest decision perhaps anyone has made in our country. He didn't want to be alone. He wanted to be fighting with the French, the Poles and the others. But he didn't quit. He didn't quit on democracy, he didn't quit on freedom.' Cameron moved around the stage, hands gesticulating, fingers pointing. 'We want to fight for those things today. You can't win if you're not in the room. You can't win a football match if you're not on the pitch.'

It was Cameron's best moment of the campaign. He was not going down without a fight. Watching from the wings, Craig Oliver breathed a sigh of relief. His man had shown some passion. That was what his debate coach Bill Knapp had told him to do. 'They've got all the emotions,' Knapp had said. 'We're defending the status quo, they've got the change. You've got to come up with an original emotional moment.' When Cameron came off stage it was to a 'tiny little dim room', with slits for windows and a couple of beers arranged awkwardly in the corner. He was the leader of the world's fifth-largest economy, and this was where they put him, in a prison cell. His team had been prepping him earlier, at a hotel near Milton Keynes, and Cameron had gone for a walk with Ed and Kate and Craig and Adam. Ed de Minckwitz was there too. There was a wedding going on, and people spotted him, but they did not come over. All very English.

'That Churchill moment, where did that come from?' Atashzai asked him when he got to the tiny green room. The journalists all thought it was prepared, but it was totally unrehearsed.

'I just thought I had to do something,' Cameron said. 'I was getting pummelled, I was getting totally nailed. I had to pull something out of the bag.'

Atashzai said, 'I thought it was a really good moment.'

The prime minister of Great Britain and Northern Ireland sat down. 'I'm glad you enjoyed it. I'm here to entertain.' Looking back on that evening, one of his aides remarked later, 'The tragedy of David Cameron is he just became really good at the job as he left it.'

Cameron reran the Scottish playbook on the final weekend. Just as he had in September 2014, he gave an interview to the *Sunday Times*, arguing that a vote to leave would be a 'one-way ticket' with 'no going back': 'Once you have jumped out of the aeroplane, you can't scramble back through the door.' Ryan Coetzee's focus group the week before had shown that this was a powerful argument with women: 'The idea that the decision of the vote next week is final, and if we leave there is no going back, really scared them,' he emailed the campaign team. But David Mundell, the Scottish secretary, thought it was all too late. He had seen how they had won in Scotland, and it felt different this time: 'I've concluded this was the big difference in the referendums. In Scotland we did in that campaign get the message over to people that this was really serious. You did not have people voting because they wanted to make a protest against David Cameron or the establishment. I think that was not achieved in the EU referendum.'

Cameron did not go without giving it his all. The previous week Andrew Cooper spoke to the former Labour minister Douglas Alexander, who told him the force of Cameron's impact was being lost because he wasn't being a prime minister, he was being a Tory politician. He suggested an event that looked like the nation's leader talking to the country. The result, on Tuesday the 21st, two days before polling day, was a speech in the street outside Number 10. Cameron's team were stretching the purdah rules to breaking point. The PM tried to make his economic message more family-friendly: 'As you take this decision whether to remain or leave, do think about the hopes and dreams of your children and grandchildren – they know their chances to work, to travel, to build the sort of open society they want to live in, rest on this outcome.'

Even as he fought for victory, though, David Cameron was preparing for defeat. George Osborne went to him with a week to go and said, 'I have a very bad feeling about the result. I'm pretty sure we've lost the campaign.' The chancellor also told his wife, Frances, 'I think we're going to lose.' Cameron and Osborne met in the flat above Number 11 Downing Street to war game their options, going into 'deep conversation' about what to do next. Could he hang on if he lost? Did he even want to? A letter was doing the rounds among MPs calling for Cameron to stay even if he lost. Both Boris Johnson and Michael Gove had signed it. Other Brexiteers like Chris Grayling and Liam Fox had been to see Cameron to tell him he must stay on. They feared the instability that would come if there was a Brexit vote and he walked away. The letter would, perhaps, buy Cameron enough time to hold on until the party conference at the start of October, to enjoy a lap of honour that would take in the G20 meeting in China at the start of September.

Osborne's view was that none of this was tenable. He believed that in Britain's parliamentary system Cameron's enemies would 'thump him'. It only needed eight or nine MPs voting with Labour to overturn his majority. The farewell tour would turn into a busman's holiday from hell. The chancellor thought it was 'not credible' that Cameron could cheerlead for Remain and then lead a Brexit government. The prime minister 'didn't need much persuading', a source close to Osborne said. The two men 'went through all the other options. And they all ended up basically with a big challenge to the leadership in October or November. In the end he might have been able to survive – if he was prepared to be absolutely ruthless and scorched-earth. A bit like Brown when he was fighting for his life in 2008, or Harold Wilson. You could do it, but your heart would have to be in it. And your heart would have to be, "I want to lead this Brexit government."' And that was the crux of the matter. David Cameron had promised months ago to put his 'heart and soul' into the Remain campaign. Maybe he had not done everything possible to win. There were some things, like declaring total war on Boris and Gove, like announcing that he would veto Turkish accession to the EU, like putting Angela Merkel on the spot and demanding more on migration, that he thought either would not work or would do more harm than good. But having put himself on the line day in and day out, David Cameron 'didn't want to lead a Brexit government'.

There was more than one conversation between the two friends and political partners. They widened the circle slightly so that Ed Llewellyn was included. Then Kate Fall and Craig Oliver too. Nothing was resolved, but they began to work on two scenarios: win or lose. When David Cameron took the stage at *Question Time* on the Sunday, when he strode into Downing Street on Tuesday, he knew he was fighting for his political life – and that the man who had been at his side throughout thought he was doomed.

There was one big moment left, the biggest debate in British history, in front of 6,500 people at Wembley Arena. David Cameron used to say he wanted his 'star player on the pitch'. That used to be a reference to Boris Johnson, but now he was on the other team. To take on Boris, with everything on the line, the two public schoolboys who had run Britain for six years sent for a working-class kid from Glasgow, the one Tory who had shown she could steal votes wholesale from Labour. Her name was Ruth.

Ruth Davidson, the leader of the Scottish Conservative Party, was a committed pro-European. She had grown up in a council house. Her dad had made whisky and textiles. 'I came off a council estate at sixteen, so every plate of food was because he made stuff and sold it abroad,' she said. That's why access to the single market was important to her. Davidson was a big prize. Daniel Hannan had invited her to a think-tank event in September, and she had agreed to speak. It was months before the deal, but she did not want to get into a will-she, won't-she 'Cameron loyalty test', so she announced that she would be backing Remain. That would not do her any harm in Scotland. Hannan had looked 'gutted'. She believed he had thought that by accepting she might declare for Brexit. She hadn't chosen to tell him she wasn't.

Peter Mandelson had tried to get Davidson on Stronger In's board that summer, but she had to put the Scottish elections first. She said the same to Cameron and Osborne: 'As soon as the election is done, I'll step up.' It had paid off: she beat Labour into third place. Her, not the Conservative Party. People voted for her to take on Nicola Sturgeon. Now she would take on Boris Johnson. The week after the Scottish election, Davidson was down in London and saw George Osborne, who reflected on how most of the cabinet, apart from David Cameron, had not done a TV debate at all since 2010, still less one in front of 6,500 people. Davidson agreed: 'In terms of a stadium debate it's only me, Nicola Sturgeon, George Galloway and [Scottish Green Party leader] Patrick Harvie that had ever done one.' That was the cast list at the debate in Glasgow's Hydro arena before the Scottish independence referendum, 'in front of eight and a half thousand sixteen- and seventeen-year-olds who had been left without wifi (but with Haribos) for two hours before the debate started'. It was, Davidson recalled fondly, 'a bloody circus'.

The morning after she met Osborne she went to see Cameron, and he said, 'George and I have had a chat about it overnight, and we would really quite like you to do it.' Tory high command regarded Davidson as 'ring-ready'. As she recalled, 'We had had two elections, two referendums in twenty-two months.' She was also keen to take on Johnson, who she felt had had a free ride: 'I am a combative Scot. I like a fight.'

After her Hydro debate experience, Davidson had valuable advice for the Downing Street team about potential technical pitfalls when talking to the BBC. Simple things like, 'We couldn't hear each other. Because it was a music venue all the speakers were at the front where the performers would be on stage.' Or, 'The audience pick was done badly. The BBC didn't make it half and half. It was really unfair, so make sure you are on them for the audience pick.' Craig Oliver was to make it his personal mission to ensure the BBC guaranteed a balanced audience.

The clincher in the choice of Davidson was a belief in the campaign that Conservatives had largely decided how they were going to vote, whereas Labour voters were still up for grabs. 'We didn't want someone with a cut-glass, received-pronunciation accent being the Tory,' a campaign source said. 'We wanted someone who had shown an ability to get Labour voters over to their side, as Ruth had just done in the Scottish elections. When you've only got one person who has ever done it before, and she speaks in an accent that's less foreign to Labour voters in the north of England, that's why Ruth was on the list.'

Later she got a call from Craig Oliver: 'We want you to be the Tory. The Labour Party are putting up Angela Eagle.'

Davidson replied, 'I think Angela's great, but are you absolutely sure that you want two short-haired, flat-shoed, shovel-faced lesbians with northern accents, because that seems to me as if you're role-casting a bit much for a UK-wide vote.'

Oliver was taken aback, and promptly 'turned into Hugh Grant', blustering, 'Yes, ah, erm, well I'll relay that back.' Davidson offered to withdraw: 'I don't mind being stepped down. I'm happy to not do this if they want her, but I'm not sure they can really have us both.'

The Labour In campaign preferred to keep Eagle. 'We wanted a woman,' a party official said. Will Straw did not want to fall out with his party again – there was a danger that Labour would turn around and say Jeremy Corbyn wanted to do it. Lucy Thomas had another idea: 'TV is my background. This was a huge set-piece event just two days before the vote, and it's really high-profile. I thought we'd got to have our absolute A-team.' Thomas phoned Robbie Gibb, the BBC's editor of live political programmes, and asked, 'Have you tried Sadiq Khan?' Gibb approached Patrick Hennessy, Khan's director of communications, and the deal was done. The BBC had originally envisaged two politicians and another public figure on each team. Vote Leave were expected to deploy the businessman and former minister Digby Jones. Stronger In would field Britain's top trade unionist Frances O'Grady, the general secretary of the TUC, as their third team member.

Wembley had been a nightmare from the beginning for the BBC. They had not intended the event to be so close to polling day, but the arena was booked. Jonathan Munro, the BBC's head of news-gathering, says, 'We didn't ever plan to go that late, but we couldn't get the arena because of a Coldplay concert.'

It was a big event and a big gamble. They met with instant opposition. Influenced by Davidson's experiences at the Hydro arena, Craig Oliver tried to scupper it from the start, briefing the media that it was wrong for the BBC to be using a pop-concert arena for a serious political debate. There was no way the Corporation could properly vet the audience to ensure balance. The whole thing would be 'a circus'. Oliver believed Remain was ahead at this stage, and a live televised event just thirty-six hours before the polls opened looked high-risk. He then claimed to have persuaded the Corporation to reduce the size of the crowd from 12,500 to 6,500. This was spin. Munro says, 'They can move a stage up and down the floor on Wembley, and we stood with the stage manager and we put our arms across the thing and said, "If we have it here, how many people is that?" And she said, "About 6,000 to 6,500," so we said, "That's more than enough." At no stage did we ever plan to fill 12,500 seats.' Munro felt this negotiation through the newspapers was 'a big mistake on their part because it made it much harder for us to change our position if we were seen to be under pressure by one side or the other. The whole purpose of doing these things privately is that you can negotiate a bit of nuance.'

The pressure to scrap the event altogether went right to the top – on both sides. 'The prime minister was definitely involved,' says a BBC source. 'They tried to put pressure on us in a very unsubtle way to pull the whole thing, and that went all the way up to [BBC director general] Tony Hall. There was discussion about "incoming from Downing Street".'

The second row was with Nigel Farage, who was furious when he heard that the BBC were not going to invite him to participate in the most high-profile television event of the campaign. Unlike ITV, which approached the participants themselves, the BBC let the two official campaigns pick their own teams. A source familiar with the exchanges says, 'Ukip sent various signals that they were threatening to take us to court. It was quite a tough period. Farage was always furious about it, because he felt that he needed to be on that platform to represent his constituency of voters, and frankly his personal following.' But BBC bosses were concerned that if Farage were invited Vote Leave would have withdrawn all cooperation. 'I think that was a real possibility,' a source involved in the planning said. The BBC offered Farage a place on Stage B, a group of less prominent politicians and commentators who had their own mini debates in the two intervals of the main debate, but he declined. Ukip put up Diane James instead.

*   *   *

Farage next fell out with Vote Leave. He could not understand why they did not want to put a businessman or a trade unionist on the stage. John Longworth, who had joined the campaign after leaving the British Chambers of Commerce, was his preferred pick: 'John knows the inside corridors of Brussels better than anybody. John sacrificed his job to campaign for Leave on principle. Vote Leave never once used him. He should have been on that stage. There were others. Mick Cash, leader of the RMT, he can make an argument. Digby's a great debater.'

Digby Jones had been Vote Leave's original choice. Boris Johnson and Gisela Stuart, the showman and the German immigrant, were locked in, but after Andrea Leadsom did better than expected in the first show-down, they had a rethink. After the ITV debate Will Walden was having a cigarette outside Westminster Tower when Matthew Elliott approached and said, 'I'm not sure we should be doing Digby.' Henry de Zoete had had the same idea, and suggested, 'Let me focus-group Andrea.' Zoot had already done Digby Jones, and he had gone down quite badly. Voters did not trust businessmen. They would say, 'What's in it for them?' After a couple of focus groups, de Zoete said, 'It's got to be Andrea.' The women liked that she talked about being a mother. Brett O'Donnell agreed: 'I really felt that they worked as a team.' They phoned the BBC and said that in the light of Jo Cox's murder, Vote Leave felt it was better to have three politicians on the stage. A fortnight later, when Leadsom had failed to back Boris Johnson for the leadership, run herself, and then edged out Michael Gove to face off with Theresa May, a few of the Vote Leave crowd regretted this decision. 'I wish we'd never put her in,' said one. 'I don't think she'd have had the gumption to run for leader. She certainly wouldn't be talked about in the same way.'

Brett O'Donnell drilled the three team-mates again. They knew the Remain team would be better-organised this time, and would try to be more positive after criticism of their Boris-bashing before. O'Donnell told them to play it cool, but 'As soon as they turn to fearmongering, you need to call that out.' He says, 'We always wanted to frame the debate as: they're selling fear and loathing, and we're selling hope.'

Stronger In's debate prep went better for the Wembley debate. Davidson and O'Grady were put through their paces by Craig Oliver, Alastair Campbell, Adam Atashzai, Ryan Coetzee, Will Straw and Lucy Thomas in rooms on Little Peter Street in Westminster, and then in a studio in

Covent Garden. Ed de Minckwitz played Boris Johnson again. 'We can sharpen that answer,' Oliver would say. 'Go in harder,' Campbell would urge. Tony Blair's old spin doctor sat above and behind the Downing Street man, and according to those present Oliver would look round to him for approval: 'Craig really did defer to Alastair Campbell quite a lot,' says a campaign source. 'It was all pretty alpha that day.'

Davidson recorded an opening and a closing statement, which Coetzee put in front of a focus group the week before the debate. They wanted to check that her accent was not too impenetrable. Coetzee emailed the senior staff: 'They responded very well to Ruth's closing statement because it used the "If you don't know, don't go" line and because it was personal: "about you and your family". He also found that Davidson's words about immigration not being a free-for-all, and EU migrants paying in to the system before they could take anything out, played well. Four months after the deal, Stronger In had finally found someone who could deliver their message script on immigration.

The debate was divided into three sections: the economy, immigration and security. 'The plan was to win on the economy, do better than expected but probably lose immigration, and win in extra time by shading it on security,' one of those present at the Stronger In prep said. The key to the immigration argument was Sadiq Khan, who turned up for the second prep session on the Monday, the eve of the debate. One of those who was present says, 'He was able to stand there and say, "Look, I don't hold a candle for David Cameron, but he's done this really good thing that means you now have to pay in for four years before you can take out." As soon as he did it we all went, "Brilliant! Why has nobody said that so far?"'

Khan became the 'glue', but initially it was not all plain sailing. At one point Campbell said, 'Can we stop, because this is shit. We're not clear about what we're trying to do here.' That was the moment at which they began to think about how to work together as a team, to make the right arguments in different ways. That was when they 'clicked'. Khan was so on-message that Adam Atashzai had to work hard to stop him spouting all of the Conservative lines. 'Mate, you sound like a Tory,' he said, though he did give Khan the line 'You've got a slogan and not a plan' to hit Johnson with when he spouted 'Take back control.' Ironically, the 'no plan' attack line had first been used at the general election against Ed Miliband, whose leadership campaign had been run by Sadiq Khan.

Frances O'Grady had been nervous at the first session – she was not a professional politician. In the second she was much better. Seeing that she was getting sucked into exchanges with Ed de Minckwitz playing Boris Johnson, Alastair Campbell told her, 'This is all about the audience, this is all about the public, this is all about people watching telly, who aren't following this as closely as we are. Every single time any of you open your mouths, you're talking to them.'

They had a third and final session on the Thursday, and by then O'Grady was ready. 'We prepped the shit out of her,' a source said. Ryan Coetzee played David Dimbleby, the BBC host. Will Straw played Gisela Stuart, and wrote what he thought would be her opening statement. Davidson was impressed later when Stuart did it for real – 'It was almost word for word right.' The moment Lucy Thomas feared the referendum was lost came when she was playing Andrea Leadsom. 'I thought, "This is so easy." You just make a positive, uplifting, patriotic case. You just say, "Of course they'll do a good deal with us," and "Vote leave, take back control." I realised that people listening to that at home – this really simple message versus a lot of complex reality – of course they were going to vote to leave, why wouldn't they?'

Her fears were reinforced by Alastair Campbell, who approached her and said, 'I'm really, really worried we've lost.' He had been at a small-business event in the Midlands, and found many of the business-men 'just gone'. In Burnley he had done another event and found the same. 'There were some from the "fuck 'em all" brigade, but there were a lot of people who had thought it through. People were just saying, "I've had enough." Those of us who did get out from time to time could never quite put what you were seeing in the polls together with what you were seeing out there.'

The debate did not pan out exactly as expected. The Remain team never quite seemed to get the audience on their side during the economy section, but on immigration they did much better than they had dared to dream. Security felt like an anticlimactic conclusion, with neither side gaining a decisive advantage.

In the opening section Boris Johnson and Ruth Davidson clashed on jobs. She accused him of 'lying' about the cost of Europe, Turkey and an EU army, and quoted him as saying 'There might or there might not' be job losses from Brexit. 'That is not good enough. How many jobs, Boris?

How many jobs?' Seeing the chance to deploy some of O'Donnell's advice, Johnson got himself out of a tight spot by saying, 'It hasn't taken them long. They began by telling us they would have a positive and patriotic case and they're back to Project Fear within minutes. They have nothing positive to say.'

Davidson, Khan and Johnson were a class apart this time, but it was Frances O'Grady who landed the most telling blow on immigration, asking Gisela Stuart whether she could guarantee that net migration would drop towards the tens of thousands if there was a Brexit vote. 'I think the Leave campaign are selling people a big con,' O'Grady said. 'Because you have never promised to reduce numbers. It's a big con, don't believe them.' Stuart floundered: 'What we said is you take back control and you can decide.' O'Grady was withering: 'So you haven't promised, you're not promising. It's a con.'

Boris Johnson sought to take the sting from the issue by saying he wanted to 'celebrate immigrants and everything they do for our country'. But Sadiq Khan had one of his most telling moments in response: 'You might start off saying how wonderful immigration is, but your campaign hasn't been Project Fear, it has been Project Hate as far as immigration is concerned.' He also hit Johnson with the 'A slogan is not a plan' line. It was the first time Stronger In had put Vote Leave's main voices under sustained pressure on immigration. Will Straw said, 'I actually thought they'd won the immigration side because they were willing to set out the positives and willing to take them head-on.'

Davidson thought Khan was 'genuinely brilliant', and Brett O'Donnell judged him the strongest opponent. Khan's performance was doubly impressive because it was the longest day of the year and he was observing Ramadan, which meant nothing to eat or drink between sunrise and sunset. At 9.24 p.m. precisely a runner came onstage with a glass of water, which he downed in one. It was the first drink to pass his lips since 5.24 that morning. Davidson leaned over and tipped her water into his glass so he could have another one.

Davidson made the final statement for Remain: 'You have to be 100 per cent sure, because there's no going back on Friday morning, and your decision could cost someone else their job.' Even John Prescott tweeted, 'Oh Lord, Ruth is good isn't she?' Davidson said later, 'I thought we were weaker on the economy than we'd hoped. We were stronger on immigration than we'd thought possible. I thought by the end we'd shaded it on security.' Alastair Campbell saw three people making a positive argument for Europe, 'whereas I felt with Cameron and Osborne, it was almost like they were being embarrassed and apologetic about their policy. And you can't do that. You have to fight for it.'

The last word and the loudest cheer, though, went to Boris Johnson. The final line of his peroration took the roof off: 'I believe this Thursday can be our country's Independence Day.' It was a line Nigel Farage had used before, but Brett O'Donnell claimed the credit: 'My proudest moment was my last time coming in to London to prep Boris, Gisela and Andrea for their Wembley debate. Everywhere were signs advertising the movie *Independence Day*, opening June 23. And so in prep I told Boris, "We've got to seize on this."'

Remain had managed to put their case in a way it had not been done before. Johnson had cemented himself in the hearts of Brexiteers across the country. At the BBC, the only feeling was one of relief that the event had not descended into controversy. One figure involved in the planning said afterwards, 'It worked. Thank fuck.'

Now the broadcasters had to prepare for referendum night, and the campaigns had to get their vote out.

24

THE WATERLOO STRATEGY

When the email dropped on 27 May it looked at first sight like a joke, or an even more ridiculous publicity stunt than usual. 'Predict the European Championships and win £50 million – the amount we send to the EU every single day,' the headline screamed. Vote Leave were offering the staggering prize to anyone who could correctly predict the winner of all fifty-one games at Euro 2016, the football tournament held that year in France. Even fans with a 70 per cent chance of picking the winner of each match were looking at an eighty million to one shot – around double the odds of winning the National Lottery jackpot. It seemed to be just a clever attempt to repackage the £350 million-a-week figure for young men who don't usually vote. But the real reason for the competition was to be found at the bottom of the message, where participants were asked to fill in their name, address and email details in order to take part. More than 120,000 people did so. With four weeks to go until polling day, that was 120,000 fresh names to add to Vote Leave's database, 120,000 people who could now be sent a text message by the campaign reminding them to vote on polling day. In total Vote Leave sent out half a million texts in the final twenty-four hours of the campaign.

They weren't the only ones who used the attractions of football in an attempt to entice fans who would not otherwise have been interested in the referendum. Britain Stronger In Europe had hired a couple of social media wizards called Tom Edmonds and Craig Elder, who had masterminded the successful Tory digital operation during the general election. Edmonds devised a product which would allow football fans to work out which players in their team might lose players from the EU if immigration controls were imposed. Edmonds sought out fans of the potentially worst-hit clubs, like Arsenal, for pro-Remain adverts on social media.

Getting someone to go out and vote for a campaign is now a highly sophisticated business. Since the dawn of radio and television it has consisted of two elements: an 'air war' and a 'ground war'. Most of this book has described the air war, the battle to convey the rival campaigns' main messages through the mass media. The air war wins the hearts and minds of voters. It is the ground war – activists knocking on doors and delivering campaign literature – that helps to drive a campaign's Get Out the Vote efforts (GOTV) on polling day, or in the weeks before for those voting by post.

Over the past twenty years two other hi-tech battlefields have opened up. The 'cyber war' is a version of the air and ground wars conducted on social media, where campaigns can advertise their message and recruit volunteers who don't get their news from the traditional media. Facebook is far and away the most influential platform, since six out of ten people in Britain have an account and they are evenly spread throughout the country, unlike Twitter, which is largely a metropolitan phenomenon. Behind all three of these battlefields lies a 'data war', where campaigns use highly sophisticated data-mining techniques to analyse the electoral roll, bought-in databases and 'scraping' information from people's social media accounts to build a model of a campaign's target voters. Once each side knows which demographic or interest groups in which parts of the country are susceptible to their message, they can then target media and social media advertising, direct-mail literature and ground campaigners towards specific households. Done correctly, all four of these operations reinforce each other. The better the information gathered on the door-step, the more accurate the targeting; the better the air-war messaging, the more effective the social media operation can be; the better the social media operation is, the more recruits can be signed up for the ground war.

When it came to digital warriors, the Remain camp had the seasoned pros who had won before. Jim Messina had run Barack Obama's re-election effort in 2012, and was one of the main reasons the Tories managed to make off with a majority in 2015. His micro-targeting of swing voters in key seats had handed the Conservatives seats that Labour and the Liberal Democrats had barely registered were at risk. Messina's data had been used highly effectively by Edmonds and Elder, who ran the digital operation for the Tories and had since set up their own firm, and they were recruited again. With Elder focusing on the London mayoral race, Edmonds was the lead man for Stronger In. Messina, though was not signed up until late October 2015. Downing Street originally asked him to wait until Cameron had secured his deal from Brussels. 'It would have looked weird, in their view, if one of their closest advisers had already gone to Remain when he was still negotiating,' a senior campaign figure said. 'Jim understood completely.' The impasse was resolved when Will Straw and Ryan Coetzee convinced Stephen Gilbert and Craig Oliver that they needed Messina. Coetzee and Straw wanted his data by the start of the year, but according to one source, 'We didn't get it until March, and the regulated period kicked in in mid-April.' A Downing Street source said, 'Jim said from the beginning of the year, "I need more time."' That meant Stronger In was not able to maximise its advantage from having a healthy campaign war chest and being guaranteed designation while Vote Leave faced a donor freeze and the debilitating battle with Arron Banks for the right to run the Leave campaign. Under electoral law, after the regulated spending period kicked in on 15 April each campaign was allowed a regulated spend of £7 million, to cover all spending apart from staff costs.

Stronger In sent a newsletter to fourteen million households in January, but Coetzee could not do this in a targeted way because he did not have Messina's data. Messina was also hamstrung because Stronger In did not get legal access to the electoral roll until 3 February, and Messina took about a month to turn around his model. Coetzee is full of praise for Messina's output, but would have liked to have been able to use it earlier: 'He did a very good job of building the model for us. But the difference with 2015 was he started much later, and as a consequence of that and as a consequence of the spending regulations, we were able to generate less bespoke data.'

Messina's work allowed the Remain campaign to make judgements about where to deploy its ground forces. In towns like Woking and Guildford, where the campaign did not have many grassroots supporters, the model showed a large number of persuadable voters, so London-based activists were sent there to leaflet commuters. The Stronger In bus spent more time in those areas where the model showed the maximum number of voters who could be won over, predominantly the east of England, the east Midlands, Yorkshire and parts of the north-west. These were not the regions where Remain was strongest, but with every vote counting in a referendum, harvesting votes in 'persuasion areas' where Stronger In might still lose was the best use of resources.

For the short campaign, Messina's model enabled Stronger In to draw up different, tailored election addresses that would be delivered to voters who were 'likely to remain', 'likely to leave' or 'likely persuadable'. Special leaflets went to pensioners and young voters. Each of these categories was then segmented again by whether the individual lived in England, Scotland, Wales or Northern Ireland. At least a hundred different leaflets went out in total. The timing of the leaflets also depended on the voter: 'If we thought you were persuadable we did leaflets quite early on,' says Straw. 'If we thought you were an In voter we sent a poster to display in the final ten days. If you were a Leaver we sent you a very simple post-card. It was much more complex than what the Leave side did. They just had their UK-wide message.'

Stronger In were hurt, though, because the referendum was very different from the general election, and data-modelling was less effec-tive. In 2015 the Tories were able to ignore most of the population. They focused on targeting just 200,000 people in one hundred marginal constituencies. Tom Edmonds was able to take a seat like Derby North and, using Messina's data, find the people who were swing Ukip voters and give them a specific Facebook message, and also locate the Lib Dem voters and give them a different message. But in the referendum campaign, with every vote counting equally across the country, they had less money with which to chase far more target voters. This time around there were nine or ten million swing voters, not 200,000. 'The model just threw up very broad categories of people who might vote Remain,' a senior cabinet minister said. 'The kind of micro-targeting you've got in a general election is not possible.'

At Vote Leave they predicted what Daniel Hannan called 'the Messina machine-gun', a wave of highly targeted get-out-the-vote material in the final fortnight: 'I was braced for it all the way through the last two weeks, and it never came.' But as Messina pointed out to his clients, data itself has no intrinsic value, it is just a tool to help other people contact voters. All campaign tactics, no matter how data-driven, can only move so many votes. Messina's major regret is that he did not press to take over the polling from Andrew Cooper, since he believes that could have thrown up different strategy and messaging options for Cameron that would have made the campaign more effective.

Tom Edmonds' first challenge on the social media side was to find Remain's supporters. While Leave could draw on Ukip, which had been around for decades, finding and mobilising people who wanted to leave the EU, there was no equivalent body for pro-Europeans. In this 'acquisition mode' the online operation was used initially to recruit volunteers and donors by running sponsored petitions, online calculators that people would click on, and Facebook ads to locate people. Those who 'liked' the Stronger In page were hooked. Edmonds then targeted them to try to get them to give money, talk to their friends or volunteer. That is known as the 'activation phase'.

Edmonds was a missionary for using Facebook in political campaigns. Beneath the social networking shopfront it is basically an advertising platform, and offers campaigns a level of targeting detail on its users that other sites do not. Stronger In pursued a two-pronged strategy, paying to get their adverts in front of the people they wanted to target while building up 'likes' and supporters into a community that would share content for free. Edmonds ran adverts targeted at parents, with children saying what they wanted to be when they grew up and why they wanted to stay in the EU. Those who supported green causes or animal charities would get adverts explaining what the EU did for the environment or animal welfare. Messages about the risk to jobs would be targeted by region, so people would know the likely effect in their area. The campaign primarily targeted people aged thirty to fifty-five, and in the final phase, when Stronger In used a video warning that Brexit would be a leap in the dark, the voiceover of each video was tailored with regional accents. 'Persuasion' voters, who still needed to be convinced to vote Remain, would get a message explaining why it was necessary to stay in. A pure GOTV advert, saying 'This is what happens if you don't vote,' would go to those who were committed to the cause, to remind them to turn out.

Edmonds was highly respected by his campaign colleagues, but he felt less effective during the campaign than he had during the general election, as the 'air war' dominated. He also had to fend off others who were not used to the amount of weight placed on social media campaigns. Roland Rudd could not understand why so much money was poured into Facebook, and he and Richard Reed called for more to be spent on billboard posters. Rudd even commissioned a report on what was not working in the cyber campaign, but nothing came of it. All three main campaigns largely ignored billboards and devoted themselves to digital campaigning. Stronger In's output was generally recognised as polished. 'I admired what they did on social media, because they were very effective,' Nigel Farage said. 'It was very professional.'

Arron Banks spent more than £11 million on social media campaigning from the summer of 2015 until polling day. Gerry Gunster provided the polling, data-modelling, and a strategy to target the voters they wanted – in this case working-class people in Labour areas who seldom voted. Banks, Farage, Andy Wigmore and Chris Bruni-Lowe then devised a deliberately outrageous array of adverts that would not only cut through with Gunster's targets but attract acres of free publicity, thus hijacking the air war from Vote Leave. 'The people that were passionate about leaving because of the way their lives were affected by the immigration issue were people that never voted before,' Wigmore said.

Leave.EU regarded Farage as the key to turning out these voters. Their aggression was a deliberate strategy to prevent him from being marginalised in the mainstream media. 'Vote Leave's view was that Nigel puts off undecideds,' said Bruni-Lowe. 'Our view was that Nigel gets the turnout high. And we need the turnout high.'

Wigmore and Banks consulted Donald Trump's advisers in the autumn of 2015, and realised that the American tycoon was using media fascination with his extreme statements to generate free publicity on a level never before seen in a presidential election. 'If you take a look at what Trump spent between July last year until he got the primary vote, it was something less than £20 million, which is nothing in a presidential race,' said Wigmore. 'Through social media, we became the provisional party of Farage. We had to do something absolutely outrageous to try and get attention. That's what Trump did as well. He didn't necessarily mean them, but the more outrageous the better. The first one we really got attention on was Poppy Day.'

On 8 November 2015, Remembrance Sunday, the official Leave.EU Twitter feed tweeted: 'Freedom and democracy. Let's not give up values for which our ancestors paid the ultimate sacrifice' alongside a picture of the sea of ceramic poppies in the moat at the Tower of London. Wigmore said, 'People just went mad for that, they really went for us – and it worked.'

Controversially, Leave.EU also sought out overt racists to hit with their messages. Facebook adverts provide a tab you can click on to see what targeting was used to reach you. Banks was caught out early on when Tom Edmonds at Stronger In set up fake profiles for far-right extremists, and found that Leave.EU adverts had been deliberately sent to supporters of the British National Party and Britain First. When the story appeared, Leave.EU stopped that.

The social media operation set up by Banks got a lot of notice. Farage says, 'I think we did very well on social media. The reach we were getting was absolutely huge. I got five million views for one video. Every day on tour we were producing videos, often within an hour of an event. The BBC were on the bus – they liked the bar on the bus – and they could not believe the speed we were turning things around.'

Banks says, 'Even though we weren't the designated campaign, we had twice as much social media reach as the two official campaigns put together. Our best did eight million views. In the end we had a million social media supporters that we've still got, reaching up to twenty million people a week. That's phenomenal reach. It's more than a newspaper. We pushed out twenty million campaign leaflets, that's almost half the population getting material from us.'

Banks hired Gunster because he had fought thirty-two referendums in the US, and won thirty of them. Gunster ran the campaign in four phases: acquiring quantitative data, segmenting the population, micro-targeting the groups he had identified, and then getting out the vote. He divided the population into hard and soft supporters and hard and soft opponents: 'You break it up into four segments. Then you're ready to start reaching out … each group is going to probably require a different message and messenger.' His work helped reinforce Farage's belief that the campaign needed to lead on immigration. 'There are three top issues,' Gunster said in November 2015. 'Border control, keeping your money, and control your own destiny so that you can make your own laws. You've got a perfect storm coming.'

Banks and Wigmore were most impressed by Gunster's polling operation. While conventional polling companies would survey one or two thousand people, Banks had the money to poll between 25,000 and 100,000 people on their mobile phones. The effectiveness of this was proven on the day of the vote, when Gunster's poll was accurate to within 0.1 per cent of the final result. As soon as Banks and Wigmore got Gunster's provisional results at 4 p.m. they decided to pay for a full-page advert in the next day's *Telegraph* thanking Farage for getting Britain out of the EU. When Farage heard what they had done he said, 'You're nuts.' Wigmore says, 'Most of the people who are polled by big polling companies are up to speed with news and current affairs. We were going for the type of people who watch breakfast TV, *Jeremy Kyle* and a bit of *Trisha*. When you put out anything on economics, we would get three or four thousand likes on a tile. If you put out something emotive you would get something like four hundred or five hundred thousand likes, and in some cases two or three million. So that's the kind of audience we knew early on that we needed to approach.'

By analysing who liked certain posts on Facebook and where they lived, Leave.EU were able to plan their ground campaign: 'We then knew off the back of our social media footprint exactly where we needed to deploy Nigel on his bus tour, because we knew there were eleven key areas that you need to convince to hopefully get you past the post in the referendum. They were all in the north of England, it was all Labour strongholds.'

Tom Edmonds at Stronger In was impressed by a lot of Leave.EU's output – if not their messaging. He recognised a campaign, like his, focused on acquisition work in its first phase, building up Facebook likes and lists of supporters to be activated later in the campaign.

Vote Leave took an entirely different approach. Upon learning that Facebook had changed its algorithms so that likes had no effect on the distribution of paid-for advertising, Cummings believed Banks was on a simple ego kick by boasting about the number of likes and video views he was getting. Zack Massingham, who eventually ran Vote Leave's social media operation, called video views 'insanity metrics', since they were poor at collecting information from an audience, or even at imparting it a lot of the time: 'You can get two or three million views, and less than 2 per cent of those people who watch it actually have the sound on.' But if likes did not help with paid advertising, they were still used by both Stronger In and Leave.EU to get millions of pounds' worth of free advertising by building a community of supporters and getting them to share the content with their friends for free. Both sides thought Vote Leave was very late to the party, for the simple reason that it was.

Dominic Cummings was clear from the beginning that he wanted to make the digital operation integral to the campaign, but for most of 2015 and the early part of 2016 Vote Leave did not have much to show for this enthusiasm. The digital team hired by Elliott were sidelined by Cummings. One campaign source said, 'We rolled from one digital calamity to another.' Tom Edmonds was surprised when he clicked on Vote Leave's early Facebook adverts to find that they were only targeted very generally, at people in the UK, rather than at specific interest groups. On one occasion an email Stronger In had sent out was copied almost unchanged and sent out shortly afterwards by Vote Leave under Matthew Elliott's name. Early Vote Leave emails often featured long, rambling disquisitions on the EU, which appeared to have come from Cummings' keyboard. The football game was imaginative, but it was the kind of thing the other campaigns had been doing months earlier to harvest email addresses. Chris Bruni-Lowe was also unimpressed: 'I don't believe they had any technical skills. They just didn't have any gifted social media people. You could see that from a mile. It was all just a bit boring. Boris has a Facebook page with 500,000 people on it. They didn't even use it.'

In the early part of 2016, Farage repeatedly called Boris Johnson and warned him that the Vote Leave digital operation was not up to scratch. Lynton Crosby passed the same message to Johnson, while Farage and Banks also disparaged the Vote Leave ground operation. Richard Murphy's decision to quit Vote Leave contributed to the sense of drift. Peter Bone and Tom Pursglove set up Grassroots Out because they believed that Vote Leave was not doing enough on the ground. In both the cyber war and the ground war, Cummings and co. were hampered by three things: initial changes of personnel, the psychodrama of the battle with Banks for designation, and the knock-on effect that Vote Leave had very little money to spend. While Banks had only to dig into his own pockets, Elliott struggled to bring in money from donors who were waiting to see who won designation in mid-April. But by then the spending cap was in place. For this reason, many in Vote Leave blame Banks for setting them back. Daniel Hannan said, 'The most damaging thing they did was to prevent us raising money before the spending limits came into effect. That was a huge, huge logistical disadvantage, because the other side had plenty of money, and used it to purchase demographic data.'

Condemned by his Leave rivals, and with his own donors doubting him, Cummings made four decisions to turn the situation around. Firstly, he appointed Henry de Zoete as digital director. Paul Stephenson and de Zoete then hired a Canadian firm of social media experts called AggregateIQ, which had most recently helped run Ted Cruz's campaign for the Republican presidential nomination in the US. 'After Henry de Zoete took over as digital director and "the Canadians" arrived, Vote Leave's digital campaign dramatically improved,' recalls Nick Varley, the head of the ground campaign. Thirdly, and in great secrecy, Cummings also signed up a group of West Coast American academics to do data analysis and modelling. Rather than hire an off-the-shelf political consultancy, he found three experts in disciplines like astrophysics, who were confident with statistics and sophisticated computing, to come at the problem from a different angle. Daniel Hannan said, 'Dominic had these astrophysicists who had found this way of scraping data off people's Google searches and feeding it into a programme to tell you, by postcode, where your voters were. And not only where your voters were, but exactly how committed they were.' The physicists and the Canadians would help Vote Leave get back in the game. Finally, Cummings decided that he would save a sizeable chunk of his £7 million budget to spend in the final fortnight on a cyber-war blitz to get out the vote. Vote Leave's digital war began weakly, but it would end strongly.

When he came aboard, Zack Massingham of AggregateIQ began, months after the other campaigns, to build up a core audience for Vote Leave adverts. These were people who had 'liked' Eurosceptic websites and Facebook pages, including those of Ukip and Farage. They tended to be over fifty-five, less well-off and non-university-educated. A small amount of money was spent each day bringing them onto Vote Leave's database. Massingham then used a Facebook tool called 'Lookalike Audience Builder', which allowed him to reach people with several similarities to the core audience, but who were not actively engaged in Eurosceptic campaigns. These he identified as 'persuadables'. He found they contained a considerable number of better-educated and better-off people.

The final stage was 'onboarding', what Tom Edmonds called 'activation' – turning sympathisers into committed supporters, volunteers and donors who would help the campaign. Every advert used on the 'persuadables' contained a call for action: first an invitation to click on the advert to be taken to the Vote Leave website, secondly entering personal details, and at level three sharing content, making a donation or volunteering. Massingham tested every advert with his target groups, and calculated how far up the ladder he could take each audience with each message. Adverts with low 'conversion rates', which failed to get 30 per cent of the audience to click on the first link, were scrapped. Once people were at level two, material that failed to get a 50 per cent conversion rate to the third stage was reworked. Each segment of Massingham's audience would receive adverts on Facebook, Google search, online display advertising and 'native' advertising (an advert embedded in news sites which appears as though it is part of the site's own content). 'Persuadables' responded better to questions such as 'Is this a good idea?' or 'Do you want to learn more?' whereas the core audience was driven by more demonstrative adverts. Massingham says, 'In the final two weeks the campaign allocated a significant portion of their advertising budget to their persuasion audiences in the hope of tipping the scales.'

The football quiz four weeks before polling day was highly successful, but Massingham also brought over an idea he had used on the Cruz campaign – a Vote Leave 'gamified' app, the first of its kind in a British political campaign. Supporters who downloaded the app got points for completing a quiz on the EU which emphasised Vote Leave's talking points ('How much money do we give to the EU?'), watching a video or sharing content with their friends, and were rewarded by moving up the levels, winning promotions as they went. Their goal was to reach the rank of Field Marshal, which Michael Gove had been awarded. The most points were given for texting campaign messages from the app to friends. In the twenty-two days it was live more than 40,000 people installed the app. Massingham says, 'The significance of that app was that it was about creating opportunities for secondary actions and instant mobilisation. We took the average volunteer onboarding process response time from something like seven to ten days down to forty-eight hours.' Vote Leave's target voters got ten emails across June 22–23, and de Zoete sent 500,000 text messages on polling day itself. People on the app sent 70,000 messages to remind their friends to vote on the big day.

De Zoete found the time difference between the UK and Victoria, British Columbia, where AggregateIQ are based, very helpful, since it meant the digital war was conducted around the clock. Ideas, new adverts and data from London or Canada were fed in as one team got up and the other went to bed, and were actioned while the other slept. Thanks to Massingham's rigorous testing of every advert, de Zoete and Cummings knew exactly which ones worked. Massingham says

Cummings was engaged in the detail of the digital operation to an unusual degree: 'Dom approached each ad as if it were its own unique poll or focus group, and would compare those results to what they had observed from the data they had already been gathering. He was seeing what was being said in the polling and focus groups, and wanted to test those assumptions online to see that everything was in agreement with everything else. And when there were things which weren't, we'd exploit them or retool. As far as campaign directors go, he was incredibly switched-on.'

De Zoete knew from his focus-group work that the people Vote Leave most needed to get to the polls were confused about which way to vote. They would say, 'I'd read something from Remain and then I'd want to vote Remain, and then I'd read something from Leave and then I'd just vote Leave.' A campaign source says, 'We wanted to use the last possible chance to get in front of someone's eyeballs. If they're seeking out information on voting day, if you're able to get in front of them with a compelling message, that's an amazing way to push them one way or another.'

This realisation caused de Zoete and Cummings to devise 'the Waterloo Strategy' to make sure they hit those voters decisively right at the end. The mythology of Wellington's victory over Napoleon has it that the decisive point of the battle took place when a Guards regiment hoodwinked the French into thinking they were weak by hiding in long grass. When Napoleon's troops advanced within firing distance, Wellington is reputed to have said, 'Up Guards, and at them!' and the French were routed. 'That was the Waterloo strategy,' a campaign source says. 'Basically spend a shitload of money right at the end. We tested over 450 different types of Facebook ad to see which were most effective. We spent £1.5 million in the last week on Facebook ads, digital ads and videos. We knew exactly which ones were most effective.' Cummings says, 'We ran loads and loads of experiments for months, but on relatively trivial amounts of money. And then we basically splurged all the money in the last four weeks, and particularly the last ten days.'

Vote Leave were so keen to throw money at social media that in the final days of the campaign they took the questionable step of donating £675,000 to a twenty-three-year-old fashion student from Brighton called Darren Grimes, who was running an online campaign called BeLeave. The timing of the donations meant they did not have to be declared until after the result was known. Grimes then spent the money with AggregateIQ. If the campaigns were working together the money would have to count against Vote Leave's £7 million spending limit – but the Electoral Commission would have to prove that Vote Leave told Grimes how to spend the money.

The physicists, by identifying likely supporters, and the Canadians, by hooking them, enabled Vote Leave to create what Douglas Carswell called a 'pop-up party' across the country. 'That pop-up party may have been brought together on the internet, but it existed on the ground in a way in which established political parties haven't existed in parts of the country for decades. I was struck by how many people who came and campaigned had never been involved in politics before. There were some Kippers there and there were some Tories. But I would say two-thirds of the people I met on the ground were members of what you might call the pop-up Vote Leave party.'

Vote Leave's field operations were run by Stephen Parkinson, a former adviser to Theresa May, and Nick Varley. Parkinson was the 'brains' of the operation, but was often busy helping Paul Stephenson or other departments, so Varley 'bulldozed everything through'. Varley says, 'The ground campaign was very good at recruiting volunteers who were already active for a political party, but the digital team were able to tap into a pretty big well of "newbie" activists with no prior experience who wanted to volunteer but hadn't really known how to get involved. Henry and his team added a significant chunk to our volunteer numbers.'

Henry de Zoete also used the physicists to locate targets for another innovative form of campaigning: 'clean graffiti', where you set out a message on a stencil and then spray-clean the wording into it. It's not like graffiti, which defaces the streets and has to be cleaned off. The only way to get rid of it is to clean the area around it. The modelling data meant Vote Leave could target low-cost supermarkets like Lidl and Aldi frequented by their target voters, or put an advert outside the gates of a school. 'We knew the precision targeting was working when the guys doing the cleaning reported that they were applauded when they did it in Middlesbrough,' a source said. The target areas where clean graffiti was used included Sunderland, the key constituency on referendum night, and Doncaster, one of the ten most Leave towns in the country.

Just like the Conservative Party's before the 2015 general election, Vote Leave's ground operation was widely disparaged in the media – and also by both Banks and Stronger In – while being stealthily effective. On 6 May, the day after the local elections, Farage met Cummings at Vote Leave's offices to express concern about the need to gear up the ground campaign in order to influence those who would be postal voting. The Ukip leader tried to make a deal, offering the services of his grassroots 'People's Army' to Cummings in exchange for a slot in the main television debates. Cummings explained that he was already targeting postal voters with a leafleting campaign. He told colleagues Farage 'looked gobsmacked' and questioned how Vote Leave could deliver all those leaflets. Cummings responded with the bold boast, 'Because we've got more volunteers who do stuff than you have.'

Farage laughed and said, 'That can't be true.'

Cummings replied, 'We've got about 11,000 people who routinely do stuff. We've got more people on the ground who do stuff in ten months than you have managed in twenty-five years.'

Farage said he did not believe Cummings, but told him to print more leaflets, 'and I'll get my people to deliver them'. They agreed on a figure of one to two million leaflets. Farage remained convinced that Vote Leave did nothing beyond the air war to contribute to the referendum win. He later said, 'Who was out there delivering millions of leaflets? Who was manning the street stalls? Who was climbing up trees to put up posters and bridges on the M25 and all the rest of it? You find that Ukip were the absolute backbone of all of those campaigns. There was no such thing as Vote Leave. Vote Leave were a group of people in London.'[1]

This approach caused most problems for Cummings, Parkinson and Varley in the run-up to designation. Parkinson and Varley met Peter Bone and Tom Pursglove in Bone's office on 16 December 2015 to hear their ideas for Grassroots Out. 'The GO situation was a nightmare at times from a ground-war point of view,' a campaign source said. 'Its entire premise was baseless – Tom, Peter and Richard [Murphy] were convinced right up to the end that Vote Leave wasn't working cross-party at a grassroots level, which was fundamentally untrue.' He added, 'Sometime in late February Farage issued a diktat that Kippers were only to work with GO, which caused Vote Leave real problems because in some areas, like Redcar, our local operation was the Ukip branch. The Farage loyalists never really came back to Vote Leave, but the entire rest of Ukip rejoined us within seventy-two hours of the Electoral Commission announcing Vote Leave as the designated campaign.'

Most activists who wanted to leave the EU did not care about the Vote Leave war with Farage and Banks, and happily worked together. Daniel Hannan says, 'The local Vote Leave and Grassroots Out people would just say, "Let's coordinate, let's have a street stall."' Iain Duncan Smith set up a network of MPs as regional directors to help the coordination. After designation, Bone and Pursglove kept touring the country, doing fifty more events of their own. They offered to hand over their data to Vote Leave, and expected to be asked to run the ground campaign, but Cummings already had what he wanted.

Varley says Farage and GO simply did not know what Vote Leave were doing – and they were happy for Stronger In to believe they had the edge. In the ground war 'We were printing, shipping and hand-delivering three million leaflets per week by mid-May. Our Get Out the Postal Vote operation on the weekend of 28 to 30 May saw us deliver over four million personally-addressed GOTPV cards. In total, our ground troops delivered over ten million pieces of Get Out the Vote literature in the final six days of the campaign.'

After the referendum, Andrew Cooper, Stronger In's pollster, concluded that this get-out-the-postal-vote effort helped Vote Leave to win: 'The Leave campaign's data analysis and modelling was, in some respects at least, more sophisticated than the Remain campaign's. I think they had a model that was specifically designed to help find people who, because of their attitude and demographic, are very likely to be Leave voters, but who also because of those demographics were very likely to be non-voters. They found them, and they got them postal votes.'

Varley says, 'Dom, Stephen, Paul and I made a conscious decision not to brief anyone on the size of our ground war because it was better that Remain knew as little as possible (a school of thinking shared very much by Lynton Crosby in the run-up to the general election) about what they were up against.'

At the heart of all these arguments over who had the best cyber war and ground war is the battle to claim credit for the referendum win. Farage is right that Ukip's People's Army provided shock troops for the ground campaign, but Vote Leave recruited activists from well beyond the Ukip clan. Nick Varley says, 'Farage and those around him were obsessed with telling everyone Vote Leave had no ground war and that it was all Ukip. Like much of what Farage comes out with, that was total bollocks. By the end of the campaign we had 12,000 regular activists across the country running good ground campaigns in about five hundred parliamentary constituencies. Our internal estimates at the time were that the party allegiance of our activists broke down as: 40 per cent Tory, 30 per cent Ukip, 15 per cent other parties, 15 per cent no party allegiance. Ukip activists made a really valuable footsoldier contribution to Vote Leave's ground campaign, but they were easily outnumbered by Tories.'

There were also frustrations for Conservatives dealing with Ukip grassroots members. The Kippers were happy to put leaflets through doors until they dropped, but they did not like knocking on those doors and finding out how people were intending to vote, vital information that could be fed back to HQ to help with the data targeting. 'They wouldn't canvass,' says Paul Stephenson. 'They were used to getting spat at on the doorstep.' Daniel Hannan recalls, 'I had to keep having this conversation over and over again, saying, "Look, there's a really, really clever guy and he's worked out a fantastic way of doing the knocking-up operation that every single house that you can feed into that system refines it and tells it where our voters are." And all the time I was saying this I had my fingers crossed, thinking, I really hope Dom knows what he is doing. But he absolutely did, and our knocking-up operation was so much better than the other side's. It was incredible.' Chris Grayling was also impressed by the field organisation: 'It was as good as anything I've ever done with the Conservative Party. There were good teams of people delivering leaflets everywhere, doing street stalls, much more visible across the country than the Remain side.'

One area of Stronger In's web strategy was hugely successful: registering up to two million people to vote. Before purdah kicked in, anyone trying to use the government's official website to renew a passport or driving licence would be greeted with a pop-up screen which would take them to the voter registration page. This was particularly important for students, since the rules had changed and they could no longer be enrolled *en masse* in their university halls of residence. In the run-up to the deadline to get on the electoral roll, Tuesday, 7 June, the official website crashed and 50,000 people missed the chance to register. The government rushed through emergency legislation to extend the deadline by forty-eight hours, and another 437,000 people signed up. Tory Brexiteer Michael Fabricant accused the government of 'desperate cheating'. Arron Banks threatened a judicial review (again) for what he called an 'unconstitutional' move, but even he and Farage struggled to muster a case against as many people as possible being able to vote. More than two million people registered between December 2015 and June 2016. Around 57 per cent of those who signed up were aged under thirty-five, though there is some evidence that a large number of younger people who registered did not go on to actually vote, whereas Vote Leave's target non-voters did turn out.

In Messina and Edmonds, Stronger In had the most experienced team in terms of British elections, but ultimately their digital strategy was not able to compensate for Vote Leave's advantages. The Leave campaign's simple messages of 'Take back control' and '£350 million a week to Brussels' were easily conveyed in viral adverts, while Remain's ideas required more explanation. Tom Edmonds believes it was the air war that was decisive. Jim Messina racked his brains after the defeat to think of what he could have done differently, but concluded that the Remain campaign was doomed by what he called the 'prevailing headwinds' of three decades of entrenched Euroscepticism.

To many working at Stronger In it was a given that they had the best ground campaign. On 16 May, staff were sent an email with two maps showing Vote Leave and Stronger In events across the country. It showed more than a thousand for Remain and just 270 for Vote Leave. The field operation was effectively subcontracted to the Labour Party, since the Tories had little or no presence in the working-class areas which the Brexiteers were targeting. Seeing these maps, Ryan Coetzee said, 'Fuck me, Labour know how to do a ground war.'

But Jim Messina had his doubts about how effective this Labour-led operation was, and those doubts were shared by senior figures in the Labour Party and the Labour In campaign. Remain's chief mouthpiece, David Cameron, was disliked by the voters they needed to win over in these areas. Alastair Campbell said, 'They knew they had a problem in that though Cameron campaigned hard, for a lot of people he was a negative. Number 10 convinced themselves Corbyn was the man to win back these voters. He wasn't. One, because his heart was not in it. Two, because he does not appeal to the kind of people we were losing.'

The problem was that many Labour events were concentrated in the wrong areas, and the constituencies where they needed to compete were safe seats in which the party organisation was moribund. A senior

Labour Party official said, 'The kind of voters who were moving away from us were in white working-class areas in the Midlands and the north. The party organisation was weakest in those areas. The existing membership was old and inactive. The level of activity on the ground was very poor, nothing like a local election, let alone a general election. We didn't have enough time to build an organisation that could do that, and we're dealing with seats that have never been marginal seats, so they've never had to do it for themselves.' No amount of good data or modelling could fix that. Afterwards Messina looked back and wished he had stood on a chair and screamed about the field operation.

Where the Labour campaign failed to tread, Labour Leave and Nigel Farage were only too happy to stomp. Kate Hoey believes Labour Leave were the key to showing the party's own voters that it was OK to vote for Brexit: 'We were finding people who were saying, "It's only Tories on television," and even though they wanted to come out, they needed the reassurance that there were Labour people who also felt that way.' Hoey lost a debate and a vote on Brexit in her own London constituency Labour Party of Vauxhall, but was greeted elsewhere in the country by delighted Labour voters. 'You would get people coming up to you after some of the rallies we did in tears, saying, "I'm so pleased there are Labour people here, why has Labour abandoned us?"'

The unravelling of Labour's influence in its own heartlands left the way clear for Farage to campaign almost unopposed in some parts of the north. Chris Bruni-Lowe said, 'We aimed all our target ads to the north of England because Nigel has massive appeal there. The lack of a Labour Remain presence was amazing for us. Nigel would go to Doncaster, Newcastle, Leeds and Bradford. He would get an extraordinary reception because they had not been hit by a Labour message on the doorstep. We could just talk about open-door migration and they'd go, "Yeah, I get that." In all the areas that Nigel went, the turnout was massive. We went to Sunderland, Newcastle, where Boris didn't.'

Most people in Vote Leave believe Farage cost them votes across the country, but even if that is true, in these areas it seems credible that he was an asset for the Brexit cause. Credit must ultimately be shared for turning out the vote. Farage and his Ukip army were a key component, but so too were a Vote Leave field operation and two sets of digital warriors who, like the Guards at Waterloo, got 'up and at them' just in time. Douglas Carswell said, 'Dominic did amazing things with data and

Facebook. He was sneered at by people over his Euro 2016 football competition, but when the results came in from Sunderland and Newcastle, I was watching and thinking, "My God, he's found his mark.'"

25

BREXIT NIGHT

Boris Johnson nearly did not vote in the EU referendum. The chief Brexiteer appeared at a final rally in Darlington on the eve of polling day, and then headed to St Andrews University to watch his twenty-two-year-old daughter Lara graduate. Another student, on spotting Johnson, unveiled a Remain poster as she was handed her degree. Will Walden had put in place a detailed plan to get him back to London to put his cross in the Brexit box, and after a celebratory lunch he said to Marina Wheeler, 'We've got to get him out of here.' They raced to the airport to find that the flight back to London was delayed due to air-traffic control problems. Nerves began to fray. As they sat on the runway at Edinburgh at 6.30 p.m. Walden thought, 'This is going to be a disaster.' He had taken the precaution of arranging a proxy vote, so someone else could cast the Johnsonian ballot on Boris's behalf, but the television cameras and dozens of journalists were already at the polling station. Vote Leave's front man would be a laughing stock if he failed to make it. The plane finally landed at City Airport in east London at 8.20. Vote Leave had booked Johnson a car, but it did not turn up. Walden said, 'This is a nightmare. I don't want you rushing around on the DLR, we'll get a cab.' At the taxi rank there was an enormous queue, so Johnson took charge: 'We'll get on the DLR. It'll be fine.'

If Johnson was confident of making it to the polling booth in time, he was not confident of victory in the referendum. On the Docklands Light Railway he got talking to a fellow passenger, Lewis Iwu, a former world universities debating champion, who promptly tweeted a picture of Johnson, rucksack on his back, saying, 'Just been asked on tube by @BorisJohnson if I voted Leave. I say no. He concedes he's lost anyway. Awkward #EUref.' A Johnson ally said, 'He had a conversation with a guy who turned out to be a Labour activist in which he was typically self-deprecating. I think he said, "Maybe we haven't won." He didn't say we hadn't. The guy then went and reported Boris had given up. He thought it was going to be close, but they probably hadn't done enough.' Johnson voted with about half an hour to spare.

There was more confidence, but also greater nervousness, in Downing Street, where David Cameron had gathered twenty-five aides and friends for moussaka and bottled beer in the Terracotta Room on the first floor of Number 10. The gallows humorists described it as 'the last supper'. Cameron joked that he had 'got my two speeches ready' – acknowledging that he might have to concede defeat. Word had spread among the PM's aides that he would resign. Andrew Cooper, who watched events unfold from his home in Oxfordshire, says, 'They were very conscious that if we lose, we're screwed.' But Cooper was hopeful. Populus had released a public poll putting Remain ten points in front, and his own final tracking poll had Stronger In 52–48 ahead. When Cooper told Cameron he thought he would win, the prime minister said, 'Lunch on me at the Wild Rabbit if you're right,' a reference to a gastropub they both favoured near their homes in Oxfordshire.[1]

The decision that Cameron would resign in the event of losing had been finalised in principle the afternoon before, and confirmed after the polls opened on 23 June. He gathered his closest aides – Ed Llewellyn, Kate Fall, Craig Oliver, Ameet Gill, Oliver Letwin, Liz Sugg and his private secretary Simon Case – in his study to discuss what he would do if he lost. He had repeatedly told the public he would not step down.

Back in January, just before his first appearance of the year with Andrew Marr, Cameron had sat down with Gill to discuss what he would say if he was asked if he would quit if he lost. 'What's your answer?' Gill asked. 'No, I'm not going to resign,' Cameron replied. Gill made the counter case that he should say 'Yes,' because it would impress upon voters the gravity of the situation: 'Put your career on the line. If the country knows you're going to go as well, they're more likely to vote Remain.' Others, including his director of external relations Gabby Bertin, felt the same way. Cameron said, 'That's very kind and very sweet of you to say that about me, but I don't think we're in that place right now.' He thought that offering himself on a plate would only encourage Labour voters to back Leave.

Six months later, the calculations were different. Having stuck to a line while he thought he was winning which he had little intention of following if he lost, Cameron now had to consider whether to reverse it. Craig Oliver expressed concern that the PM would face endless attempts to undermine his authority if he tried to cling on, and told him: 'I want to see you go with dignity, on your own terms, at a time of your own choosing.' In the Wednesday meeting, Osborne and Liz Sugg challenged that view and 'tested' the thinking, but Osborne had already decided it was the only available course of action. The team came to unanimous agreement that the prime minister should resign if he lost.

Cameron repeated the exercise after 10 a.m. on polling day with a slightly different cast. This time Oliver Letwin was present. The devil's advocates made their case again. 'The problem is all your arguments collapse in on themselves like a concertina,' Cameron said, then went off to work on his two speeches.[2] It had become conventional wisdom in Westminster that he would have resigned immediately if he had lost the Scottish referendum, but a close member of Cameron's inner circle said that is not correct: 'I was there on Scotland night, and he had an alternative speech, but it did not include resignation. He had not fully decided to resign, whereas this time he had clearly decided to resign.'

At 10 p.m. the group began watching the BBC's election coverage in the Pillared Room, a portrait of Elizabeth I gazing down at them. Cameron had been working the room with Samantha, trying to cheer everyone up. 'The PM was very nervous,' says one of his closest aides. 'George was very nervous. Dave made jokes about it – "We're fine! We're fine." George looked actually on edge.'

Aides tried to keep their spirits up by looking at the tweeted image of Boris Johnson apparently conceding defeat on the tube. Some 'pretty robust' thoughts were exchanged about Johnson. One bullish individual got in touch with Matthew Elliott over at Vote Leave: 'Just before the polls closed, I got a text message through from one of my contacts at Number 10. They were very buoyed up,' Elliott recalled. The text read 'You're toast.'[3] There were smiles when Gibraltar – not feeling snubbed by Cameron's hasty return to Britain one week earlier – mustered 19,322 votes in favour of Remain and just 823 for Brexit. But most of those who were in Downing Street that night say there was no triumphalism at all. 'At no stage were people "confident",' says one aide. 'The idea that there was an air of jubilation that was punctured by the reality is not true. There was a real sense of trepidation.'

Cameron's own nervousness became more apparent when the polls closed. He became quieter, more reflective. At around 11.30 p.m. he and a dozen or so others moved to the Thatcher Room and sat around the round table made for the G8. They included Samantha, Osborne, Andrew Feldman, Liz Sugg, Gabby Bertin, Matt Hancock and Laurence Mann, Cameron's political secretary.

Stronger In divided their resources around London. Stephen Gilbert, Jim Messina and Ryan Coetzee set up a satellite operations centre in a side room at Labour's campaign headquarters on Horseferry Road. Labour staff shared pizza with them. As the evening began, Messina took a call from a senior figure in Vote Leave congratulating him on winning: 'You ran the better campaign.'

James McGrory and Joe Carberry anchored the head-office operation at Cannon Street with a team of young staffers, preparing lines for the press and monitoring social media. Will Straw, Lucy Thomas, David Chaplin, Charlotte Todman and Amy Richards of the press team were all at the Royal Festival Hall on the South Bank for what they hoped would be a victory party but cautiously called a 'watch event'. The BBC, ITV and *Sky News* each had a reporter and cameras present.

Early in the evening, Coetzee compared Cooper's final tracking poll, which had Remain seven points ahead, with new surveys by YouGov and Ipsos MORI. He thought, 'We've probably sneaked it by a little bit. Hopefully we're scraping home here.' At Cannon Street, campaign staff were told that whatever the YouGov poll showed on the night, they should add three points to Remain, 'because YouGov had been under-ranking us for the entire thing'. In the event, YouGov had Remain ahead by 52 per cent to 48 per cent. McGrory thought, 'All right, 55–45!' That chimed exactly with the Populus poll that Cooper had chosen to publish. McGrory was confident after leafleting during the day near his home in north London: 'The response was terrific, I've never known a reception as positive in all my life in politics.' Rumours reached the office that private exit polls conducted by hedge funds had put Remain ten points in front.

*   *   *

Labour In had decamped to Ergon House on Horseferry Road with Messina and co., because they wanted to avoid Seumas Milne, who did not want any Tories in Labour's national headquarters on Victoria Street. 'Seumas was convinced there was a conspiracy,' says a party official. 'We were working with the Tories and he was really opposed, and he wanted to try and stop this thing. It had been weeks of setting up, and he was convinced there were going to be cameras and a story about collaboration.' Just as they had been throughout the campaign, Labour In and the leader's office were physically and metaphorically apart.

Brexiteers on the Tory benches had been exchanging calls all week. They did not believe what they were hearing from the pollsters. Not on their patches, anyway. Liam Fox had held a meeting in his Somerset constituency the previous Saturday, and hardly anyone had attended: 'I was getting eighty or ninety people, and then just nine people turned up.' On the Monday he spoke to Boris Johnson, Andrea Leadsom and John Redwood. They had all had the same experience. 'Oh my God,' said Fox. 'The public have made up their minds.' Fox did a straw poll in his seat and found the 'don't knows' were splitting for Leave, not Remain, as the pollsters had expected.

On polling day, Tories who would not normally canvass a council estate in a general election headed to the Labour parts of their seats to find the working-class voters they were hopeful would back Brexit. Would these traditional non-voters turn out? James Hannam, a Tory borough councillor and branch chairman for Cranbrook, a market town in west Kent, had a typical experience that day: 'Normally the people we were knocking up just don't vote. But this time, as we went around, the messages were "Went first thing this mornin', mate." "Yeah. Already done. Good luck." "Had to queue for ages, but all done now." It was also clear from the polling stations that turnout would be very high, and our target voters were turning out in droves.' In some seats MPs reported that half a council ward had voted by lunchtime, figures unheard of a year earlier. Andrew Percy, the MP for Brigg and Goole, said, 'I was having people coming up to me who'd never voted before, asking how you actually vote: "What is a ballot, what do you do?"'[4] For Peter Bone, pounding the streets of Wellingborough and in Tom Pursglove's seat of Corby, it was a case of *déjà vu* after the general election. They knew they had won on home turf again, but everyone was telling them they had lost nationally. They did not believe it.

Nonetheless, at Westminster Tower Vote Leave staff felt they were on the back foot. Ground down by months of dawn starts and the added pressures on a small number of people to deliver, most were shattered, and felt that after a spirited campaign they were not closing strongly. 'By the end of the campaign we were exhausted,' said Rob Oxley. 'Totally exhausted in a way that I've never known before. We had been doing it for a year.' Vote Leave had no party planned. Cummings considered letting a handful of journalists into the offices, but then banned all media. There were not, initially at least, many MPs present. 'They thought we'd all lost,' says a campaign source. One who did have the bottle to turn up was Iain Duncan Smith, who sat with Richard Howell, the young whizzkid. IDS was excited, an old stager who had tasted plenty of defeats in his time, reassuring a young man doing his first big campaign: 'The polls have got it wrong! The experts got it wrong!'

Matthew Elliott had known for months that if they went in at level pegging on the big night, Vote Leave could sneak it: 'Our guys were more enthusiastic, and we had a better machine to get out the vote, with more activists on the ground.' Elliott had gone to Manchester with Gisela Stuart, where the results would be collated and announced at the Town Hall. They were sitting outside a Premier Inn on a conference call with headquarters at 10 p.m. as the polls came in, discussing what Stuart would say, win or lose. The Labour MP, ever the voice of calm, said, 'Come on, the votes haven't been counted. There's everything to play for, let's see what happens.'

Nigel Farage needed a Gisela Stuart; instead he seemed to have borrowed Boris Johnson's old shopping trolley, because he was veering around all over the place: 'I got eleventh-hour nerves. I had felt the day before the referendum that we probably were going to do it, and then on the day itself I thought we probably weren't going to do it.'[5]

Whatever the result, Farage and Arron Banks were going to have a party. The insurance millionaire had hired out the Altitude restaurant on the twenty-ninth floor of Millbank Tower, and booked some of the acts from his abortive Brexit concert to perform. Bemused guests – wearing Union flag wristbands – got stuck into the champagne while listening to the likes of Kenny Thomas, Gwen Dickey and Alexander O'Neal. Someone had baked a two-foot-long cake in the shape of an exploding champagne bottle.

Farage and around twenty others, including Arron Banks and Andy Wigmore, had gathered at Chris Bruni-Lowe's house in Westminster. They were bolstered by the results of Gerry Gunster's final poll, which combined social media metrics with traditional methods. Banks said, 'We had it just after lunchtime. It had been running for three days and predicted that Leave would win 52–48. It was a huge poll. That's what gave me confidence – it was 10,000 people. So we knew it was likely to be more accurate than the others, because of the sheer size of it.' Bruni-Lowe said, 'He used all his insurance clients, called 10,000 of them, and pretty much got bang-on.' But Farage did not believe it, telling Banks, 'I think it's going to be a very narrow loss for us.'

Nigel Farage had fought for a referendum for twenty years, and not a vote had been counted, but at three minutes past ten he appeared to concede defeat. Darren McCaffrey, an enterprising political reporter with *Sky News*, had called him on his mobile while Farage was shaving. Farage said, 'It's been an extraordinary referendum campaign, turnout looks to be exceptionally high and [it] looks like Remain will edge it.' The statement was immediately treated as a concession. Banks was furious: 'Why the hell did you say that? The first result hasn't come out yet.' The Ukip leader replied, 'Oh, I have to condition expectations.' Banks said later, 'He had to do nothing.' James McGrory has an explanation of Farage's antics: 'It did make him the story for most of the night.' Having watched Vote Leave hoover up the publicity, Farage was not prepared to cede the limelight on the big night.

His behaviour was all the stranger because before he went upstairs to shave, Chris Bruni-Lowe had also received very good information suggesting that Leave were going to win: 'Someone I know was doing some quite serious exit polls. They said, "Yeah, Leave are gonna win." I told Nigel. He was like, "Really?" I was like, "Yes, we're going to win."' Bruni-Lowe said the poll he was informed about was done for 'ten different financial institutions and hedge funds' that wanted the best private information money could buy in order to construct their trading positions.

Farage's apparent concession had a dramatic effect. On the back of his remarks the pound rallied and world markets rose, in the belief that Remain were going to win. When the first results came in and the pound collapsed, some investors who had expected Brexit and had shorted the pound and companies likely to get hurt by a Leave vote – effectively betting that the currency and those shares would fall – made small fortunes. Bruni-Lowe was open about the impact of Farage's intervention: 'Nigel moved the market so much by doing that, that basically a lot of people got a lot of money. I don't think it was on purpose. I think he genuinely didn't believe what I was telling him. The market moved to such an extraordinary extent that people made an astronomical sum of money on it.' The investor and Brexit supporter Crispin Odey later revealed that he had made £220 million. After Farage had spoken, Bruni-Lowe says he got more calls from people familiar with the private poll saying, 'Why the hell did he say that? You're going to win easily.' He added, 'They rang me during the day. They rang me at ten and then they rang me at one in the morning.' He was told the exit pollsters had people on six hundred polling stations.

Asked why he made his 'concession' statement when he had been told that at least one of the financial industry's exit polls had Leave ahead, Farage said, 'They were split. There were people using the conventional polling companies, who believed that Remain was ahead. But there was another group who genuinely thought that Leave had won it. I didn't know what to think.' When the author asked him point-blank if he made his 'concession' statement to help his friends in the hedge-fund industry make money, or to make money himself, he laughed and said, 'No, no, no, no. I wasn't shorting it – I should have done!' Farage said the only bet he placed on Brexit was £1,000 at a Ladbrokes shop at the start of June, which netted him a photo opportunity and then a profit of £2,500. However, Farage's director of communications in Brussels, Hermann Kelly, may have been savvier than his boss. He gained £9,500 by shorting sterling against the US dollar on the night, doubling his money after five hours. Kelly says, 'Sterling had risen a lot on FOREX, and I judged that while it might go up a bit for a Remain vote, if there was a Brexit vote it would fall dramatically – as it did. I was not party to any hedge-fund poll, but listened to the experience of level-headed Ukip activists on the ground. The circle close to Nigel did think we were going to win, and many put bookmaker bets on.'

When Farage arrived at Arron Banks's Leave.EU party at around 11 p.m. he was instantly surrounded by a sweaty rolling maul of cameras, reporters, dead-eyed security men and increasingly drunk revellers desperate to hear his latest thoughts. Nothing else was happening. He rowed back on his earlier defeatism: 'Win or lose this battle, we will win this war, we will get this country back, we will get our independence back and we will get our borders back.' The Wembley debate might not have turned out to be the circus some had feared, but the Banks party was more than making up for it. From Westminster Tower Douglas Carswell looked on, seeing in his mind's eye what the campaign might have looked like if designation had gone the other way: 'On election night there was not a camera, or a journalist, or a punter in the Vote Leave HQ. And yet, a certain other rival campaign was tripping over itself with a media circus.'

Michael Gove was having a rather more sedate time. He spent Thursday evening hosting a dinner with his wife Sarah Vine at their home in west London. The guests included one of his special advisers, Henry Newman, Cameron's former aide Steve Hilton, who had declared for Brexit, and the television presenter Kirstie Allsopp. They dined on 'an amazing piece of beef' that had been smoked and thinly sliced by another guest, the chef Henry Dimbleby, whose father David was hosting the BBC's referendum coverage.

Hilton spread good cheer, and then left for a television studio in an Uber minicab (appropriately, as his wife Rachel Whetstone is the company's head of communications). The others enjoyed a Jeroboam of 'good red wine'. One guest was quick to declare that the booze was 'all European – a symbol that we are not turning away from good trade relations with the Continent'. Gove made it clear that he did not think the Brexiteers would win, and 'slid off to bed' before any results were declared. 'Michael knew Downing Street were confident they were winning, and he was concerned we might lose by up to fifteen points,' Newman recalled.

Given the gravity of the evening, this is one of the more remarkable acts of intellectual detachment of our times. Gove apparently slept soundly, unaware as the political maelstrom that he had helped to unleash began to unfold. His other special adviser, the softly-spoken Henry Cook, was at Vote Leave headquarters. It would be his job to rouse Gove from his slumbers later.

In Islington Boris Johnson and his team – including spin doctor Will Walden, campaign director Ben Wallace and personal aide Ben Gascoigne – dined more prosaically than Gove on 'bacon sarnies' and red wine, and watched the results on a big screen in a TV room at the back of the house.

Johnson had spent some time the day before considering what he would say when it was all over, but he had penned only a concession speech, focusing on how 'the people have spoken' and the need for the party to 'work together'. He wanted to be the first out of the blocks to try to heal the rifts in the Conservative Party, partly to protect himself from the backlash he knew was coming. Johnson was aware that pro-Remain ministers were demanding blood in a 'retribution reshuffle' – his blood, to be precise. He had seen the reports that a group of ministers planned to send a delegation to Cameron and the chief whip, Mark Harper, demanding that he be denied a cabinet post. A loyalist cabinet minister had said: 'The appointment of people who have behaved really badly is completely unacceptable.' Cameron had promised Johnson a job, and had told Wallace the pledge still stood, but Johnson did not trust his promises.

For the first two hours of the election broadcast Johnson's mood was 'reflective'. 'It doesn't look good,' he muttered to no one in particular, deep in thought, distant from those around him. 'I think he was sanguine – "We are where we are,"' one of those who was with him said. As they awaited the first results Johnson reclined on the sofa, 'snuggled up' with Marina.

Not since 'the Albanian model' had models been so important in the referendum campaign. Everyone had a model. In Downing Street and Cannon Street, at Westminster Tower, Millbank Tower, Labour head-quarters and the Royal Festival Hall, middle-aged men were hunched over computers or staring at bits of paper trying to work out what the numbers meant. It was five minutes past midnight, and the result in Newcastle had just been declared. It was very tight. Remain had won by a shade under 2,000 votes, with just 50.7 per cent of the vote.

Stronger In had three different predictive models to compare the results to: one prepared by Jim Messina, one by Andrew Cooper's Populus staff, and a third by Labour's number-crunchers. As the night went on all three models told broadly the same story, but it was Messina's the campaign looked to as the gold standard. 'Jim Messina's model very accurately predicted the results,' says Will Straw. Messina had looked at demographic data in every ward in the country, and then extrapolated it to the constituency level. By calculating which sorts of people lived where, he could work out the proportions in which a seat of that mix would have to vote for Remain to triumph by less than 1 per cent. Ryan Coetzee, who was with Messina, says, 'As soon as the numbers started coming in, we knew there was a problem.' Messina's model had predicted a 52–48 Remain win in Newcastle, but the actual lead was just 1.4 per cent. Arron Banks said, 'I knew when we saw it was nearly a dead-heat in Newcastle that we were going to have a good evening. A metropolitan town, it's Labour, it's got a university, a big student population. There's no way it should have been a dead-heat.'

At 12.16 a.m., Sunderland entered the list of places that have come to embody a seismic election result: Basildon in 1992, Enfield Southgate in 1997, Nuneaton in 2015. There was a solitary cheer when the returning officer read out the number of votes cast for Remain as 51,930. She then said, 'The total number of votes cast in favour of Leave was eighty-two thousand …' The rest was lost in a raucous bellow. Among the crowd of Leave supporters was a young woman called Sam Adamson who bounced with glee, arms aloft, on the shoulders of another Brexiteer. 'The whole room just erupted,' she said later. 'I was actually physically shaking with sheer excitement and surprise.'[6] The city had delivered for Leave by a stunning 61 per cent to 39. Messina's model said Remain needed a 60–40 loss in Sunderland to be on par. They were two points short again. 'There were a whole group of us watching the screen, and the Sunderland result came up and it led to what I will always call the Sunderland roar,' said Nigel Farage. The reaction in Westminster Tower was much the same. Daniel Hannan, watching at Vote Leave HQ, said, 'When Sunderland came, everyone knew what it meant. You could have heard the cheers in Sunderland.'

Within five minutes the pound had slumped from 1.50 to 1.43 against the dollar. By 3.45 a.m. it was down to 1.36, a fall of 8 per cent, its biggest one-day move ever.

When the Sunderland result was announced there was anxiety but not yet panic at Downing Street and the Royal Festival Hall. 'We were predicting 52–48 for Newcastle,' says Will Straw. 'It ended up being 51–49, so we ended up being a point down. We were predicting 60–40 for Sunderland and it was 61–39. We predicted Basildon bang-on 70–30.' Senior staff tried to stay positive. 'Those quite totemic results that came through shitted people up, but we were more sanguine about them because we could see that's what we were predicting on a very close outcome,' says Straw. But another problem for Remain was turnout. 'We were only 1 per cent lower than we thought we'd be in Sunderland,' says Ryan Coetzee, 'but the turnout was higher than we'd projected on the model. The problem with that is that 1 per cent therefore represents more voters than it should have.' Meaning more ground to make up elsewhere.

Up in Manchester, Matthew Elliott looked to Andrew Hood, Gisela Stuart's adviser. Elliott recalls, 'The results were better than expected, and at that point he said to me and Gisela, "I think we've won it." We had a long night to go, but on the first figures he was pretty confident.' Elliott sent a reply to the taunting text message he had received from Downing Street, but no answer was forthcoming.

Boris Johnson's position in this period was for the most part 'reclining'. But when the Sunderland result came in he 'leapt out of his seat' and said to Will Walden, 'My God, we might win this. We very well might win this.' The spin doctor kept his cool and remained cautious: 'This could be a north-east blip.' As the next few results poured in, Johnson developed a near-obsessive interest in the Betfair index on Brexit, the betting market on what the result might be. It was veering up and down like a yoyo, and so too did Johnson's mood. 'What is it now?' he'd ask Walden, who would reply, 'It's 56–44.'

There would be a pause for reflection and then, 'What is it now? Has it changed?'

'You only asked me two minutes ago.'

In Ladbroke Grove, Michael Gove slept through it all. Not all the members of his team at the Department of Justice missed out, though. When the Sunderland result came in, one of Gove's gang placed a 'four-figure sum' on Brexit at odds of 6–4, a move that would pocket him a sum in excess of £1,500 once the night was out.

Gove was not the only one trying to sleep. Ameet Gill had had a bad feeling about the night, and was no fan of big gatherings. Avoiding the Number 10 moussaka party he instead went out with one of his best friends, going home at 9 p.m. He set his alarm for 4 a.m., but at half past ten he got up, unable to sleep, and by 11.30 he was in Downing Street. He watched the early results with Adam Atashzai in his room off the Number 10 press office. When he heard the first turnout figures, which were higher than in the general election, he turned to Atashzai and said, 'This is bad.' After seeing the Sunderland and Newcastle results he said, 'We've lost.' He went home, and went back to bed. At 1 a.m. he woke up and called Atashzai. 'What's going on?' His friend replied, 'It's fucking tight, it's really fucking tight.' Gill went to sleep again.

Watching at home, the former Ted Heath aide Michael McManus studied the faces of David Dimbleby and the BBC's psephologist Professor John Curtice of Strathclyde University when the north-east results came in. On Monday he had taken part in one of the BBC's three full-dress rehearsals for election night: 'They had three scenarios. They had Comfortable Remain, Narrow Remain, and Narrow Out. I took part in the Narrow Out one, so I sat there as John Curtice's model was played out.' When McManus, a Remain supporter, 'went a bit ashen', Dimbleby had turned to him and said, 'It's all right, Michael. It's only a rehearsal.' McManus replied, 'But David, this is what's going to happen.' The anchorman, who has seen more elections than anyone else at the BBC, said, 'No, it's not going to happen.' Watching now, McManus could see it was Dimbleby and Curtice who were ashen-faced.

In the Thatcher Room, David Cameron now had a laptop in front of him. He did not want to get the information from anyone else. One of those present says, 'I'd never seen him on a computer before. A result would come up and he'd say, "Well, that's three points short," or "That's two points short." He was incredibly calm. At several points he said, "We could still pull this back."' Off to the side sat the chancellor, separated a little from those at the table. Another of those watching with the prime minister says, 'George was actually unusually quiet. All I remember him saying, when the first result came in, was "This is going to be a long night." It was clear things weren't going well.' After a while, Cameron needed a stiff drink. 'He sent someone up to get some Scotch from his personal collection upstairs,' says another friend. 'He was pouring the Scotch a bit. Nancy fell asleep at his feet.'

Andrew Cooper, Cameron's friend and pollster, maintained a lonely vigil at his home in Oxfordshire. Witney, the seat Cameron represented and where Cooper lived, was split 50–50, down the middle. The prime minister was not even delivering his own people: 'By the tenth result in, our prediction model said 52–48 for leave.'

Stronger In officials realised their only hope was to hit good vote shares in their strongholds. 'We were looking forward to seeing how we would do in the seats we were supposed to win: London seats, Scotland,' Will Straw recalled. 'We performed more or less on target for those areas, but with lower turnout than we wanted.' As the Scottish results started to come in, Coetzee thought, 'Fuck, we're in a real scrap here.' He said later, 'We started off a little bit behind, and as each set of results came in we got a bit further behind, until there came a point when we couldn't catch up.' The campaign in Scotland had been a non-event, since all of the party leaders were on the same side, but there was nothing like the enthusiasm – and consequently the turnout – that there had been for the independence referendum.

At Cannon Street, James McGrory and Joe Carberry were also following the model and pinning their hopes on the cities. McGrory said, 'A couple of London results came in, and they were massive. You're thinking, "There's still an outside chance here." There's part of you that always wants to hope.' But the axe fell on Remain's dreams when critical metropolitan areas like Sheffield and Birmingham, where Messina's modelling had put Stronger In's noses in front, began to vote narrowly for Leave. 'I knew after Sheffield that we couldn't win,' Straw recalled. The Sheffield result was also a symbolic kick in the guts for McGrory, who had worked for Nick Clegg, one of the most passionate Europhiles in Britain. Now his old boss's home town had voted to leave the European Union.

When it became clear what was happening, George Osborne texted Boris Johnson to congratulate him. Bets hedged.

Between broadcast appearances, Douglas Carswell sat quietly in the corner of the Vote Leave offices: 'The mood goes from sitting-on-your-seat nervousness to restrained optimism, and then when it becomes obvious that we've done it, it's just jubilation.'

Ameet Gill was awoken by his alarm at 4.30 a.m. He checked his phone and found a stream of texts saying 'Fuck fuck fuck fuck fuck'. He called Atashzai again and asked, 'Is it over?' 'Yeah.' For the second time in six hours, Gill went in to Downing Street.

David Cameron decided the game was up at around 3.30 a.m., and said he was going downstairs for a short sleep in his study. In the Thatcher Room everyone was in a state of numb shock: 'It was a bit like a car crash. You don't feel that bad at the time. It's only later that you feel bad about it.' Some had another drink. Others drifted off to the lavatory. When they returned they became aware that the wake was thinning out.

'Hope was abandoned at 3.30 a.m.,' said one of those present. 'I went to the loo and when I got back Ed and Kate and George and Dave weren't there. I thought I'd better go home.' Samantha Cameron had disappeared too. The quad, plus Andrew Feldman, were in the PM's study. They picked over the arguments again, but Cameron had made his mind up. The party would be uncontrollable if he stayed. 'All political lives end in failure,' he said.[7] Enoch Powell, whose phrase it was, had been a Brexiteer in 1975.

On Horseferry Road, Gilbert, Coetzee and Messina agreed it was 'basically game over'. Coetzee asked Gilbert, 'Stephen, are you OK?' and then wished he hadn't: 'It's one of those stupid questions you ask when clearly they're not OK.' He left Messina and Gilbert to make a call to Cameron. 'The mood was pretty sombre, grim-faced,' he said. After the call, Coetzee asked, 'Presumably he's going to go?' Gilbert replied, 'Yeah.'

Craig Oliver went downstairs for some fresh air and found Cameron with Liz Sugg and Matt Hancock, the Cabinet Office minister. 'This isn't going our way,' Cameron said. The group discussed his plans to resign, and how he would make the public statement. 'He knew it was another job to be done. He wanted to get it right,' said a Number 10 source. Oliver felt the foundations of his world slipping away: 'A lot of pollsters had done polling saying that we'd won, hedge funds had done models suggesting we'd won, so the sensation was really like walking across a path that appeared to be safety and then dropping into quicksand and then realising that there was nothing and nobody that was actually going to pull you out of it.'[8] Hancock and Sugg tried to talk Cameron out of resigning. 'We need you,' Hancock said. 'We are in enough chaos already. We don't need to lose a prime minister.' Cameron explained that he could not lead a government whose central policy he disagreed with. He concluded, 'OK, that's it. Final decision made. I'm going to get an hour's sleep.' They exchanged brief hugs, then watched him disappear down the corridor.

As David Cameron was going to bed, Nigel Farage was the first to declare victory. After his appearance at Arron Banks's party, the Ukip leader had watched the results from Chris Bruni-Lowe's house with his sons. 'What I knew at about quarter to four was that we were actually going to win,' he says. 'I was almost beside myself, I could barely believe it was happening.' When it became clear that victory was in the bag, Bruni-Lowe told him, 'You've got to own this.' Farage returned to Millbank and, voice shaking, declared, 'Dare to dream that the dawn is breaking on an independent United Kingdom. If the predictions now are right, this will be a victory for real people, a victory for ordinary people, a victory for decent people.' There were huge cheers as the revolutionaries of Ukip cheered their saloon-bar Che Guevara. Embracing the role, Farage said, 'We will have done it without having to fight, without a single bullet being fired.' He said later, 'I could scarcely believe the words myself. I felt pretty taken aback. I did turn away from the cameras a couple of times. I felt very emotional about it. It was an amazing night.'

The thing that struck him afterwards was that Michael Gove was asleep, and Boris Johnson was also about to go to sleep. 'Quite astonishing,' said Farage. 'They accused me of triumphalism. Well, they were in fucking bed! What were we supposed to do? They were in bed! We were at a giant Banks booze-up!' And so he was.

It was Birmingham that sealed it. Remain were supposed to win there, but Leave edged it with 50.4 per cent of the vote. To Daniel Hannan, victory there was symbolic of the campaign Vote Leave had run. The campaign's leading lights in Birmingham were two prominent locals, Saqib Bhatti and Aftab Chughtai, who ran Muslims for Britain. They had turned out the ethnic-minority vote in droves with calls for free trade with countries of origin and a fairer immigration policy, which would do more for people in Britain who had family members in the Subcontinent than for someone from Romania or the Czech Republic with no connections. Bhatti and Chughtai worked hard canvassing at mosques and community centres, suffering agonisingly long days without food or drink throughout Ramadan. 'And if you look where they were active – Bradford, Birmingham – the ethnic-minority vote where we had people making that argument was totally different from the places where we didn't,' said Hannan.

The referendum was fought in black-and-white terms, with absolutes tossed around – and never more than afterwards, when the Brexiteers were depicted as triumphing on a wave of nativism. But it was more complicated than that. When the Birmingham result came in, Farage recalled what for him was 'the absolute highlight' of the campaign, a trip to Birmingham's Bullring rag market on 31 May. 'It's a wholesale fruit and veg and fish and meat market. City centre, huge ethnic mix. And it was bloody incredible. We had 85 per cent support. These were all small traders, independent businessmen, people who get up at 4 o'clock in the morning to do a day's work. A lot of Asians, Eastern Europeans, all sorts. And you realise in the streets in Birmingham that this ethnic thing was nonsense. It was far more about class and what you do.'

At 4.39 a.m. David Dimbleby looked down at his desk and sought the words to match the magnitude of the situation. Looking up, he addressed the nation: 'Well, at twenty minutes to five, we can now say the decision taken in 1975 by this country to join the Common Market has been reversed by this referendum to leave the EU. We are absolutely clear now that there is no way that the Remain side can win.'

At Westminster Tower, Daniel Hannan jumped on a desk and began to deliver a version of Shakespeare's Henry V's speech about St Crispin's Day before the battle of Agincourt. 'From now on every year it comes round, you guys will be remembered. Our names familiar in their mouths as household words – Duncan Smith and Penny Mordaunt and Dominic and Oliver and Douglas Carswell, and Parky and Starky … What an amazing thing we have pulled off, and every year this will be our day, the day that we showed the world that this country was not yet finished. This is our Independence Day. It's your day. Enjoy it.'

There was loud cheering, but there was only one person they really wanted to hear from. In his office, Cummings heard a rumble through the wall – 'Dom, Dom, Dom, Dom, Dom!' He went into the war room, was manhandled onto a table and, shirt hanging out, delivered a more prosaic oration. 'When we started this campaign, what did we say we were going to do?' There were loud shouts of 'Win!' and 'Kill the CBI!' which was not what quite what Cummings had in mind. 'We said we were going to take back control. What are we doing?' Now with him, the chorus responded, 'Taking back control!' Cummings repeated the call-and-response, then continued: 'The reason why we've won is because of the people in this room. This is your victory. You guys did this. And you'll always be remembered. This is not because of me, it's because of you guys.' The wisps of thinning hair atop his head were already brushing against the roof, so when Cummings punched the air 'Wolfie Smith-style', his fist smashed into the ceiling, dislodging one of the tiles. 'Power to the people' indeed.

Matthew Elliott, up in Manchester, felt a sense of closure. 'I wrote an essay in sixth form on the case against the euro. I worked in the European

Parliament for a while. I was head of the Taxpayers' Alliance during the 2009 European elections. I did the NOtoAV campaign with a mind to thinking there might be a future referendum on the EU. Then I set up Business for Britain. It felt like the culmination of a lifetime's work.'

Boris Johnson was sent to bed by Will Walden at around 4.30. Walden himself stayed up with Ben Gascoigne, while Johnson's parliamentary office team went to sleep on the sofas. By 5.30 the media were outside the house in force. Walden was shaving in the downstairs loo by the front door to make himself presentable when the doorbell rang. Gascoigne looked through the spyhole and announced, 'It's bloody Kay Burley. And she appears to be broadcasting live.' The *Sky News* presenter is a force of nature. She had left the Royal Festival Hall for Islington once it was obvious Boris was going to be the big story. Walden had already had a run-in with her after Johnson's event in Darlington on the eve of the vote. Gascoigne's friend Richard Jackson had texted, 'You're all live on air in this pub and Sky have just broadcast Will bollocking Kay Burley and telling her to fuck off out of the pub.'

Walden went out to talk to the media. As he came back in Johnson was coming downstairs. It was 5.45 a.m. Walden sent him straight back: 'You need to go upstairs now, you need to talk to Michael, talk to Gisela.' Cummings had written a victory speech for Stuart to make in Manchester. She would break into her native German to reassure Europe that the UK was still an 'open society'. Johnson, though, had not prepared for the possibility of victory. He only had a 'We were close but didn't make it, Europe still needs to reform' speech mapped out. He disappeared to write a new one. Little did he know he was soon going to need a third.

Rumpelstiltskin was finally awoken at 4.45 a.m. After the broadcasters declared the referendum over, Henry Cook dialled Michael Gove's number. 'I'm terribly sorry to trouble you, Michael. I've got some good news. Guess what? We won!' Sarah Vine, lying next to him, recalled Gove's slightly Pooterish reaction as, 'Gosh. I suppose I had better get up.' She went to make tea, and could hear the press pack chattering away in the street outside. Downstairs she discovered a bomb site from the party the night before. She turned on the television, and found her home live on *Sky News*. When Gove emerged from the shower, she quoted Michael

Caine from *The Italian Job*: 'You were only supposed to blow the bloody doors off!' Gove had not expected to win either.[9]

At the Britain Stronger In Europe event in the Royal Festival Hall, the mood, once upbeat, was now that of a wake, with campaign staff in tears. Ed Miliband, Chuka Umunna and Nicky Morgan did stints with the broadcasters, and then left. By 4 a.m. the volunteers were ebbing away. Staff in 'I'm IN' T-shirts sat disconsolately on the floor. Those obviously in tears were given hugs and ushered out of camera shot.

Will Straw somehow kept it all together to give a series of broadcast interviews. 'It is clear we are in a very divided country,' he told the BBC. 'This is definitely a wake-up call for political and economic elites.' One of the staff there that night said, 'Will was a total hero. I thought he was going to cry.'

Matt Forde, a comedian who once worked for the Labour Party, summed up the evening. 'It was like going to watch your team win the Premier League and lift the trophy and then you hear that the trophy isn't coming and you haven't won it and it turns out you have been relegated as well.' At 6 a.m. David Chaplin finally managed to close up the event, dragging out ITV, who were 'being particularly difficult'.

At Labour's national headquarters on Victoria Street, it had been a surreal evening for supporters of the EU. The campaign staff had fled to Horseferry Road to avoid Seumas Milne. Jeremy Corbyn disappeared at 11 p.m., never to return. Milne, Katy Clark, Kevin Slocombe and Andrew Fisher all descended on Victoria Street. 'That changed the mood of the whole thing, because you have to be careful about what you're saying,' one staff member said. Milne and Simon Fletcher exchanged pleasantries, their first conversation for three weeks.

At around 11 p.m. Katy Clark, Corbyn's political secretary, was seen talking to Jack Bond, who did the leader's social media. Bond was upset, and said, 'What do we do if we lose this?' Clark was apparently sanguine: 'It was the right thing to do, because we distinguished ourselves from the capitalist case for leaving, and even if we leave, we'll be out of that capitalist thing.' The source who witnessed the conversation said it was 'an extraordinary thing to say – that happened'. It appeared to confirm that the Corbynistas were unconcerned about a Brexit vote.

After Sunderland 'the mood was shell-shocked', but later the atmosphere changed. 'There was anger towards Corbyn from three or four in the morning.' Staff were instructed to devise press lines blaming Tory underfunding of Labour areas for the Leave vote.

At about 6 a.m. most of the campaign staff left Ergon House to return to Victoria Street. By then markets in the Far East were in freefall, and the pound was still on the slide. Just before they left, officials from Labour In sought to get hold of Corbyn to tell him what had happened.

'Where is Jeremy?' one of them asked.

'He's still in bed,' came the reply.

'How do we get him up?'

'I don't know.'

After nearly a year of being messed around by the leadership, the usually mild-mannered Brian Duggan finally snapped. 'Are you seriously telling me the markets are crashing, the pound is falling, we've just left the European Union, the prime minister is about to resign, and the leader of the opposition is in bed?'

At Cannon Street the mood was grim. Around 3 a.m. a journalist who had been texting Joe Carberry all night, and getting positive spin, sent another message reading, 'Is there any hope?' He received the reply, 'No.' James McGrory's hardest job was to tell the young staff at HQ, who did not have access to the Messina model, that they were going to lose. He steeled himself by recalling a speech made by Nick Clegg's chief of staff Jonny Oates as the full scale of the Lib Dem election horror had unfolded the year before. At around 4 a.m. he took the group of idealistic twenty-somethings into a side room and began to speak. 'You should be proud of what you've contributed to this campaign and to your country,' he said. 'You fought the good fight, don't let anyone tell you that you didn't give everything. We'll look back and know that we did everything we could. But politics isn't always about winning. We all have some tough nights and this is, I'm afraid, going to be one of them, but nobody in this room should feel that they did anything other than make an enormous contribution to the biggest debate this country has ever had.'

McGrory said later, 'They were genuinely upset. That was one of the worst experiences of my life. I've been on the receiving end of that speech, but I've never given it before.' He and Carberry busied themselves shutting up the office. At 5.30 they led the staff through the deserted streets to Smithfield market to find an open pub.

'Dawn's coming up and you're walking by St Paul's and it looks like the most beautiful city in the world,' McGrory said. 'I remember walking through the deserted City at half five in the morning and thinking: most people don't know what's happened. My mum doesn't know, my sister doesn't know, my friends don't know. Most people in this country are in bed, and they're going to wake up and find out we've taken this terrible decision, in my view, to leave the European Union – and now I'm going to bang on the door of a pub.'

While the losers were banging on the door of a pub, one lot of winners were breakfasting at the Ritz. Arron Banks was still partying, while doing interviews for Japanese and Australian television. 'Time just flew,' he said. 'I looked at my watch and it was 5 a.m. And I couldn't believe where the four hours had gone.' He and Andy Wigmore walked back to Chris Bruni-Lowe's flat, swigging a bottle of champagne as they went. 'It was quite emotional for me and Andy. We walked from Millbank, down to Chris's flat, just as the sun was coming up. It must have been 6 a.m. The streets deserted. And we came across an old bloke. He was at an ATM trying to take all his cash out. He thought there was going to be some sort of panic! So we had quite a laugh and a joke with him.'

After a quick shower they collected Farage and a few others and headed for the Ritz. 'We went and had breakfast with [*Telegraph* co-owner] Frederick Barclay,' said Banks. 'He's a big Ukip supporter.'

Farage had just done an interview with *Good Morning Britain*, where he ran into Douglas Carswell. Chris Bruni-Lowe said, 'I could hear Carswell in the lift basically saying, "Am I going to run into Nigel Farage? I really don't want to run into Nigel Farage." So he came out of the lift and he saw Nigel and Nigel said, "Hello Douglas!" Carswell said, "Didn't Vote Leave – not you – do very well in this campaign, Nigel?" And then Nigel said, "How nice you are Douglas, what a nice bloke you are." Then he got in the lift.' The referendum was over; the battle to claim the credit was under way.

At 6 a.m. exactly, David Dimbleby announced that Vote Leave had secured more than half the votes cast. 'Quite an extraordinary moment,' he said. Britain had voted for Brexit. David Cameron had bet the farm – and he had lost the lot.

PART THREE

ALL OUT WAR

LEADERSHIP

June to August 2016

FALLOUT FRIDAY

At 7.50 a.m. David Cameron phoned Michael Gove to concede defeat. The lord chancellor was in the loo when the call came in. He emerged, and his advisers said, 'The prime minister wants to talk with you.' Gove rang the Downing Street switchboard and was patched through to the man at whose side he had risen, but who would now fall as a consequence of his actions. 'Michael, congratulations. It's a clear and unambiguous victory, well done,' Cameron said. Their conversation was cordial but brief. In a sign of how trust had waned between the two men during the campaign, Cameron did not tell Gove that he planned to resign. A Downing Street source said: 'It was a short call. Michael seemed to think he would be coming over soon to discuss the Brexit negotiations ahead.'

'I was wondering if there's anything else we can do to provide reassurance and stability at this time,' Gove said. Cameron gave him short shrift. 'We're doing the press conference at 8 o'clock, I'm sure everything will be fine. Well done.' Without further ceremony the prime minister put down the phone. He had already spoken to the queen to explain his intentions.

In Brussels, Martin Schulz, the president of the European Parliament, had phoned Jean-Claude Juncker, the president of the Commission, during the night and said, 'Jean-Claude, I think this isn't going well.' Schulz said later, 'I was shocked. In the days before the vote, I bet that the British would stay in the EU.' At that point Juncker revealed that he had actually had a bet that the UK would vote to leave: 'I put my money on Brexit. The EU Financial Stability Commissioner, Jonathan Hill from Britain, still owes me a pound.'[1] Both agreed that Britain must trigger Article 50 of the Lisbon Treaty and thus begin the process of leaving the

EU as soon as possible. Angela Merkel called the result a 'watershed' for Europe, but helpfully did not press the case for a quick Brexit. She called for 'close and fair' links between Britain and the EU.

At Vote Leave's headquarters in Westminster Tower, Gove and other leading Brexiteers were now engaged in efforts to prevent precisely that. During the campaign Cameron had threatened to fire the starting gun as soon as possible, but the Eurosceptics believed that would create unnecessary turmoil. Now Gove, Cummings and others reached out to Cameron's team, including Oliver Letwin, about the composition of the Brexit negotiating team. 'We had to make sure the PM didn't immediately declare Article 50,' a Vote Leave source said. Cummings even proposed telling Downing Street that they would demand Cameron's resignation if he invoked Article 50. But Cameron was soon to render that approach pointless.

Andrew Feldman had called Cameron around 6.30 a.m. to say that he agreed the prime minister would have to resign. Downing Street staff were in the canteen, sharing breakfast and some tears. Many still did not realise Cameron was on the verge of quitting. One of the canteen staff said to one aide, 'Why the long face? He'll be OK. He said he'd stay.' When George Osborne came downstairs he had a more realistic assessment, telling one of the PM's aides, 'Well, Dave's fucked, I'm fucked, the country's fucked.' But beyond the flippant attempt to cope, the chancellor was looking ahead. He had already been on the phone to Mark Carney, the governor of the Bank of England, to check that the stability mechanisms they had discussed in the previous weeks were in place. The aide said, 'He was talking about how the country needs to move forward, how do we handle it, what do we do next, how do we stabilise things? I actually thought that was really impressive.' Osborne had thought about resigning as well, but felt it would 'look churlish', though he knew it was 'pretty unlikely' that he could survive at the Treasury. In his discussions with Cameron they agreed he would stay on to try to help stabilise the markets.

Cameron had two speeches written. A draft of his proposed victory speech (see Appendix 3) shows that if he had won, he would have declared the referendum 'the biggest democratic exercise in the history of these islands', and sought to legitimise the Remain win by saying voters had had 'their say in a supreme act of national sovereignty'. He would then have declared, 'The British people have spoken and decided to remain in a reformed European Union.' He planned to be generous to those he had beaten: 'I also want to pay tribute to those involved in the Leave campaign. They made strong arguments about our country and what they believed was in its best interests. No one can deny that there has been vigorous debate on both sides. It has divided families, friends, colleagues – and yes, politicians, too. But it has demonstrated that there is one thing that unites us: We are *all* patriots. We *all* love Britain.' Banking his wins from the deal, he would have gone on to say, 'As far as Britain is concerned, the political project for further integration in Europe is over.'

Instead, the prime minister now put the finishing touches to the speech he had hoped he would not have to give. His study filled up with people, many of whom would normally have been preparing for the regular 8.30 a.m. strategy meeting. He addressed them all. 'We are where we are. We didn't win. We've got to get on and do what we've got to do,' he told them.[2] Then he delivered his resignation speech to the entire room. 'It was extraordinary, it was such an emotional moment,' a minister who was present said. 'He did it in front of maybe twenty people. It was a classic morning meeting crowd, civil service and ministers and spads. He treated it like any other meeting. Then he went out and did it for real. Everyone was in tears.'

The sight of Samantha Cameron at the prime minister's side as he emerged from the famous black door at 8.15 a.m. settled any doubt about what he was going to say. Once he was at the podium, a bank of television cameras crowded in front of him, Cameron said, 'The British people have voted to leave the European Union, and their will must be respected.' He called the result 'an instruction that must be delivered'. In a crisp pale-blue shirt and navy suit and tie, he was at his most polished as he proudly declared that he had fought 'directly and passionately' for 'what I think and feel, head heart and soul'. But, he said, 'The British people have made a very clear decision to take a different path. And as such I think the country requires fresh leadership to take it in this direction. I will do everything I can as prime minister to steady the ship over the coming weeks and months. But I do not think it would be right for me to try to be the captain that steers our country to its next destination.' He said there should be a new prime minister in place by the time of the Conservative Party conference at the start of October.

Somehow he got through all this as if he were making any other speech. Those who worked for him said he was driven by a rather old-fashioned sense of public service. As he reached his conclusion, those feelings welled up. 'I love this country,' he said – and that was when his voice finally cracked with emotion. 'I feel honoured to have served it. And I will do everything I can in future to help this great country succeed.' Away to his left, Samantha was dabbing at her eyes. When he had finished they went to each other, briefly held hands, then walked back together through the black door and down the corridor to the rear of the building. Staff and officials broke into applause. One of his longest-serving aides said, 'I couldn't stop weeping – and I'm not a weeper. I've grown up with the man. I've put ten years of my life into this. I just felt it was such a loss for our country.' Craig Oliver said, 'There was a lot of emotion, a lot of tears in people's eyes, and then he went with Sam to his office and closed the door.'[3]

One who was watching on the other side of that door said, 'It was like the police had come to the door and told you someone had died. You wanted to kill Michael and Boris.' Watching her husband's career come to such an abrupt conclusion was too much for Samantha, who had to be consoled by Andrew Feldman. Earlier, once the result was clear, but before the emotion had taken over, she had been 'spitting feathers'. One of Cameron's closest aides said, 'Sam is a very forthright woman and said what she thought. She was really sad and furious that her husband had been betrayed in that way.' Gove was subjected to 'the odd F-word'. The tension had been so great during the campaign that, one friend said, 'the stress drove her to cigarettes'. She was seen with a glass of wine more often too. David Cameron had impressed his staff with his calm under fire, but now he was highly emotional too. 'He was so upset,' a close aide said.

No one was pretending now that Cameron–Gove relations were fine. 'The edict went out that Michael had betrayed David in a seismic way and it was now OK to have a pop,' a source says. People were not slow to take up this offer. Samantha's brother Rob Sheffield posted a poem on Instagram: 'Goodbye EU, Goodbye Scotland, Goodbye Dave, Goodbye Tomorrow, Hello Little England, Hello Boris, Hello Fear, Hello Yesterday.' A Cameron aide said, 'There is a special place in hell reserved for Boris. He and Gove have basically engineered a right-wing coup to oust a prime minister.'

It was just 414 days since Cameron had won his historic majority – and now it was all over.

Where there is political death, so there is also new life. Many of Cameron's staff did not want to watch in the street because they knew they would become emotional. A small group had gathered in the office in 12 Downing Street shared by Adam Atashzai, Graeme Wilson, Giles Kenningham and Caroline Preston. 'There was a fair amount of holding hands. We were all crying and upset, and then everyone was kind of looking down at their feet not really knowing what to say.' Suddenly, Laura Trott said, 'So, I'm pregnant!' The mood changed in an instant. 'Everyone was immediately happy and very bubbly about it.' They lined up to give Trott hugs. Another aide said, 'Life does go on.'

Boris Johnson was standing barefoot in shorts and a South African rugby shirt when he began to realise that he might be the next prime minister. He had spent the last two hours working on a speech calling for Tory unity when Cameron announced that he was going. Johnson had had no idea his fellow Old Etonian was about to quit. 'Our view was that he was going to wait a few days, talk about stabilising the markets,' a Boris confidant said. Those present say Johnson was 'pretty emotional' at what had transpired in the past few hours. 'There was no sign of euphoria at all,' said one. 'He was drained by the magnitude of what had happened. It was a rollercoaster of emotions.'

As Cameron retreated into Number 10, hand in hand with Samantha, Johnson watched and said, 'Oh my God, oh my God, poor Dave. God, look at Samantha. Poor Dave. This is terrible.' One of those present said, 'I think it was a genuine concern for someone who he's known for years and who he counted as a friend.' Just a few hours earlier Johnson had expected to lose the referendum, and was reconciled to taking a middle-ranking cabinet job – if he was lucky. Suddenly he had another speech to write. He headed upstairs to his study and got to work. He did not immediately contact Cameron, worrying that a message of condolence would appear fake, but they did exchange texts later in the day.

Sarah Vine was taking her children to school when Cameron made his announcement. 'I felt as though I had fallen through a rabbit hole – lost in a strange land where nothing made sense any more,' she wrote later. 'This was absolutely, categorically not meant to happen. David

Cameron was not supposed to go. This was not what this referendum was about; that was not why Michael backed Leave. I felt the agony of what the business of politics had done to the people at the heart of all of this: how old friends had been wrenched apart in the most brutal of ways.'[4]

She was not the only one who was surprised. Graham Brady, the chairman of the 1922 Committee, and Chris Grayling were both live on air saying Cameron should stay when he quit. Grayling had had a meeting with Cameron a few days before the Queen's Speech in which he told him he must not go, and Cameron said he wouldn't. Over the final weekend of the campaign they had another conversation, and Grayling had said, 'It's really important you don't go.' When he saw Samantha, however, Grayling knew he had been misled. 'It rather took the edge off the event, because I'd been saying all the way through the campaign that I wanted him to stay, and I genuinely did,' he said later. 'Not just because I thought he'd had huge success as a prime minister anyway, but also because I thought it would make the aftermath of Brexit much more difficult, because it would create political instability. I think the political vacuum that the prime minister resigning created made the initial reaction in the markets and business community in terms of Brexit much worse than it should have been.'

It was an emotional morning for Steve Baker. While other Brexiteers believed they had lost, he had had 'quiet faith' in victory. He too had been in Manchester, and he found it 'painful' to watch Cameron resign. He recognised that the battle he had engaged in was 'bloody and unpleasant and carried a high price': 'There is no doubt in my mind that David Cameron is an historic and great prime minister, who held a coalition together despite cutting spending, and he managed to come back with an outright majority. He's a pragmatist and I'm more of an idealist. But there's no doubt he's a man who carried power with grace and style and dignity, and I don't doubt has sowed the seeds of public-service reform which will be looked back on in twenty years as amazing achievements. For me to have been party to events which led to him resigning is a matter of great sadness to me.' Baker confessed that he was guilty of 'a little bit of schadenfreude' as the night unfolded and constituencies like Philip Hammond's voted for Brexit. 'But I got my comeuppance, because the stone in my shoe is that Wycombe district voted Remain. I was deeply, deeply, bitterly disappointed.' When the final result was announced there was jubilation in Manchester, but Baker did not join in: 'I was happy when it was announced we'd won, but I was not elated. Other people were dancing round. The sheer price paid to win this battle has been enormous, and I knew how painful the aftermath would be.'

There was less restraint at Ukip headquarters, a dark office tucked away at the back of a house on Great Smith Street in Westminster. There were about eight people watching a flatscreen television when Cameron emerged from 10 Downing Street. When he had finished speaking, Nigel Farage said, 'Well I know how that feels. It's not a very nice feeling, losing.' There was silence for around five seconds, which was then broken by a mass outbreak of catcalls and V-signs. 'Everyone just threw stuff at the TV,' Chris Bruni-Lowe said. Nigel Farage certainly owed David Cameron no favours. He had forced the PM's hand on a referendum, and been disparaged as a fruitcake and a racist for his troubles. Now he headed to College Green, the area of grass opposite Parliament, which had been turned into a media village that resembled a refugee camp. 'In 1993 I nearly lost to the Monster Raving Loony Party,' he said. 'Now seventeen and a half million people have voted alongside me.'

At the Hope pub at Smithfield Market, the remnants of Stronger In were several pints into a marathon drinking session. When Laura Kuenssberg, the BBC's political editor, appeared on the television screens, they asked for the volume to be turned up. 'We're being called to Downing Street,' she said. In a scene loaded with allegorical meaning, David Chaplin recalled, 'All the guys from the meat market were coming in. They'd just finished their shift. They were all covered in blood, and on the TV David Cameron starts resigning.' Conservative staff burst into tears.

A while after the prime minister had disappeared back inside Number 10 an Addison Lee minicab pulled up at the Hope. Out climbed Craig Oliver, Caroline Preston, Graeme Wilson and Adam Atashzai. Chaplin said, 'Thank you, I'm glad you came.' Oliver replied, 'Where else would we be? We've just been through six months of this with you. This is where we wanted to come.' Liz Sugg, who had overseen the resignation statement, arrived later. In all there were forty people there, beginning the bereavement. James McGrory got to his feet and repeated his speech from the office, telling everyone they had fought the good fight: 'A lot of people are going to tell you the campaign was shit and are going to point out what was wrong with it, but they weren't there.' Amy Richards summed up the mood: 'Everyone cried and drank wine, so it was a fitting end somehow.'

For McGrory, the day unfolded 'like a wake – you're telling stories, you're making each other laugh, there's a lot of gallows humour, there's a lot of drink consumed'. He passed out at around 11.30 a.m., having drunk eight or nine pints. When someone tried to wake him, Joe Carberry – his new partner in crime across the party divide – said, 'Let him sleep, he deserves some rest.'

Could David Cameron have survived as prime minister? Many hoped, even expected, that he would remain in Downing Street until the end of the year, or until party conference at least. But having thrown himself so wholeheartedly into the Remain campaign his credibility was fatally damaged. If he had sought to cling on beyond the autumn he would surely have faced a leadership challenge.

As defeat gave way to reflection, his aides concluded that the only scenario in which Cameron might have been able to hang on in defeat would have been if he had stepped back from the front line of the campaign, just as Harold Wilson did in 1975. In this scenario the prime minister would have addressed the nation after the renegotiation was signed and said, 'I've got this deal. I think on balance Britain is better off in. I think it's right for our economy. But we've now got two set campaigns: Stronger In, who are going to make an argument for you, and Vote Leave, who will also make an argument for you. As your prime minister, my recommendation is that we stay in, but this is a referendum, not a general election, so these campaigns will now make their arguments to you.' He could then have taken a leaf out of Theresa May's book and made a reasoned speech halfway through the campaign. But in the event of a Leave vote he could say, 'OK, the country's made its mind up.'

The theory had some merit, but even its advocates did not think it was a viable course of action. Cameron had been too closely associated with the referendum, and the Eurosceptics had seen enough to know he was not one of them, however much he embraced Brexit. More importantly, his heart would never have been in it. 'It's not him, it's not George,' an aide said, 'because they did both passionately want to stay in.' Another aide said, 'He felt very strongly that he really believed everything he was saying during the campaign. It wasn't some made-up bollocks. For him to be the one overseeing an outcome he didn't believe in would have been wrong. Better to offer a steadying influence and then hand over to people who dig that shit.' Cameron's blunter view was that Brexit was the responsibility of the Brexiteers. To use the slogan of the American retailer Pottery Barn, 'You break it, you own it.' A Downing Street official told the *Sun* that Cameron had said on the morning of his resignation, 'Why should I do all the hard shit for someone else, just to hand it over to them on a plate?'[5] It would be for Gove and Johnson to keep the country from hitting the rocks.

Boris Johnson was already discovering that such responsibility would be a testing experience. When he emerged from his house just after 10 a.m. to travel to the Vote Leave offices, he had to run a gauntlet of furious protesters opposed to Brexit. Ben Gascoigne had been in touch with the police, and a phalanx of Met officers in hi-vis jackets helped usher Johnson into his car while people yelled 'Scum', 'Shame on you' and 'You're a cunt, Boris.' They set off, but as they approached the first set of traffic lights, the signal flicked to red. Walden, sensing trouble, said 'Jump the light,' but with so many police in the vicinity the driver, understandably, did not. The stationary car was surrounded by forty protesters on bicycles. Some banged on the roof, but Johnson stared straight ahead as they shouted, 'You've wrecked our country.' A friend said, 'There was a good deal of Remain and lefty abuse, and it was nasty when we left. I think he was a bit taken aback by it.'

At Westminster Tower preparations were under way for a Vote Leave press conference. The nation wanted to hear from the surprise victors. Chris Grayling arrived at around 10 a.m., after a doing a round of broadcasts, to find an atmosphere of 'stunned pleasure'. Some were more than stunned – they were inebriated beyond help. 'Those people who had not spent the night drinking had to organise the press conference,' a source said.

When Johnson arrived, he, Gove and Gisela Stuart talked through their speeches with the team. Will Walden, who was concerned that the attitude of some in Vote Leave was too bullish, told Johnson he needed to do a rewrite: 'This is a massive moment. Everyone will be looking to you guys for leadership. You cannot look sheepish or scared. You have to elucidate a positive vision without looking triumphalist. This is a sombre and serious occasion.' Walden had already had an argument with Dominic Cummings, who had attempted to ban ITV from the press conference. After the debate saga, Cummings said, 'I'm not having these fuckers here.' But Walden was conscious that, whether they liked it or not, the event would be seen as the first moment of Johnson's pitch for Cameron's job. 'This is not Vote Leave now,' he said. 'You kick a national broadcaster out because you don't like Robert Peston, you'll live to regret it.' ITV were allowed in.

Johnson and Walden rewrote parts of the speech, focusing on a crucial section about young people. They were still going ten minutes before Johnson had to take to the stage. 'Do it again,' Walden said. 'We've got to get this bit right. There are people up and down this country, mainly young people, thinking, "Have my parents and grandparents just sent my future down the river?"'

At 11 a.m. the three Brexiteers took to the stage, looking like a company of Tommies who had undergone a night of German shellfire. Gisela Stuart spoke first, reiterating that Britain would remain an 'open country'. Johnson, who had looked sheepish when he arrived on the low podium, affected a grave mien as he addressed the assembled hacks. He paid tribute to Cameron as 'one of the most extraordinary politicians of our age – a brave and principled man, who has given superb leadership of his party and his country for many years'. He said it was 'entirely right and inevitable' that there should have been a referendum', and sought to face down the clamour from Brussels, arguing, 'There is no need for haste,' and 'no need to invoke article 50'. Then he hit the key section. 'I want to speak directly to the millions of people who did not vote for this outcome, especially young people who may feel that this decision involves somehow pulling up the drawbridge, because I think the very opposite is true. We cannot turn our backs on Europe. We are part of Europe, our children and our grandchildren will continue to have a wonderful future as Europeans.' He concluded, 'I believe the British people have spoken up for democracy in Britain and across Europe, and we can be proud of the result.' If it was not a barnstorming vision of why he should lead the country, it did attempt to inject some sunshine in the face of a public reaction to Brexit which was becoming hysterical.

Gove spoke last, and appeared the most troubled of the three, like a man who had suffered a bereavement, which in political terms he had. He was 'very sad' that Cameron ('a great prime minister') had chosen to stand down. He was also concerned that the trio had to be seen to re-assure the markets. 'We wanted to show calmness and authority,' he said later, admitting that 'Boris struck a better note'. But the prospect of taking difficult decisions was weighing on his mind.

Matthew Elliott explained the glum faces. 'We couldn't be that joyous. This had to be a time for reassuring the country that we weren't a bunch of crazies who'd marched with pitchforks on Whitehall to take it over. So there was an intention to be serious and statesmanlike.' Elliott also felt the potential burdens of leadership were weighing heavily on both men. 'Boris in particular was thinking, "Crikey, now there's a leadership contest, the mantle's been passed to me."' Elliott also admitted that the full magnitude of what had happened was preying on the Brexiteers. 'I remember people saying, "What have we won?" It was quite overwhelming.'

Ruth Davidson, who was watching on television, put it more succinctly. 'I have seen more cheerful wakes than that press conference. It really did look like a pair of teenage arsonists that had been caught red-handed burning the house down.'

If the Brexiteers had hoped for a victory honeymoon, they were to be disappointed. Their win sparked havoc in the markets. Share values fell dramatically as panicked traders reacted to widespread fears of a recession and began a selling frenzy. The FTSE 100 plummeted by 530 points, or 8.4 per cent, within the first few minutes of trading. The pound plunged to a thirty-one-year low as investors sold sterling. Mark Carney sought to reassure the financial world by declaring that he would make an extra £250 billion available to the banks to ensure their liquidity, and that he would 'not hesitate' to intervene to steady the markets. His comments seemed to have some effect as the stock market rallied a little, closing 4.8 per cent down. By then, though, more than £100 billion had been wiped off the value of shares.

The economic turmoil enraged Remain campaigners, whose warnings had been so casually dismissed by Johnson and Gove. Craig Oliver was quick to say to journalists, 'They told us it was Project Fear, but you can see already that it is Project Reality.'

In return, some Vote Leave officials and ministers briefed against Cameron, saying that his decision to announce his resignation so soon was irresponsible. 'It was an abdication of his duty,' one senior Vote Leaver said. Speaking several weeks after the referendum, when some of the pain had eased, the same source said Cameron's doom-mongering actually conditioned the market to fail: 'He offered the people a referen-

dum where Leave was an option, and as we now know, then they did
sweet FA to plan for it. That is a total dereliction of duty of a prime
minister. Most of those things happened because they said they would
happen.'

In Scotland, the first minister Nicola Sturgeon, who is not given to
profanity, privately pronounced the result 'a monumental fuckup' – but
it was one she and her staff were well prepared for. She quickly announced
that the decision had made a second referendum on Scottish independence 'highly likely', and said it was 'democratically unacceptable' that
Scotland faced the prospect of being taken out of the EU against its will.
She and Ruth Davidson had been in touch that morning, and both spoke
to David Cameron about the need to include the Scots in any Brexit
negotiations. She also had a telephone conversation with Sadiq Khan to
discuss their common interests, as Remain supporters took to Twitter to
demand that Scotland and London, both of which had voted emphatically for Remain, declare independence from the rest of the UK as the
new EU nation of 'Scotlondon'.

Privately, senior Tories thought Sturgeon had been sincere in not
wanting a Leave vote, but they bemoaned what Davidson referred to as
the 'muted' pro-Remain campaign in Scotland. 'It felt like someone else's
referendum,' she said. David Mundell, the Scottish secretary, said, 'I
genuinely believe that Nicola Sturgeon wanted a Remain vote, because
she understands that she's much more likely to get an independence vote
for Scotland from inside the EU than outside the EU.' But he believed the
SNP were in part to blame for the defeat, because they sent 'mixed
messages' to their own voters: 'A million people in Scotland voted to
leave the EU, and 400,000 of those were SNP voters. Nicola Sturgeon and
senior Nationalists wanted Britain to remain in the EU, but they gave out
conflicting messages to their supporters by saying, "If Britain votes to
leave the EU then Scotland will have to become independent." If you're
somebody who is a fanatic about independence, that's something you're
going to pick up.'

The result created several weeks of fear and confusion amongst voters,
and particular resentment among the young, who had turned out in
record numbers to vote Remain, only to find that they were outnumbered.
The *Daily Mirror*'s splash on the Saturday spoke for many, asking, 'So
what the hell happens now?' The Plaid Cymru leader Leanne Wood

called it a 'dark and uncertain morning'. In the days that followed there were reports of ugly scenes in which Eastern Europeans and other immigrants were confronted in the streets and on public transport, with Leave supporters demanding, 'When are you going home?' A Tory MP who backed Remain and was elevated to the cabinet after the referendum said, 'I had angry elderly people making a point of being hostile in a way I never had in the general election. It did bring out emotions that normal politics doesn't bring out, and many of them are not pleasant ones.'

On the Tuesday after the referendum a German woman who had lived in Britain since 1973 called talk-radio station LBC to say, 'I have had friends of mine saying they can't be friends any more ... I have had dog turd thrown at my door, told to go back home ... My friend's grandson, seven years old, got beaten up because he had a foreign grandmother.' Cards saying 'No more Polish vermin' were left on cars near a school in Huntingdon. On 5 July the Metropolitan Police revealed that it recorded 599 race-hate incidents in the nine days after the referendum – a 50 per cent increase over a typical period. The same day, Justin Welby, the Archbishop of Canterbury, voiced his concern about 'an outwelling of poison and hatred that I cannot remember for many years'. On 8 July a Romanian food shop in Norwich was attacked by arsonists. Thankfully, the spike in these episodes was short-lived. Some 225 hate incidents were reported to the police throughout the UK on 24 June, and 289 the day after. But by the 30th they were down to 110. Media interest in the referendum may, perversely, have increased the reporting of such incidents. Liz Fekete, director of the Institute for Race Relations, told the *Independent*: 'The referendum debate and result emboldened a lot of people. They thought they could say racist things in public. They lost their shame.'[6]

The hatred worked both ways. Kate Hoey, the Labour Brexit campaigner, said, 'I had lots and lots of horrible letters from people, and emails.' Dominic Cummings had a glass of wine thrown over him, and Sarah Vine complained, 'Almost overnight, those of us on the winning side suddenly found ourselves recast as knuckle-dragging thugs, small-minded Little Englanders whose short-sighted bigotry had brought the nation to its knees.'[7]

One of the controversies of the first days after the referendum was that Michael Gove and Boris Johnson said very little about what would come next. Their advisers said they had been leaders of a campaign, not a government. With victory, Vote Leave effectively ceased to exist. In that first seventy-two hours hardly any senior Outers appeared on the broadcast media, allowing a narrative to develop that they had only won by exploiting racism and telling lies. That weekend, Chris Grayling wrote a piece for the *Sunday Telegraph*: 'I thought somebody from the Brexit team needed to be out there saying, actually we've thought about this, and this is what happens next.' But Gove and Johnson were preoccupied with leadership deliberations. Rage at the £350 million claim reached a new peak.

The issue of what had motivated Leave voters then became the subject of a row between Vote Leave and Ukip over who deserved credit for the victory, which mirrored the debate during the campaign about how hard to push immigration. Daniel Hannan said, 'Every internal poll we did showed the same as what the published polls did, which is by far the biggest issue was sovereignty, or democracy, or however you phrase it. Immigration was a distant second. And even among those citing immigration, for a lot of them it was about "Why can't we deport Abu Hamza?" "What about criminals coming in from Europe?" It wasn't about a massive cut in numbers.' This is borne out by Michael Ashcroft's post-referendum poll, that found control of laws motivated people more than cutting immigration. Chris Bruni-Lowe thought Hannan was guilty of wishful thinking: 'I think they wish people voted for them for different reasons. I think Vote Leave sleep sounder at night thinking that people voted for them because they believe it's a great injustice that 70 per cent of our laws are made in Brussels. No, they did not. They did so because they believe there are too many people coming to this country.'

While the Brexit groups were at war over the reasons they won, Stronger In entered a period of soul-searching about the reasons they lost. The focus fell immediately on Andrew Cooper's polling. His final tracker had Remain winning with 51.9 per cent of the vote. But it also showed that the campaign had failed to hold on to its early leads with the very groups it was targeting. Stronger In won only 48 per cent of 'disengaged middle' voters, and just 43 per cent of 'hearts v heads', the key group of middle-aged women. 'We lost "hearts v heads" in April and never got them back,' said Cooper. 'We lost "disengaged middle" around the 6th or 7th of June and never got them back.'

Cooper's fatal methodological flaw – which affected many pollsters – was that he dramatically underestimated turnout, more specifically turnout from people who do not usually vote. While Stronger In had been very successful at registering young voters, they were less successful at getting them to the polls. The decision not to enfranchise sixteen- and seventeen-year-olds also cost Remain 650,000 votes. Research by the LSE found that while 64 per cent of eighteen-to-twenty-fours voted, the figure rose in each age group, until it was more than 90 per cent among the over-sixty-fives.

'We assumed that the demographic profile of those voting in the referendum would be very similar to the profile of those who had voted at the 2015 general election,' Cooper explained. 'We had expected the turnout to be higher than at the general election, but expected the increase among poorer working-class voters, a clear majority of whom opposed EU membership, would be more or less offset by the increase among young, middle-class voters, who supported Remain by a four-to-one margin. That assumption proved completely wrong: 2.8 million people voted in the referendum who didn't vote at the general election, and we estimate that over 80 per cent of them voted Leave.' Cooper believes Vote Leave's data-modelling was 'more sophisticated', and enabled them to get postal votes to people who were usually non-voters: 'Among people who voted on the day it was 50–50. Among the people who voted by post, it was 55–45 to leave.'

Some at Stronger In were also sore after the result that Cooper's analysis had shackled the campaign to a rigid economic fear message, in the belief that that would trump immigration with target voters. The consistency of his polling on that issue dissuaded the Conservatives at the top of the campaign from agreeing to a change of approach. His belief, until the end, that Remain was ahead prevented David Cameron from confronting the gravity of the situation he was facing. One senior figure at Stronger In said afterwards, 'You've got to judge your contractors on their results, and other people like Craig [Elder] and Tom [Edmonds] did a superb job. Ultimately with Andrew there were two massive flaws. One was, despite people asking him repeatedly about the impact of turnout on the referendum, his view was that it would be equal for both sides. Ultimately we paid his firm a lot of money, and they got that wrong. That was the entire reason his polls were wrong. If you put all of those tracking polls four points the other way, then we'd have been behind for the majority of the campaign.' Cooper's second mistake was to convince the campaign that phone polls, which tended to give Remain a boost, were more accurate than online polls. In fact, the reverse seems to have been true. 'That gave us a bit of a false sense of security,' the source said.

In this debate George Osborne has defended Cooper, saying his errors were not significant because Tory high command knew the referendum was on a knife edge. 'The polling showed, right up until the last bit of the campaign, the last couple of days, that it was neck and neck. So we were not being misled by the polling,' says a source close to Osborne. 'Anyway, George thought we were going to lose.'

In addition to non-voters voting, there were two other major problems for Stronger In. The first was in Scotland and London, where Remain won handily but were so dominant that many of their supporters did not bother to vote, perhaps assuming the win was in the bag. Cooper said, 'The overall turnout went up by 8 per cent across the UK, but it went down in Scotland, which we needed to be one of our big regions. It was up in London – by 3 per cent – but less than we needed.' Parts of the capital suffered torrential downpours on polling day, which did have an effect, but not enough to change the result of the referendum. 'If you map London boroughs, you could see the districts flooded, and turnout was much lower,' Cooper said. 'But it was never going to be enough to make up the difference.' In Scotland Stronger In had hoped to secure between 60 and 70 per cent support from SNP voters. They actually got around 55 per cent. The Nationalists had a lot of voters who were attitudinally similar to Ukip voters, and in England would have been voting for Nigel Farage.

The final problem was the failure to win enough Labour votes, despite the media blitz in the penultimate week. 'If we were going to get at best 45 per cent of Tory voters on a 70 per cent turnout, we needed 70 per cent of Labour voters,' says Cooper. Polling analysis by Michael Ashcroft after the referendum suggested that Remain won just 63 per cent of Labour voters. According to Cooper's work, if the referendum had been a general election, Vote Leave would have won four hundred seats, and a majority of 150. While twenty of Stronger In's best twenty-five results came in Labour seats – primarily in London and university towns – twenty out of twenty-five of their worst results were also in Labour strongholds, places where Jeremy Corbyn's enthusiasm for open-door immigration would have played badly. A study by Chris Hanretty of the University of East Anglia found that 70 per cent of Labour constituencies actually voted for Leave. 'In other words,' Will Straw said, 'Labour racked up cricket scores in inner London, and then lost most of its constituencies.'

Jeremy Corbyn's evening rallies and inability to make the news appeared to have helped lose the referendum. Within four hours of David Cameron announcing his resignation, a plot was unfolding to oust the Labour leader as well.

27

JEXIT

When he was finally woken up on the morning after the vote, Jeremy Corbyn found a waiting television camera, and at 7.40 a.m., thirty-five minutes before David Cameron resigned, he declared that the government should immediately trigger Article 50 and begin the process of withdrawing Britain from the European Union: 'The British people have made their decision. We must respect that result and Article 50 has to be invoked now.' For a man who had professed to want the UK to remain in Europe, this was a curious thing to do when even the Brexiteers wanted to buy time. When he saw what Corbyn had said, Alan Johnson was furious. 'Come the day and come that result, the one person who was not upset at all was Jeremy. The party was distraught, I mean really distraught. Jeremy wasn't. And Jeremy's people weren't. Jeremy was the only person to have said we should kick off Article 50 immediately. For the party, this was a test for him.'

When the backlash came, Corbyn's spin doctors first claimed that he had not said it, later that he had misspoken. 'His own office, his own staff, didn't know he was going to say that,' said a source who was in Labour HQ that morning. 'They all looked up at the screens as he was live on telly and looked at each other in shock.' Another Labour staffer said, 'It became abundantly clear from speaking to Andrew Fisher that neither Jeremy, and possibly not him either, actually understood what Article 50 was. Corbyn never understands these things unless you ram it in his thick skull.'

At 6 a.m. Corbyn's team had sent out some 'lines to take' for MPs doing interviews, seeking to make a virtue of the leader's ambivalence about the EU. They claimed that Labour was 'far closer to the centre of gravity of the British public than other political parties', and that Corbyn was 'uniquely placed' to represent the nation's views. If that was not enough of a red rag to backbench bulls, Corbyn's Article 50 statement eliminated any lingering doubts among his critics that he was unfit to be leader of the opposition. By 9 a.m. a concerted effort was under way to remove him.

The previous week moderate Labour MPs had met Margaret Hodge, the former minister and chairman of the Public Accounts Committee, to discuss her standing as a stalking horse in a leadership contest. Hodge was prepared to put herself forward, but told a friend, 'I don't think it will work.' Barry Sheerman, whose daughter Madlin Sadler worked for David Miliband, was also considered as a stalking horse, but any leadership challenge would fail if the wrong challenger was put forward. A new plan was found. Hodge and Ann Coffey would table a motion of no confidence in Corbyn, to be debated at the Parliamentary Labour Party meeting, known to every Labour MP as 'the PLP', the following Monday. Details of the motion were submitted to John Cryer, the chairman of the PLP, and handed to the media at noon. It read simply, 'That this PLP has no confidence in Jeremy Corbyn as leader of the Parliamentary Labour Party.' By the time it went public fifty-five MPs were already backing Corbyn's removal. The shadow cabinet kept their hands clean, but support for the motion had been coordinated by several of their aides, and others working for senior figures in the faction led by Chris Leslie, the shadow chancellor during Harriet Harman's temporary leadership. The group of advisers communicated with each other on a WhatsApp group wittily entitled 'JobCentre Plus'. There was a danger that the PLP would delay the motion for a week, killing any coup momentum, so one of the aides briefed the media that the motion would be heard on the Monday, and only then began lobbying the members of the parliamentary committee to ensure that would be the case, and that there would be a secret ballot. When Margaret Hodge broke cover she was accompanied to media studios by Lisa Tremble, another former aide to David Miliband.

Two hours before the no confidence motion was made public, MP Angela Smith broke cover and called for the leader to quit: 'Jeremy Corbyn has got to take responsibility. He should consider his position. He's shown insufficient leadership.' There was heavyweight artillery support. Peter Mandelson said Corbyn 'can't cut it' as leader, and Tony Blair accused him of ignoring the voters who had backed Brexit. To keep up the pressure, Tristram Hunt – the intellectual backbone of the Leslie faction – wrote two pieces for the *Observer* and the *Sun on Sunday* saying Corbyn had to go. By the time they appeared, events had already overtaken them.

Three groups of Labour MPs had decided that Corbyn was unfit to lead. The first was the collection of moderates who had resigned from the front bench and refused to serve him when he first became leader. They included Tristram Hunt, Chuka Umunna, Rachel Reeves, Liz Kendall and Emma Reynolds, plus Siobhain McDonagh, who had been involved in an attempt to oust Gordon Brown. Their guiding force was Chris Leslie. The second group was centred around Tom Watson, the deputy leader. Watson had his own mandate, and is a skilled, union-trained backroom fixer who learned the dark arts of politics as a member of Gordon Brown's Praetorian Guard. He had allies in Lucy Powell and Gloria De Piero. In 2006 it was Watson who had coordinated the 'curry-house plot' which forced Tony Blair to name the date of his departure from Downing Street. He and three other MPs met in a Wolverhampton biryani restaurant and penned a letter telling Blair to go which was signed by a number of other previously loyal MPs. Watson resigned as a minister and six other frontbenchers jumped ship one after the other, forcing Blair to say he would be gone within a year. The final group consisted of the rest of the shadow cabinet who were not overt Corbyn loyalists, many on the soft left, who had come to see him as serially incompetent as well as unelectable. Their leading light was Hilary Benn, the shadow foreign secretary, who had enraged Corbyn by contradicting his opposition to air strikes against Islamic State in Syria with a speech of such defiant eloquence from the front bench that it had attracted applause. Seumas Milne and others had wanted Benn fired from the shadow cabinet in a 'revenge reshuffle' in January. 'That was the moment people looked at each other and thought, "If Hilary's out, I'm out too,"' said one of the rebels. Rosie Winterton, the chief whip, was a key intermediary between the frontbenchers.

The case against Corbyn was multifaceted. His views were, by any measure, at the far extreme of what had been seen in mainstream public life. He believed the West was to blame for terrorism, and had sought to do deals with the IRA. His shadow chancellor John McDonnell was a self-declared Marxist whose *Who's Who* entry boasted that he was 'fermenting [sic] the overthrow of capitalism'. McDonnell was on the record as saying, 'You can't change the world through the parliamentary system.' Corbyn himself had little interest in Parliament, preferring the direct democracy of marches and protest. To more moderate MPs this looked very like a taste for mob rule. Corbyn spoke softly and had attracted support for his apparent authenticity, but for many his performance during the referendum was typical of a man who gave cover to hardliners carrying big sticks while publicly insisting that he was a conciliator. It was axiomatic to these MPs that the British public would never choose as its prime minister someone who was so agnostic on the causes of terrorism, who appeared to believe in a 'magic money tree' to fund public spending, and who refused to sing the National Anthem at his first major public appearance as Labour leader. Then there was the question of competence. Corbyn gave Cameron an easy ride at Prime Minister's Questions, and did not develop policy, understand how to make news or seem interested in persuading voters who did not already agree with him of the virtues of his position. As a member of the shadow cabinet put it, 'Jeremy is not actually a politician. He is just a protester.'

Corbyn knew defeat in the referendum would trigger a challenge to his authority. Chris Leslie and Emma Reynolds, along with Ben Bradshaw and Adrian Bailey, had put down a marker with an article in the *Observer* on 10 April telling him to 'step up' his efforts for the Remain campaign or face the blame if there was a Brexit vote. In the run-up to the local elections in May, members of the Leslie group agreed a plan with council leaders in cities like Derby, where Labour was expected to lose control, that they would call for Corbyn to quit if the results were bad enough. A female member of the shadow cabinet was also ready to resign. In the event, Corbyn described the local election results as 'fantastic' after losing more than twenty councillors at a time in the political cycle when oppositions usually win four to five hundred seats. It was Labour's worst set of council results in opposition since 1982. But there was no appetite for a coup. During the referendum campaign, MPs say Leslie took further soundings about what might happen afterwards, but the rebels found a sizeable number still opposed to removing Corbyn. The Blairites decided that their original plan, 'to send a candidate of the right over the top to attract criticism so a candidate of the soft left could come through the middle', would be better replaced by a single challenge from a member of the soft left.

A shadow cabinet member said, 'There is a group of people around Chris Leslie who have been plotting since the moment of Corbyn becoming leader. The Parliamentary Labour Party hates Jeremy because he's useless and threatens most of their seats, so they want the same outcome as that group, but they – the bulk of the Parliamentary Labour Party – know that they cannot be associated with that group, because that group is completely doomed, as are the organisers in any coup because they cannot inherit the crown.' Tom Watson and his allies believed that no coup had a chance of success while the party membership remained sympathetic to Corbyn. Others like Vernon Coaker, Seema Malhotra, Lilian Greenwood and Kate Green shared that view.

A Labour frontbencher said, 'There had been lots of talk about leadership challenges in April and May, particularly as we ran up to the local government elections, but the local government elections basically brought that conversation to an end. The overwhelming conclusion in May and after the elections was no leadership challenge is going to succeed. The defeat in the European referendum then completely transformed the picture.'

Corbynistas regarded the attempted coup that followed the referendum as premeditated, but – like the Tory civil war that was to follow – it contained elements of chance and cock-up as well as conspiracy. 'Jeremy dragging his feet like a teenager on the campaign trail left people beside themselves,' says one of the plotters. 'Some people were very starry-eyed about Jeremy, but after the referendum defeat they looked at him differently.'

Those seeking metaphors when the shadow cabinet met on Friday the 24th did not have to look far. Corbyn's team assembled in the Boothroyd Room in Portcullis House, as the torrential rain that had depressed turnout in parts of London the day before had flooded out the shadow cabinet room. The shadow ministers took Corbyn to task for Labour's failures during the campaign. One of those present said, 'The shadow cabinet in a very impressive way expressed huge grief and anxiety about what had happened the day before. There was a very real anger expressed about how this has happened and why we were so useless, both in the campaign and now we had nothing to say about how we deal with Brexit. The only voice that was heard in Jeremy's favour was Emily Thornberry, which drove everybody in the room absolutely mad. She was uselessly awful. Jeremy responded as he always does, despite the fact that people were incredibly rude to him – "Oh, well that's an interesting point" – and as ever, failed to engage.' Those who spoke included an angry Chris Bryant, Hilary Benn and Kate Green. 'It had an air of very considerable crisis,' a source said. Despite all this rage, only Ian Murray, the shadow Scottish secretary, suggested that Corbyn might resign: 'I don't think at this moment in time that you could be prime minister, and if you do think you could be prime minister then you're talking to the wrong people.' In the face of this, John McDonnell said nothing, and left early to talk to the television cameras on College Green.

The thoughts Murray had voiced were at the forefront of everyone's minds. The publication of the motion of no confidence electrified the PLP. Here was a simple binary choice: was Corbyn up to it or not? Unlike contentious issues like Syria or the renewal of Trident, which had exposed fault lines in the party before, this was a decision everyone could make, and most knew the clear answer. Friends say that Benn, the moral leader of those still serving in the shadow cabinet, made a decision that Friday that he could not vote for Corbyn. 'Hilary is an honourable guy. He concluded that he could not do anything other than vote against Jeremy, and that meant he would have to resign. So he rang round colleagues to see how many people would be prepared to go with him.' Another frontbencher said, 'He was getting a huge lack of confidence in Jeremy. But there was no desire, at that point, to pull the trigger.' Benn's plan was to go to Corbyn and explain that there was significant opposition to him, and he should stand down. If he refused, Benn asked the others if they would join him in resigning.

Corbyn beat him to the punch. On the Saturday evening both the *Observer* and the *Sunday Times* carried front-page stories suggesting that Benn was drumming up support for a coup. A shadow cabinet source claimed, 'Corbyn will be out by the end of the week.' At 12.50 on the Sunday morning Benn called Corbyn and told him he had 'lost confidence in his ability to lead the party'. Corbyn fired him on the spot. Benn put out a statement at 3.30 a.m., saying, 'It has now become clear that there is widespread concern among Labour MPs and in the shadow cabinet about Jeremy Corbyn's leadership of our party. In particular, there is no confidence in our ability to win the next election, which may come much sooner than expected, if Jeremy continues as leader.' As Benn was issuing his statement, Tom Watson was at the Glastonbury music festival, and was photographed dancing in a silent disco.

MPs and shadow ministers awoke to find their standard bearer had been fired. Corbyn's office issued a defiant statement saying, 'Jeremy Corbyn is the democratically elected leader of the Labour Party and will remain so.' One of his spin doctors taunted the rebels: 'They don't have a candidate, they don't have a programme, they don't have the supporters to win a leadership election. He is not going to resign, and if there is a challenge he will fight it. Anyone that resigns can be replaced.' This proposition would be tested to the limits.

A member of the shadow cabinet said, 'From 6 o'clock in the morning onwards the telephone never stopped ringing. First of all with the Sunday programmes, who wanted any member of the shadow cabinet to come on to resign on air, which we didn't want to do. Between about six and nine there were a number of conference calls, involving seven or eight revolving members of the shadow cabinet.' The people on these calls included a recovering Tom Watson, Heidi Alexander, Charlie Falconer, Lucy Powell, Chris Bryant, Vernon Coaker and Rosie Winterton. 'We didn't want mass resignations, but that group was very friendly with Hilary,' a senior frontbencher said. 'The group had always agreed that we would protect each other. Our strength came from the fact that he couldn't sack one of us without sacking all of us.' After an hour of discussions the group concluded, 'We can't stay if Hilary's been fired. Heidi was absolutely determined not to be fired by Jeremy, so very early on she resigned. She's the first one out of the trap.' Alexander, the shadow health secretary, handed in her resignation at 8.22 on Sunday morning, telling Corbyn in a letter, 'I do not believe you have the capacity to shape the answers our country is demanding.'

John McDonnell was on his way to appear on *The Andrew Marr Show* when he was told he was being bumped in favour of Hilary Benn. 'He's a good and decent man but he is not a leader, and that is the problem,' Benn said. He ruled himself out of standing for the leadership. McDonnell got himself on *Sunday Politics* instead, and announced that 'Jeremy Corbyn is going nowhere.' The rebels howled with laughter. McDonnell said he would 'never stand' for the leadership himself after MPs said his friends had begun taking soundings about whether he might slip into Corbyn's shoes.

In the conference calls Tom Watson had 'not given a particularly clear lead', but when Gloria De Piero resigned at 11.23 a.m. the rest of the shadow cabinet realised Watson had given his approval for the move. De Piero is a close ally of Watson, and her husband James Robinson was his press spokesman. Less than three hours later Lucy Powell, another key Watson ally, followed suit. A Labour MP who enjoys depicting Watson as a mafia don said, 'The fat man could have stopped it and the fat man sat on his hands.' Watson waited until 6 p.m. before issuing his own statement, which pointedly refused to back Corbyn. The deputy leader said he was 'deeply disappointed' to see Hilary Benn sacked, and 'equally saddened that so many talented, able and hard-working colleagues felt they had to leave the shadow cabinet'. He announced that he would be talking to Corbyn the following day. Behind the scenes, said a frontbencher, Rosie Winterton was not pressing for resignations, but was 'organising the way it was being done'. On a remarkable day which eviscerated what remained of Corbyn's authority over his frontbenchers, eleven members of the shadow cabinet resigned, one after the other:

8.22 a.m. Heidi Alexander, health
11.23 a.m. Gloria De Piero, young people
12.03 p.m. Ian Murray, Scotland
1.02 p.m. Lilian Greenwood, transport
1.27 p.m. Kerry McCarthy, environment
1.51 p.m. Seema Malhotra, Treasury
1.56 p.m. Lucy Powell, education
5.01 p.m. Vernon Coaker, Northern Ireland
5.54 p.m. Charlie Falconer, justice
7.04 p.m. Karl Turner, attorney general
9.24 p.m. Chris Bryant, Commons leader

The last of these was the most spectacular. Chris Bryant, perhaps the most committed pro-European of them all, issued a resignation letter of withering brutality: 'If you refuse to step aside I fear you will go down in history as the man who broke the Labour Party.' The following day another twenty-eight frontbenchers jumped ship, including Angela Eagle. By the end of the week sixty-five had quit, making it impossible for Corbyn to fill all his frontbench posts. Yet he refused to resign. Hard-left MPs who had only been in Parliament for thirteen months, like Clive

Lewis and Rebecca Long-Bailey, suddenly found themselves elevated to the shadow cabinet.

Of the moderates, only three did not resign. Everyone agreed it was better to have Rosie Winterton inside the tent, keeping an eye on the Corbynistas. Jonathan Ashworth kept his head down. He had a key seat on the party's ruling National Executive Committee, and was more use to the rebels there. Andy Burnham, the shadow home secretary, issued a statement saying he had been loyal to every leader of the Labour Party he had served. He may have adopted this stance because he was hoping to be selected as Labour's candidate to be mayor of Manchester – in any case, it attracted widespread opprobrium. One MP said, 'Andy once again puts his desperation for the next job ahead of party and country.' Several days later, after the biggest mass resignation in British political history, Burnham asked colleagues, 'Do you think I should resign?' and was told, 'What's the point now?'

The second leg of the attempted coup took place on the Monday, when Hodge and Coffey's no confidence motion was put to the PLP. The anti-Corbyn mood was fuelled by a letter sent to every MP by Alan Johnson pointing the finger of blame squarely at 'the leader's office' for 'this disastrous result' in the referendum. It said, 'At times it felt as if they were working against the rest of the Party.' Johnson said later, 'They had no right to undermine the efforts of Labour Party members. But they did it with this arrogance that they possess, that they are the only true keepers of the faith. They think the socialist path to glory actually relies on us being out of this "rich man's club".'

On the Tuesday just forty Labour MPs backed Corbyn, while a staggering 172 supported the no confidence motion. Corbyn had lost the support of 81 per cent of his parliamentary party, and two-thirds of his front bench. It had been a perfectly executed coup. The rebels assumed he would resign.

He did not.

Corbyn had little concern for the party in Parliament. He derived his enthusiasm and his mandate from the membership. He refused to go. Some of those who backed him did so because they did not think it was the right time to get rid of him. Kate Hoey was one: 'The PLP had wanted to ditch him from the minute after he had been elected, so I was one of the forty who voted against the vote of no confidence, because I just didn't feel that this was the right time. I'm not saying I think Jeremy should lead us into a general election, but I think if we want to change the leader we have to do it openly and properly.'

The resignations continued through Tuesday and Wednesday. Seventy-seven Labour councillors said Corbyn should quit. All twenty of Labour's MEPs announced that they had lost confidence in him. Members of the whips' office were prepared to quit *en masse*, but stayed in order to help coordinate seditious activities. Ed Miliband said Corbyn's position was 'untenable'. 'There was an absolute consensus among sensible councillors and members that Jeremy Corbyn needed to go as soon as possible,' said one of those involved in coordinating the show of force. On the Tuesday evening, when the BBC's *Newsnight* tried to find a Corbynista to go on the programme to defend the leader, they met with resistance. Corbyn's office recommended Clive Lewis, but when a political producer phoned him he said he would not do it. Then Corbyn's team recommended Cat Smith. A BBC source said, 'She didn't get back to me until midway through the programme, when she claimed to be dealing with family stuff, which seemed to be a remarkably common problem in the shadow cabinet that night. Diane Abbott, normally the most willing of the shadow cabinet both to appear on TV and to defend Corbyn, said she couldn't do it.' Eventually Barry Gardiner agreed to appear. A BBC producer said, 'Of course, it could have been the case that the entire shadow cabinet really had arranged to meet their families that night, but from my perspective it seemed pretty clear that by about eight that evening Barry Gardiner was quite literally the last loyal shadow cabinet member standing.'

Multiple sources insisted – in the face of flat denials from Corbyn's team – that the leader had a major wobble. 'There were times when we thought he was on his way out,' a rebel organiser said. 'He was massively rattled.' PMQs was bruising. David Cameron, facing his own departure said Corbyn's refusal to resign despite losing a vote of no confidence 'might be in my party's interest, but it's not in the national interest – for heaven's sake man, go!' Some observers saw Cameron's intervention as a clever device to ensure that Corbyn stayed. But a Cameron aide insisted, 'He just said it because he believed it.'

Labour sources say Corbyn returned to his office looking like a 'broken man'. He is said to have turned to Milne and said, 'That's it, Seumas. I've had enough.' There were reports that even hardliners like

Andrew Fisher began working on a resignation plan which would have involved guarantees from the rebels that the next leader would continue Corbyn's anti-austerity economics, and that one of his far-left protégés would be allowed onto the leadership ballot. Even Clive Lewis and Cat Smith were said to have realised the game was up. But their efforts to see Corbyn, as part of a delegation that also included Burnham, were thwarted by Milne and McDonnell who kept him in isolation. Seb Corbyn, the leader's son, who was an aide to the shadow chancellor, was said to have pleaded with McDonnell, 'Let my dad go.' This was denied by the shadow chancellor's office. One MP said, 'We are not meant to mention Hitler any more, but it is just like when Martin Bormann was stopping people from seeing him in the bunker.'[1] Milne, though, had not abandoned his career in journalism to give up at the first whiff of grape-shot. McDonnell took the same view, and both refused to countenance giving any ground. Corbyn attended rallies of his supporters, and his spirits revived. Meanwhile Momentum began mobilising to recruit new party members to bolster Corbyn's chances in the forthcoming leadership election.

On Wednesday, Tom Watson attempted to speak to Corbyn about the PLP's loss of confidence in him while they were on their way to a Polish centre in Hammersmith that had been daubed with racist graffiti in the days after the referendum vote. But his plan was thwarted when Seb Corbyn and a secretary climbed into the car as well. When the visit was over, Corbyn leapt into the front seat to avoid being buttonholed by Watson. The return journey passed in silence. That evening Watson called on Corbyn to resign, but he refused, saying his legitimacy derived from the membership, not the PLP. Watson told the BBC he wanted a 'negotiated settlement' that would have seen Corbyn step aside, but added, 'I'm afraid Jeremy is not willing to discuss that with me.' He ruled himself out of any leadership contest. Extraordinarily, Corbyn's aides briefed the *Observer* at the end of the week that they had sought to prevent Watson getting a one-on-one meeting with Corbyn to prevent 'bullying' – as if a man purporting to want to be prime minister was incapable of standing up for himself. 'They want Watson to be on his own with Corbyn so that he can jab his finger at him,' said a source. 'We are not letting that happen. He's a seventy-year-old [sic] man. We have a duty of care.'[2] The story contributed to the view in the PLP of Corbyn as a feeble leader surrounded by miniature Machiavellis.

Not content with one civil war, now the rebels engineered a second over who would stand against Corbyn. The Chris Leslie group and those who believed a woman had the best chance of beating Corbyn threw their weight behind Angela Eagle. The former shadow leader of the Commons had performed better than Corbyn when she stood in for him at PMQs, and had something of a national profile after the referendum debate. But Eagle's desire to launch her challenge ran up against the continuing efforts to get Corbyn to quit. Eagle's bid was organised by Margaret McDonagh, a former party general secretary, and the Labour peer Waheed Alli. Peter Mandelson hosted a fundraising dinner. But others in the Watson circle and some of the recently departed shadow ministers feared that these backroom connections to the Blairites would doom Eagle. 'She was brave and bold, but people's noses were put out of joint,' a plotter said. While some regarded her as 'a thoroughbred stalking horse', Eagle wanted to win. Others saw it as a priority to force Corbyn out before candidates started worrying about themselves. On the Wednesday evening there was a hope that Corbyn could be forced to step down by the trade unions, and a fear that Eagle's keenness to launch could derail a deal. 'We've had to sit on Angela,' one of those trying to negotiate a deal said. 'She's going to fuck the whole thing up unless she stays out of it.' Even Jon Trickett, one of Corbyn's few shadow cabinet allies, was coming to the view that he could not go on. But in retrospect, it was those seeking to negotiate Corbyn out of a job that his closest allies would not let him relinquish who were deluded.

Meanwhile, Clive Efford, Karen Buck and Andy Slaughter began ringing round, drumming up support for Owen Smith, the former shadow work and pensions secretary. The Eagle gang cried foul. 'You can't have two fucking unity candidates,' said one. 'The clue is in the name.' On Thursday morning Rosie Winterton had Eagle and Smith into her office and made it clear that only one of them could challenge Corbyn. Eagle felt she had done her time and, as the senior woman in the shadow cabinet, should be given a clear run. But her critics did not like the way she had become the Blairite favourite. A former minister said, 'You weren't going to have a successful leadership challenge unless you had something that's convincing for the membership.' All politics is personal, and this battle was to get highly personal. 'The PLP were doubtful about Angela for two reasons: they could see it was the Chris Leslie-inspired group that was surrounding her, and Angela had been difficult with a

whole range of colleagues over the years.' Smith's supporters pointed out
that Eagle had voted for both the Iraq War and the bombing of Syria.
Eagle's team countered that Smith had been a special adviser to Paul
Murphy, the Welsh secretary, at the time of Iraq, and argued that he was
a political chameleon who trimmed his sails to the times. 'Owen was a
Blairite under Blair and a Brownite under Brown. Now he seems to want
to be a Corbynista under Corbyn,' one said.

Some of Eagle's supporters who remembered the curry-house coup
saw the hand of Watson behind Smith. One said, 'Tom taking over would
be like replacing Lenin with Stalin.' This view was strengthened when
Lucy Powell, one of Watson's closest allies, became a driving force behind
Smith's campaign. 'Tom was important in holding Angela back, because
he said to Angela, in the immediate aftermath of the shadow cabinet
resignations, "You can't announce now, and if you do, I will say that you
have frustrated the attempts that I am making to try and get Jeremy to
go." So that held her back.' Watson's action also bought time for Smith to
get organised. Eagle was certainly better prepared. She had a campaign
apparatus in place and brought in Imran Ahmed, Hilary Benn's adviser,
to help run her effort. At this stage Smith's nascent team did not even
have a bank account.

There were two dramas still to play out. The following Monday, Watson
saw Corbyn and told him the support of the membership was not enough
for him to cling on to the leadership. That evening Watson told the PLP
he would be meeting union leaders the following morning to try to find
a negotiated settlement. 'Tom knew the membership better than any
other MP. He wanted to avoid a contest against Jeremy at all costs,' a rebel
organiser said. The meeting was most memorable for a rousing speech
by Neil Kinnock. Referring to his own battles to save the party from the
Militant Tendency in the 1980s, the former party leader said, 'God
knows everybody here, no matter how old or how young, should understand the lessons, and never repeat that again. But some, for whatever
reason, are incapable of the instruction of reality, so they better wake up.'
He insisted that he would not be forced out of his own party: 'There will
be no split. There will be no retreat. Damn it, this is our party. I've been
in it sixty years. I'm not leaving it to anybody.'

Watson's talks with the unions ran from Tuesday until Saturday. The
key power-broker was Len McCluskey, the far-left boss of Unite. Watson

and McCluskey had once been flatmates. Karie Murphy, who had been on Watson's staff before she went to work for Corbyn, was close friends with the union leader. They explored the possibility of Corbyn standing down at party conference if a left-winger was guaranteed a slot on the ballot paper. But on Saturday, 9 July Watson called off the talks, saying there was 'no realistic prospect of reaching a compromise' with the now entrenched Corbyn. This action caused a rupture in his friendship with McCluskey, who said he was 'dismayed', and accused the deputy leader of 'sabotage'.

On the morning of Monday the 11th, Angela Eagle launched her leadership bid. 'I'm not a Blairite, I'm not a Brownite and I'm not a Corbynista,' she said. 'I am my own woman – a strong Labour woman.' But the same problem that had afflicted the candidates who lost to Corbyn in 2015 appeared to have infected Eagle: she failed to offer an inspiring vision to compete with Corbyn's utopian musings. When asked how she would beat a Conservative prime minister like Theresa May, she said, 'Because she's a Tory.' At 6 o'clock that evening, Owen Smith also announced that he was running.

The final throw of the dice came the following day, Tuesday, 12 July, in a seven-hour-long meeting of the NEC at which the rebels sought to get a ruling that Corbyn could not be on the ballot paper unless he secured the requisite fifty nominations from MPs – a figure the confidence motion had shown was beyond him. Corbyn's allies argued that the wording of the party rulebook meant that as leader, he was automatically entitled to fight. The meeting was long and bitter, and mired in the sort of numbing procedural arguments that Labour revels in. The first two hours were taken up with discussion about whether Andy Burnham – who had turned up to deliver a message from the shadow cabinet that a negotiated settlement was desirable – could address the meeting. The plotters became hopeful of success when the committee voted to conduct the votes by secret ballot. Corbyn faced appeals from Johanna Baxter and Alice Perry, a councillor in his Islington back yard, to back a secret ballot. A tearful Perry pleaded with him to support the motion on the grounds that she herself had faced intimidation and threats. A source who was in the room said, 'She basically talked about how she'd had a stalker, how they'd had to get him sectioned, how she was getting constant abuse about potential rape, how she was scared for her safety, and she'd heard warm words from Jeremy, but now's the time for action, and her words were something like, "Please, this is the one thing you can do, don't let me down."' But when the vote was taken Corbyn, who is seen by many as an avuncular and pleasant man, raised his hand against the secret ballot. 'I saw Jeremy's hand go up and just thought, "You bastard,"' said one NEC member.[3]

When the main discussion was reached, the two sides put forward competing legal opinions about whether Corbyn should be allowed on the ballot. Unite demanded that their QC, Michael Mansfield, be allowed into the room to address the committee. There was then a secret ballot on whether to admit more lawyers. The NEC settled against. The future of the Labour Party was effectively settled at around 7.45 p.m., when the NEC voted by eighteen votes to fourteen that Corbyn would automatically be on the ballot paper. Corbyn and Milne left the meeting and went downstairs to meet a mob of jubilant supporters waiting outside on Victoria Street. While Corbyn was gone the NEC voted to bar anyone from voting in the contest unless they had been a party member for six months, with the exception of a forty-eight-hour window in which registered supporters could sign up to vote. The cost of registering was raised from £3 to £25, to deter Trotskyite entryists and Momentum's youthful hordes. This offered some hope to the rebels, since it disenfranchised more than 150,000 new members thought to support Corbyn. In reality it was false hope. Corbyn could compete, which meant he would win. The attempted coup was over. All that remained was the counter-revolution.

The day before, Eagle's constituency office in Wallasey, Merseyside, had announced that she would face deselection, and a brick was hurled through its window. A local petition calling for her to resign had, by that point, garnered 14,000 signatures. In the previous fortnight membership of her constituency party had soared by 367, to more than 1,200.[4] An email sent to her office on 12 July read: 'If ! You become the leader of the labour party you will split it and make labour lose but also you will too have time too enjoy it, you will die your Bitch. Leave the UK … or die.'[5] A week after the NEC meeting, Eagle dropped out of the contest, bitter at the way she had been treated. She had said that she would fight on regardless, but an intervention by Yvette Cooper during hustings, warning that two rebel candidates would destroy each other rather than Corbyn, shifted the mood against her. Eagle had secured the support of seventy-two MPs, to ninety for Owen Smith.

For the next two months Smith ran a campaign that failed to catch light, tacking to the left in his efforts to portray himself as a candidate with few policy differences from Corbyn, but offering competence. It was a message that inspired neither the moderates nor defections from the Corbynistas. There were further legal challenges, with Corbyn seeking to overturn the NEC's decision to exclude those who had become party members in the previous six months. After contradictory court rulings, the decision stood. But the landscape had shifted dramatically in Corbyn's favour. In the forty-eight-hour window for registered supporters, a staggering 183,000 signed up. The moderates had a group called Saving Labour to sign up mainstream voters. They managed to round up tens of thousands of supporters, but the majority were left-wingers inspired by Corbyn.

Corbyn launched his campaign by saying that forthcoming boundary changes would mean every MP had to be selected all over again, opening the door to a purge of the rebels. Momentum activists, backed up by McCluskey, talked openly about ousting Corbyn's critics. When Owen Smith confronted Corbyn in his office in July and asked whether he was prepared to split the Labour Party, the leader refused on three occasions to say anything. John McDonnell said, 'If that's what it takes.' When McDonnell took to Twitter to deny these claims, Kate Green chipped in, 'I was in that meeting John. I heard you say it.' In public, Corbyn talked reconciliation. In private, the leader, the union boss and their acolytes held a meeting at a country house retreat in September to discuss ousting Watson and Iain McNicol, the party's general secretary. Chris Leslie's group vowed to set up their own backbench organisation, called the Clause One group, stressing Labour's commitment to the parliamentary road to socialism.

When the leadership vote was held, even Corbyn's first wife Jane Chapman voted for Smith. But on 24 September it was announced that Corbyn had won 62 per cent of the vote, 3 per cent more than the previous year. His stranglehold on the party was stronger than before.

Both David Cameron and Jeremy Corbyn contributed to the Remain campaign's loss in the EU referendum. The difference between them was that Cameron's actions were conditioned at all times by his efforts to preserve his party, whereas in the campaign and in his actions thereafter, Corbyn appeared at best careless about whether Labour would survive intact. The rebels moved against him, and two-thirds of his frontbench-ers and four out of five of his MPs declared his position untenable. 'The PLP has never done anything like this before,' one rebel leader said. 'We arranged for one person to take him on. Others put their personal ambi-tions aside for the good of the party. I'm quite proud of what we achieved.' But Corbyn had spent forty years ignoring conventional political norms, and he refused to stand down. His goal was to change the Labour Party into a nationwide movement, not to win over opponents and gain power. 'We had underestimated the degree to which the party has become a cult,' said one of the rebel leaders. 'The people who follow Jeremy are totally impervious to reason.'

Fearing the destruction of their party, some Labour MPs begged their Conservative counterparts to hold an early general election so they could be rid of Corbyn, but the leader insisted he would not quit even if Labour lost another hundred seats. Many in Labour concluded that the only way the situation would be resolved would be for Corbyn to die, since there was no way his half a million supporters would ditch him. 'The people supporting him see him as a Christ-like figure to follow,' said one Labour MP. 'If he died, those faith-based followers would not switch their allegiance to John McDonnell or Clive Lewis. There are always going to be 500,000 people in the country who are off-the-page nuts. The problem we've got is that they have all joined the Labour Party because of Jeremy Corbyn.' Another coup organiser said, 'Jeremy dying may be the only way out.'

The rebels prided themselves on a professional operation, compe-tently executed: 'In normal times it would have been incredibly effective. Tom Watson got Blair to say he was going with seven resignations. We had more than sixty. But these are not normal times. It slowly dawned on us that this man is insane, and the people around him are too. To think that you can run a political party with 172 of your colleagues having no confidence in you is insane.'

Corbyn's performance in the referendum campaign triggered pent-up sedition that for a brief moment looked as if it would bring him down. Instead, the coup and the leadership election that followed entrenched divisions in Labour from which few could see an escape. Labour's malaise was emphasised because the attempted putsch unfolded in parallel with the Conservative leadership election. While Labour was failing to oust a leader who could see his enemies coming in plain sight, the Tories were about to show the rebels how to launch a lethal strike when the victim was least expecting it, and how to pull together afterwards.

28

THE DREAM TEAM

Dominic Cummings was in the operations room of Vote Leave when Boris Johnson said, 'Come here.' It was the morning of Friday, 24 June, four hours after their referendum triumph, two hours after the prime minister had resigned. Cummings had not slept all night, and Johnson, who had managed at best an hour and a quarter of shut-eye, was tired and nervous. It was in this state of exhaustion that the two men now began talking about who should be the next prime minister. With the markets in freefall, they could have been forgiven for wondering what the prize of victory would look like. Johnson pulled Cummings into a side room and asked him whether Michael Gove was planning to run for the Conservative Party leadership. Cummings told him, 'I think the same now as I said to you three weeks ago and last weekend. I think the deal is there to be done. Michael will not run for leader, do not worry about that, that's not going to happen.' They talked a little more, and then Cummings said, 'Go downstairs and give the statement now, and when you come back up, bring Michael into this room and have the same conversation with him and talk things through.'

Gove and Cummings had had 'multiple conversations' during the campaign about the leadership, particularly after the campaign turned in Vote Leave's favour in late May. Early in June Gove said to Cummings, 'We might actually win this thing. It's going to be a nightmare for me, because a whole bunch of people say I should stand against Boris.' The same day, out on the road, Gove had a very similar conversation with Henry Cook. Gove himself appeared reluctant to stand, but was concerned that others would say Johnson was not up to the job. His special advisers, particularly Henry Newman, wanted Gove to run.

Cummings was more cautious. He told Gove, 'I think we are going to win, and I think the best thing to do would be for you to make a deal with Boris.' A reflective Gove replied, 'Yes.'

Johnson then cornered Cummings and sounded him out on whether Gove would support him around two weeks before polling day. It was the first time in the campaign that he had ever raised the leadership issue. Johnson asked, 'Do you think Michael will run for the leader? What do you think Gove's going to do?' Based on his conversations with Gove, Cummings replied, 'He will not run for leader, and my advice for him is he should support you. I think if you're sensible, you should make him chancellor and you should put him in charge of civil service reform as well, because if you're going to deliver on victory, then you're going to have to tear up the Whitehall machine. Him, me, our whole team have thought a lot about this, and we know how to do it, and there's going to be a revolution.'

The issue came up for a third time on the Sunday before the referendum. Gove went to Johnson's house in Islington, ostensibly to discuss 'what would happen if we did win'. Johnson's allies say the meeting was arranged at Gove's instigation. Both sides understood the leadership would come up. Gove said he would bring Cummings with him, so Johnson asked Will Walden to attend as well. Gove and Cummings had a drink in a pub around the corner from Johnson's home before they met Boris. Cummings left the pub completely clear that Gove would not run for leader, but would instead support Johnson.

In what was the second fateful meeting in Johnson's house between the two men, Marina Wheeler drifted in and out with snacks as they talked. Johnson asked, 'If we won and it were that Dave had to step down, would you run?' According to Johnson's advisers, Gove replied, 'I'd be minded not to.' He did not say definitively that he would not run, but his position seemed clear.

Most of the conversation was about the logistics of referendum night, and how they would handle the aftermath. But Cummings also made it clear that he had no desire to interact with MPs and would sit out a leadership contest, but was prepared to work with a new government if he could square his wife Mary, who had just given birth to their first child. The four also discussed how they could make Brexit work for Britain. Gove, heavily influenced by Cummings, was of the view that the apparatus of central government would need to be completely overhauled. He wanted to see an end to the power of Sir Jeremy Heywood, the cabinet secretary, and also sought to impress upon Johnson that a post-Brexit prime minister should not allow the Foreign Office, which was institutionally pro-Brussels, to dictate the terms on which the UK left the European Union.

'The point was made that if this was going to work, we would need to think very seriously about reforming the way in which the civil service operated and make some big changes about the way in which government went about its existence,' says a source familiar with the discussions. 'We couldn't accept the world according to Jeremy Heywood and the approach the civil service had always taken to these things. And we couldn't negotiate on the basis of what the Foreign Office thought would be a good deal.'

After their post-Brexit press conference on the Friday morning, Johnson pulled Gove into the same side room upstairs in which he had quizzed Cummings, and put his cards on the table. He wanted Gove's support in the leadership election that Cameron had now triggered. In a moment of low farce, Johnson had just commenced his courtship when the door opened and Chris Grayling burst into the room. Gove said, 'It was a bit like you're making a move on your girlfriend – or your girlfriend's making a move on you – and then suddenly, "Hello, it's Giles Gooseberry here!"' Grayling clocked what was going on, and said in his trademark deadpan, 'I don't know what you're talking about.' Then he fled. Alone with Gove again, Johnson worked through his pitch. Gove said, 'I'm pretty certain I'm going to back you, but I just need to think about this over the next twenty-four hours.' Cummings then poked his head around the door. Gove and Johnson both smiled. 'Yes, it's all agreed. We'll speak tomorrow night.'

Throughout Friday, Gove had come under intense pressure from close allies to run for the leadership himself. His advisers Henry Cook, Beth Armstrong and particularly Henry Newman urged him to throw his hat in the ring. Dominic Raab, who had worked with him at the Ministry of Justice, was keen, and Gove also took calls that weekend from three cabinet ministers urging him to stand. He told them, 'No, I'm going to back Boris.' Gove will not name them, but all three eventually ended up supporting Theresa May, remained in the cabinet, and are doing different jobs at the time of publication from those they did before. If you include Priti Patel, who attended cabinet as employment minister, seven people meet those criteria. The other six are Liz Truss, Amber Rudd, Greg Clark, Sajid Javid, Justine Greening and Patrick McLoughlin.

The most vociferous advocate of a Gove campaign was Nick Boles. The business minister, who had set up the modernisers' favourite think tank Policy Exchange years before, viewed Gove as the intellectual and moral heart of the modern Conservative Party. Just as importantly, he had recently decided that he was committed to stopping Johnson becoming prime minister. If he had not contracted cancer in 2007, Boles would have been the Conservative candidate for London mayor in 2008. His health forced him to withdraw from the race, paving the way for Boris. Restored to full fitness, Boles then helped with Johnson's transition to power, becoming his first chief of staff in City Hall. It was a chaotic and unhappy period for both men, one characterised by a lack of focus from the mayor and a series of public relations disasters that led to the resignation of several key personnel. Johnson had eventually got a grip on the levers of power and won plaudits in Conservative circles for building a strong team. But Boles remembered the worst of Boris.

Boles was a Remainer, and had 'blazing rows' with Gove during the campaign, but both had worked hard to maintain their friendship. Boles concluded, 'The things I admire most in a politician are principle, courage and consistency, which is why I admire Michael more than anyone else.' He acknowledged that Johnson was ideologically 'my kind of Tory', and that he had shown courage by backing Brexit, but felt Johnson was deficient in the other two characteristics.

Boles spent part of Friday morning 'crying' at the referendum result, and after Cameron's resignation 'throwing things at the wall', but then called Gove and said, 'You know, you should run. I'm going to put a lot of effort into persuading you to run.' Gove said he was '99 per cent against – I think Boris is good and he's a good Brexiter'. Boles had always seen his friend as not 'front of house', but believed the referendum campaign had changed him. 'His sense of himself has grown,' he told a mutual friend. 'He can see himself as a wholly independent company, whereas previously he was an almost wholly owned subsidiary of the Dave and George show.' But Gove stood his ground and instead mapped out a different role, which Boles was to characterise as a 'midfield play-maker to Boris's Cristiano Ronaldo'. Gove agreed to sleep on it.

The following morning, Saturday, 25 June, Gove called Johnson and said, 'I will support you.' He had been impressed with Boris during the campaign, and felt he had matured as a politician – as one Gove ally put it, Johnson had become an '*homme sérieux*'. They had fought together in adversity, and won. It seemed the logical next step to keep the partner-ship together. 'I think Boris did a great job during the referendum campaign itself,' Gove said. 'He knuckled down, performed well. It was a revelation. The other thing, to be fair to him, and lots of people remarked on it, was he was much nicer to people at every level than other politicians of his seniority are. He was genuinely considerate.'

The campaign had highlighted Johnson's campaigning verve, and Gove had been impressed by his ability to connect with voters. During their time on the road together, sharing unglamorous hotels, the two had bonded. 'Michael liked Boris a lot more at the end of the campaign,' a friend said. In one charmingly eccentric moment on the battlebus they were on the road with Joey Essex, a reality television star from *The Only Way is Essex*. When Essex's catchphrase 'Well reem' was mentioned, Johnson 'looked totally perplexed' according to a campaign official. 'What the hell is this?' he asked. At which point Gove, of all people, displayed the broad reach of his cultural hinterland and launched into a learned explanation of Essex-man argot.

Nick Boles called Gove on Saturday morning. Despite his doubts about Johnson, he felt that the most painful thing about the referendum campaign had been his split from Gove and had decided, 'I'm not doing that again.' He asked Gove whether his view of Johnson had changed during the campaign, and Gove replied, 'Yes, a lot.' He went on to describe how Johnson had been disciplined, taken advice and knuckled down during the debate prep. Boles agreed to 'tuck in behind' and said, 'Whatever you decide to do, I'll do with you.' When Gove said he would back Johnson, Boles told him, 'You need to talk tough with Boris. You need to basically say, "I'm going to back you and I'm going to get you the job" – but you know, Michael, you need to be the intellectual steerer of the government.'

Having made up his mind, Gove held a summit at midday on Saturday at Dominic Cummings' home in Islington with Cook, Newman,

Armstrong, Henry de Zoete and Paul Stephenson from Vote Leave. He told them, 'I've told Boris I'm not going to run.' The news was met with incredulity by de Zoete, who said, 'What are you doing? You've used your only negotiating chip.' A nonplussed Gove replied, 'Yes, but I don't want to run.' Another voice chipped in: 'Have you not made any demands?' 'No, no, no. I'm not going to run.' The special advisers then told him he should stand. After a while Stephenson, the outsider of the group, intervened, telling the others, 'If Michael says he doesn't want to run, don't force it. You can't force someone to become prime minister.'

While this was going on, Gove's wife Sarah Vine was on the sofa watching television. Contrary to the picture that was to develop of her as a Lady Macbeth figure egging on her husband, she was not pressing him to stand at this point. One of those present remembers her saying, 'I don't want to live in the Number 10 flat.' As the source put it, 'I think she oscillated like he did. Part of her was not up for it at all.' Others are clear, though, that she believed her husband was every bit as talented as Cameron and Osborne, and that it was time he showed them he was not their chattel. Emily Sheffield, Samantha Cameron's sister, was later to claim that Vine had envisaged Gove as Cameron's successor three years earlier.

Cummings, it is widely assumed, was also an advocate of Gove running. Certainly some at Vote Leave believed his game plan throughout the referendum campaign was both to win and to secure the premiership for his old boss. But those who know him best say this caricature is wrong, and that he was always more circumspect than the other special advisers. Stephenson, who spent most time with him during the campaign, thinks Cummings had 'massive reservations about it', though he believes that in 'several heart to hearts' with Gove during the campaign Cummings did 'try to talk him into it'. But when Cummings and Stephenson sat down to discuss the leadership two weeks before the referendum, they agreed that a Boris–Gove 'dream ticket thing is the way to do it'. A source close to Cummings said, 'It was completely clear before the last four weeks and during the last four weeks that there was no [Gove] leadership campaign to do.'

The key for Cummings, and Gove's other aides, was to deliver on the radical reform agenda they had mapped out. The most important element was Cummings' desire to 'blow up the current civil service system', which he believed was, 'like the EU, programmed to fail'. Explaining his vision,

Cummings said, 'It keeps out great people, it hoards power to a small number of people who are increasingly crap. And the management of the whole thing is increasingly farcical, like that of any closed bureaucracy keeping its perks. It cannot manage public services, it cannot deal with counter-terrorism, it's programmed to fail – and it does.' He believed Brexit would 'force people to think about these things rather than being in the brain-dead stupor they have been in for the last twenty years, where Whitehall just thinks about being in a Brussels meeting'.

Team Gove wanted to know that Johnson would adopt this agenda, and agree to Gove's team helping to run the operation. The problem was, in the heat of the moment Gove had offered his support to Johnson without securing any commitments to the policy agenda he wanted, still less to drafting in the personnel he believed would be necessary to win the leadership election and run the government. Team Gove would spend much of the next four days seeking to make good that omission, with mixed results. Later that week much would be made of the chaos surrounding Johnson's leadership challenge, but at its inception it was Gove's role which was chaotic.

On that same Saturday after the referendum Johnson played cricket at the home of his Oxford friend Earl Spencer, brother of Diana, Princess of Wales. The two had been close friends at Oxford, and the match was a regular fixture in the diaries of both families. Johnson's allies regarded it as a chance for some valuable 'decompression' before the big battle ahead. Later, some of Gove's allies saw a man too keen to play when there was serious work to be done. Ahead of the game, Johnson's team briefed journalists that he would use the day to make a formal decision about whether he was going to run for the leadership. This was greeted with hilarity by lobby journalists who had been chronicling Boris's remorseless progress towards the job for eight years. In fact it was an accurate description, because Johnson that day was a troubled man who was torn between his long-standing ambition, the weight of expectation surrounding the future of Brexit Britain, and the stress that leadership would place on his family.

Over lunch Johnson got talking to a woman who confided details of the conversation to a Conservative minister at a fundraising event the following weekend: 'You wouldn't believe what happened to me last weekend. I went along to this cricket match at Earl Spencer's. Over lunch,

I couldn't believe it, he turned to me and said, "Well, what do you think I should do?"' The minister said, 'It became clear at lunch Boris hadn't come to any decision about what he should be doing. He asked her about leaving the EU and about running for the leadership. She said that everybody was surprised Boris was there at all, but what was really surprising was the level of unpreparedness for this outcome. He was genuinely asking her opinion about what he should do.' The 'most extraordinary thing', the woman claimed, was what happened next. Boris's wife Marina 'leant over from the other side and said, "We really don't want him to run. And he hasn't even decided if he's going to."'

Johnson's allies have not disputed this account, but they say his concerns were the natural by-product of a big decision that they had no doubt he would take. 'I think his attitude was, "I campaigned for this, I've got to go for it,"' one friend said. 'I think Marina was understanding of that and supportive of it, and it was no more than an obvious concern of a professional mother and wife about the impact it might have on their children.' A second ally has suggested that one of Johnson's daughters also had concerns about the level of media intrusion that running for the leadership would bring.

That evening Johnson, Gove, Cummings and Johnson's spin doctor Will Walden had a conference call during which Gove outlined the price of his support: the post of chancellor and chief Brexit negotiator. Despite admitting that he didn't have any special economic expertise, he said it was important to him to be part of the central axis of the government, and that meant being in the Treasury.

Trying to make up for his initial failure to get firm assurances from Johnson, Gove now issued what even one of his allies called 'this whole ridiculous list of demands'. He said, 'I don't think Dominic should come to the Treasury with me, I think Dominic should go and work with you in Number 10.' The implication was that he wanted Cummings to become Downing Street chief of staff, with Paul Stephenson becoming Number 10's communications director – the same post he had held in Vote Leave. Walden, who had been Johnson's spin doctor for four years, was affronted, and Johnson spoke up for his own team: 'Hang on a minute, I have some talented people. I think we need to just hold off on that at the minute.' A Johnson ally said, 'Boris held firm except for agreeing in principle to the chancellor stuff.' It was also agreed that Gove would chair Johnson's leadership campaign. The following day, according to Gove's account, Boris called him up and said he was 'terribly sorry', but Gove had to be co-chair of the campaign with Ben Wallace. Johnson's camp say that was agreed in the call on Saturday.

On the Saturday night Cummings wrote an email summing up what had been agreed on the call. The message, entitled 'BoGo future – summary of discussion last night and a few random thoughts', was sent at 11.18 the following morning. In the light of what happened later, it is telling that Cummings wrote: 'important [there is] clear agreement from the start so you don't get cross with each other down the line'. The key line was 'MG to be chancellor, overseeing the renegotiation process and in charge of civil service reform. Key appointments to be agreed between Boris and MG.' It went on: 'Change the Number 10 and 11 system so it's essentially one team, not two rival power centres. There will be huge resistance from officials. One of the crucial jobs is to figure this out before getting in, so you can smash through changes fast.' It also said: 'Dom to go to No. 10 with Boris,' but went on to stress that Cummings' wife Mary was 'hostile', and that he would not take any part in the leadership campaign beyond giving informal advice, and that any move to Downing Street would depend on winning her around. The email also talked about the comms team, suggesting, 'Paul Stephenson should be comms director of the leadership campaign then take over in No. 10 … You won't get someone better to handle the media. Will W would, obviously, keep doing Boris's personal stuff. He and PS worked v well together in the campaign and this is a natural fit.'

The email compounded some concerns that Walden already had about Cummings' approach. Cummings' unsuccessful attempt to ban ITV from Friday's press conference had also left Johnson 'pretty appalled'. When the email arrived on the Sunday, Walden texted Johnson and said, 'Don't let them park their tanks on your lawn.' They had a conversation in which Walden raised the issue of whether chancellor and Brexit negotiator was too much for one person to take on, but Johnson replied, 'That's the deal I've done.' Walden said, 'That's the only thing you've agreed to, and that's the only thing you should agree to at this stage.'

While Saturday evening's four-way conference call had been going on, the rest of Team Gove went to a pub for 'a proper drink' and karaoke. Later, Stephenson spoke to Cummings, who was at home looking after his new baby, and asked, 'What happened with the call, was it all good?'

Cummings said, 'Yeah it's all good, Boris basically agrees with it all.' Stephenson was immediately suspicious. It all seemed too easy. 'That doesn't sound like a proper conversation to me,' he said. After the drama had played out, Stephenson said, 'I remember sitting there thinking, it's got massive hubris around it. Everyone's emotionally, physically knackered.' The next twenty-four hours would prove him right.

Stephenson thought Walden's irritation at the prospect that he might become Craig Oliver's replacement in Downing Street was 'totally understandable'. When he heard about the conversation, Stephenson pitched an arrangement whereby Walden would speak for Boris while he concentrated on the kind of strategic communications planning for the government that he did at Vote Leave. 'I didn't want to fall out with Will,' he said. 'He's Boris's guy, and we'd worked well together. He was interested in delivery and how to make Boris look good. I thought that could work well. I did also say I'd be equally happy to work under him, but the whole thing was badly done.'

On Sunday Johnson's campaign team from the Commons – Ben Wallace, Jake Berry, Amanda Milling and Nigel Adams – visited him at his Oxfordshire home in Thame. They intended to discuss hiring office space and plans to 'beef up' his Commons campaign team to include a wider range of lieutenants from different parliamentary intakes. Johnson's decision to back Brexit had hurt him with some one-nation pro-Europeans, but Wallace and Berry were confident he had gained parliamentary support throughout the campaign. From Friday, text messages had begun to flood in from MPs, including one Remain cabinet minister, looking to support Johnson for the leadership.

'That weekend was pre-planned, whether it had been a close thing or whether we'd won, for Boris to have some time to decompress,' a source said. Gove had not originally been invited to Thame, but he called Johnson and said he was coming with his special advisers. On their way to Oxfordshire, Henry Cook called Walden to ask if there were television cameras present. Walden said there were, but that he was going to do a deal with the broadcasters. Boris would do a 'walking shot' so they had some footage of him, after which they would leave. Cook still seemed on edge. 'Is there any way of coming in the back way?' he asked. Walden felt this was over the top, but the cameras had departed by the time Gove's team arrived.

The two sides had a long discussion about what needed to be done. There was also a conversation, to which everyone contributed, about Johnson's Monday column for the *Daily Telegraph*, in which he was to outline what he wanted from a Brexit deal. But there were immediate tensions between those who had been working for Johnson for years, who began to feel that Gove, with Cummings in the background, wanted to take over, and Gove's special advisers, who thought Johnson's retainers were not good enough. 'All three of them were horrified at how amateurish things were,' one of Team Gove said. 'Ben, Nigel, Amanda and Jake had all been working on Boris's leadership campaign for over a year. So we expected, perhaps naïvely, that a far greater degree of care and thought had gone into it.' Another Gove aide said that weekend, 'Lots of other MPs are not keen on that gang. They don't see them as the A-Team that you'd expect an incoming PM to have around him.'

There was certainly a cultural clash. Gove's team were all young, whip-smart and intense; they came armed with laptops. As anyone who has worked with Johnson would confirm, his staff found the way to get the best out of him was to build a family unit around him, in which he felt comfortable. Discussion was less ordered, more free-flowing. In the civil war that erupted four days later, Gove's people were the Roundheads, Wallace and co. the Cavaliers. Team Gove were unnerved that Johnson and his team spent too much time horsing around by the barbecue, rather than knuckling down to the serious business of planning the leadership election. They later suggested to journalists that the MPs were drinking, though all four were driving, and said they barely touched a drop. Gove's advisers were also surprised that Johnson's MPs did not have what they judged to be a comprehensive list of supporters detailing when and by whom they had been recruited. For their part, Wallace and co. saw a bunch of young advisers who might know about spreadsheets, but who did not understand MPs, or anything about how to get the best out of Boris Johnson. Cook, Armstrong and Newman were quickly dubbed 'the terrible trio'.

Tensions were clearest over who should actually run the campaign. Gove pressed the case of his team, but Johnson made it clear that he had been talking to Lynton Crosby, and that his firm CTF would be coming in to run the mechanics of the campaign. In his email that morning, Cummings had said, 'You need to let others know what his [Crosby's] role will be because people will want to know they are not being undercut.'

Another factor that unnerved Gove and sowed suspicion about Team Johnson was a report on the front page of that morning's *Sunday Times* which was the first to reveal that Gove had called Johnson the day before to offer his backing. The report came as 'a surprise' to both Gove and Henry Cook, who assumed either Walden or Wallace was responsible. In fact the detail of the phone call was texted to the author on the Saturday by a member of Gove's circle following the noon summit at Cummings' house. But the effect of the story was to forestall any further discussion about Gove running for the leadership himself. Some think Gove would have been better to bide his time and consider his options. 'The briefing that went to you that weekend was a mistake in strategic terms,' one Gove ally said two weeks later.

The distrust flowed the other way when, as they all sat down to lunch, Walden got a text from a close friend at the BBC saying that Sarah Vine had tipped the broadcaster off that her husband was having lunch with Johnson, and they were sending their camera crew back to the cottage. Vine had told them where her husband was, to get them off her doorstep in Ladbroke Grove. Walden showed Gove the message. He 'looked horrified'. Walden then suggested that if the cameras were returning, Johnson and Gove should do a joint statement. Cook vetoed the plan as liable to be a disaster without preparation. Walden says he was testing Team Gove. Remembering Cook's nervousness about the cameras, he said, 'Maybe you should go, if you're so concerned about it.' Another who was present says, 'It almost seemed like they were reluctant to get up and go. They wanted to be caught there.' Later, when the two sides fell out so spectacularly, Gove remarked that this version of events was outrageous, as 'the cameras were already there'.

By the time the barbecue wound down, little had been definitively decided. When Paul Stephenson spoke to Henry Newman that morning he had asked, 'Is this actually going to happen, am I actually going to be director of comms?' Newman had replied, 'Yeah, it's all sorted out.' Stephenson went to discuss with his wife what that might mean. But in the afternoon he had a conversation with Beth Armstrong, and the mood had changed. 'It's not going well,' she said. 'Lynton's going to run it, not us. It's not a Vote Leave thing. This is not what we agreed. Boris's people are being a nightmare.'

Johnson finished his *Telegraph* column, and it was emailed to Gove at 5.29 p.m. He made four suggested tweaks to the text, but pronounced it 'overall very, very good'. However, the piece had been written hastily, and it created confusion the following day, since it seemed to advocate both membership of the single market and the maintenance of freedom of movement, which many regarded as mutually contradictory. Eurosceptics saw it as evidence that Johnson was backsliding on his commitment to full Brexit, Remainers as proof that instead of facing up to his responsibilities as a leading Brexiteer, he still wanted to have his cake on Europe and eat it. Given that the column was the first statement any senior figure from Vote Leave had made after a weekend of silence, both sides ought to have given it more attention. Johnson was no longer writing as a journalist, but as a potential prime minister, and the piece ought to have been subjected to line-by-line scrutiny. But if Gove had spotted these problems – and he had ample time and opportunity to point them out – he did not say so. Walden was reduced to briefing journalists that Johnson had been tired.

Monday brought further teething troubles. The *Daily Telegraph* reported that George Osborne had been offered the job of foreign secretary to join the Dream Team – a claim that enraged the Johnson camp.[1] *The Times* and the *Sun* had also heard the suggestion. Boris and Gove had discussed Osborne before the barbecue. Gove was keen to have the backing of his old friend, while Johnson was concerned about how it would look to have the chancellor and some of his closest acolytes on board. According to one account, Johnson said, 'Obviously it'll be helpful to have his support, but I don't think we should be offering people jobs.' Gove apparently agreed: 'You're absolutely right, we shouldn't be making any commitments to anybody at this stage.'

Johnson, his team and even most of Gove's advisers were 'very vehemently' against offering anything to Osborne, who they saw as damaged goods, with Eurosceptics still furious at the emergency budget stunt. MPs who had been overlooked for promotion under the Cameron–Osborne ascendancy would run a mile if they thought the old oligarchy was being recreated with Boris at its head. 'They'd had a private discussion about securing George's support, but Boris was very clear he didn't want to make any offers to George,' a friend of Johnson said. 'He didn't want him near government. Boris had had no conversation with George, and adamantly refused to offer him foreign secretary. But the next morning the foreign secretary offer to Osborne was in the papers.'

Gove and Osborne confirm that they did speak that weekend, but both say their conversation was primarily of the 'Politics is a funny old game, isn't it?' variety. However, those who spent time with Gove that weekend say the conversation was much more substantive. 'On the Saturday morning Michael had a call from George saying, "I've always wanted to move to foreign secretary, I'd be happy to be foreign secretary,"' a source said. A second member of Gove's circle added, 'George went straight to Michael and tried to get Michael to lobby for him. Michael did lobby for him.' According to this account, Osborne also told Gove that as the senior Brexiteer he needed to make peace with Mark Carney, citing an attack advert on the governor of the Bank of England by Vote Leave during the campaign. Gove said the video had been put out by 'one of our Labour supporters'.

At the suggestion that the chancellor should be signed up, Dominic Cummings 'went mental', saying, 'Osborne should be dropped down the hole, good riddance. What are you thinking about? Shut up.' The email Cummings wrote on the Sunday morning contained the line, 'George Osborne: You'd be mad, mad, mad to make him foreign secretary. He's toxic,' a line that strongly suggests the issue had already been discussed.

Team Boris believed Gove or one of his people had briefed the *Telegraph*: 'Obviously what happened is Gove offered him the job, and they were keen to push that out.' It is equally possible that an ally of Osborne had done so to make him appear in demand. But Walden spent Monday fending off press enquiries and seeking to kill the story. Wallace, Berry and the team of MPs also tried to convince colleagues it was untrue. A Johnson ally says, 'That did damage to Boris because there were many who felt, certainly on the Brexit side, that Osborne was toast. There were many who felt on the Remain side that he couldn't possibly stay after his warnings. That did do a great deal of damage, because it looked like a continuation of the past.'

Osborne came under attack for disappearing from public view that first weekend – headlines asking 'Where's George?' were plentiful – but the chancellor was working hard to stabilise the economy, as well as considering his own leadership options. 'George genuinely felt a responsibility to hit the phones and speak with every finance minister and central bank around the world,' an aide says. 'He had to get on and reassure them. There was a perception around the world we'd crashed out of the EU overnight.'

The government had done a great deal of contingency planning on how to prevent another banking collapse, but since they had made no preparations for what Brexit would look like, the idea was got up in the media that they were unprepared. Osborne spoke to Mark Carney at around 5 o'clock on the morning of the referendum result, and they spoke another three or four times that day. He also convened a meeting of Treasury officials, most of whom had not slept, early that morning. Osborne and Carney had met earlier that week and the week before to go over the plan. It came in two parts. The first was to provide market liquidity if sterling became unavailable in the market. A 'swap line' was agreed with the US Federal Reserve. Also put in place were contingencies if an individual investment bank or fund got into trouble. The rules governing what funds a bank needed to hold were relaxed. 'What there was not was the contingency plan for full Brexit – it would have been impossible to do,' says a Treasury official. 'We modelled the scenarios, but producing a roadmap and a detailed plan would have been impossible.'

Osborne judged that because both Cameron and Carney made public statements on Friday, 24 June, he did not need to. He finally made a public statement on the following Monday, in which he offered assurances that the UK was 'about as strong as it could be to confront the challenge' of leaving the EU. The markets briefly stopped falling while he spoke, and then continued their downward trend, the FTSE 100 slipping below 6,000 points. Osborne believed the media carping was orchestrated by Eurosceptics. 'They are Brexit people who are trying to knock me because of a looming leadership contest,' he told aides.

Some of Osborne's closest friends believe he might have done better to stand down as chancellor at the same time as Cameron announced his resignation, since it would have saved him the humiliation of being fired later. 'He'd have been better falling on his sword,' one said. But Osborne saw that as 'walking away from the battlefield'. The only question was whether he should run for the leadership himself.

From the Friday morning, the chancellor's team – including his parliamentary private secretary Chris Skidmore and ministerial allies like Greg Hands, Matt Hancock and the whip Julian Smith – took soundings. They all found colleagues who were prepared to back Osborne but were of the view that he should not throw his hat into the ring. 'People were phoning up to say, "Of course we'll support him if he stands, but we don't think he can win." The irony is that the number of people who called would have been enough,' says one ally. Up to a dozen senior ministers offered encouragement: 'He had quite a big chunk of the cabinet telling him to do it, despite the result and the role he played.' But while other candidates could run to position themselves for the future or get a better job, Osborne could only do so if he thought he had a realistic prospect of victory. With the Dream Team in place and home secretary Theresa May organising fast, there was a danger he would finish third and seem a diminished figure.

There followed a series of meetings in 11 Downing Street, some involving Osborne's advisers Thea Rogers, Eleanor Shawcross and James Chapman. On the Saturday morning they decided not to make a final decision until Monday, but the most substantive discussions came on the Sunday. Those present say people did not take sides. 'That's not the nature of discussions with him, everyone does pros and cons,' one said. The consensus was that Osborne would easily get fifty to sixty supporters, perhaps more. Chris Skidmore said, 'I think I can get you up to one hundred votes, boss, but people don't think you should do it.' Osborne told them, 'I don't want to run and lose. I don't mind running and nearly winning, but I've been too partisan in the debate.' He was also aware that leadership elections are not always about the number of people supporting you – a second factor is the number of enemies you have accumulated who are determined to stop you at all costs. According to sources present at the meetings, Osborne was aware that he had 'a massive accumulation of enemies'. 'I think I can get a lot of votes,' he concluded. 'But not enough.'

By the time he made his speech on the Monday, Osborne knew he was not standing. 'He didn't want to announce it then, because he wanted the top line of the announcement to be about steadying the markets,' a minister said. Osborne made his decision public on the Tuesday. With the exception of Andrea Leadsom, all the other runners and riders were in touch with him, and aides confirm he would have been happy to stay on if offered the right job. 'I think he thought the Foreign Office would have worked without direct involvement in Brexit negotiations. He signalled, by getting on with the job, that he was up for staying on.'

But the job he had been working towards was gone. When one friend asked him on the Tuesday how he was, Osborne replied, 'Well, we've just withdrawn from the EU and I've just withdrawn from the leadership, but other than that I'm fine.'

On Monday night Gove invited his team to dinner at his home. This time they were joined by Dougie Smith, a long-time Conservative fixer. After the previous day's débâcle at Thame, Gove wanted to 'chew the fat'. It was a social occasion with no agenda and minimal focus. The group again discussed the need for a radical overhaul of the civil service, how best to run a government, and who should get the jobs, all issues that should have been resolved on Saturday evening. But Gove was 'in a bad place', according to a source present, saying things like, 'I can't be the chancellor and negotiator and lead civil service reform.' Dominic Cummings tried to reassure him: 'You don't have to be, you can appoint good people, but you need to have a say in this.' But Gove said, 'Well, I'm not sure I want to be chancellor.'

Dougie Smith urged him to dig in: 'You've got to make sure you've got key Vote Leave people on board, because you need your people in there. You need to be fighting for these people. You're important.' The same point was made by the others: 'Michael, think what you're asking for. You're important in all this.' Gove said he was concerned that he was demanding too much from Boris: 'I don't think I should be asking for all these things.' But the special advisers told him to stand firm.

In the end Smith suggested the way forward – a meeting of the Dream Team's mafia dons: 'You need to take Dom, because he's your consigliere, and Lynton is Boris's consigliere, and you basically need to have a meeting, the four of you, and have a chat about it all.' Cummings agreed: 'If you want me to go, I'll come.'

Listening to all this was Sarah Vine, who resolved to stiffen her husband's spine. The following morning she would write an email, urging him to pin Johnson down and get his agreement, which was to enjoy a wider readership than she intended. The email, sent first thing on Tuesday, read:

> Very important that we focus on the individual obstacles and thoroughly overcome them before moving to the next. I really think Michael needs to have a Henry or a Beth with him for this morning's crucial meetings.

One simple message: you MUST have SPECIFIC [sic] from Boris OTHERWISE you cannot guarantee your support. The details can be worked out later on, but without that you have no leverage.

Crucially, the membership will not have the necessary reassurance to back Boris, neither will Dacre/Murdoch, who instinctively dislike Boris but trust your ability enough to support a Boris Gove ticket.

Do not concede any ground. Be your stubborn best.
GOOD LUCK.

Vine was not – as some in the media assumed at the time – questioning Johnson's commitment to giving her husband a job, an issue that had been resolved at the weekend. The issue she thought Gove ought to clarify was Johnson's undertakings about how the government would operate if they were to win the keys to Downing Street – 'that Boris wouldn't import into Number 10 a team of people and an approach that did not match the challenge of the hour'. Gove wanted assurances that Johnson understood 'that we need to make sure we change the way the civil service operates', that 'we're not accepting what the Foreign Office offer us as their menu of options', and that 'you can't simply promote and prefer on the basis of who said what to whom during the leadership election'.

Vine tapped in the names of her husband's advisers in the address section of the email, but instead of Henry Newman she copied in a public relations man called Tom Newman, who specialised in fashion and had sent her a couple of emails in the past. If this was a deliberate attempt to leak the message, it was a bizarrely convoluted one. Henry Cook noticed the mistake, and called Vine to ask who 'Tom Newman' was. When they Googled him they quickly found his Twitter feed, which suggested that he was sympathetic to Jeremy Corbyn. Cook knew at once that this was potentially bad news. But, in a move that later fuelled suspicion among the Boris camp, Team Gove did not let them know what had happened. 'We hoped it wouldn't come out,' one said.

Vine's email was designed to stiffen her husband's spine, and to push him and his campaign manager into a closer understanding. In the end, the furore it caused would drive them further apart.

*   *   *

On Tuesday morning, following Dougie Smith's suggestion, Johnson and Gove went to meet Lynton Crosby and his business partner Mark Fullbrook at the Mayfair offices of their firm CTF Partners. This meeting later became another point of controversy between the two camps. Gove says he texted Crosby on the Monday night to say that Dominic Cummings would be accompanying him. But the message had not reached Fullbrook or Ben Wallace, who was surprised to find the Vote Leave man waiting when he arrived. Given that Cummings had pledged to sit out the leadership campaign, they found this surprising and irritating. For his part, Gove had no idea that Wallace would be present. The original idea had been just him and Johnson, with one aide each. Given that Wallace was the co-chair of the campaign it seems reasonable for him to have been there, but the mutual antagonisms pointed to a campaign that was in some difficulty after just three days.

Gove explained that while Cummings would sit out the campaign, he had been asked to do some work on how a revamped Downing Street would work. Cummings outlined how a Brexit government would need to bring in good people from outside the civil service to run the renegotiation, and to have far more appointees from the world of business to help run Whitehall.

In any leadership election, as the old adage goes, 'The most important thing is learning to count'. This was a lesson British politicians like Michael Gove and George Osborne had learned from Robert Caro's masterful multi-volume biography of Lyndon Johnson, a canonical text for the Cameroons. LBJ was probably the canniest legislator of twentieth-century American politics, and he knew how to line up votes. On the Monday Team Gove began to probe Boris Johnson's numbers, and concluded that he had much to learn from his American namesake. 'We asked them how sure they could be of the allegiance of some of the MPs they had on board,' said Gove, 'and it became clear some of the conversations they were relying on were conversations that couldn't be relied on from third or fourth hand. From my time in the whips' office, you cannot rely on someone till you've spoken to someone yourself and got them to come out publicly – and sometimes even then you cannot be sure. But the basics simply hadn't been done.' Nick Boles was also suspicious, believing there was 'not much substance to their numbers'. Gove was surprised to discover that little thought had been given to acquiring a campaign office or a treasurer. The response from Team Johnson was, 'Oh, Lynton will fix that.'

Ben Wallace had served in the whips' office at the same time as Gove. His approach to the leadership contest from the beginning had been 'low-key and loyal', which meant avoiding strong-arming MPs in the tea room. If Team Gove had been expecting more detailed whipping data, it is also true to say that the team Wallace had built were further down the tracks than Theresa May's operation, who were racing to get established over the weekend. On the Monday evening the Wallace–Berry team got a group of Johnson's supporters together in his parliamentary office in the Norman Shaw Building to plan the whipping operation. Those present included Conor Burns, James Wharton and Chris Pincher, who had acted as an unofficial rebel whip during the Tory rebellion over House of Lords reform. Burns said, 'I'm really pleased Chris has arrived. We absolutely need to get a grip on the canvassing exercise, because when you're whipping or canvassing Tory colleagues, you don't canvass them once, you have to have multiple approaches from multiple people. It's check and countercheck.' He also pointed out that the Lords rebellion team had a 'sleeper agent' who 'pretended to be vehemently opposed to Lords reform, who was then talking to colleagues we had down as supportive to check whether they were solid or not'. Wallace and team 'divvied up' the parliamentary party based on who knew who. They agreed to meet the following day. For all their concerns about the whipping operation, Gove's people were absent from this meeting. A Johnson ally said, 'They were nowhere to be seen on the Monday night. It was Boris's troops – about thirty – who were working out who to speak to. We had the list, we had the names.'

Michael Gove and Nick Boles also spent Monday recruiting new outriders. One of them was Oliver Dowden, who had been a political adviser to David Cameron in Number 10 before becoming MP for Hertsmere in 2015. He was also close to Gove. He saw Johnson as a colourful figurehead who had shown in London that he could build a strong team, and with the right support could be a transformative prime minister. Dowden also believed the new prime minister would need to be a Brexiteer to sell the inevitable compromises to the electorate and the party. But he was under strong pressure from his close friend Gavin Williamson, Cameron's former PPS who had gone to work for Theresa May, to back the home secretary. On the Monday morning he was talking to Gove on the phone when his wife, Blythe, put a note under his nose which said, 'Don't do it, go for Theresa.' But by then he had agreed to join the Dream Team.

Dowden attended his first meeting in Gove's House of Commons office on the Tuesday afternoon. Other new recruits included the justice minister Dominic Raab, the schools minister Nick Gibb, Gove's PPS Robert Jenrick, and Rishi Sunak, the MP who had refused to see Cameron when he decided to back Brexit.

By then, after forty-eight hours of squabbling, a deal had been done to merge the database of MPs overseen by Jake Berry with the list of those who had been approached and signed up by Gove's people. 'There was a huge bust-up,' says a Johnson ally. 'It was agreed on Sunday that the lists would be combined. We only combined the lists on Tuesday morning. It appeared they'd only spoken, in the course of those three days – Saturday, Sunday, Monday – to eighteen people. Most of them were already names we had. It made me think they were not as organised as they claimed to be. We obviously had a much more comprehensive list. They needed our list to see what the state of play was.' If the Johnsonians were disappointed by the quantity of Team Gove's data, the Goveites were disappointed by the quality of Berry's. 'They just didn't have much information at all,' a Gove aide said. 'It didn't say when people were approached, it didn't say who had talked to them, which whip was speaking to which MP.' Another of Gove's advisers claims, 'Boris said to Michael, "I know the issues with these guys, but they have been with me for years. I can't just drop them."'

More debilitating than any data problems, though, was the turf battle between the two sides, which was taking up a great deal of energy. To settle the argument it was agreed that the master spreadsheet would be held and updated by Gove's special adviser Beth Armstrong. This was seen by the original Johnson leadership team as 'another power grab', but it certainly made sense to combine the lists, and one source says Armstrong 'transformed' the data input. At this stage Johnson's allies say he had around sixty-seven supporters, a good platform to build on in the two days that remained before he would have to submit his nomination papers. Gove's people thought only about twenty-five of these were 'solid'.

All the retrospective carping somewhat missed the point. The Goveites and the Johnsonians were united in a collective endeavour. Whatever problems there were, it was the responsibility of Gove and Wallace, as co-chairmen of the campaign, and Crosby as its organising force, to sort them out. When the Goveites later claimed the operation was 'a shambles', a Johnsonian said with some justification, 'The portrayal of chaos was nonsense. They were in charge by then. Gove was the campaign manager.'

Johnson and Gove were agreed that Johnson should not be making formal job offers to anyone, but that is easier said than done in a leadership election. Johnson's aides thought Gove had dangled the Foreign Office under Osborne's nose, and in the face-to-face meetings with MPs and ministers, sources claim Johnson left others with the impression that they had been offered something – though it was not always clear precisely what: 'Boris was basically having meetings with ministers offering them jobs, and people had to call up the minister afterwards to ask them what job Boris had offered them because he'd forgotten.'

In one incident a junior minister at the Department for the Environment who is now more senior went in for a chat with Johnson. Afterwards, Conor Burns had to be despatched to find out what Boris had said. The minister replied, 'Boris was unbelievably charming. He had a wonderful first line, which was "Nothing I say to you now is worth the paper it's written on," but he painted the most beautiful picture of my importance and suggested I would get a cabinet job. I'd had both Michael Gove and Nick Boles putting me under pressure to see him, telling me how splendid he was.' The minister asked Burns, 'What exactly am I supposed to do with all of that?'

MPs who joined the Johnson campaign do not think he was deployed properly to land converts. One backbencher, who was recruited by Gove, texted Johnson to say that he was backing him, and Boris replied, 'Great! Come over and see me at any time.' The MP went to Johnson's room in Norman Shaw and found him 'charming and shambolic', but with 'his mind working very strongly'. He found it odd that he had been ushered straight in, when Johnson should have been used to land those who were more important or not yet persuaded. The MP says, 'A good whipping operation is very militarily ordered. You triage people. Typically, you'd get a whip to have a conversation, then a friendly MP. You're always trying to protect your principal's time and mindspace. In a hospital, you don't go straight to see the consultant emeritus professor of oncology

when you've got a mole on your leg. You go through a process. You see
other MPs, then cabinet ministers or the chief of staff. If no one else can
crack them, then you go to the top. But you make sure that when that
person goes, the candidate knows what their ask is going to be, and
whether they're going to grant it or not. That was not going on around
Boris, and it was going on around Theresa.'

Johnson was pitching himself as a one-nation Conservative, but he was
also the leading Brexiteer in the contest, so it was important for him to
secure the support of the main Eurosceptic groups in Parliament. Steve
Baker advised the campaign that there were three key power centres: the
traditional Eurosceptics around Bill Cash, Bernard Jenkin and John
Redwood; the Fresh Start Group under Andrea Leadsom, Chris Heaton-
Harris and George Eustice; and Michael Gove, since he had pull across
the parliamentary party. Baker believed the best leadership team would
combine Johnson's charisma, Gove's brains and Leadsom's drive.

In the week between the referendum and the Thursday of nominations, Johnson did not succeed in pinning down any of these three
groups. He did talk to the Palaeosceptics, but the meetings did not go
well. An MP says, 'The problem with Boris is that he was Boris, and he
blustered with them. You can't sit down with Bill Cash and Bernard
Jenkin and John Redwood and just bluster your way through what we're
going to do to leave the European Union. There are only two options
with those guys: either you know more about it than they do, which is
hard, or you pin back your ears and you listen to them.' The MP said
Johnson should have offered to set up a Brexit support group to draw on
their expertise on how best to leave the EU.

Peter Bone did not even get an audience with Johnson, but with Will
Wragg and Martin Vickers he did speak to Gove, urging him to recruit
Leadsom rather than seek to do all the big jobs himself: 'You can't do this
all yourself, Michael. You can't be the chancellor and lead the exit.' Bone
suggested that by hoovering up power Gove would repeat 'George
Osborne's mistake'. He also wanted to make sure that Johnson was 'the
real thing', had ditched his support for a second referendum and had no
plans to employ Dominic Cummings, with whom Bone had clashed
during the referendum campaign.

*   *   *

It was not just the Eurosceptics who had concerns about Johnson. That evening Theodore Agnew and John Nash, an education minister, visited Gove and asked his special advisers to leave the room. Both wanted Gove to run for leader. They apparently told him he needed to secure greater assurances from Johnson about how their double act would work. Gove's advisers were also wondering whether Boris was the man they had hoped he would be. That evening one of them phoned Nick Boles to say, 'We're having a wobble.' Boles realised quickly that this was 'only a staff wobble, it wasn't a Michael wobble', but the complaints were the same as they had been at the weekend: 'We just don't think they've really done any work. They're not really sharing all the information they've got. They don't really accept Michael's leadership. Boris isn't calling up colleagues. Theresa's seen everybody already.'

Boles sought to calm the situation. 'It will be fine,' he said. He remembered his time at City Hall. 'Listen, Boris is different from most politicians we've ever worked with. It's more chaotic, it's less linear, but he gets there, and you've seen how he did that in the campaign. It'll be fine.'

It would need to be, because elsewhere in the Tory Party Theresa May was building up support from a group of MPs who were calling themselves the 'ABB' group. It stood for Anyone But Boris.

ANYONE BUT BORIS

The 'ABB' movement was born in the small hours of the morning on referendum night in the Blue Boar bar at the Conrad Hotel, just across the road from St James's Park tube station. A conference room in the basement had been the scene of some of the first meetings between Downing Street and Britain Stronger In Europe. Now the wood-panelled bar, lined with political cartoons, was the scene of Conservatives In's referendum party. Ministers like Liz Truss, Greg Hands, Brandon Lewis and Robert Buckland were all scanning Jim Messina's model to follow the results. Around 1 a.m. they were joined by Nicky Morgan and Damian Green, who had come over from the Stronger In party on the South Bank. When it appeared that all was lost, Nick Herbert – the group's leader – made a speech thanking everybody for their support. But he appeared 'blown away' by the loss, and the atmosphere, according to one MP, was that of 'a slowly deflating balloon'.

Around eighty Remain-supporting ministers and backbenchers were signed up to a WhatsApp message group created by the whip Julian Smith. It was originally set up as a means of coordinating 'save Dave' activities to prop up the prime minister, but by the time defeat had become certain the group was alive with drink- and rage-fuelled 'venting' about the Brexiteers. Claire Perry, a transport minister, was particularly aggressive in denouncing Boris Johnson. A cabinet minister said, 'It was a private conversation in which every so often someone had to say, "You realise there are eighty people on this group?" when someone said something injudicious.'

It was Amber Rudd, the energy secretary and Boris-baiter from the first TV debate, who suggested, 'Let's all sit down and think of what we do next,' in a more considered fashion. Although it was around 4.30 a.m.

the bar was still busy, so a group of MPs went to a quieter area between the adjoining restaurant and the toilets, and sat on green leather benches that resembled those in the House of Commons. Liz Truss, Damian Green and Sam Gyimah were all present, and Jeremy Hunt, the health secretary, arrived halfway through the conversation. Someone said, 'Well, it's got to be Theresa, doesn't it?' But there was no agreement across the group, which was ideologically very diverse, united only by its support for the Remain campaign. It encompassed Damian Collins on the left of the party through to Therese Coffey on the right. 'There was no sense of "Right, we need a candidate to run for leader," because we knew that different people would be supporting different candidates at that stage,' one of them said. 'It was just that we wouldn't let the hard right use this referendum result as a way of seizing the party. Was it an "Anyone But Boris" movement? There were one or two people who used that phrase.' They agreed on two things: 'We need to stick together as a group,' and 'Let's all meet in the morning.' Coffey then put together a WhatsApp group with a much smaller distribution list to coordinate the planning.

On Friday morning around twenty MPs met in the flat of Robert Buckland, the Solicitor General, just off the Horseferry Road. They included Karen Bradley and Richard Harrington – both Home Office ministers – Damian Hinds and Lucy Fraser, a member of the 2015 intake. 'It was a gathering together of the moderate clan,' one said. Damian Green, who had been on the Stronger In board, was an old hand at leadership elections, so he talked through the process and how previous contests had panned out. His insight was that groups of like-minded MPs had power because they could club together and get concessions. 'He gave the example in the past of how John Hayes had managed to get David Cameron to pull out of the EPP,' one MP said. 'There was discussion about if we should group around a single candidate,' but again there was no consensus. 'Some people there were clear it was anyone but Boris, but that wasn't the collective view of the room. I would say Karen Bradley would be an example of ABB. She wasn't the only one.' There was agreement that the Remain MPs should seek to work together, but the abiding memory of one present was that it was not so much a leadership plot, 'more a venting session with Jaffa Cakes'.

A second meeting arranged by Therese Coffey and Julian Smith, attended by around forty MPs, took place on Friday afternoon in a meeting room on the ministerial corridor, but proved just as inconclusive. When it was suggested that they all back one candidate, 'there was that rumbling which amongst politicians means "No." It wasn't a Theresa May rally.' While colleagues remember Anna Soubry talking about 'anyone but Boris', the attendees also included Ed Vaizey, who had been Michael Gove's best man and was soon to be coaxed towards the Dream Team. 'It became clear again that there was no view that we should be backing any particular candidate,' a minister said. But the vast majority of those present would end up supporting May. The group agreed that they would meet again on Monday and begin to organise Remain hustings for the leadership candidates, a move that would become significant for Johnson.

Manoeuvring to replace David Cameron had begun long before he stood down. The Conservative Party's leadership rules meant it was an opportunity for birds of differing hues to show off their plumage. Candidates only needed a proposer and a seconder to get on the ballot paper. MPs would then vote every Tuesday and Thursday, with the candidate ranked last dropping out each time. When there were two candidates left, the winner would be decided by a full ballot of party members.

Boris Johnson was not alone in meeting his prospective campaign team in the fortnight before the referendum. In that period a number of ministers and MPs, from both the Remain and Leave camps, had begun to tell journalists that Theresa May might need to be installed as a 'caretaker' leader, because they believed she was the only candidate with the ability to unite the warring factions and the clout to 'stop Boris'. But May was never going to get a clear run at Johnson for the premiership. Stephen Crabb, the recently appointed work and pensions secretary, was 'on manoeuvres' as soon as he got the job, seeking to widen awareness of his background as a working-class kid raised on a council estate by a single mother who had to claim benefits after she kicked out his abusive father. Crabb was close friends with Sajid Javid, the business secretary, whose own leadership prospects had been damaged with both Brexiteers and Remainers by his grudging support for staying in the EU. The two had dinner together the week before the referendum and agreed to run as a joint ticket, with Javid as chancellor. They did not expect to win, but hoped a strong showing would give them greater clout in the party. Crabb was also close to Ruth Davidson, the leader in Scotland, and enlisted Jeremy Wright, the Attorney General, to run his campaign.

On the Brexit side, Liam Fox, who had finished third behind Cameron and David Davis in the 2005 leadership contest, had also resolved to run. He had been seen dining regularly in Westminster with Theresa May, sparking speculation that they had done a deal. He hoped to peel away enough Brexiteers from Johnson to justify a return to the cabinet. The weekend before the referendum he predicted perils ahead for the party: 'There's an earthquake coming on Thursday, and none of us knows which bits of the edifice may come down.' But he also suggested cryptically that he would be prepared to put aside his ambitions if May emerged as the unity candidate: 'More than any other leadership election I have known, we would need to see what works rather than what we want.' MPs believe he already had an agreement in place with May to row in behind her after the first round of the contest.

Others actively consulting their colleagues included Nicky Morgan, who hoped to promote the interests of the socially liberal pro-European wing of the party; Jeremy Hunt, who saw himself as the continuity Cameron moderniser; Graham Brady, the chairman of the 1922 Committee, who was asked to run by several Eurosceptics; and even George Freeman, the life sciences minister and one of the party's intellectuals. On the Saturday after the referendum he contacted the *Sunday Times* to say that he and Anne-Marie Trevelyan, from the 2015 intake, were planning to put together a joint ticket to develop ideas to tackle what he called 'the inchoate insurgency storming Westminster'. When the story appeared, he got cold feet and abandoned the idea.

Theresa May had been thinking about the top job since her days at Oxford University, where she was a contemporary of a group of future Conservative politicians that included Philip Hammond, Alan Duncan, Damian Green and Colin Moynihan, as well as the television journalist Michael Crick. May studied Geography, and was the tutorial partner of Alicia Collinson, who went on to become a barrister and Mrs Damian Green. The young Theresa Brasier was eighteen and in her first term when she told Collinson she wanted to be prime minister. Another leading light in the Oxford University Conservative Association (OUCA) was Philip May, who would be introduced to Theresa by Benazir Bhutto, the future prime minister of Pakistan. Philip May was also friends with Richard Harrington, who later became a Home Office minister under Theresa. Harrington has told friends, 'Philip was the person we actually thought would be PM – the first election campaign I got involved in was Philip against Alan Duncan.' In turn, Michael Crick used to address Duncan as 'Alan Duncan: head boy, president, prime minister' – the third prediction of which he has not wholly abandoned hopes of fulfilling. Philip Hammond was not involved in politics at the time, but he knew Damian Green through mutual friends. Green, Philip May, Alan Duncan and Michael Crick were all presidents of the Oxford Union, the debating kindergarten for future leaders.

OUCA in those days, as now, was split between the public-school fraternity, who were very right-wing, and the grammar-school pupils, who at that time were members of PEST (Pressure for Economic and Social Toryism), a forerunner of the Tory Reform Group, which was the home of pro-European Conservatives from the mid-1970s onwards. That was where the future Mrs May met Green. 'Alan Duncan wasn't a friend of ours,' one of the gang says. 'He was in a completely different set of people we disliked politically. Inevitably there were factions in the Oxford Union. The right of OUCA was public-school and the left was grammar. So there was a bit of class mixed in with the politics.'

David Cameron had irritated MPs by constructing an inner circle in Downing Street and at the apex of the Conservative Party based around his friends from Eton, Oxford and the Conservative Research Department. But when the time came to harness the nascent ABB movement into a leadership campaign, the generation at Oxford a decade earlier than Cameron's would come in pretty handy.

In March, around ten weeks before the referendum, a small group of MPs loyal to May approached her and said that if she was planning to run for leader, she would need an organisation. They included her parliamentary private secretary Michael Ellis, his predecessor George Hollingbery, and Hollingbery's fellow whips Kris Hopkins and Simon Kirby. Richard Harrington and Karen Bradley, who worked under May at the Home Office, were also supporters. May, who is cautious by nature, 'made it clear that she didn't want an operation going on in the parliamentary party, because once you have an operation everyone knows about it and that's damaging', an MP familiar with the discussions said.

May's two closest confidants, her former special advisers Fiona Hill and Nick Timothy, knew they would need to hit the ground running if there was a vacancy for the leadership. Both had been quietly waiting for the chance to promote the politician they thought head and shoulders above the rest of the cabinet. Hill had worked hard while she was in the Home Office to develop May's relations with the *Mail* newspapers and other senior journalists. A Scot who enjoyed a deep personal connection with May, she was a tenacious defender of her interests, but had a warm personality with those she trusted that belied the formidable reputation she had earned in Whitehall. Timothy, one of the brightest policy brains of his age group, never stopped helping May formulate her ideas even after he had left Whitehall, and remained a back channel between May's new advisers and the wider Conservative diaspora and senior figures in the media. Like May, he was the product of a grammar school. Once 'Fi and Nick' had left the Home Office in 2014, May had recruited another talented batch of spads including Alex Dawson, the former head of the Conservative Research Department and half-brother of Cameron's adviser Gabby Bertin, former *Mail on Sunday* journalist Liz Sanderson, and Will Tanner, another sharp and able policy man.

Under the radar and sworn to secrecy, Hill approached Damian Green and asked if he wanted to get involved. He agreed, and they began to think about what would be needed if and when May was prepared to break cover. Green was another figure in involuntary exile. Regarded by colleagues and media alike as a highly competent and likeable immigration minister, the reason for his July 2014 reshuffle, the story goes, was because Cameron held a grudge about things he believed Green had briefed to the media when he was supporting Ken Clarke during the 2005 leadership election. At that stage May's team thought Cameron would win the referendum, and there would be no leadership contest before 2017 at the earliest. As May became June, Green went to see May for a private chat. There was nothing unusual in that, but this was 'a more directed conversation', although still with no anticipation that anything was going to happen quickly. Green told May, 'I would like to support you, if and when.'

They did not begin discussing organisational issues until the Saturday after the referendum, when May, Hill, Timothy and Green met in a temporary office just off Park Lane. Stephen Parkinson, who had left the Home Office to join Vote Leave, would sign up shortly afterwards.

After the first meeting of the Remain MPs at Robert Buckland's house had broken up on Friday morning Karen Bradley and Richard Harrington found themselves in a car together, and decided to phone May. They asked what she was planning to do. Ever the practical minister, May said,

'Well, I'm on my way to the Home Office. Come round.' They could not think of another leadership contender who would have been planning to put in a normal day's work on that Friday. The two ministers told May she should stand for the leadership. Harrington had only known her well for seven months, but he said, 'There is no alternative for the party.' He told her he thought it was 'destiny that this had happened', and that she 'had to step up'. Bradley agreed that May was the only qualified candidate. 'If you do stand, I will organise the funding and organisation for the campaign,' Harrington added. May said, 'I'm going to think about it and speak to Philip.'

That evening she called Harrington at around 10 o'clock and told him she was 'going for it'. She asked if Fiona Hill could discuss the organisation with him. Hill visited Harrington at his home on the Sunday after the referendum. After their chat he organised a permanent office in Greycoat Place, in the same building from which David Cameron had run his victorious campaign in 2005, and began phoning donors to raise money. Altogether he raised £270,000, including £6,000 in small donations from the public. The biggest contributors included Mick Davis, the party treasurer, and Ami Ranger, a Tory donor. Harrington also helped hire staff, buy IT equipment, set up a website and organise a phone bank.

Those who were involved say May approached her decision to run for the leadership election in the same way she approaches everything else – with a methodical manner and an attention to detail. One of her early backers said, 'Theresa is convinced by no one. She thinks about everything in detail. There's no instinctive, impulsive thought. Her reaction was exactly what you'd have expected – considered, thinking about it all day, discussing it with Philip.' Those closest to May say those who believed she had been actively plotting for months do not understand her: 'That Friday was the moment she genuinely made her mind up. Whatever people say, I could tell by her reaction.'

The next key recruit was Gavin Williamson, who had been Cameron's parliamentary private secretary. He had talked to Oliver Dowden months before the referendum, and they had both concluded that May stood a very good chance of winning. But when the time came they were on different sides. Watching Cameron brought down by Johnson and Gove's support for Brexit was double motivation for Williamson. 'Soon after the result came in and the PM had resigned, he was very clear in his mind that he was going to help Theresa get the leadership,' a close friend said.

'I know Gavin was going around telling our colleagues, "A vote for Theresa is a vote for the prime minister's preferred candidate."' Cameron said he would sit out the leadership election – he was the only Conservative MP not to vote. But he gave his blessing for Williamson to front May's whipping operation. One close aide to Cameron did not think the outgoing prime minister had warm feelings for any of his possible successors: 'My reading of it was that he thought Theresa had badly let down him and George by not campaigning vigorously enough. Boris had let them down badly by being perfidious. And Michael had badly let them down by campaigning harder than David thought he would. I don't think it's the case he was gunning for one particularly more than another. But as time moved on he definitely moved towards Theresa.'

Williamson was a key appointment, since he knew the parliamentary party inside out, and was aware of what combination of charm and menace would work with each MP. A minister said, 'He is just an extraordinary and modest man. He is ruthless in his approach, and very well organised. He doesn't take prisoners, let's put it that way. He can do the hairdryer. He doesn't threaten people, it's just "Use your bloody common sense" type of thing.' In a move that stretched the rules, Williamson enlisted most of the Tory whips' office – which is usually neutral in leadership elections – to work for May. Only chief whip Mark Harper, his deputy Ann Milton, Jackie Doyle-Price and Steve Barclay kept their hands clean. A member of the 1922 Committee executive said, 'Many of us just thought that it was damaging to the office, and that the normal practice of independence in these matters for the whips' office was a sensible thing to do.' Williamson ran a whipping team which included Hollingbery, Ellis, Kirby and Hopkins, but also the ministers Mike Penning, who helped keep the numbers, and Brandon Lewis. They operated more quickly and cohesively than the Dream Team operation.

May's first senior Brexiteer was Chris Grayling. She and the leader of the House spoke by telephone on the Monday evening, and met up on Tuesday. He told her he had decided to support her, and said, 'I want to chair your campaign and do it properly, because I've done it before.' Grayling had run Liam Fox's campaign in 2005, which had come up on the rails and nearly made it into the run-off with Cameron. May agreed. Grayling put in calls to other Leavers reassuring them that Brexit would be safe in her hands: 'I'm comfortable in trusting Theresa with this role, you can be too.'

When he considered the leadership, Grayling said, 'I just thought Theresa was the best candidate. I've known her for a long time. I said to colleagues, "I want you to imagine the boat on the lake in Germany this autumn, with Angela Merkel negotiating our future relationships with members of the European Union. Who do you want in that boat?" When you start to think about it, there was no other candidate.' By the time he arrived on the scene, Grayling found a 'good whipping operation' under way, and a 'well-oiled machine' under Fiona Hill coordinating the rest of the campaign. The campaign's main spokespeople were Green, Justine Greening, Brandon Lewis and, eventually, Amber Rudd. They met every day at 9 a.m. and 4 p.m. in Grayling's Commons office. May never attended any of these meetings – she let people do their own jobs for her while she did hers. 'She was signing warrants and going to Cobra meetings,' said a senior member of the campaign. 'There are things a home secretary just has to do and they have to do now. So there is just no kicking off her shoes and saying, "Let's talk about how we gain another three Welsh MPs."'

Alan Duncan also pressed himself into action for the cause. He went to see May, his Oxford contemporary, at 6 p.m. on the Monday, and told her, 'We've known each other for forty years. You can do this. You must do it. Have no self-doubt, and I'll back you all the way. I've got nothing else to say.' Duncan did not become a formal member of the inner circle, but he excelled at geeing up the troops and offering sage advice from one who had helped get John Major elected in 1990 and William Hague in 2001.

The following day he phoned up Fiona Hill to see what he could do to help, and asked, 'Where are you?' May's right-hand woman was running her leadership bid from Caffè Nero. Duncan immediately invited her to work from his house in Gayfrere Street. Duncan was fond of telling colleagues, 'Leadership campaigns are like wars. They bring out the best in people and they bring out the very worst in people.' They brought out the competitor in Sir Alan, a pint-sized political pugilist. He turned himself, to the frustration of some others, into the campaign's self-appointed mascot and cheerleader, an irrepressible force with an ear for a waspish quote. One of those was an early dig at Boris Johnson, twisting the slogan Johnson's supporters liked to use about him reaching the parts other Tories could not reach. 'Boris has gone from Heineken to Marmite,' he said. On another occasion he stood up in the Commons and compared Johnson to Silvio Berlusconi, the priapic former Italian premier, christening him 'Silvio Borisconi'.

The Remain gang held their first hustings on Tuesday. Health secretary Jeremy Hunt addressed around ten other MPs, pitching himself as a liberal free marketer in the Cameron tradition who had shown leadership by facing down the junior doctors, who had been protesting about their new contract and working hours. In fact the dispute was far from over – one MP who was present said, 'I don't think the timing was right for him.'

Stephen Crabb also turned out, but only got about half a dozen people to hear him. His decision to join forces with Sajid Javid did not impress the Remain audience. Javid had backed Remain, but had also written an article declaring, 'It's clear now that the United Kingdom should never have joined the European Union.'[1] Eurosceptics felt betrayed by a man who had repeatedly gone out of his way in the months before to position himself as backing Brexit. Remainers felt Javid's conversion so churlish as to be useless to their cause. One MP who watched Crabb at the hustings said, 'They probably thought it was good to have Sajid on the ticket. But I'm afraid his credibility is somewhat evaporated.'

Nicky Morgan addressed a group of around fifteen MPs in the early evening. The education secretary was frank. She wanted to stand and represent the centre-left of the party, but would not do so if running tarnished the cause. 'I am thinking about it,' she said. 'But if I think there is no point I just won't stand.' Morgan had fewer than ten supporters at that stage, and Hunt no more than half a dozen. Neither would go for it.

Liam Fox announced on Tuesday evening that he was running, but he appeared to have only minimal support as well.

To the irritation of some on the Eurosceptic right, the leadership contest was boiling down to a late convert to their cause and a home secretary who had not controlled immigration, but would not support Brexit to give herself the power to do so. Peter Bone and Tom Pursglove had visited Fox, David Davis and Graham Brady in turn to try to persuade them all to join forces, but their mission had been in vain. A 'handful' of people had asked Chris Grayling to run, but he decided 'pretty much on the spot' not to throw his hat in the ring. As soon as Brady sat down with the 1922 Committee executive he said, 'Contrary to occasional speculation I am not a candidate.' He would run the contest instead. The hardcore Brexiteers began wondering if Andrea Leadsom should carry their standard instead.

Wednesday began with Stephen Crabb's leadership launch. Even his friends, like Ruth Davidson, felt the moment had 'come too soon' for him, but Crabb wanted to put down a marker, so that he would be a contender next time. Crabb painted himself as the blue-collar candidate whose background signalled a break from the public-school gang and would appeal to Tory and Labour voters alike. He denied that he was the 'stop Boris' candidate, and then sought to position himself as just that. Adapting Johnson's phrase that he would be interested in the leadership if the ball 'came loose at the back of the scrum', Crabb said, 'On the rainy rugby fields of west Wales I learnt that it's not a question of just waiting for the ball to pop out from the back of the scrum. If you want it, you do what's required.'

The event showed that he was not yet ready for the big stage – it started forty minutes after his aides had asked journalists to assemble. When Crabb took questions, he asked by name for several political reporters who had not turned up. He also faced awkward questions about his vote against gay marriage. 'I voted the way I did, but I'm very happy with the outcome,' he said. 'That issue is now settled.' It was to be his own sex life, not that of others, which was to cause him the greater problems.

It became increasingly obvious that the contest was a two-horse race between Boris Johnson and Theresa May. There was one abortive attempt to bring the two together. A meeting was brokered by Ann Milton, the deputy chief whip, and Justine Greening, the international development secretary, who was backing May but was Johnson's closest ally in the cabinet. Johnson and May were encouraged to turn up to the Cabinet Office on the Monday to see if a contest could be avoided. Greening had said, 'One of you will end up running this country, you need to sort it out between you.' Johnson was prepared to listen, and certainly did not want to be blamed for snubbing May. He and Ben Wallace turned up, and waited for forty-five minutes. May's representatives then received a message from Williamson saying, 'Theresa's not coming.' Her team then denied ever having agreed to the meeting. 'I don't know why Boris was sitting in the Cabinet Office – there was never going to be a meeting,' a source close to May said.

The two contenders would battle to the finish, starting with the Remain MPs' hustings on the Wednesday morning – or at least, that was the plan.

BREXECUTED

The twenty-seven hours between 9 a.m. on Wednesday, 29 June and noon the following day have some claim to being the most dramatic day in British political history since 10 May 1940. It began in Greycoat Place, where Boris Johnson's team met with Lynton Crosby to discuss the state of the campaign. The MPs present said the operation had begun, finally, to feel like 'a cohesive operation'. One of the whips says, 'My sense was that it was coming to us, but not like a tsunami. Solidly ahead of May, but not wiping the board.' By now there were more than eighty names highlighted in green on Beth Armstrong's spreadsheet, indicating that they were backing Johnson. 'We were really back on the front foot,' a Johnson ally says.

Johnson was due to address the Remain MPs at 10 a.m. Therese Coffey had texted him on the Monday afternoon to invite him, and Johnson had agreed. His PA Alice Neilson and Jake Berry had both confirmed with her on the Tuesday evening. But now his advisers took a look at the list of MPs and decided he should cancel. They had heard the 'anyone but Boris' talk, and expected an ambush from fifty or more motivated May supporters, who would brief the press on their candidate's shortcomings afterwards. Nick Boles was part of the Julian Smith WhatsApp group, and could see that many of his colleagues were 'still firmly rooted in the first stage of grief' about the referendum result, and regarded Boris as the man to blame for their distress. Boles agreed that there would be 'people out to lynch him'. Later that week he would regard this as a sign of the problems with the campaign, telling a friend, 'I just think it's quite telling that we all agreed that was the thing right to do. That we basically had a candidate for the leadership of the party who couldn't go and meet a group of MPs for fear that some of them might trip him up.' But this was not an act of overprotection from Boris's old retainers, opposed by the Goveites, but a decision agreed on by all the key players: Crosby, Gove, Boles, Wallace, Walden and Fullbrook. It may have been the last thing they all agreed on.

Announced only half an hour before the proposed meeting, the decision enraged the MPs who had been stood up. Wallace explained to Coffey that a lot of the people on her list were 'anti-Boris'. Johnson's abandonment was 'the talk of the tea room', particularly among 2015 intake MPs who were surprised to have been categorised as hostile when they had only wanted to see all the candidates in action. Coffey then received a text from Boles, saying, 'Hi Therese, sorry for the change of plan on the hustings you'd set up. Boris wants to meet colleagues individually at this stage and do hustings later. Please could you let me know who was planning to attend the hustings, I would like to reach out and offer meetings to anyone who wants, Nick.' Coffey did not regard it as her job to arrange Johnson's canvassing meetings, but she forwarded the message to the others. As she did so, she resolved to vote for Theresa May. She told fellow MPs, 'My view of life is quite simple. The national interest is best served when the Conservatives are in power, so I decided to back someone who would win the next election.'

As the day went on, Boles was accosted by fellow MPs saying, 'What the fuck!? We were there and we were all ready to meet him, and he cancels on us! Do you have any idea how much time Theresa's spending on us?' He felt a 'ripple' in the pond. MPs were accusing Boris of behaving like a Roman Emperor because he was confident he had enough support already. An MP from the 2015 intake said, 'It's just a case of get on board now or you are all fucking doomed.'[1]

At the weekend the Dream Team had been expected to get the support of Brexit ministers such as Chris Grayling and Priti Patel, as well as former leader Iain Duncan Smith. Patel stressed that the Vote Leave ministers wanted to stick together: 'We have all been such a great team. We've all been through a hell of a lot together, because we've been raging against a machine which has been trying to destroy us. We've watched each other's backs.' But by mid-week Grayling had aligned himself with May, and attention was focused on whether Johnson could land the support of the other Conservative woman with whom he had twice shared a stage during the debates – Andrea Leadsom. Many traditional Eurosceptics were waiting to see whether Leadsom would run herself before they picked a candidate. Leadsom was seeking to maximise her leverage, talking to the other leadership candidates to see what they would offer. A campaign source said, 'She wanted to be chancellor or deputy prime minister or chief Brexit negotiator.'

Leadsom's most serious negotiations were with Johnson and Gove. Her demands created a measure of awkwardness, since the posts she wanted, save for deputy prime minister, were those that had already been assigned to Gove, and the power they gave him would have made him that in all but name as well. However, Gove had already expressed concern earlier in the week to Henry Cook and Beth Armstrong that he had taken on too much. He did not think he could be chancellor, reform the civil service as he had discussed with Cummings, and oversee the Brexit negotiations as well.

To complicate the situation, unbeknownst to Gove, Johnson had dined with Leadsom earlier in the year and, as far as Leadsom was concerned, strongly hinted that he would like her to be his chancellor if he ever became leader. This was in all probability a piece of shrewd flattery rather than a definitive offer, but Leadsom appears to have banked it. When a small item appeared in the Black Dog column of the *Mail on Sunday* on 13 March she did not deny it, a stance she maintained when quizzed her about her conversation with Johnson in the spin room at *Sky News* the night Cameron was grilled by Faisal Islam. Johnson has privately called the claim 'total bullshit', but a minister who is friends with Leadsom is adamant the offer was made: 'I knew that from about February Boris had dangled chancellor in front of Andrea. I don't know exactly how he phrased it but he promised her, "I think you would make a marvellous chancellor when I am prime minister." I knew that Andrea had fallen for this.' On the Sunday after the referendum, Leadsom was so confident she even approached another minister to ask if they would work for her in the Treasury.

At 2 p.m. Gove and Johnson met in Johnson's office in the Norman Shaw North block overlooking the Thames to discuss whether to make Leadsom a firm offer. Gove had had several phone conversations with her to sound her out. Ben Wallace had repeatedly impressed on Johnson that he should not make firm job offers to win support, and Gove was of the same view, though in this case he was conflicted. Leadsom then arrived at the office for a conversation with both Johnson and Gove. They established that she, thinking the promise of the Treasury from months earlier held good, assumed Gove would be the minister in charge of Brexit. 'Andrea said she'd be happy to be in charge of Brexit if she was the DPM,' a source familiar with the discussions said. 'She'd have to be DPM and in charge of Brexit, or chancellor.' At this meeting Johnson remained non-committal, and told Leadsom, 'I've already offered chancellor to Gove.' Nonetheless, Leadsom said she was prepared to consider either post.

After Leadsom had gone, Johnson and Gove called Crosby and had a conversation on a speakerphone. By this time Johnson's personal aide Ben Gascoigne, Henry Cook and Nick Boles had arrived, since Boles was due to spend the afternoon working on Johnson's speech for the campaign launch the following morning. The team agreed that Johnson should not offer any jobs, and should call Leadsom's bluff. Johnson began to work on his speech.

As the afternoon went on, opinions changed. Before the team's regular 4 p.m. meeting, Gove spoke to Crosby, who was now firmly of the view that Leadsom had to be brought on board. 'We need to get her involved,' he said. Leadsom was a key figure for the traditional 'faith and family' Eurosceptics, and her support could be expected to persuade a couple of dozen MPs to back Johnson. If she ran for leader herself she could leach away valuable votes and weaken his hand. Gove called Leadsom and explained that while Johnson did not want to offer specific jobs, she would get either chancellor or deputy prime minister with responsibility for Brexit. The offer was a good one. It guaranteed Leadsom one of the three most powerful roles in government. At 5.25 p.m. Johnson called Leadsom himself. An ally says, 'Boris sealed the deal and agreed with her she would have a top-three position in government: essentially deputy prime minister, Brexit negotiator or chancellor.' He agreed to confirm the offer with a letter, and to make the pact public in a tweet later that evening, announcing that she would be joining him at his campaign launch on Thursday morning. According to a close ally of Gove who spoke with Leadsom that evening, 'The tweet had to be sent and the letter had to be received by 8 p.m. That, Boris did not mention. At no point did he say 8 p.m.' The Johnsonians deny there was a specific deadline.

By this point Leadsom was also being encouraged to run on her own. Harriet Baldwin, a Treasury minister who had been friends with Leadsom's sister Hayley for thirty years, spoke to her during a debate in the chamber at around 4.30 that afternoon. Baldwin was a convinced

Remain supporter, and had rowed with Leadsom the previous weekend over the economic consequences of Brexit, but now she said, 'Andrea, you really should run. I'm not going to back you, I'm going to back Theresa. But you have nothing to lose by running.'

Leadsom was a good catch for Johnson, but she had come at a high price. Nick Boles was not alone in thinking that Leadsom, who had never been more than a minister of state, was 'overbidding'. He and Gove had also lined up Nicky Morgan, the education secretary, to support Johnson. Boles arranged with her that she would come out for him during the launch speech, a move that he hoped would lead to a flood of MPs signing up. Amber Rudd too was preparing to back Boris, a move that would have been highly symbolic after she savaged him in the ITV debate.

Along with the aborted meeting and the Leadsom saga, the third strand of Johnson's campaign implosion came over his speech for the launch event. Johnson is extremely unusual among present-day politicians in crafting his own speeches. He had tried previously to employ speech-writers, but found that he could not deliver other people's lines well. Combined with a tendency to write up until the last minute, this was a state of affairs that put others in his campaign on edge. By Wednesday morning Boris had a couple of sides of handwritten talking points, but nothing formal put down. Three hours of the day during which he ought to have been phoning MPs were blocked out to work on the speech. Nick Boles figured they needed fifteen hundred words.

At the start of the speechwriting session, Johnson and Boles had Crosby on the phone and they discussed how to approach the message. Crosby said, 'Our research says that people don't want continuity, they want change. This is post-referendum. So the strong message is that you've got to stand for change.' Boles came up with a riff that Johnson could use throughout the speech to capture that theme: 'This is our chance.' It was forward-looking and optimistic. It encapsulated Crosby's demand, Johnson's sunny disposition and the sense of a key moment in the country's destiny having been reached. To Boles's surprise and delight, Crosby liked it. 'Nick, that's the first intelligent thing I've ever heard you say,' the Australian said.

Johnson had had two and a half hours to work on the speech, but when Boles returned and asked how he was getting on, he said, 'I've got nothing.' He had managed to produce just a few lines on various scraps of paper. Boles found the situation awkward. Johnson was proud of his writing skills, his way with words, and in his hour of maximum exposure they appeared to be failing him. Boles told other members of the team, 'That was when I began to panic a little.'

Those who knew Johnson best believe he was not given the space he needed to craft the speech. 'Lynton had made it very clear on Tuesday morning, and Boris had to Michael, that we needed five or six hours on that Wednesday afternoon to craft the speech,' an ally said. 'And they didn't allow him that time. They kept bringing people in there. They had the Andrea meeting.' This view highlights the difficulty of stepping up to contend for the premiership whilst writing your own speeches. It was important to land Leadsom, but it would have been better to have a speechwriting team work with Johnson – as would have to be the case in Downing Street – or to have begun work earlier.

News that the speech was not finished filtered out to the rest of the team. It unnerved Oliver Dowden, who had worked in Downing Street and knew how much effort went into a prime minister's party conference speech, for which the first draft would come in July, more than two months before the big day. Boris had just sixteen hours left to get it right. Dowden spoke to both Crosby and Boles, asking whether they were helping to feed in messaging and querying why Gove, one of the party's best phrasemakers, was not helping. He then called Gove and said, 'I'm worried about this. This man wants to be prime minister of the United Kingdom. I've worked for the prime minister of the United Kingdom. This is not how the prime minister of the United Kingdom should be behaving.' He looked at the professionalism of the May operation in the Commons under his friend Gavin Williamson and thought, 'This is not what I signed up to.'

Campaigns and governments have a tendency to take on the person-alities of their leader. Those who were used to working with Johnson had seen his approach work before, and knew that Crosby would inject rigour and discipline where it was needed. Those who were not saw a mode of working they had not encountered at the top of politics before, and worried that it was incompatible with the demands of national lead-ership. But even they believe the problems could have been ironed out by the end of the week. The problem for Johnson was that at the moment he needed to grip the campaign, he was suffering from writer's block.

It was in the midst of this swirling mistrust that Sarah Vine's email hit the internet. Its publication caused a sensation, since it revealed to the outside world the seething tensions between the two camps, highlighting how Gove was still trying to nail down a deal on Tuesday morning, three days after the Thame summit which it had been assumed was the key moment. Johnson's aides immediately smelled a rat, wondering why a wife would communicate with her husband via email rather than a text or a phone call, and why she would copy in his special advisers. 'It looked like it was written to be leaked,' said one Johnson confidant. 'It makes it look like Michael hadn't got the reassurances he needed from Boris. It was designed to destabilise him.' Some of Johnson's allies have subsequently accepted that the email was a mistake, rather than an attempt to undermine Johnson. Some have not. Gove's friends say it was common for his wife to email him. For most, the clinching argument that exonerates Vine is that had she designed the missive to be leaked she would not have included comments about the views of her editor Paul Dacre, who was furious to see his private thoughts about the Tory leadership splashed across the pages of every national newspaper.

After the cancellation of the hustings appearance, it was the second moment that caused MPs to question whether the Johnson campaign was becoming dysfunctional.

While Johnson struggled with his speech and others worried about him, Theresa May was wowing the hustings for Remain MPs. The home secretary arrived 'perfectly on time' for the 6 o'clock meeting, which was attended by around fifty MPs. She spoke for a short while and then took questions, including a charge from Ed Vaizey, the arts minister and a close friend of Michael Gove, that she was a micro-managing minister who would get too bogged down in the detail to run a country. 'She said when she was at the Home Office she thought attention to detail did matter, and she was very pleased that she got a grip,' one of the MPs present said. 'She said she recognised that as prime minister she wouldn't be able to go into that level of detail.' She also used the opportunity to take a swipe at Vaizey, making a remark about the rollout of rural broadband services as an example of a policy where there might have been more attention to detail. 'I know I won't have a job, then,' Vaizey joked. He was to be proved right about that.

The main revelation was that May could tell good jokes. Asked why she had not joined the Young Conservatives in her area, this daughter of a clergyman said, 'Because the first thing I was invited to was a vicars and tarts party.'

As she left, most MPs banged the tables. 'It definitely sealed the deal with a lot of people,' one minister said. May appeared in control, and unlike Johnson, actually seemed to be enjoying herself.

At 6.30 p.m. Boris Johnson headed off to a party thrown by the 1922 Committee at the headquarters in Golden Square of M&C Saatchi, the advertising agency long associated with the Tories, accompanied by Jake Berry and Nigel Adams. He was asked if he had the letter for Leadsom with him, and Berry saw him pat his breast pocket. But when Nick Boles called to check if he had it, Johnson realised he had left it on his desk in the office. They turned the car around and returned to Parliament, and Johnson's PA Alice Neilson brought the letter down.

At Saatchis Johnson worked the room, with Berry and Adams bringing potential recruits to speak to him. Team Boris took their lead from the 1980s comedy series *Yes, Minister*. One of the most celebrated episodes features Jim Hacker in a dry Arab country using a hand signal that involves pulling on his shirt collar to signal that he wants an alcoholic drink. A member of Johnson's team said, 'We all agreed we'd go early and fan out among colleagues and signal if we had a waverer. It was a hand movement onto the collar, slightly more subtle than in *Yes, Minister*. If someone was on the verge, Boris would come over.' Not all of those wooed that night were impressed. 'Boris was ushered around by his greeters,' said one MP. 'It was like a visit from foreign royalty.' Andrea Leadsom was also present, but it appears that she and Johnson did not speak.

Boris left the party to go to the Hurlingham Club in west London, where the Tories were holding their summer party, which had now become a farewell event for David Cameron. Mark Fullbrook, Lynton Crosby's business partner, was hosting a table at the dinner, and Johnson joined him for the evening. At 7.30 p.m. Nick Boles texted Fullbrook to say that he needed to get Boris away early because there was still work to be done on his speech, and Fullbrook decided not to drink until he had safely despatched Johnson. On arrival at the Hurlingham, Johnson gave the letter for Leadsom to Boles, who was to deliver it. When Boles asked the organisers which table Leadsom was seated at, they told him she had cancelled and never turned up. Boles sent her a text saying, 'Andrea, I've got this letter to you from Boris, where are you so I can get it to you tonight? Or do you want me to photograph it and text you the photograph?' He heard nothing back.

Johnson texted Gove, who was also at the Hurlingham event, at 8.10 p.m. to say: 'Andrea wants me to tweet something like "looking forward to campaign launch tomorrow with top team Michael Gove and Andrea Leadsom." Is that OK?' Gove did not reply, but his allies say it was already too late, as Leadsom's 8 p.m. deadline had been missed. But it seems clear from the subsequent course of events that the situation could still have been salvaged if the tweet was sent at that point. It was another hour and eighteen minutes before Leadsom told Johnson she regarded their deal as void.

Gove's failure to respond to Boris's text created the suspicion among Johnson's aides that he had sabotaged the Leadsom deal on purpose. 'There was no deadline. They obviously faked that because they obviously know that he sent a text to Gove at 8.10 p.m. Gove never got back to him deliberately,' one said later. Alternatively, Gove may simply have missed the message because he was at a noisy dinner – but neither of the principals should have left it to chance. Johnson has admitted privately that he did not attach as much significance to the tweet or the letter as subsequent events suggest would have been prudent: 'I thought she had agreed and we were all set.' Gove's allies pointed out that if Johnson had wanted to discuss the tweet with him, he could have just walked to his table. It is astonishing that the future leadership of the country was to hang, in part, on such misunderstandings.

The tweet itself appeared to have been the subject of another miscommunication. Johnson believed he had issued orders for it to be sent. Jake Berry, Johnson's House of Commons staff and Will Walden, who was at CTF at the time, had a conversation about it, but Berry had understood that Leadsom was supposed to walk on stage at Johnson's launch the following morning as 'the big reveal', and that tweeting about her role would spoil the surprise. The deal done by Johnson, Gove and Leadsom therefore made no sense to the campaign staff, and the tweet did not get sent. Johnson only discovered this a week later. In fact, Nick Boles wanted Nicky Morgan to introduce Johnson, and viewed her, not

Leadsom, as the big reveal. There is more than a whiff of 'For the want of a nail, a kingdom was lost' about all this.

Back at the Hurlingham party, one of Boris's supporters came across Will Wragg around 8.15 p.m. Wragg, the MP for Hazel Grove, was just twenty-eight, having ousted the Lib Dem veteran Andrew Stunnell at the election. A firm Eurosceptic, he was one of Leadsom's most devoted allies. He was somewhat emotional, repeatedly hitting the refresh button on Johnson's Twitter feed and saying, 'The bastard's going to betray us! The bastard's going to betray us!' When the Boris backer asked Wragg what he was talking about he replied, 'It's Boris! He promised he'd be tweeting before 8 o'clock that Andrea was going to be in his top three.' The Johnson supporter watched while Wragg called Leadsom and said, 'He's going to stitch you up, he's going to stitch you up, you've got to run.' The witness then saw Owen Paterson call Steve Baker to say, 'We've got to get Andrea to run.' Wragg left the party between 8.45 and 9 p.m. to acquire nomination papers and get Leadsom to sign them.

The MP who had been watching all this says, 'They were categorically clear that Boris had said that before 8 o'clock that evening he would tweet that Andrea Leadsom would be in his top three.' He texted Gove to say, 'We've got a problem, this is unravelling, you need to intervene.' Gove did not respond, which the MP regarded as unusual.

For Steve Baker, the events unfolding were proof that Johnson had not nailed down the three Eurosceptic power bases he had identified. The Sarah Vine email showed that Gove was not fully on board, the traditional Eurosceptics had not been impressed, and now Leadsom was about to go it alone. He texted Gove to say, 'This is a shambles, an absolute shambles.'

Since this sequence of events was to rupture the Johnson–Gove relationship beyond repair, it is hotly contested terrain for partisans on each side. 'Michael implemented Boris and Lynton's decision to bring Andrea on board, set it up for Boris on a plate – and he fucked it up,' said one Gove adviser. Even some of Johnson's close friends concede that Leadsom should not have been allowed to get away. 'Boris fucked up,' one ally involved in the campaign admitted a week or two later, using the same form of words. But Walden, Wallace and the others were furious with Gove for failing to confront the issue, signal his discontent or respond to Johnson's text about the tweet. They interpreted Gove's silence at 8.10 p.m. as proof of conspiracy rather than cock-up. Above all, having ceded much control over the campaign they had built to Gove's people, they believe he shared responsibility for failing to tie down Leadsom.

What translated this mess into one of the signal acts of betrayal in modern political history is a story that combines not just the events of that tumultuous Wednesday, but also Gove's state of mind that evening, his guilt at having contributed to Cameron's downfall, and the growing belief, nurtured by some of his closest friends, that he was quite capable of doing the job of PM himself. Ministers who know Gove well are convinced that he was driven to act, in part at least, by the speeches he heard that night at the Hurlingham Club dinner.

David Cameron gave a 'barnstorming speech' which reminded those present 'of what we are going to miss', as one minister put it. Nick Boles was not alone in being moved to tears. The prime minister praised George Osborne, while acknowledging that their relationship had had its ups and downs: 'We may have fought, but we have never let it come out in public.' Gove, whose doubts about Johnson had been growing through the week, could not have helped but wonder whether he and Boris would be able to sustain so functional a relationship. There was plenty of opportunity for Gove's guilt at his role in Cameron's demise to go to work too. Andrew Feldman, the party chairman, delivered 'a hymn of praise' to his old friend. A Downing Street aide who was there said, 'Andrew Feldman, who has taken speechwriting to new depths as a discipline, gave an extraordinary speech, the speech of his life.' But the clincher was a tearjerker by Samantha Cameron. The prime minister's wife told guests how proud she was of her husband, and said, 'Every time I go to bed at night you know he has done his best for the country and you can sleep at night.' One cabinet minister said, 'The contrast with Boris was obvious. I think Michael felt like he had betrayed him. It was a case of "Oh God, what have I done?"' Another who was present said, 'It was a lot like a memorial service.'

After the event Gove returned home to Ladbroke Grove, where Sarah was having dinner with Simone Finn, Gove's long-time girlfriend in their twenties who was now a Tory peer. He had a telephone conversation with Leadsom, who told him it was too late. 'I've put my nomination in,' she said. 'I'm running.' Gove began to 'expostulate at Boris's failure'. Vine and Finn told him, 'Get the team over.'

*   *   *

Boles and Johnson left the Hurlingham Club at 10.15 p.m., and in the car on the way back to Islington Boles confiscated Boris's mobile phone. 'Boris, we're focusing on the speech,' he said. It was now only twelve hours from the launch of Johnson's leadership bid. According to Boles, when he took the phone he found a text from Leadsom, sent at 9.38 p.m., announcing that the deal was off: 'I am very sorry Boris and Michael but it was very clear that I needed a public statement this evening. I would have been really keen to work with you but I am now going to submit my nomination papers. Best, Andrea.'

According to Boles, Johnson went into meltdown, exclaiming: 'Fuck, fuck, fuck, fuck. What do we do? Fuck, fuck, fuck.' Boles tried calling Leadsom from his own phone and then from Johnson's, thinking she might be more likely to answer that, but she did not pick up. He then texted Gove to say, 'Something's gone wrong. Leadsom's put in her nomination papers, saying something about a tweet. What was the tweet?'

When the author saw Johnson a week later, his version of events was different. He said he did not see the contents of the text at all until after Boles had left him for the evening. He also said the same text was sent to Gove. Johnson had not seen the text in his list of messages from Leadsom, in part because it was in a separate chain, since it was sent to both men simultaneously. He does recall Boles saying, 'Andrea has sent a text, there was some cock-up about the tweet,' to which Johnson replied, 'Send her a text to see if we can do it tonight or in the morning.' The text that was sent, apparently by Boles, read, 'Sorry, my cockup. I told Boles about the letter, not about the tweet. We can do the tweet now or tomorrow first thing as you prefer.' This would seem to be an attempt to placate Leadsom, since Johnson *had* actually asked for the tweet to be issued. But, crucially, Boris claims he had no idea that Leadsom was 'pulling the plug'. If he had, he would have rung her back, or sought to persuade her not to in his reply. The wording of the text seems to bear this out, as it makes no reference to Leadsom jumping ship. It makes sense if Johnson had not seen Leadsom's original text. Boles and Johnson's accounts are completely irreconcilable, but the author was able to verify the contents of both the Leadsom text and the reply on Johnson's phone.

A Johnson ally said that Boris became suspicious during the journey about the frequency with which Boles was himself texting: 'All the way to the house and afterwards while Boris was finessing his speech late at night, all the time Boles was texting, having taken Boris's phone away, isolating him from the likes of Will and others. Boris noted that he was constantly texting people.' Some MPs believed after the event that Boles even sent a text from Johnson's phone telling Leadsom the deal was off, but when Johnson's team examined his phone afterwards there was no evidence to support this conspiracy theory at all.

It may have been too late to win Leadsom round, but Johnson appears not to have tried, and none of his closest supporters, including Crosby or Wallace, was enlisted to rescue the position. If the Goveites had not engineered the situation – and even most Johnsonians later accepted that that was far-fetched – their reaction was ultimately to withdraw their support rather than call a crisis meeting or read the riot act to Boris that he needed to sharpen up his act. A close confidant of Johnson says, 'The point is that even at 9.30 p.m., everything could have been done to stop Leadsom going off on her own, and they didn't do anything to stop it. They allowed it to continue. They held the phone. Boris did not see the text until he got his phone back after Boles left.'

Afterwards, the anger of Johnson's team focused on two aspects of the evening. Firstly that Gove, who was the campaign chairman, chose to abandon his candidate rather than tackle the crisis. Secondly, that Team Gove continued to behave as if nothing was wrong for another twelve hours.

What both sides agree on is that in the car Johnson was still down about his launch speech, complaining, 'I can do funny speeches. I just don't know how to do this kind of speech.' Boles knew this was nonsense, not least because Johnson had delivered a very well-received speech at the party conference. On that occasion Wallace and Berry had helped him polish the text. They perhaps ought to have been involved this time as well. 'You don't have to be completely serious,' Boles said. 'We need to have serious intent and content, but it's got to be you, and you can put in some of your colourful language.' He told Johnson that he had a chance to bring a divided society back together.

Johnson seemed deeply affected by the abuse he was getting from the public for winning the Brexit campaign. Boles saw a man 'in a blue funk' who was 'shaken to his foundations' and operating at a less efficient level than during the referendum campaign, and less even than during his first chaotic months as mayor. Johnson talked to their driver about the abuse he had received outside his house on the morning after the referendum. He was used to jovial abusive banter of the 'Boris, you're a wanker!'

variety, but this was different. For the first time, Britain's most popular politician was having to confront the public opprobrium familiar to other politicians.

Johnson felt that during this car journey he had been speaking to Boles as a friend and collaborator. When they fell out he regretted revealing so much of himself, but denied that he had second thoughts about seeking the Conservative leadership. An aide agreed: 'I didn't see that at all.' But in an interview during the referendum campaign Johnson had admitted he was more vulnerable than the public realised: 'If you're not vulnerable and you don't care, then what use are you to anybody?' Asked if he thought vulnerability was an important attribute for a politician, he said, 'I do. But you've got to be brave, you've got to be tough. You've got to be robust and you've got to go out there and have a thick skin, which I do.'[2]

Back in Islington, Boles made coffee and took it to Johnson in his study. He tried not to sit too close, to give him space to write. When Johnson read out lines Boles would say, 'Oh, that's great! That's good! That's fine. That's fine. We can polish it later, just get it down.' Marina came home, providing a momentary distraction, and then Johnson carried on writing.

Boles had gone to the loo when he got a call from Gove, who said he had spoken to both Leadsom and Steve Baker. The politest man in Westminster 'went ballistic' about Johnson – Boles had never heard him so angry. Gove said, 'He's incompetent, he doesn't do what he says, he doesn't remember anything, he doesn't communicate with anyone, he can't make anything work.' Boles asked, 'What are you going to do about it?' Gove replied, 'I'll have a think and we will speak.' A short while later Boles got a text message from one of Gove's special advisers saying, 'We're all at Michael and Sarah's. Can you come over?' Boles replied that it was awkward because he was with Johnson, but then Boris said, 'I'm not much of a night owl, Nick. I'm going to go to bed and I'll do it in the morning.' Boles jumped into an Uber at 12.30 a.m. By then Johnson had mapped out a structure for the speech and written a third of the fifteen hundred words. He was due to announce his candidacy in just over ten hours.

* * *

When Boles arrived at Ladbroke Grove he found Gove deep in conversation with Henry Cook, Henry Newman and Beth Armstrong, with Sarah Vine and Simone Finn chipping in from the sidelines. Gove explained his 'governing view' of the past week: 'Boris has had a week to prove he can be prime minister – not that I was setting out to test him – and in the last twenty-four hours he's had the opportunity to do two things which were relatively trivial to nail it down. He couldn't even do those. I don't have the luxury of time. Tomorrow, I have to say to my colleagues and the country, "I think this man is ready to be prime minister," and be held to account forever for having made that claim – or not.' He then drew parallels with the Labour Party leadership handover in 2007, when Gordon Brown replaced Tony Blair uncontested: 'There were people in the Labour Party who knew that Gordon Brown could not be prime minister. And they kept quiet, and that is understandably held against them. I can't say I think Boris can be prime minister. That's not to say he couldn't be at some point in the future, but it's just that in the course of what I've seen in the last week and day, it's too big a risk for the country.'

Having decided that he no longer believed in Johnson's candidacy, Gove was clear that he would have to publicly withdraw support. There was never a question of fighting on in the hope of winning. 'I can't do that,' he said. A source familiar with Gove's thinking says, 'Arguably the prudent thing to do would have been to have knuckled under and assume it would crumble, or if Boris wins, great! But that's not Michael.' Gove believed it would have been odder still to just withdraw his support and then remain silent. 'Once we realised we couldn't support Boris, then running myself seemed to be the sensible thing, or the logical thing, to do,' he explained.

He went back over the previous week. 'I expended whatever credibility and energy I had trying to get people to support Boris. But I realised it was not going to work. It was the inability to focus on the task at hand – either Boris writing his article on time or people understanding what was needed in a leadership race, and I was determined to put a brave and constructive face on it.'

From there it was only a short step to concluding that he should run himself. One source who was there said, 'We just went through it all. And within about an hour Michael and Nick realised that they would not vote for Boris Johnson in the first round because they didn't want him to be prime minister. And when that realisation came, the whole deck of cards started to fall. How can they in good conscience persuade other people to vote for Boris? How can they run his campaign?' One of those present explained Gove's reasoning: 'It was, "Boris can't be prime minister. Who else is there? It can't be Theresa. Therefore it has to be me." I think it was as simple as that.'

Gove's wife Sarah urged him to follow his principles, saying, 'Since I have known you, you have always done what you think to be right.' It was not the clinching argument, but Gove also knew he could expect heavyweight newspaper backing. The previous day he had taken a call from an influential figure in the media who urged him to run. A source in Cameron's team claims George Osborne had bumped into the media power-broker earlier that day at a business event and suggested he make the call.

At 1.30 a.m. Gove turned in, saying he wanted to sleep on it. At that point Henry Cook called Dominic Cummings, who was out of London. It was the first he knew of Gove's decision. Then Cook rang Paul Stephenson's mobile. Stephenson was woken by the call, but did not answer it. Cook tried a second time, and when that was also unanswered, he tried Stephenson's landline. 'What is it?' Stephenson snapped. 'Michael's decided to run.' Stephenson thought the situation was 'mental', but said, 'OK, of course I'll come and help.' Having been excluded from a leadership campaign he had wanted to be involved in, he now had a way in. He texted Cummings to gauge his opinion, and in one of the classic autocorrect mistakes of the campaign, got the reply that it was 'batshot crazy'.

Gove's team stayed up until 3 a.m and then crashed at Simone Finn's house. They would reconvene at Gove's home at 6.30 a.m.

Gove had been sincere in believing for years that he was not cut out for the top job. But during the campaign he had begun to realise that he could deal with the pressures of leadership better than he expected, and that he enjoyed the strategic decision-making. 'During the referendum campaign, Michael put himself through – so did Boris, to be fair – what a party leader puts themself through in a general election campaign,' a friend said.

If his response to Queengate, when he had blurted out a semi-confessional statement of his culpability to the press waiting outside his front door, was Old Gove, the man who emerged from the debates was a different politician who had tapped wells he didn't know he had. He had always wanted to shield his family from the scrutiny that goes with leadership. When the *Guardian* doorstepped his elderly father and got him to say the EU had not actually finished his fish business, when Emailgate erupted, he realised that his decision to back Brexit meant he had failed in that regard. But he dealt with the crises firmly, and the family had coped. When he came to make his decision in the small hours of that Thursday morning, he thought to himself, 'I've endured it. They're throwing everything at me. I'm confident in the argument I'm making – and I'm soaking it up. What more can they throw at me?' He was about to find out.

The second aspect of Gove's character that carries explanatory force was his taste for revolution. If his politics and his leadership launch speech owed much to the nineteenth-century radical Richard Cobden, Gove's ministerial office was also decorated with a bust of Lenin. He, like Steve Hilton, had grown frustrated with David Cameron's caution on public-service reform. Cameron, in turn, had been horrified by Gove's 'Maoist' taste for 'creative destruction'. In abandoning Johnson and running himself, Gove was embracing this approach.

Nick Boles could not sleep. At 5.30 a.m. he texted Gove and said, 'We should do this.' He jumped in a cab at 6.30 a.m. and returned to Ladbroke Grove to find Gove still asleep. When he was up they went to talk in the garden. 'This is the right thing to do, isn't it?' Boles asked. Gove replied, 'Yes.' Boles looked him in the eye and asked the key question: 'Are you ready?' Again, Gove said, 'Yes.' The two old friends exchanged some personal words and then made an agreement. 'We can do this,' said Boles. 'We're in it to win it. And we give up when we win it or we're defeated under the rules, but not before.' They then embraced to confirm the arrangement. No matter how badly they did among MPs, if they were still in the running when it got to the final two, they would contest the election. With that decided, they went back inside and told the others who had by now assembled at the house.

At 7 a.m. Gove held a conference call to confirm his decision. The two dissenting voices were Henry de Zoete and Paul Stephenson, both of whom thought the betrayal of Boris would play badly for Gove. De Zoete said, 'Theresa May will be prime minister if you do this.' Stephenson warned that abandoning Boris would be compared to another notorious act of political fratricide: 'This will be Ed Miliband times one hundred.' There appears to have been little understanding of the salience of this point from most of the others, who did not think Johnson would drop out of the race, nor any comprehension that Gove would be seen to be diminished by his planned action.

Crucially, Gove had his wife's backing. 'The key thing with Sarah is: can she live with this?' a source who was present said. 'She's going to have to give up her columns, it's going to be a huge amount of pressure and restraint, and she's said, "I'm ready to do this. You know I believe in you." She doesn't have innately thick skin, but I think she's developed a thicker one. Her main role was to say, "It's OK, it's fine." But more than that, "I'm absolutely sure he's ready for it and he can do it and he's the best person to do it." So that was the permission.'

Having made the decision the team got to work, phoning around a dozen MPs like Dominic Raab and Oliver Dowden who were supporting Johnson because Gove had asked them to, and asking them to attend a meeting in Gove's Commons office at 9 a.m. Boles felt strongly that those MPs whose primary loyalty was to Gove ought to be the first to learn from them what had happened. Between 8.30 and 9, Gove personally phoned Liz Truss, who had already declared her support for Johnson, while Boles got hold of Nicky Morgan, who was due to declare that morning, and Amber Rudd, who was due to be revealed later.

Team Boris was particularly angry later that it took Gove nearly two hours from the time of his decision to inform Johnson that he was abandoning him. They regarded an email sent by Henry Newman at 7.10 a.m., detailing which MPs were due to attend Boris's campaign launch, as particularly misleading. Newman's job had been to round up attendees, and he continued to text MPs until 10 o'clock the previous evening. Another adviser said the email was an attempt to play things straight: 'It would have been dishonest to have done stuff that screwed over Boris's launch, so he sent a final list of people who said they were going. That was an attempt to be as straightforward as possible in the circumstances.' One side's attempt at morality was interpreted by the other as duplicity. In a similar vein, Gove's allies say Beth Armstrong handed back the entire spreadsheet of Boris supporters, and took herself off the distribution list.

At 9 a.m. Gove and Boles met their MPs: Ed Vaizey, Dominic Raab, Nick Gibb, Oliver Dowden, Rishi Sunak, Suella Fernandes, Jacob Rees-

Mogg, Robert Jenrick and John Hayes. Gove explained that he was going to run. Vaizey was first out of the blocks. 'OK, thank God! This is what I've always wanted you to do. You've got my 100 per cent support.' John Hayes agreed, in his trademark grandiloquent fashion. But not everyone was happy. Jacob Rees-Mogg said, 'I don't think I should commit to this. You know how much I respect you, but I need to think about this.' Oliver Dowden's reaction was the same: 'I want to think about it.' He had only signed up to the Johnson campaign because Gove was on board, but he also remembered conversations in which Gove had confessed he would not be a good prime minister. He also knew, from having family in the public sector, what a mountain Gove would have to climb to win over some voters. When the news broke, he was immediately contacted by Gavin Williamson. Dowden slept on his decision, but told Williamson on Friday morning that he would support Theresa May.

At 9.02 a.m. Westminster journalists were gathering at the Royal United Services Institute on Whitehall, where Theresa May was due to announce her candidacy in the library upstairs, when an email popped up that would turn British politics on its head.

In a statement to the media, Michael Gove began by distancing himself from David Cameron, saying the referendum result was the chance for a 'bold break from the past'. He then acknowledged, 'I have repeatedly said that I do not want to be prime minister. That has always been my view. But events since last Thursday have weighed heavily with me. I respect and admire all the candidates running for the leadership. In particular, I wanted to help build a team behind Boris Johnson so that a politician who argued for leaving the European Union could lead us to a better future. But I have come, reluctantly, to the conclusion that Boris cannot provide the leadership or build the team for the task ahead. I have, therefore, decided to put my name forward for the leadership.' Gove needed to explain why he was making one of the most extraordinary political U-turns of all time, but that had necessitated a statement so personal that it ended up wounding himself as well as Johnson.

Matt Hancock, the Cabinet Office minister, had turned his phone off between 8.30 and 9.30 a.m. because he was watching his son in a school production of *Romeo and Juliet* – playing Paris, just one of the victims of the seemingly endless Shakespearean bloodletting. 'I'd forgotten how much murder there was,' he told friends later. 'And suicide. Just death.

Paris is murdered right at the end. Lots of death. Then I came out and turned my phone on and read Michael's statement. Extraordinary.'

The first inkling Team Boris had that anything was wrong came when Ben Wallace got a text message from Dominic Raab just after 7 a.m. saying that he could no longer appear on the *Today* programme for personal reasons. Nadhim Zahawi agreed to step in. The campaign team were all due to meet at 8.15 a.m. at Greycoat Place to run through the day. When Gove did not show, one member of CTF turned to another and said, 'Do you think the bastards have turned us over?' His colleague replied, 'Stop being such a conspiracy theorist. You've been watching too many movies.' At 8.40 Johnson texted Gove: 'Call me. Need to speak to you about the speech.' Paul Stephenson says he was standing by Gove's side as he repeatedly tried Johnson's mobile but could not get through, before texting him and asking him to call at 8.53. By that point Johnson was in the shower. At 8.54 an email from Nick Boles arrived in Wallace's inbox: 'Guys, I am very sorry but I am not able to handle Boris's nomination. Here is the paper. All you need is his signature and the signature of two other MPs and then take it to Graham Brady's office by 12 noon. Best wishes, Nick.' Again, there was no proper explanation.

The first Team Boris knew for certain was when Gove called Lynton Crosby on his mobile just after 8.40 a.m. 'Lynton, I'm running,' he said. 'Running what?' replied the bemused Australian. 'I'm running for the leadership myself.' Shortly afterwards Ben Wallace arrived, and found Crosby 'ashen-faced'. At 9.02, eight minutes after Boles had handed back the blank nomination papers, Gove's statement hit the headlines.

Will Walden was travelling on a part of the tube where there was mobile reception and got a text from Ben Gascoigne saying, 'Gove, what the fuck?' Knowing immediately what had happened, he got off at King's Cross and jumped in a cab. He called Crosby and asked, 'What do you think? I just don't think it can work.'

Crosby said, 'I don't think it can either, but it's got to be his decision.' Crosby then phoned Boris and asked him, 'Have you spoken to Gove?'

'About what?'

'He's running, he's running for leader himself.'

Johnson's first reaction was disbelief. Then he said, 'Well, that's it. I can't go on. I can't run.' Crosby said, 'Don't decide anything yet. Come over here, and let's meet your colleagues and discuss.' Crosby, who had got David Cameron to move Gove from the Department for Education two years previously, was apoplectic. Asked how angry he was, a source said, 'On a scale of one to 100, I'd say 928.'

In the car on the way from Islington to Westminster, Johnson sat 'very quietly' contemplating the death of his dreams. 'I think he was shell-shocked,' one ally said. 'He was devastated about what might be about to happen. Obviously he hadn't made that decision. He just couldn't believe that somebody could act with such treachery.'

At Greycoat Place Johnson met Wallace, Crosby and his business partner Mark Fullbrook, and other MPs who were supporting him. They had already hit the phones, and found that as few as thirty-eight of his supporters were still on board. The night before Johnson was told he had ninety-seven votes, and some say it had hit a hundred that morning. The problem was not so much the numbers – it was the tone of Gove's attack. 'He'd be forever spending the campaign having to defend that accusation, when we knew it wasn't true.'

When Johnson arrived most of the MPs were asked to stay in another room while Johnson, Marina, Crosby, Walden, Wallace and Fullbrook mulled over their options. Johnson veered between wanting to fight on and admitting, 'I don't think we can do this.' Wallace articulated the view held by many of the MPs that there could yet be 'a fairy tale where you go on and fight and become the underdog and everyone flocks to you'. But Wallace did not believe that himself, and Crosby interrupted to say, 'That isn't going to happen, is it? I think we all feel "Don't do it."' Johnson said later, 'To go on would have been very bloody, and with Gove's knife in my back it would have been hard to pick up momentum again with colleagues.'

Ultimately, it was the kind of decision that a husband can only make with his wife. Boris and Marina went into an adjoining room together. They were gone for ten minutes. 'Marina just wanted to be supportive. She was very reassuring,' one of those present said. 'Nobody put any pressure on him. He took advice, but the decision was made by him.' Another said, 'I've never seen him so winded. He looked utterly crushed. It was not the realisation it might all be over, it was just the betrayal. "Why couldn't he have discussed it with me? Why has he done it?" Gove was still listed as the campaign manager on the frigging website.'

The team were adamant that Johnson should still give his speech, but with the closing remarks redrafted. He would be able to show what he would have offered as prime minister. When Johnson arrived at the St Ermin's Hotel to give his launch speech at around 11.40, about twenty MPs were present. Most had no idea what was about to happen. Just before he went in, hand in hand with Marina, a friend gave him a hug and said, 'Show them what they're going to miss. You just make them ashamed.'

Johnson gave his speech, a little subdued perhaps, but some interpreted that as statesmanlike. 'Let us seize this chance,' he said, borrowing Boles's riff, 'to stand tall in the world. That is the agenda for the next prime minister of this country.' He slapped his hand twice on the lectern for emphasis, looked down and then slowly raised his head. Jutting out his jaw in Churchillian pose, he said, 'But I must tell you, my friends, that person cannot be me.' In the stunned silence that followed, Nadine Dorries, one backer, appeared to be in tears.

Later Gove and Boles entered the House of Commons tea room to be confronted by Dorries, who marched up to the justice secretary and said, 'Why did you do it, Michael? Why?' Gove looked her in the eye and tried to explain his view that Johnson was not up to the job. 'No one believes you!' Dorries said.[3]

Also making a rare appearance in the tea room that day was David Cameron, who had his lunch among the MPs. 'It is the happiest I have seen him in a long time,' a cabinet minister said. One source who watched Johnson's speech from Number 10 said, 'It was the first time people had smiled in Downing Street for months. They felt the emotion from having lost and then the PM having resigned was given release by Boris going.' Cameron eventually texted Johnson to say, 'You should have stuck with me mate.'

George Osborne's team denied rumours that he had urged Gove to wield the knife, but not that he enjoyed the spectacle. 'I know this for a fact: George did not know Michael was going to do what he did until he heard it on the news,' a Treasury source said. 'I think he was quite highly amused.' Johnson believed that Osborne had been on the phone to Gove 'the whole time', urging him to ditch Boris and run himself. After Gove's announcement, Osborne texted Johnson to deny a story that Gove had been at Dorneywood the weekend after the knifing, or that he and Gove were planning to go on holiday together. But Johnson saw these denials as suspiciously specific.

*   *   *

In the days that followed, sadness quickly turned to rage in the Johnson camp, and then into an agonised questioning about whether things could have unfolded differently. The first impulse was to view it all as a plot from the start, in which Gove, Boles, Gove's advisers and his wife, with Dominic Cummings in the background, had manipulated events to get Johnson to back Brexit, help win the referendum, and had then sat cuckoo-like in his campaign, appropriated his list of MPs and abandoned him so late in the day that he had no option but to drop out, clearing the way for Gove to run. One ally even speculated that knifing Johnson was Gove's way of atoning for bringing down Cameron: 'It was calculated treachery. It is Gove's way back into Cameron's affections.' Jake Berry took to Twitter to say, 'There is a very deep pit in hell reserved for Michael Gove.' Another said, 'Lady Macbeth and the Dark Lord Cummings always had this planned. They knew he couldn't win on his own so he needed to back the favourite and poison the well and then do the dirty at the last possible moment.' Those who saw the hand of Vine in it referred to that Wednesday evening as 'the night of the long wives'.

There is some evidence that, despite his repeated protestations, Gove had long been interested in the premiership. One ally who worked with him for more than five years says, 'There were times when I think he wanted it in the past. When education went tits up he abandoned that. But the reason why he wanted it was to come out of the European Union.' Aides recalled a meeting late at night in the Department for Education in 2012 or 2013 when Gove was 'shooting the breeze'. He said, 'If I ever did do it, it would be to leave the EU.' During the campaign, some watching the interactions between Gove and Johnson believed he was positioning himself to run. 'We could see it,' said Nigel Farage. 'They sent Boris off in a shiny bus while Gove did all the serious stuff. We said to ourselves, "Crikey O'Reilly, it's all about him being leader of the Tories and Cummings running Number 10."'

But this analysis does not stack up. The plot theory might have resembled something from *Game of Thrones*, but it made little sense. Had Gove decided a week before that he wanted to run, he could have done so. Cummings was absent when the U-turn was made, away in Durham with his family. His wife had worked with Boris, and Cummings sent Johnson a note expressing his regret about what had happened and making it clear that he had nothing to do with it. Johnson believed him.

'Of all the things I could be accused of, being a complete moron is not one of them,' Cummings says.

Johnson himself went through agonies about whether he should have dropped out of the race, which were only salved when he was given a top cabinet job. He apologised to his supporters, saying, 'I was a fool to trust him. Some of you told me I should never have done so, and I am sorry I didn't listen.'[4]

Gove's allies say they never expected Johnson to withdraw from the race, and the view of Gove has been coloured as much by that decision as his own. 'We thought we would have a fair fight,' one aide said. Gove thought Boris's withdrawal proved his point about Wallace's organisation – that once they had lost his support, Johnson's core team did not believe they were strong enough to continue: 'I think that the sense of entitlement and therefore grievance that they have is out of all proportion.' This is an optimistic interpretation. Most journalists, on reading Gove's statement, concluded that Johnson would have to withdraw, and that Gove's decision to knife Boris would rebound on him, an opinion Stephenson had voiced that morning.

Gove, in turn, resented the fact that he was accused of having overweening ambition when his leadership rivals had all been plotting for longer: 'I was the only person who ran who, a week before running, did not think about running. Otherwise by definition I would have done things differently.' Admitting it that it was 'self-serving', he said after the event, 'I can say at every point that I was doing what I was thinking was best for the country. Obviously I wasn't engaged in a desperate desire to turn myself into a martyr. The idea that we were cuckoos in the nest, and deliberately there in order to piggyback on Boris's campaign, is preposterous. Everyone knows that we would have a better chance of getting somewhere if I'd run to start with.'

The more legitimate charge is that by waiting until the last moment to tell Johnson what he had decided, Gove stoked the suspicions that he had intended harm all along. Johnsonians looked back at Newman and Boles's emails and felt there had been a deliberate effort to deceive, giving Boris as little time to consider his options as possible. Team Gove now acknowledges that this was an error. 'The key mistake I think that was made on the Gove campaign was not telling Boris,' one ally said. 'Michael should have called Boris the night before and said, "Look, this isn't working for me, I'm going to leave unless you do this ..."' Another Gove aide questioned Johnson's commitment: 'If Michael was enough for him to pull out, it does rather make you question how much he really wanted the job. Since then it's been: Boris is the victim, Gove wielded the knife.'

Johnson's primary grievance afterwards was that he had let his guard down with people he thought were friends, and had been punished for it. 'You behave very differently with people you think are fundamentally on-side,' he said. He particularly resented the way Boles had used his references to the public abuse he had received after the referendum as proof that he was not ready to be prime minister. He also believed that by resisting Leadsom's demands for a job he had been protecting Gove's interests. He repeatedly asked his aides, 'Why did he do it? It was so unkind.'

Within days, commentators – and even Johnson himself – were wondering if he could have made a different choice and stayed in the race. But it felt to those present that he had no option but to drop out. He had lost all momentum, and Crosby believed it was better to live to fight another day than to go down swinging. One of Johnson's closest allies also thinks that if he had had more time he might have stayed in the race: 'If Michael had come to him the night before and said, "I don't think this is working, we have to make a choice here, I'm going to run," it's possible Boris would have carried on. But of course, in a strange inversion, they expected him to carry on and as a result they got crushed. They never gave him the time to react.'

The most interesting question is what would have happened if Gove had not decided to pull the plug, if he had confronted Johnson and made it clear that things needed to change, if he had even – with Crosby's help – talked Leadsom into attending the launch at Johnson's side as chancellor- or Brexit-negotiator-in-waiting. In the first round of voting, one of the MPs in the whipping team said, 'If you'd held everyone's hand to the fire, I think Boris would have been on around 120, and probably Theresa would have been more like ninety to a hundred. Boris may well not have got to the final round being ahead, but he wouldn't have been far off it.' There is no guarantee that he would have beaten May, but with both Eurosceptic and modernising heavyweights behind him, his popularity with the grassroots would have given him a very good chance.

Theresa May called Johnson on the Thursday evening. It is understood she left a voicemail message, the gist of which was, 'I'm very sorry it's ended up like this for you, you've been treated very badly.' A Johnson aide said, 'She was being genuinely kind.' Perhaps it was always in her mind that she would be the one who would ultimately cheer him up. But at that stage Johnson believed his chances of a top job were gone. 'Either he's the greatest actor in history, or he had no expectation of any job at all,' a source close to him said. 'He thought this was it. I think he'd resigned himself to it.'

Yet there is also evidence that Johnson had not abandoned his ambitions, merely put them on hold. That weekend Lynton Crosby said to a friend, 'I still expect him to lead the Tory Party at some time in the future.' Johnson was quick to console his supporters. To one MP he texted, 'Don't worry. It's not over yet.' To another he said, 'There are some twists and turns to come.'

For now, the twists and turns were focused on May, Gove and Andrea Leadsom.

MAYNIACS V LEADBANGERS

While the boys were fighting among themselves, the leading woman in the Tory Party was quietly going about her business. Theresa May was preparing for her own campaign launch when the BoGo psychodrama began to unfold. She was upstairs at the Royal United Services Institute, the same building in which David Cameron had launched his leadership bid eleven years earlier – though May chose the library rather than the achingly trendy white room where 'Dave' had first introduced himself to the world with smoothies laid on for the journalists. Gove's knifing of Johnson led to no changes by May. 'There were no last-minute rewrites of the speech,' a campaign source said. Another who was present says, 'That was what struck me. Just how calm she was. She didn't seem surprised. She was just standing chatting. We didn't spend a lot of time talking about it.'

Chris Grayling introduced May, the first time his involvement in her campaign had been revealed. The home secretary emerged wearing a tartan trouser suit. Her speech had been written by Nick Timothy – or 'Theresa's brain', as he became known, a title that does little justice to either of them. She moved swiftly to placate the Eurosceptics by declaring that 'Brexit means Brexit,' and announced that a Leave-supporting minister would front the negotiations with Europe. She ruled out a general election until 2020. Then she announced that there was no need to see a budget deficit before 2020 either, throwing George Osborne's central economic target into the dustbin. Mapping out a social agenda of her own, she said she wanted to create 'a country that works for everyone'.

At this stage Johnson was still thought to be running, so there was even time for a good dig at his expense: 'The last time he did a deal with the Germans he came back with three nearly-new water cannon.' Johnson had spent more than £300,000 on the devices only to have the home secretary ban their use in England and Wales, to her evident delight. 'It was always going to be, until Michael stabbed Boris, a Boris/Theresa contest,' one May confidant said. Asked by a journalist for her pitch, May was to the point: 'I'm Theresa May and I'm the best person to be prime minister.'

May's team had assembled more than fifty MPs in the audience, from a broad cross-section of the party. The pace of events was such that Andy Bell of 5 News asked if anyone present wished to announce that they were not backing May, and wanted to run themselves. Spying Alan Duncan in the front row, one journalist yelled, 'It's not too late, Sir Alan!' In what could have been a gaffe, Grayling left the launch to return to business questions in the Commons – the weekly discussion of scheduled debates and votes – with his microphone still attached. As he walked back he was quizzed by a lobby journalist, who said, 'Is Boris completely fucked?' Grayling made a non-committal response, but fortunately their exchange was not being broadcast back over the airwaves at May's launch.

In fact May already had more than seventy pledges lined up by the time Grayling joined her team on Wednesday morning, and she was motoring past ninety by the close of play on Thursday. Sensibly, her team were holding some of them back. From his days with Liam Fox in 2005, Grayling impressed upon the campaign the fact that they needed to show momentum, with a steady stream of declarations. Mike Penning, who had helped run Iain Duncan Smith's leadership campaign, made the same point.

The May campaign had also benefited from George Osborne's decision not to stand, since most of his supporters went straight to May. Matt Hancock, the Cabinet Office minister, told colleagues he 'felt like a released delegate' in a US presidential election, someone bound to support one of the candidates at the nominating convention who is then allowed to support someone else. 'The advantage for Theresa is she essentially inherited a machine,' one MP loyal to the chancellor said.

As soon as Gove's statement became public, Gavin Williamson put his whips into action, calling every Boris Johnson supporter they could find to get them to switch to the home secretary. Some modernisers with strong social links went to Gove, while those who had been backing Johnson because he was a Brexiteer switched to Andrea Leadsom, but

May's team managed to hoover up most of the ministers and the non-ideologically bound. With four days to go until the first ballot, May had twice the support of any of her rivals. She was suddenly the hot favourite to become prime minister, and people began to ask themselves who she really was.

At her campaign launch May introduced herself to the nation with the words, 'I know I'm not a showy politician. I don't tour the television studios. I don't gossip about people over lunch. I don't go drinking in Parliament's bars. I don't often wear my heart on my sleeve. I just get on with the job in front of me.' This chimed with the experience of many of those backing her. Shortly after the referendum two Conservative MPs had gone to her to ask what jobs they could expect in a May government. She replied, 'I don't do deals. You're going to support me because I'm Theresa May.'[1]

May was a no-nonsense politician who had survived in one of the toughest jobs in government by studying her brief, picking her fights carefully, and defending her positions, once established, tenaciously. Damian Green, who was helping to front her campaign, remembered a meeting with the former Liberal Democrat business secretary Vince Cable during the coalition years: 'One of the more memorable meetings I was at was with her and Vince, at the height of Vince's attempt to sabotage the immigration policy, where in cold and icy terms she took him apart. I had the strong impression nobody had ever spoken to Vince like that. He almost physically shrank. This was a strong woman getting her way at least partly just by force of personality.'

May had shown the same determination in deporting Abu Qatada, the man dubbed Osama bin Laden's 'ambassador to Europe', to Jordan to answer terrorism charges in 2014. When the European Court of Human Rights ruled that some of the evidence against him had been obtained through torture, May jumped on a plane to Jordan and negotiated a new treaty to guarantee that the torture evidence would not be used, clearing the way for Qatada's extradition. That incident amply demonstrated her tenacity and determination in dealing with thorny international negotiations. It would become a central element of her leadership pitch, along with her willingness to demand reforms from the police and her decision to stand up to the United States by refusing to deport Gary McKinnon, a computer hacker suffering from Asperger's Syndrome. Despite her reputation as a hardliner on immigration, May had also been one of the original Tory modernisers. She was a key supporter of the push to get more Conservative women into Parliament, and her reform of police stop-and-search powers was highly liberal.

Her perceived disadvantages were that she was secretive, and disappeared from view for long periods. Plenty of Cameron's advisers called her a 'control freak'. In its most extreme form this criticism encompassed an unflattering comparison with a Labour predecessor. A Downing Street source said, 'Having worked with Theresa, she has the potential to become a Gordon Brown. I know the bandwidth of a prime minister. It's big, but it's limited. Brexit is an enormous issue, so I worry that everything else will grind to a halt because she won't let others get on with it. She has perfected the submarine pose. You can't do that as prime minister.' Others had not forgotten May's time as party chairman between 2002 and 2003, when she told members that the Conservatives had come to be seen as 'the nasty party' – a home truth many had struggled to forgive.

Other cabinet ministers had found it frustrating that they could not do deals with her, swapping their support on one issue in return. The Conservative peer and *Times* columnist Danny Finkelstein said, 'She is not transactional. She'll take a position on something and you'll support her, but then she won't come back and support you in return. She'll just take a position on the next issue. That has given her a reputation for being non-collegiate, but also a reputation for being tough at what she does.'[2] For many, that was the clincher. David Davis, who was to become her secretary of state for Brexit, said, 'I can see her looking Merkel in the eye and if need be staring her down.'

But victory was not a foregone conclusion.

On Friday, 1 July, eight days after the referendum and a week to the day since Nick Boles urged him to run, Michael Gove stood up at the headquarters of Policy Exchange – the think tank that had launched the modernisation of the Conservative Party – and explained why he wanted to be prime minister. While Johnson had struggled to cobble together fifteen hundred words of prose, Gove had, in less than twenty-four hours, knocked out a 5,000-word opus summarising his views. It may have been the most substantial speech ever delivered at a leadership launch, but it was also one of the strangest. It had a valedictory quality, as if Gove was bringing down the curtain on a decade of reform by

preserving his world view in a political time-capsule. He channelled
Richard Cobden and Theodore Roosevelt to map out a vision of a sort of
national-greatness conservatism that would exploit the opportunities of
Brexit to put science and education at the heart of the economy, and raise
up the less well-off. But even some of his allies regarded it as a better
seminar than a leadership launch. 'It was much, much too substantial,'
one friend said. 'One of the things Michael had a reputation for across
Whitehall was meddling and sounding off. As I listened to that speech
my heart sank further and further as he had the lobby in his hands,
extemporising about the issues of the day in a way calculated to piss off
absolutely everybody. It was a great *Times* leader conference performance, but it was not someone reducing his negatives amongst his peers.'

The media and Boris Johnson's allies were immediately suspicious of
the speech, seeing its commendable breadth and buttock-numbing
length as evidence that Gove had prepared it in advance, and had been
plotting to knife Johnson all along. Since it was almost Gove's last political will and testament it flowed easily, but he had also had help from
Clare Foges, a former speechwriter to David Cameron.

When he was done, Gove took questions until the arms of the waiting
media fell exhausted to their sides. It was immediately apparent that
whatever the merits of his speech, it had been overshadowed by his
actions the day before. He was asked which *Game of Thrones* character
he now resembled, but refused to answer. Hearing this, Ben Wallace took
to Twitter and wrote, 'He is actually Theon Greyjoy, or will be by the time
I am finished with him.' Fans of the series were aware that the character
had his penis severed in one gruesome episode, though Wallace later
explained that he had been referring to an episode in which Greyjoy
returns to his native Iron Islands and is pronounced unfit to rule by his
peers.

Nick Boles, who introduced Gove, had advised him to take questions
for as long as it took, as part of a 'pure masochism strategy'. He told him,
'What do you do when you've basically done something really appalling
in most people's eyes? You take the punishment beating. What you do
when you face someone who's very, very competent, but actually quite
narrow and quite boring, is that you amaze people with your range and
brilliance.' The problem was that Gove's move against Johnson had
undermined his reputation for competence, since it seemed to have sunk
both of their chances. As a Labour frontbencher put it, 'Boris can with-

stand all of these things, because the nature of Boris is things always go wrong with him. The whole thing about Gove was he was clever. And then he showed himself to be incredibly stupid.' Boles was just delighted to be helping someone he believed in totally. He told friends, 'My view is that even if we lose I won't regret a piece of it for a second.' He regarded Gove as 'the real deal and the whole deal' in a way even Cameron was not.

Having proclaimed Britain's Independence Day a week and a half earlier, Nigel Farage chose American Independence Day, Monday, 4 July, to announce that he was resigning as leader of Ukip for the third time. Speaking at a press conference in Westminster, he said: 'During the referendum I said I wanted my country back ... now I want my life back.' His departure made Tim Farron, who had been leader of the Liberal Democrats for the grand total of 354 days, Britain's longest-serving major party leader. Irvine Welsh, the socialist author of *Trainspotting*, marked his passing by tweeting, 'Johnson and Farage – a couple of jakeys who wake up from a binge having shat the bed, then sneak out the doss house by the back door.'

Ukip's deputy leader Paul Nuttall, immigration spokesman Steven Woolfe, culture spokesman Peter Whittle, Suzanne Evans (who had replaced Farage for three days the last time he had resigned) and the party's only MP, Douglas Carswell, were all considered runners and riders to replace Farage. Pretty soon they were all out of the running too.

The Conservative candidate getting all the attention from the Eurosceptics, in both the Tory Party and Ukip alike, was Andrea Leadsom, who was fast emerging as Theresa May's main rival. Up until that point all that most of her colleagues knew about her was that she had run the Fresh Start Group, that she had told the nation in the debates that she was a mother and a grandmother – and that she had once told George Osborne to 'Fuck off.' For a sizeable minority of the Conservative Party in the House of Commons, that was not a bad prospectus. Leadsom had supposedly sent the four-letter volley Osborne's way in 2011 when he urged her not to join the rebellion of the eighty-one Tories demanding an EU referendum. She also earned the chancellor's enmity when, as a member of the Treasury Select Committee, she suggested that he should apologise for suggesting that 'people around Gordon Brown' had given Barclays Bank the green light to manipulate the Libor lending rate at the height of the financial crisis.

Leadsom's aides always denied the swearing story, pointing out that Osborne eventually consented to her taking a ministerial job at the Treasury, but it gave her a certain cachet with MPs not admitted to the Cameron–Osborne circle. Those who worked with her at Fresh Start depicted a woman who, like Theresa May, knew her own mind. 'Unlike almost every other politician I've ever known, she absolutely at all times understood what her objectives were,' one of her aides said.

Leadsom's independence of mind was in evidence in the early part of the referendum campaign, when she kept her head down until Vote Leave won designation. Dominic Raab, her Brexiteer colleague, encouraged her to do more, warning her that if the Brexiteers lost she would be just as likely to be punished by the Cameroons as if they won, so she may as well put her shoulder to the wheel.

If her background in financial services earned Leadsom respect, it was her faith, worn proudly and publicly, that made her popular with a certain faction on the Eurosceptic right. Iain Duncan Smith had got to know her several years before, when his Centre for Social Justice had done some work with the Oxford Parent Infant Project, a charity that helps families struggling to form a secure bond with their new babies, of which Leadsom was chairman for nine years. Halfway through the referendum campaign, Duncan Smith approached Leadsom and said, 'If you decide to stand I will back you.' Bernard Jenkin, who had been Duncan Smith's first shadow cabinet backer in 2001, was also keen on Leadsom running: 'With Boris's collapse and the way poor Michael became rather discredited, her candidacy became essential. But at no point did I pressure her to stand. You have to let them make their own decision.' Leadsom spoke to her husband, who was supportive. She quickly enlisted the help of her media spokesman Bill Clare, who had also advised Chris Grayling and Liam Fox.

Her campaign manager would be Tim Loughton, the former minister for children and families, who had recruited her to the Conservative Association at Warwick University during a freshers' fair in the 1980s. There were reports that the two were old flames, and that he called her 'TW'. This became a running media joke all week, as Loughton would be seen carrying a folder stamped with different slogans like 'The Winner', 'Trouser Wearer' and 'Tattoo Woman'. A journalist on a red-top newspaper even asked one of Leadsom's aides whether the initials meant her nickname in younger days had been 'Tit Wank'. This suggestion was vehemently denied. Another key recruit was Steve Baker, who was asked to get a ground operation organised, ready for the battle for grassroots support, and acted as the unofficial whip. The dedication to the cause of another recruit, Will Wragg, was such that having missed the postal deadline to send a letter to Tory MPs, he slept in his office overnight to ensure the letters got there as soon as possible the following morning. He had to be 'sent home for a shower', another campaigner said.

On the morning of 4 July, the day before the first ballot in the leadership election, Leadsom got the backing of Boris Johnson, who issued a statement laced with coded attacks on Gove. He pointedly praised Leadsom as 'kind' and 'trustworthy', and suggested 'she possesses the qualities needed to bring together Leavers and Remainers in the weeks and months ahead'. A survey on ConservativeHome, the website that monitors grassroots Tory opinion, made her first choice for leader. May's supporters looked on nervously. But Leadsom's team were all too aware that they were playing catch-up. 'Theresa has been planning this for six months,' said one aide. 'We've been planning this for about six hours.'

At times the lack of preparation showed. With prominence came scrutiny. Stories quickly circulated questioning details of Leadsom's CV. *The Times* revealed that, despite her allies saying she had controlled 'billions of pounds of funds' in the City, she had never managed funds or advised clients during ten years at Invesco Perpetual, and had only held approval from the financial services regulator for three months. Company documents showed that she had been a marketing director at her brother-in-law's investment fund, rather than managing director, as she had claimed. When her campaign issued a new CV in response to the media scrutiny it downgraded her role at Barclays in the mid-1990s and failed to repeat earlier claims – made when applying to become the Tory candidate for South Northamptonshire – that she had been the bank's youngest-ever director, and 'head of UK banking'. Critical MPs compared her to Sarah Palin, the social conservative who was the Republican candidate for vice president in 2008, who appeared flaky on contact with the media.

The Leadsom bandwagon hit the buffers at the first hustings for the candidates on Monday the 4th. Backbenchers who knew her from her debate performances or her forensic cross-examinations on the Treasury Select Committee were bemused when she started babbling to MPs about how she wanted to address 'the three Bs' – 'bankers, Brussels and babies' – before segueing from her pitch to be leader into musings on the importance of massaging babies' brains. One MP said he thought she was applying to be a 'child development officer'. Another said the performance 'went down like a cup of cold sick'.[3] Perhaps more seriously, Leadsom faced three questions about the support she was attracting from Arron Banks and Ukip. She had not spoken to Banks, or invited his support, but the Leave.EU chief was pouring money into phone banks and social media advertising urging his supporters to back her, and she did not stop him from doing so. Had her campaign lasted through the summer, it is likely that Banks would have spent far more than either of the official campaigns. He said, 'We absolutely hammered it on social media. Our first thing was seen by about 800,000 people.' May's team 'raised alarm bells' with Tory high command. Leadsom's failure to close down the issue at the hustings added to concerns about her candidacy. 'When you're asked to say you're not Ukip at a hustings to be leader of the Conservative party, you're in trouble,' said one MP. 'It was a car crash.'[4]

By contrast, when Theresa May spoke the banging of desks was sufficiently vigorous that policemen waiting in the Commons committee corridor outside rushed to the doors because they feared the glass was going to fall out. 'The thing that came across with Theresa was her sheer, icy, professionalism,' one grandee remarked. 'Margaret Thatcher without the sense of humour.' May made a point of talking about how she would restore cabinet government, distancing herself from the Cameron 'chumocracy'.

May's only sticky moment came on the question of whether EU nationals in the UK should be given the right to stay. She was the only candidate not to guarantee those rights, saying all options should be open in a negotiation, but Stephen Crabb scored some points by saying it would be 'immoral' to use people as 'bargaining chips'. Liam Fox spoke for twice as long as he took questions, and pronounced that he had 'enjoyed it'. Remarkably, Michael Gove escaped without any mention of Johnson, and instead teased Ben Wallace, who had written a piece that weekend for the *Telegraph* criticising Gove's 'emotional need to gossip, particularly when drink is taken'. Gove joked about going to watch

Queens Park Rangers with Dominic Cummings: 'I'm not sure whether Ben Wallace wants to pick up the drinks tab.'[5]

With the hustings over, the campaign whips tried to nail down the remaining waverers, and swapped notes with their rivals on MPs who were proving holdouts, or being unusually ecumenical in their favours. Keith Simpson, the MP for Broadland in Norfolk and one of Parliament's best wits, told colleagues, 'There are far more important things than principles at stake here – there are jobs.' Daniel Kawczynski, who had asked one of Boris Johnson's sidekicks for a junior ministerial post, offered to deliver the Polish vote to the other campaigns. The Foreign Office had recently acquired a new cat called Palmerston, and a minister involved in May's campaign said, 'We are lining up Daniel to become Palmerston's PPS, because he is desperate to be in the Foreign Office. We think he can be trusted with the litter tray.'

Ken Clarke upstaged everyone on 5 July, the day of the first ballot, when he sounded off in the Westminster studios of *Sky News*. Believing he was off air, he described Gove's views on foreign policy as 'wild', and predicted, 'With Michael as prime minister we'd go to war with at least three countries at once.' He then added, 'He did us all a favour by getting rid of Boris. The idea of Boris as prime minister is ridiculous.' But the *pièce de résistance* was his description of May: 'Theresa is a bloody difficult woman.' The home secretary's team rejoiced at Clarke's verbal incontinence. 'We were all thrilled,' said a senior figure. 'At the time we were thinking, what do we need to say to the membership? That is what we needed to say to the membership. Thank you, Ken.'

Gove's team spent the day of the first ballot trying to convince MPs on the left that Leadsom was too dangerous to make it into the run-off, and those on the right that only he could beat May. He told MPs, 'I've been tested in the fire, and there's nothing more that they can throw at me.' He believed that in backing Leadsom the Eurosceptic right were making their second strategic mistake, after seeking to oust Dominic Cummings from the Leave campaign in January.

Steve Baker was the 1922 Committee member on duty manning the ballot box when George Osborne came in to vote that day. It was just three weeks since Baker had helped kill the chancellor's emergency budget plans. He said, 'George Osborne did congratulate me on the

campaign. He did reflect he'd been the object of some of my campaigning. I thought it was gracious given what we did to him.' Osborne told
Baker, 'One of the high points in a dark night was seeing that Wycombe
district voted remain.' Osborne did not take sides publicly, but he voted
that day for Theresa May to take the job that, just twelve days earlier, had
looked most likely one day to be his.

Just before 6.30 p.m. Graham Brady, the chairman of the 1922
Committee, entered Committee Room 6 on the Commons committee
corridor and addressed a motley gathering of MPs, journalists and grandees to read out the results. The ballot was a triumph for May, who
secured 165 votes to Leadsom's sixty-six. Gove surprised some by securing forty-eight, with Crabb on thirty-four and Fox on sixteen.

Crabb and Fox were quick to announce that they would withdraw,
and back May. It was natural for Crabb, a fellow Remainer and member
of the cabinet, to support her, but the speed and enthusiasm of Fox's
conversion, when he might have been expected to talk to Leadsom, reinforced the view that he had done a deal with May in advance. He said she
would be 'a very fine prime minister'. One MP remarked to him that
night, 'That was such an exquisitely well-played-out game of chess.' Fox
responded, 'You're such a cynic.' May's team insisted she had offered no
jobs to anyone, but one said, 'There was one partial deal.' This was understood to be with Fox, at a stage when he was thought to be peeling votes
away from Boris Johnson. Fox's response was typically enigmatic: 'I've
never done partial anything with anyone.'

Gove insisted he would fight on. Leadsom's camp alleged that May
had loaned Gove eighteen votes to prop him up. The details were murky,
but even Gove's team believed they had received some votes from friends
of his who were formally backing May but knew she had plenty of unde-
clared votes in hand, although this was not officially sanctioned by the
home secretary's seconds. Gavin Williamson and his team met shortly
afterwards in Committee Room U in Portcullis House to decide whether
or not they should reverse this policy in the second round. Should they
recalibrate, so as to give Gove enough support to keep Leadsom out of
the run-off? If Gove had been closer than eighteen votes behind they
might have considered it, but Williamson said, 'We need to keep this
simple. As soon as we start playing silly games we're going to find
ourselves ending up in a Jeremy Corbyn situation.' The previous autumn,
Labour Party moderates had helped Corbyn onto the leadership ballot

paper out of politeness, only to see him romp to victory. There would be no deal.[6]

Celebrating her win, May said she was the only one capable of uniting the country and the party, and negotiating the best Brexit deal: 'I am also the only one capable of drawing support from the whole of the Conservative Party.'

Gove's hopes of beating Leadsom to claim second place were sunk by the second hustings on Wednesday the 6th. While most of the world was digesting the conclusions of the long-awaited Chilcot Report into the Iraq War, which condemned Tony Blair's handling of the lead-up to the conflict, Leadsom did much better than in the previous hustings. When she finished her pitch, she said, 'I'm a quick learner – note I didn't use the expression "babies' brains" once.' May also altered her pitch. On Monday she had spoken as a potential prime minister. This time she 'changed tack totally and talked about how she would lead the party', said one of her team, stressing her desire to listen to the grass-roots. This went down well. Once again, the home secretary had the most memorable line. A friendly MP, Richard Graham, asked about Ken Clarke's description of her. 'I am a bloody difficult woman,' she replied. 'The next man to find that out will be Jean-Claude Juncker.' That took the roof off.

Gove began well, humbly addressing the trust issue. 'My real name is not Michael Gove,' he admitted, winning admiration for discussing his adoption. But he was then put on the spot as first Steve Baker and then Peter Bone asked if he could guarantee that Dominic Cummings would not be employed in Number 10 if he were to win. Gove replied that Cummings would have no job, and when pressed said he would not have any more influence than a friend who he occasionally saw for a drink.

The wheels came off when the MP Nicola Blackwood asked Gove whether he had sanctioned calls for tactical voting to keep Leadsom out. Gove denied it, stressing that MPs should vote for the candidate they most wanted to be prime minister. But he was sunk below the waterline when Graham Stuart, the former chairman of the Education Select Committee, stood up and pointed out that his supporters were urging MPs to vote tactically. Within minutes a text sent by Nick Boles, Gove's campaign manager, had leaked, showing that they were doing precisely that.

The previous day the Gove campaign team had held a meeting to discuss tactics. Those present remember that everyone was clear: contacts with MPs were to be made in person or on the telephone, with nothing in writing. The order was, 'Don't send texts, don't send emails.' For the campaign manager himself to forget this was a schoolboy error. Boles had written to a dozen May-supporting colleagues:

> You are my friend. I respect the fact that you want Theresa May to be PM. It is overwhelmingly likely that she will be. And if she does I will sleep easily at night. But I am seriously frightened about the risk of allowing Andrea Leadsom onto the membership ballot. What if Theresa stumbles? Are we really confident that the membership won't vote for a fresh face who shares their attitudes about much of modern life? Like they did with IDS. I am not asking you to respond unless you positively want to have a chat. But I hope that you will reflect on this carefully. Michael doesn't mind spending two months taking a good thrashing from Theresa if that's what it takes, but in the party's interest and the national interest surely we must work together to stop AL?

One MP who spoke to Boles that week believed that in the intensity of the campaign, 'Nick went briefly mad.' He did not choose the recipients of his text wisely. They included Richard Harrington, who had introduced Boles to his husband on an Israeli beach during a Conservative Friends of Israel visit to the Middle East. But Harrington was not just supporting May, he was her campaign fundraiser. He phoned Boles and asked him if he wished him to pass the message on to May's campaign chairman Chris Grayling, but Boles said he would prefer it to remain confidential. Harrington did nothing more. But by then it was in Anna Soubry's inbox too. She did show it to the campaign, and it quickly found its way to journalists including the BBC's Laura Kuenssberg. Once again the Gove camp had been let down by an injudicious electronic communication. Once again they looked at best too clever by half and at worst duplicitous. Most seriously, they looked incompetent.

Boles tweeted an apology, but to Gove rather than Leadsom: 'He did not know about it let alone authorise it. And it does not reflect his views.' Which was half right. Gove was polite about the disaster: 'You did it because you wanted to support me – and I can't blame you for that.' Boles was very hurt by the episode, texting MPs a few days later, 'I'm not doing politics anymore.'

The Boles text was a briefly notorious episode, but it did not kill off Gove's hopes. He had never developed the momentum he needed to challenge Leadsom. 'The "Big Mo" was never there,' a friend of Gove said. 'I thought we were dead in the water when I saw the Eurosceptic old guard rowing in behind Widow Twankey.' The friend described Leadsom as 'pure panto'. Gove suspected that May had not stuck to the letter of her pledge not to offer jobs, and that the hint of cabinet posts had lured away possible supporters like Priti Patel and David Davis, who Gove tried 'amazingly hard' to win over. A campaign source said, 'I think people were told, "If you back me, you'll be in the cabinet."'

Boles and Gove, who had been present at the creation of the Conservative Party's modernisation project, were there again when it was outflanked by the forces of old Tory pragmatism and dynamic-movement Euroscepticism. For Gove, who had seen Tony Blair as 'the Master', to have his campaign hit the buffers on the very day Chilcot buried Blair's reputation was symbolic of the end of an era of centrist metropolitan liberalism that had dominated British politics since 1997. David Davis, by contrast, felt he had got his party back: 'I do think there is a bit of a return to normal politics. You've had a very extended Blairite era both sides of the political divide, a sort of managerial approach to politics. One of the things that's happened with the referendum is that the ordinary people have reasserted themselves. The same people who carried off the referendum are the same sort of people who put Margaret Thatcher in power. It was a distinctly non-metropolitan decision.'

A battle for the soul of the Conservative Party was now under way between a group of establishment pragmatists around May and an insurgency backing Leadsom, who blended support for Brexit with an appeal to party traditionalists who still resented gay marriage. The Brexiteers knew how to win an election like that, since they had just done so. One MP said, 'Andrea is a movement candidate and it may not matter how she performs. Her supporters have seen off Dave and George. They've got their party back. They won't worry about the details.'

On the morning of Thursday, 7 July, Leadsom formally launched her campaign with a brief and optimistic speech at the base of Millbank Tower. The auditorium was packed with enthusiastic right-wingers. The event had been advertised to journalists as a major speech on the economy, but Leadsom decided instead to string together a few warming bromides and get off-stage before she could be asked any tricky questions about her CV. She had asked Boris Johnson to introduce her, but her most prominent supporter did not appear, the first sign that he was beginning to pull back to a position of studied neutrality. At the end of the event, Penny Mordaunt encouraged the assembled masses to march on Parliament, which they duly did. Campaign manager Tim Loughton then led the way, bouncing around like a teddy bear with a new set of energiser batteries. Loughton decided to inject more pantomime camp by chanting, 'Whadda we want?' Some of those trailing in his wake, who included recognisable Ukip activists, responded. 'Lead-som-for-lead-er!' 'When do we want it?' 'Now!'

'Whaddawewantleadsomforleaderwhendowewantit.Now!' On and on *ad infinitum*. Some engaged enthusiastically, but Theresa Villiers, who had incautiously placed herself next to Loughton, kept her lips zipped like a captured prisoner of war reluctant even to give up name, rank and serial number. From Team May, Damian Green said, 'She looked more uncomfortable than anyone since Cersei did the walk of shame in *Game of Thrones*.' Loughton and Mordaunt had scrambled together the march idea as an eye-catching means of demonstrating Leadsom's strength, after hearing the talk that May's team would lend Gove votes to keep Leadsom off the final ballot paper. But a minister backing May added, 'There is something about MPs marching on Parliament that, apart from looking ludicrous, feels improper. It is revolutionary mobs that march on parliaments, not ministers of the crown.' Leadsom did not march, of course. She and Mordaunt were ushered into a black Mercedes and whisked back to Parliament the easy way.

Watching from Downing Street, David Cameron felt he had seen a glimpse of an alternative past. He told a close ally, 'If it wasn't for Michael and Boris, the Leave campaign would have felt like the Leadsom campaign march on Parliament.' One MP told Sam Coates of *The Times* that he had switched sides to May after watching the 'freaky' procession wend its way along the river. But to the people Leadsom was seeking to win over, the event was not a turnoff. Damian Green was among the members of the May camp who were fearful that Leadsom could gather momentum. As Hillary Clinton discovered while battling Barack Obama for the Democratic presidential nomination in 2008, beating a movement can be impossible once it gets up a head of steam. Leadsom's supporters were already deploying the Vote Leave playbook, labelling anyone who criticised her an establishment crony.

To aid her argument, the party hierarchy and the media were finding much to criticise. Tory whips, who are supposed to be neutral, urged MPs to vote for May, using the line, 'You've got to vote for Theresa, because Leadsom is an extremist.' One MP sidled up to Leadsom ally Owen Paterson, the former environment secretary, and said, 'I'm backing Andrea, but please don't tell anyone because it will be the first time I have ever defied the whips.' The same day Gary Gibbon, the political editor of *Channel 4 News*, interviewed Leadsom and asked her, 'Do you ever feel that you've been spoken to directly by God?' Gibbon had been told by a minister who had sat next to a close relative of Leadsom's at a dinner that Leadsom believed she had heard the voice of God. Leadsom complained that Gibbon was 'poking fun' at her faith, and denied that God had told her to do things – which was not quite what Gibbon had asked.

Iain Duncan Smith went in to bat for Leadsom, accusing her opponents of conducting 'black ops' against her. MPs contacted her campaign team and called on them to 'send for Lynton'. A senior figure in the campaign replied, 'We already have.' An approach had been made to Crosby's firm CTF Partners shortly after Boris Johnson dropped out of the contest. But despite Johnson's involvement with the Leadsom campaign, Crosby said, 'No. I won't work on another campaign. Boris is a friend and I help him.'

On Thursday evening, Graham Brady announced the results of the second ballot. Gove had clung on to forty-six votes, with Leadsom on eighty-four, but May had romped home with 199. May's reaction on being told the result was, 'Oh dear, one short!' A minister present said, 'That's typical of Theresa. She's never satisfied. She always wants to do better.' The home secretary had won 60 per cent of the parliamentary party. It was a commanding lead, but could still be overturned by the grassroots. As Gove's team filed out of the room where they had learned the result, one of them turned to the journalists waiting outside in the corridor. 'Enjoy Prime Minister Leadsom,' he said. 'It'll give you lots to write about.'

Among Boris Johnson's supporters there was jubilation at Gove's distant bronze medal. At 4.24 p.m., as the result was announced, Johnson's sister Rachel channelled her inner Joy Division, tweeting,

'Gove won't tear us apart again.' 'He got what he fucking deserved' was Jake Berry's blunter response. In the offices of Crosby Textor Fullbrook there was joy. 'It was justice for the justice minister,' a CTF source said.

That evening Gove kept a long-standing arrangement to give a speech at the summer party of the investment firm the Legatum Institute. One of those present was impressed by his composure. 'It was an hour after he had dropped out, and I saw him on the way in and he just said, "Interesting times." It took courage to turn up.' Gove took to the stage and channelled Andy Warhol: 'Everyone is going to be a contender for the Conservative leadership for fifteen minutes. I've just had my fifteen minutes.'

While Gove licked his wounds, Andrew Feldman was trying to ensure that David Cameron got a send-off lasting more than fifteen minutes. When the 1922 Committee executive met to draw up the timetable for the leadership election run-off, Brady and his team recommended that the whole process be completed by 2 September at the latest, so there would be a new prime minister in place by the time Parliament returned from the summer recess. They were keen for it to be finished by 25 August. But when the issue went to the Conservative Party board, Feldman mobilised his forces and got the end date changed to 9 September. It was no coincidence that this meant Cameron would be able to attend his final G20 summit as prime minister the preceding weekend. Cameron's critics saw the move as the 'worst of both worlds – you maximise instability by announcing your immediate resignation, and then provide lack of direction through to the autumn'.

After Vote Leave's victory, no one was prepared to write off Leadsom, however far behind she trailed with MPs. But she herself was already having second thoughts. She looked across the Commons chamber at Labour, where Jeremy Corbyn enjoyed the full-throated support of only one in ten of his MPs, and wondered whether winning the backing of a quarter of her parliamentary Conservative Party was enough. Graham Brady saw what might happen quicker than most. This was not just a leadership election: the Tory Party was picking a prime minister in the midst of a national crisis. In advance of the second ballot, Brady spoke to Sir Jeremy Heywood, the cabinet secretary, and Simon Case, the prime minister's principal private secretary, whose responsibilities included liaison between Downing Street and Buckingham Palace. Brady advised them that it would be worth thinking through the consequences of one of the candidates dropping out. He asked about the location of the queen, and pointed out that Cameron was due to be out of the country from Friday at a NATO summit, and was not due back until late on Saturday. 'If someone was to withdraw, it could be really quite inconvenient,' he told them. He also enquired about the constitutional niceties of one person becoming Conservative Party leader while another remained prime minister. There was a precedent under John Major, but Brady suspected there would be 'queasiness' at the royal end if the interregnum was too long. He then arranged to see Chris Grayling and Tim Loughton, the two campaign chairmen, and talked them through the process.

On Thursday evening, after the second ballot and without talking to Loughton, Andrea Leadsom called Brady. She indicated that she was close to a decision to withdraw, on the grounds that May had an overwhelming lead and a protracted election process could damage the economy. Had she dropped out there and then she might have been spared the pain that followed. But Brady advised her not to act precipitately, and to sleep on it. He also talked her through the difficulties presented by the fact that the prime minister was away until the Saturday evening. This phone call proves that what followed was not Leadsom's primary motivation for abandoning the fight – but it was certainly to make the decision she was moving towards easier.

After her call with Brady, Leadsom attended a fundraising dinner in Northamptonshire organised by Chris Heaton-Harris. Boris Johnson was there to support her, but many of those present found the event awkward. 'They were all crowding around Boris, and not her,' one MP observed. Johnson encouraged Leadsom to fight on. An ally said, 'He had discussions with her and said, "You need to be resolute and move forward." I think he felt there had to be a contest.'

Leadsom did an interview with Rachel Sylvester of *The Times* on Friday. The issue of whether to drop out was still playing on her mind. She said, 'We have to do what is in the interests of the country. As I sit here I'm weighing up, this is a very long time to go … I think the country needs to see leadership.' For unexplained reasons she met Sylvester at a coffee shop in Milton Keynes station, with no press officer or assistant to hand. It is usual for politicians to record set-piece interviews like this, in case there is any dispute over the quotes. Leadsom appeared to be in an odd frame of mind, bursting into tears when she talked about the struggles her mother had been through while raising her.

Sylvester asked her what she thought was 'the main difference between you and Theresa'. After saying that she understood the economy, Leadsom then talked, unprompted, about how she was a 'member of a huge family'. In her first campaign interview the previous weekend with the *Mail on Sunday*, May had been quizzed about her childlessness, and said that she had sought 'help', but to no avail: 'Of course, we were both affected by it. You see friends who now have grown-up children, but you accept the hand that life deals you.'[7]

Given Leadsom's decision to raise the subject of her huge family, and to portray herself as a mother and grandmother during the referendum debates it was an obvious follow-up question to ask how her family informed her politics. She replied, 'I don't really know Theresa very well, but I am sure that Theresa will be really sad she doesn't have children, so I don't want to be, "Andrea has children, Theresa hasn't," because I think that would be really horrible, but genuinely I feel that being a mum means you have a very real stake in the future of our country, a tangible stake. She possibly has nieces, nephews, lots of people, but I have children who are going to have children who will directly be a part of what happens next.'

When the paper came out that evening, Leadsom reacted with fury to its front-page headline, 'Being a mother gives me edge on May'. At 10.41 p.m. she tweeted, 'Truly appalling and the exact opposite of what I said. I am disgusted.' This was stretching things. Fifteen minutes later she had another go: 'This is despicable and hateful reporting. You must now provide the transcript – this is beyond disgusting.' At 11.13 she attacked Sylvester: 'This is the worst gutter journalism I've ever seen. I am so angry – I can't believe this. How could you?' Leadsom had seen the dangers of answering the question, which is why she said it would be unfair to May – but then went ahead and answered it anyway.

In fact, *The Times* did not even print all of Leadsom's newsworthy views. She also expressed strong views about sexual abuse, saying that she would not hire a male nanny, on the grounds that he might be a paedophile. The paper printed that line a week later. The full transcript of the interview shows that she did not stop there. In remarks that would probably have caused another storm had they been made public, she expressed the view that children who had been the victims of child abuse should be placed for adoption with gay couples: 'Look at some of the appalling things [that] happened to children who then become adopted, there's a very strong case that a child who has been terribly abused, a gay couple who are not of the sex of the person who carried out the abuse can be very therapeutic.' The comment may have been intended to demonstrate that Leadsom was not homophobic, but it was notably eccentric.

In any case, Leadsom's comments about childlessness had already offended the party's leading gay politicians. Ruth Davidson tweeted, 'I am childless. I have nieces and nephews. I believe I – like everyone else – have a very real stake in our country.' Alan Duncan, another May supporter who had had a gay wedding, called Leadsom's views 'vile'. The next morning Anna Soubry said Leadsom was 'not PM material', and 'should do us all a favour including herself and step aside'.

The following day, clearly shaken, Leadsom gave a statement outside her home, and said she was 'disgusted with the way this has been presented'. Friends say she spent most of the weekend in tears. 'She got vile texts,' one of her MP supporters said. Some of these abusive messages were from fellow MPs. The irony of 'Mothergate' was that it was Leadsom's concern for her family that had nearly kept her out of the leadership race to start with. 'Andrea agonised over running,' one friend said. 'The main reason was her twelve-year-old daughter. It's fine if you are in some middle-class private school, but in a lot of state schools it's unthinkable to have the prime minister's kid there. The fact that Theresa May has not got any children will actually make it easier for her.'

Leadsom, according to a senior campaign figure, had answered Sylvester's questions 'rather naïvely'. Tim Loughton picked up rumours that a tabloid newspaper would try to get Leadsom to discuss May's diabetes and the challenges facing someone with health problems in high office. Leadsom spent the weekend trying to 'get her head around the magnitude' of 'nine weeks of vitriol' that would have marked her path to Downing Street.

Fiona Hill ordered May's campaign not to respond to the furore. But not everyone could hide their disgust. One member of May's team said that weekend, 'I'm going to fucking kill her for this.'

Leadsom sought to get back onto the front foot with an interview for Monday's *Telegraph*, in which she said she had been left 'shattered by the criticism'. She added, 'I've already said to Theresa how very sorry I am for any hurt caused.'[8] That message was sent by text. May replied that she was 'very grateful'. But there were already signs that Leadsom's most prominent supporter was beginning to distance himself from her. On the Saturday night Boris Johnson was at a party thrown by Jonathan Marland, the former Tory treasurer who had helped fund his first mayoral bid. One of those in attendance phoned Michael Gove to tell him that Boris 'was in a very perky mood and that he indicated to people there was going to be a very big surprise over the next few days'. Johnson and May's teams both deny that they had done a deal. What is certain is that Johnson helped Leadsom decide to throw in the towel. She called Boris on the Monday morning and said she would continue if he was prepared to campaign for her around the country and Lynton Crosby would run the campaign. Crosby had already refused, and Johnson said he was not prepared to spend his entire summer on the stump. A Johnson ally said, 'I don't think he disavowed her in terms of carrying on. But he didn't feel that he would be able to play that sort of role. I think it was due to the fact he was cream-crackered more than anything to do with her. He said, "I can't do this again."' Johnson's other concern was that if he campaigned full-throttle for Leadsom, he would become the centre of attention. 'It becomes the Boris and Theresa show, not the Andrea and Theresa show,' he told an aide. 'I could end up undermining her.'

On Monday morning Leadsom's campaign team met in a house in Cowley Street belonging to former Tory MP Sir Neil Thorne. She explained to her assembled supporters – including Tim Loughton, Steve Baker, Owen Paterson, Bernard Jenkin, Will Wragg, James Morris, Justin Tomlinson, Tom Pursglove, Heather Wheeler, Andrew Murrison, Stuart Jackson and Chris Heaton Harris – that she was standing down because she believed that the country needed a prime minister quickly. A friend who was there said, 'Once she decides to do something there's no point trying to persuade her not to. It's a considerable strength of hers.'

Leadsom went outside and addressed the waiting media from the steps of the house: 'A nine-week leadership campaign at such a critical moment for our country is highly undesirable ... We now need a new prime minister in place as soon as possible.' She thanked the eighty-four MPs who had backed her, but said, 'I do not believe this is sufficient support to lead a strong and stable government should I win the leadership election. I have concluded that the interests of our country are best served by the immediate appointment of a strong and well-supported prime minister. I am therefore withdrawing from the leadership election, and I wish Theresa May the very greatest success.'

Leadsom's supporters were furious about her treatment. Bill Clare said, 'Anyone who knows Andrea and what she stands for, knows absolutely beyond dispute that the characterisation of her at times during the campaign was completely wrong.' But they were sanguine about her decision. Many still thought she could have won. Steve Baker said, 'I'm pretty sure we could have gone to the country and won even with the collateral damage of that weekend.' They accepted, however, that it was the right thing to do. 'She put up a game fight, and I think we were all disappointed but relieved when she decided not to ride through the summer,' said Bernard Jenkin. 'I think her campaign sharpened the focus about the debate about Brexit even in the short time that she was running.' Another friend said, 'Andrea is a woman who will not be bullied. But the combination of having only a quarter of the votes, plus the pure poison, led us all to know it was the right decision. A campaign of that viciousness, extending through until September, would have been appalling. Anyone who suggests she folded has not understood the woman.'

The Conservative Party got a new leader in seventeen days. Labour's malaise showed little sign of being resolved in seventeen months. At the very moment Andrea Leadsom was announcing her decision to quit, Angela Eagle was launching her bid to oust Jeremy Corbyn. Asking journalists for questions by name, she found they had fled. It was still the Tories that were box office.

IRON MAY-DEN

When Theresa May took to the stage for her formal campaign launch in Birmingham she knew she might become the next prime minister. Leadsom had called her that morning to say she might drop out, but May did not know for sure. Chris Grayling was in a meeting with the chief executive of the House of Commons when his private secretary rushed in and thrust a piece of paper into his hand saying 'Andrea's going to quit'. Grayling looked at his phone, and saw he had a text from Graham Brady, chairman of the 1922 Committee, saying 'Please ring urgently.' The two spoke, and Brady explained what was happening. Grayling rushed to Greycoat Place to speak to Fiona Hill and Nick Timothy. By the time he arrived they were both talking to May, who had finished her launch speech and was on her way back to London.

Leadsom had called Brady at 10 o'clock that morning and told him she was going to drop out. She said she would brief her own team at eleven, so Brady waited until that meeting was under way before phoning Sir Jeremy Heywood, the cabinet secretary. 'The thing we talked about hypothetically has happened,' he said. There followed 'a wonderful, eloquent silence' from Britain's senior mandarin. 'I see,' Heywood said eventually. The machine of state, as it had for May's fifty-three predecessors, whirred into action. Downing Street spoke to Buckingham Palace to alert the queen that she would soon be receiving some visitors. Heywood said Cameron would want to take cabinet for one last time on the Tuesday, and PMQs on the Wednesday, before visiting the palace on Wednesday afternoon. Brady then phoned May to congratulate her. There followed an afternoon of carefully choreographed appearances outside St Stephen's Entrance to the Commons, where first Brady, then Grayling, and eventually May herself, addressed the gaggle of waiting journalists.

Michael Gove was quick to offer May his congratulations, closing down any speculation about the contest being reopened with him in the run-off instead. Brady was clear that the rules did not permit anyone who had been eliminated from re-entering the race. Leadsom had briefly wondered if Dominic Raab could take her place, but new entries were not permitted either.

Before May could be declared Tory leader, the 1922 Committee and the Conservative Party board had to approve the termination of the contest. Andrew Feldman emailed all members of the board seeking their consent, and by about 2 p.m. he had it. Brady might have reflected that his actions the week before, in extending the length of the leadership election, had backfired: 'The irony is that when the board of the Conservative Party rejected the 22 executive's recommendation for a very rapid election, pushing the date back to 9 September, the unintended consequence was that they made it much more likely that a candidate in second place would withdraw in order to avoid adverse economic consequences for the country.'

When May got back to London after 3 p.m., Karen Bradley and Chris Grayling planted large kisses on both cheeks and said, 'Well done.' May is not given to overt displays of emotion, but someone who saw her in this period said she had assumed her 'Well I never' look: 'She took it very calmly and looked quietly pleased.' May spent a lot of time working with Hill and Timothy on her statement, while Grayling liaised with Brady. The 1922 Committee would meet at 5 p.m. Her team agreed that the leader in waiting should address the party first, and then go out and make a public statement. At the moment of her triumph she was just three weeks and a day from becoming Britain's longest-serving home secretary.

It was standing room only in the Boothroyd Room in Portcullis House when May appeared to a rapturous reception. She told MPs she was 'very honoured', repeated her pledge that 'Brexit means Brexit', and said she would do her best to lead the party until 2020. The cheering and stamping when she had finished was such that the floor outside, where the journalists were waiting, shook. Steve Baker emerged to seal the peace: 'This thunderous, passionate reception from the Conservative Party shows that Andrea made the right decision, Theresa May must now go forward to take us out of the EU.'

When May emerged outside the Commons for her first public appearance as leader, she wore her new responsibility with ease. Quentin

Letts, the irrepressible sketchwriter for the *Daily Mail*, shouted, 'Give her a kiss!' Philip May leaned over and planted a chaste smacker on his wife's cheek. The image made the front page of nearly every national newspaper the following day. When May went back inside, Alan Duncan said to her, 'I've been calling you Theresa for the last forty years, and these are the last forty-eight hours in which I can do that.' May smiled. 'No, Alan,' she replied. 'You have special permission to call me Theresa, not Prime Minister.' Having helped get Major and Hague elected too, Duncan delighted in telling colleagues, 'The kingmaker has become queenmaker.'

David Cameron's spirit was also light. He addressed the waiting cameras in Downing Street to explain that the formal handover of power would happen on Wednesday. As he walked back through the black door the microphone picked him up humming a little tune, 'Do-doo-de-do,' which sounded a bit like the theme from *The West Wing*. Then he said, 'Right, good,' and was gone.

That evening, May hosted a 'quiet' drinks party at Greycoat Place. Over glasses of wine, with laptops still open, she thanked her small team profusely, and was met with cheers. On the Tuesday evening, as she bade farewell to the Home Office, the magnitude of her achievement finally seemed to hit her. She thanked the staff and said, 'There will always be a part of me that will be Home Office. I know you will give the next home secretary ...' She paused and, with a smile, continued: '... whom I will appoint ...' The officials burst into laughter. The tension was released.

It was a day of valedictory moments. His final cabinet earlier that day had been an emotional experience for David Cameron. As May showered him with praise, his eyes moistened. When George Osborne followed suit, the chancellor detected that his old friend was uncomfortable. 'Being English, David, you'll hate all this praise,' he said.

'You're quite right,' Cameron replied. 'I am English, and I don't much like it.' Fearing a torrent of incontinent eulogies, he brought the meeting to an abrupt close.[1] 'It was all very nice and all very awkward,' said one of those present. 'Very English.' Michael Gove, normally an ebullient contributor to cabinet, remained silent throughout.

Gove held his own party to thank his leadership campaign staff on the Tuesday evening at Mosimann's dining club in Belgravia, where he was joined by ministers, MPs and advisers, including Nick Boles. Gove told the youngsters, 'If anyone in this room is considering mounting a leadership bid in future, Nick and I will be available to tell you exactly how not to do it.'

Cameron had a 'last supper' (coronation chicken with 'some nice wine provided by a donor') that evening in the Downing Street state dining room with his family, closest aides and some MPs who had supported his leadership from the start, like Hugo Swire, Greg Barker and Richard Benyon. The outgoing prime minister talked about his 'partnership' with George Osborne and thanked his wife for 'never putting a foot wrong' as his consort. He also joked about the speed with which he brought about his own downfall: 'They say all political careers end in failure. I had hoped to have a slow, gradual decline, but it has come with a juddering halt instead.' The rapidity of it all had shocked those around him, who had confidently expected him to remain as prime minister until 2018 or 2019. 'We thought we had another three years to go,' said one aide. 'Then it was another three months, and it ended up being three days.'

It was left to Samantha to cheer everyone up, thanking her husband for being able to put his work behind him when he went back to the flat, and saying 'he doesn't shout at the kids' whatever the crisis going on downstairs. She said she had not looked forward to living in Downing Street, but insisted she had been 'very happy' there. A friend said, 'Everyone thinks she's like, "Hip, hip hooray, open the bloody champagne, got this thing over and done with." But it's not really like that.'

The Cameron children ran around the dining room with their cousins. It would be a great upheaval for them too. 'Florence keeps talking about going back to the old house,' one guest said. 'David has to explain she's never actually lived at the old house. Then she went back to the old house, saw how small her bedroom was, and said, "Daddy, I want you to stay on being prime minister!"'

The evening was an opportunity for those who knew Cameron best to reflect on the man and what he had done. 'For me, I think that he was a man that had a love of family, love of country, love of the British way of life, he was a patriot through and through. That's what he was all about,' one said. 'Because he was intellectually and emotionally self-confident, he could give in a way which other politicians couldn't. He could take decisions.' The accumulated result of Cameron's decisions on the EU referendum was defeat. But he was not introspective about them. 'He said, "In the end I took those decisions and I stand by them." It wasn't like a wake. He's a big boy, and I think he's somebody who's already at ease with the decision he's made.'

Cameron's final day in Downing Street began with the usual meetings to prepare for what would be his 182nd and last Prime Minister's Questions. At noon, as ever, the first question was to ask him to list his official engagements for the day. 'Mr Speaker,' he said, 'this morning I had meetings with ministerial colleagues and others. Other than one meeting this afternoon with Her Majesty the Queen, the diary for the rest of my day is remarkably light.' When Jeremy Corbyn began to quiz him about how May would implement Brexit, Cameron took the chance to score the obvious point: 'When it comes to women prime ministers, I'm very pleased to be able to say pretty soon it's going to be 2–0.' With the Labour Party mired in arguments about who would be allowed to vote in its leadership contest, Cameron said, 'We've both been having these leadership elections. We've had resignation, nomination, competition and coronation. They haven't even decided what the rules are yet.' He then compared Corbyn's resilience in the face of blows that would have felled most leaders to 'the Black Knight in Monty Python's *Holy Grail* – he's been kicked so many times, but he says, "Keep going, it's only a flesh wound." I admire that.'

Peter Lilley said that in his thirty-three years in Parliament he had seen Cameron 'achieve a mastery of that despatch box unparalleled in my time'. But Angus Robertson of the SNP misjudged the mood of the House: 'The prime minister's legacy will undoubtedly be that he has taken us to the brink of being taken out of the European Union, so we will not be applauding his premiership on these benches.' Others, however, did. As he finished, Cameron said, 'I will miss the roar of the crowd, I will miss the barbs from the opposition, but I will be willing you on.' He went out as he came in, with a reference to the moment in 2005 when he said of Tony Blair, 'He was the future once.' Now he told MPs, 'Nothing is really impossible if you put your mind to it. After all, as I once said, I was the future once.' The Tories rose to their feet to applaud. They were joined by a dozen or so Labour MPs and some Liberal Democrats, but it was a measure of the lingering anger about the referendum that the others could not bring themselves to send him off as the Conservatives had done Blair. At the bar of the House, some Tory MPs were in tears. From the far end of the chamber, Michael Gove and Boris Johnson watched, their thoughts their own.

At 4.40 p.m. Cameron, Samantha and their three children, Nancy, Elwen and Florence, emerged from Number 10 for the last time. Downing Street staff formed a guard of honour in the lobby and Cameron went down the line giving high fives. Outside, at the lectern, the outgoing prime minister sought to write his own political obituary, ticking off a few of his achievements: the National Living Wage, the new schools and 'the couples who have been able to get married, who weren't allowed to in the past', the social change for which he will perhaps be longest remembered. He thanked his team, his wife – 'the love of my life' – and his children, recalling how they 'kicked the red boxes full of work', and that Florence 'once climbed into one before a foreign trip and said, "Take me with you."' With an apologetic look at them, he said, 'Well, no more boxes.'

All that remained was the formalities: 'We will shortly be heading to Buckingham Palace to see Her Majesty the Queen, where I will tender my resignation as prime minister and I will advise Her Majesty to invite Theresa May to form a new administration.' At forty-nine years of age and in his prime, after six years and sixty-three days in the hot seat, David Cameron uttered his final public words as prime minister. 'It has been the greatest honour of my life,' he said, voice wavering slightly. 'As we leave for the last time, my only wish is continued success for this great country that I love so very much.' This time there were no tears, just a group family hug.

Cameron drove to Buckingham Palace. At 5.19 p.m. his premiership officially came to an end with an announcement from the palace that he had tendered his resignation, 'which Her Majesty was graciously pleased to accept'. At Number 10 his aides took the back way out through the Cabinet Office, where they met Fiona Hill, Nick Timothy, Alex Dawson and the others waiting to come in the same way. Around 6 p.m. Theresa May kissed the queen's hand and accepted her offer to form a new government.

In Downing Street, the new prime minister was quick to set out her stall. 'If you're from an ordinary working-class family, life is much harder than many people in Westminster realise,' she said. 'I know you're working around the clock, I know you're doing your best, and I know that sometimes life can be a struggle. The government I lead will be driven not by the interests of the privileged few, but by yours. We will do everything we can to give you more control over your lives.' Using 'control' was a clever touch, since it acknowledged that the motivations for the Leave vote embraced discontent beyond the European sphere.

When she entered Number 10, May was greeted by another guard of honour with staff applauding. In her new office she found two bottles of red wine left behind by Cameron. Watching all this, one minister wondered if he would still have a job when the reshuffle began, but his main feelings were of pride at the way the Tories had extricated themselves from a mess largely of their own making, while Labour were descending further into theirs. With Owen Smith having announced that he would challenge Angela Eagle for the leadership, it looked as if the moderate vote would split their vote. 'There was a sense of pride that our party, when it really needs to, can get its shit together,' the minister said. 'Labour somehow managed to end up with two unity candidates.'

May had only been at her desk half an hour when she summoned George Osborne from next door in Number 11, the only minister for whom a move would mean a change of home as well. With speed and little sympathy, she told him that he was fired and she did not want him anywhere in her cabinet. She even offered him the advice, as if from an 'elder sister', that if he wanted to be prime minister he should do more to get to know the party. The manner of Osborne's despatch angered his friends, but the man himself was phlegmatic. He had been prepared to do another job, but he had held the economic brief for eleven years in government and opposition. Anything else would have been a demotion. Minutes later, Philip Hammond arrived to receive the keys to the chancellor's red box.

Then it was Boris Johnson's turn. The MP for Uxbridge and South Ruislip had phoned Will Walden around 6.30 p.m. Walden had been playing golf in Scotland, but thought he had better return to London in case Boris was offered a minor role in May's cabinet. He was shocked when Johnson said, 'They've already called. I'd better get over there.' Fearing that his man would be mobbed in the street, Walden said, 'You're absolutely not going to get on your bike.' He arranged for Downing Street to send a car for Johnson, then tipped off the BBC that Boris was on his way. That afternoon, when Johnson had spoken to members of his leadership team he had expected nothing, and said he would reject the culture department, which he had turned down before, or the party chairmanship, which some saw as an option. Now he walked out of

Number 10 as foreign secretary, his rise, fall and renaissance complete. He was 'stunned and thrilled'. May had tied in the most conspicuous alternative power in the party with generosity and cunning. Johnson's 'box-office Boris' star power would be deployed to promote Britain abroad, just as he had promoted London around the world as mayor. His audience was so brief, and Johnson so grateful, that when he came out Walden asked, 'Did you discuss your position on Heathrow?' Johnson said, 'Oh God, no. I never got a chance.'

After visiting the Foreign Office, Boris headed to a book launch, and then took Marina and their children to dinner in a modest restaurant around the corner. The reaction to his appointment was hysterical. Labour's Kevin Brennan said making him foreign secretary was 'the strangest move since Caligula appointed his horse a senator'. Jean-Marc Ayrault, the French foreign minister, said Boris had 'lied a lot' to the British people, and was 'unreliable'. But within forty-eight hours EU foreign ministers were queuing up to meet him, and Johnson's accentless French had led to a rethink at the Quai d'Orsay, where one official pronounced him '*l'homme formidable*'. Four months earlier his 'low-key and loyal' plan envisaged taking a good job, proving he could run a department and be a serious politician, and positioning himself for the future. It was game on again for Boris.

When it emerged shortly afterwards that David Davis was returning to government for the first time since 1997 to run a new department for exiting the European Union, and Liam Fox was back as international trade secretary, it became clear that May was entrusting the public face of Brexit to 'the Three Brexiteers'. There was much talk that she was setting them up to fail, and much amusement when it emerged that they would all have to share Chevening, the foreign secretary's grace-and-favour home. As one MP put it, 'Fox and Davis hate each other, and they both hate Boris.' But in truth they were all soon collaborating, and May herself would run the Brexit negotiations. Banned from several key cabinet committees by Cameron, who thought her a confounded nuisance, she immediately set up four new committees for her key priorities, including Brexit, and promptly announced that she would personally chair each and every one of them.

Michael Gove was having dinner with Justin Welby, the Archbishop of Canterbury at the offices of Marshall Wace, Paul Marshall's hedge fund, when the news came through that Johnson had been given the

Foreign Office. He immediately thought, 'That's it. I'm pretty sure if Boris is going to be foreign secretary, then I'm not going to be in the government.' In the most bitter falling-out in recent political history May had taken sides – and she had sided with Johnson.

When Gove turned up for work at the Ministry of Justice on Thursday morning, he knew it would probably be for the last time. He had done forty minutes' work when the phone rang at around 9.50 a.m. 'Will you go to see the prime minister in her Commons office?' Gove knew with '99 per cent certainty' that he was about to be fired. Ministers who are staying are invited to walk up Downing Street; the culled are given the bullet in the privacy of the prime minister's wood-panelled office overlooking New Palace Yard. Gove was ushered in by Simon Case, the prime minister's principal private secretary. He sat down, and May got straight to the point. 'Michael, as you know, I have to form a new cabinet. And I have to make room for some new faces. And I have to tell you, you won't be in that cabinet.'

Gove, embracing the polite persona that had been his trademark until the Boris betrayal, said, 'I quite understand, Prime Minister.' May made it clear that the events of the week before had been a factor in her decision: 'One of the things that's very important is loyalty, and after the last few weeks I've been speaking to people in the party ... I wouldn't say that you could never come back, but you need to take a period on the backbenches in order to demonstrate loyalty.'

'I quite understand, Prime Minister,' Gove repeated. Standing, he said, 'Congratulations again on your victory, Prime Minister, and good luck.' He walked the short distance to his Commons office, where his special advisers were waiting, and said, 'That's it.'[2] When he got back to the department for the last time, he heard that Nicky Morgan had been sacked as well. As he left the MoJ he walked past his old ministerial car, and was driven away in an Addison Lee minicab. Wits on Twitter described his new position as 'poetic justice secretary'.

May had been emboldened to move against Gove by messages from her campaign team, including Chris Grayling, that MPs did not want to see him rewarded for what they saw as his betrayal of Johnson. But concerns about Gove continuing in the cabinet went wider than that. Several of Cameron's aides still blamed him for leaking government documents to further Vote Leave's chances during the campaign, and hinted that he was a security risk. There were suggestions that Cameron might raise the same concerns with May. There was also concern among some Buckingham Palace staff about whether Gove was a suitable minister of the crown. During the 'Queen backs Brexit' saga, royal officials had not troubled to hide their belief that he was behind the leak. On the evening when Gove held his thank-you party in Mosimann's, a public-affairs man who used to work in journalism and who has close links with the Conservative Party was approached at another social event by a royal courtier. The source recalls, 'I was told by a friend who works in the palace that while it was up to the new leader of the Conservative Party and soon-to-be prime minister to form her government in any way she saw fit, they should know that it was unlikely that Mr Gove would ever be seen by the queen on her own, without a private secretary in attendance to take a note, because they are perfectly persuaded that Michael Gove was the source of that story.' The public-affairs executive has known the courtier for twenty years: 'He's a proper person. He's not a footman. It's not the queen saying, "Bloody hell, I'm not having him come to see me." It's other people guarding her back.'

When the author approached Buckingham Palace the day after Gove was sacked, a senior figure said that no such message had been conveyed to May. In Downing Street, the new prime minister's team also said that she had not been passed a warning about Gove. After he was sacked, Gove's final official duty had been to drive to Buckingham Palace to hand the Great Seal back to the queen in person. He saw her alone, without any note-taker. Whatever concerns were harboured by some at the palace, they were never made official. While refusing to discuss his conversation with the queen, Gove insists that it was 'very nice', and that the monarch has never expressed any displeasure to him. A friend of Gove said, 'A load of bollocks has been talked about the whole thing. There's never been any problem with the queen. Michael has been alone with her twice.'

The real reason for May telling Gove to cool his heels on the back-benches was more prosaic. As one Tory put it, 'She can't stand him and she doesn't trust him.' The two had clashed repeatedly. When May made a wide-ranging speech in 2013 that was interpreted as her leadership pitch, Gove condemned her openly in cabinet. May, who regarded it as a virtue that she did not gossip over lunch with journalists, saw Gove as a mischief-maker. Their relationship reached a bitter nadir in June 2014 when the two ministers clashed over who was to blame for the failure to stop the rise of extremism in schools. Gove and his advisers were accused of briefing against May, something that contributed to Cameron's decision to fire him as education secretary the following month. Fiona Hill hit back, leaking a government document to embarrass Gove. Cameron fired her and forced Gove to issue a public apology. After a period working on modern slavery – an issue close to May's heart – and a spell in consultancy, Hill had returned in triumph as joint chief of staff at Number 10. Gove's fate was sealed.

If her approach with Gove was predictable, May's ruthlessness that day was striking. Before lunch she had despatched culture secretary John Whittingdale, Cabinet Office minister Oliver Letwin and education secretary Nicky Morgan. David Cameron's hero as prime minister may have been Harold Macmillan, but he himself had disliked reshuffles, and struggled to sack people. It was May who was re-enacting Macmillan's 'night of the long knives', when a third of the cabinet was despatched in a day. Her effort swiftly became known as 'the day of the long stilettos'. After he was sacked, Whittingdale went to find a pub. 'We are going to get drunk,' he said. Morgan was furious when it was briefed that she had left May's office in tears. In return, she told friends she had to help May find the words to sack her. The new prime minister said she wanted to bring on new people, and added, 'I'm going to have to …'

'Let me go?' Morgan said.

For Stephen Crabb, his departure from the cabinet was even more personal. On the same day *The Times* had splashed with Leadsom's comments about motherhood, the paper's front page also carried a report that Crabb had sent sex texts to a woman half his age, saying that he wanted to kiss her 'everywhere', describing MPs as 'risk-takers' and suggesting, 'The public can't expect MPs to be angels.' A week earlier, and the story would have been more explosive. Unlike the others, Crabb walked up Downing Street, and May offered him the chance to stay on as secretary of state for work and pensions. But when she asked if there could be further damaging allegations, Crabb decided it would be better to spend time with his family, away from the public eye.

Those who benefited from May's patronage represented a broader spectrum of the Tory Party than under Cameron. Amber Rudd and Priti Patel, two of the most aggressive campaigners on either side of the Brexit debate, became home secretary and international development secretary. May's personal backers did well. Her old ally Damian Green got his first cabinet job, replacing Crabb at the DWP. He had been metaphorically measuring the curtains at the culture department when Crabb resigned. Green's pensions minister would be Richard Harrington, who he had signed up at a freshers' fair at Oxford forty years earlier. Karen Bradley, one of May's first supporters, got the culture job, and Chris Grayling went to transport, a long-standing interest of his. Justine Greening became the first education secretary ever to have been educated solely at a comprehensive school. In all, just five of May's cabinet were privately educated, half the number in Cameron's last cabinet.

Those she kept were interesting too. Michael Fallon, a highly competent figurehead of the right, remained at defence, suggesting that the new meritocracy would not be age-dependent. Jeremy Hunt, the health secretary, had sought out May during the leadership contest and asked, if he were to impose the new contract on junior doctors, whether she would reverse the process if she won. She said she would not, and reappointed him, signalling clearly that she was prepared to face down the doctors, just as she had once taken on the police herself.

Members of the Cameron chumocracy were let go, none with more style than Hugo Swire, one the MPs who backed Cameron in 2005, when his entire campaign team could have fitted in the back of a cab. Just before May administered the *coup de grâce*, he shouted out, 'Viva Cameron!' like a latterday South American revolutionary facing the firing squad. Those associated with Gove were also purged. Dominic Raab, who had been promised a full cabinet post by more than one candidate – Gove included – let it be known to May's team that he would serve in any minister of state post. May duly offered him a junior post, and he walked. Gove was more angry about the removal of Ed Vaizey – his best man – as arts minister, Raab and Nicky Morgan than he was about his own demise. He told friends he 'felt guilty' because their association with him had led to 'a sort of career death for some of my colleagues'.

The speed and ferocity of May's wielding of the knife impressed many MPs, and bewildered others. Andrew Bridgen said, 'Some of my older colleagues like a nap in the afternoon. They've been waking up and not recognising the world.' Even the vanquished Cameroons managed grudging admiration: 'She sat there watching everyone for years, working out who she would kill if she got the chance,' said one. George

Osborne managed to see the funny side. When someone suggested that May had carried out a purge of the Osborneites, he noted that Amber Rudd and Sajid Javid, both former PPSs of his, had survived, while his former deputy Philip Hammond was now the main man at the Treasury. 'Actually it's the Mayites who've done rather badly. Michael Ellis, deputy leader of the House, and George Hollingbery, still PPS,' he remarked drily to one friend.

However, the scale of the purge created problems for May. One minister who was fired said, 'A lot of us decided not to back her because of the way she behaves, not because of what she stands for. And the first thing she does is behave exactly like her critics have said. She's created enemies where she didn't need to.' By ditching Osborne's deficit target, giving his Northern Powerhouse the cold shoulder and talking about more state intervention in the economy, May had made an enemy of Osborne by the first week of September. The former chancellor set up a new think tank to defend his big idea, and pointedly pronounced that May was only the best prime minister 'of those who put their names forward'. The same week, David Cameron announced that he was standing down from Parliament, his wish to remain MP for Witney rubbing up against the reality that he could not vote for the creation of new grammar schools, May's first signature domestic U-turn.

Before he left the House of Commons, Cameron was a rare visitor to the chamber. He did appear for a debate on the renewal of Trident. Steve Baker glanced up and saw Cameron looking at him, a moment that brought back memories of the time, just a year before, when Baker had been to Downing Street to explain Conservatives for Britain. 'Seeing a great prime minister on the backbenches because of events which I will have played my part in driving, is a matter of great melancholy to me,' he said. 'I didn't mean to do that to him, and I don't think I did do that to him. I think he did it largely because of decisions he made himself. But I'm reminded of the quote of Wellington: "Nothing except a battle lost can be half so melancholy as a battle won."'

As a reminder to May that she had inherited the same tiny majority as Cameron, and the same sizeable contingent of Eurosceptics, the summer brought the creation of not one but two groups demanding a 'hard Brexit' that would sever links with the single market, or even the Europe-wide customs union. Even Gove's notorious 'Albanian model' was unacceptable. Change Britain, which emerged out of Vote Leave and

Leave Means Leave, run by Richard Tice of Leave.EU, ensured that the Judean People's Front and the People's Front of Judea were both still in business.

For all the upheaval, there was no turmoil on the Tory benches – in stark contrast to the other parties. Arron Banks and Nigel Farage hoped to capitalise on Labour divisions by uniting Ukip behind a new leader like Paul Nuttall or Steven Woolfe. But Nuttall decided he did not want to run for family reasons, and Woolfe submitted his nomination papers seventeen minutes too late and was barred from standing. After a campaign in which she declined to debate with the other candidates, Diane James emerged as the victor, a cut-glass Home Counties candidate when what many felt was needed was a no-nonsense northerner. To cap it all, her victory was upstaged by Banks revealing that he and Andy Wigmore had gone skinny-dipping with Farage off Bournemouth beach on the eve of Ukip's conference. When Farage insisted he kept his underpants on, it ensured that the story ran for a second day. Banks, meanwhile, busied himself with plans to create a 'right-wing Momentum' pressure group.

After eighteen days James stood down, saying she did not have the authority to make the changes she wanted. Woolfe was again tipped for victory, but found himself in a Strasbourg hospital after an altercation with another Ukip MEP. Ukip appeared to have reinvented the old adage about history repeating itself as: 'first as farce, and then again as farce'.

Meanwhile, Owen Smith tried to fight Jeremy Corbyn by emulating his left-wing stances, while arguing that he was a more competent means of executing them. This inspired neither the new Labour Party membership nor the moderates, and Corbyn sealed a more comprehensive victory than a year earlier. The attempted coup having failed, some moderates contemplated a return to the front bench, while Corbyn said that boundary changes unveiled in September would mean every MP had to be selected all over again, an open door to a purge of his critics. This time the plan was to come for the staff at Labour Party HQ as well. Neil Kinnock predicted that there would not be another Labour government in his lifetime.

Theresa May, though, reigned supreme. Yes, there were grumbles about her team exerting overbearing central control. But when she strode out to make her first appearance at PMQs on 20 July, she looked as if she had been doing it all her life. Corbyn, bizarrely for a man in the midst of a leadership challenge, asked about people who were insecure in their jobs. May closed her briefing folder and began to play with Corbyn as a cat plays with a mouse: 'I suspect that there are many members on the opposition benches who might be familiar with an unscrupulous boss. A boss who doesn't listen to his workers, a boss who requires some of his workers to double their workload, and maybe a boss who exploits the rules to further his own career.' Then she leaned over the despatch box and with an intonation that was pure Maggie Thatcher, said, 'Remind him of anybody?' If she had swiped her hand like a giant paw and yelled 'Meow,' the Tory backbenches could not have been happier.

David Cameron had held a referendum to satisfy the Conservative Party, and had led a campaign that never got out of third gear because he did not want to deepen internal divisions. In so doing he destroyed himself but saved his party, and made it possible for Theresa May to impose stability in a matter of weeks. Alistair Burt said, 'Look at the position we're in now. The other parties are flat on the floor and the Conservative Party, despite the extraordinary result, is probably in a stronger position than ever. If you are carrying the responsibility for government, as David Cameron did, party management isn't just about everyone keeping their comfortable positions. It is about running the country and doing a responsible job, and I think on that we are streets ahead.'

That may not be the political epitaph, and Theresa May may not have been the successor, he wanted; but for David Cameron, the man who gambled and lost, that would have to do for now.

Conclusion

WHY LEAVE WON

In 1972, 183 years had elapsed since the French Revolution when Chou Enlai made his famous comment that it was 'too early to say' what it meant. As I write this, we are only halfway to 183 days since the EU referendum changed British politics, and it is impossible to say with any certainty what it will mean in two years' time, let alone two centuries. Was this the great liberation the Brexiteers promised, or the beginning of an economic malaise that will set the country back for a generation? The capturing of a brave new world, or a quest for one nostalgically imagined? We know it led to the downfall of the Tory ruling class which had run the country since 2010, perhaps more broadly too of the liberal metropolitan managerialism of which both Tony Blair and David Cameron were expressions. None of the national political leaders who took their parties into the 2015 general election was still in charge fourteen months later. The referendum represented a revolt of the provincial classes – ignored, maligned and impoverished – against the cosy metropolitan consensus on Europe, the benefits of immigration and the belief that national economic prosperity trumps personal experience of hardship. If the referendum was anything it was a victory for outsiders over insiders, a dividing line that was replacing both left/right and rich/poor as the dominant split in British politics. It was appropriate, perhaps even inevitable, that the winner in this process was Theresa May, who tiptoed cleverly through the wreckage on her kitten heels. She had been an outsider in the ultimate insiders' government, a grammar-school girl disdained by the posh boys she worked alongside. It was no accident that her opening statement on the steps of Downing Street was a vow to make government work for everyone, a canny political creed for sure, but one she had lived for a decade.

*   *   *

Answering the question about why Leave won is a tale with short- and long-term explanations. It is a story of things both done and not done, strategy and tactics, planning and Macmillan's unforeseen 'Events, dear boy, events ...' Digesting defeat, many Remainers have consoled themselves with the fatalistic view that the referendum was unwinnable. They advance two arguments, one historic, the other contemporary, to which you might add the temperamental British trait of being unconvinced by grand utopian schemes.

The first is that the result was the culmination of three decades of Euroscepticism cloaking a nation in its suffocating embrace. Alistair Burt said, 'Looking back, the truth is this was lost a long time ago with the relentless drip, drip of anti-European propaganda.' Certainly that cannot be ignored, but Remainers too were responsible for this state of affairs. James McGrory said, 'With some honourable exceptions, like Peter Mandelson and Nick Clegg, the left have been reluctant to make the case for Europe.' Will Straw believes he always had an uphill task: 'I have come to the conclusion that there were factors beyond the control of the campaign. We launched in October for a June referendum. In those eight months we weren't able to turn around twenty years of sustained Euroscepticism. David Cameron was actually one of the most Eurosceptic Conservative prime ministers that we've had, until he turned on a sixpence in February.' Damian Green says, 'If no Tory leader for twenty years had said anything good about Europe, which broadly speaking was the case, then trying to turn that round in six months was impossible. It was beyond even David Cameron's campaigning skills.'

The second explanation advanced by the Remainians is that the referendum came at a time when powerful forces that assisted the Leavers were sweeping the Western world. They see Brexit as a manifestation of the same phenomenon fuelling support for Donald Trump and Bernie Sanders in the US and Marine Le Pen in France. The cocktail of ingredients included a revolt against the consequences of globalisation by those who have not benefited from it, a revolt which found its most potent voice in the anger of working-class communities about depressed wages and pressure on local services from rising immigration. It included a rejection of political elites, to the point where voters have never been less inclined to accept the arguments of recognisably establishment figures. It included too the growth of what critics call a 'post-truth' culture, in which voters are persuaded by the volume rather than the accuracy of an announcement. 'In an age of emotion we sought to fight a rational campaign,' says Will Straw. All sides in a political debate tend to believe they have a monopoly on rationality. Many winning campaigns – including Barack Obama's in 2008 and David Cameron's for the Tory crown in 2005 – have seen the benefits of running as an insurgency against more established opponents, and of deploying emotion to win an argument. But the Remainers feel these issues particularly strongly.

Ryan Coetzee believes the campaign was hurt by a breakdown of trust between rulers and the ruled, and a flourishing of conspiracy theories: 'Britain got caught up in something that is sweeping the West, and that involves distrust to the point of paranoia. It involves growing fear of the other, whether that person is foreign or black or whatever it might be. It involves a turning away from reason, evidence, logic – those ideas that have built what is called the West over the past five hundred years. What the Leave campaign did was they turbocharged that lack of trust.' Craig Oliver believes, 'We were up against a campaign that was prepared to mislead on an industrial scale.' There are some on the Brexit side, too, who believe the trends were more significant than the campaign. Chris Bruni-Lowe says, 'The public were clearly just pissed off with immigration. It's all about national momentum. All the campaigning in the world can't prevent national moods.'

This backdrop of ingrained Euroscepticism may even be the dominant cause of Brexit. It was certainly a necessary prerequisite, but it does not follow that it was sufficient explanation, or that David Cameron could not have won if he had done things differently. Fighting the Remain cause may have been, in footballing terms, an away tie against Barcelona, but Cameron had his fair share of shots on goal, had an extra player on the pitch until the half-time purdah, his opponents spent the first half kicking lumps out of each other and only deployed their star player (Immy Gration) in the second half, while Cameron ordered his own goalkeeper's hands tied behind his back as Vote Leave's striker (Boris Johnson) approached goal. Remain could certainly have won. If six hundred thousand people had changed their minds it would be the Leave campaign's numerous mistakes and infighting that are the focus of this book. Paul Stephenson admitted the Brexiteers only won by 'fine margins'.

*   *   *

What Vote Leave got right is fairly straightforward. As Andrew Cooper admitted, 'The Leave campaign had all the best tunes. "Take back control" was a brilliant slogan. £350 million a week was disgraceful in one sense, because it's not true, but I thought it was incredibly tenacious, as well as deeply cynical, that they were just sticking to it, in the face of all the criticism that it was a lie. It cut through in the focus groups.' Stronger In found it far more difficult to sell a more nuanced argument about the economic advantages of staying in. James McGrory says, 'In focus groups, unprompted, people would tell you Leave's three top arguments: "We spend loads of money on Europe," "They're making all the laws out there," and "Too many immigrants." On our side, there was a vague sense that it was good for the economy, but nothing tangible.' But Stronger In did themselves no favours by jumping from message to message – from jobs, to £4,300 a year, to security and the risk of war. When he was doing Leave's focus groups, Henry de Zoete found that Stronger In's most effective slogan was that Brexit would be 'a leap in the dark'; but even the dangers of taking a step into the unknown undermined the spurious specificity of George Osborne's economic claims, since voters wondered, if the future was unknown, how the chancellor could be so precise about the costs.

That Vote Leave stuck to their message and doubled down in the face of criticism was largely due to the determination of one man. Ask most people in Vote Leave why they won and they have a simple, one-word answer: 'Dom.' Matthew Elliott, who deserves credit for establishing the organisation, recognised that he needed a 'warrior' like Cummings to run the war room, and had Cummings been ousted in the attempted coup in January 2016 it is difficult to see the campaign being as successful with Arron Banks and Nigel Farage in charge. The MPs said they wanted Cummings' ideas, but not his leadership. But good campaigns are dictatorships, and a strategy is only as good as the campaign manager's ability to drive it through. One ally said, 'The reason the coup didn't work is that the staff backed Dom. The people who actually made stuff happen would walk through walls for Dom.'

As Paul Stephenson, Cummings' able lieutenant, put it, 'Fundamentally, why did we win it? Matthew created an organisation which allowed things to flourish. But it was down to Dom setting the strategy, sticking to the strategy, being his obstinate best. If everything went wrong, everyone was going to blame him. But that meant we had more focus.'

Cummings and a very small core team ran a nimble insurgency. 'There are huge advantages to being the big incumbent, but it makes you unwieldy,' says Stephenson. 'Whereas, we did what we needed to do.' Cummings understood what messages worked, he found a way of highlighting the immigration issue by campaigning about pressure on public services like the NHS that kept floating voters on board, and when the immigration figures dropped and purdah kicked in, he was able to persuade Johnson and Gove to sharpen their attacks on Cameron to put Downing Street on the back foot.

Vote Leave was the campaign better prepared for hand-to-hand combat. Even those who disagreed with some of his more confrontational antics believed Cummings' role was pivotal. Chris Grayling says, 'He was tactically very smart, he was really driven by the research and what people said in focus groups. He might have had some interpersonal issues, but the strategy he pursued was brilliant.' Steve Baker, who had been appalled by the CBI stunt, added, 'I'm pretty sure that we owe this victory to Dominic Cummings. His strategic insight, his willingness to pull off political operations, and his dogmatic determination to stick to a line he knew worked, however painful it may be – all of those talents undoubtedly materially influenced this referendum being won.'

The contribution of Steve Baker and his parliamentary guerrillas to the Vote Leave cause was also significant, robbing the government of key advantages. Changing the question from yes/no to remain/leave may have been worth four percentage points to Vote Leave, the eventual difference between victory and a dead heat. It is impossible to quantify the effects of a proper four-week purdah period, which Bernard Jenkin and others battled for, but it allowed Vote Leave to fight on a level media playing field at just the moment when their attacks became most potent. Similarly, the neutrality of the Conservative Party robbed Cameron and his allies of canvassing data which they could have exploited to their advantage if the government's policy had been imposed on the party. Taken together, all these factors might well have been enough to tip the balance in Leave's favour. Baker's willingness to deploy the rebels to amend the Finance Bill and the Queen's Speech undermined Cameron and Osborne's credibility at crucial moments. The insurrection on the emergency budget not only trumped the chancellor's final ace, it contributed to the end of his cabinet career.

Debate raged afterwards between the two Leave campaigns about whether Vote Leave or the Banks–Farage operation was really responsible for victory. For his part, Farage thinks the generals in Westminster Tower have claimed too much of the credit, while the infantry commanders like him have been overlooked: 'Elliott wants a peerage more than anything. The chaps back at the château getting decorated for bravery!' Farage certainly deserves credit for helping to force Cameron into calling the referendum in the first place. No one in the preceding twenty years had done more to put the issue on the national agenda or to link the issues of Europe and immigration. But Farage's repeated failures to get elected to Parliament, even in a favourable environment in South Thanet the year before, are evidence that his personal appeal is far from universal. Chris Bruni-Lowe and others make a fair point when they say that Arron Banks's dynamism after the general election encouraged Elliott and Cummings to get their act together, but it is hard to see the debilitating battle that raged between the two camps between October 2015 and April 2016 as a net gain for Leave. Had the campaign been lost, it is that civil war which would have been blamed.

The case against Banks and Farage is twofold: that their uncompromising approach repelled floating voters, and that their personal ambitions to run and front the campaign risked destroying it. A key figure in Vote Leave said, 'From my point of view, Arron Banks and the people around him's principal contribution to this referendum was to make everything vastly harder than it needed to be. Their dogged pursuit of core vote strategy, like that stupid migration poster, put off swing voters. That alone would have been unhelpful. They couldn't just get on with a Ukip campaign, they had to try to take over the whole thing. And their various attempts to do that were part of what led to the near blowing-up of Vote Leave. They made the designation process a complete nightmare.' Cummings regarded Farage as 'toxic', and Henry de Zoete found in his focus groups that in towns like Watford, the most positive thing voters would say about Farage was that 'He tells it like it is.' Cummings is in no doubt that Farage's antics cost votes: 'If Farage had disappeared in summer 2015, we'd have got more than 55 per cent. Farage alienated voters, he made it impossible for us to penetrate with the business community – one of our big failings of the campaign – which was very bad news for us. And he was a focal point for all the internal fighting.'

Rob Oxley agrees: 'His actions made me think he wasn't interested in winning it. The stuff they did was harmful to the cause.'

Yet one of the keys to Leave's victory was turning out the very people Farage was targeting. 'Our voice was utterly critical with two sets of voters,' Farage said. 'One was the Labour voters. Secondly – and I believe crucially – what pushed us beyond the line was non-voters. Vote Leave never envisaged this high turnout.' Turnout was 72 per cent, six points higher than at the general election. 'The difference was this was a once-in-a-lifetime opportunity to tell the establishment what you think,' says Farage. One of David Cameron's aides said, 'Farage was a big factor in the campaign. I don't buy for a second that Farage doesn't matter. Bullshit. He convinced a lot of people.' Arron Banks said, 'The bottom line is that we figured that in order to win this referendum, you've got to get 4.5 million Labour voters to come out and vote. We went to the north, we went to Bolton, we went to Halifax. Nigel was wildly popular in those areas. They say he was toxic. He was toxic inside the M25, in the rarefied air there. But outside of there, he was anything but toxic.' The Ukip grassroots, which Farage had inspired and marshalled over two decades, were a significant factor in Vote Leave's ground war too, though perhaps not as dominant as Farage liked to believe.

In the end, it may have been of benefit to have two 'Out' campaigns. Vote Leave was able to reassure swing voters that by backing Leave they were not voting for Ukip, while Farage and Banks were able to make a virtue of edgier messages designed to appeal to working-class voters. Banks, in his less confrontational moments, acknowledged this: 'I think Boris and Gove reassured some Tory voters. I give them credit for bringing over weak Tory voters who would have vacillated. In the end, I think Nigel connected to the north and working voters in a way that other parties hate. That's the biggest achievement of the lot. To lose several times in Parliament and be probably the most influential politician in a generation, without having ever won, it's quite remarkable really.'

Both Farage and Vote Leave were accused of pandering to the basest instincts of the electorate to win votes. A senior figure in Stronger In said, 'Michael Gove launched an all-out assault on the Enlightenment in the name of atavistic nationalism.' Gove rejects this claim: 'Their line was, "I'm not saying that everyone voting Leave is a racist, but certainly every racist is voting Leave. And we know who'll be happy the next morning: Le Pen, Putin and Trump."' Gove says many Remain campaigners refused to engage in the arguments, and chose to smear instead: 'I was put in front of television audiences, and I was given the opportunity to whip up feeling or respond with answers. And I responded with reason. I defended immigration in front of studio audiences even when there might have been easier applause to run with it. And if it is the case that people are going to put a big electric fence around arguments about the EU for fear that it will stir up these emotions, then what people are saying is seventeen million people's feelings about the future of this country are illegitimate.'

There was a strong element of identity politics in the campaign. Pollsters found that 80 per cent of people who defined themselves as 'English' voted Leave, while 80 per cent of those who called themselves 'British' voted Remain. In talking about the dangers of Turkey joining the EU and the downsides of immigration, the Leave campaign played on nationalism and uncovered some latent racism, but Stronger In's problem was that by failing to address these issues in an emphatic way their own leaders were more easily depicted as the elites responsible for the neglect of the communities left behind. It might have been an at times incoherent cry of rage, but it was one that deserved a better answer than Remain provided.

Some Remainers agree that the Leave campaign did not create these forces, it simply uncovered what was already there. They also admit that the political class had failed many of those who backed Leave. Alistair Burt says, 'I don't think the referendum divided the country, I think the referendum revealed the divisions. Areas of the country were hurting more than we realised from some of the things we had glossed over, like immigration and the pain of globalisation, job losses, low and middle incomes not rising.' Both major parties share the blame for ignoring the people with these concerns. Henry de Zoete found it incredibly humbling to sit in focus groups and listen to people talking about the impact of immigration on their lives. Typical of what he heard in town after town was a man in his late thirties who said, 'I've worked in a factory for the last fifteen years, and I'm paid less than I was fifteen years ago. All the people who I work with, who used to be mates of mine, are now Eastern Europeans. My kid's the only kid in his class speaking English. I don't know what's going on.' Brett O'Donnell sees parallels between Brexit and the forces propelling Donald Trump's presidential campaign: 'Vast numbers of the grassroots feel very disaffected from their government because they have been promised to and not delivered to. That was true with immigration, but it was also true with the economy. Because like the US, the economy in Britain is working for the top end, but it's not working for the middle.' Sam Adamson, who became the poster girl for Brexit when she bounced gleefully on another Brexiteer's shoulders as the result was announced in Sunderland, has no doubt the result was a message to the political class: 'I definitely feel that the working-class people got their voice heard. It shook our then prime minister, David Cameron. It shook the Labour Party. For the working-class people it was, "Now you've heard us; now do something about it."'

Nowhere was this shift more symbolic than in the corner of Leicestershire represented by Andrew Bridgen that Cameron had once called 'a dump'. 'I knew Leave were going to win,' says Bridgen. 'I was speaking to people who had never voted in their lives. They're not on the radar of Osborne and Cameron. They were the people living in Coalville.' Bridgen's area usually has a high turnout in general elections, over 70 per cent, but in the referendum it was pushing 80 per cent. Its council estates, which normally produce 50 per cent turnout, hit 65 per cent. 'Those people are not engaged in politics, they're not on YouGov's polling panel. When IpsosMORI ring them they say, "I've never voted in my life," so they put them down as "Won't vote" and don't count them. But they came out to vote Leave.' Coalville had taken its revenge on the prime minister who disparaged the town. 'It was never all right for someone with a very privileged upbringing who went to Eton to call my home town a dump,' says Bridgen. 'It was those same voters that cost him; the voters he had no relationship with and he didn't understand. That's what did him. The council estates and the terraced houses of all the Coalvilles across the country were the ones who put him out of office.'

After the referendum, Remainers acknowledged the concerns of these voters, but expressed fears that blaming their problems on Europe would create a false catharsis that could fuel political extremism. Ryan Coetzee said, 'When they discover that the EU bogeyman wasn't actually the cause of their problems, they're going to attach those feelings to someone or something else.' But he believed voters would have to take responsibility for their actions: 'People say, "Blame the Leave campaign because they lied." "Blame the Remain campaign because they should have done something about immigration." "Blame Corbyn because he should have done more." "Blame David Cameron because he should have done a better renegotiation." Well, you can blame all those people, but if you believe in taking the vote seriously, blame the voters. Either you treat the voters like adults or you don't. If you're an adult and you're living in Sunderland, where the motor industry and EU funding are critical to your livelihood, and you voted to leave, well, I'm sorry mate, I think that's your fault.'

David Cameron and his team made a series of decisions that contributed to his defeat. It is too simplistic to see them all as 'mistakes', in that some were virtually unavoidable, and others were a function of the cross-party coalition he had constructed. But despite the obvious prevailing head-winds it is wrong to see Brexit as inevitable. If you follow the philosophy of the Team Sky cycling team, where tiny improvements in each area ultimately contribute to a sizeable edge over your rivals, there are many changes Cameron and his allies at Stronger In might have made that could have switched the 600,000 votes they needed to win.

With Cameron's closest political ally, George Osborne, believing he should not have called the referendum and that it could have been avoided, it is not possible to insist that the referendum was inevitable. But those Tories who say that even if he had not made the Bloomberg speech Cameron would have been forced into the commitment after the 2014 European elections were won by Ukip make a persuasive case. Sceptics and Europhiles around Cameron believed he would not have won the 2015 election without the pledge. Having already reneged on the promise of a referendum on the Lisbon Treaty, once the prime minister was committed he was boxed in. The Conservative MP Nigel Evans says, 'He didn't have to offer the referendum, but the reality was once he gave that promise he had to deliver on it. One could say his biggest error was winning the 2015 general election, because had it still been a coalition, then of course the referendum, I suspect, would never have been allowed by the Liberal Democrats.'[1]

Cameron did not have to call the referendum before the end of 2017 or rush it through in early 2016. He could have tried to cast the question differently, so it was not an in/out proposition, though that would have enraged many of his backbenchers. Having selected the form and timing of the referendum, he could have done more to strategically prepare the groundwork for the Remain campaign, trumpeting his successes rather than his frustrations in Brussels. He should certainly have done more to explain what Britain got from membership of the single market, a concept many voters only encountered for the first time during the short campaign. Peter Mandelson recalls, 'Craig Oliver remarked the week after the referendum that Cameron had "called a referendum on a subject no one could understand". He was exaggerating to make a point, because many people had strong, thought-through views both ways. But probably the majority of the population simply did not grasp what was at stake in Britain leaving after forty years of integration to the EU, and the bulk of the press were determined not to enlighten them.'

Cameron also contributed to the scope of Euroscepticism and the distrust of politicians. As a leadership candidate his first action on Europe had been to give way to the Palaeosceptics on withdrawal from the EPP, a tactic of strategic retreat from which he never wavered. His U-turn on Lisbon, understandable as it was in practical terms, since the treaty had already been ratified, was politically toxic, and meant the next referendum would have to be an all-or-nothing vote on EU membership.

Cameron shares parentage of that mess with the man of whom he once pronounced himself the 'heir'. Michael McManus, the Conservative writer who worked with Ted Heath, has a theory that Tony Blair was actually the godfather of Brexit: 'Blair opened the floodgates on immigration. The country changed fundamentally in the Blair years, and that created a very ugly political climate. He underestimated the effects of the accession of these big countries in Central and Eastern Europe. Secondly, the Iraq War destabilised the Middle East and helped to create the migration crisis. Thirdly, Blair conceded a referendum on the European constitution and then, after the 2005 election, he said because it had been renamed the Lisbon Treaty this was no longer needed. It would have let all the steam out, having that referendum then. We probably would have voted against the treaty. We could have changed the direction of the European Union without jeopardising our membership. I think Blair personally bears more responsibility than Cameron or anybody, because he created the perfect storm.'

Had Blair been Labour leader in 2016, however, campaigners on both sides believe Remain would have won easily. Cameron had assumed until the autumn of 2015 that he would have enthusiastic support from the Labour Party. The election of Jeremy Corbyn, and Labour's experience in Scotland, where campaigning with the Tories had left the party vulnerable to the SNP, changed all that. Harriet Harman's decision to set up a separate Labour campaign meant Stronger In was more top-heavy with Tories than it might have been. Labour staff at Cannon Street felt George Osborne and Craig Oliver did not really understand Labour voters. On one occasion the Tories briefed two stories that would have appealed to Labour voters – on NHS bosses warning about the dangers of Brexit, and the impact on the cost of shopping – against each other in rival Sunday papers. Labour staff protested, saying both big hits were being thrown away, but Oliver refused to bend.

James McGrory says, 'I have a fantasy in which Labour were led by a moderate, coherent pro-European who could make the case. We'd be in a different world now.' Jeremy Corbyn's behaviour will never be forgiven by many at Stronger In. 'I thought Corbyn was a disgrace. He's supposed to be a man of principle,' says one senior figure. 'If he's against the EU, fine, be against it, but he did the worst of all possible worlds by being some sort of sceptic Remainer. Labour has been pro-European for decades, and their own leader refused to articulate that. It also stopped us from credibly portraying our opponents as a bunch of right-wing nut jobs. That needed to be nailed by the Labour Party, and it just wasn't.' Alan Johnson blamed the people who put Corbyn on the leadership ballot the first time around, thus undermining a system which was designed to send to the Labour membership only those candidates who had the confidence of the parliamentary party: 'The onus was on the PLP to make sure, in these new circumstances, that you were very careful about who you nominate. People who lent Jeremy Corbyn their nominations, they're the people to blame.' Once Corbyn was elected, Cameron had to rely on his sworn enemies to produce votes.

One thing Remainers and Brexiteers agreed on afterwards was that Cameron's renegotiation was not good enough. Many Downing Street staff sincerely believe that he got the best deal he could. We will never know definitively if they were right, but the decision to switch from a cap or emergency brake on migrant numbers to cuts in benefits looked afterwards like a serious error. Similarly, Cameron and Osborne's decision after the general election to ask only for what they thought they could get was lacking in ambition, even if it was politically sensible if they assumed it would still be enough to deliver victory. Ministers like Sajid Javid, Eurosceptics like Dan Hannan and Number 10 aides like Mats Persson, Daniel Korski and Ameet Gill all thought he could have asked for more, and offered ideas. Instead, efforts to fight for specifics on regulation, employment legislation, even to seek an important symbolic change by reinstating the dark-blue British passport, were all dismissed.

At almost every turn Cameron, advised by officials like Ivan Rogers and Tom Scholar, sought ways to get reform within the existing tramlines of EU law, rather than advancing the political proposition that the fundamental reform he had promised at Bloomberg involved tearing up some of the laws and conventions of the EU and ordering Rogers to act accordingly. Brussels' rules are often there to be broken. The one exception to this cautious approach was the modest benefits reforms Cameron demanded in the JCB speech. These were dismissed as illegal by the civil service on the grounds that they infringed the principle of 'non-discrimination' – yet Cameron still managed to win some of what he wanted. Had he fought on something that limited free movement, he might have been able to win concessions if he put Britain's membership of the EU on the line.

The problem was that Cameron assumed, until gone midnight on polling day, that he would win the referendum. He never forced Angela Merkel or the other European leaders to choose between compromise on Britain's borders and the UK leaving the EU. He might not have liked the answer if he pushed the matter, but he never truly put them on the spot. Demanding more and being rebuffed would also have given him an excuse to walk away from the renegotiation, as Lynton Crosby had suggested was advisable. That would have bought him time, and certainly could have extended his premiership towards its natural end date in 2018. 'We were very, very good at kicking a can down the alley with a difficult problem and letting it resolve itself,' one aide said. 'We didn't do that with the European referendum. We could have kicked that can down the alley for another three years. Dave would have still been in Downing Street. Lynton wanted that.'

Having failed to land an immigration deal which neutralised the issue, Stronger In were always on the back foot. They could not find politicians in any party to parrot their balanced script on the subject, while the suggestions of Peter Mandelson and Will Straw that Cameron make an 'I have listened' speech, or unveil a new migration fund to help affected communities, could have retrieved some votes. That, however, needed to happen before Vote Leave began hitting the issue hard in the final week of May, after which it would have looked panicky. By the penultimate week, when Cameron contemplated a Scotland-style 'vow', it was probably too late to make a difference. But the evidence is that simply ignoring the issue because it belonged to Vote Leave contributed to the sense that the Remainers did not understand public concerns. Cameron was never going to win on immigration, but he could have lost less badly on it. James McGrory says, 'If you ran the perfect campaign on immigration you still wouldn't have made the fence on the issue, but you would have been competing. And we just didn't compete.'

The primary reasons for that were that Cameron and Osborne were determined to run the same economic-risk-based campaign that had worked in the Scottish referendum and at the general election, and that throughout the campaign Andrew Cooper's polling showed that the economy would trump immigration with Stronger In's target voters. Both judgements were seriously flawed. The blueprint for victory was not followed in several important respects. Osborne had not recognised that his claims about the economic dangers of Brexit would be seen as incredible without the support of the tabloid press to amplify them. Will Straw says, 'They wanted to pursue a Lynton Crosby, strip the barnacles off the boat, relentless focus on the economy. What this referendum has shown us is that if you don't have the right-wing echo chamber you can't do that.'

The tactic of enlisting third-party support from the IMF, Mark Carney and Barack Obama backfired because it reinforced the sense of a privileged establishment dispensing wisdom to the poor benighted masses. The successful efforts to undermine Ed Miliband in 2015 were not replicated against Michael Gove and Boris Johnson, who had written enough controversial things in their pasts to have been negatively caricatured if Cameron had let their images be used in social media advertising. Ducking blue-on-blue confrontations did not kill the Conservative civil war and leadership succession as campaign themes, it just meant Vote Leave was able to stir the psychodrama on its own terms.

Perhaps the most important thing missing from the Cameron–Osborne–Crosby strategy was Crosby himself. The master strategist had given a year of his life to the Tory re-election effort, and did not want to return to the front line of a political war room. In his absence, Stronger In lacked a dominant leader in the mould of Cummings. Will Straw was widely commended for being an excellent manager of people and ensuring that cross-party relations were harmonious, but he, Coetzee and

Stephen Gilbert did not have the clout to overrule Craig Oliver or Ameet Gill, who were Cameron and Osborne's representatives on earth. Key decisions were taken in Downing Street without Straw, Coetzee or McGrory's input. Perhaps Jim Messina should have been put in charge of the whole thing. The only other figure involved who had top-level experience of campaign command was Peter Mandelson, but Cameron and Osborne were not prepared to put their political futures in the hands of a pro-European Blairite. With its split responsibilities and half a dozen chiefs, the Remain campaign resembled the failed 2010 Tory election structure, rather than the successful 2015 model.

If Remain had won, most of those who worked for the campaign believe the remarkable degree to which Tories, Labour and Lib Dems worked together would have been the reason. 'The thing I'm proudest of is that we did create this cross-party culture, which is hard in our very adversarial political environment,' says Will Straw. Some non-Tories wished later that they had been a little less consensual, more willing to challenge some of the assumptions of the campaign. Some Conservatives, too, believe a form of 'group think' developed about how the economy should be put to the fore. One of the Labour officials said, 'We never snapped out of a mode of being overly deferential to them on the economy, on blue on blue, on having nothing to say on immigration. And that is all of our faults. We should have all spoken up, but we didn't. We went with it. We can't dump it on them.' Ultimately, the senior staff believed that what Straw calls 'the two golden law of politics were going to win it for us in the end – that risk kicks in towards the end and people vote for the status quo, and secondly that prosperity trumps all other issues – and both those laws proved false in this election'. That is not quite right. Leave voters trusted the existing economic peril they could perceive to their pay packets and jobs from immigration, not the speculative risk painted by George Osborne.

Those who know Lynton Crosby say it was not only his organisational ability that was missed. He was one of the few people who could tell Cameron and Osborne that they were on the wrong track and make them do something different. With a month to go, Coetzee's focus groups made it clear that the economic strategy was not working, while Vote Leave's focus on immigration and Turkish accession was – but no changes were made. Crosby's strength is analysing data dispassionately, and responding to it. 'If Lynton had been there he would have made the prime minister say, "Turkey will never join the EU as long as I am here." Lynton's greatest strength is that he puts all political views aside when he does polling. He would have used the evidence to say, "This is killing you, you've got to do something about it." He doesn't care about policies, he cares about winning.' On Turkey, Cameron chose good statesmanship over good politics.

The main reason why Stronger In stuck with a failing strategy was Andrew Cooper's polling. Studies of the polls after the referendum suggest that Leave was ahead throughout the campaign, but until the final three weeks Cooper's tracker had Stronger In ahead, and even then he briefed Cameron that Remain would scrape home. Of the two tracking polls he produced, the more secret of the two, the one that more closely reflected his view, was the less accurate. He chose to publish a separate Populus poll on referendum night that put Remain ten points ahead. Jim Messina, who wished he had taken command of the polling himself, pointed out to friends afterwards that Cooper was fourteen points wrong on the day. Cooper's, and to some degree Osborne's, mistake was to mentally separate immigration and the economy, while impoverished voters, Dominic Cummings and Arron Banks all understood they were the same issue. One of the senior figures in the Remain campaign said later, 'We put a huge amount of time, effort and money into our polling, and were led by it throughout the campaign. It was totally and utterly wrong on most of its key assertions. Frankly, we'd have been better off having no polling at all, or going out into the street and randomly stopping every fourth person and asking them what they thought.' In Cooper's defence, he tested the possible alternative strategies on immigration and found that they would not work. When he put the suggestion of a migration-impact fund to focus groups, 'people literally laughed at the idea'.

Cooper's polls undoubtedly strengthened Cameron's belief that he would win, but there was also a degree of complacency in Downing Street about the prime minister's personal ability to charm the voters, many of whom were not Tories. McGrory says he could not fault the way Cameron and Osborne 'bent their backs' for the campaign. But he adds, 'Where they do have to bear responsibility is that they got us into this mess in the first place, and there was a large element of hubris, I'm afraid. They thought they were going to win, and it was a gamble that has not paid off, catastrophically not for us, not for them, but not for the country either.' The belief that they would emerge victorious meant that Cameron and Osborne put the future unity of the Tory Party ahead of the demands of winning the referendum. One member of Stronger In says, 'We should have been tougher with Gove and Boris. But Craig Oliver didn't want to, because he decided we were going to win, and when we won the Tory Party had to come together and heal itself.'

Cameron did have less room to manoeuvre than his opponents. While he could not commit his government to policy changes, Gove and Johnson created their alternative government on the back of an envelope.

The one thing most Remain campaign staff agree on is that being more positive about the EU would not have been a vote-winner. Will Straw says, 'If we had run an entirely positive, passionate campaign I think we would have been lucky to get 48 per cent. I think votes at sixteen would have clearly made a difference. I think in retrospect tackling immigration more head-on could have made a big difference. But whether those two things would have got you over the line, I just don't know. Certainly the other suggestions that we've had for running a more positive campaign would have set us back.'

The problem with the economic-risk campaign was not the basic concept, but the failure to join the dots between leaving the EU, lower GDP, less money for public services and the cost of living for individual families. Peter Mandelson says, 'We lost because of the mountain of anti-EU sentiment in the country, driven by Rupert Murdoch and Paul Dacre and the rest of the Brexit press over many years, the hopelessness of the Labour leadership, and our own campaign's lack of dexterity and reading of public opinion. Having said that, given the underlying drivers working against us, including the prevailing anti-politics, anti-establishment feelings in the West, the achievement of 48 per cent of the vote begins to look like a small miracle.'

George Osborne's analysis was that he and Cameron miscalculated the scale of division within the Conservative Party that left nearly half their MPs against them, had failed to predict the impact of a hostile press, which they should have recalled from the 2001 and 2005 general elections, and went blind into the strategic planning, not knowing whether two of the party's key assets, Boris Johnson and Michael Gove, would be on their side.

Johnson and Gove did not win the campaign for Leave, but they made victory possible by giving the Brexit cause glamour, publicity and intellectual heft that it would otherwise have lacked. Alastair Campbell says, 'I think if it had just been Nigel Farage and the right-wing papers and a few Tory oddballs, it would have been fine. It wouldn't have happened without Boris Johnson and Michael Gove, in my view. They took it to a different level.' Another senior figure in the Remain campaign says, 'The truth is, Johnson and Gove transformed the Leave campaign, discombobulated Cameron, terrified Osborne, who wanted to protect his friendship with Gove, and gave firepower to the Tory Brexit press which they would not have had otherwise.'

Without Gove, Johnson may well not have had the courage of his wavering convictions and made the jump for Brexit. Without Gove, the coup against Dominic Cummings might have succeeded, and the Leave campaign been thrown into a death spiral from which it may not have escaped. Without Gove's commitment, the number of Tory MPs backing Brexit might have been limited to double figures, rather than more than 140. Without Gove providing the patina of intellectual credibility to the Leave campaign it would have been dominated by Ukip and Nigel Farage, whose appeal to middle England was more limited. Without Gove getting Johnson on board, the face of the campaign may well have been the Ukip leader. Without Gove's support for and then betrayal of Boris, one or both of them might have been a viable leadership contender. Between 19 February and 30 June, it was Gove's decisions which shaped history's path. The sum total of those decisions, each of which he stood by afterwards, was a disaster for his own career and ensured that many of those around Vote Leave won the war and lost the peace.

Gove's final act ironically saved Johnson's career, which those who believe Boris only backed Brexit to advance his chances of becoming prime minister will regard as unjust reward. It may well be that, deep in the recesses of his subconscious, or in very private conversations with his loved ones, Johnson's driving motivation was his career. But it is only fair to record that this was not obvious to those who spent most of their waking hours with him while the decision was being made. He had easier options which would still have left him with a clear path to Downing Street. Backing Brexit was the riskier one, as both his campaign manager Ben Wallace and his own father pointed out to him, though it was admittedly the option with more immediate and higher rewards. Johnson saw the decision as the logical conclusion of his Eurosceptic writings, and as a one-off chance to secure the sovereignty both his wife and Michel Gove had persuaded him was the key issue. It was also a decision guaranteed to make Johnson a leading character in the defining drama of national life, and I am persuaded that was at least as important as any leadership calculation. If you think Boris was cynical and career-ist, you must also accept that he was bold and courageous. There are worse attributes in those who wish to lead us.

Johnson is a contradictory character. It is fairly clear from his texts to Cameron and his mood early on referendum night that he expected Remain to win. But equally, if he began the campaign accepting the likelihood of a heroic loss, the personal attacks he came under persuaded him to fight hard for victory, since that was his only guar-antee of survival. Johnson was profoundly shocked by Cameron's immediate resignation, which was the reason for his sombre mien at the press conference on the morning after the result. There were moments in the following week when some MPs who saw him believe that he wavered when confronted with the magnitude of the challenge that would face him if he became prime minister. Andy Wigmore of Leave.EU claims to have seen emails to that effect: 'There was a reali-sation that Boris probably didn't want the job.' Johnson and his team deny this, but the encounter over tea at Althrop House showed that he had understandable reservations about the effect on his immediate family. There are claims too that Johnson did not actually want to leave the EU. George Osborne tells friends that Johnson repeatedly said this to him before the referendum, and after it asked plaintively, 'It is going to be OK, isn't it?' But politicians ought to be judged by their actions, not their words and wishes, and Johnson made his choice and owned it afterwards, arguing as foreign secretary for a 'hard Brexit' outside the European customs union. The 'what' was so significant that it outweighs the 'why'.

Johnson can be more easily rebuked for letting things drift in the five days of his leadership campaign, but he had every reason to expect that his campaign chairman, Michael Gove, would fight to keep his challenge on track rather than turn on him. Had the show stayed on the road he would have had every chance of victory. Gove's decision to do the dirty was partly the consequence of his frustration with Johnson's actions, and more pertinently his inactions, but it escalated quickly because his advis-ers and Nick Boles had always wanted him to run himself, and were quick to encourage him to do so. It is telling that the advisers who spent least time in the bubble around Gove that week – de Zoete, Stephenson and Cummings – were the least enthusiastic about the enterprise. But for the first time in Gove's career the 'what if?' ambition that many politicians harbour for what he calls 'the big job' seemed, after his experiences during the campaign, finally to be plausible.

Relations between Johnson and Gove were slow to heal. They ran into each other in the division lobby after the vote on renewing the Trident nuclear deterrent on Monday, 18 July, eighteen days after the great betrayal. They talked for twenty-five minutes in Johnson's ministerial office, which he had inherited from Osborne. Gove offered what Johnson's camp describe as a somewhat equivocal apology, of the 'I'm sorry if you feel that I've hurt you' variety. One aide who witnessed part of the exchanges felt Gove was trying to offer an olive branch, telling Boris, 'Thank you for leading us to victory.' But Johnson was not responsive, since Gove also tried to justify his decision. Johnson made it clear that he felt personally wounded by Gove's assertions that he was not up to the job: 'I don't understand how anyone could behave like that. We've been friends for thirty years.' Gove told friends he was struck by how hurt Boris was, as he himself considered his actions logical and unavoidable. Johnson's view was more prosaic. He told another MP, 'I wanted to punch him.'

Within three months of the referendum Gove had returned to *The Times* as a columnist. Some of his friends believe he could still have a second cabinet career: 'The consoling thing about MG is that, because he'd been humiliated, he can come back. If he'd been put in a shit job, or even sent back to the MoJ, he would have this sword of Damocles hanging over him.' Others think the lure of journalism and the prospect of editing *The Times* will claim him. Gove stuck to the view that each of the decisions he made was correct at the time. But he admitted later that he could have handled things better. The accumulated effect of those decisions was ultimately disastrous for him, and for many of those around him. 'I should with the benefit of hindsight not have backed Boris so precipitately. And potentially run myself, or potentially just held back,' he said.

The events of June 2016 also shattered the Notting Hill set. Samantha Cameron was disgusted with Sarah Vine, who is godmother to the Camerons' younger daughter Florence. A Cameron family friend said: 'Sam's a very open person, and sometimes naïvely trusting in a friendship. I think she wanted to remain friends with Sarah, but it has gone too far now.' A close aide to David Cameron added, 'Sam doesn't want Sarah crossing their threshold again.' Another familiar with the situation asked wryly, 'Can you excommunicate a godmother?' Many in the Notting Hill set hope Cameron takes a more charitable view of Michael Gove. By late September 2016 there had been no rapprochement, but mutual friends were hoping to engineer one in 2017. The blue-helmet mediators are expected to include Ed Vaizey and Hugo Swire. Special rage among Cameroons was reserved for Steve Hilton, once a key member of Cameron's gang. Hilton told friends it was Cameron's 'World War III' speech that 'tipped me over the edge'. A Cameroon said, 'Steve is the Satan figure. Michael and Boris had to have a position; Steve could have easily stayed out of it, but he chose to come back home and kick us in the bollocks.'

The human cost of an intense political moment like the referendum also dragged in families. In November 2015, just as Cameron was writing to Donald Tusk, Dominic Cummings and his wife Mary Wakefield were told at the twenty-week scan that their unborn son, their first child, was not growing properly, and would not live. Mary wrote, 'My husband and I began to mourn. We sat for an hour in the hospital corridor, watching the water cooler belch, feeling panic and despair, then in the end, resigned.' Fortunately, a second prognosis pronounced the baby healthy. He was born in early March. Cummings took just two days of paternity leave.

Daniel Hannan's wife was also expecting a child. 'For six months I barely spent two nights in the same place,' he admitted. On the big night, with his wife eight months pregnant, he installed her in a hotel near Vote Leave's offices. Fortunately, Sarah Hannan was a committed Leaver, and had been a member of the Oxford Campaign for an Independent Britain.

Other homes and teams were divided. Adam Atashzai had seen a lot for a guy who turned just thirty-two during the campaign, but the toughest conversation he had was with his mother when he realised she might be about to vote for Brexit. She took him to task for the 'lies' his bosses David Cameron and George Osborne were telling, but Atashzai laid out the economic risks and won her over. He discovered on the morning of 24 June that his father had voted Leave. With the exception of Nigel Adams, Boris Johnson's House of Commons leadership team were all Remainers, none more vociferously so than Ben Wallace. He spent referendum night at Johnson's home, supporting his leadership candidate, then went home to his family in Lancashire, where he promptly burst into tears at what he feared Brexit might do to his children's futures. Wallace felt defeated twice when the Johnson campaign went belly-up, but, like his man, he was saved by Theresa May with the plum job of security minister at the Home Office. Will Walden went to join Johnson at the Foreign Office as his chief of staff and senior special adviser.

The campaign also brought people together. Paul Stephenson and Ameet Gill never stopped talking on WhatsApp across the Brexit divide. When it was all over they came together to start a PR company called Hanbury Strategy, offering businesses advice on how to cope with Brexit. Gill turned down a peerage in David Cameron's notorious resignation honours. James McGrory and Joe Carberry, bright lights of the Lib Dems and Labour, sat next to each other for six months and became inseparable friends. After the referendum they joined forces to set up a successor organisation to Stronger In, called Open Britain. Roland Rudd became its chairman. Will Straw helped them get up and running and then went off to work in the private sector, still harbouring ambitions to be an MP and consoling himself with the knowledge that his father endured four general election defeats before holding two of the great offices of state. As Liberal Democrats, James McGrory and Ryan Coetzee had both suffered two brutal losses in thirteen months. Coetzee took a consultancy job. He was more sanguine after the referendum than after the general election, but concluded, 'I came to Britain to build the centre ground. I should have come in 1995, because the centre's not holding at all.' McGrory was more upbeat: 'I'm very much of the Theodore Roosevelt school: better to be in the arena. I have worked in an age that has not been a good time for progressives. But is your answer to get out of the ring and say it's all too difficult? That's not my outlook. I think progressives will have their day again. I just hope I'm around to help.'

Some friendships flourished across the divide. During the referendum McGrory of Stronger In was dating a former flatmate of Rob Oxley of Vote Leave, and the two would see each other with mutual friends. 'Every time, we had a gossip,' says Oxley. 'He once tipped me off about something shitty someone was trying on me, and I tipped him off about something someone was trying on him.' Few made more sacrifices during the campaign than Oxley: 'I missed two close friends' weddings; I'm not speaking to one friend, because I didn't get to go on his stag do.

I basically left it too late to tell him. I ended up not going to his wedding as well.' During the period around the renegotiation announcement Oxley's grandmother in Zimbabwe became very ill. Paul Stephenson gave him permission to fly to see her, but Oxley did not feel he could let the campaign down: 'I spoke to my grandmother for the last time in the office on my mobile. The day my grandmother died was a Friday. I went into the stairwell. My mum told me. I gave her what warm words I could, and went back to my desk and worked for the rest of the day, because there was too much work to get on with.' At 9.30 p.m. Vicky Woodcock saw Oxley looking at a picture of his grandmother on his computer. 'I burst into tears,' says Oxley, 'had a bit of a hug with her and then went home.' The funeral was the following week, and Oxley's mother asked him to fly out for a couple of days, but he said, 'I can't because of the campaign.' In the cold light of day this might seem callous, but anyone who has been involved in events of this intensity will recognise the total commitment to a cause and to colleagues. 'People spilled blood, sweat and tears for that campaign,' Oxley said. He went to work as a special adviser for Priti Patel, the new international development secretary.

If victory took its toll, defeat was a pain that would not leave some people. Three months after the referendum Jim Messina still thought every day about losing the Brexit vote. He had never really been involved in a losing campaign before. Three days after the referendum his company helped win the Spanish national election for Mariano Rajoy, but Messina never celebrated that win – all he could think about was Brexit. He had been proud to work for the Remain side, he believed it was a just cause, and he felt crushed by the result. He thought Cameron's departure was bad for the world. As the post-mortems were conducted Messina figured he would get his share of the blame, while Vote Leave would be lionised. He consoled himself with the thought that he wasn't a genius when Obama and Cameron had won, and he wasn't an idiot now.

Craig Oliver wrote his memoir of the campaign, *Unleashing Demons*, and got a knighthood from Cameron, while juggling offers from consultancies. 'Part of me is waiting for the moment when you suddenly feel utterly bereft,' he said afterwards. 'I was sad to leave Downing Street. I was sad to lose the referendum. But I don't feel like my life has been blighted. I feel like there's a new chapter starting.'[2] Ed Llewellyn took a peerage and was also rewarded with the ambassadorship to Paris, which comes with an embassy and residence that are the jewels in the crown of the British diplomatic estate. He will share the red benches with Cameron's three closest female aides, Kate Fall, Liz Sugg and Gabby Bertin.

Both Dominic Cummings and Daniel Korski showed an interest in harnessing the power of data and computing for politics and government, but characteristically both kept their schemes under wraps. Matthew Elliott set up a new website, Brexit Central. Adam Atashzai went off to begin the long march towards becoming either the David Cameron or the Lynton Crosby of the 2030s. Peter Mandelson advised and chivvied Labour moderates on how to resist the Corbynista takeover of the party. Life went on. Stuart Rose, the wisest man of all, realised he had had enough of politics: 'If banging your head against the wall is giving you a headache, stop banging your fucking head against the wall.'

Arguably, no one sacrificed more for his cause than George Osborne. The chancellor must take his share of the blame for what went wrong. The emergency budget, the overly specific Treasury documents, the refusal to change tack from a failing 'Project Fear' message, are black marks. But, as one senior Number 10 source said, 'The one red tick is that he has sacrificed his political career for a referendum he thought should never have existed, and defended a "tens of thousands" figure that he always thought was bonkers.' Osborne was quick to defend his legacy, setting up a think tank to promote the Northern Powerhouse and making pointed interventions on the need for soft Brexit even before September 2016 was out. At forty-five he is fourteen years younger than Theresa May and has time for a second political life, unless the IMF or another international finance body lures him away. To anyone who asked his intentions that autumn, he pointedly said, 'I am not going anywhere.' After thirteen years' continuous service on the front bench, he had time for reflection. A close friend said, 'He can become an elder statesman, a William Hague. If something goes wrong in the next term, people will come to him rather than him coming to them.' A former Labour minister who has known the taste of defeat observed, 'The fact that he was fired will ensure his career is not over. He'll feel very incomplete.'

The hardcore Brexiteers felt more complete. '*Mission accompli*,' said Dan Hannan, vowing to move on and 'do something outside politics' once his career as an MEP is over. 'I could spend another thirty years in

politics, and I'll never achieve anything like this.' His friend Douglas
Carswell, an uneasy member of Ukip, vowed not to return to the
Conservatives: 'I feel far more protective over Vote Leave, because in a
sense, that was my party.'

The most intriguing referendum legacy project was that of the self-
styled 'bad boys of Brexit,' Arron Banks and Nigel Farage. Leave.EU had
given Banks a mailing list of around a million followers, including most
Ukip members and activists and probably a quarter to a third of Tory
members. Banks, Farage and Chris Bruni-Lowe all regarded Ukip, with
its volunteer ethos, its constitution that bans whipping and its eight-hour
NEC meetings (to which members bring packed lunches) as fundamentally unreformable. Banks mused out loud about a new party, and creating a right-wing version of Momentum, the network of the Corbynistas
on the left. The referendum severed some of the ties that bound the
working class to the Labour Party. Banks says, 'British politics will be
realigned after the referendum. The vast number of people who've never
voted before, or the Labour voters who came out against the establishment, I think people have got a taste for it. The Labour Party's ripping
itself to pieces. The Conservative Party peace is not convincing.'
Whichever party or movement Banks supports will be a player: 'I think
we've got an opportunity to win thirty or forty seats.' Nigel Farage may
no longer be Ukip leader, but he seems likely to remain the dominant
force in this world. 'Nigel might come back in another guise,' says Banks.
'I think he hankers after something like the president of the Five Star
Movement – not a party, but it could morph into it.' The web-based
movement of comedian Beppe Grillo finished second in Italy's 2013 election on a populist, Eurosceptic platform. Farage said, 'The SDP didn't
mushroom overnight. Roy Jenkins actually advertised it openly, for about
eighteen months, that he was thinking about doing it. I think there could
be some big changes between now and 2020, very big changes.' In their
hands the tone of politics could change. Banks said, 'We use a bit of sense
of humour, we use a bit of shock and awe. We changed the rules a bit.'

He and Banks may not agree on much else, but Douglas Carswell also
thought realignment was possible: 'I think it will happen. The internet
will redefine what it means to be a political party, and will remove the
barriers to entering politics. What is fundamentally happening is the
disalignment of the Labour intelligentsia from the working-class Labour
vote. The fragmentation of that alliance, which has been in place basic-

ally since the 1920s, that is what is going to reshape politics. I suspect the political ecosystem will change quite dramatically.'

The potential fragmentation of Labour might also create changes on the centre left. The proto-alliance of Cameroons and Blairites in the Stronger In offices broke up in defeat, but senior Liberal Democrats have seen a world where they might be able to lure Labour moderates into a new alliance. In early July 2016 Paddy Ashdown put together a new organisation called More United, designed to bring together progressives to recruit online and hold public meetings like those that led to the Great Reform Act, the Suffragettes and the creation of the trades unions. His model was also the Five Star Movement. Ashdown said his plan was not to create a new political party, but noted archly that the SDP emerged from differences within Labour exposed by the 1975 referendum. His plan had the tacit approval of Tim Farron, the leader of the Lib Dems, who was prepared to contemplate a rebranding of his party. A week earlier Farron had met in the Two Chairmen pub in Westminster with a Conservative special adviser, who had in turn met with a Labour MP. In these conversations a new party called The Democrats was floated, though it was idle talk rather than a serious plan.

Britain's first-past-the-post electoral system makes it much more difficult for political realignment to occur than in many European countries. Ryan Coetzee, who has experience in both Britain and South Africa, believes realignment is 'a good idea', but says, 'I think the electoral system makes it absolutely impossible. In order for realignment to work, you need both major parties to split at the same time. Otherwise, the other one will just win by default.'

Realignment or not, it is clear the referendum will have as-yet unclear implications for British politics and society. David Mundell, who saw how the fallout from the Scottish referendum still influenced everything two years later, cautioned his colleagues that a referendum is not a moment, but a process 'with a long tail': 'A referendum is very divisive, and isn't actually a very nice experience. It pits people against each other. It's not a one-off event that can just be absorbed and moved on from.' Peter Mandelson is not optimistic about the implications: 'Britain will not be finished, but we will be diminished. We will end up with a smaller economy, less to spend on public services and defence, weaker soft power, a less relevant relationship with the US, and reduced status in the world.' Alan Johnson says, 'It means turmoil and uncertainty for a long time to come.'

The upbeat case was put by Steve Baker, who compared the Brexit vote to one of his skydives: 'Jumping out of the plane is terrifying, but you've got to trust the equipment and get on with it. When the EU plane is going down and you know that free trade and self-government will make you prosperous and free, then you've just got to jump, however frightening it is. Remain people are absolutely terrified, because they didn't have the confidence to jump. Skydiving is like that; loads of people get in the plane and want to jump and at the last minute don't do it, because it's just scary. But this isn't scary. Having the dignity of governing yourself and trading freely is going to work.'

The story began with David Cameron, and it must end with him too. Ultimately, the decisions that mattered in the period covered by this book were taken by him, and he is the one who paid the ultimate political price. A close confidant said, 'I think David feels that he did what he thought was right, and you have to take decisions as PM. He took those decisions, he'll live with those decisions, and that's the way life is. Obviously he's got a strong family. He's not the sort of person who's going to be screaming at the end of the garden and twisting himself into knots about what could have been.' Many around Cameron believe his unusual and commendable attachment to a world beyond Downing Street enabled him to cope better than most with the loss of office. But there will linger a feeling that – despite the long hours and the crisis management – it did not matter enough to him that he should win. As a Labour MP said after he had resigned, 'He's the only prime minister in my adult lifetime who has treated it as just another job, rather than a vocation.'

Cameron knows already what the first line of his obituary will say. He will be for ever the prime minister who took Britain out of the EU by mistake. George Eustice, who was his director of communications in opposition and his farming minister in government, says, 'Leaving the European Union is not the legacy David Cameron wanted. I remember when I worked for him as an adviser and we were discussing his approach on the Lisbon Treaty he once joked that if we left the EU he wouldn't have to worry about his legacy.' A friend of Michael Gove compared Cameron to the prime minister who lost the American colonies: 'At the moment he looks like Lord North.'

Those who deplored Brexit were quick to apportion the blame. A member of the Stronger In board said, 'I'm afraid I don't feel sorry for David Cameron having gone, because he got us into this appalling mess. I think Cameron goes down in history as the worst prime minister since Eden, and arguably the worst since Chamberlain, because Brexit is much more serious than the Suez crisis for Britain. I think that's a very, very poor legacy.'

The Cameroons hoped that if Brexit became a success and the Tories continued to enjoy the kind of political hegemony that Margaret Thatcher enjoyed, Cameron's decision not to blow up the party to win the referendum would be vindicated one day.

The Eurosceptics always wanted Cameron to be like Thatcher. In the manner of his departure, he was. Both were brought down by a combination of Europe and poor party management. Cameron never mastered backbench operations when confronted by people with stronger convictions than his own. This, and his belief that loyalty trumped principle, caused him to fatally misread Michael Gove and to underestimate the number of Tories who would be against him, both of which might have made him think harder about calling the referendum.

In some ways Cameron was a victim of his own success. His government's economic policies led to a jobs boom which created a magnet for migrants to come to Britain. The rhetoric of toughness and cuts perpetuated by Osborne meant that few, even among those who benefited, ever noticed that income inequality declined under Cameron. When the time came to vote on the EU many of those who had done well out of his economic and welfare policies did not feel they owed him anything, and voted to leave. Cameron's insistence on sticking to the 'tens of thousands' formulation on immigration undermined public trust as much as the high numbers of new arrivals. When he asked these voters to trust him on the economic risks of Brexit they did not believe him.

The counterpoint to these criticisms is that Cameron was facing historic forces he could not control, and an almost uniquely difficult political environment. One of his Downing Street loyalists said, 'If we had actually won it would have been a stunning victory. We would have won this when populist movements are sweeping across Europe and there's huge anger and concerns about immigration; defending an institution which has been pilloried for the last forty years by the British public with a renegotiation which was shit; at a time when the Labour Party were on the floor; at a time when the tabloids were all against us.

Six hundred thousand people change their votes and we win. I think that's amazing.'

In the final analysis, Cameron showed himself to be the ultimate Macmillanite. From his hero he took an approach of centrist conciliation, a desire to be at the table in Brussels rather than away from it, and an instinct to placate rather than challenge his critics which ill-equipped him to deal with the 'Events, dear boy, events' which his own decisions unleashed. He was tactical where he needed to be strategic, confident when he should have been nervous, resolute in sticking to a campaign plan he should have changed. Ultimately, he never made the other European leaders choose between Britain in the EU and the principle of free movement. In the interests of Tory unity, he put party before what he believed to be in the best interests of the country. He embodied the establishment in an election that always favoured the insurgent. Cameron threw himself into the campaign, finally liberated to fight 'heart and soul' for British membership of the EU, in which he had come to believe wholeheartedly. His political mistakes were well-intentioned, and he put statesmanship before his role as campaign chief. But unlike his opponents, Cameron could not, in all truth, look himself in the mirror and answer 'Yes' to the question: 'Did you do everything possible to win?'

The Brexiteers were prepared to go further. Rob Oxley says, 'When it comes down to people criticising what the campaign did, we weren't out there to make friends. We weren't there to have the academic debate about the EU. We were out there to win – and we did.' Arron Banks puts it best: 'We were prepared to do almost anything to win, and sometimes did.'

No one's ends justify limitless means, but it seems to me when we look at the US, where Donald Trump makes Arron Banks or Nigel Farage look like Mary Poppins, or at much of the EU itself, where parties mine more extreme reaches of the political spectrum than we do in Britain, that we are still lucky to have the politics we do. If we are getting furious about the niceties of an overcooked £350 million a week to Brussels, or a dubious £4,300 cost to families, rather than rioting in the streets or real coups, political executions or racial apartheid, we are not doing so badly as a country.

Appendix 1

BORIS JOHNSON'S FIRST 'OUT' ARTICLE

Sent to Marina Wheeler, Will Walden and Ben Wallace at 6.32 p.m. on Friday, 19 February 2016

I was trying to explain the EU question to an 18 year old the other day and she seemed flummoxed. 'Sovereignty?' she said, and I bet she spoke for a lot of her generation, 'Who cares about sovereignty?'

As far as she was concerned, the world was pretty fine and dandy. Leaving the EU just sounded mad, to her: a bit cranky, a bit sepia-tinted, a bit of a cravat-wearing pass-the-port type affectation.

So let me give an example of why I think sovereignty matters, and what it means when you lose it. It was back in the autumn of 2013, and we suddenly started to see an increase in deaths of people on bicycles. It was a dreadful time.

Day after day (so it seemed) there was a fatal incident, often a young woman who died under the wheels of a lorry. Every time TFL officials would go to the scene. They would come back ashen-faced, and with the same broad account.

The problem was to do with visibility. The cabs of these tipper trucks were so high, and the blind spots so big, that the drivers were missing the cyclists altogether. The victims were being dragged under the wheels, often when the vehicle was turning left, with horrific results.

So we went to the Department of Transport and proposed that London should become a 'Safer Lorry Zone'. We didn't want to ban the lorries: that would have been economically damaging. We just wanted to introduce some existing types of driver's cab that had lower windows and were better designed for the city.

The Department was in principle very enthusiastic. The only trouble was that they weren't responsible for the design of lorries. All that had to be settled in Brussels.

It would take years to get the legislation through. European road hauliers would lobby against it. They weren't sure that Britain would succeed. Sorry. And that was it.

Here I was, mayor of a city clamouring for measures to protect cyclists; here was the British government, with all their plenipotentiary authority. There was nothing they or I could do, not with any speed.

That was because this thing called sovereignty – the power given to them by the British people to take decisions on their behalf – was no longer in Westminster. Sovereignty was no longer in Whitehall. It had been given away, traded away. I felt a surge of rage, and I hope you will understand my feelings when I say that I have found myself meeting or corresponding with the grief-stricken relatives of cyclists who have died under lorries.

You may say that it is very sensible to have decisions about lorry cabs taken at a European level; that it is good for the single market, all part of the great project of sewing European markets seamlessly together, so that we more closely resemble the giant single market of America.

On closer inspection, that analogy is hopelessly misplaced. Compare American rules on trucks. It is an extraordinary fact that the states of the United States have more discretion on truck sizes, weights and dimensions than the nations of the EU. They have more discretion over emissions standards.

The people of the state of Vermont have more say over the type of lorries on the roads of that tiny cow-populated state than the people of Britain have over the lorries on the roads of the fifth biggest economy on earth.

And which economy is growing faster – the American, or the European? Which is more flexible? Which is more dynamic?

Sovereignty is the ability to make our own rules when we desperately need them; and, conversely, to stop the flood of new rules that we don't want.

It is hard to gauge exactly what proportion of our law now comes from the EU. The House of Commons library puts it at anything between 15 and 50 per cent, depending on whether you count the statutory instruments as well. Those numbers strike me as already pretty high. Then there are several special features of EU law.

First, new EU laws are created for this country as a result of the Qualified Majority Vote procedure, so that Britain may be outvoted. That is happening more and more regularly – 40 times in the last five years, and over all sorts of policy areas, from the handling of migrants to the pensions of EU officials.

Next, EU law is supreme. In a conflict with any act of parliament or any other British legislative instrument, it is the European Court of Justice that must and does prevail – at least so far. Third, EU law is effectively irreversible. Because it has to be agreed by 28 countries, it can only be repealed by a similar method – which is why EU legislation is frequently compared to a one-way ratchet.

Last, any piece of law that somehow involves the EU must go for ultimate arbitration before the European Court of Justice, and that court is now massively expanding its range of interests. Following the Lisbon Treaty, the Court has taken on the interpretation and application of the European Charter of Fundamental Rights.

Among these supposedly fundamental rights are all sorts of things that never before came within the competence of the EU: rights to free education, rights to found schools, rights to 'choose an occupation', rights to pursue a 'freely chosen occupation' anywhere in the EU, rights to run a business, rights to 'academic freedom'.

Tony Blair thought he had an opt-out from this stuff at the Lisbon summit. The Court of Justice has blown it away. As Lord Denning said as long ago as 1974, 'When we come to matters with a European element, the Treaty is like an incoming tide. It flows into the estuaries and up the rivers. It cannot be held back.'

That is the thing about EU law: it is supreme, irreversible, and in danger of flooding out national discretion. Human rights law fetters the ability of the British army to fight. Employment law such as the 48 hour week makes it harder to run the NHS. It is the EU's law on free movement of citizens – not just workers – that has caused such grief across Europe.

Sometimes I think it is not the numbers of immigrants that people mind so much as the legal inability of governments to do anything; because, again, that precious thing called sovereignty has been given away.

This is leading to a dislocation in politics – a gap between the governed and the public. It is one of the factors in the general disgruntlement towards the so-called elites. It has been disconcerting, during this negotiation, to see how little this view seems to be shared by Brussels. The EU bodies have shown absolutely no spontaneous desire to help David Cameron: to give powers back to nation-states, to engage in the general devolution that is otherwise taking place.

On the contrary, they want to go forward with yet more integration, in the hope of making sense of monetary union, and defending their embattled construct. According to the 'Five Presidents' Report', which came out last year, they want a new 'fiscal union' and a budgetary union, with more centralised control of the tax and spending policies of countries such as Greece – already groaning under the servitude of the euro.

They want a new raft of social policies to go with it. They will go ahead at a new Intergovernmental conference to change the Treaties, and there is not a lot we can do about it. The fundamental problem of our relationship is getting more and more acute.

David Cameron has battled for Britain in these talks; he has achieved a great deal in a short time. He has secured some very useful language that excludes us from ever closer union, on competition, on deregulation, and on the relationship between the euro ins and outs.

There is an excellent forthcoming Bill that will assert the sovereignty of parliament, the fruit of heroic intellectual labour by Oliver Letwin, which may well exercise a chilling effect on some of the more federalist flights of fancy of the Court and the Commission. It is good, and right, but it cannot stop the machine; at best it can put a temporary and occasional spoke in the ratchet.

The reality remains: that they have an ideal that we do not share. They want to create a truly federal union, *e pluribus unum*, when most British people do not.

It is time to seek a new relationship, in which we manage to extricate ourselves from most of the supranational elements. We will hear a lot in the coming weeks about the risks of this option; the risk to the economy, the risk to the City of London, and so on; and though those risks cannot be entirely dismissed I think they are likely to be exaggerated. We have heard this kind of thing before, about the decision to opt out of the euro, and the very opposite turned out to be the case.

I also accept that there is a risk that a vote to leave the EU, as it currently stands, will cause fresh tensions in the union between England and Scotland. On the other hand, most of the evidence I have seen suggests that the Scots will vote on roughly the same lines as the English.

We will be told that a Brexit would embolden Putin, though it seems to me he is more likely to be emboldened, for instance, by the west's relative passivity in Syria.

The real risk is to the general morale of Europe, and to the prestige of the EU project. We should take that seriously.

We should remember that this federalist vision is not an ignoble idea. It was born of the highest motives – to keep the peace in Europe. The people who run the various EU institutions – whom we like to ply with crass abuse – are in my experience principled and thoughtful officials. They have done some very good things: I think of the work of Sir Leon Brittan, for instance, as Competition Commissioner, and his fight against state aids.

They just have a different view of the way Europe should be constructed. I would hope they would see a Vote Leave as a challenge, not just to strike a new and harmonious relationship with Britain (in which those benefits could be retained) but to recover some of the competitiveness that the continent has lost in the last decades.

Whatever happens, Britain needs to be supportive of its friends and allies – but on the lines originally proposed by Winston Churchill: interested, associated; with Europe – but not comprised. We have spent 500 years trying to stop continental European powers uniting against us.

There is no reason (if everyone is sensible) why that should happen now, and every reason for friendliness. The EU has changed out of all recognition from the body we joined – and which I first started writing about, for this paper, 28 years ago.

They know it; we know it. There is no harm in acknowledging that. If the 'Leave' side wins, it will indeed be necessary to negotiate a large number of trade deals at great speed. But why should that be impossible? We have become so used to Nanny in Brussels that we have become infantilised, incapable of imagining an independent future. We used to run the biggest empire the world has ever seen, and with a much smaller domestic population and a relatively tiny civil service. Are we really incapable of cutting trade deals? We will have at least two years in which the existing Treaties will be in force.

I want to end by saying something about the referendum campaign. For many Conservatives this has already been a pretty agonising business. Many of us are deeply internally divided, and we are divided between us.

We know that we do not agree on the substance, but I hope we can all agree that it would be quite wrong if the discussion were to become in any way *ad hominem* – descending to any kind of personal attack or commentary, on or off the record, about our friends on the other side of the argument.

At the end of it all we want to get a result, and then get on and unite around David Cameron – continuing to deliver better jobs, better housing, better health, education and a better quality of life for our constituents for whom (let's be frank) the EU is not always the number one issue.

It is entirely thanks to the prime minister, his bravery and energy, and the fact that he won a majority Conservative government, that we are having a referendum at all. Never forget that if it were down to Jeremy Corbyn and the so-called People's party, the people would be completely frozen out.

This is the right moment to have a referendum, because as Europe changes, Britain is changing too. This is a truly great country that is now going places at extraordinary speed.

We are the European if not the world leaders in so many sectors of the 21st century economy; not just financial services, but business services, the media, biosciences, universities, the arts, tech of all kinds (of the 40 EU tech companies worth more than $1bn, 17 are British); and we still have a dizzyingly fertile manufacturing sector.

Now is the time to spearhead the success of those products and services not just in Europe, but in growth markets beyond. This is a moment to be brave, to reach out – not to hug the skirts of Nurse in Brussels, and refer all decisions to someone else.

We have given so much to the world, in ideas and culture, but the most valuable British export and the one for which we are most famous is the one that is now increasingly in question: parliamentary democracy and the right of the people to remove, at elections, the men and women who make the laws of this country.

Reasonable people may take different views about the importance of this so-called sovereignty. I place a high premium; but I am perfectly prepared to accept that you can be a patriot (and indeed a rock-ribbed Tory) and a full-blown federalist.

In the next few weeks, thankfully, the views of politicians like me will matter less and less, because the choice belongs to those who are really sovereign – the people of the UK. And in the matter of their own sovereignty they, by definition, will get it right.

Appendix 2

BORIS JOHNSON'S 'IN' ARTICLE

Sent to Marina Wheeler at 9.04 p.m. on Friday, 19 February 2016, copied to Will Walden and Ben Wallace at lunchtime on Saturday, 20 February (Note: Johnson sent the piece with no paragraph breaks)

OK OK, I admit it. If you gave him a truth drug, or hypnotised him, I don't think even the prime minister would really deny it. This EU deal is not perhaps everything that we would have liked. It is not what we Eurosceptics were hoping, not when the process kicked off. We were hoping that he was going to get really deep down and dirty, in the way that the Bloomberg speech seemed to indicate. He was going to probe the belly of the beast and bring back British sovereignty, like Hercules bringing Eurydice back from the Underworld. I had the impression that this was going to be the beginning of a wholesale repatriation of powers – over fisheries, farming, the social chapter, border controls, you name it: all those political hostages joyfully returning home like the end of Raid on Entebbe. It was going to be a moment for the ringing of church bells and bonfires on beacons, and union flags flying from every steeple, and peasants blind drunk on non-EU approved scrumpy and beating the hedgerows with staves while singing patriotic songs about Dave the hero. I don't think we can really pretend that this is how things have turned out. This is not a fundamental reform of Britain's position in the EU, and no one could credibly claim it is. It is not pointless; it is not wholly insignificant; it is by no means a waste of time. But it will not stop the great machine of EU integration, and it will not stop the production of ever more EU laws – at least some of which will have deleterious effects on the economy of this country and the rest of Europe. Never mind the Tusk deal; look at the elephant in the room – the great beast still trampling happily on British parliamentary sovereignty, and British democracy. So there are likely to be a significant number of people – perhaps including you – who will feel that in all honour we can now only do one thing. We said we wanted a reformed EU. We said that if we failed to get reform, then Britain could have a great future outside. We have not got a reformed EU – so: nothing for it, then – ho for the open seas! Viva Brexit! That would seem to be the logic, and yet I wonder if it is wholly correct. Shut your eyes. Hold your breath. Think of Britain. Think of the rest of the EU. Think of the future. Think of the desire of your children and your grandchildren to live and work in other European countries; to sell things there, to make friends and perhaps to find partners there. Ask yourself: in spite of all the defects and disappointments of this exercise – do you really, truly, definitely want Britain to pull out of the European Union? Now? This is a big thing to do, and there is certainly a strong political-philosophical imperative leading us to the door. We are being outvoted ever more frequently. The ratchet of integration clicks remorselessly forward. More and more questions are now justiciable by the European Court of Justice, including that extraordinary document, the European Charter of Fundamental Rights. This bestows on every one of our 500 million EU citizens a legally enforceable right to do all sorts of things across all 28 states: to start a business, to choose any occupation they like, to found any type of religious school, to enjoy 'academic freedom'. I shudder to think what is going to happen when UK citizens start vindicating these new 'rights' in Luxembourg. There is going to be more and more of this stuff; and I can see why people might just think – to hell with it. I want out. I want to take back control of our democracy and our country. If you feel that, I perfectly understand – because half the time I have been feeling that myself. And then the other half of the time, I have been thinking: hmmm. I like the sound of freedom; I like the sound of restoring democracy. But what are the downsides – and here we must be honest. There are some big questions that the Out side need to answer. Almost everyone expects there to be some sort of economic shock as a result of a Brexit. How big would it be? I am sure that the doomsters are exaggerating the fall-out – but are they completely wrong? And how can we know? And then there is the worry about Scotland, and the possibility that an English-only Leave vote could lead to the break-up of the union. There is the Putin factor: we don't want to do anything to encourage more shirtless swaggering from the Russian leader – not in the

Middle east, not anywhere. And then there is the whole geo-strategic anxiety. Britain is a great nation, a global force for good. It is surely a boon for the world and for Europe that she should be intimately engaged in the EU. This is a market on our doorstep, ready for further exploitation by British firms: the membership fee seems rather small for all that access. Why are we so determined to turn our back on it? Shouldn't our policy be like our policy on cake – pro-having it and pro-eating it? Pro-Europe and pro-the rest of the world? If sovereignty is the problem – and it certainly is – then maybe it is worth looking again at the PM's deal, because there is a case for saying it is not quite as contemptible as all that. He is the first PM to get us out of ever closer union, which is potentially very important with the European Court of Justice and how they interpret EU law. He has some good stuff on competition, and repealing legislation, and on protecting Britain from further integration of the euro group. Now if this were baked into a real EU Treaty, it would be very powerful. Taken together with the sovereignty clauses – which are not wholly platitudinous – you can see the outlines of a new role for Britain: friendly, involved, but not part of the federalist project. Yes, folks, the deal's a bit of a dud, but it contains the germ of something really good. I am going to muffle my disappointment and back the PM.

Appendix 3

DAVID CAMERON'S 'VICTORY' SPEECH

The speech Cameron would have delivered on Friday, 24 June, if Remain had won the referendum (Note: The square brackets and underlining are Downing Street's emphasis)

INTRODUCTION

This referendum was perhaps the biggest democratic exercise in the history of these islands.

33 million people – from England, Scotland, Wales, Northern Ireland and yes, even Gibraltar – all having their say in a supreme act of national sovereignty.

We should remember that we're fortunate to live in a country with democratic institutions, the rule of law and this – the opportunity to ask the people on an issue that goes to the heart of Britain's place in the world.

And we will never forget that, during this exercise in democracy, we lost a true servant of democracy …

… the brilliant MP and campaigner, Jo Cox.

THANKS

The British people have spoken and decided to remain a reformed European Union.

Let me thank the people who were involved in the campaign: Everyone who worked with Britain Stronger in Europe …

… all the politicians who took the brave decision to cross party lines and argue for what they believed was in the national interest …

[[… and all the young people who took to the streets and took to social media to say: this is about our future – this matters.]]

But I also want to pay tribute to those involved in the Leave campaign.

They made strong arguments about our country and what they believed was in its best interests.

Of course, no one can deny that there has been vigorous debate on both sides.

It has divided families, friends, colleagues – and yes, politicians, too.

But it has demonstrated that there is one thing that unites us:

We are all patriots.

We all love Britain.

That is what motivated us, what made us so passionate …

… and it is now what must bring everyone back together again,

[[We all believe in Britain …

… and I know I now have a special responsibility to bring not just politicians, but our whole country, back together.]]

REFERENDUM AND RENEGOTIATION

It's worth remembering why we had this renegotiation and referendum.

It's because the status quo wasn't working properly for Britain.

We needed to fix some of the problems with the EU: Safeguarding the pound, cutting bureaucracy, ending 'Something for nothing' …

… but, above all, I don't think Britain ever felt comfortable about the prospect of deeper political integration.

So things needed to change.

And now they will.

Because we voted to stay in on a reformed basis, key elements of Britain's enhanced special status will be set in stone.

This afternoon in Brussels, new rules to protect Britain from Eurozone discrimination come into force.

From today, national Parliaments will have new powers to block EU legislation.

And – as of this moment – we are out of ever-closer union for good.

Let me put that another way: as far as Britain is concerned, the political project for further integration in Europe is over.

And next week, I'll be going to a meeting of the European Council to report the result of this referendum.

I'll be pointing out to my European counterparts that while 5x per cent of our country voted to remain, 4x per cent voted to leave the European Union altogether.

Institutions in Brussels must understand that they work to serve the people and democratically-elected governments of Europe – not the other way round.

The EU needs to recognise that this referendum was about not just making a decision but also about listening.

And they will have heard the British people's concerns, for example about the impact of migration, loud and clear.

So the work of reform doesn't end here.

And Britain's voice gets stronger, too.

In all the things we need to do together – fighting terrorism, completing the Single Market, dealing with the migration crisis, creating job opportunities for young people – Britain will now play an even bigger role.

ONE NATION GOVERNMENT

I believe it was right to hold the referendum early on in the Parliament ...

... so the uncertainty didn't hang over us.

And it was right to say ministers could campaign on whichever side they chose.

But the Cabinet will come back together ...

... we will meet on Monday ...

... and we will get on with the work set out in our manifesto and Queen's Speech.

We are servants of the people. They rightly expect us to do what we were elected to do a year ago.

So we must be one government, with one goal: building One Nation.

We want this to be a country in which everyone – whatever their background – can get on in life.

Where it doesn't matter where you come from – it's where you're going that counts.

That means a strong economy, so people can get a good job, a decent wage, a home of their own.

It means extending life chances right across our country.

And let's remember: while there were many people who felt that leaving Europe was a threat to their economic security, there were some who never felt that security to begin with ...

... worried about their job prospects, worried about the impact of migration, worried about getting on in life.

They need a government that delivers the security they crave ...

... and we will not rest until we build One Nation, in which <u>everyone</u> is a part of Britain's success.

CONCLUSION

We are on a long walk to a Greater Britain.

It's not always a straight line, or the easiest of journeys. But today, thanks to the British people, we've taken what I believe is an important step forwards.

We will continue to move ahead with a strong economy that delivers opportunity for all.

We will go further and faster in building an open, outward-looking, tolerant society – one that we will be proud to pass on to our children and grandchildren.

We will be that big player on the world stage, fighting for our national interest.

And we will do so, together, as one government, as one people and as one United Kingdom.

ILLUSTRATIONS

David Cameron's Bloomberg speech, 23 January 2013. (Matthew Lloyd/Bloomberg via Getty Images)

Boris Johnson announces that he will support Leave. (Niklas Halle'n/AFP/Getty Images)

Nigel Farage at the Ukip Spring Conference, Llandudno, 27 February 2016. (Oli Scarff/AFP/Getty Images)

The 'Six Brexiteers' at the launch of the Vote Leave campaign, 20 February 2016. (Stefan Rousseau/AFP/Getty Images)

Boris Johnson at the Gisburn cattle auction, Clitheroe, Lancashire. (Stefan Rousseau/PA Wire/Press Association Images)

Nigel Farage with the 'Breaking Point' poster, 16 June 2016. (AFP/Daniel Leal-Olivas/Getty Images)

Remain supporters including Bob Geldof shout at the Brexit flotilla on the Thames, 15 June 2016. (Ben Stansall/AFP/Getty Images)

Nigel Farage and Kate Hoey accompany the Brexit flotilla. (Ben Stansall/AFP/Getty Images)

Jeremy Corbyn before speaking to students at the Casa bar in Liverpool, 13 May 2016. (Lindsey Parnaby/Anadolu Agency/Getty Images)

George Osborne at the Bristol and Bath Science Park, 18 April 2016. (Matt Cardy/WPA Pool/Getty Images)

Michael Gove and Boris Johnson address workers during a campaign visit to DCS Manufacturing Group, Stratford-upon-Avon, 6 June 2016. (Christopher Furlong/Getty Images)

Arron Banks at the Leave.EU party at Millbank Tower on 24 June. 2016 (Jack Taylor/Getty Images)

Boris Johnson cheers Vote Leave to victory. (Photo © Ben Wallace)

Nigel Farage outside the Leave.EU party. (Geoff Caddick/AFP/Getty Images)

Dominic Cummings punches the ceiling during his victory speech. (Photos © Rob Oxley)

Daniel Hannan's victory speech. (Photo © Rob Oxley)

Boris Johnson watches David Cameron resign on 24 June 2016. (Photo © Ben Wallace)

Samantha Cameron watches as David Cameron announces his resignation. (Ray Tang/Anadolu Agency/Getty Images)

Michael Gove's victory press conference at Westminster Tower on 24 June. (Stefan Rousseau/WPA Pool/Getty Images)

Boris Johnson's speech declaring that he will not stand for the party leadership, 30 June. (Leon Neal/AFP/Getty Images)

Stephen Crabb announces his candidacy for the leadership of the Conservative Party, 29 June. (Leon Neal/AFP/Getty Images)

Liam Fox launches his leadership bid, 4 July. (Daniel Leal-Olivas/AFP/Getty Images)

The Leadsom for leader march. (Photo © Tim Shipman)

Andrea Leadsom just before dropping out of the leadership race. (Photo © Steve Baker)

Thousands marched through London in protest at the decision to leave the EU. (Michael Tubi/Corbis via Getty Images)

Theresa May, with her husband Philip, after becoming Conservative Party leader on 11 July. (Christopher Furlong/Getty Images)

BIBLIOGRAPHY

Ashcroft, Michael and Culwick, Kevin, *Well You Did Ask: Why the UK Voted to Leave the EU* (Biteback, 2016)

Ashcroft, Michael and Oakeshott, Isabel, *Call Me Dave: The Unauthorised Biography of David Cameron* (Biteback, 2015)

Bennett, Owen, *Following Farage: On the Trail of the People's Army* (Biteback, 2015)

d'Ancona, Matthew, *In it Together: The Inside Story of the Coalition Government* (Viking, 2013)

Elliott, Francis and Hanning, James, *Cameron: Practically a Conservative* (Fourth Estate, 2012 edn)

Gibbon, Gary, *Breaking Point: The UK Referendum on the EU and its Aftermath* (Haus Curiosities, 2016)

Jackson, Daniel, Thorsen, Einar and Wring, Dominic (eds), *EU Referendum Analysis 2016: Media, Voters and the Campaign* (Centre for the Study of Journalism, Culture and Community, Bournemouth University, 2016)

Laws, David, *Coalition: The Inside Story of the Conservative–Liberal Democrat Coalition Government* (Biteback, 2016)

Mosbacher, Michael and Wiseman, Oliver, *Brexit Revolt: How the UK Voted to Leave the EU* (Social Affairs Unit, 2016)

Oliver, Craig, *Unleashing Demons: The Inside Story of Brexit* (Hodder & Stoughton, 2016)

Seldon, Anthony and Snowdon, Peter, *Cameron at 10: The Inside Story 2010–2015* (William Collins, 2015)

NOTES

Introduction

1. Craig Oliver, *Unleashing Demons*, 2016

Chapter 1: 'My Lily-Livered Colleagues …'

1. Seldon and Snowdon, *Cameron at 10*, pp.258–9
2. Ibid., p.165
3. Ashcroft and Oakeshott, *Call Me Dave*, p.490
4. Seldon and Snowdon, *Cameron at 10*, pp.168–9
5. Tim Bale, 'Banging on about Europe', LSE blog, 23 June 2016
6. Seldon and Snowdon, *Cameron at 10*, p.169
7. How to win friends, *Financial Times* magazine, 23 January 2016
8. Seldon and Snowdon, *Cameron at 10*, p.174
9. Ibid., p.175
10. David Cameron, *Daily Telegraph*, 30 June 2012
11. Laws, *Coalition*, p.241
12. Seldon and Snowdon, *Cameron at 10*, p.263
13. Ibid., p.268
14. *How We Voted Brexit*, Radio 4, 23 August 2016
15. *Brexit: Battle for Britain*, BBC2, 8 August 2016
16. Laws, *Coalition*, p.246
17. Merkel: I will block PM on immigrants, *Sunday Times*, 26 October 2014
18. How to win friends, *Financial Times* magazine, 23 January 2016
19. Ministers revolt over Osborne's 'brutal' cuts, *Sunday Times*, 11 October 2015

Chapter 2: For Britain

1. Is Nigel Farage hurting the Eurosceptic cause?, *New Statesman*, 3 April 2014
2. Farage needs to take a break from UKIP, *The Times*, 16 May 2015

Chapter 3: Dom and Arron

1. PM backs Michael Gove but suggests former aide was a 'career psychopath', *Guardian*, 18 June 2014
2. A profile of Dominic Cummings, friend of Gove and enemy of Clegg, ConservativeHome, 15 May 2014
3. Tory bovver boy leads 'No' fight, *Sunday Times*, 14 June 2015
4. Dominic Cummings' blog, 30 June 2014
5. Dominic Cummings, *The Times*, 26 June 2014
6. Dominic Cummings' blog, 30 June 2014
7. Tycoon Arron Banks unrepentant for backing UKIP, *Financial Times*, 23 January 2015
8. Britain needs to get a better deal from Brussels or leave the European Union, major new study argues, *Daily Telegraph*, 21 June 2015

9. David Cameron plans EU campaign focusing on 'risky' impact of UK exit, *Guardian*, 26 June 2015
10. Tim Shipman, *Sunday Times*, 28 June 2015
11. Mosbacher and Wiseman, *Brexit Revolt*, Chapter 3

Chapter 5: Cornering Corbyn
1. Jeremy Corbyn draws fire for position on Britain's EU future, *Observer*, 25 July 2015
2. Ibid.

Chapter 6: Guerrilla Warfare
1. Why we MUSTN'T let No10 fix this vital vote, *Mail on Sunday*, 7 June 2015

Chapter 8: The Deal
1. *Brexit: Battle for Britain*, BBC2, 8 August 2016
2. PM could reject EU if it lends 'deaf ear', *Sunday Times*, 8 November 2015
3. Is That It Mr Cameron?, *Daily Mail*, 11 November 2015
4. No regrets: An insider's guide to Brexit failure, Politico, 8 August 2016
5. PM's 47-hour battle with Brussels, *Sunday Telegraph*, 21 February 2016
6. Ibid.
7. Cameron's rocky road to Brussels, *Financial Times*, 20 February 2016
8. Banging his head against a wall … Prime Minister's two days of frustration as he pleads his case for deal at EU summit, *Daily Mail*, 20 February 2016
9. Ibid.
10. Cameron's rocky road to Brussels, *Financial Times*, 20 February 2016
11. PM's 47-hour battle with Brussels, *Sunday Telegraph*, 21 February 2016
12. Cameron chomped through 23 bags of Haribo during marathon EU talks, *Sun*, 21 February 2016
13. PM's 47-hour battle with Brussels, *Sunday Telegraph*, 21 February 2016
14. Banging his head against a wall … Prime Minister's two days of frustration as he pleads his case for

deal at EU summit, *Daily Mail*, 20 February 2016
15. Ibid.
16. The 31-hour marathon destined to save the day, *Independent on Sunday*, 21 February 2016
17. Ibid.

Chapter 9: Boris and Michael
1. Gimson, *Boris*, p.70
2. 'Tipsy' Michael Gove launches an Exocet against Boris as £100-a-bottle wine flows, *Mail on Sunday*, 16 March 2014
3. Michael Gove, *World at One*, BBC Radio 4, 18 December 2015
4. The torture of watching my husband choose between his beliefs and his old friend the PM, *Daily Mail*, 24 February 2016
5. Boris in the Wilderness, *Spectator*, 3 October 2015
6. The torture of watching my husband choose between his beliefs and his old friend the PM, *Daily Mail*, 24 February 2016
7. Ibid.
8. Craig Oliver, *Unleashing Demons*, 2016
9. How Theresa torpedoed PM Cameron, *Mail on Sunday*, 25 September 2016
10. How Boris went for Brexit over tennis, *Mail on Sunday*, 28 February 2016
11. *Brexit: Battle for Britain*, BBC2, 8 August 2016
12. Ibid.
13. EU f***ing betrayed Dave, *Sun*, 26 April 2016

Chapter 10: Project Fear
1. Brexit puts Jobs at risk, say 200 business chiefs, *The Times*, 23 February 2016
2. Revealed: Queen Backs Brexit, *Sun*, 8 March 2016
3. *Brexit: Battle for Britain*, BBC2, 8 August 2016
4. Simon Walters and Brendan Carlin, Cabinet euro rebel Gove is on the

brink, *Mail on Sunday*, 12 March
2016
5. *Brexit: Battle for Britain*, BBC2,
8 August 2016
6. Ibid.

Chapter 11: The IDS of March
1. D'Ancona, *In it Together*, p.90
2. Outraged Cameron's 4-Letter Tirade
at 'Fraud' IDS, *Mail on Sunday*,
20 March 2016
3. Revealed: The blazing row between
Iain Duncan Smith and George
Osborne, *Mail on Sunday*, 22 August
2010
4. Ibid.
5. Ibid.
6. Ibid.

**Chapter 12: Designation's What You
Need**
1. Brexit: Infighting, resignations, celebs
and cock-ups as rival EU campaigns
face off, *PR Week*, 11 April 2016
2. Mosbacher and Wiseman, *Brexit
Revolt*, Chapter 3
3. Labour MP quits Brexit group in row
over 'toxic' leadership, *The Times*,
5 February 2016
4. Nigel Farage? He would be an
appalling MP, says UKIP donor, *The
Times*, 6 February 2016
5. Eurosceptic Tory MPs Paid £40,000
By Their Own Anti-EU Campaign,
Buzzfeed, 21 April 2016

Chapter 13: 'Back of the Queue'
1. Laws, *Coalition*, p.241
2. Ibid., p.244
3. *Brexit: Battle for Britain*, BBC2,
8 August 2016
4. Brexit 'would help West's enemies',
Daily Telegraph, 10 May 2016
5. Don't vote for Brexit, US defence
chiefs warn, *The Times*, 10 May 2016

Chapter 14: The Economy, Stupid
1. Gove's idea is weird, says Albania PM,
The Times, 26 April 2016
2. *Brexit: Battle for Britain*, BBC2,
8 August 2016

3. *How We Voted Brexit*, Radio 4,
28 August 2016

Chapter 15: Blue on Blue
1. Tory meltdown as Foreign Secretary
hurls four-letter abuse at anti-EU rival
after trying to hide secret, *Mail on
Sunday*, 28 February 2016
2. *Brexit: Battle for Britain*, BBC2,
8 August 2016
3. Ibid.
4. Ibid.

Chapter 17: Aunty Beeb
1. *Brexit: Battle for Britain*, BBC2,
8 August 2016

Chapter 19: Labour Isn't Working
1. Jeremy Corbyn Allies 'Sabotaged'
Labour's In Campaign On The EU
Referendum, Critics Claim,
Huffington Post, 25 June 2016
2. Ashcroft and Oakeshott, *Call Me
Dave*, 2016 edn, quoted in *Daily Mail*,
22 September 2016
3. *Brexit: Battle for Britain*, BBC2,
8 August 2016
4. Ibid.
5. Ibid.

Chapter 20: Immigration Crisis
1. Osborne wanted promise on migrants
in referendum, Balls reveals, *The
Times*, 27 August 2016
2. *Brexit: Battle for Britain*, BBC2,
8 August 2016

Chapter 22: Breaking Points
1. *How We Voted Brexit*, Radio 4,
28 August 2016
2. *Brexit: Battle for Britain*, BBC2,
8 August 2016

Chapter 24: The Waterloo Strategy
1. *How We Voted Brexit*, Radio 4,
28 August 2016

Chapter 25: Brexit Night
1. Ashcroft and Oakeshott, *Call Me
Dave*, 2016 edn, quoted in *Daily Mail*,
22 September 2016

2. Seldon and Snowdon, *Cameron at 10*, updated edn, quoted in *The Times*, 1 July 2016

3. *How We Voted Brexit*, Radio 4, 28 August 2016

4. *Brexit: Battle for Britain*, BBC2, 8 August 2016

5. Ibid.

6. Ibid.

7. Seldon and Snowdon, *Cameron at 10*, updated edn, quoted in *The Times*, 1 July 2016

8. *Brexit: Battle for Britain*, BBC2, 8 August 2016

9. 'Gosh, I suppose I better get up!', *Daily Mail*, 29 June 2016

Chapter 26: Fallout Friday

1. 'Deadly for Europe', *Der Spiegel Online*, 8 July 2016

2. Seldon and Snowdon, *Cameron at 10*, updated edn, quoted in *The Times*, 1 July 2016

3. *Brexit: Battle for Britain*, BBC2, 8 August 2016

4. 'Gosh, I suppose I better get up!', *Daily Mail*, 29 June 2016

5. REASON CAM QUIT 'Why should I do the hard s**t?', *Sun*, 25 June 2016

6. Racism unleashed: Incident by incident – the grim litany of post-Brexit hate crime, *Independent*, 28 July 2016

7. 'Gosh, I suppose I better get up!', *Daily Mail*, 29 June 2016

Chapter 27: Jexit

1. The broken man kept in a bunker as challengers circle, *Sunday Times*, 3 July 2016

2. Jeremy Corbyn aides refuse Tom Watson one-on-one meeting, *Observer*, 3 July 2016

3. Tears, threats and soggy shortbread in the battle to ditch Corbyn, *Sunday Times*, 17 July 2016

4. *Liverpool Echo*, 11 July 2016

5. BBC *Newsnight*, 12 July 2016

Chapter 28: The Dream Team

1. Britain Out Tory leadership battle, *Daily Telegraph*, 27 June 2016

Chapter 29: Anyone But Boris

1. Sajid Javid, *Mail on Sunday*, 21 February 2016

Chapter 30: Brexecuted

1. Boris gives 'two f***ing fingers' to Remain Tory MPs, *Times* Red Box, 29 June 2016

2. Blonde Ambition, *Sunday Times Magazine*, 12 June 2016

3. I was a fool to trust Gove, *Mail on Sunday*, 3 July 2016

4. Ibid.

Chapter 31: Mayniacs v Leadbangers

1. Red Box podcast, 5 July 2016

2. Ibid.

3. Andrea Leadsom's Tory leadership hustings performance was criticised with MPs saying she went down 'like a cup of cold sick', *Sun* website, 4 July 2016

4. Andrea Leadsom Didn't Go Down Well at Leadership Hustings, Tory MPs Say, Buzzfeed, 4 July 2016

5. Ibid.

6. Theresa stakes it all on a single throw of the dice … and for the sake of her party it had better work, *Mail on Sunday*, 10 July 2016

7. 'We were affected by not having children, but we coped', *Mail on Sunday*, 3 July 2016

8. *Daily Telegraph*, 11 July 2016

Chapter 32: Iron May-den

1. James Forsyth, *Spectator*, 16 July 2016

2. Tim Ross, *Sunday Telegraph*, 17 July 2016

Conclusion

1. BBC *Newsnight*, 12 July 2016

2. No regrets: An insider's guide to Brexit failure, Politico, 8 August 2016